THE WORLDS OF LANGSTON HUGHES

THE WORLDS OF
LANGSTON HUGHES

Modernism and Translation in the Americas

VERA M. KUTZINSKI

CORNELL UNIVERSITY PRESS
Ithaca & London

First published 2012 by Cornell University Press

Printed in the United States of America

Library of Congress Cataloging-in-Publication Data

Kutzinski, Vera M., 1956–
   The worlds of Langston Hughes : modernism and translation in the Americas / Vera M. Kutzinski.
      p. cm.
   Includes bibliographical references and index.
   ISBN 978-0-8014-5115-7 (cloth : alk. paper)—
   ISBN 978-0-8014-7826-0 (pbk. : alk. paper)
      1. Hughes, Langston, 1902–1967—Translations—History and criticism.   2. Hughes, Langston, 1902–1967—Appreciation.   3. Modernism (Literature)—America.   I. Title.
   PS3515.U274Z6675 2013
   811'.52—dc23   2012009952

Lines from "Kids in the Park," "Cross," "I, Too," "Our Land," "Florida Road Workers," "Militant," "The Negro Speaks of Rivers," "Laughers," "Ma Man," "Desire," "Always the Same," "Letter to the Academy," "A New Song," "Birth," "Caribbean Sunset," "Hey!," "Afraid," "Final Curve," "Poet to Patron," "Ballads of Lenin," "Lenin," "Union," "History," "Cubes," "Scottsboro," "One More S in the U.S.A.," and "Let America Be America Again" from *The Collected Poems of Langston Hughes* by Langston Hughes, edited by Arnold Rampersad with David Roessel, Associate Editor, copyright © 1994 by the Estate of Langston Hughes. Used by permission of Alfred A. Knopf, a division of Random House, Inc. Electronic rights worldwide and UK/Commonwealth, S. African and Irish print on paper rights for these poems and for materials from Langston Hughes's autobiographies are granted by Harold Ober Associates Inc.

Cloth printing   10 9 8 7 6 5 4 3 2 1

To my extended family, acá y allá

CONTENTS

Acknowledgments   ix

Chronology of Travels, Translations, and Other Key Publications   xi

Abbreviations   xvi

Introduction: In Others' Words: Translation and Survival   1

1 Nomad Heart: Heterolingual Autobiography   15

2 Southern Exposures: Hughes in Spanish   56

3 Buenos Aires Blues: Modernism in the Creole City   86

4 Havana Vernaculars: The *Cuba Libre* Project   132

5 Back in the USSA: Joe McCarthy's Mistranslations   184

Afterword: America/*América*/Americas   221

Appendix   241

Notes   257

Bibliography   311

Index   339

ACKNOWLEDGMENTS

This book has been a long time in the making, and the debts of gratitude I have incurred along the way are plentiful indeed. Even if I could recall them all accurately, it would be impossible to do them justice in writing. I do, however, want to single out those friends and colleagues who were generous enough to comment on my many drafts: Elizabeth Barnett, Hubert Cook, Paula Covington, Roberto González Echevarría, Detlev Eggers, Kathleen de Guzmán, Amanda Hagood, Justin Haynes, Robert Kelz, John Morell, Chris Pexa, Kathrin Seidl-Gómez, Daniel Spoth, Aubrey Porterfield, José María Rodríguez García, and Lacey Saborido. For invaluable help with locating translations of Hughes's poetry, I want to thank Paula Covington, Curator of the Latin American Studies Collection at Vanderbilt, Jim Toplon, Director of Interlibrary Loan Services at Vanderbilt, and Laurie N. Taylor, Digital Humanities Librarian at the George A. Smathers Libraries, University of Florida. Very special thanks go to Giorleny Altamirano Rayo, mi hermanita, and to the ever-faithful EE-gor. Without their mostly gentle but insistent prodding this book would likely never have been completed. Ange Romeo-Hall and Jamie Fuller did a splendid job copyediting my manuscript, and I am grateful to them for saving me from embarrassing infelicities. I thank Kitty Liu for making sure that everything kept moving along apace. Last but by no means least, my heartfelt gratitude goes to Peter Potter for his thoughtful feedback, his choice of engaged and helpful readers, and his unwavering support for this project over the past few years.

Earlier versions of chapters 2 and 4 were published as "'Yo también soy América': Langston Hughes Translated," in *American Literary History* 18, no. 3 (2006): 550–78, and as "Fearful Asymmetries: Langston Hughes, Nicolás Guillén and Cuba Libre" in *Diacritics* 34, nos. 1–2 (2004): 1–29. I thank Random House for the permission to reprint lines from Hughes's poems and Harold Ober Associates Inc. for granting the electronic rights to excerpts from Hughes's poetry and prose. The materials from the Langston Hughes Papers, part of the James Weldon Johnson Memorial Collection at the Beinecke Rare Book and Manuscript Library at Yale University, are also quoted with the permission of the Estate of Langston Hughes. Passages from the Alfred A. Knopf correspondence at Beinecke Library are reprinted with the permission of Random House Inc., and citations from the poems of Nicolás Guillén are reproduced with the permission of the Fundación Nicolás Guillén.

Finally, I wish to thank both Yale University and Vanderbilt for giving me the time I needed to complete this book, and the Martha Rivers Ingram Chair for providing funding for research materials, research assistance, and permissions fees.

Vera M. Kutzinski
Nashville, February 2012

CHRONOLOGY OF TRAVELS, TRANSLATIONS, AND OTHER KEY PUBLICATIONS

1902 James Langston Hughes born in Joplin, Missouri (February 1).

1903 Moves to his grandmother's home in Lawrence, Kansas. Parents separate, and James Nathaniel Hughes emigrates to Mexico.

1908–9 Starts school in Topeka, Kansas, where he lives with his mother, Carrie Mercer Langston Hughes, and then is returned to his grandmother's in Lawrence.

1915 Stays with the Reeds in Lawrence after his grandmother's death, then joins his mother and her second husband in Lincoln, Illinois.

1916 The family moves first to Cleveland, Ohio, where Langston begins high school, then to Chicago. Langston remains in Cleveland.

1919 Spends the summer with his father in Toluca, Mexico.

1920 After graduating from Central High in Cleveland, Langston returns to Toluca to live with his father. Spends weekends in Mexico City. Teaches at Luis Tovar's business institute near the end of his year-long stay. Sails from Veracruz back to New York City.

1921–22 "The Negro Speaks of Rivers" appears in *The Crisis*. Enrolls at Columbia University, only to withdraw after a term. Breaks with his father as a result. Moves to Harlem and works odd jobs.

1923–25 Signs on to the Africa-bound freighter *West Hesseltine* in June 1923. Visits Accra, the Azores, Ivory Coast, Senegal, Lagos, the Belgian Congo, Guinea-Bissau, French Guinea, Sierra Leone, and Angola. Sails to Europe on another freighter, the *McKeesport,* in December and again in February 1924. Visits

Rotterdam and stays in Paris until August, traveling to northern Italy, finally returning to the USA via Genoa on the *West Cawthon*. Arrives back in Manhattan in early November 1924.

1925   "The Weary Blues" wins *Opportunity*'s poetry contest. Lives in Washington, D.C.

1926   Publishes *The Weary Blues* and "The Negro Artist and the Racial Mountain." Enrolls at Lincoln University in Pennsylvania.

1927   Publishes *Fine Clothes to the Jew*. Meets Charlotte Mason Osgood, who becomes his patron. Travels through the South of the USA with Zora Neale Hurston. First brief visit to Havana.

1928   Fernández de Castro publishes his first Hughes translation in *Social*.

1929   Graduates from Lincoln University.

1930   Publishes *Not Without Laughter*. Second visit to Havana (February–March). Breaks with his patron. Translations of Hughes's poems appear in *Contemporáneos* (Mexico City), *Sur* (Buenos Aires), *Revista de La Habana*, and *El Diario de la Marina* (Havana). Nicolás Guillén also publishes his interview with Hughes in *El Diario de la Marina*.

1931   Together with Zell Ingram, embarks on a trip to the Caribbean (April–May). Stops over in Havana, Port-au-Prince, Cap-Haïtien, and Santiago de Cuba. Returns to Miami in July. Rafael Lozano publishes a selection of Hughes's poems in *Crísol*. Poetry reading tour of the South of the USA. Visits Scottsboro Boys in jail.

1932–33   Publishes *Scottsboro, Limited* and *The Dream Keeper*. Travels to Los Angeles, Portland, Seattle, and San Francisco. Leaves for Moscow in June 1932 and spends fourteen months in the Soviet Union. Visits Tashkent, Samarkand, Bokhara, Ashgabat, Merv (Turkmenistan), and Permetyab (central Asia). Returns to Moscow in January 1933. Departs for Vladivostok in June, then returns to the San Francisco via Kyoto, Tokyo, and Shanghai. Takes up residence in Carmel in August.

1934–35   Publishes *The Ways of White Folks*. Labor unrest in California. Travels to Mexico on the occasion of his father's death and stays for several months in Mexico City. Returns to the USA and joins his mother in Oberlin, Ohio. Visits New York. His play *Mulatto* opens on Broadway.

1936   Wins a Guggenheim Fellowship. Ildefonso Pereda Valdés publishes *Antología de la poesía negra americana* in Santiago de Chile.

1937   Spends summer in Paris for the League of American Writers. In August travels to Valencia, then on to Madrid, as a war reporter for the *Baltimore Afro-American*. Leaves Madrid for Barcelona in mid-November. Returns to the USA via Paris at the end of the year.

1938   Publishes *A New Song*. Rafael Alberti publishes his Hughes translation in *El Mono Azul*. First visit to UK in September 1938.

1939–41   Takes up residence in California again, mainly in Carmel, and spends some time in Chicago. Publishes *The Big Sea*. Moves back to New York in December 1941.

1942–43   Begins to write a weekly column for the *Chicago Defender* in November 1942. Dudley Fitts publishes his *Anthology of Contemporary Latin-American Poetry*. Gastón Figueira publishes his translations of several Hughes poems in *Nueva Democracia, Sustancia,* and *Aurora*.

1944–45   Under surveillance by the FBI. *The Big Sea* appears in Buenos Aires as *El inmenso mar* in a translation by Luisa Rivaud and in Rio de Janeiro as *O imenso mar* in a Portuguese translation by Francisco Burkinski. Ortíz Oderigo publishes a translation of *Not Without Laughter* (*Pero con risas*), also in Buenos Aires.

1947   Publishes *Fields of Wonder* and *Masters of the Dew* by Jacques Roumain. Vacations in Jamaica.

1948   Back in Harlem. Publishes *Cuba Libre: Poems by Nicolás Guillén*. Several poems appear in translation by Manuel González Flores in *El Nacional*.

1949   Teaches in Chicago for three months. Hughes and Arna Bontemps publish *The Poetry of the Negro, 1746–1949*. Tomás Blanco publishes his Hughes translations in *Asomante*.

1950   Publishes *Simple Speaks His Mind*. González Flores includes
           Hughes translations in *Una pareja de tantas*.

1951–52   Hughes publishes *Montage of a Dream Deferred, Laughing
           to Keep from Crying*, and his translation of García Lorca's
           Romancero gitano as *Gypsy Ballads*. López Narváez includes
           translations of Hughes's poetry in *El cielo en el río* (Bogotá).
           Publishes *Poems from Black Africa, Ethiopia, and Other
           Countries*.

1953   Testifies twice before the McCarthy Committee in late
           March. Poetry translations by Figueira appear in the *Revista
           Iberoamericana*. Pereda Valdés's *Antología* is reissued
           in Montevideo. Toruño publishes the anthology *Poesía negra*
           in Mexico.

1954   Gáler publishes a translation of the play *Mulatto* in
           Buenos Aires.

1955   Gáler publishes his translation of Hughes's novel *Laughing
           to Keep from Crying* (*Riendo por no llorar*). Florit publishes
           Antología de la poesía norteamericana contemporánea.
           Hughes is also included in Oswaldino Marques's *Videntes e
           sonâmbulos: Coletânea de poemas norte-americanos* (Rio de
           Janeiro).

1956–57   Publishes *I Wonder As I Wander*. Gáler publishes *Poemas de
           Langston Hughes*. Hughes's poems are included in Gandelman
           et al., *Negros famosos a America do Norte*. Hughes publishes
           The First Book of the West Indies and *Selected Poems of
           Gabriela Mistral*.

1959   Publishes *Selected Poems*. Gáler publishes his translation of *I
           Wonder As I Wander* (*Yo viajo por un mundo encantado*). Fidel
           Castro visits New York City.

1961–62   Inducted into the National Institute of Arts and Letters. Visits
           Africa twice. Publishes *Ask Your Mama*. Xavier Villaurrutia's
           earlier translations of Hughes's poems are reprinted in Mexico
           in *Nivel*. Ernesto Cardenal publishes translations of Hughes's
           poems in *Antología de la poesía norteamericana*.

1964   Publishes *New Negro Poets, U.S.A.* Alfonso Sastre publishes
           another Spanish version of *Mulatto*.

1965–66 Tours Europe for nearly two months for the U.S. State Department. Vacations in Tunis. Travels to Dakar, Senegal, to be honored at the First World Festival of Negro Arts. Visits other African countries, including Nigeria, Ethiopia, and Sudan.

1967 Dies in New York City (May 22). José Luis González publishes his Hughes translations in *Siempre! El inmenso mar* is reprinted in Havana. *The Panther and the Lash* appears posthumously.

1968 Ahumada publishes *Yo también soy América. Poemas de Langston Hughes* in Mexico City.

1970 Martins publishes *Poemas de Langston Hughes* in João Pessoa, Brazil.

1971 Bansart's students include translations of Hughes's poems in their anthology *Poesía negra-africana.* (Chile) Rivaud publishes excerpts from *The Big Sea* as *Renacimiento negro.*

1972 Ruiz del Vizo includes translations of Hughes's poems in *Black Poetry of the Americas.*

1973 Gary Bartz and NTU Troop debut their version of *I've Known Rivers* in Montreux.

1994 Random House publishes *The Collected Poems of Langston Hughes.*

1998 Fraile Marcos publishes *Langston Hughes: Oscuridad en España/Darkness in Spain* in León, Spain.

2003 Several of his translations are reprinted in volume 16 of *The Collected Works of Langston Hughes.*

2004 Cruzado and Hricko publish *Langston Hughes: Blues* in Valencia, Spain. Reprint of *Let America Be America Again* with a preface by John Kerry.

ABBREVIATIONS

BS   *The Big Sea*
CL   *Cuba Libre: Poems by Nicolás Guillén*
CP   *Collected Poems of Langston Hughes* (ed. Arnold Rampersad and David Roessel)
CR   *Langston Hughes: The Contemporary Reviews* (ed. Letitia Dace)
Essays   *Langston Hughes: Essays on Art, Race, Politics, and World Affairs* (ed. Christopher de Santis)
IM   *El inmenso mar* (Hughes, trans. Luisa Rivaud)
IW   *I Wonder As I Wander*
LHP   The Langston Hughes papers are part of the James Weldon Johnson Memorial Collection at the Beinecke Rare Book and Manuscript Library, Yale University. I reference materials from this collection by box and folder number.
Life   *The Life of Langston Hughes* (Arnold Rampersad)
Poemas   *Langston Hughes. Poemas* (ed. and trans. Julio Gáler)
PT   Public testimony of Langston Hughes, Thursday, March 26, 1953
ST   Secret testimony of Langston Hughes, Tuesday, March 24, 1953
USA   Abbreviations used to distinguish the United States of America from other countries in the Americas and from other United States. See note 11 in the introduction for further explanation.
TWB   *The Weary Blues*
YT   *Yo también soy América. Poemas de Langston Hughes* (ed. and trans. Herminio Ahumada)
Yo viajo   *Yo viajo en un mundo encantado* (Hughes, trans. Julio Gáler)

IN OTHERS' WORDS

Translation and Survival

A text lives only if it lives *on* [*sur-vit*], and it lives *on* only if it is *at once* translatable *and* untranslatable.
> —Jacques Derrida, "Living on / Border Lines"

Home's just around
the corner
there—
but not really
anywhere.
> —Langston Hughes, "Kids in the Park"

Langston Hughes is inextricably woven into the fabric of contemporary culture. Most people in the Americas and in Europe recognize his name. Maybe they have read a poem or two in an anthology. In the United States of America, more than half a century after his death in 1967, Hughes has a firm hold on the popular imagination, so much so that even the occasional politician resorts to lines from his poems. His handsome face adorns books, greeting cards, and a commemorative thirty-four-cent postage stamp. On satellite radio's Real Jazz station, we can listen to Gary Bartz's version of "I've Known Rivers" from the 1973 Montreux Jazz Festival. For anyone who prefers lighter fare than Isaac Julien's *Looking for Langston* (1989), there is *The Great Debaters* (2007). In this Oprah-produced biopic, the labor activist and teacher Melvin B. Tolson, played by a Denzel Washington intent on upstaging Robin Williams, fervently recites lines from "I, Too" to his rapt students at Wiley College. In 1959, LeRoi Jones admitted, "I suppose, by now, Langston Hughes's name is synonymous with 'Negro literature.'"[1] Even today, in an age when we hear much about the end of the book as we know it, almost all of Hughes's books are in print, many of them in new editions.[2]

Yet what do we *really* know about Langston Hughes? Thanks to the good offices of his biographers, notably Faith Berry and Arnold Rampersad, we have much information about Hughes's life, even though, as I show in the pages that follow, the record is not altogether complete.[3] What we understand less well is exactly how certain aspects of Hughes's lived experiences relate to his writing. Hughes's poems and his two autobiographies, *The Big Sea* (1940) and *I Wonder As I Wander* (1956), present themselves to us in plain language as if they were wholly transparent and self-explanatory. The more we read Hughes, however, the more it becomes apparent that they are not. In my case, the growing sense that those of us who write about literature for a living have not yet given Hughes his due became the starting point for this book.

As my title suggests, Langston Hughes moved in different worlds and, I argue, had not one life but many. What I mean by this is that Hughes lived and wrote in more than one idiom and that his writings have enjoyed active lives in others' words, that is, in languages other than English. Although we think of Hughes as writing in English, I show that his poetics are plurilingual. Because his autobiographies and his verse, to which I largely limit myself here, weave in and out of a host of cultural geographies and languages, translation quickly emerges as vital to all of Hughes's literary pursuits.

TRANSLATION AS METAPHOR AND LITERARY PRACTICE

A passionate traveler for most of his life, Hughes spent time in Mexico, the Caribbean, Africa, Europe, central Asia, and the Far East. Almost always, he carried in his luggage copies of his books to give away to those he met along the way. And if he did not carry them himself, he sent them by mail in numbers large enough to consume much of his royalties. Such generosity contributed in no small measure to the worldwide circulation that his writings enjoyed during his lifetime and well beyond. Hughes's poems, novels, short stories, and autobiographies also traveled by other means.[4] Having survived their author and taken on lives of their own, many of Hughes's texts live on in French, German, Italian, Hebrew, Japanese, Portuguese, Russian, Serbo-Croatian, Spanish, Uzbek, and Yiddish. It is their journeys into other tongues, most notably Spanish, that I track in this book, along with the routes of literary works whose afterlives Hughes himself similarly ensured. I demonstrate that reading the Spanish versions of his poems and autobiographies alongside his English texts gives us access to layers of meaning we may otherwise overlook. By the same token, Hughes's own translations from Spanish into English are always in conversation with his other writings. They also grant us valuable insights into his work as editor, anthologizer, and marketer.

The sense in which I use translation combines the act of moving oneself (*translatio*) with that of leading or carrying someone or something across some sort of divide (*traductio*).[5] Neither sense is reducible to bridging distances between diverse linguistic spaces by finding equivalents for foreign words and sentences in one's own native idiom. In fact, the metaphor of the bridge, one of the key metaphors for translation, is highly suspect.[6] The problem is that translation's expected respect for differences among cultural codes obscures the fact that it posits, and relies on, the very separation of what it purports to bridge. As a result, an understanding of translation as an act of bridging linguistic and cultural differences may well end up so-lidifying those very differences. Steven Ungar's remarks on the work of the Maghrebian writer Abdelkebir Khatibi point to an alternative. Translation, as he has described it, is less "a process leading to transparency in the tar-get language than...a confrontation in which multiple languages square off against each other and *meet without merging...without* a reconciling *osmosis* or *synthesis*."[7] Translation need not, however, be confrontation; it can be, and often is, respectful, noncompetitive play. What I am after are more precise ways of talking about such mergings and more nuanced metaphors to articulate an idea and a practice of translation that is at once performative and transformative.

Studying translation requires exceedingly close readings, a courtesy that has not always been extended to Hughes. It is inattentiveness to detail that has bedeviled Hughes's legacy at the hands of those who have dismissed his writings as "simple," even "shallow." This is a trend in Hughes scholar-ship that I vigorously contest throughout. Even though academic readers are now increasingly highlighting his "portentous ambiguities made out of simple language" and his "expert manipulation of colloquial or 'plain' lan-guage," I agree with Jeff Westover that Langston Hughes remains "easily the most critically neglected of all major modern American poets."[8] With this book, I hope to contribute my share to remedying this situation.

HUGHES AND/IN TRANSLATION

In no small measure, the Spanish translations of his work made Hughes the best-known USAmerican poet in the Hispanic Americas since Whitman and Longfellow.[9] Given Hughes's many personal connections to Mexico and Cuba, it is perhaps predictable that Spanish would be the one language into which his writings have been translated the most since the late 1920s. While some of those translations have appeared in Spain, the vast majority of them were published in the Hispanic Americas, particularly, and perhaps oddly, in Argentina in the 1930s, 1940s, and 1950s. I say "oddly" because Argentina is not a country known for its population of African descent in the way that, say, Brazil is.[10] This substantial archive of literary translations consists not only of Hughes's poems but also of his autobiographies, short stories, and novels. Neglected, this archive is part of a historical geography defined by artistic innovation, political conflict, and ideological contestation: the early-to-mid-twentieth-century Americas.[11] The African diaspora, black in-ternationalism, and modernism are three popular abstractions created to represent the cultural work of mainly transient intellectual and artistic communities during that period. My goal is to render these abstractions more tangible by showing how Hughes connects these groups, through travel and personal contacts and by way of translation.

Why were certain Hughes poems translated and not others? How were they translated? What images of Hughes did different translators construct for their readers? Since it is impossible to analyze all Spanish translations in the space of a single book, I limit myself to a series of case studies that focus mainly on two settings, Cuba and Argentina, with detours to Mexico, Uruguay, Chile, Colombia, and Spain. The basis for my discussion in chapters 2 to 4 is a systematic inventory of the poems that were translated into Spanish between 1928 and 2004 (see appendix). During that time, more than three hundred translations were printed and reprinted in journals, newspapers, anthologies, and poetry collections, as well as in the Spanish versions of Hughes's two autobiographies on which I comment in the first chapter— Luisa Rivaud's *El inmenso mar* (1944), her translation of *The Big Sea*, and Julio Gáler's *Yo viajo por un mundo encantado* (1959), his Spanish version of *I Wonder As I Wander*.

Especially prior to the early 1990s, USAmerican academics have tended to divide Hughes's verse into two groups: black "folk" poetry, which generally covers the blues poems, and "social protest," or "revolutionary," verse.[12] While Hughes's early poetry on racial topics was usually embraced as culturally "authentic" in the USA, the so-called protest poetry, written mainly in the 1930s, has generally been deemed an aberration. A third grouping that has more recently emerged is that of Hughes's "modernist" verse, mainly around *Montage of a Dream Deferred* (1951) and *ASK YOUR MAMA: 12 Moods for Jazz* (1961).[13] Both folk and protest labels subordinate the formal aesthetics of Hughes's poems either to ethnographic or to ideological criteria,[14] and the creation of a separate modernist category around his later poems implicitly confirms the validity of those criteria. Many of Hughes's translators from the Hispanic Americas seem to have made similar distinctions. Surprisingly perhaps, the majority of them, like many of Hughes's readers in the USA, turned away from his radical verse, despite the fact that his socialist politics formed a significant part of his reputation in the Spanish-speaking world. Contrary to what one might expect, Hughes's Hispanic American translators also rarely touched his vernacular verse, including the widely admired blues poems. I reflect on why this might have been so by exploring differences among the literary avant-gardes in the Americas.

Another key concern of this book is how well, or poorly, racialized identities anchored in the history of the USA traveled from Harlem south to other parts of the Americas and vice versa. Is a Cuban or Uruguayan *negro* the same as a Negro in the USA in the early twentieth century? I think of them as false cognates along the lines of "America" and "América," homonyms that signify differently in their respective languages. English-language translations, especially of literary vernaculars such as Afro-Cuban, have tended to reproduce the effects of the same racially based cultural homogeneity that academic diasporic theories have typically championed.[15] In addressing this effect of sameness and related identity issues, I scrutinize some of the theoretical and ideological expectations in African diaspora studies by contrasting them with what the actual translations manifest. Many scholars who have written about the literary discourses of blackness in the Hispanic Americas have put too little pressure on the assumption that these discourses are culturally rooted and ideologically unified, both within themselves and across languages.[16] More recent work on the francophone and transatlantic "stirrings of black internationalism" by Brent Edwards, Anita Patterson, and others offers welcome alternatives to the usual commonplaces about "the African American literary experience" and "black diaspora."[17] I happily build on their insights.

Analyzing how Hispanic American writers engaged with Langston Hughes's texts and tracing the trajectories of their translations open an important window onto Hughes's own work as a translator. As Brent Edwards points out, "Hughes is the most prolific black poet-translator of the twentieth century...and at the same time a prodigious and groundbreaking anthologist in his own right."[18] He translated the work of other writers, chiefly from Africa and the Americas, whose work, he felt strongly, should be accessible to English-speaking readers in the USA and elsewhere. Although the fact that some of Hughes's poems and essays survive only in languages other than English has rekindled some scholarly interest in his literary translations,[19] little has been written about linguistic migrancy, or nomadism, in relation to Hughes's poetics. That Hughes himself rarely talked about translations, including those of his own writings, probably has not helped matters.

Hughes's career as a book-length literary translator began in 1938 with Federico García Lorca's play *Blood Wedding* (*Bodas de Sangre*, 1933), followed by Jacques Roumain's novel *Masters of the Dew* (*Gouverneurs de la rosée*, 1994) in 1947, *Cuba Libre: Poems by Nicolás Guillén* a year later, García Lorca's *Gypsy Ballads* in 1951 (*Romancero gitano*, 1928), and *Selected Poems of Gabriela Mistral* in 1957.[20] Although the translations of García Lorca and Guillén have seen some critical attention in recent years, there has on the whole been little scholarly engagement with Hughes's own translation aesthetics.[21] I show in chapters 3 and 4 how one can reconstruct important facets of that process by examining archival material, including corrected drafts of translations and correspondence.[22] These materials also provide evidence of the aesthetic *and* political concerns that motivated decisions about what material to translate and how. The choices Hughes made—whether to translate one vernacular idiom, say, Afro-Cuban, either into another, supposedly parallel, register, such as so-called Negro dialect or Black English, or into a more standardized version of USAmerican

English—tell us much about how perceived cultural similarities and differences are linguistically encoded.[23]

All these translations of and by Langston Hughes raise the question of whether and how modes of translation found their way into his literary practice more broadly. Shifts in location, be they from one textual genre to another or from one linguistic, cultural, or historical space to another, change how we perceive and read any text.[24] For example, a Hughes poem in the pages of *New Masses* or *Opportunity* accrues meanings quite different from what the same poem might mean to readers who encounter it either as part of *The Weary Blues* in 1926 or in the chronologically organized *Collected Poems of Langston Hughes* in 1994. Additional interpretive possibilities come into play when a given Hughes poem is rendered in Spanish and printed in the conservative *Diario de la Marina* in Havana, in the avant-garde literary journal *Sur* in Buenos Aires, or in the radical *El Mono Azul* in Madrid. Hughes himself was well aware that relocating a text—his own or that of another writer—from one cultural space to another would alter it in important ways. For Hughes and his colleagues, certain textual repositionings also had financial benefits: being translated was a way of earning royalties or other fees from multiple sources. For literary scholars, they have intriguing historical and theoretical implications, especially with respect to ideas about cultural and political identity.

Such textual relocations are also forms of translation. I apply this logic to the poems that appear in the official records of the hearings of Joseph McCarthy's infamous Senate Permanent Subcommittee on Investigations, at which Hughes testified in the early spring of 1953—not once, as is commonly believed, but twice (see chapter 5).[25] The publicly broadcasted hearing made Hughes out to be a witness who was far too cooperative, renouncing his political radicalism far too readily. His public appearance, however, did not reveal the whole story. The transcript of the secret, or "executive," hearing, released in 2003, shows how expertly Hughes refused to be translated into someone else's terms.

TRANSLATION AND MODERNISM'S LOOSE ENDS

It is neither inevitable nor logical that movement in literature and of literary texts would occur only between cultural centers and their peripheries. There is a great deal of cross-linguistic and cross-cultural traffic that connects the world's peripheries with each other. One case in point is *Changó el Gran Putas* (1983, 1985) (*Changó, the Biggest Badass* [2010]), an epic novel by the Colombian Manuel Zapata Olivella. *Changó* includes a rather remarkable homage to Hughes that I analyze in more detail at the end of chapter 1. While there are many who dedicated poems to Hughes—I have used some of these tributes as epigraphs—Zapata Olivella went so far as to make his friend a minor character in a novel. My point is that in fictionalizing Langston Hughes, Zapata Olivella renders the very idea of a literary afterlife in translation quite literal.

Such movements across cultures and languages notwithstanding, translation theories, including more recent ones, are almost invariably based on situations where foreign texts are ferried to politically dominant linguistic and cultural settings either in Europe or in the USA.[26] This scenario applies, at least in part, to Hughes's own translations. Special caution is in order, however, when examining the Hispanic American translations of his work.

Acts of "domestication" occur in all literary translations, regardless of the direction in which a text travels, which makes all translations treacherous terrain.[27] Yet it is quite unjustified to speak of "appropriation" when texts travel from south to north—in this case from Spanish into English—and of literary "influence" when the direction is reversed. Translation has historically meant something quite different in the literatures that have been placed at the margins of Europe and the USA. Postcolonial literatures—including those in the Americas—have done much to unsettle assumptions about the convergence of language and culture in the figure of the nation. Analyzing these literatures opens myriad possibilities for breathing new life into the worn idea of "world literature"—Erich Auerbach's *Weltliteratur*—in the context of the past and present migrations that have largely unloosed the idea of human community from its nineteenth-century linguistic and ideological moorings. I especially stress that cross-linguistic literary traffic occurs not just between center and periphery but also—and this is particularly significant in the context of the Americas—between different local and global peripheries, however they may be defined.[28] The conceptual opposition between the local and the global obscures three important dynamics: one, that center-periphery relations are historical phenomena that exist in a given locale at a specific time; two, that cross-hatching exists between diverse manifestations of the local on a hemispheric and even global scale; and three, that peripheral alliances can develop independently of and bypass the centers of colonial and neocolonial power. Translational exchanges on the global fringes, as I think of them, are characterized by different dynamics than are those in a center-margin model. To track the movements of their multiple vectors requires far greater flexibility than most translation theories permit.

My main goal in piecing together the overlapping stories of Hughes's travels, his translations, and his translators, has been to show how different modes of translation come together in a poetics that situates itself along the edges of the linguistic, cultural, social, and political geographies of what we know as "high modernism." I argue that Hughes's writings, notably his early poems and his two autobiographies, exemplify this poetics and that his translators added noteworthy local variations. In the work of his translators, for instance, Hughes's Harlem joins similarly imaginative extensions of actual places such as Buenos Aires, Bogotá, Madrid, Montevideo, and Mexico City. Despite the fact that these metropoles were cosmopolitan hubs for modernist writers from across the Americas and different parts of Europe, they have rarely been stops on academic grand tours of modernism in the English-speaking world. With a nod to Gayatri Spivak, Chana Kronfeld, Iain Chambers, and Beatriz Sarlo, whose work on the intersections of modernism and postcolonialism does take us to these and other neglected areas, I provisionally call this poetics "fringe modernism."[29]

The metaphor bears some consideration as a thought experiment, less so perhaps as yet another label. What I think of as the *fringes* of modernism as traditionally conceived are spaces worldwide in which we find avant-garde literary practices typically excluded from modernist studies for being too "transparent," too "realistic," too "ethnic," or too "political" — or simply for using languages other than English. Although the concept of a fringe has the disadvantage of reviving narratives of marginalization, it also has the benefit of not tying modernist literary practices to a single language, country, or region, making them at once comparable and incomparable in their local specificity. Fringe also suggests the selvaged edges a fabric may have to keep it from fraying. Even if they do not make the entire fabric unravel, some selvages do fray, causing the threads to hang loose so that they can tangle, much like the decorative fringes on a scarf or sweater. It is the idea of loose ends and their entanglements that I find appealing about this metaphor, despite its seeming two-dimensionality and its potential for falling back into a center-margin model.

The kind of cloth I have in mind is heavily textured. It is created when loose ends from pieces of fabric with fibers of different lengths and thicknesses intertwine unevenly. The result is bumpy and far too asymmetrical to have a clear center, and it has rough edges that look and act like an irregular coastline in that their true dimensions are impossible to measure. I see the different garments that may be tailored from such material, to continue a thought inspired in part by Zora Neale Hurston's "tight chemise" in her introduction to *Mules and Men* and the clothing metaphor in the journal title *El Mono Azul* (Overalls), as correspondingly crooked.[30] But being uneven and jagged does not necessarily make them any less significant or beautiful. Wearing such unfamiliar garb may be a bit uncomfortable at first, but the hope is that it will allow for more freedom of movement.

TRANSLATION AND MIGRANCY

If migrancy, real and imaginary, is the condition of taking up residence in multiple linguistic and cultural homes, Langston Hughes was a migrant in the truest sense of the word. He moved in and between various worlds and wrote at length about their relative distances and proximities. As an African

American who grew up during the early decades of the twentieth century, he was uncomfortably conscious of the racial chasm separating people in the USA. No less acute was his awareness of the class and color divides among peoples of African descent in the Americas. A polyglot and world traveler, Hughes felt deeply that more than geographical distances separated Africa from the USA, Europe from the USA and the other Americas, and the various countries in the Western Hemisphere from each other. Because of his brush with McCarthyism, the ideological enmities that pitted the USA against the Soviet Union before and during the Cold War became a painful reality for him.

Throughout his life, Hughes tried to understand these multidirectional tensions by carefully taking the measure of actual and perceived distances between people(s) and by imagining ways of inhabiting remoteness and strangeness both emotionally and intellectually. In the process, he fashioned often unexpected connections between an array of linguistic and cultural fields in the USA, the Americas, and indeed the world. In doing so, Hughes remapped home—"America"—by exposing to "lexical shock" all sorts of pieties and proprieties, whether they pertained to race, color, sexuality, or class.[31]

Hughes dwelt and traded in multiplicities, donning countless costumes and taking on many voices in his poetry and prose. Among these masks are the conventions of various literary and nonliterary genres that are liberally strewn throughout Hughes's prose and poetry. His ventriloquizing ranges from the accents of the personae he creates in his autobiographies and characters such as the notorious Jesse B. Semple (from the *Simple* stories) to the nameless and ungendered figures that proliferate in his lyrics. Although these voices typically speak in more and less standardized versions of English, Hughes's repertoire is not limited to those. It also includes a host of other languages, among them Spanish, French, German, and Russian, which he weaves into his writings with some frequency, at times translated, at others not. Hughes's literary polyvocality is vital to his ability to take up residence in varied cultural and linguistic settings. Such dwelling, however temporary, is as inescapable a feature of Langston Hughes's poetics as it was an inexorable reality throughout his life. I illustrate in this book how Hughes's "translation sensibility"[32]—that is, positioning himself on the fringes of competing social and symbolic systems—led him to encode in his writings both lived and imagined truths that have frustrated many readers' expectations of what a black USAmerican author should be and do.

TRANSLATION AS "WORLD CONSCIOUSNESS"

While it is important that "another language [French]...awakened him to his literary vocation," moving between worlds, for Hughes, was never just a matter of learning French, Spanish, German, and a smattering of other languages, including Russian and Cantonese.[33] It was a matter of taking other languages and cultures into the fibers of his very being. Of multiracial heritage, he was a Negro who was not black, or not black enough, who looked and sounded like a Mexican to some and like a white man to others.[34] He had relationships with women but seemed to have preferred the company of men.[35] He was educated and wrote poetry but usually had little patience for the literary establishment and the New Negro elites, fraternizing instead with the working poor in word and in deed. Unwilling to share anyone's values and beliefs unquestioningly, Hughes, it seems, was always pulled in several directions at once. Belonging to different races and classes and yet at the same time to no particular one completely complicated his desire for an emotional and intellectual home. Disconcertingly to him, America was, in many respects, as unhomely as faraway Africa. The feeling of being in perpetual exile, of being misrecognized no matter where he went, instilled in Hughes a profound sense of being "in-translation," to use Emily Apter's term—of being at home nowhere.[36] At the same time Hughes also realized that he himself had to engage in intricate acts of translation to survive as a person and a writer.[37] Clearly, in the terms of discourses on race, nationality, sexuality, and class that insist on fixed subject positions, Hughes's multiple lived and imagined truths are neither possible nor intelligible.[38] Discerning these truths and fully grasping their strategic slipperiness requires us to tune our scholarly tools to the ideological and historical frequencies of the languages and discourses in which we constitute our own senses of identity, place, and belonging.

Virtually all of Hughes's writing encodes spatial and temporal displacements in tropes of travel and memory. "Rendering a 'foreign' language into a 'native' language," Stephanos Stephanides avers, "finds its equivalent in our 'translation' of the past."[39] The connective filament here is repetition, a figure for memory in which restatement and recovery combine. While repetition is most visible in the formal devices through which Hughes's poems, most obviously the blues- and jazz-based poems, situate themselves in relation to literary, vernacular, and musical traditions, it is no less evident in his prose, notably in his autobiographies. In both *The Big Sea* and *I Wonder As I Wander*, Hughes explicitly figures memory and self-writing as acts of "wandering" and "crossing," and these movements always lead to scenes of translation. Whether he writes about Mexico, Senegal, France, Haiti, Russia, or Harlem, speaking in other—and others'—words is always an overriding concern. It is through actual and represented acts of translation that Hughes connects all these different sites into a global geography that extends well beyond early-twentieth-century pan-Africanism and even beyond more recent critical conceptualizations of the African diaspora.[40] The transatlantic legs of this global geography—that is, Hughes's ties to France, Spain, Russia, and central Asia—have received a good deal more attention than the hemispheric spokes I map out in this book. Even though the hemispheric reach of Hughes's work has elicited some scholarly commentary, much uncharted territory remains.[41]

Langston Hughes spent much of his life trying to come to terms with the codes of other cultures—including those of the USA—and with what Walter Benjamin called "the foreignness of language" as a representational system.[42] Contemplating layers of foreignness means running up against the limits of what is translatable, and therefore representable, in the first place. One possible definition of translation, then, is "expressing without representing" as a way of addressing, in William Scott's words, "the incommensurability of language as such in relation to historical experience." Another is hearing in the silences between words what Iain Chambers describes as "the potential murmur of a dialogue barely begun."[43] It is in the dialogue between different languages of an original and a translation that many significant details emerge, details that neither text by itself can articulate.[44] Reading Hughes requires us to think of translation not as a set of exchangeable and reproducible meanings but epistemologically, "as a cognition and a recognition," and hence as a function of the "diverse inhabitation" of the medium of language.[45] To translate is "to set language against itself," which, Chambers explains, "is to wrest from language itself the truth that it is always partial and partisan: it speaks for someone and from a specific place, it constructs a particular space, a habitat, a sense of belonging and being at home."[46] Because of this partiality, translation generates questions about where one belongs and what can and cannot be carried across linguistic and other cultural divides.

Such questions, many of them quandaries, seem never to have been far from Hughes's mind, whether he contemplated the cultural relations between, say, Cuba, Mexico, Haiti, and the USA, or between Anglo, Jewish, and African America. In these contemplations, he was alert to what eludes representation but might still be felt and expressed otherwise. And "otherwise" for Hughes is always a mode of translation, of "assuming in the openness of our language other inscriptions, further sense."[47] Borrowing from another famous traveler, Alexander von Humboldt, I think of this openness to other meanings and perspectives as a form of "world-consciousness" (*Weltbewusstsein*), which is an awareness of translation writ large. Tracing how this sensibility shaped Hughes's writings requires recourse to translation as a literary practice and a multilayered metaphoric system. For it is translation that helps bring into sharper focus overlapping movements across all sorts of political and conceptual borders.

Since linguistic multiplicity is inevitably part of all discourses that are truly transnational, research on the literary aspects of these discourses, no matter what their assigned social color, would do well to consider the practical and theoretical dimensions of translation. With some exceptions, however, processes of translation themselves have rarely moved to the forefront of attention in scholarly work informed by (Black) Atlanticist paradigms.[48] Yet translation's metaphors proliferate in and animate those very academic discourses: we read about ideas that "carry over" more or less well, successful and unsuccessful "border crossings," and all sorts of directional "routes" and "routings." It is hardly a secret that translation is one of the necessary vehicles for globalization and has been for a long time. Ironically, its very ubiquity in our scholarly and quotidian lives seems to have made us almost entirely oblivious to its workings.[49]

Literary translation, a form of cultural mediation that is not as easily consumable as most of the amalgamated information with which the popular media envelop us, has fared no better in this respect. I have attempted in this book to make a case for why translations and translators need to be more visible in scholarship on literature and in other cultural exchanges. Those engaged in translation studies have done that for some time now. More important, however, translation theorists have yet sufficiently to consider situations in which "foreign" texts are ferried to what is now known as "the global South," that is, postcolonial settings and languages—despite the fact that this is the direction in which most translations travel.[50] There is no question, for instance, that the work of translators is a fundamental part of the vast international networks we vaguely term modernist and that translation connects African American modernists from the USA with postcolonial writers in other parts of the world.[51] Without analyzing in some detail when, where, and why translations came about and how they transformed both literary texts and writers' reputations, we have only very limited access to the processes of literary history as they unfold across languages. Translation studies, reception history, and literary history have no choice but to work hand in glove.

TRANSLATION AND/AS "WORLD LITERATURE"

Where, then, does a text in translation *belong*? Like Hughes's own translations, this body of literature has largely disappeared in the cracks between different literature and language departments and in the territorial gaps between various interdisciplines and area studies, such as African American, USA/North American, and Latin American studies. As is typically the fate of literary translations, the organization of academic specialties around the literatures and languages assigned to nations has made it difficult to figure out which field should claim responsibility for these texts and their "*effective* life as world literature," as David Damrosch has it.[52] Comparative literature has been of relatively little help because it, too, has tended at least implicitly to hold fast to the idea of national literatures by fetishizing original literary production. Working around the static opposition of national and world literatures to which even theories of "migration literature" still tend to subscribe, I take seriously the idea that translation does not just *produce* world literature but in fact *is* world literature. It is world literature by being actively present in multiple literary systems *at the same time*. Important is not movement from one fixed place definable as a point of origin to another but movement among many changing locations—what might be called "translocation."[53]

The movement and direction of translations help us recognize the work of individual writers as something that is constituted at the intersection of worldwide intellectual and artistic trajectories, or vectors.[54] As David Johnston has noted: "The existence of a text is not a bounded site, but rather an itinerary between there and here, then and now, and that itinerary is configured by a series of translations that take place in and across the various temporal and cultural engagements.... [Translation] is a way of thinking about time and space that privileges movement rather than stasis, transformation rather than belonging."[55] The very existence of translations has fundamentally shifted the national or ethnic borders within which writers such as Langston Hughes have traditionally been enclosed. Such shifts suggest that it is more fruitful to regard Hughes as a nexus than as a solitary author who wrote in a single language identified with a particular nation. By reading Hughes's life and texts as moving parts of a global network, I eschew the conventions of the single-author study in favor of writing comparative literary and cultural history. My model is Langston Hughes himself. To be able to dwell in transnational residences, Hughes broke the established rules of autobiography and lyric poetry alike. Following his lead, I work against the pronounced trend in New Americanist inquiry to privilege a specific genre (usually the novel), a single geocultural location (usually the USA), and a language seen as somehow unified (usually USAmerican English). I focus instead on the irregular historical imbrication of autobiography, poetry, literary translations, and oral testimony to reconstruct important chapters in the story of literary modernism as an international formation.

At issue in this book, then, is not literary influence as a formalist textual phenomenon but the human dimensions of literary history and the material circumstances in which acts of writing and reading are always embedded. I want to know how avant-garde writers interacted with each other and what transient artistic, intellectual, and political communities formed at certain historical moments at certain crossroads. As Hughes creates shifting, and shifty, autobiographical and lyrical personae to pry apart the discursive manifestations of ideologies that would have either assailed or altogether denied his existence as a writer and a nonheterosexual male, he often foregrounds situations in which the process of translation either falters or breaks down altogether to strip away the veneer of shared assumptions about racial and sexual identity and national community.[56] Rejecting the simple *appearance* of shared cultural and political values, he portrays himself as a migrant whose desire for belonging leads him to create provisional communities.

I think of them as open communities that are fundamentally, and perhaps paradoxically, based on accretion, not exclusion. For Hughes, these mobile spaces are intellectual and emotional alternatives to the home he did not feel he had in the USA. The communities I construct as I retrace Hughes's own itineraries and those of his texts in translation also and not infrequently lead us to places he himself never visited in person.

The "geography of crossing points" in which I am most interested here is located in Harlem, Havana, Madrid, Mexico City, and Buenos Aires, not the well-explored modernist hubs of London and Paris.[57] These intellectual way stations or crossroads are (on) the fringes of modernism as we know it in the English-speaking world, geographically, linguistically, and aesthetically. That neither Spanish nor Portuguese is typically considered a major language of modernism shows just how sharply the history of modernists' intellectual and artistic exchanges diverges from their marginalization in relation to assumed European and Anglo-American centers. The linguistic dimensions that these sites, and the itineraries that connect them, add to Atlanticist inquiry skews more familiar triangles into jagged polyhedrons. The irregular shape of these sites is all the more precarious for incorporating "the cuts in and interruptions of the existing modalities of historical knowledge" that postcolonial studies have brought into view during most of the twentieth century.[58] Hughes's hemispheric networks, then, do not exist in isolation from larger global currents. Whatever impact Hughes may have had on other writers in the Americas and elsewhere, "influence" does not begin to describe the reciprocity and multidirectionality that characterize the literary affinities that make up global modernism. That postcolonial writers from different parts of the planet continue to pick up loose ends that lead back to marginalized modernists may well account for the long afterlife Hughes's writings continue to enjoy in other worlds and in others' words.

CHAPTER ONE

NOMAD HEART

Heterolingual Autobiography

> Tu as promené ton cœur nomade, comme un Baedeker, de
> Harlem à Dakar
> La mer a prêté à tes chants un rythme doux et rauque, et
> ses fleurs d'amertume de écume.
>
> [You carried your nomad heart, like a Baedeker, from / Harlem to Dakar /
> The sea gave your songs a sweet, rasping rhythm, and / its bitter flowers
> opened up in the spume.]
>
> —Jacques Roumain, "Langston Hughes"

How does a person such as Langston Hughes, who lived in and between worlds, write an autobiography in the first place? How does one write a self when that self is perpetually displaced, put at risk, and not just by actual travel? Autobiography is an exceedingly vexed literary genre with ill-defined boundaries that tends to raise a host of expectations about what subjectivity is and how it is to be represented. Autobiographies that stray into fiction by blurring the line between imagined and lived experience create problems for most readers. These days, they are readily deemed fraudulent and censored publicly. Add to this the fact that readers' requirements for black autobiography have historically been quite specific and inflexible.[1] Writing almost a hundred years after Frederick Douglass penned his paradigmatic 1845 *Narrative of the Life of Frederick Douglass*, Hughes had considerably more freedom to reshape autobiographical convention. What it meant to him to "tell a free story" was unlike what it had meant to Douglass even in his later autobiographical writing, for what Hughes had to contend with in the 1940s and 1950s were different politics and strictures. There were substantial pressures on a black autobiographer in the USA to construct himself as a subject that would *represent* African Americans in just the right ways: as valued citizens and loyal patriots. Hughes faced this issue not just in one but in two autobiographies, *The Big Sea* (1940) and *I Wonder As I Wander* (1956). The second one was, for the most part, written after his testimonies before the McCarthy Committee, whose members subjected Hughes to their own autobiographical misreadings. I analyze those hearings at length in chapter 5. In this chapter I lay the groundwork for extending to Hughes's writings, which I consider intercultural by definition, Japanese comparatist Naoki Sakai's notion of "heterolingual address."[2] My path is not a straight one but a weaving together of texts and a host of intertexts, including the Spanish translations of Hughes's autobiographies, around scenes of translation.

NOT IN KANSAS ANYMORE

When Langston Hughes arrived in Moscow in 1930 to write the dialogue for a Meshrabpom movie about Negro workers in Birmingham, Alabama, he encountered some unforeseen stumbling blocks.[3] For one, the German director, "especially imported from abroad for this film," spoke neither Russian nor English or French well (*IW*, 79, 90). For another, and to make matters worse, everything was written in Russian. As Hughes relates in *I Wonder As I Wander*,

> The script of the film we were to make consisted of an enormous number of pages when I first saw it—entirely in Russian! Just like my contract, it had to be translated. This took two or three weeks. . . . At first I was astonished at what I read. Then I laughed until I cried. And I wasn't crying really because the script was in places so mistaken and so funny. I was crying because the writer meant well, but knew so little about his subject and the result was a pathetic hodgepodge of good intentions and faulty facts. With his heart in the right place, the writer's concern for racial freedom and decency had tripped so completely on the stumps of ignorance that his work had fallen as flat as did Don Quixote's valor when good intentions led that slightly demented knight to do battle with he-knew-not-what. (*IW*, 76)

Hughes leaves us with the impression that the ill-fated feature, "a kind of trade-union version of the Civil War all over again" (*IW*, 79), might have been a fascinating part of film history. At the time, however, the various mishaps surrounding its production were sources of seemingly endless frustration for the cast and, for Hughes, the stuff of hilarious anecdotes. But the "pathetic hodgepodge" of misunderstandings and mistranslations does much more literary work for Hughes here. Although the writing seems wholly monolingual, Hughes plays with several layers of significance that revolve around the acts of (failed) translation he thematizes. In this way, he makes his readers aware that the premises of his own writing are heterolingual and heterocultural. For instance, the film script Hughes might have written but did not in the end would have been an American translation of the English translation from the initial Russian, and the distance between these three texts would not just have been marked by time. Doing such literary work in the first place also depended on the satisfactory completion of another translation, that of Hughes's contract. Once we consider the implications of all the translations that quixotically proliferate in this brief passage, it dawns on us that, for Hughes, the very act of writing is always a translation whose sources are prior translations. Does this sound like Jorge Luis Borges? Russia may not, in the end, be as far away from Argentina as we think, especially not with Cervantes mediating our passage.

My brief excerpt is one of the many droll tales with which Hughes regaled readers in both *I Wonder* and *The Big Sea*. It was precisely because of such passages that reviewers have quite consistently showered Hughes with deprecatory adjectives such as "shallow and slick" and "pedestrian and thin" (*CR*, 274). The reception of *The Big Sea* was overall more generous than that of *I Wonder As I Wander*, which reviewers targeted for proffering little beyond an affable "smiling surface," with Hughes telling us "about himself but not of his self" (*CR*, 275).[4] Writing for the *New Masses* in 1940, Ralph Ellison carped about Hughes's "avoid[ance] of analysis and comment" (*CR*, 261). "One wishes that more of life had irked him," Alain Locke scoffed when he reviewed *The Big Sea* for *Opportunity* in 1941, adding that "important things are glossed over in anecdotal fashion, entertainingly but superficially" (*CR*, 274). Worse yet, Milton Rugoff patronizingly opined in the *New York Herald Tribune* that Hughes's autobiographical prose was "characterized by a tolerance, simplicity and unpretentiousness that borders on the naïve" (*CR*, 241). The only African American writer who raised his voice in Hughes's defense was Richard Wright. "Hughes is tough," Wright wrote in the *New Republic* in 1940, "he bends but he never breaks, and he has carried on a manly tradition in literary expression when many of his fellow writers have gone to sleep at their posts" (*CR*, 269). While it is difficult to say exactly what Wright meant by "manly," I suspect that his idea of masculinity was rather at variance with Hughes's. The notion of "manliness" recurs in Henry Lappin's review for the *Buffalo Evening News Magazine*, in which he calls *The Big Sea* "the first attempt by a Negro to write a full and manly account of the recent history of Negro literature in the United States" (*CR*, 237). What is drowned out by this nearly unanimous chorus of detractors is the fact that in both autobiographies Hughes does tell plenty about himself as a person and a literary artist. This is not to mention the fact that both autobiographies also put in evidence plenty of "modernist complexities" beneath seemingly tactful surfaces.[5] One simply has to know where to look or how to listen. I argue in this chapter that early reviewers and many later scholars have let their own expectations of what an African American autobiography should be get in the way of reading how and what Hughes actually wrote.

On the one hand, then, Hughes's literary artistry as an autobiographer has been neglected and misrecognized due to readers' unwarranted insistence that knowledge of the text give them access to knowledge of the autobiographer's private self. On the other hand, that self had to have the shape of a distinctively "black" identity. Zora Neale Hurston's *Dust Tracks on a Road* (1942), which Robert Hemenway admits can be "a discomfiting book," also fell victim to this peculiar version of the autobiographical fallacy. Reviewers' criticisms of Hurston's "folksiness" and her "raceless" posture are echoes of the charges of naïveté leveled at Hughes. But Hurston's case is not strictly analogous to Hughes's, in part because much was edited out of *Dust Tracks* after the Japanese attack on Pearl Harbor, especially Hurston's not-so-tactful criticisms of USAmerican foreign policy.[6] Ironically, what the expectation of a self revealed disregards is an author's concern with audience. The question of audience was particularly fraught for African American writers in the USA prior to the civil rights movement and the defeat of Jim Crow legislation. His remarks in "The Negro Artist and the Racial Mountain" (1926) notwithstanding, Hughes was no less sensitive to and at times apprehensive about audience expectations than were other New Negro writers: "What can he [a black writer in the USA] presume about an audience, however liberal or even progressive, that is not predominantly black? What is the appropriate discourse for an audience whose power he distrusts but must nonetheless respect? And what is the relation of one's subjective vision to a public sphere in which every word can be (mis)judged?"[7] John Lowney poses these questions specifically for the 1940s, "the era of incipient anti-Communist hysteria" and "red smear" campaigns. They apply equally to earlier and later decades.

Why, then, would anyone expect an African American autobiographer living in the USA in the early 1930s, and especially in the mid-1950s when the so-called Red Scare was in decline but by no means over, to reveal his innermost thoughts for all the world to see? Given antiblack racism, red-baiting, homophobia, and other pressures that existed during Hughes's lifetime, would it not be perfectly understandable that *The Big Sea,* as one reviewer noted, has an "odd quality of seeming to be written in two moods—one that is explicit and another that follows through like an undercurrent"? Could we not expect that parts of *I Wonder* might seem "strangely evasive" and that, along with the value of frankness, Hughes also knows "the value of reticence"?[8] To Hughes, being reticent about his personal life would have been a matter of sheer survival.

Reserve might also help explain why *I Wonder As I Wander,* which commences roughly where *The Big Sea* leaves off, did not extend the later volume's time frame into Hughes's then present. Although *I Wonder* is twice the length of *The Big Sea,* it ends at the start of 1938, covering barely seven years, whereas the first autobiography spans twenty-nine, from Hughes's birth in Joplin, Missouri, in 1902 to 1931. Arnold Rampersad attributes this disparity to the fact that "the second volume of autobiography presented challenges and opportunities that Hughes had not quite anticipated," veteran writer though he was (*BS,* xi). It is more plausible, however, that Hughes, in the immediate wake of his broadcast testimony before the McCarthy

Committee—he began to work on *I Wonder* in 1954—might have responded to this harrowing experience by turning to his earlier travels to make certain political points. Notably, Hughes devoted a great number of pages to his stay in the Soviet Union in 1932–33, leaving few doubts about his positive, though by no means uncritical, impressions of a Soviet-style government.[9] If what had initially motivated Hughes had been a desire to set his own political record straight in ways that he could not have during that testimony, his defiance did not last long. Only two years later, he excised the same Russia chapters from *The Langston Hughes Reader* (1958). Most significant about the writing of *I Wonder* is that Hughes took imaginative recourse to travel writing to work through what was clearly a personal and political crisis of major proportions (see chapter 5). He did so in ways that allowed him to come away with his dignity intact, at least for the most part.[10]

The historical exigencies impinging on Hughes's acts of self-writing are linked to broader theoretical concerns about autobiography as a literary genre. The usual premise of autobiographical referentiality is that life-writing is a more or less transparent record of an already completed and hence fixed subject, a self, and that we can therefore move from knowing the text to knowing that self without any obstructions.[11] What if the autobiographer constructs a self that would not exist otherwise, that is more than a more or less mimetic representation of the external reality we call life?[12] Since the very act of writing is "an integral and often decisive phase of the drama of self-definition,"[13] an autobiographer's may well not represent the kind of self we expect, or perhaps not even a self at all. This is very much so in Hughes's case. Stubbornly refusing to turn self-inscription into self-revelation, Hughes put pressure on the "two universals—truth and the first-person 'I'—that [popularly] define the genre of autobiography."[14] As a result, *The Big Sea* and *I Wonder As I Wander* redirect readers' attention to the very obstructions themselves, that is, to Hughes's *literary* strategies, which displace the figure of the author and set it in motion, making it a point of departure, not perpetual arrival.[15]

Some reviewers did notice "style" in *The Big Sea* but complained, as Ellison rather unreasonably did, about "too much attention…given to the esthetic aspects of experience at the expense of its deeper meanings."[16] But it is precisely in the "esthetic aspects" that the "deeper" meanings reside, as the future author of *Invisible Man* (1953) would have been well aware. Straddling the fact-fiction divide, Hughes's autobiographies should be read as we read his verse: by paying close attention not to the obvious narrative line but to the elements that disrupt that line, throw it off course. The pattern of these breaks creates an *implied* beat over which Hughes tends to linger, as any experienced musician or poet would.[17] Ellison would have called this communicating on the "lower frequencies."

Ellison's metaphor alerts us to the importance of sound as a vehicle for knowledge in Hughes's writing, where the interplay between phonetics and visual representations is always troubled, not infrequently leading to some form of violence when thematized. Iain Chambers's point about the problematic of the visual as a privileged vehicle for knowledge applies directly to the role of sound in Hughes's poetics: "[W]e have inherited the centrality of visuality as the hegemonic modality of humanist knowledge, leading, via cartography, writing, and visual representation, to the continual reconfirmation of the I/eye in every corner of the globe. *The gaze is rarely able to attend to listening, is unable to accommodate a reply.*"[18] Hughes's autobiographies, like his poems, require that we *listen*, not just look, for what he calls, in yet another turn of the figure of the sea, "the *undertow* of black music with its rhythm that never betrays you, its strength like the beat of the human heart, its humor, and its rooted power" (*BS*, 209; my emphasis).

The concept of the implied beat—the undertow of black music—confers upon Hughes's prose the rhythmic qualities of what Amiri Baraka has famously called the "changing same."[19] Hughes himself connects his autobiographical writing with African American music when, in "Jazz as Communication" (1943), he riffs on the poetic metaphor from which *The Big Sea* takes its title—"Life is a big sea/ full of many fish. / I let down my nets / and pull" turns into "Jazz is a great big sea. It washes up all kinds of fish and shells and spume and waves with a steady old beat, or off-beat."[20] Hughes's repetitions turn life ("Life is a big sea"), literature ("Literature is a big sea," *BS*, 335), and jazz into intertranslatable terms; that is, they are perpetually translated into one another. Through this process of intertranslation, "jazz seeps into [Hughes's] words." I agree with Anita Patterson and others that jazz appealed to "Eliot and other avant-gardists during the 1920s, in part because the music affirmed their cosmopolitan outlook, enabled their struggle against conformity with tradition, and aided their engagement with vernacular sources."[21] Jazz, however, did something more for Hughes, whom Patterson also includes in her statement. It made his words move differently, inflecting their overtones and undertones to convey gradations of delight and despair at the same time.[22] That Hughes also applied the words "overtones and undertones" to "the relations between Negroes and whites in this country [the USA]" points to an aesthetics awash in the history of race relations (*Essays*, 33).

In Hughes's prose, no less than in his poetry, proximity to the formal structures of jazz results in privileging diachronic movement and sound over stasis and visuality. "Music," Larry Scanlon explains, "defines its formal elements precisely by their *movement through time*. To highlight the affinities between music and poetry is to highlight the diachronic aspect of poetic form."[23] Diachrony, of course, does not mean linearity or unidirectionality. Hughes tends to encode movements through time in tropes of transit, that is, movement through space. By aligning spatial movement with the formal properties of jazz, Hughes creates poetic patterns that emphasize cyclicality and reversibility. Layering these patterns in writing creates the effect of multidirectional movements across spatial geographies and temporal grids. Pasts, presents, and futures are no longer arranged along a single vector that points in one direction; instead, they are *locations* from which one can move in different directions and to which one can return at will and repeatedly. In this way diachronic patterns work together with synchronic arrangements. In Hughes's texts, their copresence always makes available histories of musical and literary forms as destinations in the past linked with particular actual and symbolic geographies. For Hughes, the rural history of the blues is always already inscribed in urban jazz, so that the question is never whether Hughes's is a blues or a jazz aesthetic. It is inevitably both.[24]

A brief excursion to W.C. Handy, a Memphis musician whom Hughes admired tremendously, helps clarify how this jazz/blues aesthetic might work in Hughes's writing. Handy's celebrated and beautifully illustrated *Blues: An Anthology* appeared in print the same year as Hughes's *Weary Blues*. In *Father of the Blues*, his own autobiography, W.C. Handy talks about how he transformed "bits of music or snatches of song" into fully fledged blues compositions "embellished by my harmonizations and rhythm."[25] Jürgen Grandt astutely concludes from this passage that "[t]herefore, Handy's blues are a product of pastiche and collage and result from the collisions of the snatches of folk songs, field hollers, and other vernacular musics on the one hand, with his classical training and inclinations on the other, and are thus thoroughly modernist." Hughes's autobiographical anecdotes work in the same way that Handy's "snatches" of different tunes do: they are blues composition in the making. For "all its eclecticism," Grandt continues, Handy "sees his music standing firmly within a greater African American tradition. The arc of this tradition, in the case of his famous 'St. Louis Blues,' reached from Africa to Argentina and Spain to Cuba (via the tango) and then to St. Louis."[26] This is the arc Hughes himself imagined. If he did not complete its full span in his actual travels, his books, as we shall see, went the rest of the way for him.

By the same logic, setting out also implies a return, or returns, to history and tradition. The relationship between what we tend to see as two separate movements is fluid in Hughes's writing, but it is not shapeless. The concept of syndesis, which Edward Pavlić has transplanted from anthropology to African American literary scholarship, explains this process well. Building on Robert Plant Armstrong's use of syndesis to describe "[Yorùbá] cultural systems organized by aligning voices or rhythms in multiple layers of repeating cycles," Pavlić suggests that "syndesis creates a fluid and dynamic relationship between repetition and variation, as well as between past and present. The interplay between repetition and variation situates the past emerging in the consciousness of the participants in a fluid but structured milieu."[27] To Pavlić, these insights about the participants in Yorùbá ritual ceremonies can be applied to African American literature from the USA as well. The challenge he poses for what he calls "syndetic criticism" in the context of African American studies "is to describe how the [symbolic] spaces [of North and South] overlap, how the social patterns shape the contours of personal space and vice versa." He adds that "the best theoretical exploration of these issues often occurs in the literature itself."[28] While I concur with both statements, I find that analyzing Hughes's work makes it necessary to enlarge the range of symbolic spaces, or "ritual grounds," relevant to African American literature.[29]

While repetition as a literary trope tends to be most palpable in the formal elements through which Hughes's poems situate themselves in relation to literary, vernacular, and musical traditions, it is no less evident in his autobiographies. The effect of Hughes's lingering over the implied or offbeat in his autobiographies opens up textual spaces in which selves can multiply. These selves are not simply mimetic extensions of the historical Hughes, even when the narrated events reflect on his lived experiences. Rather, they are the result of repetitions with a difference at the level of theme and character. I argue that the proliferating selves in Hughes's autobiographies and verse are closely linked to human and textual interactions that involve more than one language. When Hughes's selves engage with each other and with presumed Others they encounter as a result of travel, they create possibilities for communality out of what I call translational performances. Such performances model—*sound* out, if you will—relations among humans that work against, and as a result render audible and visible, "conditions of dialogue in which the different powers, histories, limits and languages that permit the process of 'othering' to occur are inscribed."[30] That is, possible communal relations are tested out without necessarily being resolved. Unlike identity, which is an unmoving social delimiter, selfhood—being a person—is crucially a function of *being in translation*,[31] of translating and being translated in turn. The same ontology applies to the kind of human community that acts of translation make possible, even if only for a limited time. Translation, then, is always at least implicitly at issue in any multilingual literary practice, even, and especially, when mutual understanding remains either elusive or is not, in the end, an exclusive function of language. What makes the translational performances in Hughes's autobiographies especially valuable for inquiring into how "social patterns shape the contours of personal space and vice versa" is their status as highly self-conscious acknowledgments of the possibilities *and* limits of creating communities across languages and cultures.

Since this issue of subjectivity connects Hughes's autobiographies with his verse, it is odd that until quite recently academic readers have virtually ignored *The Big Sea* and *I Wonder As I Wander*. It is as if Arnold Rampersad's remarks about Hughes's "honest, water-clear prose" (*BS*, xxv) have left most scholars with little more to add.[32] Few have explored Rampersad's suggestion that "deeper meaning is deliberately concealed within a seemingly disingenuous, apparently transparent, or even shallow narrative"

(*BS*, xvii). What appears to have escaped notice altogether is that both of Hughes's autobiographies teem with tales of linguistic adventures and misadventures in both domestic and foreign settings, settings in which one translates oneself and is being translated in turn. While some have commented on the use of different languages in Hughes's poetry, even the sheer frequency of multilingual scenes in his autobiographical writings has gone almost entirely unnoticed.[33] The insistence with which Hughes draws attention to translation in all sorts of settings is indeed striking. Whether traveling to closer or more remote areas of the world, including the outer reaches of the former Soviet Union, Hughes always, and repeatedly, remarks on the linguistic "bedlam" that was going on around him—conversations in Haitian Kréyòl, Uzbek, Tajik, Russian, Georgian, and Tartar (*IW*, 17, 149). I propose to read the tales of linguistic adventures and misadventures in *The Big Sea* and *I Wonder As I Wander* as traces of "syndetic cultural patterns [that] resist the stable and ordering influences of modern rationalization."[34] The passage I quoted at the outset of this section is but one of countless instances that show Hughes's keen awareness of the ever-present potential for cultural misunderstandings across languages and cultures. In the case of the unfortunate film script, the reasons for misapprehension are not linguistic incompetence but a lack of cultural knowledge. The hapless Russian writer had produced "a script improbable to the point of ludicrousness" because he had—unsurprisingly at the time—never traveled to the USA, relying instead on the "very few books about contemporary Negro life in our country [that] had been translated into Russian" (*IW*, 76). The film script, then, is already a translation of a translation even before being rendered in English: "Imagine the white workers of the North clashing with the southern mobs of Birmingham on the road outside the city, the red forge of the steel mills in the background, and the militant Negroes eventually emerging from slums and cabins to help with it all!" (*IW*, 79). "It would have looked wonderful on the screen," Hughes admits, "so well do the Russians handle crowds in films"—"Russians" meaning director Sergei Eisenstein, who threw a party for the cast in Moscow. There is only one small problem: superimposing a Soviet future upon a USAmerican past creates a clash of cultural sensibilities that, to Hughes, distorts the present almost beyond recognition. Like the movie scene in which a "hot-blooded white aristocrat" from Alabama would ask the "lovely dark-skinned servant" to dance at a party, "it just couldn't be true. It was not even plausible fantasy—being both ahead of and far behind the times" (*IW*, 78, 79).

While Hughes's recourse to Cervantes's "slightly demented knight" is a suitable response to this travesty, invoking *Don Quixote* also has another effect. As a literary reference, Cervantes represents the undercurrent of another generic mode in this autobiographical narrative: not the *Quixote*'s parody of courtly love but the picaresque whose tricky legacy—*fictional autobiography*—is one of the keys to Hughes's episodic inscriptions in both

I Wonder and *The Big Sea*. None other than a rather paternal Carl Van Vechten points us in this very direction when, in his introductory remarks on Hughes's "picturesque and rambling" life in *The Weary Blues*, he projects how Hughes might set up his autobiographical writing: "[A] complete account of his disorderly and delightfully fantastic career would make a fascinating *picaresque romance* which I hope this young Negro will write before so much more befalls him that he may find it difficult to capture all the salient episodes within the limits of a single volume."[35] Van Vechten was right; one volume did indeed prove insufficient. Given that both of Hughes's autobiographies lay claim to a far-flung literary genealogy in which Cervantes and Lazarillo de Tormes sit gleefully with Frederick Douglass and Brer Rabbit, it is no accident that trickster figures akin to the wily pícaro populate Hughes's autobiographies.[36] Gatesians would probably prefer the figure of the "Signifyin' Monkey," a trope that comes to life in the seemingly extraneous story of Jocko, the riotous monkey Hughes brings back from Africa only to have him defecate on a pool table (*BS*, 131–37).[37] The pícaro, who signifies in similar textual ways, is surely a branch of a family tree that sprouted in very close proximity to North Africa. Yet simply conflating the Spanish pícaro with the West African figure of Esu-Elegba on which Henry Louis Gates bases his theory has the serious disadvantage of rendering imperceptible Hughes's allusion to the picaresque novel. This allusion enables a discussion of narrative structure here in ways that Gates's theoretical framework does not. A wonderful example of the pícaro in *The Big Sea* is the sailor named George (no last name) on whom I will comment below. In *I Wonder*, there is Emma, the former actress who presumably makes a living as a translator but is really too busy *playing* a socialite "Kentucky Mammy" in Moscow (*IW*, 83–84). There are also "Yeah Man," the woman chaser—whose "Russian was far worse than mine when he would try to speak it at all.... most of the women never knew a word that he said"—and Yusef Nishanov aka Nichan, who "knew about a hundred words of Russian—our only language in common" (*IW*, 112, 144). This is not to mention the ubiquitous *besprizorni*, the street urchins who lurk at every corner (see *IW*, 152–53). And let us not forget Sylvia Garner, the only one of the movie's USAmerican cast to defy "that old cliché that all Negroes just naturally sing—without effort" (*IW*, 80). Sylvia's antics deserve a close look.

Sylvia, who "became an American folk-song star on the Moscow radio" (*IW*, 81), in many ways exemplifies the figure of the translator-as-trickster. Hughes recounts that because of Soviet restrictions, when spirituals were sung, "the words *God, Lord, Christ*, or *Jesus* were not to be used... Sylvia would substitute whatever word came into her head" (81). Because her Russian listeners presumably did not understand English, or not well enough, she could get away with substitutions that were quite comical and perhaps as heretical as Lazarillo's would have been in sixteenth-century Spain: "My God is so high, you can't get over Him, you can't get under Him," came out as "Old mike is so high, I can't get over it, I can't get under it! Oh, this mike is so high! Hallelujah!" (*IW*, 82). The most compelling scene for my purposes is the one prompted by Sylvia's stubbornness: "I'm tired of faking. I'm gonna get God into my program today." Her friends are understandably skeptical.

All of us had our ears glued to the radio receivers in the Grand Hotel. When Sylvia came on the air that night, she opened with, "Oh, rise and shine and give God the glory." Only what she actually sang was:

> *Rise and shine*
> *And give Dog the glory! Glory!*
> *Rise and shine!*
> *Give Dog the glory.* (*IW, 82*)

This episode resonates with the earlier scene not because it performs or thematizes translation as such or because Sylvia modifies the original song lyric by using wordplay worthy of Ezra Pound. More important is that Hughes shows here how the linguistic distance between Russian and English can be strategically exploited to circumvent censorship. In the case of the botched movie script, that distance is more cultural than linguistic, and the attempt to cross it produces the effect of a "burlesque" (*IW*, 76), an unwitting hybrid. In Sylvia's performance of the spiritual, the comic effect of her substitutions is entirely lost on her Muscovite listeners, as "Them Russians don't understand English." Had they understood English, they, as presumably good Stalinist comrades, might have actually appreciated her sacrilegious humor. Initially, Sylvia's ingenious anagrammatic solutions are lost even on her American friends, who seem slow to comprehend exactly where God is in that song. "Where He ought to be,' said Sylvia. 'What is d-o-g but God spelled backwards?'" While the joke may not have been lost on Hughes's English-speaking readers—clearly, puns such as this one do not translate into another language[38]—they nevertheless seem to have missed the fact that Sylvia functions as a foil for the autobiographer himself here. It is plausible that Hughes would use this anecdote to call attention to the sly strategies he employs in his own writing, including in this very text.

As a picaresque trickster figure whose African American literary pedigree includes memorable characters such as Hughes's own Jesse B. Semple[39] and Charles Chesnutt's resourceful Uncle Julius in *The Conjure Woman* stories, among many others, Sylvia throws the proverbial monkey wrench in the gears of the Soviet government's authority by feigning compliance with its restrictions on free expression. As autobiographer, Hughes confronts not Soviet censorship but the entrenched racial and social biases of his USAmerican readers and the presumed unavailability of "true self-consciousness" to African Americans who, according to W.E.B. Du Bois, were stuck with an ironically lesser version: "double consciousness." I quite agree with Kate Baldwin that Hughes's goal as a writer was not "*proper* self-consciousness" (my emphasis), that is, the idea of an integrated, immutable, and supposedly unreachable self. Baldwin's related point, that Hughes refused to link African American art with lamentation and victimhood, is equally valuable.[40] Hughes shared this rejection with Zora Neale Hurston, who was similarly opposed to being classed with what she, in 1928, rather unkindly dubbed the "sobbing school of Negrohood who hold that nature somehow has given them a lowdown dirty deal."[41] While Baldwin makes her case by focusing mainly on Hughes's writings in and about Russia — notably the pieces about central Asia he purged from *I Wonder* and from *The Langston Hughes Reader* after his brush with McCarthyism in 1953 — Hughes's lack of desire for a proper self, or any *one* self for that matter, is evident well before then. Hughes's resistance to Du Bois's idea of "double consciousness" as both African and American went very much against the grain of dominant discourses about black male identity during and after the Harlem Renaissance.[42] The literary articulations of his opposition, however, follow the strategy of outward compliance that we see in Sylvia's circumventions of political restrictions. As Hughes shows, such subtle tactics are easy to miss or to misread.

Through the kinds of sundry spaces that translational performances allow him to create, Hughes, like Sylvia, hides his political moves in plain literary sight. Hughes's prose teems with words and phrases from an array of languages; some are translated, most not. The effect of this textual cohabitation is that the linguistic fabric of English becomes marvelously flexible. Like Hughes himself, at least in Richard Wright's estimation, Hughes's brand of American English bends, but it does not break. Significantly, translation is a function of marvel, or "wonder," that, for Hughes, is always part of his Whitmanian physical and spiritual roaming the world: wandering *is* wondering; such movement becomes wondrous through the simple substitution of a vowel. Hughes's purported poetic realism notwithstanding, the literary strategies he employs in his autobiographies are much closer to Alejo Carpentier's *lo maravilloso* (the marvelous) and Gabriel García Márquez's *realismo mágico* (magical realism). Like them, Hughes unexpectedly defamiliarizes what is familiar, though his slanting of reality is slighter. In Iain Chambers's words, "the taken for granted is turned around, acquires an unsuspected twist, and, in becoming temporarily unfamiliar, produces an unexpected, sometimes magical, space."[43] Hughes's purpose in creating such spaces is to bring to the fore the unexamined assumptions that all systems necessarily include, be they linguistic, literary, social, or political.

One way in which Hughes destabilizes the presumed linguistic integrity of USAmerican English is by calling attention to the multiple mediations in his own writing. Linguistic layering characterizes Hughes's stories about his stays in France and Haiti, both places where his "high school French didn't work very well, and...I understood nothing anyone said to me" (*BS,* 144; also *IW,* 20). A Haitian fisherman translates for Hughes a dirge from patois to French, which Hughes quotes together with his own English version (*IW,* 23). Similarly, when speaking of the notebooks he kept in Russia, Hughes acknowledges that "a great many words and figures were translated by Kikilov [head of the Turkoman Writers Union] from Turkoman into Russian to Koestler, and by Koestler from Russian into English to me"; some notes he took "were [even] fourth hand—from Baluchi to Turkoman to Russian to Koestler to English to me" (*IW,* 115, 129). The Hungarian-born Arthur Koestler, whose phobia of contagion Hughes ridicules more than once in *I Wander,* is the only one of Hughes's travel companions in remote central Asia to speak any workable English at all, and Koestler is happy to share the notes that would become the basis for his 1934 travel account, *Von weissen Nächten und roten Tagen (Of White Nights and Red Days).* Their shared language and partially shared politics notwithstanding,[44] Hughes points to fundamental differences between Koestler's perspective on central Asia and his own: "To Koestler, Turkmenistan was simply a *primitive* land moving into twentieth-century civilization. To me, it was a *colored* land moving into orbits hitherto reserved for whites" (*IW,* 116). This remark goes a long way toward explaining Hughes's affinity for the people he encountered in these parts of the world. Tellingly, Hughes's note taking ceases with the departure of his fastidious friend (see *IW,* 138). Left in Bokhara without a translator, Hughes engages in other kinds of translational performances.

Whether enacted or thematized, translation for Hughes is a way of simultaneously registering cultural differences and searching for common ground—*not* necessarily similarities. Stuart Hall has fittingly called what Hughes models "a conception of identity which lives with and through, not despite, difference."[45] As the following episode from *I Wonder* demonstrates, understanding and common ground can be created in all sorts of ways. In Hughes's writing, translations that we would typically regard as failed usually involve recourse to jazz.

[My Mongol-looking friend of the unknown tongue] was a very outgoing fellow,..., lots of fun, intensely active, crazy about my Ooo-wee Harm-Strung records (as he termed Satchmo), a stout vodka drinker, good at wine, a woman chaser and an acrobat....I never did get his name straight, but it sounded like Yeah Tlang, or Yaddle-oang, or Ya-Gekiang. He said it so fast and matter-of-factly, as if I must be familiar with it, that when I slowed him down, it didn't sound the same at all. As nearly as I could gather, it had two and a half or three syllables. I finally settled for a nickname of my own coining. *Yeah Man,* and he called me *Yang Zoon* which seemed to be the best he could do with Langston. Yeah Man was a bright fellow, though I think he was allergic to languages [his Russian was far worse than Hughes's]. But after a while each understood everything the other said—or implied—without strain, and with laughter. (*IW,* 111–12)

Yeah Man and Yang Zoon are, of course, not translations proper. They are phonetic approximations that signal the creation of a linguistically mixed common ground mediated by the undertow of jazz. Here the musically inflected phrase "Ooo-wee Harm-Strung" serves as a springboard for similar onomatopoeia in the space between Mongol and English, as does the shared appreciation for Louis Armstrong's playing.[46] In this act of translation, layers of cultural differences are not erased but respectfully and humorously flaunted; they are amalgamated into an unstrained form of implicit understanding that reaches beyond language. Shared laughter is always a catalyst for successful communication in Hughes's autobiographies, marking the point at which a group of total strangers come together in a makeshift community. Here is an earlier encounter in Turkmenistan, a former Soviet republic.

> A stream of musical inflections filled my ears—but I had not the least idea what he [the bright-eyed, grinning Oriental youth in a spick-and-span Red Army uniform] was saying.... Since he kept right on talking in his musical tongue without a word of Russian mixed in, I began to talk in English. Thus we carried on a conversation in which neither understood the other.... I would have thought understanding under such conditions impossible, but I learned differently. Later, when the teacher came to call on me, it turned out that he spoke *not* English but Flemish. There was at that time no one in Ashkhabad who spoke English—not a human soul. My Red Army friend came from the high Pamirs away up near the Sinkiang border, and spoke only his own strange language. He was a captain of the border guard, and looked like a Chinese Negro, very brown, but with Oriental eyes. He was my friend for weeks, in fact my boon buddy, yet I never knew a word he said. However, when the ear gives up and intuition takes over, some sort of understanding develops instinctively. (*IW*, 110–11)

This passage shows how reciprocal communication requires that one acknowledge the existence of cultural differences and a lack of understanding in the first place ("I had not the least idea what he was saying"). Hughes admits to the limitations of his linguistic skills almost as a matter of course, regardless of whether he is in Moscow, Mongolia, Italy, or Haiti. The fascinating thing, however, is that he never lets linguistic obstacles impede contact. A fitting exception that may prove the rule is Hughes's memorable "blind date" with a Tartar woman, one of the "amatory" episodes of whose frequency some reviewers of *I Wonder As I Wonder* actually complained![47] "I had no idea what language a Tartar spoke," Hughes confesses to his readers. What further compounds the problem is that he and his new friend Hajir, who had arranged the double date, "had no language in common for me to tell him how strangely that Tartar woman had behaved" in resisting what Hughes considered expected sexual advances (*IW*, 158, 163)

Particularly revealing of the different ways in which Hughes uses translation in his autobiographies is the following carefully crafted scene set at a rail depot in Uzbekistan, clearly a figure of the crossroads. Abandoned by the rest of his party, Hughes is waiting for the next train to arrive.

> "*Drasvoti, tovarish.*" I said to a young Uzbek in half-European, half-native clothing—and English-type coat, a tibeteka cap of bright embroidery, and soft, heel-less boots. "Good morning."
>
> He answered in a flow of guitarlike syllables that certainly weren't Russian. I grinned and shook my head. We began with signs. Hand to belly: *hungry.* Fingers pointing down the track with a frown: *disgust, train late.* Hands across brow, then pretending to fan: *hot, sun getting hotter.* He pointed at my face, then at his: *Brown, same color.* But myself, *ni Uzbek.*
>
> "Russki?" he asked.
>
> "Niet," I said, "No. Me, Americanski."
>
> He shrugged. More guitarlike syllables. I thought I might as well speak English since it really didn't matter. Neither of us understood a word but it was fun to talk....He knew two Russian words anyhow. Then back into his own tongue, *king-ting-a-ling-ummm-ding,* which is about the sound of the Uzbek language—a kind of musically tinkling tenor speech, as decorative to hear as Persian script is to see. (*IW*, 141)

Hughes frames the image of cultural hybridity in his description of the young Uzbek's attire with utterances in both Russian and English, the latter being a partial translation of the former. The narrator's Russian greeting, which sets him apart from English-speaking readers much like Yang Zoon does in the previous passage, initiates a dialogue that detours into sign language upon contact with the Uzbek's "guitarlike syllables." Language as the space for communication is displaced onto the body. Once the bodily exchanges reach the issue of identity by way of shared skin color, it is necessary to return to speech to articulate different cultural and political affiliations. Interestingly, Hughes is first identified as "Russki," not as American. Hughes again represents this speaking as a mixture of Russian and English. English phrases that translate gestures to the reader are now cast in italics, usually reserved for unfamiliar languages in an English text. As in other passages from *I Wonder*, the narrator never once pretends to understand the Uzbek, whose words are literally music to Hughes's ears. The young man's shrug, in turn, suggests that he has absolutely no clue what this stranded "Americanski" might be saying. Rather than eliding a tongue he does not comprehend, however, Hughes incorporates it into his text, rendering its musicality through the onomatopoeic approximation *king-ting-a-ling-ummm-ding*—elsewhere he refers to it as "*tinga-a-ling-gong-ling* language" (*IW*, 156). A surprising simile reconciles ear and eye via synesthesia, translating the Uzbek's radical linguistic otherness into aesthetic appeal: to Hughes, this "musically tinkling tenor speech" is "as decorative to hear as Persian script is to see." Although English is the language that mediates this comparison, the culture it represents is not a point of comparison here. The centers of cultural power represented by English are thus sidestepped. It is not just the comparison itself that confers aesthetic pleasure but also the very act of circumventing other political frames for this encounter.

As in the earlier scene with the Oriental-looking youth in a Red Army uniform, no meaning is being transacted between the two speakers once they abandon using gestures. As a result, the simultaneous flow of English and Uzbek—"neither of us understood a word *but it was fun to talk*" (my emphasis)—must be interpreted as a performance in which speech acts signify not so much an effort at comprehension but simply *play*. Important is the mutual engagement in a play with words that is actually far from simple. Such play, once represented in writing, has aesthetic value beyond the element of "fun." Play, which is ritual performance, returns us to repetition. "In nearly all the higher forms of play," writes Johan Huizinga in *Homo Ludens* (1950), the classic study of play in culture, "the element of repetition and alternation...are like the warp and woof of a fabric." The play in this translational scene signals not misapprehension but understanding at a different level: this is mutual understanding, a new form of order, achieved amid cultural and other differences in which the dynamics of play prevent those differences from congealing into otherness. According to Huizinga, play not only "adorns life, amplifies it," but "is in fact freedom."[48]

CALIBAN'S COMPANY

In Hughes's writing, translational scenes of this sort always occur in special places and almost always outside the USA. It was in rented quarters in Uzbekistan that "[c]onversations in Uzbek, Tajik, Russian, Georgian and Tartar flowed around [him] continually. At times, bedlam could hardly have been more linguistic than this room in the former Tszarist—but now Soviet— hotel in Tashkent" (*IW*, 149). Other such spaces include rooms in hotels across the world, train depots in central Asia, Paris nightclubs, and, of course, freighters bound for Africa and Europe. These spaces are important in that they are cultural crossroads of one sort or another: they are temporary locations inhabited by transients from elsewhere who often share "the quick friendship of the dispossessed" (*BS*, 150). Hughes himself is one of those transients and self-consciously so: "Most of my life from childhood on has been spent moving, traveling, changing places, knowing people in one school, in one town or in one group, or on one ship a little while, but soon never seeing most of them again" (*IW*, 101).

Even though Arnold Rampersad suggests that Hughes "craved the affection and regard of blacks to an extent shared by perhaps no other important black writer" (*BS*, xv), Hughes's autobiography shows that his sense of home and belonging is highly conflicted and not cast in familial, national, or racial terms. Here Hughes represents his well-known wanderlust as a direct response to acutely felt anxieties that disturb assumptions about expected affiliations. Both physical dislocation through travel and imaginative displacement through (self) translation—Paul Gilroy calls it "intercultural positionality"—become survival mechanisms for Hughes.[49] In *The Big Sea*, he encodes personal and cultural anxieties about belonging in scenes of misrecognition in which prior assumptions about familial, cultural, or political identities and ties are rendered unstable and often severely ruptured. More often than not, figures of travel and translation enable Hughes to draw out the assumptions behind the identities others readily assign him. In his writing, he replaces assigned identities, be they national, racial, or sexual, with the multiple and shifting truths he ultimately holds dear—truths about himself as a person and about the worlds in which he lived. In response to crises of belonging, such as his lie about being "saved" at Auntie Reed's church (*BS*, 18–21) and his visits with his father in Mexico, Hughes creates provisional communities as contexts in which to assert and safeguard the multiplicity of human values and behaviors that discourses of nation, blackness, and compulsory heterosexuality work hard to deny. This is entirely consistent with the dynamic patterns of divergences and convergences that surface in *I Wonder As I Wander* and especially *The Big Sea*, where tears in the fabric of belonging alternate with the creation of provisional communities through which the original terms of belonging—assumptions about and ascriptions of identity—can be emotionally reevaluated and aesthetically rearticulated.

What most immediately connects travel with writing in Hughes's autobiographies is that both are ways for him to take some measure of control over his life; for him, aesthetic rearticulation is a way of coping emotionally. We should not take lightly that writing itself had a therapeutic function for Hughes, which is clear from repeated admissions that he did most of his writing when he was utterly miserable and lonely: "[M]y best poems were all written when I felt the worst. When I was happy, I didn't write anything" (*BS*, 54; also see 56). Hughes is quite explicit about this relationship when, at the end of the first part of *The Big Sea*, he repeats the text's well-known opening scene on the S.S. *Malone* in which he divests himself of "all the books I had had at Columbia, and all the books I had lately bought to read" (*BS*, 3). This retrospectively melodramatic gesture of divestment is as obviously modernist as it is postcolonial.

> It was like throwing a million bricks out of my heart—for it wasn't only the books that I wanted to throw away, but everything unpleasant and miserable out of my past: the memory of my father, the poverty and uncertainties of my mother's life, the stupidities of color prejudice, black in a white world, the fear

of not finding a job, the bewilderment of no one to talk to about things that trouble you, the feeling of always being controlled by others—by parents, by employers, by some outer necessity not your own. All those things I wanted to throw away. To be free of. To escape from. I wanted to be a man on my own, control my own life, and go my own way. I was twenty-one. So I threw the books in the sea. (*BS*, 98)

This scene benefits from being read with Hughes's dramatic sensibilities as a playwright in mind. In the years leading up to the publication of *The Big Sea*, for instance, Hughes enjoyed quite a bit of success in the theater, starting with the Broadway production of *Mulatto* in October 1935.[50] The Karamu Theater in Cleveland staged three other plays, *Little Ham, Troubled Island*, and *Joy to My Soul* in 1936 and 1937, and *Don't You Want to Be Free?* premiered at the radical Harlem Suitcase Theater in April 1938.[51] Although Hughes was not known for writing melodrama, the self-reflective adjective "melodramatic," with which the autobiographer distances himself from his younger persona's coming-of-age scene, functions as an invitation to read this framing as a carefully staged performance. At the same time that the narrator asserts that "[he] felt grown, a man, inside and out. Twenty-one" (*BS*, 3), Hughes works against the conventions of black *male* autobiography for which Frederick Douglass's 1845 *Narrative* served as prototype.[52] In fact, with his departure from the USA, Hughes places himself beyond the reach of these conventions. This move brings *The Big Sea* closer to postcolonial writing than we have come to expect from an African American text from the USA.[53] Such proximity to postcolonial literatures allows for a host of new affiliations and readings. Hughes casts himself in the role of Caliban seeking to divest himself of Prospero's apocryphal books and the imperial and racist shackles they represent. On the other hand, Hughes's dramatis persona also resembles Shakespeare's Prospero in that he, too, departs an island—Manhattan—tossing his books into the "moving water in the dark off Sandy Hook." (Perhaps he holds on to his magic wand.) Hughes's variations on the Shakespearean plot are not entirely unfamiliar. Rather than being left behind, his Caliban follows in Prospero's footsteps, or so it seems, sailing to Europe but via Africa, where he is ironically misrecognized as a white man. Liberia, also Marcus Garvey's destination (see below), "was the only place in the world where I've ever been called a white man. They looked at my copper-brown skin and straight black hair–like my grandmother's Indian hair, except a little curly—and they said: 'You—white man'" (*BS*, 103). Giving the figure of Caliban the ability to move, to travel and reenact both the Grand Tour and a Middle Passage in reverse is the first of many imaginative revisions of literary and historical sources in *The Big Sea*.[54] Unlike Prospero, an exile on his way back home to Italy, Hughes's Caliban is a nomad for whom home remains elusive on both sides of the Atlantic. By setting Caliban in motion, Hughes maximizes the potential of the figure's cultural and linguistic mixture and multiplicity.[55] Being set in motion here means to travel *and* to inscribe one's own self. For Hughes's Caliban writes his own books, and it is in writing that he seeks to recover his mother tongue. Although he writes in English, it is an English that suffers certain sea changes, as indeed the language we still call English had when it was previously ferried across the Atlantic. What transforms Caliban's English into something rich and strange is the undercurrent of a vernacular voice that engages English in a perpetual state of heterolingualism best described as a state of translation. Bill Ashcroft has specified this dialogue as a "dialogue in difference," arguing that this form of literary contact, typically identified as a characteristic of postcolonial writing, produces "a translated reader, just as it produces a translated/translating writer."[56] Clearly, Hughes's maneuvers in this scene align the cultural and linguistic engagements that characterize African American literature from the USA with the translational situations in other postcolonial writing.

The way in which Hughes initially constructs his autobiographical persona, which strongly suggests an amalgam of Caliban and Prospero, places his literary and cultural sensibilities in close proximity to those of writers from other postcolonial islands, notably C.L.R. James, George Lamming, and Aimé Césaire, who would take issue with the figure of Caliban in their own versions of *The Tempest*.[57] The above passage makes clear that Hughes's younger self, like Shakespeare's Caliban, acts out of a "deep sense of betrayal."[58] The intense psychological and physical pain that Hughes experiences when confronted with betrayal—from his father, his white patron, and some of his fellow writers, notably Hurston[59]—is surely akin to the aches with which Shakespeare's Prospero threatens the monster repeatedly as a punishment for disloyalty, which we can easily read as nonconformity in Hughes's case. Instead of plotting murder, Hughes's Caliban exacts his revenge by making these tales of betrayal part of his autobiography, digesting them for his own purposes of resignification. What concerns him is not revenge but, above all else, his own survival.

I am hardly proposing that *The Tempest* serves as an explanatory matrix for *The Big Sea* as a whole. What I am suggesting, however, is that recourse to Shakespeare's comedy helps illuminate salient features of Hughes's autobiographical self-fashioning. The reason that his personae seem to lack psychological depth is that Hughes's goals in *The Big Sea* are more performative than mimetic. Hughes the dramatist represents aspects of himself as "character-masks,"[60] stylized and highly symbolic figures of memory that multiply and move through his autobiography as if they were actors upon a stage. The performance of which they are part may well be called a *ritual* of self-fashioning.[61] In a sense, Hughes's character-masks become his joint authors. By controlling the movement of these figures, Hughes controls his narrative, deciding what to reveal and what to withhold and how. This control is just as important to Hughes the autobiographer in the late 1930s and the mid-1950s as assuming control over his life is to his twenty-one-year-old persona in 1923. Just how tight Hughes's controls are over his narrative is plain right from the start of *The Big Sea*, where he withholds the fact that his younger self did not, in fact, toss all his books to the sea. He kept one, and not just any one: Walt Whitman's *Leaves of Grass* (see *Life*, 1:xxx).[62] Consider also that the image of radical divestment he constructs here clashes with the figure of the baggage-laden traveler in *I Wonder As I Wonder*. There we encounter Hughes in war-torn Madrid and at a small train depot in the middle of central Asia, surrounded by what appears to be a veritable mountain of luggage, including not just books and a typewriter but also a Victrola and a record box. "It took three trips," he laments, "before I had all my luggage inside the station" (*IW*, 108; also see 394). Although, astonishingly enough, this baggage does not seem to encumber his movements, the self Hughes invents here differs markedly from that of the earlier autobiography. In 1954 he no longer casts himself as a happy-go-lucky vagabond but as a professional writer: "This is the story of a Negro who wanted to make his living from poems and stories" (*IW*, 3).

Through its emphasis on the figure of the writer as working-class itinerant, *The Big Sea* parodies the Grand Tour in ways that once again affiliate Hughes's autobiography with the picaresque genre. The picaresque's peripatetic narrator, always a member of a lower socioeconomic class, is a confidence man. Typically male, he functions as trickster in relation to varied representatives of both sacred and secular authority, notably the Spanish monarchy and the Roman Catholic Church.[63] The loosely episodic structure of the pícaro's narrative encounters with such forms of political and social authority is one of the models for *The Big Sea* and its chronological jumbling of events in which the persona confronts power in many guises and in situations that range from familial to religious and economic.[64] It is a model Hughes continued to utilize in *I Wonder As I Wander*, where stories persistently interrupt a narrative line that seems otherwise fairly linear. Conflict invariably prompts the crises I mentioned earlier, whose narrative function is to keep the personae moving both backwards, through memories, and forward, through Hughes's modernist desire to leave the past behind him. Hughes's opening reference to Columbia University, for instance, makes us instantly aware that we are not at the beginning of a chronology here but at the start of a new departure that is also the aftermath of a personal predicament that had occurred a year earlier and is narrated some eighty pages later. This crisis culminates in Hughes's intense dislike for Columbia, where, after having battled with his father to get him to pay for attending this college, he spends only a term. Hughes's decision to move down to Harlem and into a life of precarious financial independence marks the final break with parental authority and his father's oppressive acquisitive ethos: "I felt that I would never turn out to be what my father expected me to be in return for the amount he invested. So I wrote him and told him that I was going to quit college and go to work on my own, and that he needn't send me any more money. He didn't. He didn't even write again" (*BS*, 85). At this point in the text, all that is left of James N. Langston, whose name Hughes drops from his genealogy, is a waning echo of his favorite exhortation—"Quick now! Hurry!"(*BS*, 89). This echo, also a form of repetition, marks an emotional distance Hughes achieved at great cost. The young Hughes's departure from New York is a way of translating that emotional distance into bodily movement.

The Big Sea always returns to metaphors of setting out and transit, out of which Hughes builds up the narrative frame for the first part of his autobiography. Each return repeats and reinflects the metaphors and adds to their cumulative meaning. The text's larger frame, which opens with the epigraph and ends, or pauses, with its qualified restatement in the narrative's final sentences, weaves together images of movement in a figure of networking that is decidedly not a closure but another opening: "Literature is a big sea full of many fish. I let down my nets and pulled. I'm still pulling" (*BS*, 335).[65] The tense change in the second sentence turns the act of writing into a mnemonic figure that pulls in things from the past, while the addition of a third statement—"I'm still pulling"—turns writing into an ongoing process of recovery and innovation. The substitution of literature for life—"Life is a big sea" becomes "Literature is a big sea"—signals the transformation of life (*zoê*, not just *bios*) into literature that is at the heart of all autobiography. Self-writing as a function of continuous movement thus folds back into the text's travel metaphors. The sea here is not just history, as Derek Walcott has it, a space of remembrance across which one floats. It is an what Chambers dubs an "intricate site of encounters and currents" where the self knowingly exposes itself to the risks and pleasures of being culturally translated by voluntarily relinquishing recourse to any prior culture and the essentialism that might come with it.[66] Self-writing, no less than fiction, renders the autobiographer vulnerable to self-estrangement, a process in which the "proper" self is broken up and constituted anew by the strangers that become part of it. There are losses and gains. "What we lose," suggests Chambers, "is the security of the starting point, of the subject of departure: what we gain is an ethical relationship to the language in which we are subjects, and in which we subject each other."[67] In Hughes's autobiographies, the strangers that come to inhabit the self as a result of its being in transit and in translation assume the shape of fictional characters, be they personae or understudies. Transit, for Hughes, marks the desire for distance from oppressive situations and discourses that insist on his being or projecting a unified self. His desire—indeed, his need—is for creating alternative spaces of belonging in which writing not only articulates belonging but itself *becomes* a form of belonging to the world.

Among the spaces I discuss above, all of which are either explicit or implicit crossroads, one stands out because of the prominent position in which

Hughes places it in *The Big Sea*. Once Manhattan has melted into the darkness of the night, the narrative moves down into an airless mess boys' cabin in the freighter's capacious hold, which, at first glance, resembles a prison cell more than anything else. The location of this cabin, which the young Hughes shares with two other sailors, anticipates the better-known underground spaces from Richard Wright's "The Man Who Lived Underground" (1942) and Ralph Ellison's *Invisible Man* (1952). In both Wright's story and Ellison's novel, descending into such a space signifies a withdrawal from history into contemplative solitude and, at times, hallucinatory revelry. Hughes's underground space is cut from the same cloth, though it is far from solitary; the narrator identifies it as a communal site from the start: "I went down a pair of narrow steps that ended just in front of *our* cabin" (*BS*, 4; my emphasis). That the freighter is bound for Africa makes the collective quarters take on aspects of a Middle Passage in reverse. It turns the cabin into a time capsule in which geographical movement literalizes and reinforces processes of memory that reconnect present freedom with past enslavement, to people and ideas.

This space, tellingly located aboard a ship that sails the pages of *The Big Sea* under an invented name, is not a stage for mimetic realism.[68] It is a textual and cultural vortex repeated in the image of another floating stage: the afterdeck on a cargo vessel in Port-au-Prince harbor where a nearly penniless Hughes, here in the company of Zell Ingram, is "caught greasy-handed, half-naked—and soxless—by an official delegation of leading Haitians." Jacques Roumain, whom Hughes had met earlier that day—conversing with him "[f]or an hour, in French—mine halting, and in English—his bad"—had assembled that distinguished group "to pay me honor at the last moment and to present me with bon voyage gifts" (*IW*, 30, 31). When the boat lifts anchor, Hughes describes himself "standing on the poop deck over the churning rudder to wave farewell to the folks on the dock—Jacques Roumain, who was to become Haiti's most famous writer, the elegant gentlemen of his delegation, and the girl of the town who had come to see me off" (*IW*, 32). Paul Gardullo notes that "Hughes's construction of a particular space—floating, nationless, transient [one might add classless]—in which this strategic identity [a complex form of pan-African identity] emerges,...rais[es] questions about how constructions of identity and constructions of space may be mutually constituted and enacted performatively."[69] This space, however, does more than raise these questions; it *models* the mutual constitution of space as a secular ritual ground and identity as performance. Edward Pavlić, from whom I borrow the term "cultural vortex" above, describes the dynamics of the underground space with admirable precision. He also pinpoints an important difference between Hughes's representations and those of Wright and Ellison: "In this [communal underground] space, people perform (Jamesian) aspects of their subjectivity which remain off limits, or abstracted, in secluded contemplation. In this way, the diasporic modernist self becomes an *accumulating repertoire of presences summoned from personal depth and communal interactions both past and present.*"[70] The difference is one between abstraction and embodiment or action.

Hughes wrote the Haiti episode almost twenty years later than the cabin scene from *The Big Sea*. What remains constant in both, however, is his unflagging fascination with how people who barely know each other come to form a community, if only for fairly brief moments in time. The cabin scene is the first of the many provisional communities Hughes creates in his autobiographies. It is also the most complexly layered and deserves to be read with care.

Inside the hot cabin, George lay stark naked in a lower bunk, talking and laughing and gaily waving his various appendages around. Above him in the upper bunk, two chocolate-colored Puerto Rican feet stuck out from one end of a snow-white sheet, and a dark Puerto Rican head from the other. It was clear that Ramon in the upper bunk didn't understand more than every tenth word of George's Kentucky vernacular, but he kept on laughing every time George laughed.

George was talking about women, of course. He said he didn't care if his Harlem landlady pawned all his clothes, the old witch! When he got back from Africa, he would get some more. He might even pay her the month's back rent he owed her, too. Maybe. Or else—and here he waved one of his appendages around—she could have what he had in his hand.

Puerto Rico, who understood all the bad words in every language, laughed loudly. We all laughed. You couldn't help it. George was so good-natured and comical you couldn't keep from laughing with him—or at him. He always made everybody laugh—even when the food ran out on the return trip and everybody was hungry and mad. (*BS*, 4–5)

Here the autobiographical I, which had commanded the reader's attention with its melodramatic opening gesture, disappears behind the voice of a third-person narrator who recounts the banter inside the cabin. "Puerto Rico," whose other name is Ramon, has limited English, and George's Kentucky vernacular presents rather a challenge to his mate's comprehension. George's Spanish, in turn, is nonexistent, his "only 'foreign' language" being "pig-Latin" (*BS*, 5). Because Hughes's narrator does not directly report anything of what is said, as he does elsewhere ("'*Largo viaje*,' said Ramon," *BS*, 5), he has no need to insert himself into the scene as a mediator who translates George's every word to Ramon or Ramon's responses to George. There may well not have been any verbal replies, since, as we later learn, Ramon "didn't talk much, in English or Spanish" (*BS*, 6). Nor can readers who know nothing about Hughes immediately assume that he could even function as a translator here, for that assumption depends on autobiographical events yet to be narrated. Hughes's description focuses not on language but on his cabin mates' bodies—one naked and racially unmarked,[71] the other covered by a sheet that exaggerates the skin's darkness—and on sexual gesturing understood without translation, at least among the banterers themselves. Translation enters when the narrator shifts to a paraphrase of George's vernacular antics, steering readers away from interpreting the men's interactions as homosexual: "George was talking about women, of course." Or so, at any rate, it seems. By adding the mildly exasperated yet indulgent "of course," Hughes asserts the heterosexual default precisely in order to debunk it. "Of course," a phrase that appears in *The Big Sea* with some regularity, signals Hughes's taking control of a discourse that constitutes itself by denying or abjecting the possibility of the multiple readings that this scene enables, including—of course—homosexual ones. Brian Loftus, in one of the few attentive readings of *The Big Sea*, rightly calls this passage "multiracial, polylogic, and sexually ambivalent." He adds that "by virtue of its structural position, at the beginning of the text, it serves as a model to allow readings that implicate the sexual, the racial, and the linguistic in an overdetermined relation."[72]

By positioning himself as third-person narrator of this scene, Hughes can both be part of the spectacle in the cabin and at the same time stand aloof. What hints at his involvement in the scene he describes is a sudden explosion of shared laughter: "We all laughed." The laughter catalyzes a mutual understanding that depends less on language—"all the bad words"—than on the materiality, albeit euphemistic, of bodies, on the men's physical presence to each other across linguistic divides. On one level, the characters cackle at George's obscenities, which are all the more powerful for being withheld from us. On another level, the narrator chuckles—or grins—at readers who do not recognize George's paraphrased comments about women as a heteronormative red herring. If we as readers join in the laughter, as Hughes invites us to do by opening the "we" onto an even more inclusive "you" ("You couldn't help it"), we should at least know why. For laughter can signify understanding and intimacy just as it can indicate unease. We can easily find this scene funny without being entirely able to appreciate the different layers of its humor. While there is room for a homosocial interpretation of this scene, in which a female figures mediates the relations between the men, this mediation is purely rhetorical. George is not exactly expressing an interest in having sex with his landlady; he simply indicates that he would like to tell "the old witch" to go fuck *herself*. Using the now popular expletive to which I resort here would, however, have deflated the scene's power of suggestion, turning it into mere salacious anecdote. Loftus's reading of sex and sexuality in *The Big Sea* as "that which is withheld from representation" usefully suggests that "[t]he erotics of bodily and racial display are not entertained, rather they are *translated* into their economic significance" (152–53; my emphasis). In this case, it is the rent money George owes and does not have. Elsewhere in *The Big Sea*, it is prostitution, or "dancing." Sonya, the Russian dancer with whom a broke

Hughes temporarily shacks up in Paris, sums it up beautifully: "I have no mon-ee nedder" (*BS*, 150).

There is yet another dimension to the laughter in the cabin scene. George's mirth and his ability to incite mirth by "making up fabulous jokes" and "playing pranks" (*BS*, 7), even in near-desperate situations, is a survival strategy Hughes himself adopts throughout. As a survival strategy, Hughes's humor taps self-consciously into the blues, and George, not coincidentally, "knew plenty of blues" (*BS*, 7). It is worth remembering that the blues, like jazz, is about movement, about wanting to move or the consequences of somehow having moved, that is, of crossing boundaries of race, class, culture, and gender. As a consummate performer, George has much in common with certain aspects of Hughes himself, "the ever-smiling, often-laughing boon companion," as Rampersad calls him (xiv). More important, however, is that Hughes emphasizes George's talent as a storyteller whose prodigious talent makes him resemble a New World Scheherazade[73]: "George had a thousand tales to tell.... And several versions of each tale. No doubt, some of the stories were true—and some of them not true at all, but they sounded true. Sometimes George said he had relatives down South. Then, again, he said he didn't have anybody in the whole world. Both versions concerning his relatives were probably correct. If he did have relatives they didn't matter— *lying* there as he was now, laughing and talking in his narrow bunk on a hot night, going to Africa" (*BS*, 6; my emphasis). In the context of an autobiographical narrative, this commentary cannot be passed over as mere character description. George is not just "lying" on his bunk; he is also telling "lies." This pun is a highly self-conscious reminder that autobiography, much like the travelogue and the picaresque novel, is a literary genre that happily, purposefully, and productively straddles the fact/fiction divide. This is something well worth recalling, given the contemporary public excoriations of autobiographers who stray too far into fictional territory. Can we really be sure about the line that separates fiction from nonfiction, let alone truth from lies? I think not.

This is not to say that Hughes simply makes up tall tales about himself but that his truths take the shape of stories that may or may not use a first-person narrator. Some of them, like George's anecdotes, have multiple versions, all of which are equally true, and some of these versions are stories not about Hughes but about others who stand in for him. George, who "always referred to himself as brownskin" rather than as "black" (*BS*, 103), is one of Hughes's understudies, or character-masks. This is why "[e]verybody knew all about George long before we reached the coast of Africa"(*BS*, 5), and why readers of *The Big Sea* seem to know much about George and comparative little about the autobiographer himself. What about Ramon, who says little and does not care for women? "The only thing that came out of his mouth in six months that I remember is that he said he didn't care much for women, anyway [this is not strictly true; he also talks about his mother].

He preferred silk stockings—so halfway down the African coast, he bought a pair of silk stockings and slept with them under his pillow"(*BS*, 7). Along with George, the boisterous talker with whom Hughes becomes "pretty good pals" (*BS*, 7), the quiet Puerto Rican who likes silk stockings also embodies facets of Hughes's self. As I argued earlier, Hughes is well aware that to write within the conventions of autobiography—compulsory truth telling and first-person narrative voice—does not give him any standing as a speaking subject who does not easily fit prevailing norms and identities. This awareness makes him a resistant autobiographer who often prefers the distance of an impersonal narrator and first-person plural pronouns to representations of individual subjectivity. In Hughes's autobiographies, no single and singular narrative voice has the final claim to truth. Producing meaning is always an ongoing process. Hughes's vision of dispersed and "improper" selfhood exists within translational dynamics akin to Creolization.[74]

The passage that immediately follows the cabin scene exemplifies the shifts in narrative voice through which the "I" is constantly formed and reformed: "Then it was ten o'clock, on a June night, on the S.S. *Malone*, and we were going to Africa. At ten o'clock that morning I had never heard of the S.S. *Malone*, or George, or Ramon, and anybody else in its crew of forty-two men. Nor any of the six passengers. But now, here were the three of us laughing very loudly, going to Africa" (*BS*, 5). Hughes marvels here at how quickly a series of unforeseen circumstances have welded a group of total strangers into a new community, and he insists on the collective pronoun. "We are going to Africa" is the refrain that echoes throughout the chapter. This refrain also sets the reader up for the denouement at the end of the section when Hughes is excluded from the one community he had assumed to represent unquestioned belonging: "[T]here was one thing that hurt me a lot when I talked with the people. The Africans looked at me and would not believe I was a Negro" (*BS*, 11). This peremptory expulsion from "the great Africa of my dreams" provides Hughes with an opening for meditating on racial identity and misrecognition back home: "You see, unfortunately, I am not black. There are lots of different kinds of blood in our family. But here in the United States, the word 'Negro' is used to mean anyone who has *any* Negro blood at all in his veins. In Africa, the word is more pure. It means *all* Negro, therefore *black*. I am brown" (*BS*, 11).[75]

That the misrecognition Hughes experienced and wrote about is also a form of exile, or better, a mark of the condition of migrancy, comes into clearer focus when he recounts his conversation with the Japanese stage director Seki Sano in a café in Montmartre on New Year's Eve 1937. Hughes placed this espisode in the final chapter of *I Wonder As I Wander*.

> "There are too many people wandering around the world now who can't go home," [Seki Sano] said, "Lots of them are in Moscow. More are in Paris—people from the Hitler countries, from the South American dictatorships, from China,

from my own Japan. No exiles from America—though I wouldn't be surprised if the day didn't come."

"That's one nice thing about America," I said, "I can always go home—even when I don't want to."

"*Bonne année!*" said the waiter bringing our drinks. "It's the New Year." (*IW*, 404)

Having been forced to leave Japan in 1930 because of his Marxist politics, Seki Sano had good reasons not to share Hughes's optimism. Unlike Hughes, he would never return to his homeland but would spend the rest of his active and quite influential professional life in exile in Mexico and other parts of the Hispanic Americas, until his death in Mexico City in 1966.[76] Hughes, by contrast, although he could physically reenter the country of his birth, was in a similar position. In psychological terms, could he really go home? Although his response to Seki Sano may appear naive at first glance, Hughes's words carry more than a hint of doubt. The final sentences in *I Wonder* apply here directly: "But worlds—entire nations and civilizations—do end. In the snowy night in the shadows of the old houses of Montmartre I repeated to myself: 'My world won't end.' But how could I be so sure? I don't know. For a moment I wondered" (*IW*, 405). For my part, I wonder whether Hughes also recalls Toussaint L'Ouverture in his snowy prison in the French Alps on this occasion. After all, his play about Haiti, *Troubled Island*, had premiered not long before, in 1936.

Hughes's is a book-length moment of wondering, called out here to turn closure into another opening.[77] The story, then, is by no means over, only temporarily halted. By repeating to himself the phrase "My world won't end," Hughes is in fact acknowledging that his world is about to end. The repeated words do not, however, simply spell denial; they are invocations that create a lifeline at a time when Hitler and Mussolini were about to "finish their practice in Ethiopia and Spain to turn their planes on the rest of us" (*IW*, 405). At the beginning of 1938, large parts of the world as people knew it before World War II were on the brink of being destroyed, physically and psychologically. Although the USA, unlike its European allies and certainly unlike Japan, appeared largely unaffected during the war's aftermath, at least outwardly, the country was hardly the same place in 1945 as it had been before the war. Even in 1937, the time of his conversation with Seki Sano, Hughes's point of departure (America) is no more certain than his return which the interjection of the untranslated French "*Bonne année!*" in place of the English "Happy New Year!" emphatically suspends. When Hughes sat down to draft *I Wonder As I Wander* during the initial decade of the Cold War, the doubts he had had at the end of 1937 were even more tangible. We ourselves would risk naiveté if we did not consider, as contemporary reviewers did not, that Hughes probably wrote this scene not long after his encounter with McCarthyism in 1953, in which his loyalty to the country of his birth had been harshly questioned. We might think of what transpired during these hearings as yet another misrecognition (more on this in chapter 5). At the time, potential measures for denaturalizing USAmerican citizens were actually being debated in Congress. Other than the fear of being deported from Japan as persona non grata, Hughes might not have had any compelling political reasons for not wanting to return to the USA in 1938, though there would have been ample reasons in the 1940s and 1950s. Either way, there was no homecoming for Hughes. Chambers elucidates that, unlike travel, migrancy "calls for dwelling in language, in histories, in identities that are constantly subject to mutation. Always in transit, the promise of a homecoming—completing the story, domesticating the detour—becomes an impossibility."[78] The way in which Hughes dwells in language in this scene is by lingering on the repeated phrase "my world won't end" long enough to turn it into a veritable blues motif.

SWOLLEN TONGUES

The fact that Hughes's narrative building of what Homi Bhabha has called "differentiated communities" never occurs in the USA or in places where "the American color line stretched out its inconvenient prejudices"(*BS*, 197) speaks directly to this impossibility. Unlike the scenes set on the Africa-bound vessel or on the Genoa waterfront (*BS*, 116 and 192), episodes that focus on provisional and mixed communities rarely involve whites, especially white USAmericans. When such Anglos do appear, as in the case of the pregnant young woman who oddly insists on bearing her child in Moscow, they become occasions for different sorts of interactions or no interactions at all. Despite his initial sympathy with her, Hughes's final diagnosis of the girl's sudden, unexplained physical affliction is also a biting commentary on Anglo-Americans' inability to communicate with people who are unlike them: "This speechless American's tongue was swollen as thick as a sausage—*salivated*! I could diagnose that" (*IW*, 209). There are numerous scenes in both autobiographies in which racial and class biases foreclose linguistic and cultural translation, producing patterns of radical divergence. Racist incidents range from Hughes's frustrating experiences at Columbia (*BS*, 83–85) and his vexing rail journeys across various southern states (see *BS*, 50) to his problematic relation and ultimate break with his patron, Charlotte Osgood Mason, and his being refused entrance to a Havana beach leased to an "American concern" (*BS*, 11–15). Yet criticisms of color prejudice and classism also abound in Hughes's interactions with Washington's black bourgeoisie, on whom he comments rather disapprovingly: "They all had the manners and airs of reactionary, ill-bred nouveaux riches—except that they were not really rich. Just middle class" (*BS*, 207).

An especially resonant, indeed paradigmatic, episode comes near the end of the first part of *The Big Sea*. Here Hughes describes his encounter with a new teacher at the school in Toluca, Mexico, where he taught English after his second visit with his father in 1920. Important to this scene, which is worth revisiting at some length, is the characters' displacement, their location in another country, and the fact that the young Hughes was about to return to the USA, where he had previously been mistaken for a Mexican (see *BS*, 50).

Professor Tovar had neglected to tell the new teacher that I was an *americano de color*, brown as a Mexican, and nineteen years old. So when she walked into the room with him, she kept looking for the American teacher. No doubt she thought I was one of the students, chalk in hand, standing at the board. But when she was introduced to me, her mouth fell open, and she said: "Why, Ah-Ah thought you was an American."

I said: "I am American."

She said: "Oh, Ah mean a white American!" Her voice had a southern drawl.

I grinned.

She was a poor-looking lady of the stringy type, who probably had never been away from her home town before. I asked her what part of the States she came from. She said Arkansas—which better explained her immediate interest in color. For the next two days, she sat beside me at the teacher's desk.... [S]he kept looking at me out of the corners of her eyes as if she thought maybe I might bite her.

At the end of the first day, she said: "Ah never come across an educated Ne-gre before." (Southerners often make that word a slur between *nigger* and *Negro*.)

I said: "They have a large state college for colored people in Arkansas, so there must be some educated ones there."

She said: "Ah reckon so, but Ah just never saw one before." And she continued to gaze at me as her first example of an educated Negro.

I was a bit loath to leave my students, with whom I had had so much fun, in charge of a woman from one of our more backward states, who probably felt about brown Mexicans much as my father did. But there was no alternative, if they wanted to learn English at all. Then, too, I thought the young ladies from Señorita Padilla's academy might as well meet a real *gringo* for once. Feminine gender: *gringa*. (BS, 78–79)

Right away Hughes takes discursive control by embracing a translated identity: *americano de color* is what his Mexican colleagues call him. (Being part of North America, Mexicans would not call USAmerican citizens *norteamericanos*.) *Americano de color* is a phrase that signifies the respect that the woman, who is described in terms not of her skin color but of her regional origins, will not grant Hughes in the exchange that follows. Naming himself an *americano de color* is a way for Hughes to place himself outside a familiar frame of reference before someone else can put him in what she presumes his place is by excluding him from America. *Americano de color* has, of course, a referential range that is hardly limited to the USA, and it allows Hughes to make himself into a citizen of the Americas in a gesture that might be termed hemispheric cosmopolitanism.[79] To the woman, however, it is the young teacher's skin color, "brown as a Mexican," along with his youthful appearance, that renders him perfectly invisible. She expects both an American and a teacher and sees neither. When she is finally forced to acknowledge his presence, she immediately tries to impose her very precisely defined, yet unspoken, expectations of what an American is. Hughes represents her words in a southern vernacular that makes her embarrassed stutter rupture her idea of her own selfhood and subjectivity. The standard signifier of a self, the I, dissolves in an inarticulate "Ah-Ah" as the presumptive authority of being a teacher of English founders on the rocks of regional grammar: "I thought you was." Hughes shrewdly gives her utterances inflections of race and class that call into question both her cultural whiteness as a southerner and the level of her education. Adding the seemingly needless observation that "her voice had a southern drawl" is tantamount to a discursive grin, with which Hughes slyly indicates that he has got her. Indeed he has. Instead of defining the woman in racial terms, Hughes's (to her) confusing assertion "I am American" forces her to spell out as yet unspoken racialist assumptions about the restricted meaning she gives that adjective and to name herself as white by implication. Sitting next to him at the teacher's desk, she is made to grant Hughes respect after all but very grudgingly and warily, as her fearful sideways glances betray. Hughes plays here on the myth of white women's fear of being physically assaulted by black men—a myth that gave rise to cruel historical reality through so many lynchings. He takes literally the metaphor of being "bitten" to bring to the surface the psychological remnants of a discourse of animalizing African Americans through which white USAmericans tried to safeguard their own racial difference as the default of humanity.

A sign of the woman's reluctantly evolving respect is that she calls Hughes "an educated Ne-gre." Hughes's parenthetical comment is more of an extension of the earlier textual smirk than it is an explanation of this apparent neologism based on the French *nègre*.[80] The broken-up noun "Ne-gre" is not really a word at all, not even in a southern USAmerican vernacular. Neither French nor English, this word exists only in the space between an insult and a somewhat more benign racial label. It fills the catachrestic space of the impossible and the unintelligible that the figure of the educated Negro already occupies. To his interlocutor, an educated Negro is a contradiction in terms. Once she is presented with the reality of such a contradiction in the flesh, her attempts to represent and contain it end up as a mere stammer that echoes her earlier "Ah-Ah." In her vernacularized part of the dialogue, which contrasts sharply with Hughes's own standardized, more educated diction, English—the USAmerican version of it—visibly comes apart at the seams. Once made to confess to the tenuousness of its underlying assumptions about racial and national identity, the normative discourse on race that the woman's language represents struggles in vain to maintain coherence and authority. In the end, this discourse, like her own language, loses its ability to produce meaning, disintegrating into nonsense syllables. Representing a normative discourse as regionally specific—"southern" in this case—further adds to its loss of authority.

By perforating the rigid surface of a discourse that would define him as non- or un-American, Hughes can name the woman for what she is *where* she is, in Mexico. Calling her a *gringa* from his perspective of an *americano de color*, he in turn withholds from her an identity as American, which his text had granted her prior to this scene. It is significant that even Hughes's father, whose sentiments about "greasers and niggers" this woman might well have shared, is accorded more respect than a *gringo (BS, 42)*. By the end of the passage, the woman has been stripped of any pretenses. The only thing that remains is her feminine gender, along with her status as an outsider, a despised foreigner. By the end of the passage, the woman effectively finds herself in the very place she had wanted to assign to Hughes.

By using another nameless white southerner who "frequently made unkind remarks about spicks and niggers," Hughes consciously connects that episode with another incident whose setting aboard the *S.S. Malone* also ties it to the earlier cabin scene. The character in question is the ship's "Third Engineer [who] was from Arkansas, the same state, strangely enough, as the lady who had taken my English courses in Mexico" (*BS*, 114). What makes the following excerpt resonate with the Toluca episode are the verbal replies; what makes them different is the threat of physical violence.

> They [the customs men and the clerks] were entirely Negroes that day, Africans in European clothes, four or five of them, very clean and courteous in their white duck suits. They were in the midst of their meal at a single long table, when the Third Engineer came in.
>
> He ordered: "Get these niggers out of here. I haven't eaten yet."
>
> I said: "You can eat with them if you like. Or I'll serve you afterwards."
>
> "I don't eat with niggers," he said. "And you know damn well an officer don't have to wait for no coons to be fed." He turned on the startled Africans. "Get out of here!" he shouted.
>
> "You get out of here yourself," I said, reaching for the big metal soup tureen on the steam table.
>
> The Third Engineer was a big fellow, and I couldn't fight him barehanded, so I raised the tureen, ready to bring it down on his head.
>
> "I'll report you to the Captain, you black—!"
>
> "Go ahead, you—and double—! I said, raising the soup tureen. He went. The Africans finished their meal in peace. (*BS*, 115)

Note that the engineer does not initially address the African officials directly, although "they spoke English." He only stares at them in Conradian horror, resorting to a familiar racial slur, the verbal equivalent of his gaze, as he addresses the mess boy who, he assumes, shares his sense of racial hierarchies ("you know damn well"). The mess boy's replies, conciliatory at first, reject this assumption and put the engineer in a place wholly unfamiliar to him: that of an intruder whose conduct is highly inappropriate. Unaware that the social rules aboard the ship are different from what he is used to, the incensed engineer escalates the situation into a shouting match, in which Hughes leaves the invectives that are traded up to the reader's imagination, much as he elides verbal obscenity in his narration of the cabin scene. Once again Hughes reworks the discursive terrain of antiblack racism, here replete with potential physical violence, to create an alternative sense of understanding, in this case with the shocked Africans at the table and in fact, the rest of the nonwhite crew. Confronted with signs of verbal and physical opposition, the engineer is effectively expelled from the scene and forced to adjust his future behavior: subsequently, "he kept quiet and never referred to the day of the soup tureen" (*BS*, 116).

The briefly rendered aftermath of this confrontation confirms the existence of a differentiated community with its own understanding of race relations. This understanding is marked if not by respect for foes then at least by tolerance. In this community, the disgraced officer is silenced and put in his place, but he is not completely cast out. When mess boy Hughes informs the chief steward of his refusal to wait on the engineer ever again, the "grave little Filipino" replies "forlornly," "Mess boy, in this my life things is not always *easible*. Sometimes hard like hell! I wish you please *help me out* and feed the Third" (*BS*, 115; my emphases). That Hughes predictably relents — "because I liked the steward" — is less interesting than the remarks that prompt his acquiescence. What stands out is the neologism "easible," which sounds like English but, as the nonstandard grammar and syntax imply, is not. It is not hard to gather that what the Filipino means is that "life hasn't always been kind to me," or that "life hasn't always made things easy for me." Realizing that "easible" does not just mean "easy" attunes our ears to the Spanish underneath the English words. It is as if the steward were saying: *la vida no me ha sido facilitado*. "Easible," then, is his English version of *facilitado*, from *facilitarse*, "to help out," which reappears as what would have been *facilítame, por favor*, "please help me out" — had the steward spoken in Spanish. The reason why this little word is so remarkable here is that "easible," occupying as it does a space between English and Spanish, encapsulates the ethos of mutuality that underlies the provisional communities Hughes assembles in both autobiographies: helping one another out. Adding to this ethos the element of (linguistic) play brings out important ritual dimensions in this scene. If, "[a]s a sacred activity play naturally contributes to the well-being of the group,"[81] it does so in a secular context as well. In this sense, the communities Hughes models are ludic communities, even if some players are unaware of themselves as such and hence unaware of the changed rules of the game. It is no accident that the drunken brawl in which "crew solidarity outweighed race" (*BS*, 116) follows hard on the heels of a confrontation in which racial epithets had taken on rather less playful connotations.

In *I Wonder As I Wander*, the principle behind Hughes's own drunken yells in *The Big Sea*—"Get them niggers! Get them limeys!" (*BS*, 116)— finds its counterpart in the traveler's frustrated ranting at his less adventurous fellow travelers, who have left him standing at yet another train depot in the middle of nowhere:

> You don't need to stop with me in Ashkhabad, you low-life Negroes! You dirty Russians! Double-crossing movie-makers! You trade-union Communists! I'll get along! I damn sure bet you I'll get along! Right here in the middle of this Godforsaken desert, I'll make it! (*IW*, 109)

Even in the absence of interlocutors and the usual derogatory references to female family members, Hughes's flood of mock curses brings to mind the dialogic play of the dozens, that ritualized insulting of "yo' mama." He used the cultural matrix of this performative trading of insults elsewhere to good effect and most memorably in *ASK YOUR MAMA: 12 Modes for Jazz* (1961).[82] The logic of defiant play may be extended to many of the other performative situations I have analyzed in this chapter, where humor almost invariably serves as springboard for engaging with pressing issues of physical and psychological survival. In *I Wonder*, it is the little Russian word *nichevo* that assumes the function of the more familiar generic incantation "yo' mama," announcing the translational adaptation of African American ritualized play to different linguistic and sociocultural circumstances:

> "*Nichevo*," he [the Turkoman station master] said with a grin.
> *Nichevo* can mean a hundred different things in Russian, depending on the inflection. In this case, there in the middle of the desert, I gathered that it mean, 'So...Well?...What's the difference?...Anyhow, to hell with it!
> "*Nichevo*," I grinned back at him.
> We both laughed. (*IW*, 109)

From this point forward, Hughes uses the virtually untranslatable *nichevo* so freely that it becomes part of his regular vocabulary, leaving his readers to figure out which inflection he prefers at any given time in any given place. This is the kind of translation that disrupts and reworks the real, to the extent that the real typically insists on more clear-cut distinctions between concepts and identities. In his autobiographies, Hughes routinely sabotages the operations of dominant discourses. Instead of a counterdiscourse, however, he offers us the "the enigmatic present of language that attempts to reveal an opening in ourselves and the world we inhabit."[83] To wit, we need not know any Russian to appreciate the myriad possibilities of *nichevo* in all sorts of cultural settings.

SPANISH ACCENTS

The discourses of race, gender, and nationality that Hughes takes to task are often quite specific to the conventions of USAmerican English. As such, they are quite distinct from other forms of English spoken and written in the Americas—for instance, the New Orleans Creole and the British West Indian "brogue" Hughes mentions in *The Big Sea* (92, 195)—and sometimes used in his plays.[84] Given the linguistic cultural diversity of his autobiographical voice, it is well worth asking how his autobiographies have fared in translation. Both *The Big Sea* and *I Wonder As I Wander* make it abundantly clear that learning Spanish was vital for Hughes, even more important than learning French (see *BS*, 33–34). Knowing this particular language was his passport to the other parts of the Americas, notably Mexico and Cuba, and it mattered to him that "people in far-away lands" would be able to read his work (*BS*, 34). Indeed, his poetry and prose would be translated into a number of languages, even during his lifetime, among them French, German, Japanese, Russian, Portuguese, and, of course, Spanish.[85] Since I discuss the Hispanic American translations of Hughes's poems in the next chapter, I conclude my commentary on his autobiographies by taking a brief look at passages from two Spanish translations from Argentina: Luisa Rivaud's *El inmenso mar* (1944) and Julio Gáler's *Yo viajo por un mundo encantado* (1959).[86] I reserve more detailed comments on these two translators for chapter 3.

There is no question that the nuances of Hughes's rhetorical maneuvers, his puns and linguistic admixtures, and his insistence on a multilingual texture in which Spanish plays an important role make his autobiographies a formidable challenge for any translator, much more so even than his short stories and plays.[87] And it is clear that both Gáler and Rivaud struggled with these issues, resolving them more or less successfully. Take, for instance, Hughes's emphasis on sound and musicality, which is no less vital in *I Wonder As I Wander* than it is in *The Big Sea*, starting with the title's homophony. This shared sound is entirely lost in Julio Gáler's choice of a title, *Yo viajo por un mundo encantado*, an English retranslation of which would be "I am traveling in an enchanted world." Hughes's title would be more effectively rendered as "Erro maravillando"—"I wander wondering"—which better captures the sense of an incomplete and uncertain movement (in *errar*, to err or roam), as opposed to traveling (*viajar*), which implies having a destination and the expectation of returning home.

Not surprisingly, Rivaud encountered related problems in *El inmenso mar*. While Gáler had to navigate languages other than Spanish in *I Wonder*,

Rivaud was confronted with a situation in which the contrast between varying inflections and linguistic registers too easily fades in Spanish. In her rendition of the voice of the chief steward, for example, the quality of Hughes's Spanglish disappears entirely behind flawless, unaccented Spanish, and clearly it would not have done to imitate the character's Filipino English in what would have been his native tongue, or one of them. Similarly, the two voices in the Toluca scene become indistinguishable but for different reasons. Although vernaculars are notoriously difficult to translate, and philosophies differ widely about whether a black vernacular from the USA should be turned into, say, a black Colombian or Cuban dialect, the absence of an orthographic contrast makes it impossible to discern Hughes's careful play on language and the layers of intralingual translation. The ironies with which Hughes ruptures the normative discourse in English are largely invisible and inaudible in this Spanish version. We catch only a residual glimpse of them when Rivaud distinguishes *negro instruido*, or "schooled Negro," from *negro educado*, meaning an educated or learned Negro—her not very satisfying rendition of Hughes's "educated Ne-gre." There are many missed opportunities in *El inmenso mar* that are more likely the result of the inevitable cultural disparities between an African American from the USA and a European Jew in Argentina than a matter of outright mistranslation. In the same scene, we also no longer hear the woman's utterances break down into stutter. "Why, Ah-Ah thought you was American" becomes "Ah! Yo creí que era usted americano" (*IM*, 90)—"Oh! I thought you were American." It would have been fairly easy at least to render the stutter as "Y-yo" or even "Yo-yo." That Rivaud chose not to do so makes one wonder if she, coming from and living in countries (Spain and Argentina) without significant populations of African descent and without comparable racial and racist lexicons, fully grasped the significance of this scene. It is not that Rivaud's translation does not make any sense. The problem, rather, is that it often makes almost too much sense, that is, it is too comfortably readable for Spanish-speaking audiences. In Spanish, this key scene becomes mere anecdote instead of a disturbing reflection on racial and national identity.

Without overstating the significance of Hughes's use of italics and other kinds of typeface, it is fair to say that they do modulate his meaning, often to a significant degree. Although fonts are visual markers, they also change how we *hear* words in our heads and require close attention from translators, especially in texts with linguistic overlap. Both Rivaud and Gáler tend to italicize and footnote words and phrases that are in Spanish in Hughes's texts, although Rivaud is more inconsistent about this fairly standard practice and does not seem entirely comfortable with Hughes's multilingual practice. While *Americano de color* is both italicized and footnoted in *El inmenso mar*, possibly because it would have been an unusual locution in Argentina, the more ubiquitous *gringo* and *gringa* are allowed to blend into the Spanish text. English book titles and lines from poems by Hughes and others are routinely kept in English, with Spanish translations supplied in footnotes. One noteworthy example is Rivaud's clunky translation of the title *Not Without Laughter*, Hughes's first novel, as *No sin regocijo* (*IM*, 313), which the musicologist Nestor Ortíz Oderigo wisely chose not to adopt for his own Spanish version of the novel. His alternative, *Pero con risas*, gives the title a more graceful poetic turn. In other places, Rivaud is hesitant to retain English words in her translation, not even when Hughes foreignizes them in his own text by placing them in italics, as he does with "nigger" and "Negro" in the Toluca episode. It would have been perfectly plausible to have kept both of these words in the Spanish text, perhaps even with a footnote about the history and usage of "nigger." Rivaud might have considered at least a reference to the later section "Nigger Heaven," where Hughes himself uses Carl Van Vechten's oft-maligned novelistic title as an occasion to comment on the word that "to colored people of high and low degree is like a red rag to a bull....The word *nigger* in the mouths of little white boys at school, the word *nigger* in the mouths of foremen on the job, the word *nigger* across the whole face of America! *Nigger*! *Nigger*! Like the word *Jew* in Hitler's Germany" (*BS*, 268–69). Somewhat confusingly, Rivaud does not translate "nigger" at all in this section except in her version of Countee Cullen's poem "Incident" in the footnote: "but he poked out / his tongue and called me, "Nigger," becomes "pero el sacó / la lengua y me gritó, 'Negro.'" But the Spanish noun *negro* does not render "nigger" as it is used in the *Estados Unidos*. As we shall see in the next chapter, there can be a world of difference between the two, as there is between *negro* and *gente de color*. Rivaud is not particularly sensitive to such nuances, nor does she seem to realize that the word "Jew" (*judío*) needs not quotation marks but italics to complete the link to the Third Reich (see *IM*, 279). That Rivaud refrains entirely from any interpretive annotations might be regarded as a virtue, but it also perhaps shows that she is being pushed to the limits of her cultural understanding. Gáler, by contrast, is a more confident translator who does not shy away from informing his Spanish-speaking readers that "Yeah Man" is a "Deformación de 'Yes-man,' que significa: 'hombre que obedece ciegamente'" (deformation of "Yes-man," which means: "a man who agrees or obeys silently"). He is also flexible and astute enough to turn Hughes's "Ooo-wee Harm-Strung" into the equally comical "Uuu-i Jarm-Strang," adapting the sound of the phrase to the phonetic requirements of Spanish (*Yo viajo*, 89, 118).

BLACK INTERNATIONALISMS

Despite the challenges that Hughes's autobiographies present for translators and even despite the often scathing reviews each received, *The Big Sea* and *I Wonder As I Wander* are the only autobiographies by a Harlem Renaissance writer to be translated into Spanish shortly after their initial publication. To be sure, Hughes was already very well known in the Hispanic Americas from the earlier translations of many of his poems, which I examine in the next two chapters. But that, I contend, was not the only reason. Hughes's heightened sensitivity to being always in translation was rather unique among the New Negro intellectuals who gathered mainly in Harlem and Washington, D.C. The literary sensibility that grows out of such sensitivity to translation does not necessarily have anything to do with how many languages someone knows. Rather, it is a matter of what precise role other languages play in self-perception and in (self-) writing. James Weldon Johnson, Alain Locke, W. E. B. Du Bois, Claude McKay, and others certainly had linguistic competencies in languages other than English. Yet few of their literary writings have inspired translations.[88] This is not insignificant in light of Brent Edwards's argument that "the cultures of black internationalism can be seen only in translation. It is not possible to take up the question of 'diaspora' without taking account of the fact that the great majority of peoples of African descent do not speak or write English."[89]

I wrap up this chapter by amplifying Edwards's point. To this end, I offer a condensed commentary on a text that pays homage to Langston Hughes in a rather unusual way: Manuel Zapata Olivella's epic novel *Changó el Gran Putas* (1983, 1985), which Jonathan Tittler, a bit stuffily, translated as *Changó, the Biggest Badass* (2010). While there are many who have dedicated and addressed poems to Hughes—some of these tributes serve as epigraphs to my chapters—Zapata Olivella went so far as to make his friend a novelistic character. In a scene from *Changó*'s fifth and final section, Zapata Olivella grafts his own encounter with Hughes in 1940s Harlem onto a fictionalized meeting between Hughes and the Jamaican pan-Africanist Marcus Garvey.[90] Garvey is the historical mask that Ngafúa, the messenger of the titular Yorùbá deity, has donned for the occasion. Changó-Ngafúa-Garvey, in turn, is recounting the exchange with Hughes for Agne Brown, a character that strikes me as a cross between Zora Neale Hurston and Angela Davis. I quote the passage at some length because it situates Langston Hughes at several important crossroads, some already familiar, others yet to be explored.

El viento frío no lograba descapotar los muelles de Sandy Hook, en New York.... Y esa mañana, Agne Brown, el vapor "S.S. Malone" atracó inesperadamente en la punta de Manhattan. Langston Hughes desembarca con el envoltorio de su ropa bajo el brazo. La visera de su gorra o las noches le han oscurecido la mirada. Hasta sus viejos zapatos necesitan un poco de luz. Anduvo buscando los libros que diez meses atrás arrojara a las aguas estancadas del puerto como si aún estuvieran allí esperando su regreso.

Años después me confesará que en aquella partida lo embargaban los temores:

—Marcus Garvey, yo tenía veintiún años como tú, cuando embarqué en este mismo puerto rumbo al África. Me he lavado la cara en los ríos del Níger y del Congo donde cazaban a nuestros abuelos. Conozco a Francia, Alemania, Italia, Holanda y España. En aquel entonces partí con siete dólares. No sé si regreso enriquecido o mas pobre.

Miró hacia los rojos edificios de Harlem y en voz alta, como si se confesará ante sus Ancestros, recita aquel poema:

> He contemplado ríos,
> viejos, oscuros, con la edad del mundo
> y con ellos, tan viejos y sombríos
> el corazón se me volvió profundo...

[The cold wind did not manage to blow the top off the covered docks of Sandy Hook, in New York.... And that morning, Agne Brown, the steamer *S.S. Malone* moored at the tip of Manhattan. Langston Hughes disembarks with his clothes bundled under his arm. Either the brim of his hat or the late nights have darkened his gaze. Even his old shoes could stand a little light. He walked about searching for the books that he had thrown into the port's stagnant waters ten months earlier, as if they would still be waiting there for his return.

Years later, he will confess to me that fears engulfed him during that departure.

"Marcus Garvey, I was twenty-one years old like you when from this very port I set sail for Africa. I have bathed my face in the Niger and Congo Rivers, where the traders hunted down our grandparents. I know France, Germany, Italy, Holland, and Spain. At the time I left I had seven dollars in my pocket. I don't know if I return wealthier or poorer."

He looked toward the red buildings of Harlem and, as if confessing to his Ancestors, recites aloud this poem:

> *I have contemplated rivers,*
> *old, dark, the world's age,*
> *and with them, so old and somber,*
> *my heart grew deep...*][91]

This scene can be read as a conjoined translation of *The Big Sea* and "The Negro Speaks of Rivers." Zapata Olivella invokes the opening frame of *The Big Sea* to peg Hughes as a transatlantic traveler, not setting out but returning home in this instance. At first glance, Hughes seems to be the weary voyager situated squarely in the Europe-Africa-USA triangulation that we easily recognize as a version of the Black Atlantic. Garvey's Jamaica is an implicit part of this configuration; so is Hughes's own encounter with "Mother Africa." The Atlantic triangle, however, is but a partial shape here. By transplanting the erstwhile poet laureate of the Negro race into a Colombian novel, Zapata Olivella repositions Hughes in time and space, extending the poet's travels in the Hispanic Americas to a place he never visited in person.[92] Zapata Olivella thus makes the hemispheric Americas a directional axis that intersects with that of the Atlantic world. We might say that the Black Atlantic meets the Black Americas in the playfully fluid temporalities of the novel that also encompass the time of its own publication in the late twentieth century and the place where it was written and published, Bogotá.[93] Their junction and overlap are as vital to Zapata Olivella's grand Afro-diasporic literary project as they are to my own scholarly endeavors. The main difference—other obvious differences aside—is that my focus is not exclusively on the African diaspora.

Translation is at issue in this extract from *Changó* in several ways. Indeed, Zapata Olivella explicitly posits the need for translation a bit later in the novel by having his narrator excitedly tell Hughes about a new journal entitled "el Nuevo Negro"—*The New Negro*—which, unlike Alain Locke's celebrated 1925 collection, has "secciones en francés y español para aquellos de West Indies y América Hispana que no conocen el inglés" (sections in French and Spanish for those from the West Indies and Spanish America who don't know English).[94] Most conspicuously, however, translation moves into the foreground when the fictional Hughes recites a poem by the historical Hughes, arguably his most famous verse, "The Negro Speaks of Rivers." He recites it in Spanish, of course. This is not the first time that Zapata Olivella pays homage to Hughes by using this very poem in one of his novels.[95] On neither occasion did he use a translation of his own. The unacknowledged translator whose work Zapata Olivella quotes in both *Changó* and the autobiographical *He visto la noche* (I've Seen the Night), is the Colombian poet Carlos López Narváez, who included "EL Negro habla de los ríos" in his 1952 anthology of French- and English-speaking writers, *El cielo en el río* (The Sky in the River).[96] López Narváez took considerable liberties with Hughes's text that find their way into Tittler's English version as well. What Tittler offers is a retranslation of the poem that displaces Hughes's English text. It is worth comparing Tittler's translation of López Narváez's to Hughes's prior version of his poem's final stanza:

> I have contemplated rivers,
> old, dark, the world's age,
> and with them, so old and somber,
> my heart grew deep...

> I've known rivers:
> Ancient, dusky rivers.
> My soul has grown deep like the rivers.

> (CP, 23)

I will have more to say about other Hispanic American translations of "The Negro Speaks of Rivers" in chapters 3 and 4. For now, suffice it to point out that having "contemplated rivers" is clearly not the same as having "known rivers," neither in English nor in Spanish. As if representing the act of growing more ponderous, the stanza in López Narváez's poem is now a syntactical unit that takes up the space of four lines rather than three, regularizing the shape of Hughes's unrhymed stanza by turning it into a quatrain with an abab rhyme scheme. Unable to render the Spanish rhymes in English, Tittler only follows López Narváez's lead in loosening up Hughes's notably denser diction and clipped syntax and in unifying Hughes's three discrete statements, one per line almost like a syllogism, into a single sentence. In this way, the stanza acquires an ungainliness quite untypical of Hughes's tighter modernist verse.

Because it is a translation of a translation, Tittler's version of López Narváez's Spanish adaptation of Hughes's poem raises the question of how a translation relates to a presumed original, and it does so with greater emphasis and urgency than most other translations would. In this case, which is admittedly more complicated than a more typical translation from one language into another, the presumably unidirectional flow of translation is reversed such that the Spanish text assumes the status a new "original." When transferred (back?) to English, that new, other original becomes a new poem. Neither the Spanish nor the new English version is identical with, or equivalent to, Hughes's poem. What Tittler gives us, then, are lines that Hughes, in fact, never wrote. It is unclear whether Tittler deliberately offered his own translation of these lines or whether he simply did not recognize "The Negro Speaks of Rivers" in *Changó*. Either way, it seems oddly logical to have the imagined Hughes recite a poem that the historical Hughes actually did *not* write. After all, Zapata Olivella's character is *both* Hughes *and* not Hughes; the historical Hughes was no more of a Garveyite than Sandy Hook is in New York. Analogously, a translation is both a version of another text and a *new* text in its own right.

It is fitting that Zapata Olivella should choose to retool a key scene from *The Big Sea* to move the poet into closer ideological proximity to Marcus Garvey's Pan-African project. In *The Big Sea*, Hughes does, after all, focus on what connects *people of color*—not only African Americans from the USA—worldwide. Hughes, unlike his fictional counterpart in the novel, did not support Garvey, and he may never even have met the charismatic orator outside the pages of Zapata Olivella's novel. And unlike Garvey, Hughes had been to Africa. Hughes was also hardly unaware of the Jamaican's tremendous—and to some, frightening—popularity among USAmericans of African descent at or near the bottom of the socioeconomic ladder. Many attended his famed rallies in Harlem, and many bought stock in the Black Star Line, an investment enterprise that was to become the instrument of Garvey's political undoing. These were of course the same people who stomped to the blues of W. C. Handy, Ma Rainey, Bessie Smith, and later Muddy Waters, the low-down, often criminalized black folk after whom

Hughes modeled many a character in his poems. Hughes's internationalism, however, went far beyond the racial essentialism that continues to cling to terms such as "Pan-Africanism," "Afro-centrism," and even "African diaspora."[97] In *The Big Sea*, as in his poetry, Hughes shows us how black internationalism as a discourse emerges in the multiple mediations and refractions that occur when people who speak in different languages interact with each other, often generating meanings several times removed from the original utterances, meanings that also take on lives of their own. In *I Wonder As I Wander*, his sense of belonging reaches well beyond the expected areas of the African diaspora—Europe, Mexico, South America, and the Caribbean—to include Russia and what are now the central Asian republics. It is through metaphorical and literal acts of translation that Hughes knits together these varied sites into a global cultural network that extends far beyond the still largely anglophone idea of an Atlantic world.[98]

Modeling the dynamics of cross-cultural and cross-racial communities, Hughes's autobiographies stand as remarkable reminders that the intersecting discourses of black internationalism and international modernism do not come into being as fully formed abstractions. First and foremost, they exist as layers of the fundamentally chaotic conversations people carried out in different places at overlapping points in time. A literary artist such as Hughes reimagines the formless chaos of lived experience, reworking it into distinctive shapes and patterns in which multilingual, translational processes become visible on the page and audible in the reader's mind. To read Hughes's work attentively means to participate in the process of negotiating linguistic, cultural, and ideological differences; to experience what it is like to straddle the divisions between them; and, above all, to keep moving. To keep moving, in the context of Hughes's autobiographies, means that there is no closure, only more openings. It also means that acts of translation do not overcome or resolve cultural differences. Translation is a process of reimagining those differences that lays the groundwork for mutual respect. It is worth noting that decades before Stuart Hall, Paul Gilroy, and others started to theorize diaspora as a frame for cultural identity determined by dispersal and difference, Hughes had already put into literary practice a plurilingual, heterocultural poetics that articulated "the knowledge of [one's] moving."[99]

CHAPTER TWO

SOUTHERN EXPOSURES

Hughes in Spanish

> Langston Hughes hermano,
> hermano de raza
> y también por ser hombre
> y humano,
> mi admiración te alcanza.
>
> [Langston Hughes, brother, / brother in race, / and it is also for being a
> man / and human, / that my admiration takes hold of you.]
> —Pilar Barrios, "Voces"

> Y canto esa día,
> Langston, Langston,
> Para todos esa día,
> Langston, Langston!
>
> [And I sing of a distant day, / Langston, Langston, / For all, a distant day,
> / Langston, Langston!]
> —Alejo Carpentier

One need not to subscribe to Walter Benjamin's view of original and translation as so many shards of a greater language to imagine some semantic overlap between the Spanish noun *negro* and its English counterparts.[1] Such overlap has invited much theoretical speculation on kinship relations among the cultural formations of the African diaspora in the Americas. But can a "spic" really be a "Negro," even a "nigger," and vice versa? Is there, for instance, such a thing as a black Cuban?[2] Nicolás Guillén, who is often credited with having started "a movement known as Afro-Cuban poetry," struck a different note when he wrote in *El Nacional* (Caracas) in 1951 that the interest in Afrocubanism was something that came entirely from outside Cuba:

"Poesía afrocubana," "música afrocubana," "arte afrocubana"...Que quiere decir esto? A mi juicio...no quiere decir nada. Es en todo caso una manera rápida de hablar, una convención que no responde a ninguna realidad en el panorama de la cultural nacional. Considerar que existe lo "afrocubano" como expresión independiente y parcial del alma de Cuba, es falso, pues estamos hechos de una conmixtión profunda de dos sangres.

["Afro-Cuban poetry," "Afro-Cuban music," "Afro-Cuban art"...What does this mean? In my estimation...it means nothing. It is in all cases a sleight of hand, a convention that does not correspond to any reality in the national culture. To think that "Afro-Cubanism" exists as an independent and partial expression of the Cuban soul is wrong, since we are the product of a profound admixture of two bloods.] [3]

When one tries to determine, then, just how similar the word *negro* in, say, early-twentieth-century Cuban literary and popular usage is to racial epithets such as "Negro," "black," "darky," "boy," or "nigger," as they have circulated in the USA at different points in time, it quickly becomes apparent that claims to cultural equivalence are far more complicated in historical and literary practice than they appear in theory. In this chapter and the next one, I analyze Langston Hughes's poems in their Spanish translation to try to untangle some of these complications.

A NEGLECTED ARCHIVE OF TRANSLATIONS

Langston Hughes's reputation in the Hispanic Americas is the stuff of legend. Maribel Cruzado and Mary Hricko, translator-editors of *Langston Hughes. Blues* (2004), even claim that Hughes was the "Afro-American writer most widely read in the world."[4] Translations of a few of his poems first appeared in Cuba between 1928 and 1930. Others quickly followed, notably Xavier Villaurrutia's and Jorge Luis Borges's, which in 1931 found their way into two leading avant-garde journals, Mexico's *Contemporáneos* and Argentina's *Sur*.[5] From there, Hughes's fame spread swiftly and not just among fellow writers. To many, Hughes was "uno de los poetas negros más interesantes del momento" (one of the most interesting black poets of his time).[6] Even after his death in 1967, Hughes remained the best-known and most admired USAmerican poet in the Hispanic Americas since Longfellow and Whitman.[7] Along with Cuba's poet laureate, Nicolás Guillén, Hughes continues to be regarded as the most important "Negro poet" of the twentieth century in many parts of the Hispanic world, including Spain.[8] What accounts for this immense popularity, which has been unmatched not only by any of Hughes's African American contemporaries but also by any of the canonical Anglo-American modernists?[9] What was it about Hughes's poetry that so compelled Hispanic Americans?

Unless they had access to the English versions of Hughes's poems and could read them in that language, Hispanic Americans would have come into contact with what at first glance seems a relatively small portion of his poetic corpus: to date, 164 out of a total of 856 poems have been translated into Spanish.[10] With the help of an Excel spreadsheet and Mullen's 1977 landmark bibliography of translations of Hughes's work into Spanish,[11] I began by mapping the trajectory of every single known Hughes poem translated into Spanish and printed in either a book or a periodical (see appendix). Between 1928, the year of Hughes's first official visit to Cuba, and the end of 2004, more than three hundred translations of Hughes's poems were published in Argentina, Brazil, Chile, Costa Rica, Cuba, El Salvador, Mexico, Puerto Rico, Spain, Uruguay, and Venezuela. They were printed in no fewer than eleven anthologies, twenty-nine periodicals, and the Spanish versions of Hughes's autobiographies. Although perhaps not as important to the overall circulation of Hughes's poems in translation, three stand-alone poetry collections—Julio Gáler's *Langston Hughes. Poemas,* Herminio Ahumada's *Yo también soy América,* and Cruzado and Hricko's *Langston Hughes. Blues*—significantly boosted the number of poems available in Spanish at different points in time.[12] That this substantial archive of translations has gone largely unexamined has blurred both the broad contours and the specifics of Hughes's reputation in the Hispanic Americas.[13] My work here is meant to begin the process of providing firmer ground for such speculations.[14]

To his translators, as to those who wrote poems in celebration of him and used his verse in their own writings, Hughes was not one poet; he was many.[15] My analysis of the corpus of Hughes's work disseminated in Spanish translation shows both broad trends among Hughes's translators south of the USAmerican border and significant individual variations. Which poems his translators chose to carry over into Spanish, and which they omitted, also speaks to what each considered representative of either Hughes the New Negro poet or Hughes the revolutionary. Equally telling is how translators from different countries treated individual poems. There are fascinating differences among multiple translations of the same poem, some of which I explore in detail here. Hughes's translators across the Americas—be they poets, journalists, or academics—had varied reasons for being interested in his verse, and the ways in which they rendered his verse in Spanish gives us access to some of their motivations.[16] In this and the following chapter, I explore what Hughes, the man and his literary corpus, came to mean to audiences in Cuba, Chile, Mexico, Uruguay, and Argentina, to name but a handful of the countries in which translations of his poems saw print. Was Hughes the "darker brother" with whose predicament those in the long shadow of their northern neighbor identified, regardless of their own ethnicity or race? Was he a political radical offering up poetic versions of the revolutionary sentiments of the Internationale? Or was he the rebellious vanguardist whose poems they admired for their formal daring? In particular, I scrutinize translations by José Antonio Fernández de Castro (1887–1951) from Cuba, Ildefonso Pereda Valdés (1899–1996) from

Uruguay, Xavier Villaurrutia (1903–50) from Mexico, and (in chapter 3) Jorge Luis Borges (1899–1986) and Julio Gáler from Argentina. All these translations provide historical and textual testing grounds for theories of black internationalism that relativize assumptions about cultural and political sameness and equivalences often so deeply lodged within the academic discourses of African American and African diaspora studies that they have become virtually invisible. Brent Edwards's excavation of the intellectual history of the term "diaspora" is an important step in "remind[ing] us that 'diaspora' is introduced in large part to account for *differences* among African-derived populations, in a way that a term like 'pan-Africanism' could not." [17] I add to his work close-ups of how Hughes's poems were reframed as they passed from English into Spanish.

Considering both larger trends and the texts of individual translations, I argue that several distinct regional and international discourses, notably anti-USAmerican imperialism, socialism, and modernism, provided the triple lenses through which Hughes's poems were refracted in the Hispanic Americas. While it is often difficult cleanly to separate these interlocking lenses, I foreground the connections translators made between antiblack racism and imperialist oppression in this chapter and defer my remarks on comparative modernisms and the politics of different modernisms in the Americas until the next chapter.

THE POLITICS OF TRANSLATION

There is strong evidence that translators frequently appropriated Hughes's verse for their own nationalist agendas rather than using it to spread the seeds of black political awareness across the Hispanic Americas.[18] The discourse of anti-USAmerican imperialism flooded the Hispanic Americas during the aftermath of the Spanish-Cuban-American War (1895–98). It proved quite inseparable from nascent nationalist ideologies in a number of countries, providing translators and literary commentators alike with fertile ground for analogizing external and internal colonization: that is, they likened the USA's neocolonial encroachments in the Hispanic Americas to the antiblack racism that Hughes scorned in so many of his poems. Such analogies also facilitated the absorption of Hughes's poems about racial oppression into the discourse of revolutionary class struggle radiating outward from the Soviet Union, especially during the 1930s. Taken together, these two refractions add up to substantial reformulations of an English-language discourse of blackness—New Negro-ness, if you will—that, though often regarded as international, reflected and was part of the peculiar history of USAmerican race relations during the early twentieth century. To argue that translations of the poems associated with the discourse of New Negro-ness played a crucial role in making Hughes an unofficial USAmerican cultural ambassador in the Hispanic Americas has countless implications beyond the academic fields identified with the study of race and blackness, most immediately for comparative New World or hemispheric studies and for conceptualizations of literary and cultural influence more generally.[19]

Hughes's fame in the Hispanic Americas is inconsistent with what Guido Podestá calls "the cultural blockade actively promoted by intellectuals after [José Enrique] Rodó" and with Rodó's critical pronouncements, in *Ariel* (1900), in "response to the expansion of United States cultural [and, one might add, ideological] habits in Latin America."[20] Podestá's argument that Rodó's vision of the USA as a "barbaric" nation discouraged Hispanic American scholars from engaging in comparative studies of Hispanic American and USAmerican literatures makes good sense. "To the advocates of the cultural blockade," he writes, "a comparative study of this nature would have meant acceptance of 'affinities' with a society portrayed as the negation of truly cultural European (French) values." His claim that "the pervasive consumption and construction of prejudices against African-Americans, even among indigenistas, deterred even more a cultural and political appreciation [among Hispanic American intellectuals] of what was being written by African-Americans in the United States" does not, however, easily follow from Hughes's example.[21] Just the opposite seems to be true. In many parts of the Hispanic Americas, postwar Europe's *vogue nègre* translated into a more than faddish awareness of the local importance of racial topics which, in the 1930s and 1940s, produced numerous collections of *poesía negra americana* in Cuba, Chile, Uruguay, and elsewhere, along with scores of new journals and professional societies devoted to Afro-Hispanic American cultures.[22] The work of W. E. B. Du Bois, Walter White, and other New Negro artists and intellectuals appeared regularly in Hispanic American magazines and newspapers.[23] The criticisms of internal colonization that they voiced loudly during the early decades of the twentieth century appear to have resonated with Hispanic Americans of many colors and ethnicities.[24] The marginal position that African American writers and thinkers occupied within the USA became a ready analogue for how many Hispanic Americans perceived their own countries' situations vis-à-vis what José Martí had famously dubbed the "monster" in whose entrails he had lived when in exile in New York.[25] Such hemispheric resonances may also explain why one finds Hughes's poems in Hispanic American anthologies of USAmerican poetry in the company of Anglo-American modernists such as Eliot, Pound, Stevens, Frost, and Hart Crane just as often as one encounters him in major anthologies of *poesía negra,* such as Ildefonso Pereda Valdés's *Antología de la poesía negra americana* (1936) and Emilio Ballagas's *Mapa de la poesía negra americana* (1946).[26]

To some extent, then, Hughes's marginalization at home made him all the more popular among artists and intellectuals from the Hispanic Americas. Hughes's position as a Negro writer in the USA does not, however, sufficiently explain his popularity in the Hispanic Americas. Other writers in this category—notably Countee Cullen, Claude McKay, and James Weldon Johnson—appeared with some frequency alongside Hughes in both sorts of anthologies. But their poems rarely made it into journals, and no one ever translated enough of them for a book-length collection. The same is true of most other twentieth-century USAmerican poets, including white modernists. Hughes was also neither the only New Negro who had ever lived in or visited the Hispanic Americas nor the only one who spoke Spanish. Johnson, William Carlos Williams, and Hart Crane are notable examples of modernists with contacts south of the border of the USA.[27] Like the work of other USAmerican Negro writers included in Hispanic American anthologies, Hughes's poetry stood outside mainstream literary canons, including the incipient canons of modernism. Not a few Hispanic American anthologizers remarked on this exclusion. On this point, the Mexican poet Salvador Novo wrote in 1931: "Pocas antologías poéticas [en los Estados Unidos] se atreverían a incluir en sus páginas producciones de poetas negros. Y cuando lo hagan, como lo hace Louis Untermeyer, escogerán poesías en dialecto de Paul Laurence Dunbar, patriarca de los poetas negros de América, cuya mayor preocupación era precisamente la de no concentrase en el dialecto" (Few poetry anthologies [in the United States] dare include in their pages works by Negro poets. And when they do, as Louis Untermeyer has, they choose dialect poetry by Paul Laurence Dunbar, the patriarch of American Negro poets, whose main worry was precisely not to limit himself to dialect).[28] As late as 1955, Eugenio Florit, who was teaching at Barnard College when he compiled his *Antología de la poesía norteamericana contemporánea,* remarked that, with the exception of Hughes, Dunbar, and Cullen, "no ha aparecido ningún poeta de significación nacional entre los de la raza de color" (not a single poet of national significance has emerged among the poets of color) in the USA.[29] Florit includes a total of thirty-eight poets in his bilingual volume, ranging from Masters, Sandburg, and Stevens to Pound, Eliot, Williams, Auden, Lowell, and Wilbur. Hughes stands out as the only African American contributor. Notes Florit:

A pesar de todo ello y de esa universalidad que creo ver en los poemas de Hughes, me parece que *esta poesía se mantiene aparte, muy mezclada aún con lo pintoresco, y sin incorporarse como poesía a la corriente nacional.* Esta situación es evidente si observamos que en casi ninguna de las excelentes antologías que se publican en los Estados Unidos aparecen poemas de poetas negros.

[Despite all this and despite this universality I believe I see in Hughes's poems, it seems to me that this poetry exists apart, very much mixed up with the picturesque, and without being incorporated as poetry into the national mainstream. This is evident when one considers that no poems by Negro writers are included in almost any of the excellent anthologies that are now being published in the United States.] [30]

In fact, if one constructed a USAmerican literary canon from Hispanic American anthologies between 1936 and 1976, it would differ markedly from that of the USAmerican academy for that same period. The same is true when one compares collections of black poetry from James Weldon Johnson's *The Book of Negro Poetry* (1922 and 1931) to Robert Hayden's *Kaleidoscope: Poems by American Negro Poets* (1967) with the anthologies of *poesía negra americana*.

BLACKNESS AND UNIVERSALITY

Given the substantial number of translated Hughes poems, a closer analysis of this archive logically begins with those poems translated with the greatest frequency and printed in the widest array of venues, both during the early years and later on. Some provisional patterns emerge quickly. The single most translated poem of Hughes's in Spanish is "I, Too" from 1925, the "Epilogue" from *The Weary Blues*. It circulated in the Hispanic Americas in no fewer than fifteen different translations, with four additional versions published in Spain. "I, Too," typically under the title of "Yo también," appeared in nine anthologies and fifteen periodicals; it was also reprinted numerous times. Gastón Figueira attributes Hughes's popularity in the Hispanic Americas specifically to this poem and "la intensidad de su sentido social" (the intensity of his social sentiments).[31] The next most translated of Hughes's poems, though a distant second to "I, Too," is "Negro," an earlier lyric from *Crisis* (1922), which appeared in Spanish nine times. "The Negro Speaks of Rivers" and "Cross," also from *The Crisis* (1921 and 1925, respectively), generated nine and seven different translations each.[32]

The four most-translated Hughes poems are all part of *The Weary Blues* (1926), as are the majority of his other lyrics translated during the 1920s, 1930s, and 1940s—a total of seventy-six poems. In fact, all but one of the Hughes translations that Villaurrutia and Borges, along with Rafael Lozano and José Antonio Fernández de Castro, published between 1928 and 1931—respectively in *Contemporáneos, Sur, Crísol, Social* (see figure 1) *Revista de la Habana,* and the *Diario de la Marina*—were of poems from that collection.[33] Poetry anthologies published during the next two decades also selected some poems from *Fine Clothes to the Jew* (1927), as well as from journals such as *Opportunity* and *New Masses*. But this was not enough to alter a clear preference for *The Weary Blues* that has persisted until today.[34]

A glance at the group of twenty-six poems translated during the 1920s and 1930s reveals surprisingly common choices on the part of very different translators. Even if not all of these poems fit the category of what Edward

La cabeza de Paul Robeson, en bronce, ejecutada por el famoso escultor judío-norteamericano Jacobo Ep-stein, quien en su reciente viaje a su país—después de 20 años de deliberada ausencia—quiso servirse de Robeson como modelo del hombre más interesante de la hora actual en los Estados Unidos.
(Foto Wide World.)

POR
LANGSTON
HUGHES

Yo, también, honro a América
Soy el hermano negro.
Me mandan a comer en la cocina,
Cuando vienen visitas...
Pero me río,
Como bien
Y así me fortalezco.

Mañana
Me sentaré en la mesa
Y aunque vengan visitas
Nadie se atreverá
A decirme
"A la cocina, negro."
Al mismo tiempo
Se darán cuenta
De lo hermoso que soy
Y se avergonzarán.
¡Yo soy también América!

YO,
TAMBIEN...

30

Figure 1. Page from *Social*, 1928, with José Antonio Fernández de Castro's translation of "I, Too."

Mullen rather disparagingly calls "nostalgic portraits,"[35] their selection alone—independent of the specifics of a given translation—shows a penchant for emphasizing aesthetics over politics. To most of these translators, *la raza negra* was a valuable cultural commodity that could serve the cause of nationalism *and* provide an important link with European literary modernisms through which Hispanic American intellectuals could affirm ties with the cultural elites of France and Germany.[36] In the Hispanic Americas, even in countries with significant numbers of citizens of African descent such as Cuba and Brazil, it was quite common at the time to separate blackness as a cultural commodity from the social and political realities of racial conflicts. In literary contexts, terms such as *negro, mulato,* and *negrista* were often used interchangeably, regardless of a writer's perceived or claimed racial identities. In this way, blackness could be rhetorically integrated with nationalist and anti-imperialist causes quite regardless of the marginalization of darker-complexioned populations that existed, and exists today, throughout the Hispanic Americas.[37] The Afro-Antillean movement, which flourished in Cuba and Puerto Rico in the 1930s and exemplifies transatlantic modernisms' strong investments in blackness as a revitalizing aesthetic, is but one example of such contradictions.[38]

With few exceptions, then, the poems Hughes's translators chose did not emphasize the contradictions between culture and politics that led to political crises at home, among them the banning of the Partido Independiente de Color in Cuba in 1910 and the Partido Autóctono Negro in Uruguay in the late 1930s.[39] Their selection of poems and their actual translations constructed Hughes's verse in Spanish as a vehicle for nationalist and transnational anti-imperialist alliances. His poems were appealing because of their presumably restorative "primitivism"—evident in rhythms that some described as "eminentemente espontánea," "desliteraturizada," and "un poco sincopados, como la música de jazz" (extremely spontaneous, unliterary [or deliteraturized], a bit syncopated, much like jazz is)—without being politically limited by race.[40]

Sencillez, "simplicity," is a related term that keeps recurring in commentaries on Hughes's style, linking him to Martí. In the eyes of these commentators, *sencillez* was a prime poetic vehicle for what some called truth, others "excesiva franquesa" (excessive candor). The Chilean scholar and teacher Andrés Bansart, in his posthumously published *Poesía negra-africana* (Santiago de Chile, 1971), described Hughes's lyrics as "obras maestras de sencillez: ninguna palabra rebuscada, pero palabras verdaderas" (masterful works of simplicity: not mannered words but truthful words). The Spanish poet Rafael Alberti, in the brief unsigned note about Hughes's poetry that prefaces his 1937 translation of "I, Too" in *El Mono Azul* speaks admiringly of "sus sencillos poemas, que no sólo los negros de su país aman y repiten, sino que también los escritores y lectores del Mundo han sabido ya valorizar" (his simple poems not only beloved by the blacks in his own country who repeat them but also already praised by writers and readers in the rest of the world).[41] Juan Felipe Toruño, who greeted "el arte poético negro" as a welcome alternative to what he regarded as the stylistic contortions of certain vanguardist movements such as *Ultraísmo*, summed it up well in his prefatory remarks to *Poesía negra* (Mexico City, 1953): "No tiene secretos esa poesía"—this poetry has no secrets.[42] Similar language, in English of course, can be found in Rampersad's introduction to the 1993 edition of *The Big Sea*, where he refers to Hughes's "honest, water-clear prose" that is "utterly devoid of affectation" (BS, xxv).When one reads Hughes's lyrics side by side with their Spanish-language versions, one readily realizes that these poems are neither simple nor direct. Even lyrics such as Hughes's "Negro" offered Hispanic American (and other) readers multiple points of nonracial identification concurrent with the opening line, "Yo soy negro" (I am a Negro)—notably "worker," "singer," and "victim" (*CP*, 24). "He conocido ríos," as Borges rendered the first line of Hughes's "The Negro Speaks of Rivers"—"I've known rivers" (*CP*, 23)—is especially effective for its use of a first-person pronoun that could easily be separated from the "Negro" in the poem's title (for more on this poem see chapter 3).

Not only did Hughes's translators tend to select poems that allowed Hispanic Americans to imagine unity along nationalist lines and around international causes. They also, in the actual translations, strategically reinforced certain areas of identification at the expense of others to ensure that that *all* Mexican—or Cuban, Uruguayan, or Argentine—voices could "acompaña[r] la voz de Hughes para decir a coro: 'Yo también soy América'" (join Hughes's voice in proclaiming, in unison, "I, too, am America").[43] Ildefonso Pereda Valdés's version of "Mulatto" ("Mulato"), one of Hughes's most confrontational early poems about racial mixing, exemplifies such efforts. Like most of Hughes's Hispanic American translators, the Uruguayan was attracted to the racial elements in Hughes's verse, and "Mulatto" was one of the Hughes poems he selected for his anthology to represent "la rebelión de la raza."[44] That Pereda Valdés himself was not only a professor of literature but also a poet and editor of some note who had two volumes of *poesía negra* to his credit—*La guitarra de los negros* (1926) and *Raza negra* (1929), both published in Montevideo—makes it all the more remarkable how little his translation attempts to capture the source poem's texture.[45] Omitting Hughes's indents, italics, and exclamation points, all of which further the poem's dramatic form, Pereda Valdés transforms passages such as

> *I am your son, white man!*
> A little yellow
> Bastard boy.
>
> (*CP*, 101)

into lines that fail to create any sense of the poem as a drama of lyric voices locked in a bitter quarrel:

Yo soy tu hijo, hombre blanco,
Un pequeño bastardo amarillo.[46]

Compare this with the energetic version of this poem that Julio Gáler published in his *Poemas de Langston Hughes* in Buenos Aires in 1952. His final lines also omit the italics, but at least they remain centered and emphatic: "Soy tu hijo, hombre blanco! / Un pequeño, turbio, bastardo rapaz" (*Poemas* 69). One might say that Pereda Valdés's translation, to use his own words, "pales" by comparison with its source text.[47] This sort of structural and tonal flattening-out makes the translation static on the page, yielding verse entirely bereft of the intensity of racial confrontation and of what Florit called the "delicioso sentido del humor y la ironía" (delicious sense of humor and irony) that marked Hughes's poetry for so many of his admirers.[48]

Pereda Valdés was also among the first to tout Hughes as "el poeta de la revolución social," linking his poetry explicitly to international socialism.[49] In his introduction to the same anthology in which "Mulato" appeared, he moves from lauding Hughes as "un gran poeta que canta con el alma de su raza" (a great poet who sings with the soul of his race) to stressing that Hughes "[s]e hace un poeta revolucionario y *canta como el más universal de los poetas de su raza:* al sentimiento racial se une la solidaridad con todos los explotados del mundo" (becomes a revolutionary poet and *sings like the most universal poet of his race:* racial sentiment is joined by solidarity with all of the world's exploited peoples).[50] These remarks show how carefully Pereda Valdés constructed Hughes's "universality." He firmly aligned a discourse of blackness that might spell cultural and political separatism with the more inclusive rhetoric of political solidarity among *all* the victims of capitalism. To illustrate this joining in Hughes's own poems, Pereda Valdés selected "Union" ("Unión"), first printed in *New Masses* in 1931, and "Always the Same" ("Siempre lo mismo"), which had appeared in *Negro Worker* in 1932 (*CP,* 165).[51] He might have made bolder choices. For instance, he might have selected "Good Morning Revolution" or "Advertisement for the Opening of the Waldorf-Astoria" (*CP,* 162, 143), both of which had appeared in *New Masses* in 1931–32 and were, in fact, translated by Miguel Alejandro for *Nueva Cultura* in 1936 (see figures 2 and 3), the same year that saw the first edition of *Antología de la poesía negra americana* (it was reprinted in Uruguay in 1953).[52] It is especially telling that Pereda Valdés did not pick Hughes's "Scottsboro," published in *Opportunity* in 1931 (*CP,* 142–43). Afro-Hispanic American authors may well have "shared Hughes's hatred of Fascism as exemplified in his comments on Scottsboro."[53] Yet Hughes's translators, especially in Chile, Argentina, and Uruguay—countries with relatively small populations of African descent—favored inclusive abstractions such as "todos los oprimidos / del pobre mundo" ("all the whole oppressed / Poor world," *CP,* 138) over

2 LANGSTON HUGHES

POR MIGUEL ALEJANDRO

Langston Hughes, el poeta negro de la Revolución

EL ESCENARIO

«*El problema del siglo XX es el problema de la línea de color.*»—W. E. W. Du Bois.

«*El corazón no es una rodilla para ser doblado.*»—PROVERBIO NEGRO.

«Ahoga a un blanco y se convertirá en negro también», ha dicho Waldo Frank, regalándonos una diapositiva nítida, universal y definitiva.

Se le podría oponer un «NO» rotundo y ecuménico, si no fuera verdad:

1.º Que B. Anderson, del Chase Bank,

Arrancados a la primitiva vida de sus aldeas africanas, los seres «inferiores» van a amasar con su sudor y con su sangre la riqueza y el esplendor del mundo capitalista que nace

contestó a una demanda informativa sobre la situación de la U. S. A.

—No sabemos nada —dijo modestamente—. Estamos estudiándolo.

2.º Que Wáshington, es la capital de las estadísticas y que ocupa en estos menesteres a 28.000 individuos (que algún día harán su propia y cruenta estadística).

3.º Que el «Empire State» tiene habitaciones vacías.

4.º Que Ford, de 100.000 obreros, tiene ya menos de 10.000.

5.º Que hay parados en Bowery.

6.º Que la crisis americana, y la mundial, se deben a un inmenso error de contabilidad.

6 Se podrá juzgar esto como una bagatela, como un rasgo de humor latino, pero los más

autorizados voceros nacionales no lo desmienten, sino lo confirman acumulando datos.

Por Upton Sinclair, sabemos que la industria de materias primas en Norteamérica *está muerta* y que significa que hay 10.000.000 de obreros que no trabajan, ni trabajarán mientras dure el sistema actual, y que como *ellos* no «consienten» en morir de inanición, se han de alimentar con dinero del erario público, lo que significa que nunca se podrá equilibrar el presupuesto. El 90 por 100 de las transacciones se realizan por medio de créditos.

La carga estadounidense de intereses se ha vuelto absolutamente intolerable y no obstante soportan esta carga abrumadora, colectivamente, por medio del Gobierno. Sistema singularísimo de la economía superada que permite que uno se preste dinero a sí mismo. Algo así como una dolorosísima broma de Marc Twain.

«Si pretendiéramos librarnos de estas calamidades, ¿qué deberíamos hacer? La única solución de la crisis se conseguiría distribuyendo las fuentes naturales de la riqueza, cesando de producir mercancías para provecho de una clase reducida y fabricándolas para uso de todos los trabajadores útiles, sean intelectuales o físicos.

No trato de acusar a nuestros hombres de negocios con esta solución, sino inducirlos a pensar en su propio interés. ¿Por qué no ordenar y organizar las enormes fuerzas de la producción, en bien de la seguridad y comodidad de todos los habitantes de los Estados Unidos?»

También podrían tomarse estas palabras como ejercicio literario, si no las confirmaran los que buscan soluciones paliativas con sus panaceas librescas y financieras.

Rumbo a las Américas. El gráfico demuestra el horrible hacinamiento de la mercancía humana en las calas de los buques negreros

Mister W. E. Woodward, ha escrito un libro titulado «Dinero para mañana», en el que propone una ruta restauradora al capitalismo norteamericano, basándose en proposiciones sugeridas por la Cámara Norteamericana de Comercio para la estabilización económica, la idea de un Congreso de Comerciantes de la Federación Cívica Nacional, el proyecto de «Soviets Capitalistas», de Genard Swpoe y el plan de Stewart Chase. La mayor parte de estos planes tienden a proteger los intereses de la oligarquía financiera e industrial compuesta por minorías selectas.

A pesar de las cadenas y de un horizonte cerrado de oscuridad, los pobres esclavos conservan con triste sordina la antigua alegría de sus almas

La situación angustiosa sirve de plataforma para un nuevo tipo de escolasticismo que resuelve todos los problemas con «dádivas». Con este libro, se refuerza el capitalismo vacilante que ese ha ido descomponiendo por sí mismo durante 25 años y que ahora está al borde de la bancarrota.

Esta confesión de parte, evita el comentario.

Si todo esto es verdad para los trabajadores blancos, ¿qué será para los trabajadores de color?... Aunque, si hemos de reconocer la verdad, los blancos, hoy en día, son también negros, y bien negros, por sus miserias. Por esta razón, «la línea de color» es más extensa de lo que se cree. Tan extensa, que se ha convertido —por su génesis geométrica— en una dilatada superficie negra, con la pez de una «confesadas y evi-

[154]

Figure 3. Title page from *Nueva Cultura*, 1936.

more disquieting lines such as "8 BLACK BOYS IN A SOUTHERN JAIL. / WORLD, TURN PALE!" (*CP*, 143).[54]

There were two ways in which translators such as Pereda Valdés could make Hughes's poems more universal. One was to select poems without precise references to the USA, be those geographical, cultural, or political. The other was to suppress such contextual references, including distinctive musical traits, such as the responsorial form of blues lyrics and other repetitions suggestive of blues or jazz. This would explain, for instance, why none of Hughes's blues poems were translated prior to 1952, the date of Julio Gáler's *Poemas*,[55] even though Hispanic American reviewers had celebrated those very poems from the beginning. The closest we get to a translation of a blues poem is "Canto de una muchacha negra," a version of "Song for a Dark Girl" from *Fine Clothes to the Jew* (*CP*, 104) by one G. Caparicio, which was included in Pereda Valdés's *Antología*.[56] This poem, also printed in Emilio Ballagas's *Mapa de la poesía negra americana*[57] as "Canto de una joven negra," is one of two Hughes poems in the *Antología* with geocultural references to the USA. The other one, also from *Fine Clothes to the Jew*, is of course "Mulatto." In "Mulato," the place name in the phrase "Georgia dusk" is retained in "Crespúsculo de Georgia." But the more charged and rather conspicuous "Dixie" in "Canto de una muchacha negra" — conspicuous because it is part of the refrain "Way Down South in Dixie" — finds itself folded into the translation's more generic "south": "Allá lejos, en el sur," or, as Ballagas has it, in his enhancement of the poem's rhythms, "Fué allá en el Sur, en el Sur."[58] The elision and transmutation of such specific reference points were a translational strategy that facilitated the north-south passage of certain Hughes poems.

Richard Jackson contends that Hughes's "radical image" among Afro-Hispanic American writers "also helped account for [his] popularity outside the Black Diaspora in Latin America."[59] That Hughes spent a year in Russia and was on friendly terms with known Hispanic American Communists — notably the Cuban Nicolás Guillén, whose poems he would translate in the late 1940s, but also the Chilean Pablo Neruda and the Argentine Raúl Gonález Tuñón — no doubt made him a politically appealing figure for many members of the Hispanic Americas' intellectual elite.[60] Yet if the poems that circulated most in translation are any indication, Hispanic Americans, though they praised Hughes's political radicalism often enough, were apparently less attracted to the actual poetic manifestations of his politics. Pereda Valdés's *Antología* is a case in point. It was the most influential collection of *poesía negra americana* for the better part of three decades. When it was reprinted in 1953, its editor made no changes in his lineup of Hughes's poems, nor elsewhere in the volume, even though, by then, he surely would have seen a far greater number of poems than he had in the mid-thirties, including those in Hughes's *A New Song*, rejected by Knopf for its radical politics and finally published by the International Workers Order in 1938.[61]

Pereda Valdés's unchanged selections no doubt contributed to maintaining a pattern that was well established by the early 1950s among Hughes's Hispanic American translators: admiration for his leftist politics coupled with a conspicuous avoidance of his radical poetry.

This paradoxical pattern ran parallel to the treatment Hughes's blues poems experienced in the Hispanic Americas. Although this practice shifted somewhat first with Julio Gáler's *Poemas* and then Herminio Ahumada's *Yo también soy América* (1968), later anthologizers still tended to stay away from Hughes's revolutionary poems, regardless of whether they thematized racial or political subjects.[62] One example is the 1971 Chilean anthology, *Poesía negra-africana,* published posthumously by the students of Andrés Bansart, who regularly taught courses on the subject at the Pontífica Universidad Católica de Chile in Santiago in the 1960s. (Pereda Valdés also taught courses on African American literatures in Chile but at the Universidad de Santiago and the Universidad de Concepción.) The editors offer this anthology not only so that Hispanic Americans may be more aware of the plight of African Americans but "también para que los latinoamericanos se sientan más solidarios de sus hermanos de Tercer-Mundo en la lucha contra todos los tipos de imperialismo" (also so that Latin Americans feel greater solidarity for their Third-World brothers in the struggle against all types of imperialism).[63] Yet, with the exception of "Yo también," none of the Hughes poems they include—"Poema" ("Poem 1," *CP,* 22), "Tener miedo" ("Afraid," *CP,* 41), and "Nuestra tierra" ("Our Land," *CP,* 32–33)—have much to say about the so-called Third World or imperialism. But labels such as "social revolutionary," "radical," and "militant" stuck, and they followed Hughes for decades to come. Even in 1971, when the Black Arts Movements in the United States had produced any number of younger radical poets, the Bansart anthology still presented Hughes as the premier voice against black oppression.

It was broader ideas and concepts, then, not cultural particularities that facilitated the construction of parallels between Hispanic Americans' neo-colonial situation in relation to the USA and the domestic plight of African Americans in the USA. My epigraphs to this chapter suggest this to be true of Hispanic American writers as different as the Cuban Alejo Carpentier and the Uruguayan Pilar Barrios, who paid homage to Hughes in their own verse by evoking generalized sentiments of brotherhood and shared hope. Through their preference for particular poems and their formal choices, translators made Hughes's verse compatible with their own and their readers' cultural values and political agendas.

WHO SINGS AMERICA?

The Hispanic American career of "I, Too" is perhaps the best example of exactly when and how this happened. Two well-known anthologies, Pereda

Valdés's *Antología de la poesía negra americana* and Ballagas's *Mapa de la poesía negra americana,* were the first to feature translations of "I, Too."[64] In fact, the only two Hispanic American anthologies in this genre that did not include "I, Too" were Hildamar Escalante's *Breve informe de poesía norteamericana* (Venezuela, 1947) and Hortensia Ruiz del Vizo's bilingual *Black Poetry of the Americas* (1972).[65] In 1953, the Nicaraguan writer Juan Felipe Toruño included his version of "I, Too" in *Poesía negra: Ensayo antología* (Mexico). Other versions followed, in Bansart's *Poesía negra-africana* and José Luis González and Mónica Mansour's *Poesía negra de América* (Mexico, 1976).[66] In addition to being included in both Gáler's and Ahumada's collections, the poem was also printed in a 1955 Mexican anthology of USAmerican poetry, Eugenio Florit's *Antología de la poesía norteamericana contemporánea.*[67] Perhaps even more important, however, is the fact that years before being anthologized, each of these translations of "I, Too" had made their way into many different journals and other periodicals, including *La Nueva Democracia* (Uruguay, 1938), *Sustancia* (Argentina, 1942), and *El Diario de la Marina* (Cuba, 1930), where they would no doubt have reached many more readers than the books did. All told, publishers printed fourteen different versions of "I, Too" in eighteen Hispanic American periodicals.

"I, Too" proved unusually versatile in the hands of its Hispanic American translators. In what follows, I consider entire poems rather than only exemplary lines, analyzing in close detail four of the earliest translations of "I, Too": one each by Jorge Luis Borges and Xavier Villaurrutia, both avant-gardists, and two by José Antonio Fernández de Castro, the politically progressive editor of the Sunday Literary Supplement that Cuba's leading newspaper began to carry in 1926.[68] Unlike Villaurrutia and Borges, Fernández de Castro had an interest in African American cultures that went well beyond the literary uses of blackness we find in the poetry of fellow countryman Emilio Ballagas. In fact, Fernández de Castro appears to have been something of a Cuban Carl Van Vechten.[69] I will return to his translations in this chapter, using Borges's and Villaurrutia's versions only as initial benchmarks and points of contrast and comparison. Borges's other Hughes translations are the focal point of the next chapter.

I begin with "I, Too" as it appeared in the 1925 *Survey Graphic* issue that became *The New Negro,*[70] followed by Villaurrutia's and Borges's translations, which appeared within months of each other in Argentina and Mexico in 1930. Here and throughout the chapter, I also use boldface to flag noteworthy discrepancies in diction and structure, and I point to minor variations across the different Spanish versions in the notes.

I, too, sing America.

I am the darker brother.
They send me to eat in the kitchen

When company comes,
But I laugh,
And I eat well,
And grow strong.

Tomorrow,
I'll be at the table
When company comes.
Nobody'll dare
Say to me,
"Eat in the kitchen,"
then.

Besides,
They'll see how beautiful I am
And be ashamed—

I, too, am America.

(*CP*, 46)

Yo también canto América	Yo también canto a América.
Soy el hermano oscuro.	Soy el hermano oscuro.
Me hacen comer en la cocina	Me mandan a comer en la cocina
Cuando llegan visitas.	Cuando llegan visitas,
Pero me río,	Mas yo me río
Y como bien,	Y como bien
Y me pongo fuerte. [71]	Y crezco fuerte.
Mañana	Mañana,
Me sentaré a la mesa.	Me sentaré a la mesa
Cuando lleguen visitas.	Cuando lleguen visitas.
Nadie se animará	**Entonces,**
A decirme	Nadie se atreverá
"Vete a la cocina"	A decirme
Entonces.	–"Ve y come en la cocina."
Y tendrán vergüenza—	**Además,**
Además, verán lo hermoso que soy.	Verán que soy hermoso
	Y se avergonzarán.
Yo también soy América.[72]	Yo también, soy América ...[73]

Placing these texts side by side reveals how closely both translations follow Hughes's format and where they adjust the source poem's shape. Apart from the fairly minor differences in diction between these translations, we see that Borges alters some of Hughes's punctuation, moving the dash to the end of a different line and adding an ellipsis at the very end. He also drops a line, throwing off the poem's structure slightly. Changes like these will assume greater weight in the context of my more detailed discussion of Fernández de Castro's two versions below. For the time being, I only want to point to one major variation: the rendition of Hughes's "darker" as "oscuro" — rather than "*más* oscuro" — which has two noteworthy effects. First, replacing "darker" with a less overtly racialized adjective implicitly places greater emphasis on skin color's metaphoric value than on its so-cial and political significance.[74] Second, eschewing the comparative fixes the persona's (racial) identity rather than making it relational. Villaurrutia's grammatical change of "They'll see *how* beautiful I am" to "They will see *that* I am beautiful" (Verán *que* soy hermoso) further stabilizes the relative states of social existence on which Hughes insists in English.

Fernández de Castro's more complicated translations employ similar strategies to very different effect: they make Hughes's poem more, not less, black. Fernández de Castro first met Hughes in Havana in 1930. During Hughes's visit, the journalist-editor introduced the young poet to prominent writers and artists *de color*, among them Gustavo E. Urrutia, who edited "Ideales de una Raza," a special page on black culture in *El Diario*'s Sunday supplement, and the national-poet-to-be Nicolás Guillén. Both Fernández de Castro and Urrutia, whom Hughes called "one of the leading journalists of Cuba," read USAmerican newspapers and journals fairly regularly, includ-ing the *Amsterdam News* (New York), *Crisis,* and *Opportunity.*[75] Ramp-ersad suggests that Fernández de Castro first came across Hughes's poetry in Countee Cullen's *Caroling Dusk: An Anthology of Verse by Negro Poets* (1927), which included "I, Too" (*Life,* 1:178). The Cuban clearly owned a copy of *The Weary Blues* by 1928, since seven of the eight Hughes poems he translated then and in 1930 were part of that volume: "Soledad," "The White Ones" ("Los blancos"), "Sea Calm" ("Calma en el mar"), "Poem [2]" ("Poema"), "Suicide's Note" ("Nota de un suicida"), and "March Moon" ("Luna de Marzo"). "Afraid" ("Miedo"), from *Fine Clothes to the Jew,* is the only exception.

Given Fernández de Castro's keen interest in poetry and black culture, translating Hughes was not a passing fancy for him.[76] The renowned journalist produced the very first Spanish version of "I, Too" — "Yo, tam-bién..." — which appeared in the Cuban journal *Social* in the fall of 1928. Between 1928 and 1930 he translated a total of eight Hughes poems, as well as excerpts from *Not Without Laughter.* In March and April of 1930, he published another version of "I, Too" in *La Revista de la Habana* and *El Diario de la Marina.*[77] "I, Too" was the only Hughes poem that Fernández de Castro translated and published twice within a short period of time; it is also the only one of Hughes's lyrics translated into Spanish more than once by the same person.[78] His translations stand out from the rest for the formal decisions he made as he carried this poem across to Cuban readers, many of whom, like his fellow editor Urrutia, were *mulatos.*

In Fernández de Castro's hands, Hughes's poem became more explicitly "militant" in each incarnation. On the one hand, Fernández de Castro claimed that "en la traducción han perdido a veces toda la fuerza e intensidad que poseen siempre en el original" (in translation we sometimes lose all the force and intensity that the original always has). [79] On the other, perhaps to compensate for this loss, he grafted onto Hughes's poem his own expectations of what would constitute such force and intensity, remaking Hughes into more of a protest poet than he actually was at this early stage in his career. While this view is consistent with perceptions of Hughes's politics at the time—Cubans and Mexicans had already begun to identify him with the Left by then[80]—the political sympathies that led him to spend a year in the Soviet Union in 1932–33 were not easily discernible from the early poems translated into Spanish. If "I, Too" could be read as more combative than contemplative, on the surface at least, the other brief Hughes lyrics that Fernández de Castro also translated were not exactly clear articulations of either black pride or radical-Left politics. For instance, no translator could have turned lines about the damaging effects of white dominance such as "O, white strong ones, /Why do you torture me?" and "So deeply scarred, / So still with silent cries" (*CP*, 37, 57) into ready expressions of black pride.[81] In fact, none of the usually pithy lyrics circulating in Cuban and Mexican periodicals by the end of 1931, twenty-two in all, show Hughes in the role of the "poeta militante negro" in which Fernández de Castro would cast him five years later in *El Nacional*.[82] Even if we grant that Hughes's early blues poems may have been received as politically radical in their day, other poems in *The Weary Blues* and especially what some saw as the "unsanitary, insipid, and repulsing" ones in *Fine Clothes to the Jew* would have much more readily carried sentiments of black pride or militancy.[83]

Rather than choosing a different poem, Fernández de Castro created with "Yo, también…" the kind of poem he thought Hughes should have written. I compare Fernández de Castro's two versions of "I, Too," both titled "Yo, también…," this time side by side with my own retranslations back into English to highlight structural and rhetorical changes.

Yo, también, **honro a América**	I, too, **honor** America
Soy el hermano **negro.**	I am the **Negro** brother.
Me mandan a comer a la cocina,	They send me to eat in the kitchen,
Cuando vienen visitas…	When visitors come…
Pero me río,	But I laugh [to myself],
Como bien	I eat well
Y así me fortalezco.	And so strengthen myself.
Mañana,	Tomorrow,
Me sentaré a la mesa	**I will sit [seat myself] at the table**

Y aunque vengan visitas	**And even though** visitors will come
Nadie se atreverá	No one will dare
A decirme	Tell me
"A la cocina, **Negro**."	"Off to the kitchen, negro."
Al mismo tiempo	**At the same time**
Se darán cuenta	They will realize
De lo hermoso que soy,	How beautiful I am
Y se avergonzarán.	And they will feel ashamed
¡Yo, también soy América!⁸⁴	I, too, am America!

Yo, también, honro a América.	I, too, honor America.
Soy el hermano **Negro**.	I am the **Negro** brother.
Cuando vienen visitas	When visitors come
me mandan a comer a la cocina.	they send me to eat in the kitchen,
Pero yo, río,	But I, laugh [to myself],
como bien	I eat well
y así, me fortalezco.	and so, strengthen myself.
Mañana,	Tomorrow,
me sentaré a la mesa	I will sit [seat myself] at the table
aunque vengan visitas.	although visitors will come.
Nadie se atreverá a decirme:	No one will dare tell me
"a la cocina, negro!"	"off to the kitchen, negro!"
Entonces	**Then**
verán lo hermoso que yo soy,	**they will see how beautiful I am,**
Y se avergonzarán.	and they will feel ashamed.
Yo, también soy América.⁸⁵	I, too, am America.

There are two remarkable differences between the source poem and the two target texts. One is structural. Note that Hughes wrote this poem in three, not two, stanzas framed by a one-line refrain. As we will see, adjustments to the poem's overall structure in both these translations resonate with smaller, similarly startling alterations that Fernández de Castro made throughout. The other difference is far less obvious: it is the accent in "América" that prevents it from reflexively collapsing into the English "America," better known by many in the Western Hemisphere as Los Estados Unidos, the United States of America. Unlike its famous historical precedent, José Martí's "nuestra América," the "América" in these translations potentially encompasses *all* the Americas.⁸⁶ The small accent that Spanish supplies changes dramatically what and how this noun signifies to a

non-English-speaking American, then and now. In a sense, "América" functions as a false cognate. It eases the poem's transfer to a different linguistic
and cultural context without, however, reconciling multiple and divergent
meanings.[87]

Of course, all Spanish translations of "I, Too" share the inescapable dia-
critical difference in *América* when compared to "America." The disparity
assumes greater significance in this particular case because Fernández de
Castro also decided to translate "I…sing" as *honro* instead of *canto,* the
verb all other translators preferred. There are two typical variations of this
line. Borges's "Yo también canto América" and Villaurrutia's "Yo también
canto a América."[88] The latter personifies the grammatical object to in-
voke Whitmanian multitudes. Replacing "sing" with *honro* prepares the
path for rendering "I, Too" much more equivocal than Hughes's own verb
choice would allow. The sounds of alliteration link *honro* with *hermano*
more strongly than the verb *canto* would have and thereby tonally under-
score the persona's desire for equality and brotherhood. More important,
however, the shift from "sing" to *honro* infuses the persona's singing with
a specific purpose: that of honoring an object that has now also shifted,
namely from "America" to *América.* The substitution of a univocal verb
also dulls Hughes's irony, making the poem more praise song than social
critique, at least initially. This opening note is inconsistent with choices
Fernández de Castro made later on in his translation(s). At the outset, it
is the persona's *presence,* rather than his singing, that honors America. Because the persona in Fernández de Castro's version need not be a bard, the
poem's so-called message can be more easily detached from its aesthetic
value. The ambiguous quality of singing that sounds at once criticism *and*
praise is at the root of Hughes's layered irony in "I, Too."

To the extent that Fernández de Castro's translation retains some of
Hughes's irony, that irony now serves a different purpose. Within the translation's contrastive two-stanza format, the "I" moves smoothly from a state
of social and political exile (stanza one) to one of inclusion (stanza two).
Although, as in Hughes's poem, the ability of the *hermano negro* to honor
and hence become *América* stems from the very stumbling blocks in his
path, Fernández de Castro offers more certainty about the persona's ability
to overcome obstacles. Like Hughes's "too," the adverb *también,* wedged in
between subject and verb, announces the existence of such hindrances before the poem details them. Part of the persona's identity resides within this
appositive, whose grammatical position is analogous to the persona's social
position: he has to make a place for himself in a situation that does not, but
should, include him—grammatically and socially. In Hughes's poem, writing
poetry ("I sing") creates the possibility for social acceptance *through* self-
acceptance ("I am"). Poetry, then, is not a vehicle for social inclusion but a
medium in which the poet can imagine such a state. While "I, Too," posits
that singing confers being, it does not show actions to produce predictable,

measurable effects, in this case, remedies for racial discrimination. Structurally, Hughes's poem does not suggest a course of action beyond singing. In the second stanza, Hughes relocates the persona from the kitchen to the dining room without explaining that sudden change from being hidden away on public occasions— "when company comes" —to the future possibility of grudging social acceptance (through embarrassment or shame) and eventual respect (appreciation for beauty).

The 1930 "Yo, tambíen..." entirely dispenses with the wistful note of uncertainty on which Hughes ends his second stanza ("then"). In Fernández de Castro's earlier version, the added *negro* already appears in an emphatic position at the end of the line. In the 1930 translation, that word also moves to the end of a stanza, which causes the adverb "then" to be pushed to the beginning of the next sentence to connect it grammatically with the last stanza. In the process, Hughes's "besides" drops out altogether, so that "*Besides,* / They'll see how beautiful I am," which had initially been rendered as "*Al mismo tiempo* / Se darán cuenta / De lo hermoso que soy" (*At the same time,* / They'll take note / Of how beautiful I am) turns into "*Entonces* / verán lo hermoso que yo soy" (*Then* / they will see how beautiful I am). The change is literally more visible here than in the earlier version, which also retains Hughes's capital letters at the beginning of each line. Like the addition of the second *negro,* this revision in the translation is willful, and the effect it produces, especially when combined with other interpretive decisions, is substantial. The second version restores Hughes's original three-stanza shape, but added line spaces after "mañana" and "entonces" force a formal symmetry that does not exist in Hughes's poem. Thematically, what results from this symmetry is an unproblematic progression from present discrimination to future acceptance, with two, not three, stops along the way: "tomorrow" and "then," rather than "tomorrow," "then," and "besides." The shorter third stanza is now the direct outcome of an earlier action on the part of the persona to which all *reactions*—fearful silence, apperception of beauty, and resulting shame—are directly attributable. In both translations, the act of seating oneself at the table ("me sentaré a la mesa") rather than simply staying there or being invited to sit,[89] *causes* others to take note of the speaker and to experience shame at the same time (*avergonzarse* is closer to feeling humiliated). The reflexive verb *sentarse* registers a sense of rebellious action more strongly than its English counterpart "to sit" can. This is very different from Hughes's "I'll *be* at the table," which is silent on how that state of being will have been achieved.

A fundamental divergence between "I, Too" and "Yo, también..." comes into view here: the difference between ontology and politics, that is, a state or quality of *being* versus a social *position* one assumes. "I, Too" values the speaker's being, not his actions; singing, for Hughes, is a mode of being more than an action. That Hughes in his *Selected Poems* (1959) changed "I'll be at the table" to "I'll sit at the table" (*CP,* 625) does not much alter this stasis. Withholding directional, kinetic verbs, Hughes allows us no certitude on how equality is achieved, or even what it might mean. In his poem we know neither how the speaker moves from one social space to another nor what precise roles his actions and the acknowledgment of his beauty play in such a movement. Hughes's placement of "besides" at the opening of the third stanza suggests that aesthetics, though they might precede ethics—the speaker is beautiful *before* he is perceived as such by certain others—do not *prompt* moral behavior; the speaker's beauty, be it innate or perceptual, is not the *reason* that he sits at the table. "Besides" separates equality, a possible result of the ethical choice to abstain from racial discrimination, from the perception of just how beautiful the speaker is, implying that he is *already* aware of his own beauty. The final measure of the singer's darker beauty is, of course, the poem itself.

"I, Too" also leaves us unsure about the exact source of "their" shame: does it come from not having noticed the darker brother's beauty before or from having denied him equal standing in spite of his beauty? Does sudden awareness of beauty cause feelings of shame, or have those at the table been humiliated into seeing, and appreciating, the persona's beauty because he refused to leave the table at the appointed time? By avoiding causation, allowing only for a spatial and a temporal movement—"tomorrow," "then"—that trail off into the contemplative "besides," Hughes poses poetry's ethical and political efficacy as a question. Related to this question is the doubt Hughes sows through the relational comparative "darker," both about the persona's racial identity and about who "they" might be. Although the opposite of "darker" is, of course, not "white" but "lighter," USAmerican readers, conditioned by a specific history of race relations, would have tended to resist a comparative that, in addition to unsettling racial binaries, also opens up the no less discomfiting possibility of color and class distinctions *within* racial groups.

Apparently dissatisfied with the poem's searching philosophical mode, Fernández de Castro tried to streamline its political message. In his versions, conscious acts of resistance to racial injustice result in equality *and* "at the same time" force the acknowledgment of the *negro*'s beauty: "Al mismo tiempo / Se darán cuenta / De lo hermoso que soy." In this scenario, action, or activism, becomes the only possible guarantor of political and social equality because it produces shame, humiliation, and guilt. The translations' insistence throughout on stark contrasts and active confrontations also cements the implicit sense that repetition is stasis. Doing so invalidates repetition as an aesthetic principle and an imaginative vehicle for social change. Eschewing subtlety, Fernández de Castro substitutes "y aunque" (and even though) for Hughes's repeated "when" in the second "when company comes," which bolsters the notion of variation-as-change by rendering it literally visible. Yet in the end the pervasive adversarial mood this translator creates as he systematically infuses the poem with undertones of conflict puts literary form at odds with political content, making the visions of brotherhood he had initially projected less than convincing. The final declaration, "Yo, también soy América," now stripped of its exclamation point, rings hollow, especially after the translator has dispensed with the dash that dangled the final line from the rest of the poem to avoid conveying a sense of simple fait accompli.

Fernández de Castro's repeated use of *negro* in place of Hughes's "darker" is, to me, the strongest sign of this Cuban translator's discontent with the young Hughes's poetics and his politics. This problematic adjective apparently gave all Hughes's translators considerable pause. Oddly enough, only post-1950s translators chose the most literal option, *más oscuro*.[90] Fernández de Castro's version is unusual not because it forgoes the comparative. Other translators did this as well; in fact, Lozano, Gáler, and Toruño used the same adjective, *negro*. Nobody else, however, repeated the word in the poem.[91] Fernández de Castro not only repeats it but also adds an exclamation point in his second translation. "Nobody'll dare / Say to me, / 'Eat in the kitchen,'/ then" becomes, first, "Nadie se atreverá / A decirme / 'A la cocina, negro'" and then, with the first line break removed, "Nadie se atreverá a decirme: / 'a la cocina, negro!'" Although this echo adds thematic emphasis, as a formal device, it is inconsistent with the erasure of other repetitions.

The adjectival *negro* stands out even more in the *Diario* version because of the now-restored line space after *América*. In its new location, the adjective increases the poem's sting, creating a harsher tone than Hughes's poem has. This harshness in turn sharpens the contrast between the adjectival and the nominative uses of *negro* so that the poem's opening reclamation of a loathsome racial epithet, and the stereotype that goes along with it, can come into relief as a triumphant assertion of racial pride. The choice is that much more significant because Fernández de Castro's interest in racial issues and Afro-Cuban culture made him well aware that the Spanish *negro* would have had a far more offensive ring to a Cuban than to an African American from the USA, who at the time would have preferred the term to "black."[92] The more acceptably permeable color line in the Hispanic Americas, especially in the Caribbean, accounts for such different responses.

In the absence of the infamous one-drop rule and Jim Crow laws, racial taxonomies in the Hispanic Americas, which focus on color and phenotype more than on blood, have remained more elastic. This does not, however, make their effects any more benign. Even in "a distinctly Negroid country" such as Cuba, one cannot disregard the existence of what Hughes called a "triple color line" (*IW*, 10). During the early twentieth century in particular, an educated dark-complexioned member of the Cuban middle class would not have identified as *de raza negra*. He or she would likely have preferred terms such as *de color* or *mulato/a* to *negro/a*. Although also used as a colloquial term of endearment by Cubans of all hues, this label still spelled lower-class economic and social status. Fernández de Castro pushes the (Spanish) *negro* into close, and troubling, proximity to its seeming English cognates, the capitalized *Negro* in "hermano Negro" and the lowercase *negro* in "'vete a la cocina, negro!'" Another English source text surfaces here. This text, if we can call it that, is not Hughes's poem but consists of the USAmerican discourses *of* blackness and *on* race in which his poem is embedded. In the former, "Negro," as in the phrase New Negro, symbolizes racial pride; in the latter, "negro" is closer to "nigger." Both discourses mediate the transition from Hughes's poem, which employs neither word, to Fernández de Castro's translations.[93] The latter's choices, however, do not make his translations any less Cuban; in fact, the Spanish *negro* accomplishes quite the opposite. By the time the word resurfaces, it has brought about an unexpected darkening of the poem's implied, and silent, interlocutors. The Cuban setting loosens and shifts racial categories assumed to be more rigid and predictable in Hughes's poem. They remain so despite the fact that Hughes's own language, especially the comparative "darker," worries assumptions bound up in the racial dualities that most USAmerican readers would almost reflexively supply. Any darker brother would automatically have been coded as black rather than perceived as a darker shade of white. What USAmerican readers at the time would likely have apprehended as a black/white conflict, Cubans would more readily have understood as an *intra*racial situation in which the lighter implicit in darker would signify *mulato*.

By insisting on *negro* and inviting readers to supply the silent *mulato*, Fernández de Castro effectively cubanized Hughes's poem. In the same way, Guillén cubanized Hughes by calling him a "mulatico" (little mulatto) who, more than anything, wanted to be "negro de verdad" (really, truly black).[94] What Guillén's affectionate appellation implied is that, in Cuba, Hughes was a *mulato* rather than a *negro*, someone who would already have sat at the table, to be sent off to the proverbial kitchen only when certain *foreign* company came. In *I Wonder As I Wander*, Hughes actually recounts being denied entrance to a USAmerican-controlled Havana beach and being arrested when he resisted (*IW*, 11–15). The incident, quite an embarrassment to his Cuban hosts, was also reported in "Ideales de una Raza."

WHO INFLUENCED WHOM?

One of these hosts was Nicolás Guillén. Like Hughes himself, the Cuban poet was a *mulatico* and of the same age. Although Guillén, who is at the core of my fourth chapter, did not translate any of Hughes's poems, he is worth mentioning here because many have taken his poetry, most notably his "Motivos de son" from 1930, as exemplary of the influence Hughes's early verse supposedly exerted on Afro-Hispanic American writers. These kinds of influence studies are chiefly built on suppositions grounded in precious little historical and textual evidence. Faced with a lack of concrete historical evidence and armed with comparisons that liken Guillén's *poemas-son* (*son* poems) to Hughes's blues poetry, critics have made much of the largely unrecorded conversations Guillén and Hughes had in March of 1930.[95] Maribel Cruzado and Mary Hricko have even gone so far as to declare that Guillén himself translated Hughes's poems, which he decidedly did not.[96] His personal interactions with Hughes in the spring of 1930 were probably what finally motivated Guillén to put pen to paper and produce eight poems that differed dramatically from his earlier verse. But what *literary* influence Hughes's poems had on Guillén's was unquestionably mediated by Fernández de Castro's translations, especially of "I, Too." What I have called the cubanizing of Hughes prepared the textual ground on which the two different sets of cultural values and sensibilities that Hughes and Guillén embodied could and did meet. It is not coincidental that the *Motivos* were first published in the same *página negra* in the *Diario de la Marina* that would feature Fernández de Castro's second translation of "I, Too" only weeks later, in April of 1930. That Guillén's poem had appeared in "Ideales" before that retranslation may also explain some of the formal changes in the second version of "Yo, también...," notably the looser strophic arrangement and the added exclamation point.

Guillén, in fact, dedicated the *Motivos* to Fernández de Castro, not to Hughes. This, to my mind, is a resounding tribute to the fact that Fernández de Castro was the one who introduced him to Hughes's poems not once but twice, in 1928 and again in 1930. By the time he met Hughes in person, also through Fernández de Castro, Guillén was already well aware of this and other Hughes poems in translation, having no doubt seen the journalist's first version of "I, Too" in *Social* two years earlier. Guillén likely reencountered the translation in March of 1930 in the short-lived *Revista de La Habana*, along with Fernández de Castro's article "Presentación de Langston Hughes." In that article, the journalist attributed to Hughes's poems "un *vigoroso orgullo racial,* una *combatividad* desconocida hasta el momento presente por parte de los productores intelectuales de esa raza" (a strong racial pride, a combativeness heretofore unknown among the intellectuals of his race).[97] In his final translation of "I, Too," then, Fernández de Castro tried to encapsulate in a single word — *negro* — the political energy of the militant racial pride that he had imputed to Hughes's poetry only a month earlier.[98] That Fernández de Castro's translations of "I, Too" resonated with Guillén is evident from certain thematic and textual affinities between these translations and the poems from the *Motivos* that explicitly stage conflicts between *negros* and *mulatos* or, more often, *mulatas*. One of these poems, "Ayé me dijeron negro," is of particular interest because in it Guillén plays on the same racial theme as "I, Too" does: hiding from

view dark-skinned family members "when company comes." (More on this in chapter 4.) This
social practice was familiar to Cubans from well
before the USAmerican military occupation after
the Spanish-Cuban-American War.

Like Fernández de Castro's translations and
unlike Hughes's "I, Too," "Ayé me dijeron
negro"—which Hughes published as "Last Night
Somebody Called Me Darky" in *Cuba Libre:
Poems by Nicolás Guillén* (1948)—hinges on the
word *negro*. Hughes himself may have remembered Fernández de Castro's unorthodox translation of "darker" as "negro" when he rejected,
though not without considerable hesitation, both
"Negro" and "black" as desirable options for
rendering that poem's title and opening line in
English. To the extent, then, that Guillén's *poemas-son* were influenced by Hughes's early lyrics
and in their turn affected Hughes's own thinking about race and color years later when he set
out to translate those very poems, Fernández de
Castro's translations of "I, Too" played a decisive
role in shaping that influence.[99] They refracted
"I, Too" in the prism of a Cuban discourse on
race and color at whose core resides the figure
of the *mulata*. As they insinuate themselves into
Fernández de Castro's translations, the discursive
properties of this feminine icon unsettle gender
along with racial categories. In "Yo, también…"
the persona is *negro*, unlike Hughes himself, who
looks very *mulato* in the photograph printed
above the translations in the *Diario* (see figure 4).
Once author and persona appear as more distinct
than they would in "I, Too," because they share
neither the same color nor the same language, it
also becomes less plausible to postulate shared
gender.

That most of Hughes's Hispanic American
translators, including Fernández de Castro, were
not black according to racial standards in the
USA further complicates the points I have made
about mediation and literary influence by adding into the mix the cultural differences that exist

Figure 4. Page from *El
Diario de la Marina*,
April 27, 1930, with
José Antonio Fernández
de Castro's translation's
of three Hughes poems.
Courtesy of George A.
Smathers Libraries,
University of Florida,
Gainesville.

within, as well as between, individual nation states. One need only think of languages such as Brazilian Portuguese, Misquito, or Quechua to appreciate the existence of myriad linguistic differences within the Hispanic Americas. The geopolitical entity typically known as Latin America (among English-speaking North Americans and Europeans) is by no means as homogeneous as surface appearances, produced by the use of the once-imperial Spanish as the region's major lingua franca, might suggest. Because the legacies of slavery are unevenly and unequally shared throughout the Americas, the racial categories and social practices to which slavery gave rise during and after the nineteenth century can differ widely across the Hispanic Americas, not just between the USA and the rest of the hemisphere. The cultural and political valences of blackness were and are significantly different in parts of the Hispanic Americas, such as Cuba and Brazil, where the de jure and de facto abolition of plantation slavery occurred late in the nineteenth century and was thus not a distant memory during the early twentieth. The fact that there are notable differences in how racial distinctions have affected Hispanic American societies internally, in relation to each other and to the USA, has still not taken sufficient hold in comparative literary scholarship originating in the USAmerican academy. In that academy, as-sertions of cultural equivalence have been key constitutive elements in the formation and legitimization of academic fields such as African American and African diaspora studies.

The fact that Hispanic Americans appreciated Hughes's poems—in the form of translations, essays, and other kinds of approbation—says little about the relative presence or absence of antiblack prejudice in those parts of the Americas. What it does suggest is that both Hughes's poems and his politics were quite compatible with the anti-imperialist sentiments that had flared up again after the Spanish-Cuban-American War and contin-ued to simmer in many parts of the Hispanic Americas for much of the twentieth century. In countries that preferred to see antiblack racism entirely as an import from the USA, what fell through the cracks, however, was due attention to local racial tensions and disparities. Ironically, Hispanic Ameri-cans' interest in black literature from the USA, more so than from either the anglophone or francophone Caribbean, did not necessarily translate into greater attention to racial conflicts in their own backyards. Nor, for that matter, did it invariably make Hispanic Americans more aware of artis-tic efforts by the writers of African descent in their midst. This disconnect might explain why Hughes's work could be embraced by so many different groups in the Hispanic Americas and yet that embrace did not translate into any lasting support for Afro-Hispanic American writers across color lines. Hispanic Americans may have included Hughes and a smattering of other New Negro poets in their anthologies. But in the end, they did at home the very thing they criticized abroad: they excluded from accounts of

Hispanic American literature the work of writers who explored race relations critically.

Comparisons of the sort that I proffer in this chapter inevitably prompt a reexamination of the concept of diaspora. As valuable as this idea has been to African American and postcolonial studies, it has also left in its wake a host of unexamined theories about cultural equivalences across national borders. Although the rhetoric of racial origins and essences has largely been replaced, in literary studies and elsewhere, by a more dynamic emphasis on shared historical experiences, the latter has spawned no less problematic assumptions about, and indeed expectations of, cultural homogeneity among the various parts of African, Asian, and other diasporas.[100] In academic theory and practice, such assumptions have begun to flatten out the historical dimensions of diasporas' local communities, refashioning them into less varied cultural geographies than they actually are. What has been lost, at least to some extent, in the rush to assert transnational links between cultures is the very commitment to exploring the racial and ethnic heterogeneities that had energized diaspora studies in the first place and had offered ways to imagine communities in other than national configurations. Diaspora studies have developed their own protocols for erasing or suppressing "cultural asymmetries" (in Venuti's suggestive phrase from *The Scandals of Translation*) and for rendering invisible local "foreign" elements that would produce incoherence. Homogenizing protocols have left their imprint on most comparatist projects, mainly in the form of transhistorical analogies that presume misleading degrees of likeness and equality among local diasporic constituents.[101] For example, that African slavery was a colonial practice throughout most of the New World does not justify the assumption that discourses on race, literary and otherwise, function in similar ways in different languages and social contexts across the Americas. Because translation can be "uniquely revealing of the asymmetries that have structured international affairs for centuries," it offers a particularly useful framework in which to rethink comparisons based on the belief that race, culture, and class interact in analogous ways in various American contexts or that kinship always involves likeness.[102]

That USAmerican comparatists would be the ones to have produced most critical narratives of literary blackness in the Americas is a reflection that "the economic and political ascendancy of the United States [has] reduced foreign languages and cultures to minorities in relation to its language and culture."[103] Ironically enough, diaspora, in these narratives, becomes "an effective way of disseminating the legitimacy of the nationalist form itself," that is, of upholding nationalism "along racial and ethnic lines."[104] Instead of considering intellectual traffic in the Americas as a two-way street, most USAmerican scholars have drawn patterns of cultural influence that spread in one direction only: from north to south. The field of African American (literary) studies is no exception to this rule. In inquiries into the "the shared cultural forms used by black writers to reconnect to a common, ancestral resonance," which started to multiply in the 1970 and 1980s, it is a critical commonplace to assert that African American writers based in the USA were instrumental in disseminating ideas of literary blackness across the Americas and particularly in the Hispanic Americas.[105] In his role as an inter-American cultural broker, Langston Hughes has been an especially popular example of such cultural exports. What has been largely ignored, however, is the likelihood that Hughes's work as a translator and his sustained contact with Hispanic American authors affected his own views on how racial politics aligned with literary aesthetics.[106]

That Fernández de Castro's mediation of the literary relationship between Hughes and Guillén went in both directions shows that one cannot simply assume "*deeply rooted* interconnections among writers of the black diaspora."[107] Unless we wish to posit that such interconnections are essentially nondiscursive, a possibility that Mullen's figure of deep roots implies, we have little choice but to concede that literary relationships and the national and international communities that form through and around them are always mediated by larger discursive formations. This fairly basic point has special significance in international settings where texts cross not only political but also linguistic borders. The discourses of blackness that spread worldwide alongside imperial discourses on race are a case in point. Discourses of blackness flourished during the early decades of the twentieth century as writers of African descent and their writings traveled, jointly or separately, between destinations such as Paris, New York, Madrid, Havana, Montevideo, and Buenos Aires. What Brent Edwards has termed black internationalism was constituted by a plethora of writing in English, French, Spanish, Portuguese, and Dutch, among the better-known languages. The specifically literary discourses of blackness that evolved in the context of the African diaspora not only intersected with but were vital parts of the historical avant-gardes we call modernist in English. Hughes's poems in Spanish translation exemplify the intense heterolingualism that makes it impossible to conceive of, let alone analyze, often far-flung correlations between writers and literary texts without taking careful measure of the role of translation.

CHAPTER THREE

BUENOS AIRES BLUES

Modernism in the Creole City

Au centre, une logique urbaine occidentale, alignée, ordonné, forte
comme la langage française. De l'autre, le foisonnement ouvert de la
langage créole dans la logique de Texaco. Mêlant ces deux langues, rêvant
de toutes les langues, la ville créole parle en secret un langage neuf et
ne craint plus Babel. Ici la trame géométrique d'une grammaire urbaine
bien apprise, dominatrice; par-là, la couronne d'une culture-mosaïque à
dévoiler prise dans les hiéroglyphes du béton, du bois, de caisses et du
fibrociment. La ville créole restitue a l'urbaniste que voudrait l'oublier les
souches d'une identité neuve: multilingue, multiracial, multi-historique,
ouverte, sensible à la diversité du monde. Tout a changé.

[In the center, an occidental urban logic, all lined up, ordered, strong
like the French language. On the other side, Creole's open profusion
according to Texaco's logic. Mingling these two tongues, dreaming of all
tongues, the Creole city speaks a new language in secret and no longer
fears Babel. Here the well-learned, domineering, geometrical grid of an
urban grammar; over there the crown of a mosaic culture to be unveiled,
caught in the hieroglyphics of cement, crate wood, asbestos. The Creole
city returns to the urban planner, who would like to ignore it, the roots of
a new identity: multilingual, multiracial, multihistorical, open, sensible to
the world's diversity. Everything has changed.]

—Patrick Chamoiseau, *Texaco*

Mostradme un blanco más poeta que Langston Hughes.
Traedme un Duke Ellington.

[Show me a white man who is more of a poet than Langston
Hughes. / Give me a Duke Ellington.]

Raúl González Tuñón, "Ku Klux Klan"

In 1938, after having spent several months in Valencia and Madrid as a correspondent for the Baltimore *Afro-American,* Hughes, along with most of
the other "internationals," decided to leave the war-torn capital. The city

had been under siege since November of 1936, and provisions and ammunition were running low. In *I Wonder As I Wander,* Hughes recounts how, in "an alcoholic fog," he hastily stuffed his bags and pockets full of books, manuscripts, banderillas, shrapnel, and other souvenirs. A wine bottle from the farewell party Hemingway and others had given for him still dangling from his neck, the inebriated Hughes had to rely on the good graces of one of his friends to help him cart his belongings to the bus station in the wee hours of the following morning. That friend, who did "not object to being a pack mule," was none other than the Cuban poet Nicolás Guillén. The comedy with which Hughes invests this exit scene relieves the sense of emergency that had been building for pages.

> I was so tired, so sleepy, and so unsteady on my legs, and the things I had in my hands, under my arms, and in my pockets were so heavy that I had to stop every few hundred yards and put everything down to rest. Guillén declared that we were going to miss the bus if I didn't hurry. To get another permit for another bus on another date from the military authorities might take weeks. I replied that I didn't care — to go ahead if he wanted to — just drop my stuff on the ground and leave me.
>
> "*Caramba, chico,*" Guillén cried, "Madrid might be cut off from the rest of the world soon — you might never get out."
>
> "*Nichevo,*" I said. "*Que le hace.* Damn if I care! I can't walk any faster with this stuff — and I'm not going to leave my typewriter here, and these books that the writers have given me, nor my banderillas and my few clothes I've got. So go ahead."
>
> But Guillén stuck with me. (*IW,* 394)

Another image flickers here, ushered in by the incongruous Russian word Hughes flings at Guillén, who would have been much more likely to use the expletive "¡coño!" than "caramba": that of an abandoned, cursing traveler sitting atop a mountain of luggage at a train station in the midst of central Asia. There is, however, a significant difference. Unlike his earlier travel companions, the Cuban stayed with Hughes, and they caught the bus to Valencia together.

Nexus Madrid

During the Spanish Civil War, Madrid was a place bustling with travelers, journalists, and expatriates, much like Paris had been in the 1920s. For African Americans such as Hughes, the city of "[f]lamenco and explosives" (*IW,* 391) was a place where it was possible to "embrace both the Communists' internationalism and their own vision of pan-Africanism simultaneously."[1] Hemingway was there on the same reporting mission as Hughes and Nicolás

Guillén, and so were many others. They mingled with Spanish writers at the Madrid chapter of the Alianza de Intelectuales Antifascistas para la Defensa de la Cultura over suppers of beans and onions, the sound of explosions and antiaircraft fire only occasionally interrupted by Guillén's singing. Members of the Alianza included the poets José Bergamín, Rafael Alberti, Miguel Hernández Gilabert, León Felipe, and Manuel Altolaguirre, all of them members of the Generation of '27, which had also included Federico García Lorca before he was murdered by Nationalist militia in 1936, days before the outbreak of the Spanish Civil War. The Hispanic American artists whom Hughes mentions meeting in addition to their Peninsular colleagues include the composers Amadeo Roldán (Cuba) and Silvestre Revueltas (Mexico), the musicologist Vicente Salas Viu (Chile), Alejo Carpentier (Cuba), and the young poets Octavio Paz (Mexico) and Pablo Neruda (Chile) (*Essays*, 150–51; *Life*, 1:345–55).[2] As Franco's siege went on, Madrid became a veritable haven for modernist artists of all stripes, brought together by the fight against fascism. Many of them were avowed communists, some, like Guillén and Neruda, card-carrying comrades. Hughes had already met some of them, notably Neruda, at the International Writers' Congress in Paris in 1935, to which he makes brief reference at the end of chapter 7 of *I Wonder*. Naturally they all read one another's work. Hughes recounts that he "was busy translating, with the aid of Rafael Alberti and Manuel Altolaguirre, the 'Gypsy Ballads' of Federico García Lorca, and his play, *Bodas de Sangre*" (*IW*, 388).[3] Alberti, in turn, paid tribute to Hughes by translating his poetry. In August 1937, he published Spanish versions of four of Hughes's poems in *El Mono Azul*, the Alianza's journal: "Yo Soy Negro" ("Negro"), "Estoy haciendo un camino" ("Florida Road Workers"), "Hombre convertido en hombres" ("Man into Men"), and "Yo también" (I, Too"). These poems followed Miguel Alejandro's translations of "Good Morning, Revolution!" ("¡Buenos Dias, Revolución!") and a section of "Advertisement for the Waldorf-Astoria" ("El Waldorf-Astoria [Fragmento]") in *Nueva Cultura* (Valencia) in 1936 (see figures 2 and 3 in the previous chapter).

One of the more extraordinary products of this congregation of poets and soldiers was the pamphlet *Romancero de los Voluntarios de la Libertad* from 1937, which collected verse written and sung by soldiers in the trenches and at the graves of fallen comrades. Their songs, some of which had been scribbled on parts of uniforms, followed Alberti's "A las Brigadas Internacionales" and Hughes's "Song of Spain," which opened the collection.[4] The pamphlet was edited by the German novelist Gustav Regler, then the political commissar of Garibaldi Brigade. Perhaps the most unusual aspect of this publication is not just that it was illustrated with various unidentified drawings but that it featured poems in all sorts of different languages—from Spanish, French, and English to Russian, Polish, Italian, and German. Sometimes the authors identified themselves by their full names; others used only first names (Adam, Ilja, Fred) or initials (E. B. and H. G.)

or preferred to remain anonymous. Among the better-known writers who contributed to his collection were Edwin Rolfe, who befriended Hughes while the latter was in Spain,[5] and the German Communists Erich Weinert, Hans Marchwitza, and Ludwig Detsinyi, as well as the Italian Giorgio Braccialarghe.

Compared with the fleeting contacts Hughes made at the International Writers Congress in Paris, which he attended right before setting out for Spain in 1935, the interactions he had with major modernists from both Europe and other parts of the world in Barcelona, Valencia, and especially Madrid were far more intense and sustained. Yet these connections have spurred surprisingly scant comparative scholarship. What little work there is on Hughes's time in Spain has concentrated either on Hughes and García Lorca, whom Hughes had never met face to face, or on Hughes's contact with the International Brigades.[6] If Hughes's collaborations with Alberti and other members of the Generation of '27 were productive, his associations with the Hispanic American writers he also encountered in Spain proved even more so. In addition to Neruda, Paz, and Carpentier, Hughes also met the Argentine poet Raúl González Tuñón, who had arrived in Spain in 1935 and published *La rosa blindada* to great acclaim the same year García Lorca was executed.[7] Although Hughes himself does not mention Tuñón, Guillén does, and Tuñón himself remembers Hughes.[8] The Argentine occupies an important place in my critical narrative on the reception of Hughes's writing in Buenos Aires later on in this chapter. Although Tuñón never translated Hughes, at least as far as I know, the chapter epigraph indicates that he had read Hughes's poetry even before traveling to Spain. Indeed, as I argue, the two were kindred spirits in many ways: two modernist globetrotter-poets on the fringes of their respective countries.

I noted previously that some of Hughes's later poems, especially *Montage of a Dream Deferred* and *ASK YOUR MAMA*, are now being discussed within literary modernist frameworks. With few exceptions, however, the poems from *The Weary Blues* and *Fine Clothes to the Jew* continue to languish in the critical limbo of ethno-poetry, while the poems and poetry collections from the 1930s, such as *A New Song*, have been largely dismissed as too political to qualify as lyric poetry. The poems that fall outside both categories—many of them imagist poems—have typically been consigned to silence. In this chapter, I pick up the threads of my argument from chapter 1 in connection with Anita Patterson's contention that "even [the] simplest, most documentary and most historically engaged [of Hughes's] poems evince a characteristically modernist preoccupation with the figurative implications of form."[9] Rather than focus on poems that place Hughes in the context of transatlantic modernisms, as both Edwards and Patterson do, I continue to situate his verse in the hemispheric context of the Hispanic Americas.[10] My focus in what follows is on Argentina, where the majority of the Spanish translations of Hughes's writings were published. Extending

my discussion beyond historically engaged poems to Hughes's politically engaged verse, I argue that not all modernist writers separated the aesthetics of
language art from their political convictions. Such partitioning, which Newcomb rightly identifies as "subterranean formalism," occurred far more frequently on the part of their readers.[11] Is it only out of sheer neglect that,
until quite recently, the politics of fascism in Anglo-American modernism
have been tacitly swept under the rug of formalist poetics? How is Eliot's
notorious anti-Semitism, preserved in published drafts of *The Waste Land*,
any less a form of political engagement than Hughes's antilynching or pro-
socialist poems? It is Guillén who reminds us of these disjunctions within
modernism in his 1967 eulogy for Hughes:

> ¿Por qué no recordar que este siglo es también el de Proust o el de Joyce? ¿Por
> qué no va a ocupar el artista negro un sitio en la cultura americana y universal,
> abandonando o reduciendo las fuentes del arte nacional y folklórico? Ni digo
> que no.... Pero difícilmente hubiera podido ese artista—y no ya en los días en
> que Hughes surgió, sino ahora mismo—escrito algo como *Ulises* o *En busca
> del tiempo perdido,* dos obras maestras de la literatura universal, es cierto,
> mientras los negros eran asados vivos en el Sur, no sé si por lectores de Proust
> o de Joyce, pero sin duda por salvajes de la peor naturaleza, que había—que
> hay—que exterminar a balazos tanto como a poemas.

> [Why not remember that this is also the century of Proust and Joyce? Why
> won't the black artist occupy a place in the culture of America and the world
> after abandoning or exhausting the founts of national art and folklore? I am not
> saying that he won't.... But only with great difficulty could such that artist—
> and not just when Hughes grew up but also today—have written anything on
> the order of *Ulysses* or *Remembrance of Things Past,* surely two masterpieces
> of world literature, while blacks were burned alive in the South not, I suppose,
> by readers of Proust or of Joyce but no doubt by low-life savages that had to be
> wiped out with bullets and poems; they still do.][12]

Guillén points here to the continued necessity for poetry as a weapon
against antiblack racism in a register that anticipates the political rhetoric
of the Black Arts movement, notably in the poetry of Amiri Baraka. His
remarks also imply that societal exigencies and political engagements might
have compromised the status of black artists' work in relation to the so-
called masterpieces of world literature. There is no question that this has
been the case. Academic scholarship, certainly in the USA, has almost always
greeted politically committed literature with disdain. The division of modernisms into high and low, which is a symptom and a measure of this scorn,
is indicative of two kinds of problematic innovations. The first one is topi-
cal. Socially and politically committed modernist poets turned to spaces
located outside of the walls of what Nietzsche once disparagingly called

"the garden of knowledge."[13] These modernist fringe spaces are distinctly urban, populated by individuals and groups whom our varied societies have preferred to consign to invisibility and even criminalize. They have been called "low-down," in Hughes's words, or Harlem, *arrabales* (suburbs or barrios), *baldíos* (wastelands), or *hampas* (underworlds).[14] In the 1920s and especially the 1930s, modernist poets such as Hughes insisted that such public spaces were distinctive *cultural* settings, not sites bereft of any form of culture, as they were for Eliot and other elite modernists. The second, equally troubling novelty was that poets themselves were turning away from privileged spaces, among them lyrical interiority, and toward what one might call public intervention. They were actively looking for new ways in which poetry might address audiences beyond the intellectual elite. Poetry was written to be recited, read out loud, and circulated in the form of pamphlets and leaflets or in inexpensive editions.[15] Beatriz Sarlo has called the increasing public role of literature one of the most vital cultural phenomena of this period: "La función de la poesía es pública de un modo desconocido hasta entonces" (Poetry's function was public in a manner heretofore unknown).[16]

MODERNISMS HIGH AND LOW, NORTH AND SOUTH

Modernist studies have been dominated by formalist methodologies since their inception. This scholarly bias has resulted in the wholesale marginalization of those poets—black, white, and anything in between—whose writings combine aesthetics with social or political critique. Most of the Harlem Renaissance writers have thus been an uncomfortable fit for studies of literary modernism.[17] Until quite recently, Hughes's work was no exception. In the last two decades, there have only been a handful of book-length studies that place Harlem Renaissance writers alongside USAmerican modernists of other ethnicities. Most notable among them are Michael North's *The Dialect of Modernism* (1994), George Hutchinson's *The Harlem Renaissance in Black and White* (1995), Charles Scruggs and Lee Vandemarr's *Jean Toomer and the Terrors of American History* (1998), and Anita Patterson's *Race, American Literature and Transnational Modernisms* (2008).[18] Hutchinson not only rejects the black / white divide within modernist studies but also emphasizes that Anglo-American modernists did not exactly constitute an aesthetically and ideologically unified group, a point that is often neglected.

> It is still the case that discussions of modernism and the Harlem Renaissance often pit black writers against white writers like Eliot, Pound, and Stein, who inhabited a very different space (literally!) in the modernist landscape, while ignoring or giving little careful attention to the forms of uncanonical, "native" (white) modernism with which the African American renaissance was

intimately related.... One reason for the superficial appeal of assertions of a radical disjunction between black and white modernisms is that traditional definitions of modernism that have excluded African American artists have also excluded the white artists with whom they associated. By and large, African Americanists have taken Eurocentric conceptions of modernism as representative for so-called Anglo-American modernists generally.... Indeed, since the late 1930s the institutionalization of "high" and "lost generation" brands of literary modernism has done much to obscure the affiliations between white American modernism and the Harlem Renaissance.[19]

Racial difference was by no means the only, and perhaps not even the most significant, dividing line among USAmerican modernists in the inter-war years. Eliot, Pound, Stein, and other "high" modernists did indeed in-habit spaces that were quite unlike those in which we find Hughes, Waldo Frank, John Dos Passos, and Edwin Rolfe. The difference was not just a matter of geography—Paris and London versus Manhattan, Moscow, or Madrid, for instance. There was obviously some overlap, since Hughes and other not-so-high USAmerican modernists also visited Paris. The dif-ferent travel routes were also closely linked to personal political beliefs and commitments, notably to international socialism, then called Commu-nism, which—and this is not a coincidence—virtually none of the canonical Anglo-American modernists shared.

The same apprehensions that have created and maintained color lines in literary and cultural studies seem to extend to the idea of hemispheric modernisms and the kinds of forays it would prompt into more unfamil-iar linguistic and cultural territory. As I show in my previous chapter, this has not always been so, and there is no good reason why it should con-tinue to be so. Studies of USAmerican modernism that cross color lines may well create momentum in the direction of exploring how race functions in modernist writing from across the Americas.[20] What obstacles there are to such hemispheric comparisons are today mainly the results of inflex-ible disciplinary organization and bias. Foremost among these hindrances are sometimes bewildering variations in terminology and periodization. Contrary to what some of the contributors to the *Cambridge History of Latin American Literature* suggest, *modernismo* does not unproblemati-cally translate as literary modernism, certainly not of the Anglo-American variety. In fact, *modernismo* is in many ways a false cognate.[21] Typically placed between 1880 and 1916, Hispanic America's *modernismo* predates the modernisms that emerged in Europe and the United States of America. Although many Hispanic American *modernistas* were of the same genera-tion as the now-canonical proponents of Anglo-American high modernism, their major writings barely reached beyond the first decade of the twentieth century. By the time Eliot published "The Love Song of J. Alfred Prufrock" in 1917 and "The Waste Land" in 1922, few of the canonical *modernista* poets—among them Cuba's José Martí (1853–1895), Nicaragua's Rubén Darío (1867–1916), Argentina's Leopoldo Lugones (1874–1938), and Uruguay's Julio Herrera y Reissig (1875–1910) and Delmira Agustini (1886–1914)—were still alive.[22] While one might work around this chronological disjunction by dividing *modernista* writing into early and late phases, it is quite clear that the Hispanic American writers who are most comparable to the Anglo-American modernists and their formal concerns are those usually grouped together as a *vanguardia,* or avant-garde, that Hugo Verani plausibly situates between 1916 and 1935.[23] The kinds of artistic and ideological transgressions that the English-speaking world places under the terminological umbrella "modernism" are all part of transatlantic networks that connect the Americas with Africa and Europe. Significantly, these networks also connect the various parts of the Americas (north, south, central) and the Caribbean with each other, with *and* without routing such communications through Europe. While these avant-garde networks are global cultural formations, studying them historically does not produce universals. On the contrary, tracing continuities and discontinuities among the literary avant-gardes that came into being roughly during the first half of the twentieth century enables us to see how phenomena that might otherwise appear discrete and isolated—that is, merely local—are also the moving parts of a vast transnational topography. Borges and Guillén are as much part of this cultural landscape as Hughes, Hemingway, and Waldo Frank. Even though these writers did not always move in the same literary circles, events such as the Spanish Civil War drew them to the same place in their fight against fascism. And even if they never met in person, their writings—thanks to the efforts of fellow artists, scholars, translators, publicists, and publishers—circulated in and around cultural hubs such as Buenos Aires, Havana, Madrid, and New York.

What comes into sharper relief in comparative scholarship on transatlantic and hemispheric literary networks is that the Hispanic American *vanguardia* was no more unified than its counterparts in the USA or Europe. The proliferation of countless "isms" is hardly a surprise. What is astonishing, however, is the extent to which Hispanic American literary history has also been ghettoized along color and, implicitly, class lines. The *Cambridge History of Latin American Literature* is a recent example. Given perceptions and claims that the Hispanic Americas have not been torn apart by racial conflict and discrimination, or certainly not to the extent that the USA has and still is, one might not have expected to find similar practices of exclusion in both popular and academic settings. Yet in the Hispanic Americas, as in the USA, writing about the black diaspora in the 1920s and 1930s has shared the fringes with Communists and others concerned about sociopolitical issues. Scholars have rarely addressed racial and ethnic rifts that existed within the *vanguardia,* often in concert with political ones. If the persistent racial segregation of New World modernisms is the reason that "Jean Toomer [is] never cited" in discussions of Anglo-American modernism, it is also the reason that Nicolás Guillén, Ildefonso Pereda Valdés, Pilar Barrios, Jorge Artel, and many others are quoted far less frequently in scholarly work on Hispanic American avant-garde poetry than Borges, Neruda, or Vicente Huidobro.[24] If they are discussed at all, they tend to be pigeonholed (via Renato Poggioli) into what Hugo Verani calls the "sociopolitical Avant-Garde."[25] So-called *indigenista* writers—Tace Hedrick has called them "mestizo modernists"— have been similarly marginalized in literary histories.[26] This ghettoization has left us with rather distorted perspectives on writers whose contacts with each other—through personal communications, translations, or both—have historically crossed the very lines that scholarship upholds. Take, for instance, the insistence that Guillén's *poemas-son* most resemble Hughes's blues poetry, which has hardened into an orthodoxy in Afro-Hispanic studies.[27] Once Guillén's *poesía mulata,* by sleight of translation, turns into "black poetry," the presumably most natural point of comparison becomes the "Aframerican" poetry of the New Negro movement or, in the case of some of Guillén's later poems on black subjects (such as the *Elegías*), the Black Arts movement. On the one hand, this critical narrative recognizes that Guillén was in conversation with New Negro artists, including of course Hughes. On the other hand, however, it has also had the effect of separating Guillén's "Motivos de son" and *Sóngoro cosongo* not only from the verse of so-called *negrista* poets throughout the Hispanic Americas but also from the mainstream (or elite) *vanguardistas.*[28] Why not, however, compare Guillén's poetry with that of Borges and Neruda, or, crossing different boundaries, William Carlos Williams or Sherwood Anderson?

Historically, all these marginalized ethnic and political modernisms are interconnected. Points of contact between the historical avant-gardes and their writing in various parts of the New World are the moving parts of a larger phenomenon that takes shape from publications (books and, often more important, journals and newspapers) and personal papers and correspondence. As a discursive phenomenon, what we call modernism resides in a host of intertextualities, including translations. On the one hand, it is important to recognize that the New Negro Renaissance occurred more or less at the same time as the Afro-Antillean movement, Haitian *indigenisme,* and similar artistic phenomena throughout the Hispanic Americas.[29] On the other hand, however, the precise nature of the ideological and aesthetic overlap that such simultaneity implies comes into full view only when those literary events are also connected with (now) more canonical modernist writing from across the Americas. How else, for instance, could one explain why Borges, not exactly a member of the African diaspora, translated Hughes's "The Negro Speaks of Rivers"? The same holds true for the Mexican vanguardists Xavier Villaurrutia, Rafael Lozano, and Salvador Novo, whose poetry is never placed in any proximity to the work of Afro-Hispanic American writers; yet they translated and published Hughes's poems in their literary journal, *Contemporáneos.*[30] There are times when discussions of race and ethnicity in literature can be as profoundly limiting as ahistorical formalist readings, especially when the critical focus is solely on literary thematics amplified by biographical and phenotypical factors.[31]

The close contact that authors such as Langston Hughes and Waldo Frank cultivated with a variety of Hispanic American authors is a case in point here. Another is the fact that Alfred A. Knopf, Hughes's main publisher, was the first USAmerican press actively to seek out South American manuscripts.[32] Until the 1960s, the sorts of translations that Knopf, which has been distributed by Random House since the 1950s and is now a division of the latter press, published were mainly from French, German, and Italian. Notable among these early translations were Oswald Spengler's *The Hour of Decision* (1934) and Kafka's *The Castle* (1956) and *The Trial* (1955). Knopf's list at the time also included Swedish, Danish, Norwegian, and Hungarian authors. Blanche Knopf also made her first trip to South America in the early 1940s, and on November 30, 1950, Hughes wrote to her that "it is nice to read about the appreciation the Latin Americans have for what you have done for their literature there."[33] Translations from the Portuguese and Spanish began to appear from Knopf in the late 1950s and early 1960s.[34]

WALDO FRANK AND SUR

Between the late 1920s and the 1950s, significant numbers of Hughes's poems, along with his autobiographies, short stories, and a novel, circulated in the Hispanic Americas in translation. During that time, no fewer than seven volumes of Hughes's poetry and prose were translated and published in Buenos Aires alone. It was in Argentina that both of his autobiographies, *The Big Sea* and *I Wonder As I Wander,* were published in Spanish translations in 1944 and 1959, along with his first novel, *Not Without Laughter* in 1945; a collection of short stories, *Laughing to Keep from Crying* in 1955; and a generous assortment of poems, *Poemas de Langston Hughes* in 1952. What makes this fact noteworthy is that Argentina—unlike Colombia, Venezuela, Brazil, and even Uruguay—had a relatively small population of African descent at that time, despite the fact that Buenos Aires had been one of the main ports for the transatlantic slave trade in the sixteenth century. That the Afro-Argentine population in Buenos Aires declined dramatically during the nineteenth century (though it grew in other parts of the country) may in part account for the absence of *poesía negra* and *poesía negrista* from Argentina during the 1920s and 1930s, despite immigration from the Cape Verde islands during the same period. Even today Argentine artists and intellectuals are not known for their interest in a part of the population that seems to have been either "forgotten" or "disappeared."[35]

What, then, might account for such plenitude of publications in the case of Hughes? After all, he never traveled to Argentina, and he appears to have had direct contact with only one of his Argentine translators, Julio Gáler. Interest in Hughes's work seems to date from 1931, when Jorge Luis Borges published his translations of three Hughes poems in the second issue of the fledgling journal *Sur*. How did Borges come to translate Hughes? To be sure, there were certain affinities and, as Sergio Waisman has pointed out, translation is fundamental to Argentine literary history.[36] As a poet, the younger Borges, who had not yet emerged as a major writer by the time these translations appeared, shared Hughes's passion for Whitman and his interest in the poetic uses of colloquial language. Although Borges was involved in national politics in those days, sociopolitical themes did not find their way into his poetry, which, unlike Hughes's, tended to be sentimental and nostalgic.[37] How and when Borges would have come into contact with Hughes's early poetry is unclear. I see two equally plausible possibilities. The first one is Waldo Frank, self-styled prophet of hemispheric cultural wholeness. The other is the Argentine poet Raúl González Tuñón, a contemporary and erstwhile friend of Borges's, who had met Hughes in Spain.

Frank traveled to Argentina in the late 1920s, at about the same time that Hughes visited Cuba. He embarked on a lecture tour throughout Central and South America in 1929 and 1930 in the wake of President Herbert Hoover's not-so-successful tour, delivering numerous well-attended lectures in Mexico, Brazil, Uruguay, Argentina, Chile, Peru, Bolivia, Colombia, and Cuba. The following year, Frank, like Hughes, visited the Soviet Union. Some considered the author of *Our America* (1919) and *The Re-discovery of America* (1929) "the only serious North American author who exercised a direct influence" on Hispanic American letters in the 1920s. Indeed, both books were reviewed favorably by Hispanic American intellectuals, who saw in Frank a kindred spirit, and they were eventually translated into Spanish.[38] Frank first arrived in Buenos Aires in September of 1929. Through Eduardo Mallea, literary editor of *La Nación* and a proponent of Frank's belief that "America will be created by artists," Frank met Victoria Ocampo, a member of Argentina's social and cultural elite.[39] Ocampo, already quite well known by the time Frank encountered her and "perfectly trilingual," came from a prominent liberal aristocratic family that had considerable financial resources at its disposal.[40] It was to his new friend that Frank, committed as he was to cultural union and spiritual harmony within the Americas, pitched the idea of a Pan-American literary review, "a cultural bridge between the Americas, a forum for the best thinkers of both continents."[41] In his history of *Sur*, John King quotes María Rosa Oliver, a close friend of Ocampo's, to the effect that Frank wanted "algo totalmente distinto" (something completely different) from the literary journals that existed then, "algo más continental" (something more continental, or hemispheric). He argued that "o desentrañamos la América oculta por mentira, mitos, lugares comunes y propagandas chillonas, o las relaciones entre no-sotros se deterioran de más en más" (either we disembowel the lies, myth, commonplaces, and the shrill propaganda that obscure America or the rela-tions among us will deteriorate further).[42] The rhetoric of (re)discovery is unmistakable in Frank's speeches and throughout his writing. Ocampo was quite taken with his idea of a "viaje de descubrimiento" (journey of discov-ery), a quest for what she, following Frank, called the "América del oculto tesoro" (America of secret treasures). She was intrigued enough to throw her personal fortune behind *Sur,* which was to become one of the leading literary journals in the Hispanic Americas for decades to come.[43]

As King points out, Ocampo was an incorrigible Europhile, and it was clear from her editorial in the first issue in 1931 that *Sur*'s "dominant ma-trix would continue to be Europe."[44] As Ocampo explained at some length in her editorial, significantly entitled "A Letter to Waldo Frank," one could hardly "volver la espalda a Europa" (turn one's back on Europe); to do so would be, well, "ridiculo." At the same time, however, she saw *Sur* as "el lugar constante de nuestro encuentro...testimonia de mi admiración por esa obra, mi absoluta adhesión a lo que la inspiró. Seguirá en cuanto a su orientación un camino paralelo" (our shared meeting place...testimony to my admiration for your work, my absolute devotion to what it has in-spired. The journal will follow a path parallel to that of your own work).[45] Frank continued to support *Sur*'s development, and not a few translations of his own work appeared in the journal during the 1930s. But he wistfully noted in his *Memoirs* that the "ideational" rift between Ocampo, Oliver, and Samuel Glusberg (aka Enrique Espinoza), who had organized his trip to Argentina, symbolized that "the 'parts' of America were not yet ready to grow together."[46] The "cultural union" Frank had envisioned between Ocampo and Glusberg, "the dynamic immigrant Jew with a Prophet's Amer-ican in his heart," did not become a reality. "My concept of the magazine as an organism," Frank wrote in his *Memoirs,* "meant nothing to Victoria for whom most of the American and Hispano-American authors, loved by Glusberg more for promise and intent than for complete achievement, also had no meaning. The elegant *Sur* published many a good piece, but it was remote from what I wanted and the hemisphere needed."[47]

I offer this radically abbreviated version of the founding of *Sur* for two reasons. First, Hughes could not possibly have wished for a more visible venue for some of the early Spanish translations of his poems. To become "a magazine for everyone with an interest in the Americas and [that] would serve as a bridge between America and Europe,"[48] *Sur* published transla-tions of those who were considered major European and North American writers at the time. In fact, translation was at the core of *Sur,* clearly a way for the editors to build cultural capital in a Europhile Argentina.[49] It is quite likely that Borges's translations of Hughes's poems for *Sur* stimulated interest in Hughes's other works in Argentina and elsewhere in the Hispanic

Americas. My second reason for talking about the (pre-)history of *Sur* is that it is quite conceivable—even if there is no hard-and-fast evidence—that it might well have been Waldo Frank who first brought Hughes's poems to Borges's attention, either directly or indirectly. Although Frank does not mention Borges in the context of his visits to Buenos Aires, it would have been highly unlikely that they did not meet, given how close Borges was to Ocampo and his involvement in *Sur* from the start. By 1942, when Frank was writing *South American Journey*, the account of his second "campaign" in the Hispanic Americas, he did include Borges among those whom he considered "the country's leading writers." The others were Lugones (whom Frank himself translated), Horacio Quiroga, Alfonsina Storni, Mallea, and Ezequiel Martínez Estrada. He seems to have done so somewhat grudgingly. True, Frank gave Borges his due as "his generation's finest stylist." But calling the Argentine, who had left his mark on the country's literary scene by then, someone who "brazenly devotes his genius to a literature of fantasy and utter escape" does not suggest that he saw this literary genius, who "incidentally lift[ed] the detective story to a new height of literary excellence," as much of visionary fellow traveler.[50]

When considered in the context of "the politics of cultural alliances" in the Americas, the publication of Hughes's poems in *Sur* may well be called "paradigmatic."[51] Important here are not just Frank's avowed Pan-American ideals but also his interest in African American culture. He supported New Negro writers, notably his friend Jean Toomer, while at the same time proving quite comfortable ignoring African Americans' cultural contributions to the multitudinous hemispheric "Whole" he envisioned with Whitman's help.[52] Frank's friendship with and influence on Jean Toomer is as well known as Toomer's affair with Frank's wife. By contrast, Frank's relationship with Hughes was far more superficial and may not have extended much beyond their common interest in Communism. If Frank did indeed introduce Hughes's poetry to his Argentine friends, he would likely have done so because Hughes's early lyrics may have reminded him of what he valued about Toomer's *Cane* (1923): that these were poems in which "a land...suddenly [rose] up into the eminence of song."[53] Frank, of course, was talking about the USAmerican South, where he had traveled, disguised as a Negro, in the company of Jean Toomer in 1921. The "Southland" is also the site of some of Hughes's early poems, although Hughes hardly wrote in Toomer's pastoral and Gothic key. Hughes was also far more fascinated by urban life, something he shared with Borges.[54] Even in Hughes's urban poems, Frank would at least have appreciated "the struggle" of so-called folk forms "toward literary expression."[55] And there is one thing that Hughes's poems did that Toomer's haunting lyrical prose did not: they spoke not just to the USA but to the Americas and, indeed, to the kind of hemispheric cosmopolitanism that Frank embraced and advocated. Frank's idea of a New World that had yet to be discovered was probably what also attracted Borges to Hughes's verse. But, as his translations of Hughes show, Borges's Americanism was far more abstract than Frank's. It was an aesthetic concept rather than a political or religio-philosophical plan.

Given his proclivity for such abstractions and his aloofness from social issues, Borges's interest in racial issues was predictably slight. In fact, in his only published statement about "la literatura negra" from 1937, Borges wrote that "[s]alvo a ciertos poemas de Countee Cullen, la literatura negra, hoy por hoy, adolesce de una contradicción inevitable. El propósito de esa literatura es demostrar la insensatez de todos los prejuicios raciales, y sin embargo no hace otra cosa que repetir que es negra: es decir, que acentuar la diferencia que está negando" (except for certain poems by Countee Cullen, black literature today suffers from an inevitable contradiction. The goal of this literature is to show the senselessness of all racial prejudice, and yet it does nothing but repeat that it is black: that is, emphasize the very difference it is negating).[56] Borges's comments open a brief introductory note to Hughes's poems in *El Hogar,* where, in February of 1937, he published a slightly revised translation of one of the three Hughes poems he had done for *Sur* six years earlier: "The Negro Speaks of Rivers." His remarks resonate with Waldo Frank's sense that "the whole will and mind of the creator must go below the surface of race. And this has been an almost impossible condition for the American Negro to achieve, forced ever[y] moment of his life into a specific and superficial plane of consciousness." What Frank was after was "direct and unafraid creation," as he called it, not "sentimentalism, exoticism, polemic, 'problem' fiction, and moral melodrama."[57] Borges's singling out some of Cullen's poems of course raises the question of why he did not translate Cullen instead of Hughes. The answer, I believe, is that Cullen's Keatsian poetry was ultimately too staid for Borges's incipient Ultraist tastes, which is another way of saying that Cullen was not enough of a modern stylist for him.[58] More significant, however, is that Borges, like Frank, would have heard in Hughes's lyrics the cadences of Whitman, whose poetry Borges had loved since his youth. Borges would not, however, publish his translation of Whitman's *Leaves of Grass* until 1969, despite the fact that he had already announced this translation as early as 1927.[59] Borges would certainly not have shared the opinions of Rafael Lozano and Juan Felipe Toruño, to whom the "primitivism" and "vitalism" of Negro poetry, and particularly the rhythms of Hughes's poems, provided a welcome relief from French symbolism and from "las estructuras que presentan otras, en las que se nota la preocupación por pulir, depurar, sutilizar, perfeccionar o aglomerar duples, triples o cuádruples figuras en metáforas que fusionan contenido y continente, como en el Ultraísmo. En la poesía negra compruébese lo contrario" (the structures we find in other modernist or ultramodernist movements, in which there is obsessive polishing, purifying, subtilizing, perfecting, and combining double, triple or quadruple figures into metaphors that fuse content and continent, as in Ultraísmo. In Negro poetry, it is just the opposite).[60]

Borges would quickly become the best-known and most prolific translator among *Sur*'s initial contributors. As André Waisman has noted in his
study on Borges and translation, Borges "led his generation in renovating
Argentina's literature by effecting a series of dialogic crosses between local
/ criollo and cosmopolitan / international tendencies and by demonstrating
that such intersections have always been at the core of Argentine literature.
In the 1920's and 30s, the local and the European [and, one might add,
the USA]—intralingual and interlingual translation—coexisted in a tension
that was experienced as deeply problematic, but also produced important
cultural innovations." Translation was at the heart of this formal and ideological tension and as a result was at the core of the literary innovations that
Borges himself pursued and supported. For him, literary translation, like
all literary writing, was "a matter of a displacement towards the margins,"
which he claimed as a privileged site for innovation. Criticizing Lawrence
Venuti, Waisman points out that "the ethics and aesthetics of translation are
fundamentally different in the periphery than they are in the center.... Techniques that in the center contribute to projects of cultural imperialism can,
in the periphery, function as a form of resistance, as a redrawing of political
as well as literary maps."[61] On the one hand, then, Borges redrew Argentina's literary map by translating European writers such as James Joyce,
T. S. Eliot, Virginia Woolf, Oscar Wilde, Franz Kafka, André Gide, and Paul
Valéry, among others. Most of these translations were published by the *Sur*
Press.[62] On the other hand, Borges also furthered Frank's hemispheric vision by translating USAmerican writers, especially in the 1930s and 1940s.
Among them were Edgar Allen Poe, Nathaniel Hawthorne, Herman Mel-
ville, Edgar Lee Masters, and Carl Sandburg, along with William Faulkner,
E. E. Cummings, Hart Crane, and, of course, Hughes.[63]

Borges's theoretical writings on translation, especially "Las dos maneras
de traducir" (1926), which date from around the same time that Walter
Benjamin penned "The Task of the Translator" (1923), "present a complete
reformulation of how the relationship between source and target texts and
cultures is usually understood."[64] The Argentine modernist emphasized,
well in advance of Roman Jakobson's famous essay "On Linguistic Aspects
of Translation" (1959), that intralingual translation obtains whenever post-
(or neo-)colonial writers carve out for themselves a space for innovation
based on their cultural differences, a space from which they can define their
own writing in relation to dominant metropolitan traditions, be they European or USAmerican. For Borges, writing from the margins is always,
inevitably, a form of translation that challenges the authoritative original-
ity of metropolitan scripts from the secondary, merely mimetic position of
postcolonial literatures. In such scenarios, postcolonial writers function as
irreverent translators whose strategies of deliberate mistranslation generate

an aesthetics of theft and infidelity, in which even a so-called original can betray its translation.[65] What links writing and translation—indeed, what makes writing translation—is their analogous position in relation to source texts, be they originals or other literary precursors. Although a translation may seem to have only one source text, other texts always mediate the translational process and connect seemingly disparate cultural geographies in unexpected ways. For Borges, the original is always what he calls an "hecho móvil" (moving event), a phrase that I am inclined to translate as a "movable feast."[66] Borges's emphasis on infidelity, his outright rejection of the idea of a privileged original, and his complication of the figure of the literary precursor as something that each text invents rather than inherits all stem from his realization that the spatiotemporal displacements that characterize translation similarly affect all other acts of writing and reading.[67] For Borges, this made translation "an ideal metaphor for writing [and reading], as well as a perfect point of departure to consider issues of aesthetic value and cultural difference," an idea he worked to the fullest in a story such as "Pierre Menard."[68]

In the early 1930s, Borges seems to have been more receptive to the politics of cultural difference than he was at later stages in his career, when he condemned literary realism and any type of social and political purpose for literature. Frank's diatribe against "the vile current realistic novel [that] has spoiled all minds for the essential and pure lines of aesthetic form" would have struck a familiar chord in the later Borges.[69] At this earlier point in his life, however, Borges "display[ed] a surprising number of influences and interests: the gauchesque tradition, the *malevos* of Buenos Aires...and even the condition of the suffering blacks."[70] The three Hughes poems that Borges chose for *Sur* were "I, Too" (on which I have already commented at length in the previous chapter), "Our Land," and "The Negro Speaks of Rivers." *Sur* printed the translations together with the English texts. Two of these poems were hardly unusual choices: along with "I, Too," "The Negro Speaks of Rivers" from 1921 was among the most frequently translated Hughes poems in the Hispanic Americas. What is noteworthy about all three poems is that they do *not* exemplify the "lyric realism" that some have associated especially with Hughes's early blues poetry.[71] In fact, all three poems enact, at least to some extent, a familiar modernist break with historical referentiality, which is what would have made them appealing to Borges. This is most evident in Hughes's "Our Land (Poem for a Decorative Panel)" from 1923, which opened the final section of *The Weary Blues*, also entitled "Our Land."

> We should have a land of sun,
> Of gorgeous sun,
> And a land of fragrant water
> Where the twilight

Is a soft bandanna handkerchief
Of rose and gold,
And not this land where life is cold.

We should have a land of trees,
Of tall thick trees
Bowed down with chattering parrots,
Brilliant as the day,
And not this land where birds are grey.

Ah, we should have a land of joy,
Of love and joy and wine and song,
And not this land where joy is wrong.

(*CP*, 32–33)

In his introduction to the first edition of *The Weary Blues,* Carl Van Vechten remarked on Hughes's "nostalgia for color and warmth and beauty," which, he adds, "explains this boy's nomadic instincts."[72] Van Vechten quoted lines from two poems to illustrate what Anita Patterson calls Hughes's "poetics of migration:"[73] "Our Land" is one of them. Any reading of this poem depends significantly on how one identifies the first-person plural pronoun, which is far from unambiguous. The two lines Hughes added when he included the poem in *The Weary Blues* in 1926 take us back to one of his communities of migrants and the emotional bonds they share: "Ah, sweet away! / Ah, my beloved one, away!" (*CP*, 33, *TWB*, 99). We may say that these bonds are the product of outwardly directed movement away from a place, a "civilization," whose frostiness suffocates. There is a close link—indeed, a formal and emotional symmetry—between "Our Land" and "Poem," which is subtitled in a similar way: "For the portrait of an African boy after the manner of Gauguin" (*CP*, 32). The imagined painting in "Poem" has the same status as an objet trouvé as the decorative panel. The subtitles accentuate each poem's status as a representation of a representation, which locates their exoticism outside any external reality. "Poem" is also part of the same section in *The Weary Blues;* in the *Collected Poems,* which presents Hughes's poem chronologically, "Poem" lands right before "Our Land" on the same page. Both poems eschew historical specificity to stage a clash of civilizations. Exotic imagery associated with the African jungle and related equatorial spaces collides with figure of frigidity, colorlessness ("grey"), and the general absence of pleasure and delight. Indeed, there is a moral injunction against them ("wrong"). In the case of "Our Land," the entire poem contradicts the title, for what characterizes "this land" is that it is precisely not *ours,* that it is *not home.*[74] *Our land* is thus a projection, a "sweet away," an elsewhere that might be located in either the past or the future. This poem can thus be read in terms of exclusion, marginalization, and "minority rhetoric" with respect both to race and sexuality. Nicholas Evans is right to suggest that "'Our Land' dramatizes the conflict between the desire to root in nationalist formations of identity (American, African American and even homosexual) and the need to disavow such formations and continue to roam in new routes of identification. The fact that this necessity derives from the exclusion of those with 'vagrant' desires manifests a bitter critique of USAmerican and African American nationalist formations—of their insufficiency to accommodate alternative subject positions like those of black homosexuals."[75]

The idea of vagrant desires and the critique of nationalism may both have resonated with Borges in 1930. His translation of "Our Land"—"Nuestra Tierra"—omits the last two lines and appears to be based on the first version of the poem Hughes published in *World Tomorrow* in 1923.[76] Borges also drops the parenthetical subtitle, thus moving the poem both into closer ideological proximity to *Nuestra América*—José Martí's essay and Waldo Frank's journal—and, ironically, further away from modernist aesthetics.[77]

> Deberíamos tener una tierra de sol,
> De lujoso sol,
> Y una tierra de agua fragante
> Donde la tarde es un pañuelo suave floreado
> De rosa y de oro,
> Y no esta tierra
> Donde la vida es fría.
>
> Deberíamos tener una tierra de árboles,
> De alto, espesos árboles,
> Agobiados de loros charlatanes
> Brillantes como el día
> Y no esta tierra donde son grises los pájaros.
>
> Ah, tendríamos un país de alegría,
> De amor y alegría y vino y canción,
> Y no esta tierra donde la alegría está mal.[78]

There are two other Spanish translations of this poem, one by Miguel Alejandro from 1936, the other by Ahumada from 1968 (see figure 5). In *Yo también soy América*, Ahumada's collection of Hughes's poems "en memoria de Martin Luther King," "Nuestra tierra. Poema para un panel decorativo" is flanked by "Trabajadores en un camino de Florida" ("Florida Road Workers") and "Orgullo" ("Militant"), both from 1930 (*YT,* 89–93).[79] Their company renders the abstractions in the earlier poem more socially concrete, as well as situating them geographically in the USAmerican South. The bitter ironies of "Florida Road Workers" specify the absence of joy,

Figure 5. Cover of Herminio Ahumada's *Yo también soy América*, 1968.

or better, its class-bound prohibition: "Sure, / the roads helps everybody. / Rich folks ride—/ And I get to see them ride" (*CP*, 159) (Sí, / un camino ayuda a todos! / Los ricos transitan / y yo alcanzo a verlos transitar.)[80] "Militant," which Hughes had initially titled "Pride," shows a response to a joyless existence that is rather at variance with the desire for getting away: "For honest dreams / Your spit is in my face / And so my fist is clenched / Today—/ To strike your face" (*CP*, 131) (Por mis honrados anhelos / me escupes en la cara, / y así, mi puño está cerrado / ahora, / para golpear tu rostro). Alejandro's translation in *Nueva Cultura* has a comparable politicizing effect: a fragment of the poem appears right above "¡Buenos Días, Revolución!"

Perhaps more remarkable even than the varied company this poem keeps in its Spanish versions are the differences in imagery in the translations. Borges mixes the mundane (*tarde* instead of *crepúsculo* or *alba*) with splashes of extravagant metaphor. The land is one of "lujoso sol" (luxurious sun),[81] where dazzling parrots "overwhelm" (*agobiar*) rather than just weigh down the trees. Borges intrepidly turns a dreary afternoon into a "pañuelo suave floreado / De rosa y de oro," a soft scarf flowering resplendently in rose and gold. Ahumada's simile, by contrast, is fairly conservative: "tan suave como un pañuelo de hierbas / De oro y rosa"—as soft as a scarf of leaves of gold and rose. Alejandro's translation offers an even starker contrast to Borges's by ignoring Hughes's conditional tense and folding his metaphor into the overly precise entomological verb *eclosar* (to metamorphose). Just as oddly, the suggestive splendor of Hughes's opening figure now yields to rather incongruous images of excess and exhaustion whose negative connotations blur the contrast the English poem sets up. Now life is no longer just cold but, to fit a rhyme scheme that Hughes eschews and echoing Eliot-like ennui in the process, also boring or dull ("aburrida"). Alejandro's choices are all the more puzzling because he translated the poem in the politically charged context of the Spanish Civil War.

> Precisamos nosotros un derroche de sol,
> de sol agotador
> y aromas de flor.
> Donde alba eclosa
> en oro y rosa.
> No este país, donde la vida
> es fría y aburrida!

[We need a surfeit of sun, / of draining sun / and flowery fragrance. / Where dawn metamorphoses / into gold and rose. / Not this land where life / is cold and boring!]

There are also pronounced differences in how each translator interprets Hughes's emphatic "where joy is wrong." Ahumada turns it into "en que la alegría es *equívoca,*" using the conjunction ("in which" rather than "where") to accent the inventedness of a place that his tense choice locates in the future: "fuera tan suave," "inclinaran," will be as soft, will bend down (*YT,* 91). Ahumada makes the final lines Hughes added to the poem oddly inconsistent with the projected vision of a distant land by making the beloved distant instead: "Ah, sweet away! / Ah, my beloved one, away!" becomes "¡Oh, dulce, lejana! / ¡Oh mi amada lejana!," that is, "O, sweet, away! O, my far-off [female] beloved!" Alejandro in his version prefers the religious register in "donde la alegría es pecado," (where joy is a sin), while Borges's line, "donde la alegría está mal" (where joy is evil) echoes Baudelaire. The allusion to *Les Fleurs du Mal* is fitting given Hughes's own familiarity with Baudelaire on the one hand and Borges's worries about the imminent rise of a political dictatorship on the other.[82]

The idea of (time) travel, to which the allusion to Baudelaire gives a transatlantic direction, links "Our Land" with "The Negro Sings of Rivers," the second poem Borges translated. What is particularly interesting in the case of Borges's "El Negro Habla de los Ríos" is that he published a second translation of this poem in *El Hogar* in 1937. The two versions are almost identical, except for the penultimate line, on which I comment below. In the following stanza, I have marked the differences between them by using brackets. For additional comparisons, notes 83–85 provide two other versions of each stanza, one by Gáler, the other by Lozano.

He conocido ríos...
He conocido ríos antiguos como el
mundo y más antiguos que la
      Fluencia de sangre humana por las humanas venas.
Mi espíritu se ha ahondado como los ríos.[83]

Me he bañado en el Eufrates cuando las albas eran jóvenes.
He armado mi cabaña cerca del Congo
y me ha arrullado el sueño,
He tendido la vista sobre el Nilo y he levantado
las pirámides en lo alto.

He escuchando el cantar del Mississippi
cuando [Abe] Lincoln bajo hasta Nueva Orleans,
Y he visto su barroso pecho dorarse todo con la puesta del sol.[84]

He conocido ríos:
Ríos envejecidos, morenos. [Ríos inmemoriales, oscuros]
Mi espíritu se ha ahondado como los ríos.[85]

Hughes opens his poem, published in *The Crisis* in 1921 and subsequently placed as the title poem of the third section of *The Weary Blues,* with one of his many ungendered voices. In Spanish, the poem's speaker is male almost by default: *el negro.* Hughes's speaker contemplates the past from his or her position in the present: "I've known rivers:" / I've known rivers as ancient as the world and older than the / Flow of human blood in human veins" (*CP,* 23). Hughes's simile shifts in the third line from body to soul to introduce depth as another dimension: "My soul has grown deep like the rivers." Hughes repeats this and the first line at the end of the poem, varying only the middle line:

> I've known rivers:
> Ancient, dusky rivers.
> My soul has grown deep like the rivers.
>
>   (*CP,* 23)

Following Hughes's figurative conjoining of age, experience, and blackness, Borges initially translates "ancient, dusky rivers" as "ríos envejecidos, morenos." The dark or brown rivers have grown old much like the soul has grown deep. Six years later, he would change the line to "ríos inmemoriales, oscuros." Unlike *envejecer,* which emphasizes the passing of time in relation to a human life, the adjective *inmemorial* places the rivers in the poem beyond human time and memory: "ancient" and "deep" are no longer a function of human experience but are metaphysical qualities whose presence in Borges's second translation minimizes the historical dimensions Hughes implies. By the time we reach Abraham Lincoln and the Mississippi in Hughes's poem, we have traversed the distance from what appear to be signs of faraway time to the more proximate memory of specific historical situations—lynchings and race riots—that prompted Hughes to write this poem in 1919.[86] The point is that rivers are vehicles for or induce memory.

Hughes recounts in *The Big Sea* that he formulated his first ideas for "The Negro Speaks of Rivers" as his train to Mexico was crossing the Mississippi. What results is a poem about travel and translation, in which dislocation represents the mnemonic process and functions as what Stephanides thinks of as "an agent for reshaping tradition."[87] Crossing the river in St. Louis, Missouri, "slowly, over a long bridge" (*BS,* 55), the young poet is literally suspended over the Mississippi. As the sound of the train's wheels on the bridge is in his ears and the train's rhythm involuntarily becomes part of his own body, Hughes imagines himself on the edge of two worlds. The rhythms of poetry render the movements of train and body *in time,* repeating them with a difference. Hughes's autobiographical journey from east to west becomes a movement not just across different geographies but also into a collective past.[88] The poem's rhythmic repetitions synchronize all these different locations, making them available to the reader at the same time and in the same space: that of the poem itself. To have known rivers, then, is to have felt that synchronizing rhythm. This feeling is an intellectual and emotional understanding of origins, historical experiences, and the gaps in one's own memory. It is best called *cultural* memory, with all its imperfections. As the poem plumbs the depths of intellect and emotion, history comes closer to home, as it were, and audible. The "singing of the Mississippi" is of course the remembered sound of slave songs. It is also an echo of Handy's famous "St. Louis Blues."[89]

> I bathed in the Euphrates when dawns were young.
> I built my hut near the Congo and it lulled me to sleep.
> I looked upon the Nile and raised the pyramids above it.
> I heard the singing of the Mississippi when Abe Lincoln
>   Went down to New Orleans, and I've seen its
>   muddy
> Bosom turn all golden in the sunset.
>
> (*CP*, 23)

Hughes's autobiographical retelling of the poem in *The Big Sea* should not, however, tempt us into thinking that Hughes himself is the poem's speaker. The poem represents someone else's speech: that of the titular "Negro," whose oral incantations are distant, depersonalized utterances. Far from being a transcription of those utterances, which belong to a different semiotic system, the poem seeks to appropriate that very system and its codes for its own purposes: to create a collective *voice* as a vehicle for cultural memory. But that voice, like the figure of the speaker, must remain an abstraction; though audible, it is intangible. As a poet, Hughes seeks emotional reassurance in an imaginative projection of cultural memories that are not altogether his own. He seeks to translate speech into writing that would communicate this quality of feeling as a vital part of knowledge of past survival and for future survival.[90] What Hughes also shows, however, is that he cannot completely collapse the distance between himself and the Negro any more than he can fully translate speech into writing. Both orality and the figure of the Negro are part of the frame that leaves the poet as if on the outside looking in. We encounter an analogous situation in "The Weary Blues." Since these are not *his* memories, Hughes must create a *proxy* through which to call up the resources of deeper cultural memory. It is precisely this gesture that makes the speaker a poetic persona.

Borges's second translation of the poem hints at an awareness of the poet's quandary in this lyric. *Inmemorial* poses the question of memory more directly, and more categorically, than Hughes's "ancient" does, while *oscuro*, a racially less charged term than *moreno*, extends the line's referential range beyond race. That Borges was aware of African American political and cultural history "up and down the Americas" is amply evident

from "El espantoso redentor Lazarus Morell," a 1933 short story known
in English as "The Dread Redeemer Lazarus Morell." The paradoxical ap-
pellations in the title of each of the stories that comprise Borges's *Historia universal de la infamía* (1935) (*Universal History of Infamy*), together
with the brevity of the book, suggest that his chief purpose here is aesthetic
rather than political. Borges has no interest in casting aspersions on Morell
or any other of the odd crew of characters in this book; in fact, he seems
rather to delight in stereotypes. His purpose here is not to moralize but to
intertwine historical with fictional events and translate the fragments into
what ultimately amounts to a travesty of realism. The opening paragraph of
"Lazarus Morell" exemplifies this process of assembling fragments and can
be read as a mise-en-abîme.

En 1517 el P. Bartolomé de las Casas tuvo mucha lástima de los indios que se
extenuaban en los laboriosos infiernos de las minas de oro antillanas, y propuso
al emperador Carlos V la importación de negros, que se extenuaran en los
laboriosos infiernos de las minas de oro antillanas. A esa curiosa variación de
un filántropo debemos infinitos hechos: los *blues* de Handy, el éxito logrado en
Paris por el pintor doctor oriental D. Pedro Figari, la buena prosa cimarrona del
también oriental D. Vicente Rossi, el tamaño mitológico de Abraham Lincoln,
los quinientos mil muertos de la Guerra de Secesión, los tres mil trescientos
millones gastados en pensiones militares, la estatua de imaginario Flucho, la
admisión del verbo *linchar* en la decimotercero edición del Diccionario del
Academia, el impetuoso film *Aleluya,* la fornida carga a la bayoneta llevada
por Soler al frente de sus *Pardos y Morenos* en el Cerrito, la gracia de la señorita
de Tal, el moreno que asesino Martín Fierro, la deplorable rumba El Manisero,
el napoleonismo arrestado y encalabozado de Toussaint Louverture, la cruz y la
serpiente en Haití, la sangre de las cabras degolladas por el machete del *papaloi,*
la habanera madre del tango, el candombe.

[In 1517, **the Spanish missionary** Bartolomé de las Casas, taking great pity
on the Indians who were languishing in the hellish workpits of Antillean gold
mines, suggested to Charles V, king of Spain, a scheme for importing blacks,
so that they might languish in the hellish workpits of Antillean gold mines. To
this odd philanthropic twist we owe, **all up and down the Americas,** endless
things—W.C. Handy's blues; the Parisian success of the Uruguayan lawyer and
painter **of Negro genre,** don Pedro Figari; the solid native prose of another
Uruguayan, don Vicente Rossi, **who traced the origin of the tango to Negroes;** the
mythological dimensions of Abraham Lincoln; the five hundred thousand dead
of the Civil War and its three thousand three hundred million spent in military
pensions; the entrance of the verb "to lynch" into the thirteenth edition of the
dictionary of the Spanish Academy; **King Vidor's** impetuous film *Hallelujah;*
the lusty bayonet charge led by **the Argentine captain Miguel** Soler, at the head
of his **famous regiment of** "Mulattoes and Blacks," in the **Uruguayan** battle

of Cerrito; the Negro killed by Martín Fierro; the deplorable Cuban rumba "The Peanut Vender"; the arrested, dungeon-ridden Napoleonism of Toussaint Louverture; the cross and the snake of Haitian **voodoo rites** and the blood of goats whose throats were slit by the *papaloi*'s machete; the *habanero,* mother of the tango; **another old Negro dance, of Buenos Aires and Montevideo,** the *candombe.*][91]

Borges's references to Abraham Lincoln and especially W.C. Handy are clearly nods to Hughes. Borges was no doubt well aware that the arc of the African American musical tradition in the case of Handy's "St. Louis Blues" spanned the distance from Africa via Spain to Cuba (the habanero) and to Argentina (the tango), then on to St. Louis.[92] The story's next section confirms that "The Negro Speaks of Rivers" in particular is indeed an intertext for the travels of "Lazarus Morell," especially for the story's English version. So is "I, Too." The Mississippi River, which plays a crucial role in the story's setting, helps Borges connect North with South America so as to universalize his own distinctive location: "El Padre de las Aguas, el Mississipi, el río más extenso del mundo,...es un infinito y *oscuro hermano* del Paraná, del Uruguay, del Amazonas y del Orinoco. Es un río de aguas *mulatas*" (The Father of Waters, the Mississippi, the largest river in the world an infinite and *dusky brother* of the Paraná, the Uruguay, the Amazonas, and the Orinoco. It is a river of *muddy* waters.).[93] Anyone as aware of linguistic nuance as Borges was would not have employed these adjectives lightly. Calling the Mississippi an "oscuro hermano" echoes Hughes's "darker brother" in the phrase that Borges had translated as "hermano oscuro" in 1931 (see chapter 2). "Oscuro hermano" also anticipates the "ríos inmemoriales, *oscuros*" in Borges's revised 1937 translation of "The Negro Speaks of Rivers." By rendering *oscuro* as "dusky" (rather than simply "dark") in the English version of Borges's story from 1979 and *aguas mulatas* as "muddy waters," which echoes Hughes's "muddy bosom," the two translators close the circle. I am tempted to add the Mississippi blues musician Muddy Waters into the equation, for that reference would also have been available to Borges and his cotranslator, Norman di Giovanni, in the 1970s. Although Hughes's poems stand at the chronological beginning of this sequence of translations and retranslations, the lines one might draw between originals and translations have now been, well, muddied.

Detecting in "Lazarus Morell" echoes of Borges's earlier translations of Hughes's poems does not necessarily make their relation one of literary influence. It does, however, point to a common literary ancestor: Walt Whitman. "The Negro Speaks of Rivers" would have appealed to Borges precisely because it relies on repetition to build catalogs of fragments and uses visual mirror effects to achieve depth. For Borges, this would have recalled Whitman above anyone else. And Hughes does not inscribe one-sided ideological or even moral judgments in any of these poems, another element that Borges would have appreciated. But, as we shall see, Borges's Buenos Aires, however much of a cosmopolitan edge it has, does not in any way resemble Hughes's Harlem or any of the other spaces to which Hughes carries pieces of Harlem during his travels.

HARLEM IN ARGENTINA

In a series of interviews conducted in 1973, Raúl González Tuñón told fellow poet Horacio Salas that he had in his library a copy of *Luna de enfrente* (1925), which Borges had inscribed to him in his tiny (*chiquitita*) handwriting: "al otro poeta suburbano."[94] Although the inscription literally translates as "to the other suburban poet," suburban has entirely different class inflections in English. The middle-class suburbs that began to encircle USAmerican cities after World War I did not have much in common with the *favelas* that grew at the outskirts of many metropoles elsewhere in the Americas, including South America and the Caribbean. It would be more precise, then, to tag Tuñón the poet of the *other* Buenos Aires, the one for which Borges himself had little literary use: the areas on the fringes of the port city that Tuñón labeled "los baldíos," an expression best rendered, with a wary nod to Eliot, as wastelands. Tuñón opens his "Blues de los Baldíos" (Wasteland Blues), one of six blues poems in *Todos bailan* (They All Dance, 1935), with the following lines:

> Solo allí los chiquillos recogíamos la influencia telúrica.
> A la orilla
> pasaba la ciudad como un circo.
> Canto el fervor oculto de los baldíos, su clima universal,
> su geográfica síntesis, el hilo de agua, los montículos, el
> musgo y los gatos flacos y los papeles inútiles y los ruidos y
> los ruidos.[95]

[It is only here that the kids would sense telluric power. / At the edge / the city wanders like a circus. / I sing the hidden passion of the wastelands, their universal climate, / their geographical synthesis, the filament of water, the heaps, the / moss and the emaciated cats and the useless papers and the clamor and / the racket.]

Tuñón was hardly alone in his obsession with the idea of borders and edges. The "orillas" (edges), as Borges called them, were not, however, the same for everyone. Tuñón's *baldíos* are not the same well-lit neighborhood streets that Borges's flâneur roams in *Fervor de Buenos Aires* (1923) and *Luna de enfrente*. This was not the Buenos Aires Borges had "felt" (*sentí*) upon his return from Europe: "Esta ciudad que yo creí mi pasado / es mi porvenir, mi presente" (this city which I believe is my past / is my future, my present).[96]

In neither case, however, are these urban perimeters anything other than invented literary spaces. Although related to specific urban geographies, they are not realistic representations of actual places. It is significant that before these places on the margins could become literary references whose value was at once aesthetic and ideological, they first had to be thought of as cultural spaces rather than as places devoid of culture. Invention, then, means to imagine a perspective from which these edges — which may or may not be on a city's actual outskirts — can be seen, from which they become visible. Borges's literary suburbia is at once local and universal, and it is a bohemian quarter that belongs to the intellectual elites.[97] By contrast, Tuñón's Buenos Aires, especially in the poems he wrote after he broke with the vanguard group around the journal *Martín Fierro* (which also included Borges),[98] is perhaps best described as an alternate universe that is global in a very different sense: the characters, objects, and itineraries that define this space are associated with an entirely different class of people, that of an urban proletariat. Although Tuñón's *baldíos* seem to occupy the same geographical place, in cultural terms they could not be any farther removed from the streets in Borges's poems, "las calles desganadas del barrio, / casi invisibles de habituales" (the listless streets of the neighborhood, / almost empty).[99] In fact, the closest global neighborhood with which Tuñón's *baldíos* intersect is Hughes's Harlem, "the quarter of the Negroes," as Hughes calls it in *ASK YOUR MAMA* (*CP,* 477).[100] Both are landscapes of dreams deferred. James DeJongh notes that with *The Weary Blues,* "Hughes initiated a commitment to the theme of Harlem as a landscape and dreamscape of the blues, a theme that for over half a century has been since the 1920s a principal force shaping the development of the Harlem motif among three generations of Africana poets.... [They produced] black identity delineated in the tensions and resonances in the trope of the Harlem landscape itself, and advanced beyond the kind of twoness characterized by Du Bois."[101] The only attribute that perhaps distinguishes the downtrodden, transient denizens of Tuñón's *calles sin nombre* (nameless streets)[102] — immigrants from different parts of the globe, prostitutes and pimps, drug addicts, sailors, tramps, and circus folk — from Hughes's Harlemites is their skin color, and sometimes not even that:

> Te acuerdas de María Celeste?
> Pues hoy María Celeste es una
> Prostituta.
>
> . . . . .
>
> Te acuerdas de Juan el Broncero?
> Pues Juan el Broncero es hoy,
> Un ladrón.
>   ("Blues de los pequeños deshollinadores")[103]

[Remember María Celeste?/ Well, she's a prostitute now./ . . . / Remember Juan el Broncero? Well, today he is/ a thief.]

En las encrucijadas de ansias y de fracasos,
en los hoteles internacionales donde se encuentran rostros conocidos
de estafadores, prostitutas, prestidigitadores y judíos.

. . . .

En las tabernas cuando cantan los marineros
y en las mujeres canallas y en los sótanos fumadores.

. . . .

Esperar, esperar en una esquina,
encender un cigarrillo
y escuchar con asombro, con miedo, con nostalgía
la música amontonada del mundo.

("Recuerdo de A. O. Barnabooth")[104]

[In the cracks between worry and disappointment,/ in the international boarding houses where one finds the familiar faces / of con men, prostitutes, magicians, and Jews. / . . . / In the taverns where the sailors chant / and in sleazy brothels and smoky basements. / . . . To wait, to wait on a corner, / to light a cigarette / and listen with wonderment, with fear, with nostalgia / to the piled-up music of the world.]

The proximity between the urban fringes that attract Hughes and Tuñón and compel their poetic attention is not a matter of simple surface resemblances. The Buenos Aires Tuñón re-creates is a multinational space made up of the mixed-up sounds of social and economic differences that we also find in Hughes's Harlem, and what I would call his Harlemized spaces.[105] Iain Chambers's observations about the Mediterranean fit these urban spaces as well. "The history of place," he points out, "is itself an archive of sound, a collection of musical accidents, an accumulation of historical notes, an orchestration of cultural traces."[106] What distinguishes these poetic spaces, associated as they are with such different locations in the Western Hemisphere, is not that they are ghettos or barrios but that they are *de-provincialized*: these are peripheral spaces made up of fragments of other cities. In the first epigraph to this chapter, the urban planner in Patrick Chamoiseau's *Texaco* beautifully calls it "une culture-mosaïque" (a mosaic-culture), a "ville créole" (Creole City) with a grammar all its own.[107] Such Harlemized spaces are all locally anchored global microcosms connected to vast systems of circulation and translation. Tuñón's intense multilingual and multihistorical space is the stomping ground of Juancito Caminador, named after world-famous Johnny Walker, the persona of the traveler-magician from *Todos bailan* who comes straight from the circus to the modern city. Juancito Caminado is a magical alter ego that would stay with Tuñón for the rest of his literary career. A mock-epitaphic poem from 1941 ironically testifies to his longevity.

Juancito Caminador...
Murió en un lejano puerto
el prestidigitador.
Poca cosa deja el muerto.[108]

[Juancito Caminador.../ he died in a faraway port / the magician. / The dead man left little behind.]

Although Tuñón's poetic illusionist may be read as a counterpart to Borges's flâneur, Juancito Caminador is much closer kin to García Lorca's gypsies from *Romancero gitano* (1928) and especially to the itinerant tricksters Hughes conjures up in his poems and autobiographies.

At the risk of reading biography back into poetry, it is worth mentioning that Hughes and Tuñón led somewhat parallel lives. They were roughly the same age (Tuñón was born in 1905, Hughes, like Guillén, in 1902), they were from similarly humble backgrounds, and they both wrote prize-winning poetry quite early in their careers as writers. In 1926 Tuñón's first book of poems, *El violín del diablo* (The Devil's Violin), won first prize in the competition held by the publishing house Gleizer; the poet Alfonsina Storni was one of the three jurors. Two years later, *Miércoles de ceniza* (Ash Wednesday) was awarded a Premio Municipal. The twenty-three-year-old Tuñón promptly used the prize money to travel to Europe. While Hughes was roaming the Caribbean, Tuñón spent 1929–30 in Paris. Both men visited the Soviet Union and Cuba, though at very different points in their lives. Tuñón did not travel to the USSR until 1953; he visited central Asia in 1958.[109] And he did not go to Cuba until after the revolution, in 1963.

For Hughes and Tuñón, traveling is neither a pastime nor even an option. It is sheer necessity and, in fact, an ineluctable condition of modern life and literature. Theirs are different kinds of voyages to similar kinds of places. The gritty neighborhoods of the Buenos Aires that Tuñón's poet frequents seem closer to Hughes's not-so-affluent Harlem, as distinct, for instance, from the more proper, respectably middle-class Harlem whose cultural and political institutions James Weldon Johnson chronicles in *Black Manhattan* (1930) and also in *Along this Way* (1933). Tuñón's figures recall the cast of characters from Hughes's early poetry: "Yellow girls" who become "workin' girls," like Ruby Brown and Clorinda; the "ruined gal" in "Beale Street Love"; booze hounds like Gin Mary. *Fine Clothes to the Jew*, which might be read as a long poem,[110] in particular features a motley array of characters with "low-down ways" (*CP,* 62), many modeled on blues women like Ma Rainey and Bessie Smith, whose performances were quite unabashedly (homo)sexual. There are characters who let white boys look at their legs ("Red Silk Stockings") and sometimes even wield knives and stereotypical razors to fend off their "bad, bad" men, characters like "Do Dirty" who beat and cut them. For one reason or another, all of them are "deep in trouble." Like Juancito Caminador with his "[t]ruco mágico, ilusión, / canción, barja y paloma" (magic trick, illusion, song, deck of cards, and dove), [111]they are "dream singers," as Hughes writes in "Laughers":

> Rounders,
> Number writers,
> Comedians in vaudeville,
> And band-men in circuses—
> Dream-singers all,—
> My people.
>
> (CP, 27)

Striking also is Tuñón's preference for the blues, at least in *Todos bailan,* although he also offers the occasional *poetango,* a poetic form reminiscent of Nicolás Guillén's *poemas-son* (see chapter 4).[112] This choice, combined with the direct mention of Hughes in the lines from "Ku Klux Klan" in the second epigraph to this chapter, leaves little doubt that *Todos bailan* is (also) an homage to the USAmerican poet, whom Tuñón would not meet in person until several years after the collection appeared in print. Another unexpected reference to "Langston" appears in "Nuestra rosa, rosa de América," a long poem Tuñón first published in 1953. In that poem, in which the *rosa* of Borges's early verse is proudly wearing a full metal jacket, Tuñón characterizes the USA as the land of "los imperialismos mordiendo el Continente / y a su cabeza el yanqui biznieto del pirata /—no la tierra de Lincoln, de Whitman y de Lansgton [sic]" (the imperialisms chewing up the Continent/ and at their head the Yankee great-grandson of the pirate /—not the land of Lincoln, Whitman, and Langston).[113] What resonates here as well is Hughes's "Our Land" but minus the mythological slant that Borges gave it in his translation. Tuñón's American roses, like Hughes's, grow quite well in political manure.

Geographical and linguistic differences notwithstanding, Hughes's interest in what one might call socioaesthetics provides more fruitful grounds for comparing his poetry to Tuñón's verse than to Borges's and even to the work of Tuñón's close friend and fellow Communist Pablo Neruda, with whom he collaborated in Chile in the early 1940s. By the same token, the pioneering aesthetics of Hughes's poetry—even before he wrote "Advertisement for the Waldorf-Astoria," which some have oddly taken to mark the beginning of his career as a "political" poet—have much less in common with the lyrics of Countee Cullen, who shared Johnson's sense of public propriety, and even with those of the more combative Claude McKay. That the shared thematics of blackness and race relations may be enough to establish singular lines of cultural descent to the exclusion of a host of others must neither be underestimated nor undervalued. The same applies to the political expediency of doing so during the Harlem Renaissance and the Black Arts movement in the USA. Those shared topoi do not, however, justify cordoning off political and aesthetic affinities that existed both across the color line in the USA and well beyond national boundaries. In fact, I use the term "socioaesthetics" to signal the impossibility of separating politics from aesthetics when analyzing the poetry of the avant-gardes to which both Hughes and Tuñón *chose* to belong. These avant-gardes were critical of socioeconomic divisions and the institutions—be they literary, political, or religious—that either tacitly reinforced or openly policed those lines of separations. Race and color were obviously not secondary concerns for Hughes. How could they be? At least through the 1930s, Hughes was also not worried about propriety in either political or aesthetic terms. Had he been, he would never have written and published the poems in *Fine Clothes to the Jew* or *Scottsboro Limited* or, for that matter, any of the controversial verse he penned during the 1930s. I suspect that he probably never would have written anything worth reading. We should take to heart Hughes's reply to the reviewers who sneered at *Fine Clothes.* "My poems are indelicate," he retorted. "But so is life" (*Essays,* 39).

For Hughes to write about blues singers and their African American audiences, both of which were perceived as lower-class by the Negro elite in the 1920s, was no less a conscious act of transgression than it was for Tuñón to write about prostitutes and opium addicts in Buenos Aires's less respectable neighborhoods.[114] Both men were and created a new type of writer who was at once traveler and witness. And unlike Borges and his attentive idler, their poetic personae not only observed and invented, as Sarlo notes; they also cast judgments and shook things up.[115] Although the respective political climates in which Hughes and Tuñón wrote were ones in which anarchists, socialists, Communists, and other "writers on the left"—as Daniel Aaron would call them in his classic study—were accepted in intellectual circles, their poems pushed the limits not just of good taste but of what lyric poetry might sustain when written in a social and political key. Creating what Beatriz Sarlo called a "nuevo pintoresquismo, diferente de los costumbristas y de la mitologia urbana que Borges esta inventando" (new picturesque different from the costumbristas and the urban mythology that Borges invented), they rescued politics from the generic realism of so-called social literature and brought it into the previously safe aesthetic spaces of the lyric.[116]

Consider the issue of propriety in Hughes's "Ma Man" (initially "My Man"), one of the poems he modified for inclusion in *Fine Clothes,* in a way translating it from standardized English into an African American vernacular. If we follow Lawrence Venuti in assuming that translations "involve the inscription of domestic values in the foreign text," we find that "Ma Man" works with a very different notion of the "domestic" from what Venuti has in mind.[117] Here is the opening stanza of this blues poem:

When ma man looks at me
He knocks me off ma feet.
When ma man looks at me
He knocks me off ma feet.
He's got those 'lectric-shockin' eyes an
De way he shocks me sho is sweet.

(*CP*, 66)

If dialect in English, as Venuti argues, "exposes the hierarchical values in Anglo-American culture," African American vernacular in Hughes's poems also brings to the fore salient class differences among USAmerican Negroes.[118] If we posit a reader who does not readily identify with this language and the class position it denotes, which would have been true of many of Hughes's readers in the 1920s regardless of their race and color, we can see how the vernacular actually renders the text less rather than more familiar. This estrangement effect would also work with a different set of readers, those more apt to listen to the blues than read it on the page, for Hughes transforms the lyrics and musical structure of the blues into a poetic performance *related* to the musical performance but not identical with it. Either way, this poem does not position any reader in familiar "domestic intelligibilities." Instead, Hughes makes his readers uncomfortably aware of their distance from the poem's language and the situation the poem represents, which is anything but domestic. In fact, it is quite the opposite. The poem's persona is a female blues singer who confronts readers with an unabashedly sexualized, public account of her man's prowess as a banjo player—"he plays good when he's sober / An' better, better, better when he's drunk and a lover"—and as the "eagle-rockin'" lover to whom her seductive voice calls out in the final stanza.[119] The combination of raunchy sex and alcohol would have carried distinct lower-class inflections, and the poem, unframed and thus uncensored by a distant poetic voice, flaunts them quite unapologetically.

The figure of the blues singer in "Ma Man," like that of the prostitute in other poems, also functions as a fragment of the domestic relations in which black vernaculars emerged.[120] The originators of these mother tongues were not just mothers but also slaves who, in the antebellum Americas, took over the socializing and educational function of biological mothers while, especially in the USA, remaining on the outside of the white families they served. In the domestic sphere, slavery combined with racial oppression produced a structure of simultaneous closeness and distance that compromised the integrity of dominant languages in the same way that the historical realities of miscegenation compromised purportedly white lineages. Both compounded the problem of accessing intergenerational memories, including linguistic memories, that had begun with ruptures in African families caused by the slave trade. The persistence of racial oppression well after emancipation caused additional ruptures in African American families. We should not assume that this situation was limited to the USA. Set adrift by racist and economic pressures, the prostitutes in Hughes's poems represent the displacement of the black family. Like Hughes's female blues singers, these whores are potential maternal figures recovered from the morass of sexual and racial taboos in which African American womanhood was mired in the early twentieth century. As maternal figures, they are purveyors of a lost or displaced mother tongue but one stripped of all nostalgia. Their language is fiercely sexual in its insistence on having a body rather than being a body that can be used and abused. "Ma Man" is transgressive, then, not just because it represents underworld characters but also because it flouts the injunction against literary representations of black sexuality, female *and* male. There is, after all, no compelling reason to read the ungendered persona in this poem only as female, especially if we place "Ma Man" in the context of poems such as "Dream" and "Desire" from *Fields of Wonder* (1939):

> Desire to us
> Was like a double death
> Swift dying
> of our mingled breath
> Evaporation
> Of an unknown strange perfume
> between us quickly
> In a naked room.

(CP,105)

"Ma Man" is but one example of how Hughes's first books of poetry, like Tuñón's, functioned as "un verdadero laboratorio de transformaciones ideológico-literaria donde se verifica el impacto productivo de los grandes temas sociales sobre los mundos referentiales de la literatura....El thesaurus del poeta se amplia incorporando nuevas referencias culturales que se cruzan con las referencias anteriores" (a veritable laboratory for ideological-literary transformations where the productive impact of the great social themes on the referential worlds of literature could be validated....The poet's thesaurus becomes more extensive, incorporating new cultural references that cut across and mingle with older references).[121] Sarlo regards the changes that began during the 1920s in Argentina and the USA as two-pronged: on the one hand, writers who themselves came from the socioeconomic margins entered the intellectual arena; on the other, they thematized the fringe in their writings. In literature, these combined factors set in motion "un proceso de expansión tópica que se traducirá también en un sistema nuevo de cruces formales entres diferentes niveles de lengua y diferentes estéticas" (a process of thematic expansion that also translated into a new system of formal crossings between different levels of language and different aesthetics).[122] The result is not poetry that thematically strains against expected aesthetic enclosures and interior subjectivity—as it does, for instance, in Claude McKay's sonnets—but poetry that explodes those frames into many swirling atoms that can then recombine with each other into unexpected and highly unstable shapes. Here thematic crossings produce formal transgressions. An excellent example of how figures of miscegenation assert multiple and conflicting origins is Hughes's poem "Cross" from *The Weary Blues* (see *CP*, 58), which Rafael Lozano translated into Spanish as "Cruz" (1931) and Julio Gáler as "Mulato" (1959).

The reactions to Hughes's and Tuñón's respective transgressions of political and literary pieties were immediate and unforgiving. Most reviewers of *Fine Clothes* were aghast and quick to demote Hughes from the poet laureate to "poet low-rate."[123] Some even called him a "sewer dweller." If the tenor of Tuñón's poetry from the 1920s could be encapsulated in the lines "[a] la mentira de arriba / prefiero la cruel verdad de abajo" (to the mendacity of high-up / I prefer the brutal truth of the down-low), his tone sharpened even more in the 1930s, known in Argentina as the Infamous Decade.[124] Tuñón was "el testigo de la Década Infame" (the witness of the Infamous Decade) in more ways than one. In his work as a war correspondent for *Crítica*, the journal edited by his older brother Enrique, he reported on the horrors of the war between Bolivia and Paraguay (or, effectively, Standard Oil and Shell) for control of the Chaco Boreal. In his poetry, he chronicled the devastating effects of authoritarian politics and economic depression in what was then known as "the City of Hunger." "Las brigadas de choque" (The Shock Brigades) marked a point of unbearable pain and frustration at which his lyric poetry becomes a cry for solidarity and revolutionary action. Through innovation, poetry itself becomes a form of public resistance, not just a tool for it. Tuñón published his lengthy "antipoema" in 1933 in the journal *Contra,* which he had founded earlier that same year. Lines such as the following excerpts of this twelve-part poem did not endear Tuñón to the Argentine authorities.

> Formemos nosotros, cerca ya del Alba motinera,
> las Brigadas de Choque de la Poesía.
> Demos a la dialéctica materialista el vuelo lírico de nuestra fantasía.
> ¡Especialicémonos en el romanticismo de la Revolución!
>
> . . . .
>
> Contra
> Contra
> Contra las putas espías de Orden Político.
>
> . . . .
>
> ¡Abajo la inteligencia burguesa!
> Es tiempo de ocuparse del hombre.
>
> . . . .

Hablemos de esta ciudad sucia como su río.
Aquí todo está prohibido.

. . . .

¡Yo arrojo este poema violento y quebrado
contra el rostro de la burguesía![125]

[Already close to the mutinous Dawn, let us set up / the Shock Brigades of
Poetry. / Let us give dialectic materialism the lyric flights of our fantasy.
/ Let us specialize in the romanticism of Revolution! /.../ Against / Against
/ Against the fucking spies of the Political Order. /.../ Down with the bourgeois
intelligentsia! / It is time to attend to human beings. /.../ Let us talk about this
city as dirty as its river. / Here everything is forbidden. /.../ I hurl this violent
and blazing poem / into the face of the bourgeoisie!]

This poem can easily be read as a harsher version of Hughes's "Our Land,"
in which the response to tyranny and injustice is now not flight but fight.
"Las brigadas de choque" earned Tuñón instant detention and made him
subject to legal proceedings in which he was charged with inciting public
unrest and rebellion. The trial concluded with a verdict of a two-year prison
sentence with "juratory caution," meaning that his freedom was conditional
on the promise that he would abstain from the very conduct that had led to
his arrest in the first place.[126] After being released on his own recognizance,
Tuñón departed for Spain, where he would spend the better part of four years
(1935–39) exercising a right he did not have in Argentina: freedom of speech.
Upon his arrival he became something of a cause célèbre for the Spanish and
Hispanic American writers there. In June of 1935, they issued a public protest against the sentence Tuñón had received in Buenos Aires. Among the
signatories were García Lorca, Neruda, Felipe, and Hernández.[127] Ironically,
especially given the assassination of García Lorca, it was in civil-war Spain
that Tuñón wrote some of his best poems, including *Todos bailan*.

To readers of Hughes, the sentiments in "Las brigadas de choque" are
not unfamiliar. Tuñón's poem echoes many of the poems Hughes wrote and
published between 1932 and 1935, after he had returned from the Soviet
Union. Most notable in this context are "Wait," "Revolution," "Always
the Same," "Chant for Tom Mooney," "Letter to the Academy," "Song
of a Revolution," "A New Song," "Open Letter to the South," "Good
Morning, Revolution," "One more 'S' in the U.S.A," and the poems of
Scottsboro Limited. Tuñón would also evoke the Scottsboro trials in his
"Los negros de Scottsboro," a poem that disturbingly captures how the
animalistic brutality of the lynch mob is transferred to the bodies of the
incarcerated.

Oh como relucen los Nueve Negros de Scottsboro.
Los Nueve Negros de Scottsboro

aúllan esperando la muerte,
aúllan y muerden las rejas
los Nueve Negros de Scottsboro.

. . . .

Ya nunca nos olvidaremos
de los Nueve Negros de Scottsboro. [128]

[Oh, how the Nine Scottsboro Negroes glow. / The Nine Scottsboro Negroes,/ they howl waiting for death, / they howl and bite the prison bars / the Nine Scottsboro Negroes. /.../ Now we will never forget / the Nine Scottsboro Negroes.]

Among 1930s socialist intellectuals, such remembrances functioned as fuses for social and political action, whereas in 2010 they have become popular entertainment: *The Scottsboro Boys*, a Broadway musical—of all things![129] As the following excerpts from Hughes's poetry show, revolution, for Hughes as for Tuñón, was the very basis of literature's political, moral, and aesthetic value.

Better that my blood makes one with the blood
Of all the struggling workers in the world—

. . . .

Until the Red Armies of the International Proletariat
Their faces, black, white, olive, yellow, brown,
Unite to raise the blood-red flag that
will never come down!

("Always the Same," *CP,* 165–66)

Speak about the Revolution—where the
flesh triumphs (as well as the spirit) and the
hungry belly eats, and there are no best people...

("Letter to the Academy," *CP,* 169)

Revolt! Arise!
    The Black
    And White World
    Shall be one!
    The Worker's World!

The past is done!
    A new dream flames
    Against the
    Sun!

("A New Song," *CP,* 171–72)[130]

The function of poetry in these passages is to project the spectacle of public solidarity, not to contemplate the predicaments of solitary subjects. The poet here is not a lyric "I" that observes and chronicles from the outside but a fractal consciousness dispersed into the active verbs that perform public acts of collective defiance.

Like Tuñón, Hughes would be accused of spreading Communist propaganda but not until almost twenty years later (see chapter 5). It is not that external circumstances and key experiences in the lives of Hughes and Tuñón transformed their poetry into political propaganda during the 1930s. Rather, both, along with a host of other writers who came together in Spain because of what quite literally was a state of emergency, felt the need to write poetry that circulated in public spaces—as something to be read out loud, recited, sung—and that could insert itself into public discourses more directly than most printed books of poetry could. The places where this avant-garde poetry was read and heard were the same liminal spaces that had spawned it: the fringes of the world's great cities, in this case Madrid, New York City, and Buenos Aires. In other, related, contexts, they have been called contact zones (Pratt) or borderlands (Anzaldúa), but those terms have lost their initial precision. Taken together, these diverse quarters and wastelands constitute global regions: "Baldíos de las cosas—recuerdos, voces, gestos, / escenas, despedidas—, ayer, hoy y mañana" (debris or trash heaps of stuff—memories, voices, gestures,/ scenes [flashbacks?], farewells—yesterday, today, and tomorrow).[131] The metaphor Tuñón develops in these lines from "El mercado de pulgas" (The Flea Market) connects quite effortlessly with the images of the many objects and remembered voices that are cast off, pulled out again, and ultimately recycled and revitalized in Hughes's writings and, for that matter, in Chamoiseau's Creole City. For Hughes and Tuñón, writing poetry was a process of continually sorting through what others had left behind. Likewise, picking up some part of Hughes's work at this global flea market—a poem, a line, an image, or even just his name—and making it part of one's own writing in some different part of the world is surely a form of literary translation, in all possible senses of that word.

BEYOND BORGES

Although Borges's translations no doubt did their initial share to make Hughes known among Argentine intellectuals, his own literary interest in Hughes's poetry was short-lived. So was his admiration for Raúl González Tuñón's writing when politics proved too much of a dividing line to sustain their earlier friendship and collaboration. The interest in Hughes's writing did, however, continue without Borges and most likely with the support of Tuñón, who returned to Buenos Aires in the 1940s. Even though he had been away for years, first in Spain and later in Chile, where he teamed up with Neruda, Tuñón was at least as well connected in the Buenos Aires publishing scene as his former colleague at *Martín Fierro* and *Proa*.[132] And Argentina's publishing industry was booming in the 1930s and 1940s. Scores of new journals were launched, some short-lived, and exiles from Franco's Spain moved publishing houses to Buenos Aires and founded new ones.[133] Having just returned from Spain, Tuñón would have known, at least casually, the next generation of intellectuals who started to translate Hughes's poetry and prose in the early 1940s.

In 1944, Editorial Lautaro, one of several small presses organized by Argentina's Communist Party to disseminate translations from Russian and other languages, published *El inmenso mar,* Luisa Rivaud's version of *The Big Sea.* [134]Ildefonso Pereda Valdés, whose name Hughes had sent to Blanche Knopf in 1940, likely paved the way for this book, and I strongly suspect that Guillén was the one who arranged to have *El inmenso mar* reprinted in Cuba in 1967.[135] The following year, 1941, Editorial Futuro published *Pero con risas,* Nestor R. Ortíz Oderigo's translation of the novel *Not Without Laughter.* In 1952, Lautaro still had an interest in Hughes and also put into print Julio Gáler's *Poemas de Langston Hughes,* while Fabril issued Gáler's translation of Hughes's second autobiography under the title *Yo viajo por un mundo encantado* in 1956. In the intervening years, Quetzal and Siglo Veinte had printed Gáler's versions of Hughes's play *Mulatto* (1954) and *Riendo por no llorar* (1955), a translation of Hughes's story collection *Laughing to Keep from Crying.*[136] Then as now, translations were frequently negotiated through literary agents and publishers with little involvement by the authors. As a result, Hughes appears to have had no direct contact with Argentine translators and presses until after the publication of *El inmenso mar,* for which Hughes received a contract in 1945.[137] That same year, he sent *The Ways of White Folks* to Lautaro, along with a copy of *Not Without Laughter.* They liked the stories but argued, rather unconvincingly given the success of Borges's stories, that their readers "prefiere[n] siempre la novela al cuento" (always prefer novels to short stories). Admittedly, given the racial emphasis of the topics and the unsettling tenor of the stories themselves, *The Ways of White Folks* would likely have been a tough sell in Argentina. In the end, Lautaro did not take the novel either, but Futuro did. The founding director of Futuro was Raúl Larra, a militant member of the Communist Party who knew Raúl González Tuñón well.[138] Hughes hoped that Futuro would also publish his stories, but it politely declined.[139] Then, in June of 1948, Hughes asked Knopf to send a number of his books to one Julio Gáler in Argentina. The request seems to have come out of the blue but was evidently in response to Gáler's having sent Hughes drafts of several poems in translation.[140]

Who were these new translators? The anthropologist, ethnomusicologist, and folklorist Nestor Ortíz Oderigo stands out among Hughes's Argentine translators for being the only one with a sustained personal interest in African American culture—in his case African American music from the United States, where his earlier work was reviewed regularly in *Phylon* and the *Journal of Negro History*.[141] Ortíz Oderigo, who is described as *mestizo*, also worked on and had connections to Ildefonso Pereda Valdés in Montevideo and thus indirectly to Hughes himself. There is no evidence that Hughes ever met Ortíz Oderigo or, for that matter, Rivaud or Gáler.

Given their shared political and literary interests, it is difficult to imagine that Abraham Julio Gáler, who shortened his name to Julio Gáler in his publications, did not cross paths with Raúl González Tuñón. Gáler had studied languages and literatures at the National University of Córdoba, Argentina, from which he graduated in 1943.[142] In addition to being a founding member of Fabril in 1958, Gáler, a committed Communist, had worked as senior editor at Jacobo Muchnik in Buenos Aires.[143] In those days he also contributed to the Marxist journal *Cuadernos de Cultura*.[144] Although he produced an impressive list of translations from English, French, German, and Russian—in addition to Hughes, Gáler translated works by Clifford Odets, Arthur Miller, Carl Sandburg, and Friedrich Dürrenmatt, among others—Gáler is now better known for his work with the International Labor Organization (ILO), which he joined in 1959 as a member of the editorial and translation division.[145] There is no information about any connections between Gáler and Rivaud. What we do know, however, is that they were both Jewish and moved in the same literary and political circles. Rivaud's given name was Lucie Lipschutz. Born in Paris of Russian Jewish parents who relocated to Spain and fled to Argentina, she published most of her translations under the pen name Luisa Rivaud.[146] What might have attracted both Gáler and Lipschutz to Hughes's writing was their own sense of otherness, exacerbated in Lipschutz's case by exile and persecution. It was hardly a coincidence that Lipschutz adopted a different professional name upon moving to Argentina in 1939, the year Hitler's troops invaded Poland.[147] Lipschutz was most prolific as a translator in Buenos Aires during the 1940s and 1950s, when she published Spanish versions of writings by J. B. Priestley, Marian Anderson, Eddie Rickenbacker, and Upton Sinclair with some of the same publishing houses as Gáler, notably Muchnik, Fabril, Lautaro, and Losada.[148]

While Hughes apparently did not meet either Lipschutz or Gáler, Nicolás Guillén most likely did during his political exile in Buenos Aires in the late 1950s.[149] Nor are there any specifics in Hughes's papers about how the connection with Gáler came about. It is most plausible that either Lautaro's editor—Sara Maglione de Jorge, who was close to Gáler (as well as to María Rosa Oliver and Victoria Ocampo)—or Gregorio Weinberg—the press's director, who was also a friend of Gáler's—would have suggested Gáler as a possible translator to Blanche Knopf. Gáler himself recalls that he went to Buenos Aires in 1949 to offer his friends at Lautaro his translation of

Hughes's poems.[150] Gáler had started translating Hughes's poems early in 1948. Beginning in June of that year, he published a number of these translations in several relatively short-lived literary journals in Buenos Aires and Córdoba. Almost all of the typed drafts Gáler had sent Hughes a month earlier were of poems that had never been translated into Spanish: "Jazz Band en un cabaret de Paris" ("Jazz Band in a Parisian Cabaret"), "Luna Nueva" (New Moon"), "Deseo" ("Desire"), "Sueños" ("Dreams"), "Hombre" ("Man"), "Silencio" ("Silence"), and "Mulato" ("Mulatto").[151] The same is true of the poems Gáler had already published in *Cabalgata, Tiempo Vivo,* and *Continente:* "Canconcillo" ("Little Song") and "Uno" ("One"), "Amor que pasa" ("Passing Love"), "Alegría" ("Joy"), and "Canción de la lluvia abrileña" ("April Rain Song"). He sent those to Hughes in 1949 (see LHP, 443:9945 and 9946). Although there are gaps in their correspondence, we can surmise that by April 1952, Hughes had authorized Gáler's book, and its title page carries the note "Antololgía autorizada y aprobada por el autor" (anthology authorized and approved by the author). On June 19 of that same year, Hughes finally received his first copy of *Poemas de Langston Hughes* from Gáler himself.[152]

Even compared with more recent volumes of Spanish anthologies of Hughes's verse by Ahumada (Mexico, 1968) and Cruzado and Hricko (Spain, 2004), Gáler's *Poemas* remains by far the most comprehensive collection of Hughes's poetry in Spanish. Its eighty-three poems include selections from *The Weary Blues, Fine Clothes to the Jew, The Dream Keeper* (1932), *Fields of Wonder* (1939), *Shakespeare in Harlem* (1942), *One-Way Ticket* (1949), *Montage for [sic] a Dream Deferred* (1952), and eight poems published elsewhere, among them "Christ in Alabama" ("Cristo en Alabama") and a fragment of "Advertisement for the Waldorf Astoria" ("Un Aviso para el Waldorf Astoria"). Gáler celebrates the latter poem, together with the epic "El Tren de la Libertad" ("Freedom Train"), as "uno de los más finos líricos norteamericanos de su generación. Arna Bontemps dice de él que es los más aproximado a un Shelley americano" (one of the finest North American lyrics of his generation. Arna Bontemps says that Hughes most resembles an American Shelley) (*Poemas,* 9).

Gáler's volume opens with a fairly lengthy introduction, in which he details Hughes's biography and the historical context of the Harlem Renaissance, "el Renascimiento Negro" or "Movimiento de los Nuevos Negros" (*Poemas,* 14–15). The image of Hughes he projects is unequivocally that of a poet of the people. What Gáler does seem to equivocate about, however, is exactly who Hughes's people are. He claims that it was the publication of "The Negro Speaks of Rivers" in *The Weary Blues* that "le hizo de inmediato un lugar en *la poética norteamericano* y lo identifico como el primer poeta de su pueblo" (immediately earned Hughes a place in North American poetry and identified him as the foremost poet of his people):

Desde su poema inicial, "El Negro," pasando por las dulces baladas de Harlem, hasta el reciente "Tren de la Libertad," Langston Hughes es *un poeta de su pueblo,* de sus pocos alegrías y sus muchos dolores, de sus luchas, sus desazones, su brillante esperanza. Y precisamente su *distintivo carácter nacional,* por paradójico que ello resulte, lo que da a este poeta carácter y validez universal. (*Poemas,* 7, my emphasis)

[From his first poem, "Negro," to the sweet ballads of Harlem to the recent "Freedom Train," Langston Hughes has been *a poet of his people,* of their few joys and many woes, of their struggles, their worries, their bright and shining hope. And it is precisely, and paradoxically, *his distinctive nationalistic character* that gives this poet his universal character and meaning.] (*Poemas,* 11, my emphasis)

Gáler's notion of the national dimensions of Hughes's poetry is perhaps less confusing when we think of it more specifically as *cultural* nationalism, even though Gáler's reference below to the USA as "Norteamérica" does make one wonder if he is intentionally blurring the line between black and white North Americans—the two worlds that Hughes struggled to reconcile with each other.

Langston Hughes buscó la síntesis de esos dos mundos, y la hallo en la poesía. La hallo en los poemas exuberantes de Carl Sandburg, el trovador de Chicago, el cantor de las grandezas y las miserias de la América imperialista, el más genuino heredero del gran Viejo de Manhattan en la Norteamérica de hoy....Pero no fue este su único maestro. También incidió en él la herencia telúrica de Paul Laurence Dunbar, prácticamente el primero de los poetas negros de los EE.UU., el que incorporo al lenguaje poético el dialecto quebrado de los negros en las plantaciones. Ellos fueron sus primeros maestros. Puede decirse que de Dunbar derivo su sentido nacional y de Sandburg su tono social y protesta. (*Poemas,* 9)[153]

[Langston Hughes was searching for a synthesis of these two worlds, and he found it in poetry. He found it in the exuberant poems of Carl Sandburg, the troubadour of Chicago, the singer of the greatness and the misery of imperialist America, the most authentic heir to the great Gray Poet of Manhattan [Whitman] in today's North America....But Sandburg was not his only teacher. He was also influenced by the telluric heritage of Paul Laurence Dunbar, virtually the first of the Negro poets in the United States to incorporate into his poetry the broken dialect of the plantation blacks. These were Hughes's principal teachers. One might say that he derives his nationalism from Dunbar and his tone of social protest from Sandburg.]

While Gáler does mention Hughes's translations of Jacques Roumain's novel, Guillén's verse, and García Lorca's poems, he says nothing at all either about his contact with Hughes or about his own translations (*Poemas,* 18). This lack of self-reflectiveness on the part of a literary translator is not untypical for the times. In fact, neither Hughes's translators in the Hispanic Americas nor, for that matter, Hughes himself commented on the actual process of translation.

What is remarkable about Gáler's anthology is, first of all, the breadth of his selections, which clearly attempt to give readers as varied an impression of Hughes's poetry as possible—more varied, in fact, than Gáler's own introduction suggests. In this respect, Gáler was much more thorough than, for instance, Ahumada would be in his 1968 collection, which does not strive for such broad coverage and includes about one-third fewer poems than Gáler's. In both *Poemas* and *Yo también soy América,* roughly half of the translated poems are drawn from Hughes's early verse, an unsurprising choice on the part of either translator, given that Hughes's reputation in the Hispanic Americas (and elsewhere) rested mainly on *The Weary Blues* and, to a lesser extent, *Fine Clothes to the Jew.*[154] What is perhaps unexpected is that Gáler's selection went well beyond what one might consider the usual suspects in these two volumes, such as "I, Too," "The Negro Speaks of Rivers," "Negro," "Brass Spittoons," "Po' Boy Blues," or even "The Weary Blues" itself, even though he was actually the first to translate Hughes's famous title poem.[155] Gáler included a total of twenty-two of the sixty-one poems in *The Weary Blues* and only nine from *Fine Clothes.* Of these twenty-two, sixteen were the first (and thus far the only) translations into Spanish.[156] Although Gáler left intact the original frame of *The Weary Blues,* opening his selections with "El Negro" ("Negro" or "Proem") and ending with "Yo también" (the "Epilogue" to Hughes's volume), he changed the order in which Hughes had placed the poems. As a result, "Fantasy in Purple," for instance, which Hughes had placed in the section "Dream Variations," now appears face to face with "Caribbean Sunset" (from "Water Front Streets"), and "March Moon" (also from "Dream Variations") sits side by side with "Suicide's Note" (from "Shadows in the Sun"). This makes for stark but often productive contrasts.

The grouping of "Fantasy in Purple" and "Caribbean Sunset," for instance, which Julio Gáler translated as "Fantasía en Purpúrea" and "Atardecer en el Caribe," respectively, is one of those contrasts. Both the translations themselves and the placement of these two very unlike poems point to similarities that might otherwise have remained more veiled. In Gáler's "Fantasía en Purpúrea," Hughes's "drums of tragedy"—"Beat the drums of tragedy for me. / Beat the drums of tragedy and death"—become "los tambores del drama," generalizing Hughes's generic reference and enhancing the poem's performative qualities. The choir, whose "stormy song" is to drown out the death rattle, seems to have multiplied: "Canten *los coros* canciones de tormenta / Para ahogar con su ruido mi estertor" (*Poemas,* 48). Amid the tempestuous songs of the now plural choirs, the individualizing trumpet sound stands out even more. At Gáler's hands, the "one blaring trumpet note of sun" turns into a veritable stroke of lightning that transports rather just accompanies the dying speaker. In fact, Gáler's rendering of "note of sun" as "nota de luz" connects with his choice of "rayo de luz," a redundant and thereby emphatic way of expressing "stroke of lightning," in his translation of Hughes's imagistic poem "Birth" ("Alumbramiento").

> Like a stroke
> Of lightning
> In the night
> Some mark
> To make
> Some word to tell.
>
> <div align="right">(<i>CP</i>, 323)</div>

> Como un rayo de luz
> En las tinieblas,
> Para trazar un signo
> Decir una palabra.
>
> <div align="right">(<i>Poemas,</i> 75)</div>

Jahan Ramazani singles out "Fantasy in Purple" as the one poem among Hughes's usually "compressed death lyrics" that "makes room for Keatsian abundance"—such as extravagant colors and lavish sound.[157] To readers of Hughes's short story "Home" from *The Ways of White Folks,* the appearance of the "white violins" in "Fantasy in Purple" would be more startling, and unsettling, than the "one blaring trumpet note of sun" because the violins resonate cruelly with the ending Hughes would fashion for that story. In Gáler's translation, the "whir" of Hughes's "white violins" in the second stanza is no longer just "thin and slow" but also shaky, tremulous— "Toquen los blancos violines sus notas aguadas y trémulas." Like most of its companion pieces in *The Ways of White Folks,* "Home" is a death story with a distinctly Gothic flavor. More specifically, it is a story about a lynching: "And when the white folks left his [Roy's] brown body, stark naked, strung from a tree at the edge of town, it hung there all night, *like a violin for the wind to play.*"[158] The eerie whir of the white violins haunts the story, as it does the poem, with the specter of categorically inconsolable racial violence. The real tragedy, we come to understand, is not just the speaker's dying, which is horrific enough, but the brutal deaths of so many before him. "Caribbean Sunset" focalizes the same racial violence in the figure of internal bleeding externalized, that is, of coughing up the blood of the Middle Passage and spewing it across a tourist's postcard image of the darkening sea.

> Es Dios que ha tenido una hemorragia
> Y está escupiendo sangre por el Cielo,

Manchando de rojo el mar oscuro.
Es, un atardecer en el Caribe.

(Poemas, 49)

God having a hemorrhage,
Blood coughed across the sky,
Staining the dark sea red,
That is sunset in the Caribbean.

(CP, 98)

Shifting to the imperfect past tense in the opening line, Gáler's translation places the visual spectacle at more of a distance than Hughes's present participle does. Still, when placed next to "Fantasy in Purple," the minimalist "Caribbean Sunset" makes the "undertones" and "overtones"[159] of violence more audible in what appears to be a fairly conventional elegy at first glance. What makes this poem a rather unusual elegy, however, is that it foreshadows rather than commemorates. In this respect, "Fantasy in Purple" is not so far removed from the self-epitaphic "Suicide's Note," which returns us to the space of river and from there to "The Negro Speaks of Rivers."[160] Hughes's odd prolepsis finds further resonances in the combination of sunset with wondering in "Hey!," whose poetic rhythms Gáler renders quite effectively in his standardized Spanish version. Spanish also allows Gáler to incorporate the audience—"les cantaré" (I will sing *to them*)—while retaining Hughes's brevity:

Sun's a settin',
This is what I'm gonna sing.
Sun's a settin',
This is what I'm gonna sing:
I feels de blues comin',
Wonder what de blues'll bring.

(CP, 112)

El sol se pone,
y de eso les cantaré.
El sol se pone,
Y de eso les cantaré.
Y siento llegar los blues,
Qué me traerán esta vez?

(Poemas, 54)

Remarkable about Gáler's overall choices in *Poemas*, especially when they are compared with what we find in the earlier anthologies and journals I discuss in the previous chapter, is that he translated many of the poems that have since fallen through the cracks of Hughes scholarship and have not been considered representative of Hughes's (early) poetry. "Fantasy in Purple" and "Suicide's Note" are among them.[161] Such choices of course raise the question of which poems are to be regarded as representative of Hughes's verse and poetics. The varied plenitude of poetic and nonliterary forms and possible generic affiliations throughout Hughes's poetry and even in *The Weary Blues* alone—ranging as they do from odes, sonnets, and elegies to epistolary fragments, fliers, statistics, and snippets of conversations—makes this a difficult question to answer. If there is any one constant in Hughes's writing, it is that of mixing genres and discourses.[162] In this regard, connections between the poems Gáler selected and links with other lyrics come into view when we place them in the context of my earlier discussion of socioaesthetics and urban fringe spaces. Both categories easily accommodate poems such as "Negro Dancers" ("Bailarines Negros"), "Ruby Brown," and "The Cat and the Saxophone" ("El Gato y el Saxofón"), all of which are micronarratives of subcity life. Other poems that fall into this category are "Lenox Avenue" ("Avenida Lenox: Medianoche"), "Parisian Beggar Woman" ("Mendiga de Paris"), "Vagabonds" ("Vagabundos"), "The Jester" ("El Juglar"), "Suicide's Note" ("Nota de una suicida"), "Desire" ("Deseo"), and even "Youth" ("Juventud") and "April Rain Song" ("Canción de la lluvia abrileña"). All take us back to the very same Harlemized quarters on which I remark above in connection with Raúl González Tuñón.

One poem that stands out from the rest of Gáler's translations is "Árbol" (Tree), not because of any formal or thematic oddities but because it seems to have no counterpart in English:

> Tengo miedo
> de ese árbol
> sin hojas
> en la noche
> contra el cielo.
>
> Quiro llorar.

(Poemas, 135)

[I am afraid/ of that tree/ without leaves/ in the night/ against the sky. // I want to cry.]

As far as I was able to ascertain, Hughes himself never wrote a poem by this title, or if he did, it no longer exists. Nor are these lines a fragment of another poem. The only lyric that has similar ingredients is "Afraid," first published in *The Crisis* in 1924 and translated by José Antonio Fernández de Castro as "Miedo" ("Fear") in 1930.[163]

> We cry among the skyscrapers
> As our ancestors
> Cried among the palms in Africa
> Because we are alone,
> It is night,
> And we're afraid.
>
> (*CP*, 41)

Had "Árbol" been loosely based on Hughes's "Afraid," Gáler would have included it in the section on *The Weary Blues,* which he did not. It appears, then, that the English source text of "Árbol" is indeed lost. Given its absence, it is tempting to argue that this is an instance of a translator's inventing his source poem, which would be the ultimate affront to the presumed primacy of an original or literary precursor—and the ultimate Borgesian gesture. In Hughes's own words, we might take this orphaned translation as an uncanny example in which the poet runs into himself as a character in someone else's book, a fate Hughes would then share most prominently, and quite appropriately, with Don Quixote.[164] As Hughes writes in "Final Curve," a short poem from *One-Way Ticket* (1949) that Gáler also translated,

> When you turn the corner
> And you run into *yourself*
> Then you know that you have turned
> All the corners that are left.
>
> (*CP*, 368)

> Cuando al doblar una esquina
> Te encuentres a ti mismo,
> Sabrás que ya no quedan
> Esquinas por doblar.
>
> ("Curva final," *Poemas*, 100)

The very existence of Gáler's "Árbol" instantly disproves what Hughes's own poem seems to suggest: that there is an end, a final curve. This, however, is not the case for a writer. Once you run out of corners, there are always more pages to turn.

CHAPTER FOUR

HAVANA VERNACULARS

The Cuba Libre *Project*

> I enjoy translating but...it is much more difficult than writing original
> material. Unfortunately too, it does not pay as well.
> —Langston Hughes to Bernard Perry at
> Indiana University Press

> Coge tu pan, pero no lo pidas;
> coge tu luz, coge tu esperanza cierta
> como un caballo por las bridas.
> Plántate en medio de la puerta,
> pero no con la mano abierta....
>
> [Take your bread, but do not beg for it; / take your light, take your firm
> hope / as a horse by the reins. / Stand in the middle of the doorway, / But
> not with an open hand....]
> —Nicolás Guillén, "Sabás" (1934),
> dedicated to Langston Hughes

After Spain, Nicolás Guillén stuck with Hughes in more ways than one. In December of 1948 the Ward Ritchie Press of Los Angeles released *Cuba Libre: Poems by Nicolás Guillén* in a limited edition of 250 copies. This magnificently produced book consisted of fifty poems in translations by Langston Hughes and Ben Frederic Carruthers; it was the first book-length edition of Guillén's poetry in English.[1] The story of how *Cuba Libre* evolved over the course of almost two decades is a key chapter in the history of hemispheric cultural relations, testifying to the continued exchanges between Hispanic Caribbean and USAmerican intellectuals that had begun early in the nineteenth century. Handsome though it was, this folio volume did not popularize Guillén in the USA as much as Hughes had initially hoped.[2] What it did accomplish, however, was provide readers with a lens through which to reexamine the interactions of two internationally acclaimed figures, both with each other and with those who mediated what I call, more broadly, the *Cuba Libre* project. Among those mediators were the Cuban journalist José Antonio Fernández de Castro, his fellow countryman and editor Gustavo E. Urrutia, the Howard professor Ben Carruthers, the publishers Blanche and Alfred Knopf, John Farrar (of Farrar Straus), and Caroline Anderson, the head of the Ward Ritchie Press. As the project began to take shape, Hughes made pointed decisions about translation, editing, and marketing that, like his relations with these friends and acquaintances, can be traced in his personal correspondence and in his revisions of drafts.[3] The choices Hughes made as the project went on—which poems to translate, how to divide them up between himself and Carruthers, how to translate them, which English versions to publish and in what order—reflect his growing sense of being politically embattled. As we shall see in the next chapter, he had good reasons for feeling that way.

Rather than revive arguments for or against influence relations between Hughes and Guillén,[4] I take analytical stock here of what gets lost *and* added in this important example of intercultural translational commerce between Cuba and the USA during the first half of the twentieth century. One of my principal concerns in doing so is to scrutinize the *effects* of cultural homogeneity that English-language translations of African diasporic texts published in the USA have tended to create. Some of Hughes's own translations of Guillén's poetry follow this tendency, but others decidedly do not. The poems at the center of this chapter come from *Cuba Libre* and also *The Poetry of the Negro 1746–1949*, a hemispheric anthology on which Hughes started to work with Arna Bontemps in early 1947 and which I consider an offshoot of the *Cuba Libre* project. This anthology, which went to press in late 1948 just as *Cuba Libre* was on the verge of being launched, was to be the first of its kind in English, because "las otras son solamente de poetas de la raza Negro" (all the others include only poets of the black race).[5] The first edition of this anthology, which Doubleday published in 1949, devoted no less than 75 of its 386 pages to poets from the francophone and Hispanic Caribbean.[6] My readings show that even a writer who had been hailed as a literary innovator would embrace a rather guarded approach to translation when it came to the work of writers of color from the south of the USAmerican South. The choices Hughes made as translator and editor provide useful insights into how and why he came to value certain cultural differences over others.

Hughes's friendship with Nicolás Guillén, which continued almost until Hughes's death, has occupied a prominent place in critical studies. Hughes had first met Guillén during a much-popularized second visit to Havana in March of 1930, and the two poets had spent a good deal of time together in Spain in late 1937 (see chapter 3).[7] Although Hughes and Guillén met in person only on a handful of occasions between 1930 and 1949, face-to-face encounters are not an adequate measure of a friendship that unfolded mostly in letters.[8] Hughes's second trip to Cuba also marked the beginning of his career as a translator. As early as July 1930, Guillén had expressed his enthusiasm about the possibility of Hughes's translating some of his poems: "Me encanta la idea de que traduzcas algunos de los 'sones.' Ellos ganarían mucho en tus manos" (I am enchanted by the idea that you might translate some of the "sones." They would gain much indeed from your touch).[9] Indeed, just a few months after he returned from Cuba, Hughes published his first translation of a poem by Guillén in *Opportunity,* the National Urban League's journal: "Black Woman" ("Mujer negra").[10] Around the same time, Spanish translations of Hughes's own poems were appearing in Havana's *El Diario de la Marina* (see chapter 2).

According to Hughes, *Cuba Libre* collected "the best and most famous of the Guillén verses," and this volume may well be regarded as the literary culmination of the two poets' long-standing and cordial friendship.[11] *Cuba Libre* includes English versions of poems originally written in Afro-Cuban literary vernacular and extends Hughes's efforts at creating a literary vernacular in his earlier poetry.[12] Although *Cuba Libre* includes poems from later Guillén volumes as well, up to the collection *El son entero* (1947), Guillén's "Motivos de son" (*Son* Motifs), published on April 20, 1930 on the *Diario*'s "Ideales de una Raza" page, occupy a special place of interest: they were the only poems written in Afro-Cuban vernacular—Guillén calls it *criollo*—and based on a distinctively Cuban musical form. A critical analysis of these poems and their translations in *Cuba Libre,* however, does not support claims that Hughes and Guillén shared a cultural poetics. José Antonio Fernández de Castro and Gustavo E. Urrutia were the first to suggest that they did in 1930 when they had explained to Hughes that these poems written in Cuba's "very popular slang"—that is, Guillén's "Motivos"—"are the exact equivalent of your 'blues.'" Soon after, they started calling Guillén "the Cuban Langston Hughes."[13] Later scholars have too readily embraced this analogy without sufficiently examining its terms, implications, and limitations.

The translations on which Hughes worked for *Cuba Libre,* especially unpublished drafts and previously printed versions revised for inclusion in this volume, deserve more than passing attention. For one thing, the drafts show how very different Hughes's approach to translation was from his academic collaborator's. Unlike Ben Carruthers, Hughes seems to have understood and appreciated the Cuban texts' irreducible strangeness, and he sensed how tenuous it might be to make claims about a shared African American poetics when faced with textual situations in which even *negro* did not comfortably translate as either "black" or "Negro."[14] Add to this the fact that Hughes's grasp of Afro-Cuban vernacular was limited. For another, Hughes's awareness of how foreign Guillén's poetry might be to USAmerican audiences was much keener in the 1940s, after his youthful enthusiasm about his friend's lyrics had given way to the realization of just how difficult it was to publish literary translations in a country that was too focused on inventing its postwar identity as a nation to be paying much attention to foreign authors. New Directions had published Dudley Fitts's hefty bilingual anthology of Hispanic American poetry in 1942, and the press's editor, James McLaughlin, had included Lloyd Mallan's "Little Anthology of Afro-Cuban Poetry" in *New Directions 1944,* the press's "Annual Exhibition Gallery of Divergent Literary Trends." Hughes was therefore fairly confident that *Cuba Libre* could similarly be placed with a major publishing house.[15]

MARKETING TRANSLATIONS

Between 1930 and 1960, Hughes also hatched several other translation projects. By the mid-1940s, his fame in the Hispanic Americas rested not only on his poetry but also on his efforts to promote work by Afro-Hispanic American and other writers in the USA. Although it is beyond the scope of this book to discuss all of the projects with equal care, let me at least mention them. Best known are Hughes's translations of Jacques Roumain's *Les gouverneurs de la rosée* as *Masters of the Dew,* a collaboration with Mercer Cook, and of poems by Federico García Lorca. His translations of verse by the Nobel laureate Gabriela Mistral, contracted by Indiana University Press, was virtually buried.[16] But not all his translation projects found a publisher; some of them never did. Knopf, Hughes's main publisher since the 1920s, showed little interest in any of his translations. On March 1, 1937, for instance, Hughes wrote to Blanche Knopf: "If we ever did a new book of poems, they could include my translations of several poets somewhat known in this country, but whose poetry has appeared only in magazines where my translations of the work has [sic] been printed: Louis Aragon, Regino Pedrozo and Nicolás Guillén of Cuba,... as well as a number of Mexican poems, that I translated down there last year." He also mentioned "some thirty Mexican and Cuban short stories that have appeared in magazines" such as *Esquire, Pacific Weekly,* and *New Masses* and available for publication in book form. In her reply of March 5, 1937, Mrs. Knopf did not think "that the short stories are a good idea either for sales or for your reputation at the moment" (LHP, 97:1825).[17] Even ten years later, Knopf still had no real interest in Hughes's translations and turned down his English version of Lorca's *Romancero gitano.*[18] Blanche Knopf hemmed and hawed about *The Poetry of the Negro* anthology until Hughes went with a contract from Doubleday instead.[19]

Hughes had clearly overestimated his own clout as a translator. At the same time, he had also miscalculated existing interest in Hispanic American writing, which was brought home to him when Farrar Straus, Knopf, Putnam, and other major houses all rejected his proposals for translation projects. Herbert Weinstock, senior editor at Knopf, summed up the situation in 1952, when he turned down yet another one of Hughes's translation projects: "I have come to believe that the sad fact is that for most people in this country, Latin America and its history simply do not exist."[20]

Weinstock's pessimism, however, should not be taken as an exact barometer of audience interests and publishing trends at the time, for a good number of early-twentieth-century Hispanic American works were actually available in English translations from both academic and commercial USAmerican publishers by the 1950s.[21] It is no coincidence that literary translations, including the publishing and marketing of such translations, had picked up intellectual and commercial momentum in the USA during the first half of the twentieth century. Along with transatlantic modernism's fascination with certain non-Western languages and cultures went a growing interest in modernist work in other languages, mostly French and German, which USAmerican publishers fueled by making translations of major works more widely available. The problem may not have been that USAmerican readers were categorically not interested in things Hispanic American but that this was not an especially good time to promote stories of black revolutionaries, including Cuba's celebrated General Maceo. More than anything else, Weinberg's response to Hughes reflected the tense political climate of the incipient McCarthy witch hunts.

What further complicates any discussion of Hughes's role in fashioning *Cuba Libre* is that he occupied a dual position in relation to this "public object." On the one hand, he was a translator; on the other, however, he was an editor-anthologizer—positions in the literary field that, according to Pierre Bourdieu, are "structurally contradictory" to the extent that "the makers and marketers of works of art are adversaries in collusion."[22] Particularly in the case of *Cuba Libre,* the lines between making and marketing were often blurred. Because he ended up dealing with a small press, one that specialized more in graphic arts than in avant-garde poetry, Hughes's role as editor-anthologizer of *Cuba Libre* involved him much more directly in marketing decisions than would have been the case with a larger publisher such as Knopf.[23] This was not unfamiliar territory for Hughes, who, as Karen Ford has shown, was a "relentless marketer of his own poetry" with "the good business sense to understand that a poem could be 'used in many ways.'"[24] His business sense attuned him to all factors that would affect literary reputations, the ability to publish, and, of course, book sales. Even though the sales of *Cuba Libre* do not reflect this, Hughes actually worked very hard to promote the book.[25] Concerns with literary legitimacy were an inevitable part of his work as editor-marketer of *Cuba Libre,* which led him to minimize the poems' foreignness and that of their authors to make them more appealing to the educated African American readers Hughes imagined for this book (see next section). Pitching *Cuba Libre* to this audience meant creating the impression of shared racial codes and taxonomies by limiting the dissonant impact of distinctively Cuban locutions on USAmerican English. More broadly, it also meant leaving unexamined the Cuban republic's prerevolutionary political status as a de facto USAmerican protectorate even after the 1901 Platt Amendment establishing this status was repealed in 1934.[26] The vehicle for creating the impression, or effect, of shared racial codes was black vernacular represented as Negro dialect but only to a limited extent. As we shall see, it is in the handful of poems in *Cuba Libre* that are rendered in variations on this vernacular mode that the conflict between the positions of translator and editor-marketer becomes most pronounced.

THAT AFRO-CUBAN FEELING

Originally written in what Nicolás Guillén called *criollo*—"la forma en que todavía hablan—piensan—muchos de nuestros negros (y no pocos blancos también)" (the idiom in which many of our blacks [and not a few whites] still talk—and think)—these short poems known as the "Motivos de son" posed a formidable challenge to any translator.[27] In fact, most translators at the time stayed away from so-called dialect poetry, Afro-Cuban and other.[28] To translate the "Motivos" would have been a particularly tricky task for Hughes, whose mastery of Cuban Spanish was less than perfect, as Guillén noted half-jokingly but insistently—not by any means as limited as Guillén's own English but tenuous nonetheless. The poems' linguistic difficulty notwithstanding, Hughes, wearing his editorial hat, insisted on including most of the "Motivos" that had first appeared in the "página negra" of Havana's *Diario de la Marina* in April 1930, about a month after Hughes's second visit to Cuba (see figure 6). Guillén had sent Hughes a copy of the pamphlet, the form in which the "Motivos" were disseminated prior to being included in the 1931 collection *Sóngoro cosongo*.[29] And not only did Hughes include these poems; he decided to open *Cuba Libre* with them. This gesture is particularly striking in the case of a poem on whose English versions I comment in detail below: "Ayé me dijeron negro," one of the poems Hughes especially admired. It was published in English as "Last Night Someone Called Me Darky." Although this *poema-son* had disappeared from Guillén's collections by the late 1940s, Hughes still kept it in *Cuba Libre*, presumably as a representative example of Guillén's poems.[30]

A more theoretical reason for my interest in the translations of these particular poems is that the literary modes of both so-called Negro dialect and black vernacular are probably the most pronounced instances of what Guido Podestá (*pace* Roland Barthes) calls "ethnic effects."[31] Until fairly recently, ethnic effects in texts by African American authors were still read as markers of racial "authenticity" incompatible with literary experimentation, unless we follow José María Rodríguez Garcia's definition of "authenticity" as "the condition of a representation that never hides the fractures, collusions, and erasures that have gone into its own construction."[32] Such readings, combined with a preference for an aesthetics based on high-modernist standards of literary innovation, presumably justified excluding

Figure 6. Page from *El Diario de la Marina*, April 30, 1930, with
Nicolás Guillén's original eight "Motivos de Son." Courtesy of
George A. Smathers Libraries, University of Florida, Gainesville.

New Negro literature from accounts of USAmerican modernism.[33] Because of their assumed association with "primitivism," Podestá argues, African American writers in the USA—including Jean Toomer, who was touted as the most experimental of the Harlem Renaissance writers—"were not allowed to enter into the realm of modernism since they were supposed to respond only to ethnic paradigms." " 'Primitives' were not allowed to go primitive," so they went "ethnic." They "were encouraged or instructed (among others, by patrons and publishers) to play the role assigned to them by…ethnopoetics," which Podestá describes as "a hermeneutics specialized in the conceptualization of artifacts whose magnified ethnic component constrained any academic exegesis and displaced artistic judgments."[34] In literary texts associated with racialized cultural differences by way of either subject matter or authors' perceived ethnic or racial identities, the pioneering aspects of vernacular writing have tended to go unrecognized.[35] The fact that so-called Negro dialect as represented in poetry and fiction is clearly a hyperstylized discourse has not prevented it from being systematically naturalized as an authentic index of racial otherness. Even though literary representations of black vernacular are orthographically less conspicuous on the page, they have suffered similar misreadings. There are, for instance, no compelling aesthetic reasons why Gertrude Stein's "Melanctha," Toomer's *Cane,* and Hughes's blues poems, to give but a few prominent examples, ought not to be read either as equally ethnic or as equally experimental or, indeed, as both. The same is true of the *poesía negrista* that characterized much of the so-called Afro-Antillean movement, of which Guillén is often called the unwitting founder (see *CL,* ix).

The translations of Guillén's *criollo* poems that Hughes chose to include in *Cuba Libre* are telling examples of how modernist experimentation— Guillén calls it "un modo de estar en la 'avanzada' (a way of being in the "vanguard")—is pressed into the mold of ethnographic realism in order to confirm dominant literary values and thereby satisfy certain audience expectations.[36] Hughes's worry in the 1940s about how his political reputation as a former (?) "Communist sympathizer" (in the infelicitous language of McCarthyism) might affect his literary reputation was an additional reason that he opted for this sort of assimilation when he prepared the first editions of *Poetry of the Negro* and *Cuba Libre.* When Hughes was not beset by such worries, which impinged on his editorial activities in countless ways, he also seemed more willing to take risks as a translator. His earlier versions of Guillén's poems, including unpublished drafts, often concede—whether intentionally or not cannot always be ascertained—the limitations of US-American dialects, standard and nonstandard, in rendering discourses on race that fell outside the purview of USAmerican domestic ethnocentrism. Hughes was far more prepared to test linguistic and political limits in his drafts than he was in his published work.

Starting in the early 1940s, Hughes's anxiety about audiences, reputation, and political acceptance made him decidedly more wary. One immediately senses his caution in the short introduction to *Cuba Libre,* and it comes in fuller view when compared to Carruthers's initial, lengthy draft entitled "Nicolás Guillén, Proconsul of Cuban Poetry." Caroline Anderson had requested that Hughes either write a new introduction or condense the existing introduction to "no more than one page." Commenting on the fact that Carruthers's original draft had been written in 1945, she also worried that some of the material in it might have been printed elsewhere, which was not the case.[37] Hughes cut and edited the draft, keeping Carruthers's name as author of the introduction.[38] The changes Hughes did *not* make are as revealing as the ones that he did. Most surprisingly, he left intact Carruthers's opening paragraph. It begins as follows:

> *Cuba Libre* was originally a cry for freedom and in these poems it still is. Since the days of the Cuban struggle for independence, however, we *yanquis* have come to know it as a delightful drink concocted from the best of light Cuban rum, a dash of *limón* (lime to you) and cola poured over ice. Cuba's rum is the symbol of its fiery passion, its lifeblood, its livelihood. In these poems it must represent the white blood in the veins of our mulatto poet, Nicolás Guillén. As in the perfect *CUBA LIBRE,* it is fused with the dark cola which for us is the symbol of his African heritage. (*CL,* ix)

Here, Carruthers situates the book's title by referencing the revolutionary pedigree of that popular mixture of rum and Coke known as a Cuba Libre, which, legend has it, was born when the USA entered the Spanish-American War after the sinking of the battleship *USS Maine* in February 1898. Once a marker of the cause of political liberation shared between Cuba and the USA, the phrase "Cuba Libre," as Carruthers reimagines it, comes to stand for cross-cultural contact well beyond USA-Cuban good-neighborliness. By racializing the drink's brownish hue, Carruthers makes Cuba Libre signify *mulatez,* the racial mixture to which he appeals to characterize both Guillén the person and the hybrid essence of his poetry. Since the cocktail's color results from adding Coca-Cola to light, not dark, rum, Carruthers's logic is that if light rum represents "white blood" (because of the historical connection between sugarcane cultivation and slavery?), then Coca-Cola would *have* to stand for Cuba's African heritage. This makes about as much sense as saying that drinking Coke darkens one's skin. Carruthers's odd analogy between brown Coke and black skin founders even further as he goes on to conflate Africanness with USAmerican corporate capitalism, of whose global successes Coca Cola, first introduced in 1886 in Atlanta, is surely one of the premier examples. The effect of this conflation is not a racialization of Coke, although its production, like that of rum, required sugar that probably came from Cuba, at least before sugar beets, high-fructose corn syrup, economic embargoes, and Diet Coke. Carruthers's vexing rhetoric implicitly pegs Guillén's and his poetry's Africanness as a product of the USA's economy. Ironically, this is true enough, given the history of USAmerican imperialism in the Caribbean and the production of Cuban "blackness" in northern academic discourses.

The rest of the introduction, however, makes it hard to read this irony as deliberate. This might have been less so had Hughes not edited out what follows as Carruthers's draft developed. "Strangely enough," Carruthers wrote,

> Nicolás Guillén's favorite drink is not the CUBA LIBRE. He prefers the exquisite *mojito* (literally: little moisture) which is the ingenious combination of light rum, lime and mint with a dash of sugar.
>
> On one occasion in Havana my young son and I heard Nicolás protest when the café waiter served a *mojito* which had a pink color.
>
> "Don't you know how to make a *mojito*?" Nicolás demanded curtly.
>
> "Well," replied the waiter, "that's the only *mojito* we know about."
>
> "On the side, old boy," said Nicolás with finality, and with that he dashed behind the bar to make his own *mojito* as it should be made. (LHP, 424:9438).

Carruthers went on to explain the significance of this anecdote: "This is typical of Guillén. He will never accept a substitute when he knows what the real thing is. I have heard him denounce with unprintable profanity the phony night-club rumbas dished up in Havana for the tourist trade. He considers them an affront to the dignity of the Cuban Negro and, indeed, to the nation's folklore." The implication is of course that, like the *mojito*, Guillén's verse is the real thing, not something dished up for Yankee tourists. In cutting the anecdote, Hughes removed any incoherence from the titular metaphor and left unquestioned its ability to cast Cuban-USA relations in anything other than an amicable light. Hughes's promotional description of *Cuba Libre* as "an ideal Christmas gift for all lovers of poetry, of Spanish, or of *our good Neighbors to the South*" (my emphasis) resonates loudly here.[39] Such editing constructs for readers of *Cuba Libre* a fiction of easy access to another nation's culture, grounded in the assumption that *Cuba libre* meant the same thing to both Cubans and Yankees. The *mojito*, even more than *limón*, would have disrupted that fiction by asserting its "ingenious," and indigenous, foreignness, thus blocking the mildly exotic familiarity and the symbolic possibilities that the more familiar cocktail offered the volume's readers.

Another notable effect of Carruthers's strained homologies—some are almost surrealist in their disjunctions—is the virtual disappearance of the

"African heritage" as an active ingredient in the mixture that the Cuba Libre, and *Cuba Libre,* represents. This erasure would have encouraged US-American readers to disconnect cultural hybridity from racial mixing—that is, *mestizaje* or *transculturación* (in Fernando Ortiz's coinage) from what was still officially known as miscegenation under more northern skies. Literary *mestizaje,* it seems, did not need to remind readers of actual practices of racial mixing. It is well worth remembering here that the category of "mulatto" was removed from the USAmerican census in 1910, so the "mulatto millions" for whom Guillén was appointed spokesman in the introduction to *Cuba Libre* were quite invisible at the time.[40] That they continued to be hidden away until the 2000 USAmerican census—which, once again, made it possible to affirm one's racially mixed origins officially—is a measure of the political anxiety that images of racial amalgamation could still generate in the 1940s. Hughes's revisions of the introduction tried to defuse such anxieties and social phobias among his Euro- and African American readers alike by safely separating Guillén's literary mulattoness, with its "pronounced rhythms of Africa," from his supposed *"mestizo* parentage." This is no less of a rhetorical sleight of hand than Guillén's "dabbling in politics"(*CL,* ix–x). Hughes adds to the confusion by using the adjectives "mulatto" and "mestizo" interchangeably when connecting Guillén with the legacy of José Martí: "The spirit of Cuba is, like that of most of Latin America, mestizo. And as one famous Cuban put it, 'The Negro is Cuba's Indian.' From the mulatto spirit comes the future skin color of the island. Such is Guillén's conviction. 'Some day,' says he, 'there will be such a thing as a Cuban color. I'd like my poems to help this along.'" The complex process of substitutions that characterizes the relation between *mulatez* and *mestizaje,* based on the problematical transformation of the African slave into the (disappeared) Caribbean native, is all but obscured here. This is especially so since in other Hispanic American countries such as Mexico or Nicaragua, *mestizo* decidedly does *not* signify residual Africanness. Having spent considerable time in Mexico, Hughes was surely aware of the difference.

Hughes's oddly erroneous dating of Guillén's birth may qualify as a related avoidance of the lingering realities of past associations. Guillén was born not in 1904, "virtually with the republic itself," but in 1902, precisely the year of the creation of the Cuban republic and the same year as Hughes himself. This is an odd mistake to make, given the symbolic possibilities of such a coincidence. In the end, Hughes probably would have been better off had he incorporated into the book's introduction a portion of the marketing prospectus he had written for Anderson earlier in 1948.

> Nicolás Guillén is not only famous throughout Latin America as Cuba's greatest living poet, but he is one of the few poets in any country whose verses have caught the popular fancy of his compatriots and who is more than a "literary figure." Nicolás Guillén is a popular poet whose poems are widely recited and

sung by the ordinary people of the Spanish-speaking Caribbean, not appreciated only by the intelligentsia, but loved by the masses. Perhaps this entry into the people's consciousness has been achieved because Guillén often employs in his poems the rhythms of the *rumbas* and *sones* of the Cuban popular song, and because the subject matter of his work is close to the everyday problems and perplexities of the people.[41]

Either way, Hughes's image of Guillén as "citizen of the world and the champion of its inarticulate masses" blots out potentially troubling local color and smoothes rough political edges. Such messy details also include Guillén's comments about racial politics in Cuba, which Carruthers paraphrased: "Guillén, himself, has said that many of his verses are mulatto verses which he maintains are typical of Cuba although many Cubans disdain to admit it. He is especially scornful of those who would quiet the claim of the Cuban Negro to recognition in the field of art. These persons, says Guillén, for the most part are those who reached the aristocracy through the kitchen...and are now afraid of the sight of a soup-pan." The paragraphs that Hughes cut—in which Carruthers situates Guillén's poetry within Iberian and Hispanic American literary history—would have been more appropriate for the scholarly edition Hughes had envisioned at some point. The overall effect of Hughes's shortened introduction is a conspicuous depoliticization of Guillén, his poetry, and Cuban-USA relations, so conspicuous that it is jarring. Hughes's evasive euphemism is "popular," an adjective that also helps him move Guillén closer to Whitman in readers' imaginations.[42] On the whole, it is easy to read the noncommittal, noncontroversial tone of this circular as a sign of Hughes's acquiescence to Cold War politics in the USA.

THE VAGARIES OF NEGRO DIALECT

The translations in *Cuba Libre* continue Hughes's editorial efforts to guard against the domestic specter of racial mixing. This is precisely why the opening poems stand out in the volume. They comprise a section titled "Cuban Blues" rather than "Mulatto Poems," a subtitle reserved for a group of non-*criollo* poems rendered in more standard USAmerican English dialect. Hughes had initially named the section "Blue Notes," which he crossed out and changed to "Cuban Blues" on July 26, 1945 (LHP, 424:9430). In addition to seven of the eight original "Motivos," "Cuban Blues" also includes the poems "Curujey" and "Me bendo caro" from Ramón Güirao's anthology *Orbita de la poesía afrocubana* (1938).[43] Although it may be tempting to read the choice of a black vernacular evocative of Negro dialect for these poems—there are nine of them in all—as an exoticizing pitch to a predominantly white readership, we know from Hughes's letters that his target audience for *Cuba Libre* was the African American intelligentsia in the USA, inside and outside academia, especially after the project had failed to excite the interest of larger publishing houses that did not believe there was anything in it for them.[44]

It is also significant that Carruthers at the time taught at Howard University, one of the historic centers of the black elites in the USA, where he would have had his hand on the pulse of prevailing academic tastes.[45] Educated African Americans in the 1940s would surely have looked askance at the Negro dialect of the plantation tradition as a suitable literary vehicle for representing their own lives and views. In that, their response would have been no different in kind from the disdain with which Havana's colored elite had greeted what editor Urrutia called Guillén's "real negro poetry" two decades earlier. Commenting rather patronizingly "on the language and feelings of our dear negroes made most noble by the love and talent of our own poets," Urrutia wrote to Hughes in 1930:

> I am only sorry that you will be unable to translate and even understand what these poems mean, but you must know that the spirit of them is [the] same as the blues; some ones are sad, some are ironical, others are sociological, viz *Ayé Me Dijeron Negro*. This is the first time that we have real negro poetry and they have [sic] a big hit with the public. Of course there is a bunch of high-life negroes which condemns this kind of literature, same as in the states.[46]

Urrutia, himself a *mulato* and part of Havana's professional elite, was rather unkindly alluding to the members of Havana's Club Atenas. Many of them were troubled by Guillén's portraits of Havana's blacks, which they read as embarrassing racial stereotypes. Guillén himself wrote a letter addressed to "mi querido Langston" the day after the "Motivos" had initially appeared, remarking happily "que los poemas de son han gustado extraordinariamente, y han formado un verdadero escándalo, por tratarse de un género completamente nuevo en nuestra literatura" (that the *son*-poems have been extraordinarily well received, and that they have caused a veritable scandal for having been written in a genre entirely new to our literature).[47] Guillén also knew that for many of Havana's lighter-skinned elite, his poems represented "una deshonra 'para la raza'" (a dishonor for the race), as he wrote in "Sones y soneros," his satirical piece about the bourgeois "enemigos del son" (enemies of the *son*).[48]

When Hughes selected the poems for *Cuba Libre*, he was no doubt aware that a response of this sort might be a problem in the USA. Despite the success of Sterling Brown's *Southern Road* (1932), Negro dialect poetry had never quite recovered from the blow that James Weldon Johnson and Countee Cullen had dealt it in the early 1920s when they shunned it as an anachronism.[49] Johnson in particular rejected the idea that Negro dialect was part of a "living language," defining it as a throwback to the plantation tradition so embarrassingly represented by Paul Laurence Dunbar's popular poems and Charles Chesnutt's short stories.[50] Hughes did not see the world quite that way. In "The Negro Artist and the Racial Mountain," for instance, he lamented that "[t]he fine novels of Chesnutt go out of print with neither race noticing their passing. The quaint charm and humor of Dunbar's dialect verse brought to him, in his day, largely the same kind of encouragement one would give a sideshow freak (A colored man writing poetry! How odd!) or a clown (How amusing!)" (*Essays*, 34). That, however, had been twenty-odd years earlier. In the 1950s, Hughes, who actually never wrote dialect verse à la Dunbar, would even be careful to excise most of his own vernacular poems in his *Selected Poems* (1959). With Guillén's *poemas-son*, however, he was caught in a bind. Not turning these *poemas* into vernacular verse might have made them too alien to African American readers from the USA, while using a mode reminiscent of Negro dialect made them potentially all too familiar. Hughes no doubt speculated that if the black bourgeoisie and the black intelligentsia were hostile to USAmerican Negro dialect poetry because of its association with minstrelsy and even to vernacular poetry because of its class inflections, they might be more accepting of either mode when it was used to represent other parts of the African diaspora, especially those outside the USA. Such speculations would have been based on Hughes's familiarity with the fact that anointed modernist poets such as Eliot, Pound, Williams, and Crane not infrequently used US-American racial idioms either as exotic markers or as a form of slumming.[51]

Hughes was the one to make the final selections for *Cuba Libre,* and critics typically credit him with most of the translations as well. "No point would be served," wrote William Harrison of the Boston *Chronicle* on February 12, 1949, "by enquiring about what was the actual division of the labor [of] translation. Mr. Carruthers will pardon the observation that there is a great deal of Hughes in the spirit and letter of these poems." And he adds confidently, "Undoubtedly this circumstance arises from the strong kinship of feeling between the Negro American and Afro-Cuban artificers in choice of material and in the ability to use the idom [*sic*] of the unsophisticated." This may well be so, but the draft manuscripts show clearly that Hughes translated only half of the poems; he did, however, revise and edit Carruthers's versions.[52]

It is unclear exactly when and how Carruthers and Hughes met and how they decided to collaborate on *Cuba Libre.* Carruthers had written his doctoral thesis at the University of Illinois on the nineteenth-century Cuban poet Gabriel de la Concepción Valdés, better known as Plácido. While at Illinois he had also "endeavored to interpret Guillén in public gatherings and over the radio—station W.I.L.L. the University of Illinois' station."[53] Carruthers himself offers the following account of the collaboration: "Upon my return to Howard in 1941 I began my own translations and when I moved to New York in 1944 I met Langston again and began to compare notes. We found that a few but not many of our translations were of the same poem but that there were many which I had finished which Langston thought good enough to stand as they were and many others which Langston had completed without my having touched them. We collaborated completely on the final editing and polishing and Langston secured a publisher and the artist, Gar Bilbert [Gilbert]."[54] This account is not entirely consistent with Carruthers's correspondence with Hughes, according to which they decided to divide up work on the translations in October 1941. Having just returned to Washington, Carruthers wrote to Hughes: "I shall continue to work on the Guirao anthology 'Orbita de la Poesia Afrocubana' (1938) if you prefer to work on 'Cantos Para Soldados' and 'West Indies Ltd' of Guillen."[55] There is a gap in their correspondence between 1941 and 1947. By the time that Caroline Anderson, who had read the Guillén poems included in Dudley Fitts's anthology, inquired about his translations, Hughes had not looked at the *Cuba Libre* manuscript in two years.[56]

It was Carruthers whose translations were most closely identified with Hughes's "professional proletarian" poetic touch. [57] Hughes himself focused on non-*criollo* poems from later volumes. He did, however, try his hand at a few of the *poemas-son*, such as "Mulata" and especially "Ayé mi dijeron negro," finally published as "Last Night Somebody Called Me Darky." Most of Hughes's drafts are fragments, and none of them made it into the final manuscript. In the case of "Mulata," which Carruthers translated as "High Brown," Hughes changed Carruthers's version only slightly. For instance, the lines "Yo' mouf' is awful big fo' me, / an' yo' naps is short an' red" (*CL*, 6) became "Yo' mouf is *mighty* big fo' me, / An' yo' *hair* is short an' red" in Hughes's revision.[58] John Matheus, himself a translator, claimed that Hughes translated Guillén's poetry into the "Negro folk idiom," whereas Carruthers rendered it in "American Negro dialect."[59] Although Matheus does not elaborate on how these two might differ, he implies that dialect features more frequent elisions and changes of consonants, while folk idiom is closer to more standardized forms of English, as in "hair" instead of "naps." Matheus's argument, however, rests on shaky foundations, and not only because it is meant to apply to the entirety of *Cuba Libre* rather than just the first section. More important, Hughes was interested in the evolving urban vernaculars, not in the folk idioms associated with the more rural areas of the USAmerican South. Furthermore, Matheus clearly did not know who in fact translated what, who revised whom, and which translations were not included at all. He simply assumed that Carruthers had translated only the poems in "Cuban Blues," which is incorrect.[60]

Perhaps more significant yet, drawing a distinction between dialect and folk modes, which are not analogous to Negro dialect and black vernacular, bypasses the larger questions that the translations of the *poemas-son* raise: what are the relative positions of Negro dialect and Cuban *criollo* as nonstandard languages both vis-à-vis the dominant lects of their respective major languages *and* vis-à-vis each other? A (now) marginalized source language such as Spanish does not, in cases where the target language is USAmerican English, occupy the same position in relation to the standard lect of that English as do "minoritized" sociolects such as Negro dialect and black vernacular and their literary representations. Nor does the position of nonstandard versions of American Spanish, such as Afro-Cuban *criollo,* correspond exactly to either Negro dialect or black vernacular in the USA. That each is marginalized in relation to one or more ethnocenters does not mean that one is therefore *like* the other. This is precisely the sort of false comparison that has tempted not a few critics and translators to regard the transfer of poetry and fiction written in Afro-Hispanic idioms into various representations of black USAmerican English as a self-evident, supposedly natural process somehow exempt from the multilayered mediations that affect translation in other, nonracialized, situations.[61]

It may be useful to think of African American vernaculars in English as "peculiar English-language remainder(s)" that "expose the hierarchical values in Anglo-American culture."[62] A caveat must be added: Negro dialect and black vernacular can function in this way only in historically specific situations when readers either embrace or explicitly discredit them as literary vehicles. As mediums for translation, such modes can expose inequalities in non-English-speaking cultures only through distorting analogies: *criollo* is to Cuba as Negro dialect (or vernacular) is to the USA. In relation to Cuban *criollo,* Negro dialect functions much like a false cognate would: *negro* does not equal Negro.[63] Unlike Negro dialect as a written form, the linguistic practice of what Guillén calls *criollo* and its literary renditions both are and represent an acknowledgment of racial mixing, and the social and linguistic uncertainties it produces, as an inescapable historical reality at the very core of Cuban culture. In the postwar USA, a cultural and political environment still steeped in racial binarisms and anxieties about intermarriage—this is still well before the last antimiscegenation law was repealed in Virginia—the very idea of conceding, let alone celebrating, the impact of racial mixing on the national culture would have been anathema to prevailing sensibilities on both sides of the color line. To include in *Cuba Libre* prominently placed translations in USAmerican Negro vernacular was a compromise as much designed to alleviate domestic anxieties about unpalatable racial politics as intended to dispel fears of foreign threats. Whatever black vernacular infused with Negro dialect signified to different groups of domestic readers, it was something eminently recognizable to all of them, for better or worse.

In the case of Cuban *criollo,* there is no one (standard) source language, and a translator has to negotiate the often troublesome interplay of multiple source languages. Carruthers's choice of a Negro dialect in the plantation tradition severely limits this interplay, in part because this form of literary language would have represented blackness, not mulattoness, to USAmerican readers. In fact, because it was coded as black, and *only* as black, Negro dialect modes could simply not signify the processes of racial and cultural mixing so integral to the concept of Cubanness. At best, Negro dialect could be used to signal some sort of premodern otherness that would relegate Cuba to the outer margins even of African America, at least in the USA. In this scenario, Guillén's poems, and his *poemas-son* in particular, could be classified as late-modernist primitivist artifacts, precious objects of aesthetic appreciation that existed outside history, especially the history of USAmerican neocolonialism in Cuba. The relatively pricey limited edition in which *Cuba Libre* was issued — it retailed for up to $5.00, double the price of some of Hughes's own poetry books — amplified this sense of timelessness by linking value to beauty in formal design.[64] More than one reviewer commented on this discrepancy between content and format. The Boston *Chronicle* writer William Harrison observed on February 12, 1949, that the volume's typography and expensive paper "may create the erroneous impression that Guillén's poetry is the property of aesthetes." "It is a contradiction not easily understood," we read in the *Daily Worker* from 1948, "that these poems which bristle with anti-imperialist sentiment, set to African, Spanish and calypso [?] rhythms, should be read by a literary elite. I am certain after reading the poems that Nicolás Guillén has been done a disservice by thus limiting his audience.... *Cuba Libre* contains songs which should be published on leaflets and spoken at mass meetings." The literary elite, and not specifically the black intelligentsia, was certainly the audience Caroline Anderson had in mind when she asked if Hughes had "access to [the mailing lists] of 'New Directions' or any groups interested in contemporary poetry."[65]

NOT CALLING THE KETTLE BLACK

To explore in more detail the profoundly dehistoricizing effect of residual Negro dialect in the translations of Guillén's "Motivos," I first turn to "Ayé me dijeron negro," a poem that was part of the eight original "Motivos de son" and which the same *The Daily Worker* reviewer singled out to comment on the difficulties of "transcrib[ing] Cuban Spanish accents into Negro American English accents." I am quoting Guillén's poem in its entirety from its first printing in the *Diario de la Marina* from April 20, 1930 (see figure 6 above), which was most likely the basis for its English versions.[66]

> Ayé me dijeron negro
> pa que me fajara yo;
> pero e'que me lo desía
> era un negro como yo.
> Tan blanco como te bé
> y tu abuela sé quién é.
> Sácala de la cosina,

> sácala de la cosina,
> Mamá Iné.
> Mamá Iné, tú bien lo sabe,
> Mamá Iné, yo bien lo sé,
> Mamá Iné te llama nieto,
> Mamá Iné.

Here, as elsewhere in this chapter, my own English versions of Guillén's poems are mainly intended as a crutch for non-Spanish speakers. I have inflected the language as little as possible to maintain a distance between this prop and the translations by Hughes and Carruthers.

> Yesterday someone called me a darky
> just to get me into a fight,
> but the one who said this to me
> is just as dark as I.
> As white as you look,
> and your grandmother knows who you are.
> Call her out of the kitchen,
> call her out of the kitchen,
> Mamá Iné, you know very well.
> Mamá Iné, I know very well.
> Mamá Iné calls you grandson,
> Mamá Iné.

Like Guillén's other *poemas-son,* this short poem is a minidrama set in Havana and played out across the antiphonal rhythms of the Cuban *son.* Within this frame unfold metatheatrical performances of identity in which the relations between cultural origins, skin color, and social class shift.[67] A nameless speaker recounts a scene familiar to readers of nineteenth-century Cuban antislavery novels, notably Cirilo Villaverde's *Cecilia Valdés:* one *mulato* calling another *negro.* As in most of the other "Motivos," the speaker is unambiguously gendered as male and visible only through his account of the other: "era un negro *como yo*" (my emphasis). The speaker's informal tone signals that he is addressing a social equal, an insider. The poem's representation of his diction features an orthography brimming with elided consonants and other shifts in which *ayer* becomes *ayé, ves* turns into *bé,* and *cocina* into *cosina.* The insulting party is initially obscured behind a plural—*dijeron,* "*they* called me"—but assumes greater individuality with the introduction of the personal pronoun *e'* (*él,* he). If *e'* is indeed like the speaker, he would have to be of mixed race and fair skin, someone who crosses color and class lines with impunity, for what makes the insult possible in the first place is the gap between physical appearance— "epidermalized" being, in Charles Johnson's phrase[68]—and descent. The speaker seeks to redress the wrong done to him—that is, the other's verbal misidentification with him on the basis of race—by reminding his white-looking assaulter of his family. He taunts his insulter and challenges him to bring out of the kitchen and into the light of day "Mama Iné," that prototypical signifier of African slavery in Hispanic Caribbean cultures. Typically, this grandmother is hidden when company comes.[69]

In the poem's opening stanza, then, the speaker frames his verbal attack on his (now absent?) opponent by addressing a familiar audience of bystanders, whom he presumes to be sympathetic to his complaint. In the stanzas that follow, the line "Mamá Iné" functions as an *estribillo,* or refrain, in which speaker and bystanders join as they engage in the verbal ritual of putting the offender back in his place. This *estribillo* has the effect of creating a bond between speaker and audience, as well as, in another layer, the poem's Cuban readers, in the construction of a cultural community for whom Mamá Iné is more than an irritating allusion to the history of slavery. For them, Mamá Iné is not just an individual. The phrase also, or more specifically, refers to Cuba's history of aesthetic production represented here by the popular *guaracha* from 1868 known as "Mama Iné." The original song's theme is the sugarcane harvest:

> Aquí etán todo lo Negro
> que benimo a sabé
> si no consede pemmiso
> pa ponenno a molé,
> ¡Ay, Mama Iné!…[70]

These lines may be translated as "Here are all the Blacks; / we've come to find out / whether you'll give us permission / to start milling the cane." The song's second stanza moves into the singers' complaint about having been cheated by the "mayorá" (overseer), and one might, not unreasonably, link this to the topic of deceit in Guillén's poem. Yet the orthographic and structural resemblances between the song lyric and "Ayé mi dijeron negro" are far more pronounced, and far more important, than any thematic overlap. What these resemblances imply, however, is not a conception of either *criollo* or Cuban music as a timeless vessel of cultural kinship. Rather, Guillén's poem uses both *criollo* and antiphonal song as historical references that call attention to similarities *and* differences. The *guaracha*'s rural cane cutters are precisely not the same as the urban *mulatos* in Guillén's poem; each group exists in a discrete geographical and temporal location. What connects them is not a shared origin—synecdochically evoked by tonic stresses imitating drumbeats—but elements of different languages and musical forms woven into a dynamic, ever-evolving system. This underlying movement in Guillén's poem is what prevents *criollo* from hardening into a surface crust of racial stereotypes and biases.

The point in Guillén's poem is that neither the speaker nor his detractor, both of whose bodies are invisible to the reader, are reliably identifiable in racial terms, that is, by their skin color. What racially marks the poem's speaker is not physical appearance but the single word "negro," whose meaning, as the poem goes on to show, is highly unstable. It can no more confer a social identity than skin color or phenotype can. (This, incidentally, has nothing to do with the word's lack of capitalization in the body of the poem.) The poem's written representation of spoken *criollo* does serve to identify the speaker to the extent that his linguistic performance makes him audible to us, identifying him as *Cuban* without giving any dependable clues as to his race—unless, of course, we want to read Cuban as equaling black. For Guillén, however, to be Cuban meant to be *mulato/a,* which signifies a state of cultural hybridity that denotes color without being reducible to race.[71] This idea of cultural mixing would have been—and still is—exceedingly difficult to articulate in a USAmerican language environment with its historical insistence on imagining the color line as virtually impermeable and on conflating cultural with racial identities. That *negro,* in Cuban usage, can function both as a class insult and as a term of endearment, as in *mi negro,* further enhances the *choteo*-like ironies in Guillén's poem.[72] Because it can generate such layered ironies in the poem, the seemingly uncomplicated word *negro* causes the poem's translators the most trouble.

That "Ayé me dijeron negro" is the only one of Guillén's *poemas-son* that Hughes actually translated in its entirety is a good measure of the trouble these poems caused him. As a result, we have two full translations of this poem, one published, the other a manuscript version. First, there is Carruthers's translation, which was printed in *Cuba Libre;* second, there are two drafts by Hughes, one handwritten and dated July 26, 1945, the other typed, corrected, and marked as "Omitted" in his handwriting. Each translator offers a very different approach to the intricate relations of race, culture, and class that converge in the irksome word *negro.* As far as we know, neither translator even entertained the notion of translating the Cuban *negro* as "nigger," which, at least in the context of this poem, might have been the closest approximation of its social sting in a USAmerican context.[73] Carruthers opted for "darky" in the poem's opening stanza, but he apparently shied away from using the noun in the poem's title, resorting instead to "Last Night Somebody Called Me Negro."

> Last night somebody called me darky
> jes' to make me fight,
> but de one who said it to me
> is a darky, too, all right.

(CL, 4)

This is hardly the affected diction we find in the dialect poetry of a Paul Laurence Dunbar or even a Sterling Brown. Carruthers employs the conventions of Negro dialect writing much more sparingly than they do, creating the effect of a speaker who code-shifts in midsentence without the poem's supplying any motivation for why he would do so. This haphazard switching appears to be the product of the Cuban interfering with English, resulting in the impression that the poem cannot comfortably settle down into either standard or nonstandard modes of USAmerican English. We see the same sorts of inconsistencies in Carruthers's other Negro dialect translations in *Cuba Libre*, for instance in "Thick-Lipped Cullud Boy" ("Negro bembón"):

> How come you jumps salty,
> When they calls you thick-lipped boy,
> If yo' mouf's so sweet,
> Thick-lipped cullud boy?
> Thick-lipped as you is
> You got everything.
> Charity's payin' yo' keep.
> She's givin' you all you need.

(CL, 5)

Compare these two stanzas with the draft version of the poem "Thick-Lipped Cullud Bo'" that Carruthers had sent to Hughes, along with a handful of other translations, before they embarked on their collaboration:

> Why fo' ack so tuf
> Wen dey calls yo 'thick-lips,' bo'?
> Ef yo mouf's so sweet,
> Thick-lipped cullud bo'?
> Thick-lipped as yo' is
> Yo git it all;
> Sis' Charity's payin' yo keep,
> She gives yo' 'tall.[74]

This earlier version is an extreme example of the extent of Carruthers's attempt to make the diction in Guillén's poems conform to USAmerican expectations, turning them into something they were not. This was by no means as terrible as translational taming could get. The "Little Anthology of Afro-Cuban Poetry" that Lloyd Mallan edited for an issue of New Directions was to bring together "the most promising non-conformists and experimenters," and included several of Guillén's "Motivos" in translations by Mallan himself.[75] Even the titles he chose suggest the direction of his translations: "Muh Price's High" ("Me bendo caro") "If'n Yo On'y Knew" ("Si tu supiera") "High Yellow Stuff" ("Mulata"), "Satchel Mouf" ("Negro bembón"), "Muh Chick Sticks" ("Mi Chiquita"), and "Dig for the Dough" ("Búcate plata").[76] Compared with these versions, Carruthers's choices—"Thick-Lipped Cullud Boy" for "Negro bembón," "My Gal" for

"Mi Chiquita," "High Brown" for "Mulata," and "No, Sirrie!" for "Búcate plata" — sound positively plain.

Even though Carruthers makes more limited use of Negro dialect in his later drafts, his translations for *Cuba Libre* still insist on restoring precisely the sorts of unambiguous racial markers that Guillén's poem subjects to destabilizing irony. In the company of "jes'" and "de," the almost archaic "darky," resonant with half-affectionate echoes of antebellum racism and blackface minstrelsy, defaces Guillén's Cuban *negro* beyond all recognition. The only hint at dissonance here is the somewhat jarring difference between the title's use of "Negro" and the first line's "darky." But that, too, disappeared when Hughes, who had initially changed Carruthers's "Negro" to "black," settled on "darky" for the poem's final title. While Carruthers, in this case, stayed away from Negro dialect's typically dehistoricizing verb forms — "call" instead of "called" and "say" instead of "said" — he still ends up situating his speaker's language in an atemporal present when he changes Guillén's past tense in *era* (was) to "is." In Guillén's poem, the part of the poem in which *negro* still signifies racially is located in the past; it is a grammatically completed action whose present usage the rest of the poem challenges. Carruthers's unexpected injection of the present tense erases this important distinction along with the visual separation of the first stanza from the following verses. The alternating end rhymes and the fairly regular meter that places tonal stresses at the end of each line both aid in Carruthers's attempt at creating a formally unified poem — the better to block out any foreign noise between the lines. The verbal exclamation point "all right" at the end of what is now a quatrain confirms the extent to which Guillén's relational uncertainties have been displaced by the translator's desire to assert absolutes: the speaker is no longer a "darky" *in relation to* his interlocutor. Their being "darkies" has become far less contingent.

Hughes, by contrast, steered clear of this sort of Negro dialect altogether. His vernacular version of this poem is much more literal, and thus less controlling, even to the point of rendering *ayé* as "yesterday" instead of "last night," which is strictly Carruthers's interpretation. Hughes's revisions show that he changed his mind about the present tense, following Guillén's poem more closely in how it uses grammar to structure, and comment on, the characters' interactions.

> Yesterday somebody called me black
> Just to make me mad —
> But the one who said it
> **Was** ~~is~~ just as black as me. (LHP, 424:9430)[77]

The diction of Hughes's speaker seems virtually uninflected here. At first there appears to be no evidence of conflicting languages or codes. While the adjective "black" does not deface and domesticate Guillén's *negro* as irretrievably as the noun "darky" does in Carruthers's version, it also does not help create a sense of referential instability or irony. What comes across as a weak translation, however, is really an example of failed assimilation into USAmerican English. Once we consider what these lines signify, we arrive at the conclusion that for one Negro to insult another by calling him black actually makes little sense in the USA. This is what signals the presence of a foreign text that pushes Hughes's English version of this stanza to the limits of a USAmerican reader's comprehension. That the language in this stanza resembles the more dominant or standardized ("white") dialect of USAmerican English makes it no less foreign to itself. The language looks as though it ought to be meaningful, but it is in fact not readable solely within the conventions of the standardized dialect. This radical unreadability may explain why Hughes, in the end, decided to go with Carruthers's version instead of his own, with the difference of placing "darky" in the body and the title of the poem and despite the fact that he was uneasy about using a term that might strike an all-too-familiar servile chord for certain readers.

Hughes's discomfort is plain from a letter to Caroline Anderson, in which he addresses changes that the press had made in the order of the poems in *Cuba Libre*. These changes, Anderson explains, "were entirely typographical. We are trying to get title lengths of a sameness."[78] Hughes addresses the problem after congratulating her on the "BEAUTIFUL" proofs.

> I notice that you have changed the order of the poems about in the CUBAN BLUES section, which is O.K.—except that I would not start the book with, "Last Night Somebody Called Me Darky." Some colored people (especially "intellectuals") are often over-sensitive about the word "darky," and since I would expect this book to have a certain sales appeal to Negro colleges and libraries, I don't believe it would be wise to start the volume right off the bat with this particular poem. In fact, I request you, PLEASE DON'T....(I have gone through this minority sensitiveness with my own poetry and know it can affect sales if not tactfully handled.).[79]

Unlike Guillén, Hughes clearly did not thrive on the sorts of scandals that the "Motivos de son" had set off in Havana. Anderson obliged without argument and moved "Don' Know No English," on which I comment in detail below, back to the volume's beginning.

Because "Ayé me dijeron negro" itself is concerned with the interactive dynamics between speaker and audience, Hughes's attention to audience was not limited to marketing issues. It also had literary dimensions. While all of Guillén's "Motivos" are dramas performed for the benefit of an internal audience, "Ayé me dijeron negro" is the only one of these poems in which an audience of cultural insiders becomes an actual part of the performance by joining the speaker in his appeal to "Mama Iné" to settle the mock dispute. Both Carruthers's and Hughes's respective translations are conspicuously at variance with Guillén's poem, first in how they position the figure of the *abuela* in relation to the speaker and second in how closely they attend to the audience's role in the poem. Carruthers continues in modified Negro dialect mode, which even includes the requisite verb forms, with the typical added "s" in the first personal singular.

> Can't fool me, dat white face of yours
> 'cause I knows who your grandma is.
> Call her out de kitchen,
> call her out de kitchen,
> Mamá Inez, you knows all about it.
> Mamá Inez, I knows, too.
> Mamá Inez calls you grandson,
> Mamá Inez.

Hughes's translation also remains consistent in extending the uninflected voice he uses in his opening stanza to the rest of the poem.

> As white as you look,
> I know **who** ~~who's~~ your grandma-! **Is.**
> Bring her **on** out of the kitchen,
> Bring her **on** out of the kitchen,
> Mamá Iné!
> Mamá Iné, you know her all right!
> Mamá Iné, I know her, too. Sure do!
> Mamá Iné, ~~call you grandchild~~ says you're her grandchild—
> Mamá Iné!

"Y tu abuela sé quién é" might be understood either as "and your grandmother, I know who she is" or "your grandmother knows who you are." Changing the structure of this sentence in English creates a subtle but crucial difference. It puts the speaker in a position of authority that he does not quite have in Guillén's lyric, where the emphasis remains on *tu abuela* by virtue of her being positioned prominently at the beginning of the line. This position is reinforced by the absence of the personal pronoun *yo*, which, though not needed in Spanish, does efface the knowing subject. It is as if knowledge of an other renders the speaker invisible, and his own invisibility enables an implicit pronouncement about that other's phenotype and associated racial identity by contrast with the insulter's own apparent whiteness ("As white as you look"). In the Cuban poem, the contrast between them is more immediate because of the proximity between *te bé* and *tu abuela*. In both translations, the pronoun "I" more explicitly mediates the contrast than it does in the Spanish version. The poem's speaker is presumptuous in both linguistic situations. In Guillén's poem, by contrast, the speaker does not claim to know that "Mamá Iné knows" and what she *is* in racial terms. He does not necessarily presume to know *what* she knows beyond what her physical appearance suggests to him. Guillén's speaker still defers to Mamá Iné's authority as the keeper of historical knowledge: she knows "it" (*lo*), and "it" includes the insulter's secret.

By placing the speaker's "I" emphatically at the beginning of both the sentence and the line instead of taking a cue from Guillén's syntax, both translators cast the grandmother as more of a knowable, and known, object that now more closely resembles the stereotype of the Southern plantation Mammy who is perpetually frozen in a posture of domestic loyalty. Although Carruthers translates *lo* more properly as "it," rather than "her" (an eccentric choice on Hughes's part on which I comment below), his choices in the earlier line have notable implications for how we read the partly anglicized figure of Mamá Inez. Carruthers's emphasis on what his speaker knows directs the reader away from the confounding incongruity of the accent and the added "z" (instead of the expected "s") to the question of race—"it," which now represents both what the grandmother knows and what she is. Race is knowable to the extent that it becomes visible on the female body once she steps out of her domestic enclosure into the light of public scrutiny.

Carruthers's language implies that phenotype renders cultural history readable in racial terms and that such a reading is unequivocal. Perhaps he takes his cue from the poem "High Brown," where another male speaker employs clearly racialized language to describe a female body (*CL*, 6). More likely, however, he remembered a version of this very stanza from Juan José Arrom's introduction in Mallan's "Little Anthology of Afro-Cuban Poetry," to which Carruthers himself had contributed.[80] This rather free dialect translation, which leaves little to the reader's imagination, is likely Mallan's translation of Arrom; the source poem is not identified.

> O take her outen de kitchen,
> Take her offen de stove,
> Mama Inay,
> Old Mama Inay,
> You know darn well,
> Ah knows it's true,
> Mama Inay, she call you gran'son,
> An' dis sho 'nough makes you a niggah too.[81]

Although Carruthers does not resort to adding a line to render the poem's racial implications crassly explicit, his approach to representing blackness is still not that different from Mallan's. While the old lady is not a "niggah" in Carruthers's translation of this stanza, his version nonetheless suggests that race is all there is to know about "grandma," a familiarizing appellation that strips Mamá Inez of the complex referential dimensions she has in Guillén's poem and leaves her in the simple garb of stereotype. Carruthers assumes that Mamá Inez actually emerges from her kitchen when the speaker shifts his address to her, so that being called *out* is tantamount to being called *black*. It is as if hers is the black body that belongs to the deceptively white face. The speaker knows what grandma knows ("I knows, too") because he can *see* her (although we cannot). This interpretation avoids the fact that there is nothing in the Cuban poem to suggest that the relationship between seeing, knowing, and being, which Guillén's encodes in his end rhymes, is anything other than precariously asymmetrical. That *bé* (*ves*, from *ver,* to see) resonates both with *sé* (from *saber,* to know) and with é (*es*, from *ser,* to be) does not establish a causal relationship between these actions; thus Carruthers's "because," which replaces Guillén's *y* (and), is unwarranted. In "Ayé me dijeron negro," seeing does not equal knowing, and the kind of knowledge achieved in the act of perception is not a dependable ground for social being. Carruthers picks up on this momentarily through his verb choice in the lines "Can't *fool* me, / dat white face of yours" (my emphasis), which signals the fickleness of physical appearance. At the same time, however, his translation continues to elide relative states of existence, turning race, in this case whiteness, into much more of an absolute category than Guillén's own formulation would support: "tan blanco como te bé" means literally "as white as you look" — to yourself? to others?

Hughes's version seeks diligently to avoid the pitfalls of such causalities and racial absolutes. I have found no conclusive evidence that Hughes had read Carruthers's version before embarking on his own, but I suspect from certain coincident phrasing that he had. Hughes also adds an intriguing twist to the poem by translating the neuter pronoun *lo* as "her," which changes the speaker-audience dynamics of the poem's last four lines. Hughes's willful mistranslation — and it is much too willful to qualify as a mere error — enables an alternate reading in which the speaker, having called out to Mamá Iné, now turns to an audience, "you," "who know *her* all right!" The fact that the English pronoun "you," unlike *tú*, does double duty as both singular and plural separates "you" from "her," another ambiguous pronoun whose antecedent is either Mamá Iné or, possibly, the speaker's nemesis. In the former reading, the speaker addresses an audience with whom he shares a particular knowledge of Mamá Iné. What exactly speaker and audience know about her remains unspoken. Yet the fact that Mamá Iné stays invisible throughout this poem implies that that knowledge goes beyond race and racialized bodies. With the line "I know her, too. Sure do!" the speaker emphatically identifies himself as part of a community formed around that unspoken cultural knowledge: what they know is that Mamá Iné refers at once to a (mythical) progenitress and to a song, to a cultural genealogy *and* to a history of aesthetic production. Compared with this, the question of racial identity becomes secondary. No translation can make these multiple local cultural references available to a monolingual English-speaking readership. Hughes at least draws attention to their existence by retaining the name Mamá Iné in its unaltered form. His fourth line, then, constitutes a joint effort in which speaker and audience together remind the prodigal insulter that "Mamá Iné says you're her grandchild," and the final line confirms both that statement and the fact that speaker and audience have now merged into a collective voice (note the added exclamation marks). This joining of knowing voices serves as a final homage to the female ancestor's cultural authority, which also limits the speaker's earlier claims to knowledge.

Hughes's prominently placed dash, which may be read as a representation of collective convergence or consensus, also guards against the sort of closure that this image of unified voices might suggest. Not everything is resolved at the end of his poem. Most conspicuous among the remaining loose ends is Hughes's rendering *nieto* as "grandchild" rather than as the more precisely gendered "grandson."[82] The gender-neutral noun has the advantage of being acceptable to multiple cultural constituencies without sharing the exact same meaning for each. In the context of USAmerican black vernacular, "child" would signal a specific cultural kinship rather than referring to biological descent. Along different lines, "grand*child*" also invites a reading of the poem's earlier feminine pronoun, which unsettles the masculine identity of the insulter in Guillén's poem, and, by implication, that of the speaker. Hughes's choice resonates with his loose translation of Guillén's masculine pronoun *e'* as "the one" ("de one" in Carruthers), and he appears to take this looseness as an opportunity subtly to worry the fixity of gender identities at the very point that readers might finally feel reassured of the characters' racial makeups. Whatever Hughes's intent, the effect is a reminder that race cannot be fixed in the eyes of a beholder any more unfailingly than gender can. By not corroborating the masculinity of Guillén's characters, which Carruthers underlines in his preference for the verb "fight," Hughes creates a different kind of speaker. His speaker's verbal "madness" — "Just to make me mad" — displaces masculinized physical aggression by conjuring up familiar associations of femininity and madness. That "mad" does not serve here indirectly to endorse popular concepts of racial pathology is clear from Hughes's tinny rhyme of "mad" with "black" which dissociates the two words. What it does do is show that blackness is as much of a construct, something that is *made,* as femininized madness. However minor they may seem, Hughes's interpretative adjustments significantly change the way in which racial and national identity is typically imagined in Guillén's poetry, and in Cuban literature more broadly: as a symbolic transaction among and between men, and only men.[83] Hughes's feminine pronoun belongs to a context in which national culture is constructed very differently.

Hughes's translation of "Ayé me dijeron negro" carries across a strong sense of the uncertainties and turbulences that Cuban literary *criollo* creates when brought together with USAmerican English, at the linguistic and conceptual levels. This effect, though artificially enhanced by the revision in the lines I have quoted, distinguishes Hughes's from Carruthers's translations in most cases. Unlike his academic collaborator, Hughes was not a translator skilled, or even interested, in dominating another idiom. As we have seen in his autobiographies, Hughes's attitude toward foreign languages and cultures was rather one of humility and respect. In the case of Guillén's *criollo* poems, Hughes's typical modus operandi was compounded by his imperfect knowledge of Afro-Cuban Spanish, although, all things considered, that idiom would have been considerably less alien to him than Russian or Turcoman. Still, even some lack of familiarity would have made Guillén's "Motivos" more radically strange linguistic constructs to him than to Carruthers, who had spend far more time in Cuba and other parts of the Hispanic Americas. Guillén's Afro-Cuban poems pushed even Hughes's solid written comprehension to its limits, as Guillén and others reminded their budding North American colleague and friend on various occasions. Guillén, for one, wrote in his "Conversación con Langston Hughes" on March 9, 1930, "Hughes's Spanish is not the best, but he makes marvelous use of it."[84] When Gustavo Urrutia wrote to Hughes about Guillén's "Motivos," he interjected: "I am only sorry that you will be unable to translate and even understand what these poems mean."[85] Guillén struck a similar note when he sent Hughes a copy of the poems:

> Por más que me temo que a usted le cueste un poco de trabajo entender estos versos: están escritos en nuestro lenguaje criollo, y muchos giros, locuciones y frases escapan a su conocimiento actual—creo yo—del castellano. De todos modos, me parece que allá debe haber alguna persona que conoce bien a Cuba y que, además, domine el inglés para que se los explique.[86]

> [But I fear that it will be a bit of work for you to understand those poems: they are written in our Creole language, and many turns, locutions and phrases will—I believe—escape your actual knowledge of Spanish. In any case, it seems to me that there has to be someone who knows Cuba well and who also is fluent enough in English to be able to explain them to you.]

He closes by urging Hughes, "¡Aprenda a hablar criollo!" (Learn to speak Cuban!). While Hughes apparently did not learn *criollo,* he responded to Guillen on July 17, 1930, that he had found a young Cuban in Washington, D.C., to help him translate the "Motivos."[87]

Between 1930 and 1940, when Hughes began to work seriously on *Cuba Libre,* he did not spend more than a few weeks in Cuba, even though Guillén always encouraged him to return for longer periods of time and "git some cash"—as Carruthers would later translate the line "Búcate plata" from one of the *poemas-son.* That Hughes was sensitive to the difficulties these poems posed for non-Cuban speakers, including him, is evident from his reply to Caroline Anderson's request to omit the Spanish titles of each poem in *Cuba Libre,* "since we are not offering the Spanish translation of the poems." "Certainly, you may leave out the Spanish titles of the poems, if you choose," Hughes responded. "We were originally thinking of a university press as a possible publishers [*sic*], so I reckon we put them [the Spanish titles of the poems] there for academic purposes to help students find the originals quickly (in case their Spanish was only school-bookish and the couldn't otherwise identify the poems in the original language)."[88] In light of this remark, it is somewhat surprising that Hughes never seemed to have considered a bilingual volume, especially given that Dudley Fitts's bilingual anthology of Hispanic American poetry, to which Hughes contributed a handful of translations, had been published by a major press in 1942. It is reasonable to assume, however, that doubling the size of the book in this manner would have been far too costly for a small press such as Ward Ritchie.

For his part, Guillén faced a similar linguistic predicament in reverse. Although Guillén professed much admiration for Hughes's talents as a poet, he also readily admitted that he could not read the poems in English. On July 11, 1930, Guillén, for the first time addressing Langston informally as "tú," writes in a somewhat different vein and without the earlier apprehensions about Hughes's access to Cuban Spanish:

> Me satisface extraordinariamente que te hayan gustado tanto los poemas míos. Tu sabes mucho de estas cosas y, además, conoces lo suficiente la mentalidad cubana para interpretarlos. Tomaría yo estar en las mismas condiciones respecto de las cosas tuyas y de tus compatriotas. Pero pienso muy pronto saber bastante "english" y leer en tu propia lengua tus bellísimos poemas. Recibí oportunamente la traducción de algunos de mis versos, que te agradezco sinceramente, pues eso es un gran honor para mí. Creo que todas están muy bien, como hechas por tí. Urrutia me las estuvo leyendo y me dio su opinión favorable. [89]

> [I am absolutely delighted that you liked all my poems. You know much about these things and also know enough about the Cuban mentality in order to interpret them. I wish I were in the same position vis-à-vis your work and that of your compatriots. But I think that very soon I will know enough "English" to read your beautiful poems in your own language. I received the translations of some of my poems, and I thank you with all my heart, for it is a great honor for me. I believe that they are very good, since you did them. Urrutia read them to me and gave me a very favorable opinion of them.]

In fact, Guillén made repeated reference to his "precario inglés" (precarious English) and to the fact that he had to rely on friends, mainly Urrutia and

Fernández de Castro, to translate what Hughes sent him.[90] "I hope," he wrote to Hughes in September 1930, "que tan pronto aparezca tu novela me enviaras un ejemplar. En ella voy a practicar bastante inglés" (that as soon as your novel [*Not Without Laughter*] appears you will send me a copy so I can practice enough English).[91] Guillen, however, seems to have practiced his English about as much as Hughes did his *criollo*.

It remains unclear exactly how much English Guillén did understand and speak at this or any later point. Fernández de Castro, for one, claimed in 1930 that Guillén is "alleging that he is not able to understand English," and there is a curious bilingual postscript in Guillén's hand to one of Urrutia's letters to Hughes: "I will write you cuando tenga time. Recibí your letter que me alegro mucho....[92] This is the closest Guillén ever comes to writing a letter in English. Even as late as early 1949, when he thanks Hughes for having sent copies of *Cuba Libre*, Guillén regrets that he still does not know enough English to judge the quality of the translations:

> Es una edición espléndida: un alarde de primor tipográfico, que me llena de alegría y orgullo. Les pongo aquí un fuerte abrazo, con mi más viva gratitud. Pero lamento no conocer el suficiente inglés para juzgar las traducciones: pero siendo ustedes los responsables, estoy seguro de que ellas han seriados los originales míos. Además, muchos amigos me dicen que son muy buenas.[93]

> [This is a splendid edition: the typography is just exquisite, which fills me with joy and pride. I give you both a big hug, with my deepest gratitude. But I regret that I don't know enough English to judge the translations: but since I know that you both are responsible for them, I rest assured that they follow my originals closely. Also, many friends tell me that they are really fine.]

Was Guillén just being politely evasive? Was he possibly hiding his disappointment at *Cuba Libre's* failure to improve his economic situation behind his "precario inglés"? We will never know. What we do know, however, is that, unlike Jacques Roumain, whose novel Hughes also cotranslated, Guillén never wrote a poem in tribute of his friend.[94] Exactly why Guillén dedicated "Sabás" to Hughes remains an open question, at least to me.

TRANSLATING CUBAN BASEBALL

In contrast to Hughes, Carruthers preferred assimilating the source language of Guillén's *poemas-son* as much as possible into the conceptual and linguistic structures of USAmerican Negro dialect. While the results are often disappointing, there is one noteworthy instance in which Carruthers's translation achieves perhaps inadvertent transculturation. This instance is his version of Guillén's poem "Tú no sabe inglé," in which Carruthers succeeds in expanding and deepening his own language though the foreign medium, registering the difference of Afro-Cuban culture in the English translation. The reason for this may well be that Cuban-USA cultural relations are already very much at the core of this short poem which, like the "Ayé me dijeron negro," paints a deft dialogic portrait of two Cuban men. Once again, the scene is specific to a place and time: not just Cuba but a black neighborhood in 1920s Havana.

> Con tanto inglé que tú sabía,
> Bito Manué,
> con tanto inglé, no sabe ahora
> desí ye.
>
> La mericana te buca,
> y tú le tiene que huí:
> tu inglé era de etrái guan,
> de etrái guan y guan tu tri.
>
> Bito Manué, tú no sabe inglé,
> tú no sabe inglé,
> tú no sabe inglé.
>
> No te namore má nunca,
> Bito Manué,
> si no sabe inglé,
> si no sabe inglé.[95]

[With all that English you used to know, / Bito Manué, / With all that English, now you can't even / Say yes. // The American comes looking for you / And you just flee: / Your English was just strike one! / Strike one and one, two, three. // Bito Manué, you don't know any English, / You don't know any English. / You don't know any English! // Don't fall in love anymore, / Bito Manué, / if you don't know any English, / if you don't know any English.]

Like all of Guillén's "Motivos," this poem is a dramatic monologue written in a dialect or vernacular—*criollo*—that immediately identifies the speaker as an Afro-Cuban with little formal education. If we regard vernaculars as specific cultural inflections rather than simply substandard uses of a standardized language—in this case, Spanish—then translation is at issue in this poem in more ways than one, and not only because the poem thematizes the knowledge, or lack thereof, of another language: English. Jean-Jacques Lecercle notes that "when we speak of 'English'"—and, one might add, any other major language—"we speak of a multiplicity of dialects, registers, and styles, of the sedimentation of past conjunctures, of the inscription of social antagonisms as discursive antagonisms, of the coexistence and contradiction of various collective arrangements of utterance, of the interpellation of subjects within apparatuses embodied in linguistic practices (schools, the media)."[96] It follows, then, that translation occurs in both *inter*lingual and *intra*lingual settings, in which different discourses or linguistic registers function much as "natural" languages do.[97] Translation not only moves *across* the linguistic borders associated with nations but also crosses discursive boundaries located *inside* those very borders. One might term the latter movements *interdiscursive.*

Like translations that dwell at the intersections of so-called major languages, European and otherwise, their interdiscursive counterparts are cross-cultural in that they move across the boundaries defined by racial, sexual, and class differences within the space of a single nation-state supposedly founded on a shared language. What marks these cultural differences linguistically are vernaculars represented as dialects and sociolects, which we find in abundance throughout Hughes's work. In Hughes's vernacular poetry, for instance, the perplexities *and* possibilities of translation within what is commonly perceived as a single language alert us to the cultural multiplicities into which that language breaks down upon closer scrutiny. Consider, for example, the effect of spontaneity, for which many have praised Hughes's early verse, and his desire to erase the line between a written literary language and the spoken common (or vulgar) tongue. Such spontaneity is not a marker of cultural or racial authenticity, of speech or singing brought effortlessly to the written page. Unlike most of his contemporary reviewers, Hughes was well aware of this.[98] Rather, such seeming artlessness is a *literary* effect achieved through translations that move within the same language but between cultural layers or fields whose differences are defined by race, sexuality, and economics. These cultures are variously identified with either written or oral expressions, and they may share neither inflections nor meanings. Yet literary and other situations in which cultural differences do not align neatly with linguistic differences are frequently misrecognized as not in need of translation. Here, it is the existence not just of a dominant language but of a dominant *discourse*—a set of assumptions about how language affects cultural identity—that masks cultural differences by recoding them as linguistic and cultural similarities. As a result, interdiscursive situations often *appear* monolingual, despite the fact that translation occurs whenever and wherever meanings and usages are not culturally shared but are simply *assumed* to be shared.

The word "vernacular" describes more than relations between different language situations. Its historically accrued meanings suggest the imbrications of linguistic with sociocultural relations.[99] Vernacular, especially when transferred from an oral to a literary setting, already implies translation to the extent that a vernacular is "not a language as such, but a *relation* between one language situation and another."[100] Derived from the Latin *vernacularis* (of a slave), the term describes a local language or style "often associated (negatively or positively) with the vulgar, the provincial, the rustic, the rudimentary, the natural, or the carnal, and sometimes more specifically with a social underclass, or with women."[101] It is the dynamic layering of social relations—be they inflected by race, gender, sexuality, or economics— that makes vernacular writing so tricky to render in another language. In literature, vernaculars typically function as ethnographic intertexts. As presumably realist representations of others' spoken (or sung) words, they represent a "condition of *vernacularity*" that "a national language aspires to transcend, whether by standardizing and codifying its phonology, morphology, and spelling or by generating a literature worthy to stand comparison with the classics."[102] While "Tú no sabe inglé" itself is not ethnography, ethnographic discourse is what mediates the relation between this poem and its readers and inserts itself between reader and speaker. The poem itself reflects on this mediation. While the poem's direct interlocutor, the silent Bito Manué, is presumably *like* the speaker, the implied reader is situated at a significant distance from both. Consistent with the conventions of ethnography, this distance identifies both speaker and Bito Manué as linguistically, though not necessarily culturally, other in relation to the reader. This distinction between language and culture is vital to the poem.

Let us first consider what happens on the surface of this poem. The speaker himself probably knows as little or even less English than the object of his mockery, whose linguistic and romantic forays he playfully mocks. *Sabía*, a past tense of *saber*, to know, refers more to a boastful claim on Bito Manué's part than to something he actually knew and has somehow forgotten. This is consistent with the fact that his lack of English did not prevent him from *enamorarse* with the *mericana*, that is, falling for an American girl or woman who, it is safe to assume, does not speak a word of Spanish, let alone Cuban. Apparently, the specialized idiom of USAmerican baseball, with which Bito Manué apparently *is* familiar—"strike one, and one, two, three"—does not lend itself to romance. We can barely even recognize his Cubanized English in the poem: "etrái guan, de extrái guan y guan tu tri." In fact, there is no English at all in this poem. What is identified as "inglé" is already broken or transculturated—in short, it is Cubanized.[103] In a gesture that might also be read as refusal or even resistance to foreign incursions, Bito Manué takes flight, from the nightclub where he probably met the attractive female visitor from the USA, back to his neighborhood on the fringes of Havana, the *hampa afrocubana*, or Afro-Cuban underworld.[104]

The verb Guillén's speaker employs here, *huí* (a shortened version of *huir*, to flee or escape), derails the poem's narrative. It makes relatively little sense that this Cuban Don Juan would flee when the only issue is that he does not know how to say yes to the woman's advances. Why would he suddenly be afraid? What produces a break in the logic of the poem's romantic narrative is the presence of a different mediating discourse: ethnography gives way to political history, meaning both slavery and more contemporary USA-Cuban affairs. The verb *huir* supplies a metaphoric connection to Cuban slavery by invoking the heroic figure of the runaway slave, or *cimarrón*. Guillén uses the same verb elsewhere, notably in "El abuelo" ("The Grandfather"), a translation of which is also included in *Cuba Libre* (*CL*, 83). This allusion in turn prepares the ground for a heavy-handed allegory about USA-Cuban relations, in which Bito Manué represents Afro-Cuba and the "mericana" a larger-than-life Anglo mistress who recalls Lady Liberty. Both figures are allegorically overdetermined so that the poem can now also, and perhaps mainly, provide an ironic commentary on how the USA "liberated" Cuba in 1898. At the same time, it can aestheticize Cuba's resistance to a history of political and cultural encroachments by its northern neighbor. Guillén's poetic adaptation of the Cuban *son* is an important part of this resistance, which introduces yet another intertext, this one specifically cultural. The Cuban *son* is the quintessential (musical) form of *transculturación*, the *son*'s cultural parentage being African, European, and Arawak/Taíno. In "Tu no sabe inglé," this marker of transculturation facilitates the poem's passage from cultural nationalism (Afro-Cuban) to political nationalism (Cuba as *mulato* nation). Guillén himself describes his *poemas-son* as *poemas mulatos,* mulatto poems.

While the history of USA-Cuban relations, including of course slavery, is no doubt significant to "Tú no sabe inglé," Guillén makes readers jump to the allegorical level too quickly, short-circuiting more complicated readings of the interpersonal, interlingual, and intercultural relations in this poem. Most notably, an allegorical reading does not include the speaker, whom we can only conflate with Bito Manué or with Guillén himself in a symbolically simplified scenario. Yet it is the speaker whose language mediates both Bito Manué's relationship with the *mericana* and the reader's perception of that relationship. This speaker also offers up what might be understood as a moral to the story, which, though different from the one in "Ayé me dijeron negro," still has to do with racial mixing and its consequences. Specifically, he issues a warning about likely intercultural misapprehensions by appealing to language differences: if you don't know any English, don't fall in love (anymore). While the conditional "if" allows for the possibility that linguistic differences might be bridged, intercultural and especially interracial differences are quite a different matter. Though no doubt appropriate, the speaker's advice is also quite limited: Bito Manué's problem is not that he does not know enough English but that his linguistic competence, his Cubanized baseball English, does not confer any broader cultural knowledge about the divergent meanings of race in other parts of the Americas.

In the poem's English version, the speaker's warning is much stronger, and it focuses less on linguistic differences. This in part results from the fact that *any* translation of this poem into English, *any* English idiom, has to change the source poem's premises fundamentally. That is, in order for the poem to work as a dramatic monologue in English, it requires a speaker who *knows* English and who also knows what Bito Manué does not know, which is more than just English. Through the (inevitable) use of English and the necessary knowledge of a different cultural and, in this case, historical context, the translator has no choice but to force the original poem into a "structural lie."[105] Here is "Don't Know No English," which I regard as Carruthers's most successful translation of a Guillén poem, in part because he resists pushing *criollo* into some of the more egregious orthographic contortions of Negro dialect.

> All dat English you used to know,
> Li'l Manuel,
> All dat English, now can't even
> Say: *Yes.*
>
> 'Merican gal comes lookin' fo' you
> An' you jes' runs away.
> Yo' English is jes' *strike one!*
> *Strike one* and *one-two-three.*
>
> Li'l Manuel, you don't know no English
> You jes don't know!
> You jes' don't know!
>
> Don't fall in love no mo',
> Li'l Manuel,
> 'cause you don't know no English,
> Don't know no English.
>
> (CL, 3)

Like the Cuban text, this poem is a dramatic monologue. In contrast to Guillén's poem, however, Carruthers's translation is rhythmically quite clunky. Clearly, English-language meter and rhyme schemes are not a good fit for the *son.* The resulting clumsiness is a first indication of a linguistic context in conflict with the source poem's Cuba. Another sign of conflict is the notable difference between what are now two USAmerican idioms, one standard (the baseball lingo in italics),[106] the other not. In the translation, this difference creates a shift from intercultural to *intra*cultural concerns. Both forms of English are set off against what little Spanish remains in Bito Manué's modified name: Li'l Manuel, although Bito is actually short for Victor. The poem plays on these differences, creating a dense web of social and cultural relationships inside and beyond the text. Because both speaker and addressee are visible to us only through representations of their voices, as in "Ayé me dijeron negro," how they speak and are spoken about determines how we perceive their respective cultural positions and identities, in the translation no less than in Guillén's poem. How different cultural identities and sensibilities play off each other in the translation is, however, rather different from how they do in the source poem, which uses allegorical representations of Cubanness to set one national community against another rather than imagining a different sort of community altogether.

Carruthers's speaker, who chuckles at the foundering romance between Li'l Manuel and the "'merican gal" and chides Li'l Manuel for not having enough English to know what he has let himself in for, is unambiguously marked as lower-class African American, and the poem's setting has now moved to somewhere in the USAmerican South. The speaker's voice has all the familiar trappings of literary representations of the vernacular I have called USAmerican Negro dialect, but it is less emphatic and insistent than in "Ayé me dijeron negro" and other Carruthers translations in a similar vein. The hushed interlocutor is no doubt Hispanic, but there is nothing to identify Li'l Manuel as Cuban, except perhaps his knowledge of baseball (although he could easily be Dominican, too). His name retains a hint of foreignness, but he is otherwise assimilated into the poem's vernacular environment—except, of course, for what little English Li'l Manuel does speak, which is now represented in standard orthography. The effect is an almost comical correctness that masks, rather than reveals, Li'l Manuel's cultural identity. This strategic withholding of identity invites readers to imagine the character(s) in different ways.

One way to picture the Li'l Manuel in Carruthers's translation is as a young Cuban baseball player in the USA during the 1940s, a *mulato* or *negro* who is being pursued by and finds himself attracted to a white American "gal." It is easy to imagine Li'l Manuel along the lines of the pitcher Ramón Bragaña, aka El Profesor, whom Roberto González Echevarría describes as "a six-foot, bronze colored mulatto, who weighed 195 pounds in his prime." Or perhaps he was more like the darker-complexioned Orestes Miñoso, who was signed by the Cleveland Indians in 1947 (he was twenty-four at the time) and was "the best known of the black Cuban players whose careers began in the early to middle forties."[107] They likely faced similar dangerous temptations in a country where the last antimiscegenation state law was not repealed until 1967.[108]

But Cubans' cultural sensibilities were different on that count. Although they were certainly color conscious when it came to social contact, Cubans were far less phobic about racial mixing—in literature and in life. Although realities in Cuba hardly conformed to the image of the racial paradise that it had acquired among black USAmericans during the nineteenth century, race relations in Cuba did differ from those in the USA: "There was no random racist terror to speak of, and although the elite in Cuba remained separate and white, race-based segregation among the lower classes was rare. Interracial dating, while not encouraged by whites, did happen, and it was almost never the cause for murder. African American soldiers, baseball players, artists, and activists visited Cuba and maintained that blacks were better off there."[109] While historical realities do not entirely square with such perceptions, in the poem, Li'l Manuel is cautioned not to assume that the "'merican gal" shares his cultural sensibilities.[110] It is not by coincidence that Guillén's poem invokes baseball. As an "expression of Cuban nationality," both "a means to nationhood and a metaphor for action," Cuban baseball ties directly into Guillén's cultural nationalism. In many respects, baseball brought Cuban and USAmericans, especially African Americans, closer.[111] "By the time of Jackie Robinson's 'integration' of baseball in 1947, hundreds of rural and working-class players and tens of thousands of African-American and Cuban fans had come to know each other through baseball."[112] This was the first time that Cuban and other Caribbeans of color could play in the major leagues without passing for white.

Clearly, baseball is played according to the same rules in Cuba and the USA, and players from different countries and cultures shared the game's special idiom, all that English Li'l Manuel "used to know." There were also salient differences. While Cuban baseball had no color line, the USAmerican leagues were very much segregated, and darker-complexioned Afro-Caribbean players were relegated to the Negro leagues until 1947, when the previously all-white major league was opened up to black players. Yet in those days, according to one Ossie Bluege from the Washington Senators, "all Cuba ball players were called niggers"—even players who were (or looked) white. As an anonymous USAmerican ballplayer put it to Preston Gomez in 1944, "You may be Cuban, but you're a nigger sonuvabitch to me."[113] Effectively, then, "as young Cuban men—black, mixed race, and white—ventured into American baseball, they shared not only in the black community's pride but also in its struggle against the indignities of racism and segregation." They played in small, often very white towns off season, in Arkansas and other southern states, "where they slept on cramped buses, ate crackers and sardines, were often forbidden to use bath and toilet facilities, and might be threatened or attacked if they happened to beat the local white team."[114] The 2008 film *Sugar* recalls some of these settings, albeit in a more contemporary context and with reference to Dominican players whose experiences in the USA were similar to Cubans'. Filmed in two small towns in Iowa, the movie follows the short-lived career of Dominican Miguel "Sugar" Santos, played by Algenis Pérez Soto, himself an amateur baseball player. This character, who lands a job with a USAmerican minor league team after attending the baseball academy in the Dominican Republic, is a more modern incarnation of Li'l Manuel as Carruthers seems to have imagined him: handsome and dark-complexioned, unquestionably a *negro* and one who barely speaks English. Miguel is depicted as exotic to small-town Iowans, who are perfectly cordial and supportive of him as a ballplayer for the local team. The film also makes clear that his hosts, the pious Higginses, are opposed to any closer relations between Miguel and their daughter Anne (played by Ellary Porterfield), who is attracted to the young Dominican.[115]

That the color line in the pre-civil rights USAmerican South would have been very much on the mind of Ben Carruthers, a middle-class African American living in Washington, D.C., is beyond doubt. In "Don't Know No English," the situation the translation creates might initially be envisioned as a contest of sorts, not about who speaks or doesn't speak English or whose English is better but about who can or cannot have the "'merican gal" — really, the white girl — and why. The lack of an explicit reference to her whiteness is quite unusual for an African American speaker in this USAmerican context. Let us posit, then, as I think we must, that Manuel's English is good enough to explain his predicament to the speaker. What creates the intercultural bond that would make such an intimate conversation possible is a particular relational perception of racial differences. Even in her absence, the invocation of the "white" American woman makes both speaker and interlocutor "black" — meaning *not* American — in relation to her. The speaker's advice in this imaginary conversation, then, might go something like this: "If you think that you can go after white women in this country, think again. I'm a black USAmerican citizen who can't even so much as look at a white woman without risking my hide. You're a foreigner, or at least foreign enough, and even if you are light-skinned, you're still black here. You can play baseball in the USA, but you can't play *that* kind of ball here, no matter what language you speak."

The speaker's shift from "you don't know no English" to the emphatically repeated "You jes don't know!" is tellingly at variance with Guillén's poem. What Li'l Manuel could not have known is that the same dark-skinned ball players who could be part of the major leagues after 1947 might also be brutally murdered for even so much as whistling at a white woman. This is precisely what happened to Emmett Till in 1953 in Mississippi, one of the states with antimiscegenation statutes. Also worth mentioning is the case of the Martinsville Seven in Virginia in 1949, which is likely less remembered because the actual crime of sexual assault and rape was not in question. Each of the seven young men, six of them barely out of their teens, was sentenced to death. Despite growing protests and the fact that no white man had ever received the death penalty for rape, they were executed in 1951. The Supreme Court repeatedly refused to hear the case.[116] What seems to have been on Carruthers's mind in this translation is not *language* difference but the construction (indeed imposition) of a cultural identity through assumptions about race based on skin color, regardless of language. The change Carruthers makes in the poem's final stanza points to a logic quite different from Guillén's: "Don't fall in love no mo'...'*cause* you don't know no English," rather than "*if* you don't know no English," as Guillén has it. Language difference is a red herring, then; it makes, as it were, no difference to the existing social order. Color lines are as firmly drawn as ever, even at a time when certain institutions in the USA were being desegregated. What applied to major league baseball had not yet happened in other areas, such as education. In 1947, the Orval Faubuses of this world were quite active in many southern states, and the Supreme Court ruling in *Brown v. Board of Education* that declared segregated public schools unconstitutional was still seven years away.

I mentioned in my discussion of "Ayé me dijeron negro" that Guillén shapes his "Motivos" as the literary equivalent of the transculturated musical form of the Cuban *son*. This is relevant here because the *son* represents a community that is (linguistically?) distinct but whose origins, like those of the *son* itself, are a cultural and racial mixture of Spanish, Arawak/Taíno, and African elements. The blues has often been taken as the closest US-American counterpart to the *son*. In fact, as we have seen, Hughes pushes this comparison by giving the title "Cuban Blues" to the section that Carruthers's translation opens. Like "Last Night Someone Called Me Darky," "Don't Know No English" is far from being a blues poem, even though the latter poem does offer an ironic twist of the "my (wo)man left me" theme of many blues lyrics. Its mood, however, is comical rather than dejected. Nevertheless, Hughes used his editorial frame to appeal to the blues, likely as a way of containing the specter of interracial romance for a USAmerican readership. Unlike "Don't Know No English" and its companion pieces, traditional blues lyrics tended to steer clear of interracial topics.

Carruthers's translation eschews Guillén's static transnational allegory—Cuba vs. the USA—and its penchant for symbolic caricature. Instead, he represent humans beings in the process of figuring out how to live together by negotiating their cultural and racial differences. This scenario is quite reminiscent of the kinds of provisional communities Hughes himself creates in his autobiographies and many of his poems. In "Don't Know No English," we hear how the speaker and Li'l Manuel negotiate their differences to create common ground. In Guillén's poem, by contrast, common ground between speaker and addressee is assumed: they are familiars, possibly even kin. Most importantly for Guillén, they are both Cuban, part of an imperiled national community that has to be protected from outsiders. What makes Carruthers's translation so intriguing, and perhaps surprising for its time, is that here common ground does not yet exist; it has to be gained. We see in this poem how community results from the willingness of two relative strangers to take risks: they are not part of the same national, racial, or linguistic group, yet they choose to trust each other enough to seek advice and care enough to give it. In doing so, they create a transcultural and transnational space in which they can test out the limits of their differences and how best to live with them. The translation, more so than the source text, is an imaginative testing ground for knowledge about and for living together in peace and difference. It is hardly an overstatement to say that this kind of knowledge is crucial for human survival in the USA and elsewhere in the world, and now perhaps more than ever.

Human communities, even provisional ones, always seem to be founded on exclusions. There is one figure that both poems equally exclude: the female American, who is both a shared reference point and a shared source of anxiety. Whatever her specific racial and cultural attributes in each situation, intimacy with her is perceived as perilous and potentially fatal; at best, it is stereotypically unproductive. Her exclusion in both Guillén's and Carruthers's respective poems shows up the limitations of the gendered, racialized, and nationalistic communities that both texts either assume or construct. The woman is an object of desire in both poems. In "Tu no sabe inglé," she stands for another language, USAmerican English, knowledge of which would presumably make her (more) accessible to Bito Manué, or so he wrongly assumes. The solution to the amorous misadventure in Guillén's poem is for the speaker to redirect Bito Manué's desire. He points him away from the foreigner and toward a different sort of communion, and community, one that already exists or at least is posited: the Cuban nation. In Carruthers's translation, the woman stands for something that is desired by and inaccessible to all, including the reader. The respective reasons for that desire, however, and the simultaneous lack of access differ. What she represents is decidedly not English or any form of linguistic competence. The translation is, after all, written in English, different versions of it, and speaker, interlocutor, and reader all have access to English in some measure. To the extent that the "'merican gal" stands for a nation, America, romancing her would represent a desire for assimilation. Yet as the poem makes clear in no uncertain terms, Li'l Manuel's desire to assimilate into a setting that marks him as a racial, not just a linguistic, other is fraught with considerable peril. At least in the translation's historical context, the promise of a community called "'merican" is uncertain at best, for both the speaker and Li'l Manuel. Being "'merican" does not confer a national identity on any of these characters. The "'merican gal" is an object of desire whose specific attributes remain undefined. While the diminutive prevents her from representing Lady Liberty in any conventional manner, she still embodies a version of the American dream, much as Daisy Buchanan, another white "gal," does for Jay Gatsby. The truncation "'merican," which Carruthers chose to retain, unsettles a strictly binary view of racial categories by offering a glimpse of the Cuban source text. It is the continued interaction with that text that deforms and defamiliarizes "American" as a guarantor of a national identity in ways that Guillén's poem does not.

Intentionally or not, "Don't Know No English" breaks down the original poem's (trans)national allegory by making available to the reader additional knowledge about matters that the source poem simplifies. What the *mericana* represents in Guillén's poem (the USA) is not, in the translation, a culturally or even politically unified place but encompasses a multiplicity of languages and perspectives. Carruthers calls attention to this multiplicity by using black vernacular, through which the speaker signals that he both does and does not fully belong to that America. His perspective is one already located between at least two worlds that exist in the space of a nation, even before he comes into contact with Li'l Manuel's Cuba. In other words, the speaker's identity is effectively as multiple and as uncertain as Li'l Manuel's. Through this uncertainty, which is a function of the "minority" discourse of USAmerican black vernacular, the translation makes available in the figure of the nation a space in which the characters can enact, though not necessarily resolve, their perplexities.[117]

The same might be true in Guillén's poem, especially when we consider the formal dimensions of transculturation that the Cuban *son* and its literary equivalent represent. But Guillén's poem arrests the movement of the transculturative process. Transculturation stands for Cuba alone; it is not a process that extends to the USA. Because using English forces Carruthers and his readers into a structural lie, his translation puts the lie, as it were, to the original's (trans)national allegory. The fact that his translation opens up possibilities for interpretation that had not been thought of in Guillén's poem implicitly challenges the reader's desire for the original, which Goethe posits when he writes: "Übersetzer sind als geschäftige Kuppler anzusehen, die uns die halbverschleierte Schöne also höchst liebenswürdig anpreisen: sie erregen eine unwiderstehliche Neigung nach dem Original" (Translators must be regarded as busy matchmakers who offer us a beautiful semiveiled woman as the loveliest of them all; they create an irresistible desire for the original).[118] Goethe's metaphor of the veiled woman both feminizes and orientalizes the original-as-other. The metaphor returns critical discourse on translation to an ethnographic register that eschews precisely the possibility for developing transcultural perspectives. By taking for granted that readers have a quasi-erotic desire for an unreachable original, translation studies based on Goethe's precepts—most notably among them the Benjaminian strain—curtail an important potential that translations hold: the potential for encouraging readings that imagine a multitude of possible relations between selves and others and between one text and another. In "Don't Know No English," Carruthers realizes this potential. Compared with the Cuban poem, Carruthers's poem has no one place but moves between places, not just between languages. The translation sets the Cuban poem in motion variedly and in doing so opens up its intra- and interlinguistic play to other hemispheric contexts, such as the USA and the Caribbean.[119] This does not mean that the context of late 1920s Cuba is suddenly irrelevant, just that it is not the only possible and plausible context for the English translations. In this play of possibilities, the Cuban poem is but one text. It is not the privileged original, just the first version whose referentiality the translation changes and extends. To be sure, Carruthers's translation brings out an element already latent in Guillén's poem. But this aspect is overshadowed by Carruthers's insistence on creating what he perceives as a distinctly Cuban poetic sound from the voices of a marginalized group. Critical readers have too often shared his insistence on the poem's Cubanness.

THE POLITICS OF TRANSLATION

My discussion implies that Carruthers's "Don't Know No English" is more successful than his translation of "Ayé me dijeron negro" in opening up interpretive possibilities not available in the Cuban poem. To make such a value judgment is useful, however, only to the extent that it draws attention to the gap that opens up between aesthetic and ethical criteria in attempts at evaluating translations. On the one hand, Carruthers's "Last Night Someone Called Me Darky" may be a more satisfying poem in formal terms. On the other hand, it may also be offensive to certain readers' political sensibilities. Hughes's draft, while more appealing to me because it does not erase the source poem, employing subtly experimental "textual features that frustrate immediate intelligibility, empathic response, interpretive mastery," might be judged as weaker when it comes to conventional poetic values such as meter, rhyme, and structural symmetry.[120] My reading, however, also runs the risk of imposing on the text of the translation a narrative of modernist resistance to literary convention that it, unlike some of Hughes's own poems, cannot finally sustain. Depending, then, on which set of criteria I favor, I might deem one or the other poem either good or ethical but, oddly, not both at the same time.

In a gesture that has considerable theoretical appeal, Lawrence Venuti has tried to bring together both sets of values by proposing good translation to mean ethical translation — the kind of translation, in other words, that "manifests in its own language the foreignness of the foreign text. This manifestation can occur through the selection of a text whose form and theme deviate from domestic literary canons. The most decisive occurrence, however, depends on introducing variations that alienate the domestic language and, since they are domestic, reveal the translation to be in fact a translation, distinct from the text it replaces."[121] What underlies the idea of "alienating the domestic language" is hardly new. In fact, Venuti's call for "registering the foreignness of foreign cultures in translation" echoes Benjamin, who quotes Goethe to the effect that the translator "muss seine Sprache durch die Fremde erweitern und vertiefen" (must expand and deepen his own language through the foreign medium).[122] If one reads Benjamin's "The Task of the Translator" through the lens of postcolonial theory, which would bring out the dual contexts of Goethe's intellectually expansive orientalism and Oswald Spengler's theories of the West's decay and of global cultural cycles, it is not difficult to see how ethics might enter the study of translation, even if it does not for Benjamin himself.[123] It is also easy to understand why ethics would readily attach itself to discussions of USA-Caribbean-Hispanic

American relations, cultural and otherwise. Yet it nevertheless strikes me as incautious to embrace uncritically the values that ethics represent in such discussions, which is what Venuti does when he formulates a moral imperative akin to a professional code of conduct for translators. He insists that translation should register foreignness in ethical ways so as to correct the effects of international colonial and neocolonial domination. The danger here is that the category of ethics, unless carefully calibrated to specific historical settings, may too easily become just one more imposition of contemporary identity politics on the work of earlier translators.[124] This unidirectional imperative also has the serious disadvantage of not being applicable to the practice of translators who work in languages other than English. Venuti largely ignores this issue, despite the fact that the largest number of literary translations are into languages other than English.[125]

It is, then, not simply evasive to propose that both Carruthers and Hughes were conservative translators with different ideological agendas that, at least in part, influenced the decisions they made in their respective translations. Carruthers's use of a nonstandard American vernacular (Negro dialect) only appears to violate the literary values of his time, which were based on the elitist exclusion of dialect writing from the realm of the literary. It actually reinforces those very values. The translations that result conform to ethnopoetic standards, through which external cultural differences, in this case between Cuba and the USA, are rendered as internal divergences between black and white USAmericans. Such divergences fall under the ideological governance of what we now know as multiculturalism. In a so-called multiculturalist atmosphere ethnopoetry can, as Podestá demonstrates, exist quite comfortably alongside modernist poetry as long as each remains in its own separate sphere. Carruthers's Negro dialect translations of Guillén's verse do register cultural diversity only along racial lines. By conflating cultural differences at the margins—that is, between USAmerican Negroes and Cuban *negros* or *mulatos*—Carruthers's translations tend to guarantee the margins' cultural and political separateness from imagined centers. This at least holds true in "Last Night Someone Called Me Darky." As I have shown, it is rather a different story in "Don't Know No English."

While Hughes escaped the trap of ethnopoetry by refusing Negro dialect, he fell right into another one by using what looks like a more standardized vernacular, making his translation seem transparent and univocal. We may say that whenever he employs the vernacular in his own poems and in these translations, Hughes translates a displaced and marginalized "native" language—the vernacular mother tongue—back into the standardized lect of what is, for all intents and purposes, a dominant "foreign" language: English. As a result, the dominant version of English is made to "function in another register."[126] Hughes's translations tend to give even less of an impression of discursive heterogeneity than Carruthers's. Still, as I have argued, appearances are deceptive in both cases. Whatever foreignizing techniques Hughes adopts in his draft are smuggled in under the cover of prevailing linguistic transparency. It is true that Hughes gestures in the direction of cross-culturation but never to the point of open dissidence with multiculturalist, or cultural pluralist, doctrine.[127]

What commends Hughes's translations is that they, unlike most of Carruthers's, cannot reasonably exist without Guillén's original. They are, in the end, not successful poems in their own right, certainly not by the standards of a revered translator such as Dudley Fitts, who held that "the translation of a poem should be a poem, viable as a poem and, as a poem, weighable."[128] Ironically, Fitts was enough of a cultural elitist not to have approved of Carruthers's translations precisely because of Carruthers's use of a substandard idiom. Hughes's own draft of "Last Night" could in no way be confused with, or take the place of, the Guillén poem, and it would have worked well in a bilingual edition. The same holds true for Carruthers's "Don't Know No English," which Hughes approved without any changes. As testimony to the ultimate untranslatability of Guillén's *poemas-son* into any register of USAmerican English, both of these poems are revealing guides to the intricacies of the process of translation in a neo-colonial setting.

Even if Hughes's subject matter in *Cuba Libre* was controversial for his time, his approach to translating poetry was in step with the political conservatism of midcentury Anglo-American literary culture. As we have seen from his decision not to use his own version of Guillén's "Ayé me dijeron negro," Hughes, in the mid- to late 1940s, became increasingly less willing to test linguistic and political limits in his published writings, including his translations. This reluctance is even more pronounced in other translations of his that he did include in *Cuba Libre*. Earlier versions of four poems from other sections of the book had been published in Fitts's 1942 *Anthology of Contemporary Latin-American Poetry/Antología de la poesía americana contemporánea,* and Hughes revised each substantially for inclusion either in *The Poetry of the Negro* or *Cuba Libre* and in some cases both.[129] These four poems are "Fusilamiento" ("Execution"), "Soldado muerto" ("Dead Soldier"), "Velorio de Papá Montero" ("Wake for Papa Montero"), and "Cantaliso en un bar," a poem that Hughes first titled "Cantaliso in a Bar" and then modified to "Song in a Havana Bar."[130] The earlier texts show some of the same kinds of linguistic disturbances that we encounter in Hughes's unpublished drafts. The later ones, by contrast, exhibit a distinct preference for the fluency of colloquialisms and less jarring metaphors. Compare, for instance, the 1942 and 1948 versions of the following stanza from Hughes's "Wake for Papa Montero":

> But brighter than the candles
> is the red shirt

> that lighted your songs,
> *the dark salt of your music,*
> your glossy straight hair.[131]

> But the red shirt
> that once lit up your songs
> *and the brownskin laughter of your music*
> *and your gleaming straightened hair,*
> make more light for you now
> than any candles.
>
> (CL, 119).

> ¡Y aún te alumbran, más que velas,
> la camisa colorada
> que iluminó sus canciones,
> *la prieta sal de tus sones*
> *y tu melena planchada!*[132]

While the discrepancies between the two English stanzas are hardly as pronounced as the differences between Carruthers's and Hughes's respective translations of "Ayé me dijeron Negro," Hughes's revisions are still telling. Here it is the second version that seems more literal. This is in part because Hughes tones down and streamlines his diction, as he does throughout that version of the poem, turning, for instance, "tenement" into "flat" and "brawl" into "fight." In the excerpts above, I have italicized the two lines that seem to have given Hughes the most trouble. He revised them several times, changing "your glossy straight hair" first to "your black, gleaming hair" and then to "your gleaming straightened hair."[133] Similarly, "the dark salt of your music" first turned into "the dark flavor of your music" and subsequently became "the brownskin laughter of your music." "The dark salt of your music" is far more effective in conveying the presence of another language than the phrase on which Hughes settled, which takes recourse to the cliché of the "happy negro" instead of offering a more daring metaphor with a less obvious appeal to familiar racialized diction. For purposes of contrast, I offer Lloyd Mallan's Negro dialect version of the beginning of the same poem.

> An' today, Papa Montero,
> Dat ol' moon dawned right back my house
> An' slah de ground eif her dagger-edge
> An' quiver awhile an' jist stick there.
> Some black kids come along an' pick it up;
> Dey shine it till it bright, an' now
> Ah brings it t'lay it like a pillow
> Under you sorry head tonight!

Mallan adds a footnote that encapsulates his approach to translating these poems without really explaining anything: "The translator to maintain the true Afro-Cuban feeling in English felt it necessary to translate the poem into dialect in spite of its having been written in pure Spanish."[134]

Hughes's own translations are also excellent examples of how a translator's desire for greater linguistic transparency may extend to structural considerations. The fluid syntax in Hughes's final version, evened out with the help of parataxis ("and...and"), calls much less attention to itself than it does in the first version. There the grammatical relation between the last two lines, and between them and the rest of the stanza, is ambiguous. The reason for this is that Hughes chose not to include the *y* (and) that identifies the verb *alumbran* (they illuminate) as the antecedent of all three lines, not just of one. Hughes's second version produces precisely the "illusory effect of transparency" that, according to Venuti, "the popular aesthetic of translation" requires: "this means adhering to the current standard dialect while avoiding any dialect, register, or style that calls attention to words as words and therefore preempts the reader's identification."[135] We can see similar principles of absorption at work when we compare "Cantaliso in a Bar," again from Fitts's anthology, to "Song in an [*sic*] Havana Bar" from *Cuba Libre*. The alternative closing stanzas serve as my final example of how Hughes's values as a poet-translator diverged from his interests and politics as literary editor.

> I'll give them my hand,
> and I'll sing with them,
> because the song they know
> is the same that I know.[136]
>
> I can shake hands
> with poor folks
> and sing *with* them swell—
> for the same song they know,
> I know as well!

(CL, 38)

> A ellos les daré la mano,
> y con ellos cantaré,
> porque el canto que ellos saben
> es el mismo que yo sé.[137]

More than anything else in these two examples, the jarring adverb "swell" asserts Hughes's different priorities as editor in *The Poetry of the Negro* anthology and *Cuba Libre*. "Swell" can be read as a Lecerclean "remainder" that announces, rather than conceals, an imposing overlay of a USAmerican colloquial idiom.[138] By being a minor variable of the dominant dialect, the word testifies to the existence of heterogeneity within that linguistic setting. To most readers in the USA at that time, "swell" would not have registered as a minor but as a dominant mode, much like the noun "gal" in Carruthers's "Don't Know No English." Neither word belongs strictly to an African American vernacular, which works to create uncertainty in Carruthers's case. In Hughes's translation, however, which is more in keeping with his editorial commitment to assimilating Guillén's work to the cultural conventions of USAmerican English, "swell" sounds hackneyed. In Hughes's systematic revisions of already published poems, we can see even more clearly than in the differences between his unpublished drafts and Carruthers's versions how distinct political priorities assert themselves and begin to take precedence over other concerns. The conflict in these versions is not between different personal aesthetics, which is one way to read the divergences between Hughes's and Carruthers's translations. Instead, the clash, to use Bourdieu's language, is between the "field of cultural production" and a larger "field of power." In the field of cultural production, Hughes and Carruthers occupied notably different positions. Hughes himself even occupied contradictory positions *at the same time.* The field of power exerted steady but uneven pressure on these cultural producers to participate in the construction of a national political consensus, especially with respect to race.

The shifting alignments of these fields become even more evident when one compares translations by the same author but from different points in time. It is not that Hughes's approach to translation changed radically, certainly not within a few years. But it, like his politics, became increasingly more cautious, to the point of affecting his choice of subjects. Hughes's decision, in 1956, to translate "cradle songs" and other politically innocuous poems by the Chilean Nobel Prize winner Gabriela Mistral for Indiana University Press is an apt example of his growing political expediency.[139] And he chose the poems for the Mistral volume very carefully. Not a single one even implicitly addressed racial or any other politically controversial topics. Nor did his brief introduction.

It also was more important to Hughes in the late 1940s than it had been earlier that his translations not challenge the ways and the terms in which African American audiences in the USA tended to think about race in relation to national culture. In a political climate of increasing anti-Communist retrenchment, things foreign were all too readily equated with things un-American. That Hughes, wearing his editorial hat, settled for Carruthers's Negro dialect versions of some of Guillén's "Motivos" shows a notable preference for linguistic and literary conventions that favored a maximum overlap between race and culture in the construction of "literary blackness." Such overlap was also more compatible with the linguistic and referential transparency that literary realism required even from poetry. Hughes's concern was, I suspect, with not worrying the racial divisions that dominant cultural institutions such as publishing houses and universities upheld rather rigidly for middlebrow literary consumers, such as the black bourgeoisie, and more elite readerships such as the black intelligentsia. It was one thing to show continuity among African American cultures across the Americas by highlighting literature's function as a vehicle for authentic folk resources. It was quite another to associate black literature with political *and* formal innovation and as result with dissidence.

In inviting readers, notably African American audiences, to approach Guillén's "Motivos" primarily as ethnopoetry, Hughes implicitly adopted the high-modernist attitude toward poetry written in nonstandard vernacular as mere ethnography.[140] Even if suppressing much of Guillén's distinctive Afro-Cubanness was probably less of a conscious choice on Hughes's (and on Carruthers's) part and more of a reflexive alliance with Cold War cultural politics, the Negro dialect translations insistently cover cultural specificity with a veneer of worn ethnic formulas. These formulas are little different in their effect from the tropicalizing shacks, palm trees, and sugarcane stalks in the accompanying line drawings by Gar Gilbert. There are eight drawings in all in *Cuba Libre*, one at the beginning of each section (see figure 7).[141] Almost inevitably, this resolute foregrounding of ethnic effects all but erased the avant-garde qualities of Guillén's *poemas-son*. For instance, in its orthographic stylization, his Cuban *criollo* is at least as akin to César Vallejo's modernist inventions in *Trilce* (1922) as it is to the onomatopoeic Africanism, or *jitanjáfora*, other Antillean poets favored at the time.[142] But avant-gardes, as Bourdieu notes, have a short half-life. It would have been quite impossible to convince literary critics that an African American poet availing himself of nonstandard vernacular forms was offering anything radical or new in 1948, even though Ezra Pound won the Bollingen Prize for his *Pisan Cantos* that same year. What poets such as Sterling Brown and Guillén himself had done with nonstandard vernaculars in the early 1930s did not excite much interest nearly two decades later, certainly not among academic readers. Even Guillén was no longer writing *poemas-son* then.

In *Cuba Libre,* literary and visual iconographies work together to forge a sense of shared political purpose in an emblematic synecdoche of liberatory struggle: a pair of rope-bound hands raised in a gesture of (impotent?) defiance is featured at the very center of the title page (see figure 8). Miniatures of the same image trace diagonal columns across the volume's chocolate-brown cloth covers. Much as the translations in *Cuba Libre* employ American Negro dialect in an attempt to make Cuba part of a racialized cultural geography, the visual image of struggle seeks to synchronize two very different political environments by erasing their discordant histories. What the volume's packaging accentuates is that Hughes in fact mistimed *Cuba Libre*. For one thing, Guillén's poems, especially the *poemas-son,* would likely have had a very different impact in the USA even fifteen years earlier,

Don't Know No English

All dat English you used to know,
Li'l Manuel,
all dat English, now can't even
say: *Yes*.

'Merican gal comes lookin' fo' you
an' you jes' runs away.
Yo' English is jes' *strike one!*
strike one and *one-two-three*.

Li'l Manuel, you don't know no English
you jes don't know!
You jes' don't know!

Don't fall in love no mo',
Li'l Manuel,
'cause you don't know no English,
don't know no English.

Figure 7. Page from *Cuba Libre*, 1948. From the author's collection.

Cuba Libre

Poems by Nicolás Guillén

Translated from the Spanish by
Langston Hughes *and* Ben Frederic Carruthers
Illustrated by Gar Gilbert

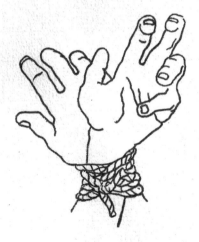

Anderson & Ritchie : The Ward Ritchie Press
Los Angeles, California : 1948

Figure 8. Title page of *Cuba Libre*, 1948. From the author's collection.

in the immediate wake of the blues poems by Sterling Brown and Hughes himself. For another, Guillén's membership in the Communist Party might have been a selling point rather than an embarrassment in the 1930s, when European and USAmerican intellectuals, in step with prominent modernist artists, were still looking to Soviet Russia, as well as to Africa and the Hispanic Americas, as energizing repositories of cultural and political values. *Cuba Libre* came too late to ride this wave. And it came too early to benefit from the renewed interest in the southern Americas after the USAmerican military response to the Cuban revolution put the lie to the rhetoric of good neighbors with common political causes.

THE ECONOMICS OF TRANSLATION

All things considered, *Cuba Libre* probably did better than expected, though compared with the sales of Hughes's own poetry, its success was unremarkable. And even the sales of Hughes's books were relatively unremarkable when compared with those of Knopf's other authors, including Willa Cather and Kahlil Gibran.[143] By May 15, 1950, *Cuba Libre* had sold a mere 273 copies, and Anderson wrote Hughes in early 1960 that she still had copies on hand.[144] The sales figures for some of Hughes's own books (by 1938) are *The Weary Blues*, 4,356 copies; *The Ways of White Folks*, 2,483 copies, and *Not Without Laughter*, 6,113 copies.[145]

Cuba Libre did, however, win a prestigious award, though not a literary one, and the prize did not seem to affect sales much. Encouraged by Hughes's repeated compliments—"CUBA LIBRE is one of the most beautiful books I have ever seen and I am delighted with it"[146]—Anderson entered the book in the American Institute of Graphic Arts contest. She reported proudly to Hughes on January 25, 1949, that *Cuba Libre* had been selected as one of the institute's fifty Books of the Year, which would be exhibited in several cities, starting with New York "sometime in February at the A.I.G.A. headquarters 115 W 40th."[147] Barely a week later, Hughes sent Guillén copies of *Cuba Libre* and his own anthology and told him about the prize. He also asked Guillén to write a letter to Mrs. Anderson, "telling her how much you like the book."[148] Meanwhile, Hughes wrote to Anderson, who was understandably anxious to hear Guillén's response, that he had known Guillén "for about fifteen years and [had] not received more than a dozen lines from him in all of that time."[149] While Hughes was trying to console Anderson in advance should she not hear from Guillén, both statements are odd: at that point, Hughes had known Guillén for close to two decades, during which time Guillén had written him regularly.

When he did write, Guillén frequently complained to Hughes that, because of the worsening economic situation, "en Cuba nadie compra libros de poemas...ni ninguna otra clase" (nobody in Cuba buys books of poems...nor any other books, for that matter).[150] Having one's writings translated into English and published in the USA was an attractive source of revenue for Hispanic American writers even if, as Hughes knew from his dealings with Editorial Lautaro in Argentina, financial transactions between the USA and many Hispanic American countries were often difficult and perplexing.[151] Cuba was an exception, at least until 1960, and so Guillén did not have any trouble receiving a wire transfer for his share of the royalties for *Cuba Libre* in 1951. It amounted to $64.50.[152] By comparison, Hughes's annual royalties with Knopf on December 31, 1936, totaled $126.28, which did not even cover the cost of the books he had ordered from the press that year. In 1949 the amount had risen to a whopping $970.73![153] As Caroline Anderson emphasized repeatedly in those of her letters to Hughes that concern royalty arrangements for *Cuba Libre,* "no one ever gets rich on poetry!"[154] On one occasion, when there was some confusion about the initial agreement with Guillén, which stated that he was to receive 50 percent of the royalties after the cost of the book had been covered, Hughes explained to her that

> [t]he reason for the Cuban agreement being that way is in Latin America (with the possible exception of Rio and Buenos Aires) writers usually have to pay for the printing of their own books. Or if they are VERY famous, maybe a publisher (or printer) might put the book out on the basis mentioned in the Guillén agreement—no money to the author until the cost of publication is paid back! But I know Guillén (in fact his representative so assured me when here last year) will be very pleased with our royalty arrangement. He is a very amiable fellow who does not expect to make a living from poetry anyhow.

And Hughes adds, "Neither do I."[155] Hughes's final remark must strike one as somewhat disingenuous given that Hughes was one of very few Negro poets—very few USAmerican poets, for that matter—who did manage to eke out a living from writing poetry.[156] Hughes had recognized quite early "that promoting his poetry involved handling both the product and the consumer."[157] He applied to the production and marketing of *Cuba Libre* the lessons he had learned when organizing his poetry reading tour in the US-American South almost twenty years earlier. The difference was that this book had an entirely different purpose. In the late 1940s, Hughes no longer made as much of "an effort to reach the great masses of the colored people" as he had in the 1930s.[158]

CHAPTER FIVE

BACK IN THE USSA

Joe McCarthy's Mistranslations

> I thought you just said I was a Red Russian. Now here you go calling me a Negro. Which is I?
>
> —Langston Hughes, "When a Man
> Sees Red"

> Words may be the instruments by which crimes are committed, and it has always been recognized that the protection of other interests of society may justify reasonable restrictions upon speech in furtherance of the general welfare.
>
> —Judge Harold Medina in 1949

Near the end of *The Big Sea*, Langston Hughes recounts how his early political verse "Advertisement for the Waldorf Astoria" earned him the thinly veiled scorn of his patron: "It's not you....It's a powerful poem! But it's not you," Charlotte Osgood Mason sighed, concluding that her New Negro protégé "had written nothing beautiful" since the completion of his novel, *Not Without Laughter* (1930) (*BS*, 323, 325). Shortly after her rebuke, the gap between what "Godmother"—as Zora Neale Hurston called her with a mixture of ambivalence and affection—wanted and what Hughes felt he could deliver proved unbridgeable. In a section ironically titled "Diagnosis," Hughes recounted rather bitterly,

> She wanted me to be primitive and know and feel the intuitions of the primitive. But, unfortunately, I did not feel the rhythms of the primitive surging through me, and so I could not live and write as though I did. I was only an American Negro—who had loved the surface of Africa and the rhythms of Africa—but I was not Africa. I was Chicago and Kansas City and Broadway and Harlem. So, in the end, it all came very near the old impasse of white and Negro again, white and Negro—as do most relationships in America. (*BS*, 325)

His disappointment with Mason did not wear off quickly. It resurfaced as late as 1939 in "Poet to Patron," a thinly veiled autobiographical lyric that appeared in *American Mercury*:

> What right has anyone to say
> That I

Must throw out pieces of my heart
For pay?
. . . .
A factory shift's better,
A week's meager pay,
Than a perfumed note asking:
What poems today?"

(*CP*, 212)

Like the caustic "Advertisement for the Waldorf-Astoria," published in
New Masses in 1931, Hughes's even more explicitly leftist poetry has fared
little better among academic readers since Mason's disapproval, which threw
him into a severe bout of depression and physical illness. As James Smethurst
reminds us, in the USA, "[n]o portion of Hughes's literary career has been
more commonly dismissed than that of the 1930s."[1] Those who had praised
the "authentic rhythms" of *The Weary Blues* and, far more reluctantly, of *Fine
Clothes to the Jew* were rather taken aback by the so-called red poetry Hughes
penned in the 1930s. Many of Hughes's contemporaries regarded poems
such as "One More 'S' in the U.S.A." (1934), "Good Morning, Revolution"
(1932), and "Black Workers" (1933) as unfortunate aberrations. This was
not the kind of Negro poet they, like Mason, wanted Hughes to be. Reviewers
virtually ignored the collection *A New Song* (1938), which included a number
of these poems. Even now, academic readers, with few exceptions, prefer either the blues poetry or the more visibly neomodernist poetry from the 1950s
and 1960s, notably *Montage of a Dream Deferred* (1951) and ASK YOUR
MAMA (1961).[2] Hughes's radical lyrics, which are rarely anthologized, figure
prominently among what Cary Nelson has called the modern poems that English professors in the USAmerican academy, have wanted to forget.[3] As we
have seen, even in the Hispanic Americas, where Hughes was widely admired
for his leftist politics, few of his radical poems were actually translated.[4]

TRANSLATION AND THE McCARTHY HEARINGS

It is precisely Hughes's "red" poetry, which was also spurned by English
departments across the nation, that caught the attention of the U.S. Senate
Permanent Subcommittee on Investigations of the Committee on Government Operations chaired by second-term junior senator Joseph (Joe) Mc-
Carthy of Wisconsin.[5] Cary Nelson is quite right in suggesting "that there
are more intricate relationships between the academic disavowal of Hughes
and his public harrowing than we would like to admit," and he likens "the
restricted and depoliticized canon of modernism" to "our discipline's testimony before HUAC."[6] Extending the comparison to McCarthy's Senate subcommittee, which was distinct from the House on Un-American

Activities Committee with which McCarthy is often erroneously associated, I build on Nelson's provocative insights as I explore Hughes's testimony and the poems that the committee took as evidence of his "subversive" ways.

Contrary to what is commonly believed, there was not one hearing in late March of 1953 but in fact two: the public hearing was preceded by a lengthier interrogation during a so-called executive session, which was not only closed to the public at the time but held in secret. No one, it seems, knew that these meetings even existed. I will work my way backwards from what we know—that is, the transcript of the public hearing—to what we did not know until early 2003 when the written records of the so-called executive sessions were released. The latter transcripts tell a very different story about Hughes than the one with which we have been familiar. The fact that the Hughes of the executive session is anything but cooperative makes it necessary to reassess the prevalent picture of Hughes as a "friendly" McCarthy witness and inquire more into the reasons for his apparent friendliness.

What, then, does translation have to do with reading these congressional records? My logic is that a poem or a part of a poem that becomes part of an official government document by being either quoted or entered into the record undergoes a displacement and transformation analogous to what happens in a translation. In this case, the translation is not *inter*cultural but, as with the vernaculars I discuss in chapter 4, *intra*cultural. Speakers use what appears to be the same language, in this case English, but make that language signify differently. The salient differences we witness in these hearings are between the languages of literature and literary interpretation and the language of the law. Translation is at issue, I argue, because committee members tried very hard to translate Hughes the poet into Hughes the former, and repentant, Communist. We observe in the secret hearing what amounts to a breakdown in communication between Hughes and his questioners. Especially when debating questions of literary interpretation, it is as if they were speaking different languages. In a way, they were. For the committee, the key question was that of *intent*: what did Hughes mean to say in his radical poems? My contention is that by focusing on intent, the committee willfully mistranslated Hughes's poems into the register of political propaganda, with the goal of turning his verse into *evidence* of unlawful conduct, that is, advocating the overthrow of the government of the United States of America. Can a literary text, any literary texts, be constructed as evidence of this sort, and if so, under what precise circumstances?

A TWICE-TOLD TALE

Much of what we know today about the McCarthy era (1950–54)—and especially the hearings in 1953 and 1954—from radio and television broadcasts, newspaper reports, official congressional records, and countless scholarly studies is not new.[7] Although McCarthy did not discover a single Communist, he was extremely successful in capitalizing "on the fears in American society—fear that the Russians had stolen the atomic bomb, fear of spies in government, fear due to the loss of China, and fear of the Korean war. His party was the party of fear. He mobilized the masses of the alarmed."[8] And he did so with breathtaking recklessness and ruthlessness. Rather than being a demagogue, however, as many have portrayed him, the Wisconsin senator actually knew little about Communism. For McCarthy, anti-Communism was not a moral or ideological cause but simply an "issue" that would advance his short-lived political career and give him the opportunity to exact revenge on personal enemies.[9] Many McCarthy-era historians have since regarded the widespread worries about Soviet Communism, which had steadily grown in the USA after the October Revolution in 1917, as exaggerated, even baseless excuses for a political witch hunt. In the immediate aftermath of the toppling of the Berlin Wall, however, it turned out that such might not have been entirely the case. In the 1990s, the Russian government made available to select USAmerican historians documents about the Soviet Union's Comintern, which supervised Communist parties worldwide. The second set of highly classified records released in 1995 was the so-called Venona documents, decrypted cable messages by KGB agents showing that, since 1942, the USA "had been targeted by an intense and widespread Soviet espionage program that had utilized numerous professional Soviet agents and hundreds of Americans, often from the ranks of the CPUSA's so-called secret apparatus."[10] This new evidence, legal scholar Martin Redish points out, brought a new perspective to arguments that USAmerican historians had previously made about the McCarthy era as the sole product of widespread paranoia about Communism, with no tangible threat in sight. Yet, as Redish remarks, "[t]he most important point to be emphasized about Senator McCarthy today is that...nothing in the dramatic revelations of the 1990s concerning espionage activity by American communists in any way historically vindicates either who he was or what he stood for"[11]—or, for that matter, what he and his committee *did* with such gusto: destroy careers and lives.

In May 2003 came additional news, this time from the USAmerican government archives: McCarthy and his staff had also conducted 160 so-called executive sessions behind closed doors, for which there were also detailed transcripts that had been sealed for fifty years.[12] It appears that the committee held these secret meetings to stage-manage the public admission of witnesses' alleged Communist activities. "The closed hearings," Ted Morgan explains, "were dress rehearsals for productions that sometimes never saw the stage. Even when they led to open hearings, some of the witnesses in the close hearings did not make the grade, if they defended themselves effectively or failed to advance the chairman's case. In 1953, 117 [*sic*] executive sessions were held behind closed doors, and 395 witnesses were heard. To bring in these hundreds of witnesses, McCarthy was said to be signing blank subpoenas like traffic tickets. Many witnesses had no time to prepare or find a lawyer."[13] The proceedings of McCarthy's closed sessions exemplify some of the extremes to which an overly anxious democratic society will go at a time of perceived crisis. To protect itself from real and imagined dangers, such a society will, without hesitation, sacrifice certain of its core values, in this case, the First Amendment protection of the freedom of speech and expression. In this particular crisis, the Red Scare years of the Cold War, expression could only have two forms: affirmation, that is, "propagandization" of "the free world, the free system,...the American system" (PT, 75), or dissent in the form of advocating the Soviet form of government—Communism, for short—which implied the destruction of the government of the USA. "Communist infiltration" was thus the very evil that the House on Un-American Activities Committee (HUAC) and then the Senate subcommittee were to root out by exposing the political associations of certain individuals.[14] The opening salvo of HUAC, which had been formed in 1938, was aimed at the entertainment industry (in 1947),[15] while McCarthy's subcommittee was to focus mainly on government employees—which, of course, it did not. For those engaged in this ideological war on the home front, USAmerican citizens could occupy only one of two possible positions or spaces: that of the loyal patriot or that of the traitor. This rigid polarity created a particular dilemma for many of those whom the McCarthy committee interrogated in 1953 and 1954. The transcripts of the closed sessions allow us to look at this particularly ugly part of our national history and come face to face with the kinds of accusations, arguments, and threats that the committee used to create compliant witnesses. Among the most prominent—and publicly cooperative—witnesses was Langston Hughes, "the well-known poet" (PT, 74), who was unfortunate enough to make the grade in his closed hearing.

The Senate subcommittee subpoenaed Hughes on March 21, 1953, barely two months after the beginning of McCarthy's second senatorial term. In fact, Hughes was questioned twice, first in an executive session on March 24 and again in a public hearing two days later, on March 26,[16] and he had very little time to prepare. Presumably Hughes was subpoenaed because some of his books were lodged in the overseas libraries of the United States Information Agency, but no specific reason was mentioned in the document itself.[17] Given Hughes's international renown, the presence of his books in foreign libraries was not surprising. That, however, was not the whole story. The "Poet Laureate of the Negro Race" was a likely candidate for such treatment because his popularity in the USA, combined with his well-known Communist sympathies, made him potentially a very useful witness.[18]

Even before he was compelled to appear before the subcommittee on very short notice, Hughes had been faced with "red smear" campaigns in the press, which gave him good reasons to be worried about his political reputation.

Allegations surfaced as early as 1943, the year of the so-called Zoot Suit Riots in which white Marines and Latino youths clashed in Los Angeles and the race riots in Detroit, Michigan, when Hughes had signed a message to the California House of Representatives opposing the Dies Committee's inquisition and when he began a series on the Soviet Union for his *Chicago Defender* weekly column.[19] In October of 1944, the *New York Sun* columnist George Sokolsky called Hughes the model joiner of Communist-front organizations, which frightened some school boards away from him during his 1944 tour for the Common Council for American Unity (CCAU).[20] Accusations multiplied as the 1940s drew to a close. On August 31, 1947, a front page article in the *Chicago Tribune* called Hughes "a member of the Communist Party," to which the poet responded in the *Chicago Defender* two weeks later, on September 13: "I am not now, nor have I ever been a member of the Communist Party, *but I believe in equality.*"[21] Still, a few months later, on November 28 of that same year, the *New York Journal American* published an article about Hughes by Chicago red-baiter Howard Rushmore, entitled "Leftist Poet Opens Educator Parley." There were also two WOR (Chicago) radio broadcasts, one on December 12, 1947, the other on March 8, 1948, recommending that scheduled lectures by Hughes be canceled, and an article in the *Pittsburgh Courier* from March 13, 1948, "Called 'Commie' Langston Hughes Rapped in Akron."[22] There were public disclaimers from Hughes and others,[23] but the damage had already been done. An entire series of lectures and readings in Illinois, Missouri, and Southern California, which had been scheduled for February and March 1948, was canceled. The same publishers and (black middle-class) readers who had applauded Hughes's revolutionary poetry in the 1930s, when Communism was de rigueur among African American intellectuals, did not find the combination of blackness with political radicalism as appealing during the Cold War as they had during the Depression years. During the 1940s and 1950s, it was also becoming difficult for Hughes to find publishing venues for work consonant with his earlier calls for a revolution, since, as James Smethurst notes, "the institutions, whether *New Masses* (which under the pressures of the period had retrenched from a weekly journal to a monthly and merged with the journal *Mainstream* in 1947) or the National Negro Congress (which folded in 1946), that had provided both a forum and form for such sentiments had collapsed or were becoming increasingly isolated."[24]

In the years leading up to the rampages of the McCarthy Committee, Hughes had already become vigilant about how he constructed his public persona. Yet even in the face of such public adversity and the threats it posed to his livelihood as a writer,[25] he had not let go of the *Cuba Libre* project and of his long-standing role as a cultural ambassador—at least not yet and not without a measure of resistance. The published and unpublished versions of *Cuba Libre* have already given us a good sense of Hughes's struggle to navigate increasingly treacherous political terrain, as a result of which his public persona became more and more of a protective armor, eventually bringing him to the point of utter silence on certain issues. While it is not entirely unreasonable to see in Hughes's writings from the late 1940s evidence of the adjustment he would make to his own political profile several years later, the image of the repentant Communist and zealous patriot that emerged from his public testimony before the McCarthy Committee is well worth revisiting in light of the transcripts of the executive session, which were unavailable to any of Hughes's early biographers.[26]

THE COMPLIANT WITNESS: THE PUBLIC HEARING

Before taking a closer look at what certain committee members—notably Senator Everett McKinley Dirksen of Illinois, the future Republican minority leader, and especially the committee counsel Roy Cohn—did to make Hughes so cooperative (McCarthy himself was not present at the closed hearing),[27] let us first consider the end product of their efforts: the figure of the compliant witness. The following is a representatively genial exchange between McCarthy and Hughes from the congressional record of the public testimony before the subcommittee.

> THE CHAIRMAN: Let me ask you this. You appear to be very frank in your answers, and while I may disagree with some of your conclusions, do I understand that your testimony is that the 16 different books of yours which were purchased by the information program did largely follow the Communist line?
>
> MR. HUGHES: Some of those books very largely followed at times some aspects of the Communist line, reflecting my sympathy with them. But not all of them, sir.
>
> THE CHAIRMAN: Now, let us take those that you think followed the Communist line. Do you feel that those books should be on our shelves throughout the world, with the apparent stamp of approval of the United States government?
>
> MR. HUGHES: I was certainly amazed to hear that they were. I was surprised; and I would certainly say "No." (PT, 79)

To Roy Cohn's follow-up question—or better, his suggestion—that "[v]ery frankly, you are not particularly proud of them at this stage?" Hughes replied, "They do not represent my current thinking, nor my thinking for the last, say, 6 or 8 years, at any rate" (PT, 79–80). Throughout the hearing, Hughes obliged his questioners to the point of being commended twice by John McClellan, Democratic senator from Arkansas and one of the "most ardent red- and black-baiters of the era":[28] "I want to commend anyone as frank about their errors of the past as you are being before this committee and before the public. It is always quite refreshing and comforting to know that any Communist or Communist sympathizer has discovered the error of his ways and beliefs, and changes" (PT, 80). When asked by Roy Cohn whether he still held "any of the views expressed in ["Goodbye, Christ"]," the only poem that was entered into the record on this occasion (and to which I will return later), Hughes recanted: "No; I do not. It is a very young, awkward poem, written in the late 1920s or early 1930s. It does not express my views or my artistic techniques today" (PT, 82). Speaking of "a complete reorientation of my thinking and emotional feelings" about Soviet ideology around 1950 (PT 74–75), Hughes disowned his radical poetry and implicitly disavowed his leftist sympathies and friendships with prominent Communists at home and abroad, among them Nicolás Guillén and Jacques Roumain, to name but a few.[29] Hughes was also given the opportunity to use his later writings as evidence of his political change of heart. To emphasize his patriotism, he cited the poems "Freedom's Plow" from 1943, "Mystery" from *Montage,* and the short story "One Friday Morning," and he read a passage from *The First Book of Negroes* (1953). Hughes followed Cohn's lead in dating his change of heart to around 1950 (PT, 74–75),[30] which is far too close to the publication of *Cuba Libre* not to raise questions about what really might have motivated Hughes's public testimony. At the end of this hearing, Hughes returned the committee's favors by claiming that far from having been "mistreated in any way by the staff or by the committee," he had been "agreeably surprised at the courtesy and friendliness" with which he had been received (PT, 83). The session concluded with McCarthy reportedly winking at his obliging witness.[31]

It cost Hughes plenty to get McCarthy's wink. While under oath in the closed session, which was chaired by Cohn, Hughes had stalled, fenced, and fought with his inquisitors, and there is evidence of barely suppressed anger on both sides. There is no evidence in this earlier testimony that Hughes's cooperation with the committee was in any way voluntary. Although he was not as confident and bluntly impatient as Paul Robeson would be at his HUAC appearance in 1956, Hughes certainly stood his ground, sparring with Cohn over the definition of Communism, pointing out "misstatements," and refusing to be bullied into simple yes-or-no replies. And Hughes did not cede any ground easily. It was only under the thinly veiled and repeated threat of a perjury charge if he did not tell a straight story that Hughes at length conceded that he had in fact "desired the Soviet form of government in this country," as Cohn put it to him (ST 990). Hughes added, however, that he had never advocated violent means to this end. This forced admission apparently allowed Hughes to strike some sort of deal with the committee on March 25, the day before his public testimony. Unsurprisingly, there are no records of what would likely have been a private meeting with McCarthy and Cohn, not even anecdotal ones. Faith Berry comments that "[t]he whole scenario of their behind-the-scene interrogation…was not a story Hughes liked to tell," and there is no evidence that he ever did. We also know from Berry's interview with Frank Reeves, Hughes's legal counsel at both hearings, that McCarthy "was anxious that a renowned American author should not become a 'hostile witness,'" and "he had worked out an agreement whereby Hughes would not be asked to 'name names' of known Communists" but only "to admit tacitly his own pro-Communist sympathies and writings."[32] Hughes agreed to this deal very reluctantly, "after much private discussion with Reeves," and only after he was assured that his poems would not be read over the air.[33] In fact, McCarthy himself stated during the public hearing, "I have been asked to put in the record a poem written by Mr. Hughes while he was, as he says, following the Communist Party line and believing in it, for the purpose of showing the type of material that was written by those who did believe in the Communist cause. I do not believe it is necessary to read it" (PT, 81). Berry further notes that Hughes "feared the worst if he didn't consent to the deal."[34]

What was the worst for Hughes? When one reads the transcript of the closed hearing, a contentious and increasingly tense interrogation that went on for several hours, it is easy to see why Hughes would not have been fond of recollecting it. He might have derived some satisfaction from putting up a good fight had it not been for two things: the fact that Cohn in the end tripped him up and what apparently resulted in the private meeting in McCarthy's office prior to Hughes's public testimony the following day. That private meeting, I suspect, is the story that Hughes really did not like to remember, let alone tell, because it would have provided evidence that his public testimony was little more than a carefully staged drama. Frank Reeves, the only witness to this deal, even if he were still alive, would still be bound by confidentiality rules to his former client. Given these circumstances, exactly what transpired between Hughes and McCarthy behind closed doors on March 25, 1953 can be only a matter of conjecture.

The transcript of Hughes's formerly secret testimony, however, provides considerably more information than had previously been available, forming a solid basis for some educated speculation. This first interrogation on March 24, 1953, was considerably longer than the public session, and the differences not just in what was said but also in *how* it was said are striking. We will see that unlike the public Hughes, whose comments sound flat and almost scripted, the Hughes of the closed session is rather feisty, challenging his inquisitors as much as they did him. The men who did most of the questioning on that occasion—Cohn and Dirksen—also merit attention as part of the context for these hearings, as do the ties between Communism, homosexuality, and the beginnings of the civil rights movement that not a few politicians imagined and voiced in those days.[35]

SECRETS AND LIES: THE CLOSED HEARING

Questions of citizenship and loyalty arose from the very start of the hearing as an implied result of Hughes's foreign travels. Dirksen pursued them before even explaining to Hughes, who was of course under oath, the purpose of the hearing. Dirksen's initial statement, "I assume you travel and lecture?," followed by "You are a single man?" (a remark to which I shall return), quickly turned more specific:

SENATOR DIRKSEN: Now, with respect to your travels have you traveled recently in the last ten or fifteen years?

MR. HUGHES: In the country?

SENATOR DIRKSEN: Outside.

MR. HUGHES: No, sir. I have not been out of the country if my memory is correct since 1938 or 1939.

SENATOR DIRKSEN: Would you care to tell us whether you have traveled to the Soviet Union?

MR. HUGHES: I have, sir, yes.

SENATOR DIRKSEN: For an extended period?

MR. HUGHES: I was there for about a year. (ST, 974)

Hughes derails this line of questioning when Dirksen asks him to spell "Meschrabprom," the ill-fated film company under whose auspices Hughes had initially visited Russia: "I am sorry I can not tell you. I don't read Russian" (ST, 975). Hughes's diction is very discriminating here because he certainly did *speak* Russian. Dirksen then shifts to the hearing's purpose: the State Department's purchase of "books that allegedly delineate American objectives and American culture, that would be useful in propagandizing our way of life and our system" in other countries (ST, 975).

As is typical of the committee's presumptive rhetoric, which implies that the logical or right answers were foregone conclusions, Dirksen's statements, like his earlier remarks to Hughes, are declarative and conclusory rather than interrogative: "So we have encountered quite a number of your works [purchased by the State Department], and I would be less than frank with you, sir, if I did not say that there is a question in the minds of the committee, and in the minds of a good many people, concerning the general objective of some of those poems, whether they strike a Communist, rather than an anti-Communist note" (ST, 975). With this declaration, Dirksen cedes the floor to Roy Cohn, who uses the standard "Have you ever been a Communist?" to gloss over Hughes's request that Dirksen identify the books he had mentioned earlier. Hughes replies in the negative: "No, sir, I am not" (ST, 976). But note the shrewd shift in tense here, which seems to escape Cohn's notice because Hughes distracts him with a presumptive remark of his own: "I presume by that you mean a Communist party member, do you not?" (ST, 976). When the sparring over a definition of Communist makes Cohn rephrase his question first as "Have you ever believed in communism?" and then as "Have you ever believed that there is a form of government better than the one under which this country operates today?" Hughes comes across as calm and emphatic: "No, sir, I have not." The latter is the question that would come back to haunt him later on in the session, when Cohn confronts him with several lines from the poem "One More 'S' in the U.S.A." which, Cohn later admitted, was not even included "in any poems in the collection in the information centers." Cohn is adamant: "I would like to know right now whether you ever desired the Soviet form of government in this country, and I would like it answered." Hughes's attempt to stall—"Would you permit me to think about it?"—is fruitless, and an increasingly impatient Cohn moves in for the kill:

> MR. COHN: Pardon me? Mr. Hughes, you have belonged to a list of Communist organizations a mile long. You have urged the election to public office of official candidates of the Communist party. You have signed statements to the effect that the purge trials in the Soviet Union were justified and sound and democratic. You have signed statements denying that the Soviet Union is totalitarian. You have defended the current leaders of the Communist party. You have written poems which are an invitation to revolution. You have called for the setting up of a Soviet government in this country. You have been named in statements before us as a Communist, and a member of the Communist party. Mr. Hughes, you can surely tell us simply whether or not you ever desired the Soviet form of government in this country.
>
> MR. HUGHES: Yes, I did.
>
> MR. COHN: The answer is yes. I think if you were a little more candid with some of these things, we would get along a little better, because I think I know enough about the subject so I am not going to sit here for six days and be kidded along. (ST, 990)

This is the point to which the entire meeting had been building up: a simple yes to signal Hughes's defeat. It is worth noting that Cohn's assertions were not exactly accurate, and his claim to sufficient knowledge of the subject was just bluster and bullying, something for which he was well known. Hughes had, in fact, never been named before this Senate subcommittee, nor had he ever been a member of the CPUSA.[36] Why, then, did Hughes capitulate at this point in the closed hearing?

An answer, I believe, can be gleaned from the treatment to which the committee subjected his writing, especially his poetry. "One More 'S' in the U.S.A.," which had first been published in the mass-circulated Communist newspaper the *Daily Worker* in 1934,[37] was not the only poem on which the committee pounced. Other poems that Cohn and Dirksen cited as evidence of Hughes's unpatriotic politics, including his alleged anti-Semitism, were "Good Morning Revolution" (1932),[38] "Ballads of Lenin" (1933),[39] "Hard Luck" (1926),[40] and "Goodbye, Christ" (1932). Hughes was also questioned about *Scottsboro Limited* (1932), which Cohn kept calling "the Scottsboro thing," and "When a Man Sees Red" from *Simple Speaks His Mind* (1950). Yet the fact that the committee, ostensibly concerned about what Cohn called "all these Communist books" lodged in other countries' libraries—"approximately 13 books, 161 copies altogether in 60 Information Centers" (PT, 77)[41]—chose to focus on these particular poems would have been odd had it not been for the fact their real targets lay elsewhere.[42] At the time, only three of these poems had been included in any books: "Goodbye, Christ" in Nancy Cunard's *Negro* anthology (1934), "Ballads of Lenin" in *A New Song* (1938), and "Hard Luck" in *Fine Clothes to the Jew* (1927). The rest had been published in journals and not been included in any of Hughes's poetry collections. Nor would they be reprinted in *The Langston Hughes Reader* (1958) or in Hughes' *Selected Poems* (1959). While red journals such as the *New Masses,* the *Daily Worker,* and *Anvil* also circulated outside the USA, they would not easily have found their way onto the shelves of the various United States Information Centers known as America Houses. Nor, for that matter, would Granville Hicks's 1935 anthology *Proletarian Literature in the United States,* which included several of Hughes's poems.

Translation is mentioned exactly once during both sessions. At the public hearing, a now more affable Roy Cohn remarked: "And a good many of your works have been published not only in English but in other languages throughout the world. Is that right?" (PT, 74). Although the committee's lack of interest in translations confirms that the focus of the hearings was not on traitorous political ideas being disseminated in other countries but on the circulation of such ideas in the USA, translation is a relevant subtext in these interrogations in at least two ways, and the cliché *traduttore, tradittore* (translator, traitor) assumes unexpected dimensions of significance. For one, the committee regards Hughes as someone who translated his radical political ideas into his poetry, assuming that there is no mediation, that meaning is univocal and self-evident, and that authorial intent is easily discernible. During the closed session, Cohn's and Dirksen's comments consistently exhibit a blatant disregard for the hermeneutics of literary interpretation and for processes of creativity through which a literary "liar" can speak (or write) true. For another, the committee members themselves can be said to have engaged in acts of translation, producing what we usually perceive as mistranslations, in which there is a stark imbalance between the deficits and surfeits of meaning that accrue during the process of any literary translation, the task of the translator being to balance these meanings carefully.

Although "bad" or mistranslations can be the result of sheer incompetence on the translator's part, they can also be ideologically motivated, with the two not being mutually exclusive. Such is the case with the McCarthy Committee's rereading of Hughes's poems as Communist propaganda for the sole purpose of branding Hughes a traitor to his country. The committee's recastings of Hughes and his poems as disloyal to the state, under whose auspices the committee functioned, are examples of interested and

reductive *translations* of poetry into political propaganda by fixing meanings that remain unfixable and indeterminate. At issue here are not linguistic
differences but a radical divergence of assumptions about *how* (literary)
language signified in the context of the Cold War USA. The transcript of the
executive session shows an intractable clash over meaning and interpretation that can be analyzed through the hermeneutical lens of translation as
a power struggle analogous to the dynamics between dominant languages
and dominated ones. I examine the assumptions at work in this struggle in
the pages that follow.

At the end of his public testimony, Hughes singled out Senator Dirksen,
who was not present on that occasion, as "most gracious and in a sense
helpful in defining for me the areas of this investigation," and he excused
"the young men [Cohn and David Schine, his sidekick] who...of course,
had to interrogate me" (PT, 83). Anyone who reads the exchanges in the
transcript of the closed hearing will find it hard to overlook the biting irony
in these remarks. Dirksen was the one to question Hughes closely about the
controversial "Goodbye, Christ," a poem that had already been a problem
for Hughes in 1940 (see *Life,* 1:392–95). At the closed meeting, Dirksen
read out loud two stanzas from "Goodbye, Christ" as evidence of Hughes's
antireligious and hence seditious sentiments. Dirksen's source was an unauthorized reprint from the *Saturday Evening Post* from November 15, 1940.
The poem was also reprinted on a mass-distributed flyer entitled " 'Hate
Christ' Is the Slogan of the Communists," which identified Hughes as a
"Notorious Negro Stalin lover."[43]

> Listen, Christ, you did all right in your day, I reckon,
> But that day is gone now.
> They ghosted you up a swell story, too,
> And called it the Bible, but it's dead now.
> The popes and the preachers have made too much money from it.
>   They have sold you to too many. [44]

To Dirksen, blasphemy — "Do you think that Book is dead?" — is clearly a
form of social deviance that runs afoul of his own more comfortable "familiarity with the Negro people for a long time" and his belief "that they are
innately a very devout and religious people" (ST, 980). Rejecting Hughes's
explanation that "Goodbye, Christ" "is an ironical and satirical poem"
about "racketeering in religion and misuse of religion as seen through the
eyes at that time of a young Soviet citizen,"[45] Dirksen, who "fancies" that
"it was not so accepted...by the American people," remains unyielding:
"*Of course* when all is said and done a poem like this *must necessarily speak
for itself,*...its impact on the thinking of the people is finally what counts"
(ST, 980–81, my emphases). But if a poem — and not just a poem like this —
does speak for itself, then why ask the poet what it means? Despite Hughes's

efforts to argue that there are as many interpretations of his poem as there are of a Shakespearean sonnet and that "you cannot take one line" out of context (ST, 982), Dirksen is undeterred. Finally returning the poem to its context, Hughes offers the following interpretation, giving an example Dirksen himself has used earlier. "If you read the twelve-year old the whole poem, I hope he would be shocked into thinking about the real things of religion, because with some of my poems that is what I have tried to do, to shock people into thinking and finding the real meaning themselves" (ST, 982).[46] Dirksen, however, persists in claiming "that this could mean *only one thing* to the person who read it" (ST 982, my emphasis), a phrase that Cohn later repeats. "This" specifically refers to the poem's third stanza:

Goodbye, Christ Jesus, Lord of Jehovah,
Beat it on away from here now.
Make way for a new guy with no religion at all,
A guy named Marx communism, Lenin, Peasant, Stalin, worker, me.

Dirksen never clarifies exactly what he means by "only one thing," assuming that every "right thinking American" (a phrase from then FBI director J. Edgar Hoover) would implicitly know.

I have italicized various phrases in my citations above to highlight the slipperiness of words spoken from a position of power. It is that very imprecision that safeguards power's notorious invisibility and makes its discursive attributes difficult to pinpoint. This invisibility is also a function of the recoding of political dissent as nonconformity and thus as *social* deviance. The state's enemies become visible as black, red, and indeed both, by being strategically constructed in terms of their deviation from assumed standards of thinking and acting.[47] As a black USAmerican citizen and an educated one to boot, Hughes—much like Paul Robeson, who had studied law—would already have been under suspicion for disloyalty at a time when HUAC, under the leadership of a Georgia congressman, took it upon itself to conduct "Hearings Regarding Communist Infiltration of Minority Groups" to certify African Americans' political trustworthiness and patriotism.[48] Robeson's career was systematically destroyed by the combined efforts of various government agencies, including the FBI and the Department of Justice, although he had sworn under oath in 1946 that he was not a member of the Communist Party.[49] It is no accident, then, that his name comes up at this hearing as well.[50] When Hughes declares that he "would not be able to say if he [Robeson] ever was a Communist," Cohn's reaction supplies a key word of the conservative political discourse of the day: "Are you a little bit *suspicious*?" (ST, 982, my emphasis). The way in which Cohn, the darling of conservative Republicans, phrases it, "suspicious" applies not just to Robeson but also to Hughes. While neither Cohn nor Dirksen were southerners, Dirksen's claim of familiarity with African Americans gives an added edge to his questions and comments. The idea that African Americans were easy prey for Communist propaganda was hardly limited to the south of the USA. As Jeff Woods explains: "The southern red scare had taken shape in the years between 1948 and 1954, but it rested on traditions stretching back to the antebellum period. Massive resisters, like their conservative southern predecessors, equated dramatic social reform, particularly in race relations, with the conspiratorial design of outsiders. The long-held racist assumption that African Americans were easily duped into supporting un-American causes served as a linchpin to their argument. Reacting to the changing social and political conditions of the early cold war, they counted black and red cooperation among the greatest threats to domestic tranquility."[51] Hughes's critical stance toward what he saw as a debased, hypocritical Christianity and its mainstream institutions would not have sat well with religious conservatives such as Dirksen, who would have received any such criticism from a black intellectual, or his pen, in precisely this frame of mind.

By far the most colorful and controversial figure in these hearings was Roy Cohn, the "whirling dervish" of a lawyer from the United States district attorney's office in Manhattan, whom McCarthy had appointed as his chief counsel when Cohn was barely twenty-six. The other candidate for that job had been Bobby Kennedy, Cohn's nemesis, who served as the committee's minority counsel early in 1953 and whose name still appeared on the roster as an assistant counsel even after his resignation.[52] Though by all accounts not particularly well prepared for his new job, the ambitious and literary-minded Cohn quickly became the senator's alter ego. Cohn's antics with David Schine, for whom he secured preferential treatment in the military, would in no small measure contribute to McCarthy's undoing during the Eisenhower presidency.[53] It is fair to assume that Cohn's role for the public hearings was that of playwright and stage manager rolled into one. During the public hearings, McCarthy appears to have done little more than ventriloquize Cohn's questions and comments from the closed sessions. It is unsurprising that McCarthy did not hesitate to take Cohn's lead. "Despite his quick intelligence," writes David Oshinsky, the former Wisconsin judge "seemed remarkably uncurious about the world beyond his immediate ambitions and physical needs. He knew nothing about history, literature, music, art, or science. And he had no desire to learn. 'As far as I know,' said Van Susteren, 'Joe looked at only one book in his life. That was *Mein Kampf.*'"[54]

In fact, many of the executive sessions, including Hughes's, were held in the senator's absence.[55] During the secret interrogation conducted by Cohn and Dirksen, with the consultant Schine in the odd posture of legal adviser, Cohn was the one to question Hughes most closely about his radical poems, mainly "Ballads of Lenin" and "One More 'S' in the U.S.A." Cohn's strident tone is entirely consistent with his reputation as the most aggressive, rabidly hostile of the committee's questioners. From the moment that Cohn takes over the questioning from Dirksen, the tension is palpable from the transcript of the two-hour session (from 3:00 to 5:10 p.m.). The image of Hughes that emerges is hardly that of a cooperative, amiable witness.

Hughes is guarded from the very beginning. Unlike the composer Aaron Copland, for instance, who testified to the committee that same day, Hughes does not declare that he had never been a Communist, only that he had never been a "Communist party member," challenging Cohn to define what he meant by Communism (ST, 976). Throughout the session, Hughes tries to stall and dissemble, asking that questions be broken down or rephrased and claiming that he has forgotten a question only minutes after it has been asked. His repeated requests to be presented with written evidence are not honored. Consider the following exchange in which Cohn systematically elides any distinction between "writing" and "saying."

MR. COHN: Did you know what you were doing on February 7 [1949], when you gave a statement to the *Daily Worker* defending the Communist leaders on trial and saying that the Negro people too are being tried?

MR. HUGHES: Could I see that statement, sir?

MR. COHN: Did you ever hear of something called the *Chicago Defender*?

MR. HUGHES: I certainly have.

MR. COHN: Did you write in the *Chicago Defender,* "If the 12 Communists are sent to jail, in a little while they will send Negroes to jail simply for being Negroes, and to concentration camps simply for being colored."

MR. HUGHES: Could I see it?

MR. COHN: My first question is did you say it?

MR. HUGHES: I don't know.

MR. COHN: Could you have said it? That was a pretty serious thing to say in 1949....

MR. HUGHES: I would have to see it to see if it is in context....I don't know whether I said it or not. (ST 983–84)[56]

Hughes, of course, knows full well that he wrote these lines in "A Portent and a Warning to the Negro People," published in the Chicago *Defender* on February 5, 1949. Cohn does not care to add the sentence that followed in the actual essay, and for good reasons. Hughes had written: "Maybe you don't like Reds, but you had better be interested in what happens to the 12 Reds in New York City—because it is only a sign of what can happen to you."[57]

What probably unsettles Hughes to the point of being even more keenly conscious of how he answers Cohn's questions about his writings is not so much the quotation from his own essay as Cohn's reference to the notorious 1949 trial of twelve top leaders of the American Communist Party, who had been arrested in 1948. The trial was presided over by Harold Medina, federal district judge for southern New York. Medina was the earliest-known Hispanic on any federal district or circuit court and had been one of Paul Robeson's law professors at Columbia in the early 1920s. I quote from Medina's instructions to the jury in the second epigraph to this chapter. Eleven of the twelve defendants were charged with violating the antigovernment conspiracy provision of the Smith Act (explained below), found guilty on October 13, 1949, after an eight-month trial, and sentenced to five-year prison terms and $10,000 fines.[58] There can be no doubt that Cohn's reference to what became known as *Dennis v. United States* veiled a threat perhaps more disturbing to Hughes than any perjury charge.[59]

CRIMINAL INTENT

What was the Smith Act, and why would Roy Cohn have alluded to it? Named after Representative Howard W. Smith of Virginia and signed into law by President Franklin D. Roosevelt in 1940 as the rather innocently named Alien Registration Act, the Smith Act is a criminal statute that makes it unlawful to advocate the overthrow of the government of the USA.[60] Important for my discussion is how the statute defines the process of "knowingly or willfully" advocating. Its language posits a direct link between speech or writing and unprotected—that is, criminal—action (*actus reus,* "the guilty act"). It does so by way of "intent," also a key word during Hughes's closed-session questioning. Here are the relevant paragraphs from the statute, which is still in force.

> Whoever *knowingly or willfully advocates, abets, advises, or teaches* the duty, necessity, desirability, or propriety of overthrowing or destroying the government of the United States or the government of any State, Territory, District or Possession thereof, or the government of any political subdivision therein, by force or violence, or by the assassination of any officer of any such government; or
>
> Whoever, with *intent to cause* the overthrow or destruction of any such government, prints, publishes, edits, issues, circulates, sells, distributes, or publicly displays any written or printed matter advocating, advising, or teaching the duty, necessity, desirability, or propriety of overthrowing or destroying any government in the United States by force or violence, or attempts to do so; or
>
> Whoever organizes or helps or attempts to organize any society, group, or assembly of persons who teach, advocate, or encourage the overthrow or destruction of any such government by force or violence; or becomes or is a member of, or affiliates with, any such society, group, or assembly of persons, knowing the purposes thereof—Shall be fined under this title or imprisoned not more than twenty years, or both, and shall be ineligible for employment by the United States or any department or agency thereof, for the five years next following his conviction. (My emphases.)[61]

Until 1957, when the U.S. Supreme Court under Chief Justice Earl Warren would reinterpret the Smith Act more narrowly,[62] this USAmerican federal criminal statute was a popular vehicle for prosecuting Communists at the federal and state level. It also paved the way for the large-scale harassment of writers and artists first by HUAC and then by the Senate permanent sub-committee. The fact that the outcome of Judge Harold Medina's Manhattan district court trial was upheld on appeal and that the Smith Act was held constitutional by the Supreme Court in *Dennis v. United States* in 1951 clearly emboldened Cohn as he questioned Hughes. Earlier that same year, Cohn had also helped Irving H. Saypol, U.S. District Attorney for the South-ern District of New York, successfully prosecute Julius and Ethel Rosenberg as Soviet spies, "a crime worse than murder," according to the sentencing judge Irving Kaufman.

The Smith Act made the entire witch hunt possible in the first place by giv-ing it a legal foundation. Collapsing the distance between *mens rea* and *actus reus*, intent and action, the Smith Act, especially as Judge Medina applied it in the *Dennis* trial, made it possible to charge *and* convict someone simply on the basis of his or her political beliefs and projected intentions without having to muster actual evidence—that is, that something had actually been caused by such beliefs and intentions. As Redish notes, "[i]n light of the total absence of evidence presented by the government to demonstrate even the remotest beginnings of an active American communist plan to attempt to overthrow, the 'subversion' for which communist leaders were prosecuted in the 1940s and 1950s effectively amounted to very little more than *punishment for the holding of unpopular ideas*. From a constitutional perspective, such suppres-sion is therefore far more invidious than punishment for espionage."[63] It is for this reason that Redish calls *Dennis v. United States* "one of the most troubling free speech decisions ever handed down by the United States Su-preme Court"—indeed a "constitutional monstrosity" that was more remi-niscent of a totalitarian society than a democratic one.[64] Redish's worries go back to the words of a rather appalled Justice William O. Douglas, one of the two dissenting judges in *Dennis v. United States*. Douglas wrote in 1951:

> The opinion of the Court does not outlaw these texts [books that contain the Marxist-Leninist doctrine] or condemn them to the fire, as the Communists do literature offensive to their creed. But if the books themselves are not outlawed, if they can lawfully remain on library shelves, by what reasoning does their use in a classroom become a crime? It would not be a crime under the Act to introduce these books to a class, though that would be teaching what the creed of violent overthrow of the Government is. The Act, as construed, requires the element of intent—that those who teach the creed believe in it. The crime then depends not on what is taught but on who the teacher is. That is to make freedom of speech turn not on *what is said*, but on the *intent* with which it is said. Once we start down that road we enter territory dangerous to the liberties

of every citizen.... We then start probing men's minds for motive and purpose; they become entangled in the law not for what they did but *for what they thought;* they get convicted not for what they said but for the purpose with which they said it.[65]

Justice Douglas did not mince words, insisting on the distinction between spoken intent and actual conduct or action: "[N]ever until today has anyone seriously thought that the ancient law of conspiracy could constitutionally be used to turn speech into seditious conduct. Yet that is precisely what is suggested. I repeat that we deal here with speech alone, not with speech plus acts of sabotage or unlawful conduct. Not a single seditious act is charged in the indictment. *To make a lawful speech unlawful because two men conceive it is to raise the law of conspiracy to appalling proportions.... We might as well say that the speech of petitioners is outlawed because Soviet Russia and her Red Army are a threat to world peace."*[66]

Although he did not quite put it in those terms, Justice Douglas implied that it is not possible to conflate *mens rea* with *actus reus.* Doing so would contradict the very premise of a criminal statute in Anglo-American law, for which one needs speech *plus* acts of sabotage or unlawful conduct. Alan Filreis explains the stakes cogently:

> The high court [in *Dennis v. United States*] thus used an abstract notion of proximity, that is, of language to action; of *language intended to lead to action* to the action itself—but tried to look *away* from the intention in the language and as exclusively as possible *at* the action, and in this way demanded the relevance of external evidence to the interpretation of language. Investigators and attorneys working on behalf of the American government in 1951 had no choice but to reshape the doctrine of clear and present danger[67] if they wanted to define American communist language as suggesting illegality.... Lacking the external evidence that seemed required by the *Schenck* interpretation, the prosecutors, aides in the executive branch (guided by Truman and his attorney general), the FBI, the lower court, and eventually the high court succeeded in shifting the test from the relation between language and the world to the *intention* of the language itself—that is, from external evidence of a powerful state imminently endangered by subversive language to internal evidence offered in a text which "meant" future illegal action.[68]

Speaking and writing take on the role of "specified" behavior ("intent") that, coupled with a state of mind called unlawful "intent," may in and of itself constitute a guilty act. As a contemporary textbook of criminal law notes, in cases of "specified intent"—for instance, overthrowing the USAmerican government—"[t]he future events contemplated by the defendant...need not occur in order for the crime to be complete."[69] I have placed the legal terms in quotations marks here because the legal locution "intent" may not necessarily have the same meaning as intent in a hermeneutic context (as in "authorial intent"). In fact, they may well be regarded as false cognates in the same way that Negro and *negro* are (see chapters 2 and 4). As any law student knows, legal terms, even and perhaps especially when they resemble so-called natural language, require translation. The same textbook tellingly compares legal language to a foreign language: "Just as one begins the study of a foreign language by learning the English equivalent of the words to be used...it is useful to treat common law *mens rea* terms, and indeed much of the language of the law, as words that must be translated into ordinary language. [70]

My question, then, is not whether the Smith Act is flawed as a criminal statute that collapses the guilty act into the guilty mind. I could not possibly even begin to engage in a satisfactory discussion beyond pointing out that the statute appears never to have been challenged on these grounds. More important here is whether legal terms such as "intent" and "specific intent" can be applied to literary writing. Writing a novel or poem about murder is clearly not the same as committing murder, and Hughes's point throughout the hearing is that writing about revolution even in approving ways is hardly the same as exploding a bomb. Literature does not represent an author's intent, certainly not beyond a reasonable doubt. Even if it could, what we mean by intent in a literary context is altogether different from the word's legal meaning, which depends on a degree of specificity that literary interpretation renders impossible. Literature and the law work very much at cross-purposes when it comes to how each produces meaning in language. For the law, the irreducible multiplicity of meanings in a literary text can only lead to confusion and is thus eminently undesirable. This variance makes translation in either direction difficult in the extreme. What we see enacted in the exchanges during the executive session is a breakdown in communication attributable to the denial, most clearly on the part of the questioners, that there are discursive differences that require translation in the first place. Although all parties involved appear to converse in the same language, there is no common ground.

However problematic from both a legal and a literary perspective, the implications of presuming the proximity of a speech act to a potentially ensuing (violent) action, even conflating them, would have been profoundly disturbing for writers, including Hughes. Although he—unlike Richard Wright, for instance—had never been a dues-paying member of the Communist Party, he could easily have been pegged as a fellow traveler. Filreis's example is Arthur Miller, whom HUAC succeeded in forcing "to concede the harmlessness of certain [literary] genres" even as he defended "the right of the author to advocate." "If literary language congeals around life's action," Filreis comments, "then it fell into the government's widening net of established subversives and subversive material. The only alternative was to make a substantial retreat and concede that some literary genres—poetry: harmless, it would commonly seem—entail less absolutely than other genres a responsibility for what the writer says about the world. Thus the 'absolute' right specifically of the poet to write anything he or she wants about, say, bloody revolution, implies for the writer the evaluation of more or less dangerous genres."[71]

Roy Cohn surely did not perceive poetry as a harmless genre, although he himself was known to have written some verse on occasion.[72] Like Dirksen, Cohn tries hard to force Hughes to incriminate himself by sidestepping the complexities of literary interpretation, reducing poetry to messages, personal beliefs, and especially authorial intent—"How did you intend it to mean?" (ST, 978). Hughes, in turn, flatly rejects the assumption that any poem, no matter what its subject, carries a specific message, that it "could mean only one thing." A poem, he insists, must be taken seriously as a work of art that "means many things to different people." This assertion should have been sufficient to invalidate the intentional fallacy. It implies, as Redish puts it, that "because words may have a force or impact wholly apart from the speaker's [or writer's] intentions, it is just as conceivable that the neutral exposition of the ideas could lead to action as would their advocacy."[73] Neither Dirksen nor Cohn, however, was prepared to regard poetry, or any form of literary writing, in this way, even though doing so would quite ironically have enabled them to make a far more convincing case for subversion: the ability of poetry-as-performance to develop a collective consciousness in readers through participation.

The arrogance for which Cohn was generally feared is plain not just in his insistence on turning mere assumptions into facts but also in his general disrespect for Hughes's work. As Cohn becomes more agitated during the closed hearing, he does not even deign to get the titles of the poems right, turning "Goodbye, Christ" into "Goodbye to Christ," *Scottsboro Limited* into "the Scottsboro thing," "One More 'S' in the U.S.A." into "Put One 'S' in U.S.A.," and "Ballads *of* Lenin" into "Ballads *to* Lenin." The differences are not negligible. Witness the following exchange about "Ballads of Lenin," the only time when Cohn actually calls the poem by its correct title.

MR. HUGHES: Sir, I don't think you can get a yes or no answer to any literary question, so I give you...

MR. COHN: I am trying, Mr. Hughes, because I think you have gone pretty far *in some of these things,* and I think you know pretty well what you did. When you wrote *something* called "Ballads of Lenin," did you believe *that* when you wrote it?

MR. HUGHES: Believe *what,* sir?

MR. COHN: Comrade Lenin of Russia speaks from marble:
On guard with the workers forever—
The world is our room!

MR. HUGHES: *That* is a poem. One cannot state one believes every word of a poem.

MR. COHN: I do not know what one can say. I am asking you specifically do you believe in *the message carried and conveyed in this poem*?

MR. HUGHES: It would demand a great deal of discussion. You cannot say yes
or no.

[...]

MR. COHN: Mr. Hughes, is it not a *fact* now that this poem here did represent
your views and it could only mean one thing, that the "Ballads to Lenin"
did represent your views? You have told us that *all of these things* did, that
you have been a consistent supporter of Communist movements and you
have been a consistent and undeviating follower of the Communist party
line up through and including recent times. *Is this not a fact?* (ST 978 and
983, my emphases)

As before in Dirksen's remarks, the emphases I have placed in this passage are
to draw attention to the lack of specificity in Cohn's rhetoric. What, for instance, does it mean to "have gone pretty far in some of these things"? Typically, Cohn reduces the "something" Hughes had authored to a single stanza
or line, trying to extract from a poem a singular message that would stand as
evidence of Hughes's subversive intentions. When Hughes reproaches Cohn,
reminding him that "that is a poem," he opens up a gap between art and
politics that seems to be in line with Sir Philip Sidney's "Defence of Poesie":
unlike politicians, poets do not lie.[74] Each time Hughes insists that "you
can't get a yes or no answer entirely to any literary question," he sounds as if
he were quoting Sidney — except that Hughes would not, in fact, have agreed
with Sidney that the poet does not "affirm" anything. Yet yes-or-no answers
were all that the committee was willing to countenance, and Cohn's inter-
ruption in this passage stands as a reminder of that shortsightedness.

That Hughes's remarks fell on deaf ears raises the question of what line
of defense was available to him under those circumstances. Filreis suggests
that "American writers had two options when facing investigators in search
of subversive language. They could dissociate literature entirely from the
political world by disconnecting texts from the acts of people who have
civil rights worth defending; thus, for instance, they could seek refuge from
the committee's intentional fallacy — subversive writings when interpreted
invariably lead back to subversive writers — by hiding behind uncharacter-
istically formal readings of irony or ambiguity." The second option Filreis
cites "was to invite the committee back into the business of the historical
interpretation of texts (which in reality ignored texts and focused on the
writers' opinions) and so to allow the committee to reiterate its author-
centered simplicities."[75] Hughes tried both options to no avail. Are these
really the only available options? Granted, they may have been for Hughes
at the time, and neither argument would convince those who today persist
in reading his radical poems as uncritical leftist propaganda devoid of any
aesthetic merit. If, in the 1930s, "writing poetry became a credible form
of revolutionary action," if only for a brief time, it did so not primarily

because of a thematic shift but because it abandoned the forms of interior lyric subjectivity—the fictions of selfhood that Hughes also challenged in his autobiographies—that academics came to value in poetry. Cary Nelson argues that "[p]oetry became a form of social conversation and a way of participating in collaborative political action. Poetry was thus in the immediate materiality of its signs dialogic—engaged in a continuing dialogue both with other poetry and with the other discourses and institutions of its day."[76] To understand the political poetry from this era, we cannot take poetic discourse as unproblematically monologic and therefore as self-enclosed or self-absorbed as the New Critics proposed in the waning days of the Great Depression. There is no question that the New Criticism has profoundly shaped our understanding of modernist writing as high modernism and continues to do so in many quarters. The historical proximity of the passage of the Smith Act (1940) and the publication of Cleanth Brooks's *Understanding Poetry* (1939), one of the monuments of the emerging New Criticism, speaks volumes. Although a number of convictions under the Smith Act were thrown out as unconstitutional in 1957 (see below), the statute remains on the books even today.[77] Likewise, the New Criticism, along with other formalisms, has continued the work of censorship by effectively depriving political poetry of any aesthetic value.

Hughes's "Ballads of Lenin" is a case in point. To arrive at his reductive reading of the poem's language both as subversive and as representative of Hughes's own views, Cohn had to ignore several facts: one, that Hughes titled the poem in the plural—"ballads" rather than "ballad"; two, that poem's stanzas are ballads *of* and not *to* Lenin; and three, that the repeated epithet "Comrade" does not carry over into the poem's title. Here is the poem in its entirety:

> Comrade Lenin of Russia,
> High in a marble tomb,
> Move over, Comrade Lenin,
> And give me room.
>> I am Ivan, the peasant,
>> Boots all muddy with soil.
>> I fought with you, Comrade Lenin.
>> Now I have finished my toil.
> Comrade Lenin of Russia,
> Alive in a marble tomb,
> Move over, Comrade Lenin,
> And make me room.
>> I am Chico, the Negro,
>> Cutting cane in the sun.
>> I lived for you, Comrade Lenin.
>> Now my work is done.
> Comrade Lenin of Russia,
> Honored in a marble tomb,

> Move over, Comrade Lenin,
> And leave me room.
>   I am Chang from the foundries
>   On strike in the streets of Shanghai.
>   For the sake of the Revolution
>   I fight, I starve, I die.
> Comrade Lenin of Russia
> Speaks from the marble tomb:
> On guard with the workers forever—
> *The world is our room!*
>
>   (*CP*, 183–84)

Cohn also had to disregard the fact that the poet who writes about the figures of the workers in the first person is not one of those who address Lenin here, or at least not directly. That Hughes reports other voices, something that is hardly alien to the traditional lyric form of the ballad, would have been evident even from the final quatrain Cohn misquotes, disregarding the rhyme on "tomb" and "room." Much like Hughes's "Ballad of Roosevelt" (*CP*, 178–79) from 1943, this poem is not an ode, a ballad *to* someone, if you will, and Cohn's persistent confusion of the title seems generic in origin: he wants to read this poem as the ode it is not. Similarly, Ivan, Chico, and Chang are not lyric personae but generic names that represent three distinct yet parallel situations in which political resistance is embedded in exploitation and social injustice.[78] Their voices function in the poem much as dramatis personae would in a play. They, not Hughes, address their individual ballad stanzas to Lenin, who comes back to life and responds in the two italicized lines at the end. The italics signal a citation and work almost as a chorus would. Thinking of these voices in dramatic terms helps us realize how important the idea of dialogue is in this poem, in a way that it is conspicuously not in the poem "Lenin," which Hughes published in *New Masses* in 1946:

> Lenin walks around the world.
> Frontiers cannot bar him.
>
>   (*CP*, 318)

Even though they do not address each other, the three voices in "Ballads of Lenin" are all part of a conversation in which proximity is created by the near repetition of the opening stanza, which becomes almost a refrain—but not quite. Not quite because salient differences remain in what Ivan, Chico, and Chang convey about their specific historical circumstances. These differences account for Hughes's retort to Cohn that this poem "symboliz[es] what I felt at that time Lenin as a symbol might mean to workers in various parts of the world" (ST, 978). Hughes imagines the possibility of a world in which Lenin is alive through his writings, which speak to others as they do here, while at the same time making room for workers worldwide to communicate and benefit from the knowledge of one another's conditions, so that they themselves might imagine the community that the pronoun "our" in the final stanza suggests (*"The world is our room"*). More than five decades ago, Hughes imagined the transformative potential of a conversation that, in our present world, Cohn surely would have supported: the truly revolutionary changes that the Internet—a new kind of "room"—has brought to modern Russia, China, and, more recently, the role that digital texting has played in the so-called Arab Spring in North Africa and the Middle East. Clearly, such a global vision would not have been available to Cohn in his time, which makes Hughes's point: that his poems mean different things to different audiences at various times in history and cannot be reduced to a single message.

Hughes and his questioners did not share any common ground from which to acknowledge, let alone find and make use of, the transformative insights that a poem or any work of art might offer. For Cohn and Dirksen, "revolution," for instance, had only one meaning in this context, one that eclipsed even the American Revolution: the October Revolution that created Soviet Russia. The idea that a poet might not write about himself but instead use the voices of others whose beliefs he might or might not share is incompatible both with the intentional fallacy that undergirds the very concept of subversive language and with the requirements of poetry as interiorized subjectivity. The differences between Hughes and his interrogators become starkest when an annoyed Dirksen poses an explicit question to Hughes about why he writes poetry: "May I ask, do you write poetry merely for the *amusement and the spiritual and emotional ecstasy* that it develops, or do you write it for a *purpose?*" (ST, 981, my emphases). Hughes's reply broadens the question's reach: "You write it [poetry] out of your soul and you write it for your own individual feeling of expression. First, sir, it does not come from yourself in the first place. It comes from *something beyond yourself,* in my opinion.... There is something more than myself in the creation of everything that I do. I believe that is in every creation, sir" (ST, 981, my emphasis). "Something beyond yourself" can be understood not as a mysterious transcendental origin or impulse but as a precise reference to the dialogic dynamics that characterize "Ballads of Lenin" and most of Hughes's other verse and that rely heavily on the call-and-response patterns of musical forms such as the blues and jazz.

Hughes's poems self-consciously communicate a strong sense of contributing to wider discursive fields in which his poetry becomes part of a multilayered, more encompassing literary and historical conversation. The poem "Union," published in *New Masses* in 1931, exemplifies this sense of connectedness. Rather than enclosing the "I" and what it knows, the dashes placed at the end of the first two lines reach out toward the world.

> Not me alone—
> I know now—

But all the whole oppressed
Poor world,
White and black,
Must put their hands with mine.

(CP, 138)

It is a sense of purposefully participating in history that animates Hughes's poetry: "I want to make my country as *beautiful* as I can, as *wonderful* as a country as I can," he testified further on in the closed hearing (ST, 988, my emphases). The little poem "History" from *Opportunity* (1934) encapsulates both purpose and beauty in four succinct lines that organize around the emphatically placed noun "mint," allowing its connotations and denotations—money, government authority, abundance, and perfection—to attach to "blood and sorrow" in a disquieting metaphor:

The past has been a mint
Of blood and sorrow.
That must not be
True of tomorrow.

(CP, 179)

An important effect of Hughes's careful negotiations of the relationship between aesthetics and politics is that he rewrites "the imagist fragment as social text,"[79] pulling into his verse material from a variety of socioeconomic contexts, from restaurant menus in "Advertisement for the Waldorf-Astoria" to the dollar signs at the end of "Elderly Leaders" (*CP*, 194). He also does this in *The Big Sea*, where he interrupts the narrative with ads for Saturday rent parties and signs barring access to African Americans (see *BS*, 229–32 and 287).[80] He arranges these nonliterary fragments into motile shapes—such as scattering dice in "Cubes" (*New Masses*, 1934)[81]—that violate the integrity of the lyric line.

d

    i

s

  e

    a

      s

  e

(CP, 176)

Such shapes, plus the use of different fonts, font sizes, and vertical columns (as in "Wait" from 1933, *CP,* 174) to create a highly differential semiotic field, are quite familiar to readers of T.S. Eliot, William Carlos Williams, Ezra Pound, and H.D., to name but a few other, more canonical modernists. Smethurst is certainly right in noting that "[w]hat has also generally been missed in Hughes's revolutionary poetry is the continued connection with modernism formally and thematically as Hughes, like nearly all other radical poets of the 1930s, writes quite consciously with the legacy of earlier modernists' art and literature in mind."[82] Another object of the committee's scorn, "Scottsboro," which Hughes published in *Opportunity* in 1931, echoes Williams's famous poem "Great Figure" from 1921 and its visual representation in Charles Demuth's 1928 painting *I Saw the Figure 5 in Gold.*

8 BLACK BOYS IN A SOUTHERN JAIL
8 WORLD TURN PALE!
8 blacks boys and one white lie.
Is it much to die?

(*CP,* 142)

These resonances remind us that the subject of Williams's poem about glimpsing an ornate number on a fire truck is also a state of emergency—"siren howls / and wheels rumbling / through the dark city"—though the precise reasons for it remain unspecified.[83] Williams, who was also a fellow traveler of the greater New York Left and, like Hughes, frequently published in Communist journals, would have been quite familiar with the conversational vernacular idiom Hughes used in "Good Morning, Revolution"—You're the very best friend / I ever had. / We gonna pal around together from now on" (*CP,* 162).[84] Cary Nelson points out that it was "partly in response to his politics," which cost Williams his position as poetry consultant at the Library of Congress in 1948, that USAmerican academic critics did not induct him into the modernist canon until the 1970s, and then with reluctance and misgivings.[85] Could this have been the reason that Harold Bloom did not include Williams in his early studies of poetry?

"One More 'S' in the U.S.A.," the poem that apparently most disgusted Cohn, had initially been composed for a Scottsboro rally and employs what Dawahare calls "a working-class vernacular [Hughes] believed has multiracial mass appeal." Hughes's diction, he continues, "has much in common with that of Carl Sandburg, who was one of his early literary influences. Hughes's poetic language is informal, often intimate, not unlike speech one might hear between friends. It is devoid of philosophical or political abstraction, like much proletarian poetry, in order to appeal to the average worker unschooled in Marxist theory."[86] The poetic frame contrasts significantly with the informality of the diction. Hughes uses two balladlike quatrains as a "chorus" to be repeated after each of the four varying sestets, the combination of each set of fourteen lines creating the shadowy outline of a sonnet. This outline is even fainter in the sections where the chorus is not actually repeated but just imagined.

> Put one more s in the U.S.A.
> To make it Soviet.
> One more s in the U.S.A.
> Oh, we'll live to see it yet.
> When the land belongs to the farmers
> And the factories to the working men—
> The U.S.A when we take control
> Will be the U.S.S.A. then.

(*CP*, 176)

This is hardly the first time that Hughes riffs on the sonnet form. He does so most visibly in "Seven Moments of Love: An Un-Sonnet Sequence in Blues," printed in *Esquire* in 1940, to chronicle a mundane love affair turned sour. One might read "One More 'S'"—in which the sonnet form is far more effaced than in "Seven Moments" or even in E. E. Cummings's famous sonnet sequences—along similar lines as the account of a political love affair between USAmerican workers and the Communist Party, especially when one adds into the equation another poem Hughes published in *Esquire* in 1936: the Whitmanesque "Let America Be America Again." The Great Depression and its aftermath were hardly times in which to write love poetry to Lady Liberty, but, for Hughes and others, there was still room, as it were, for expressing hope and the desire for change. Adding an extra "s" to "U.S.A.," which is subsequently capitalized in the poem's chorus, in addition to rhyming "Soviet" with the proleptic "yet," stands as an articulation of possibilities for positive transformations that might bring an end to injustice, poverty, repression, and racism. Unlike "Let America," "One More 'S' in the U.S.A.," which emulates the rhythm of a work song and combines it with the catchiness of political slogans and advertising jingles, takes readers beyond a national framework, declaring the nation to be as inadequate an object of one's political affections as the sonnet form is an insufficient vehicle for such declarations.[87] In the later poem, Hughes returns to a canvas of more staid imagery but also projects against that canvas the dream that "used to be" a figure of "America" (not the USA) as "the land that never has been yet":

> Let America be America again
> Let it be the dream it used to be.
> Let it be the pioneer on the plain
> Seeking a home where he himself is free.
>
> . . . .
>
> O, let America be America again—

The land that never has been yet—
And yet must be—the land where *every* man is free.

· · · · · · · · · · · · · · · · · ·

O, yes,
I say it plain,
America never was America to me,
And yet I swear this oath—
America will be!

(*CP*,189–91)

It is quite evident, from this poem and from others that I discuss in earlier chapters, that America exists in a very different discursive space for Hughes than the USA. The line "America was never America to me," which is initially bracketed in the poem as if whispered, points to a recurring topic in Hughes's writing, from "I, Too" to his essays in the *Chicago Defender*: "The most dire thought we are holding in our deep hearts is a dream of a real AMERICAN America.... Shall we, who are the Negro people of America, have no great dreams? Shall we only ask for the half-freedoms that move nobody to action for the great freedoms that this war is supposed to be about?"[88] The essay from which these lines are drawn, "No Half-Freedoms," was written in 1943, when *Brown v. Board of Education* and desegregation were not even on the legal horizon. At the time of Hughes's testimony before McCarthy, however, *Brown* had been argued before the U.S. Supreme Court for the first time, on December 9, 1952, and there was palpable hope that the separate-but-equal doctrine of *Plessy v. Fergusson* (1896) might actually be overturned. The case would be reargued on December 8, 1953, and finally decided in favor of the *Brown* plaintiffs on May 17, 1954.

Hughes took up the case for an "AMERICAN America" when he delivered a lengthy autobiographical monologue—approximately two thousand words in the transcript, which he may have read from a prepared script[89]—as part of his closed testimony. The purpose of his statement was to give a "full interpretation" of the poems under attack by demonstrating that poetry, as an act of the imagination, "goes out of a very deep background" and that it is precisely the fact that "it does not come in a moment" that gives it substance.[90] The committee initially indulges him—"Take as long as you want" (ST, 982)—but soon grows impatient. Arguing that "[t]o give a full interpretation of any piece of literary work one has to consider not only when and how it was written, but what brought it into being. The emotional and physical background that brought it into being," Hughes intones words reminiscent of the beginning of classic slave narratives: "I, sir, was born in Joplin, Missouri. I was born a Negro. From my very earliest childhood memories, I have encountered very serious and very hurtful problems" (ST, 986).

Was Hughes simply trying to buy time, or did he hope to garner the committee's sympathies? Neither seems very likely. It is hard to believe that

Hughes would have misjudged his listeners so badly on this occasion. What resounds is Hughes's undaunted reply to Cohn, who proposed to "save a little time" by "conced[ing] the background which you wrote it from was the background you wanted to describe." "I would much rather preserve my reputation and freedom," Hughes responds, "than to save time" (ST, 986). It is worth doing what the committee did not: take the time to listen to what Hughes tells us in this autobiographical account, which is very different from anything we read in his two autobiographies, where he spends little time and emotional energy recounting events from his childhood. In fact, the first childhood memory he recalls here is not even mentioned anywhere in *The Big Sea:*

> One of my earliest childhood memories was going to the movies in Lawrence, Kansas, where we lived, and there was one motion picture theater, and I went every afternoon. It was a nickelodeon, and I had a nickel to go. One afternoon I put my nickel down, and the woman pushed it back and she pointed to a sign. I was about seven years old. [Continues after an interruption from Cohn.] The woman pushed my nickel back and pointed to a sign beside the box office, and the sign said something, in effect, "Colored not admitted." *It was my first revelation of the division between the American citizens.* My playmates who were white and lived next door to me could go to that motion picture and I could not. I could never see a film in Lawrence again, and I lived there until I was twelve years old. (ST, 986–87, my emphasis)

The point for which this episode in Jim Crow Kansas around 1910 shrewdly prepares more attentive listeners is one Hughes develops carefully in narrating the second incident, which, though familiar from *The Big Sea* (see 14)—which he calls *The Deep Sea* (ST, 988) in mockery of Cohn's infelicities—is cast there in rather different language:

> They did not let me go to the school [in Topeka]. There were no Negro children there. My mother had to take days off from her work, had to appeal to her employer, had to go to the school board and finally after the school year had been open for some time she got me into the school.
>   I had been there only a few days when the teacher made unpleasant and derogatory remarks about Negroes and specifically seemingly pointed at myself. Some of my schoolmates stoned me on the way home from school. One of my schoolmates (and there were no other Negro children in the school), a little white boy, protected me, and *I have never in all my writing career or speech career as far as I know said anything to create a division among humans, or between whites and Negroes,* because I have never forgotten this kid standing up for me against these other first-graders who were throwing stones at me. I have always felt from that time on...that *there are white people in America who can be your friend,* and will be your friend, and who do not believe in

the kind of things that almost every Negro who has lived in our country has experienced. (ST, 987, my emphases)

Hughes's point here—that he had never been divisive even though he might have had good reasons to be so—is far more specific and focused on *America* than what he writes about the same experience in *The Big Sea,* where he expresses a faith in humanity in words similar to those Anne Frank uses in her famous diary: "So I learned early on not to *hate* all white people. And ever since, it has seemed to me that most people are generally good, in every race and in every country where I have been" (*BS,* 14). Here national specificity serves as a springboard for the almost desperate appeals to his patriotism that follow. Mentioning his father, James N. Hughes—who plays such a problematic role in *The Big Sea*—now becomes an occasion for marking progress on the civil rights front:

> My father as a young man, shortly after I was born, I understand, had studied law by correspondence. He applied for permission to take examination for the Bar in the state of Oklahoma where he lived, and they would not permit him. A Negro evidently could not take the examinations. You could not be a lawyer at the time in the state of Oklahoma. You know that has continued in a way right up to recent years, that we had to go all the way to the Supreme Court to get Negroes into the law school a few years ago to study law. Now you may study law and be a lawyer there. (ST, 987)

Although Hughes does not refer to *Brown v. Education* directly, he is very probably alluding to two of the Supreme Court cases that prepared the path to it: *McLaurin v. Oklahoma* (1950), which held that public institutions of higher learning could not treat students differently because of their race, and *Sweatt v. Painter,* which desegregated law schools in Texas. Hughes deploys the legacy of these cases, which were surely known to Cohn, as evidence of the gradual abolition of Jim Crow laws and argues that because of such changes, he lacks "the kind of bitterness, the kind of utter psychiatric, you might say, frustration that has been expressed in some Negro novels" and that also characterized his father's feelings toward his native land. Hughes may well have been thinking about Richard Wright's *Native Son* here. "I love the country I had grown up in," he continues. "I was concerned with the problems and I came back here. My father wanted me to live in Mexico or Europe. I did not" (ST 987). Noting that his own father was "rabidly anti-American, anti-United States," Hughes states that "I did not sympathize with that viewpoint.... My feeling was, this is my country, I want to live here. I want to come back here I want to make my country as beautiful as I can, as wonderful as a country as I can, because I love it myself" (ST, 988).

The strategy backfired, and Hughes's declarations of loyalty proved as ineffective as his attempts to defend his poetry. The committee responded with indifference to Hughes's emotional account, telling him that he had provided "enough background" and ordering him to cease what they took as evasive maneuvering (ST, 989). There was nothing left for Hughes after this failed defense strategy—it failed because Hughes appealed to a version of the same autobiographical or intentional fallacy to which the committee subscribed, and he could not beat them on their own ground. Hughes's failure also puts into evidence a sentiment that James Baldwin would express in 1963: "It is perhaps because I am an American Negro that I have always felt white Americans, many if not most of them, are experts in delusion—they usually speak as though I were not in the room. *I*, here, does not refer so much to the man called Baldwin as it does to the reality which produced me, a reality with which I live, and from which most Americans spend all their time in flight."[91]

When Hughes, near the end of the session, tries to return to earlier issues, David Schine is quick to remind him that he is risking perjury. "[I]t is only fair to reemphasize to you," Schine interrupts, "the danger that you face if you do not tell the truth to this committee, and to ask you to reconsider as to whether you wish to change any of your testimony here." Hughes declines the offer, adding that "I have never been a member of the Communist party, and I wish so to state under oath" (ST, 997). When Schine reminds him that what is at issue here is not just that one question but "your entire testimony before the committee," Hughes, after conferring with Reeves, equivocates and stalls: "The truth of the matter is, sir, that the rapidity with which I have been questioned, I don't fully recollect everything that I might have said here. If a complete review of the testimony were given me, it might be possible that I would want to change or correct some" (ST, 997–98). Then Schine goes on to ask Hughes to name "some Communist party members whom you have known." Hughes refuses, stating that he does not know who was or was not a member of the party, prompting another not-so-veiled threat from his interrogator about the accuracy of his earlier testimony: "Do you not think it is important when you are asked a question concerning your conversations with Communist party members that you try to be accurate?" Among those whom Hughes might have protected on this occasion were not only W. E. B. Du Bois, who had already been indicted for being a Communist sympathizer in 1951, but also his long-time Knopf editor Maxim Lieber, who had fled to Mexico.[92] When Hughes again asks to confer with counsel, Dirksen adjourns the meeting, requesting that Hughes return "at 10:15 on Thursday morning" for his public hearing.

We do not know whether McCarthy, in a private meeting on Wednesday, March 25, once again conjured up for Hughes the specter of perjury charges against him unless he cooperated with the committee the following day. Given the very contentious nature of Hughes's first hearing, such a threat strikes me as a likely possibility. Although perjury charges might not have led to an actual jail sentence, they would still have resulted in some form of blacklisting,[93] which was the last thing Hughes would have wanted at a time when the difficulties he was beginning to experience with publishers and agents were already endangering his reputation and livelihood (see *Life*, 2:207). Perjury charges might also have opened the door for charging and prosecuting Hughes under the Smith Act, which is precisely what would happen to the Marxist poet and editor Walter Lowenfels on July 29 of that same year.[94] Still, what most worried Hughes was continued public humiliation for having promulgated political ideas that were quite unpopular with most black USAmericans at the time. As we have seen in his editorial decisions for *Cuba Libre*, Hughes did not want to alienate that audience. Another possible avenue of coercion for McCarthy and Cohn might have been to expose Hughes as a homosexual, which would have made matters even worse. The Republicans had opened up the issue of "perverts" in the Truman administration in the late 1940s, and the persecution of homosexuals continued well into the 1950s. For not a few politicians at the time, homosexuality and Communism were close bedfellows. Senator Dirksen was one of them. Given that, during the 1952 presidential campaign, Dirksen had delivered speeches targeting what he called "the lavender lads" in the State Department, his question to Hughes about being "a single man" was not as innocent as it might otherwise have seemed. Cohn himself, who had sex with men but did not consider himself a homosexual, was also well known for his homophobia.[95] It is by no means unbelievable that members of McCarthy's subcommittee would have stooped to such slander, or at least to the threat of it.[96]

After his public hearing, Hughes wasted no time distributing partial transcripts to five hundred friends and business acquaintances,[97] and he sounded a note of relief in a letter to Frank Reeves dated April 8, 1953: "All of my publishers are pleased with the outcome of the hearings, have backed me up beautifully, and are going ahead with their publishing plans in relation to my work" (LHP, 136:2525). Yet even as late as 1959, the year when his *Selected Poems* was published and the Red Scare had largely passed, Hughes felt the need to use his public appearance before McCarthy's committee to vindicate himself, as in the following note appended to a contract with CBS News.[98]

> I am not now a member of any of the organizations or groups listed on the back of this sheet [groups that the attorney general had designated "Totalitarian, Fascist, Communist, or Subversive"]....I have explained in full for the record my own personal, political, and artistic activities under oath on March 23 [*sic*], 1953, at a public hearing in Washington of the Senate Committee on Permanent Investigations headed by Senator McCarthy. At the close of the hearings I was commended by Senator [John] McClellan, thanked by Senator McCarthy, and since that time my books to which Schine and Cohn had objected have been replaced in the U.S. Information Service's overseas libraries. Subsequently, a

number of my books have been published and distributed through the United States Information Agency—the latest being my FIRST BOOK OF JAZZ (Poetnica Jazza) in a Serbo-Croatian translation, Belgrad, May 30, 1959. The Agency has contracted for the right to translate various of my books into some 80 languages. And the State Department has sent a number of distinguished foreign visitors to interview me. My work is used on radio and television throughout the world, particularly in England, France, Italy, and other countries of Europe—much more so than here where the work of writers of color has had a pretty hard time getting on the airwaves or breaking into the mass media. (LHP, 365:5861)

That Hughes takes pains to emphasize the (now state-sponsored) presence of the translations of his work into other languages recalls the glaring absence of references to such translations during the McCarthy Committee hearings. One might say that Hughes strategically inserted his later remarks in the space left blank on McCarthy's original subpoena. Flaunting the fact that people in other countries were, and had been, reading his work in languages other than English, Hughes reasserts his international stature along with the ultimate ineffectiveness of the committee's attempted suppression of his written words. His remarks, in which we reencounter "the sly voice inhabiting the poems," stand as a final reminder that his capitulation at the public hearing had indeed been staged.[99]

It would appear that the staged surrender that appeased most of Hughes's political critics did not entirely stem the flow of skepticism, if not of outright accusations. Although Hughes had claimed during the hearings that he had officially ended his support for Communism, he would, "only seven months later, continue to attack in the pages of the *Defender* the governmental practices [of political censorship] that caused him so much trouble."[100] Given Hughes's resistance at the closed deposition, I agree with Rampersad that "certain questions about Langston's true feelings toward radical socialism remained unanswered" and that "the magma of political indignation in Hughes remained, below the placid surface, red-hot" (*Life*, 2:219–20). Regardless of whether the bitterly satiric poem "Un-American Investigators," published posthumously in 1967 in *The Panther and the Lash*, was written before or after Hughes's McCarthy experience, it renders his feelings about the process palpable.

> The committee shivers
> With delight in
> Its manure.
>
>   (CP, 560)[101]

There is one important thing, however, that Rampersad did not know, could not have known, at the time he wrote his autobiography of Hughes: the Hughes we see in the executive session was clearly *not* the person who "had come to Washington...to negotiate an honorable surrender" (*Life,* 2:211). To be sure, Hughes seemed largely composed and polite. Still, there are signs of suppressed anger and also of a growing, at times barely contained, alarm at the realization that his strategies were failing, that the story he was telling about being black, about being a writer in the USA, and about the difference between art and political propaganda was not one that the committee could and would credit. That panic seems to have spread to Reeves, who, near the end of the meeting, surprisingly interrupted the "rapid fire process" of Cohn's questioning and was promptly called to order (ST, 994). Nonetheless, the Hughes whom we see in the closed hearing had come to fight with words. Given the failure of his frequent signifyin(g) on his questioners' rhetoric and his attempts to insert a human dimension into their willful acts of mistranslation, it would be reasonable to expect a thoroughly defeated Hughes by the end of the hearing. Yet Hughes, still undeterred and with his feelings of panic under control, insists on turning the hearing to practical matters of survival. He bluntly asks Dirksen, "Would you tell me, sir, about expenses?" The question is unforeseen and perplexing to the senator.

> SENATOR DIRKSEN: About expenses?
> MR. HUGHES: Yes, sir. They are covered by the committee while I am here?
> SENATOR DIRKSEN: Under the rule the transportation is paid and there is an allowance of $9 a day while you are here.
> MR. HUGHES: From whom do I get it here?
> SENATOR DIRKSEN: From the Treasury. (ST 998)

With this seemingly mundane exchange about expenses, Hughes returns the hearing to the economic implications of his earlier autobiographical remarks, allowing him to end with an assertion of some measure of agency and human dignity. In my book, pointing out that one has certain basic needs, including economic ones, and that those needs have to be both acknowledged and fulfilled does not qualify as surrender.

DENOUEMENT: PLEDGING ALLEGIANCE

In the years that followed, Hughes became exceedingly cautious about having his name associated with anything and anyone from the 1930s Left. In 1954 he even agreed, at the request of his publisher, Dodd, Mead, to drop the entry on Du Bois from his essays in *Famous American Negroes*.[102] The following year Hughes also excised Paul Robeson from his *Famous Negro Music Makers*.[103] Not surprisingly, Hughes's *Selected Poems* from 1959 did not include a single one of the disputed poems—or any other radical poems—and ended with "Freedom's Plow," the very lyric from *Opportunity* that Hughes had used in 1953 to prove his supposed political conversion. Also in 1959 Hughes sent a copy of *Selected Poems* to Frank Reeves, in remembrance of "how you once 'saved my life.'"[104] In the years to follow, Hughes revised several of his controversial poems in later editions, effectively producing what he had earlier criticized as "a saleable tissue of conscious lies."[105] *The Langston Hughes Reader* (1958), however, still included a translated poem by Guillén, whereas the excerpts from Hughes's autobiographies conspicuously omitted all sections on his sojourn in the Soviet Union.

On September 18, 1960, in the midst of rapidly deteriorating USA-Cuban relations, Fidel Castro arrived in New York City to deliver a speech before the United Nations General Assembly. *Time* magazine reported on "the rumpled Cubans in their greasy green army fatigues" in less than glowing terms two weeks later. After causing chaos at the East Side Shelburne Hotel, Castro and his entourage relocated to the "dowdy old Theresa, which ha[d] brooded over Harlem's 125th Street and Seventh Avenue since pre-World War I days." There, according to *Time*, "Castro had a steady stream of visitors. Negro Moslem Leader Malcolm X, Beatnik Poet Allen (Howl) Ginsburg, Columbia Professor C. Wright Mills (who [was] writing a book on the Cuban Revolution) and Left-Wing Poet Langston Hughes dropped in to pay their respects. A couple of hours later, Nikita Khrushchev himself drove up to the Theresa in a skirl of sirens."[106] Hughes was not pleased to be included in this list of distinguished visitors. On September 30, 1960, the irate poet sent the following letter to the editor of *Time*:

Sir:
Since I do not know Fidel Castro and have never had any sort of contacts with him or communications from him, I would very much appreciate a retraction of the statement on page 16 in the October 3, 1960, issue of TIME to the effect that "Left-Wing Poet Langston Hughes dropped in" at the Theresa to pay respects. I have not been in the Hotel Theresa for several weeks, and was certainly not there during Mr. Castro's stay. Leonard Lyons, in his NEW YORK POST column of September 27, erroneously stated that I was a guest at a Castro dinner at the Theresa. Mr. Lyons was, however, gracious enough to make a retraction in his POST column the following day. I trust TIME will be equally gracious—for both my sake and Castro's.
Very truly yours,
Langston Hughes[107]

Clearly, Hughes was very sensitive—perhaps overly so—about being called "left-wing" even seven years after his encounter with McCarthy. While his desire to distance himself publicly from Cuba's new revolutionary regime may not be surprising, the fact that he turned a deaf ear even to his old friend Nicolás Guillén is. Six months after Castro's visit, on April 18,

1961, Guillén sent Hughes a Western Union telegram. This telegram, signed "Asociación de escritores y artistas. Nicolás Guillén presidente," seems to have been the last written communication between the two men, who had met in Havana in 1930 and had exchanged many letters over the years. The telegram reads, "Nuestro territorio ha sido invadido por fuerzas del imperialismo norteamericano brutal agresión nuestra soberanía nos permitimos esperar de usted y amigos de esa únanse protesta universal contra estos vandálicos hechos" (LHP, 70:1366). (Our territory has been invaded by the forces of North American imperialism. Because this is a brutal attack on our sovereignty, we allow ourselves to hope that you and friends of our sovereignty will join in issuing a universal protest against these vandalistic deeds.) Hughes did not respond to Guillén. Nor did he issue a public protest or participate in any demonstrations against the Bay of Pigs invasion.[108]

When Guillén's plea confronted Hughes with the reality of having to choose publicly between nationalist loyalty and the kind of transnational solidarity that Hughes's history as a New World cultural broker might have suggested, as surely it did to Guillén, he came down in favor of the former. In 1961 both Guillén and Hughes pledged official allegiance to their respective countries' governments, Hughes by severing the last of his ties to a radical political past, Guillén by embracing Cuba's revolutionary regime. Ironically, the very actions, or inactions, that divided the two poets at this crucial point in history were cut from the same nationalist cloth. Even their rewards bear some similarity. Guillén received public recognition for his political choices by being appointed to a high-level bureaucratic post as president of the National Writers' Union. He also, at long last, became Cuba's poet laureate. Hughes, in turn, "earned the gratitude of the Senate Subcommittee on Internal Security" for his resounding silence. Even more embarrassingly, the committee would later "mention him favorably in noting that American blacks had shrewdly resisted Cuban schemes 'to popularize Cuba among Negroes'" (*Life*, 2:330–31). Those who had known the Langston Hughes who, for nearly thirty years, had actively promoted Cuban and other Hispanic American writers in the USA, would surely have felt the painful irony with which this commendation must have been received.

Afterword

America/América/*Americas*

> It is awkward to speak of peoples who play such an important role on the world scene, but who lack collective names. The word *American* may no longer be applied exclusively to the citizens of the United States of North America, and it would be desirable if this nomenclature for the independent nations of the New Continent could be fixed in a way that would be at once convenient, consistent, and precise.
>
> —Alexander von Humboldt, *Political Essay in the Island of Cuba*

> I would really like to find another word for "American." When someone says "American" they mean someone who lives between New York and Los Angeles, and not someone who lives between Montevideo and Santiago.
>
> —Jean Luc Goddard in a 2004 interview

I take this afterword as an occasion to reflect on the major assumptions that underlie my book. Doing so also leads me to address some of the theoretical and practical implications of what I have proposed about heterolingual literature, modernism, and translation in the context of perhaps the most challenging and exasperating of all false cognates: "America" and *América*—challenging because alternatives in English seem needlessly cumbersome, exasperating because there is so little awareness that there is a difference and that it matters.

READING FOR SURVIVAL

This book rests on two fundamental beliefs. The first is that literature matters to life; it is an intellectual and emotional resource crucial for human survival on this planet. Literature, according to Ottmar Ette, is a storehouse of knowledge on which we can draw as we contemplate how individuals and groups can live together in mutual respect for, not just tolerance of, each other's diversities, whatever those may be. If this is so, then William Carlos Williams's cautionary reminder that "aesthetically, morally, we are deformed unless we read" applies as much today as it did in 1925, perhaps even more.[1] Since my scholarly concern for some time now has been how people, ideas, and objects share and contest the space of the Americas, I decided to put Ette's dual emphasis on respect and survival to the test in this book by inquiring into the kinds of knowledge that texts from the Western Hemisphere might encode and store. What do they have to say about how to live and write in a world where differences in color, sexuality, politics, and language, more often than not, become occasions for social and legal discrimination?

Specifically, I wanted to know what sorts of cultural exchanges are possible in spite of such perceived barriers. Langston Hughes quickly emerged as an almost inescapable focus for such a project because of his worldwide travels, his knowledge of other languages, his work as a literary translator, and the fact that his own writings have been translated widely throughout the Americas. Most important, however, was the fact that his poems, autobiographies, and translations are exemplary explorations of what it might mean to live and write, as the title of my introduction suggests, "in others' words." This circumstance—some would call it a predicament—had special salience for Hughes as an African American poet from the USA who was part of the Harlem Renaissance and, like many other New Negro writers at the time, flirted extensively with Communism.[2] Although Hughes is no doubt a popular cultural icon, a favorite certainly of the Academy of American Poets, as a *writer* he has hardly been taken seriously enough. My way of taking Hughes very seriously has been to read his literary representations of actual and imagined movements across racial, political, and other cultural divides as strategies for survival through translation. It is, after all, no coincidence that survival is such a frequent topic in his poems and autobiographies and that tropes of survival modulate what might otherwise appear to be an obsession with death.[3] I have argued that knowledge of and for survival was precisely what Hughes wanted to pass on to his readers and that the extent to which he succeeded in doing so has varied greatly. The degree to which he failed is perhaps most obvious in his Senate testimonies, but it is also evident in much academic scholarship on him. Taking the reception of Hughes's work beyond the context of the USA gave me a springboard for tracing in detail how specific texts changed as they were ferried across linguistic, cultural, and political borders and acquired literary lives that proved quite independent of their author.

My second precept is that "[a]ll theories are ultimately masks for hidden diversities," as Wilson Harris phrased it so succinctly.[4] Critical theories in academia are no exception. To the extent that the afterlives Hughes's writings attained deserve to be called "world literature," one might argue that what I have done in the preceding chapters is put flesh on the bones of the concept of world literature as something that, in David Damrosch's words, is "formed by the interactions of two or more national literatures within a given cultural space."[5] This is true only to the extent that I imagine Damrosch's given cultural space as the space of translation, which he does not. And I do so rather grudgingly, since I see such a space not as given but as something always under construction—recall Emily Apter's "in-translation."[6] I also do not regard either Hughes or his Hispanic American translators as representative of any national literatures. If anything, they illustrate the fact that not all literary works that fully or partially inhabit the linguistic space associated with a nation can be unproblematically identified with that nation as a political construct that Wilson Harris would call a "closed world."[7] A nation is a political construct without a necessarily coincident cultural entity. Rightly or wrongly, we tend to regard the latter as changing far more rapidly than the former, which seems to stay relatively static, changes in geographical borders notwithstanding. Culture pulls at politics, at institutions of all sorts, while politics tries to bring perceived cultural chaos back in line, violently if need be. The trouble that nationalisms cause, both practically and theoretically, has to do with the fact that the political entities we call nations are indeed never static but change all the time, both in relation to each other and internally, as previously hardened borders become ever-more permeable. In response, nations try to limit their citizens' ability to imagine kinship "beyond a boundary," as C.L. R. James put it.

Literary translations are a case in point, but they are hardly the only example of texts that interrogate forms of national identity by dwelling in perpetual homelessness. Repatriation is as much beside the point for translation as it is for any literatures that have multiple points of national origin, or perhaps none at all. In this regard, I find Ette's concept of "Literatur ohne festen Wohnsitz" (literature[s] without a fixed abode) hospitable and theoretically productive because it "crosses the divide between national literature and world literature with impunity, without being beholden to the exclusive and exclusionary logic" of either.[8] Any viable definition of world literature(s) for the present and the last century, it seems to me, would have to be formulated around the conditions of actual and linguistic migrancy and cultural homelessness rather than exile, a term that has been as overworked in cultural studies as "hybridity."[9] I also agree with Ette that we have more than enough spatial concepts by now. What we lack is "a sufficiently exact terminology for *movement, dynamics, and mobility* . . . ways of rendering more conceptually precise the relations between culture and language, space and time, medium and discipline." [10]

Yet we are lacking something else in our theories if we are to chart real movements within real or virtual space and time, in this case the hemispheric space of the Americas roughly during the first half of the twentieth century: we need ways of not screening out the human dimension as that which produces movement in the first place. What troubles me about both and indeed most theoretical formulations is the notion that literatures can somehow interact without human input and agency, clearly a rhetorical function of the quasi-anthropomorphic investments we make in our objects of study. Such investments tend to dehumanize most current humanistic modes of inquiry—including, ironically enough, Ette's.[11] Despite the fact that my own scholarly locutions remain implicated in this perhaps unavoidable dehumanization, at least to some degree, I cannot help but ask where the lives of authors and readers are in all this. After all, literatures can interact precisely because they have readers and because some readers become authors, translators even, who create texts for different audiences. Books sit on shelves or, these days, online in silence until someone opens them—brings them, as it were, to life by making them part of her own life. We—professional readers with or without homes in various academies—know this reflexively, even without having to call to mind the humans-as-books in Ray Bradbury's *Fahrenheit 451* (1951) or its recent lackluster cinematic remake, *The Book of Eli* (2010). The problem is that we take the act of reading and the existence of readers as simple givens, much as we take for granted the unobtrusive workings of translations. It is certainly the case that "[t]hese days, the practice of translation is culturally taken for granted to such a degree that its conscious perception requires what the Russian Formalists called a deautomatization. Literary translation is so much a part of the network of our daily translation activities that we have to make an effort to recognize its fundamental and, at the same time, exceptional value."[12]

To me, the fundamental value of studying literary translation is precisely such deautomatization. "Thanks to translation," Octavio Paz writes, "we become aware that our neighbors do not speak and think as we do"—whoever our neighbors are.[13] Most importantly, then, translation makes us reconsider common ground too easily assumed or posited. It does so by drawing attention to degrees of incommensurability, which, according to Natalie Melas, "[opens] up the possibility of an intelligible relation at the limits of comparison."[14] That translations, much like critical theories, are to produce sameness is an expectation whose logic follows the construction of equivalent value within capitalist economics. The important point here is that equivalent value, in contrast to what Marx calls "relative value," seeks to hide the fact "that some *social relation* is at the bottom of it."[15] Incommensurability, however minimal, makes us sit up and take notice of the existence of social and cultural differences *and* relations that, if left unnoticed and unattended, will likely harden into ideological calluses—one possible form of relation to which one might apply Marx's term "reification" (*Verdinglichung*). Many of them already have. One of the ways of preventing such undesirable coagulation is to construct provisional, nonhierarchical similarities that, as Melas (*pace* Edouard Glissant) rightly proposes, need not unify, at least not in any totalizing sense. Not all similarities automatically spell sameness. Like the proverbial devil, degrees of incommensurability in cultural transfer reside in the details. In comparative literary and cultural studies, details thus amount to far more than flotsam and jetsam in vast theoretical oceans of "world systems" and "deep time."[16] Whatever the benefits of Franco Moretti's "distant readings," which eschew analytical close-ups and make distance *"a condition of knowledge,"* they cannot help us access the intricacies of textual details.[17] Only close-up readings do, though clearly not the sort of formalist readings that insist on the aloof autonomy of a literary work, relegating its historical, political, and cultural situatedness to mere background noise. Insofar as translation returns our attention to language, it helps restore a philological dimension to a cultural studies discourse in which literary analysis has largely been replaced by sociology.[18]

With Harris, Williams, and Ette foremost in mind, I wrote this book as a reminder, to myself and to others who profess literature, that we make far too many unchecked assumptions and take too many things as simple givens. Our own human and professional identities too often rest in the category of givens. At the same time, it goes largely unrecognized that all of us live in other, and others', words virtually all the time. This is so regardless of whether we imagine the words we speak and write as awash in large discursive formations that submerge all subjectivity or as speech acts in which we self-consciously refract all linguistic and discursive conventions. This is so regardless of the number of languages in which we think, dream, speak, and write. Like most naturalized USAmerican citizens, I have more than one language at my disposal, and my scholarly fascination with translation likely derives in some measure from having lived with and in the sounds and cadences of several languages for as long as I can remember. The German I learned as a child was suffused with my grandmother's Polish phrases and East Prussian inflections, my mother's native Russian (though she spoke it rarely), my father's occasional *Plattdeutsch,* a regional dialect, and the English of my parents' British friends, which in time was to become Americanized and almost more familiar to me than my native tongue. Eighth grade brought French, recently revived by my work on Alexander von Humboldt, and graduate school Spanish, not to mention the motley assortment of vernaculars I inevitably acquired along the way. They have all stuck with me to varying degrees as (mostly) welcome reminders of the extent to which different languages, even those believed to be relatively proximate to each other, often encode cultural knowledge in radically different ways. Living-in-translation, then, amounts to residing in pluriverses that make code switching a modus vivendi.

Perhaps unavoidably, self-consciously navigating the flux of linguistic and discursive differences also creates a peculiar sense of being out of place. What is original, or native, and what translation blend together in a condition of linguistic homelessness that has complicated cultural consequences. This sense of homelessness, which is hardly unique to our times, affects all private and public interactions, among them self-representations and cultural identification that frequently do not match socially and professionally ascribed identities. For me, being pigeonholed as an American and an Americanist trained in African American studies speaks to vexations many share and few acknowledge.

The question of what can and cannot be thought and articulated in different languages and discourses extends to academic knowledge production more broadly. It makes all types of knowledge by definition local and partial, and it acknowledges untranslatability as a fact. Untranslatability flags gaps between so-called natural languages and discourses that cannot be closed, not easily or not at all. Taken to their outer conceptual reaches, these gaps belie claims to the universality of knowledge that have been passed down to us from the European Enlightenment.[19] Although we (scholars) pay tribute to epistemological partiality in theory, practice lags lamentably behind. For instance, we (Americanists) assume that we all know exactly what we mean when we speak about English, America, or race, the latter invariably defaults to black in the USA, the rise of whiteness studies notwithstanding.[20] The possibility of gaps in mutual understanding, culturally based misprision, and areas of untranslatability in our disciplinary languages and discourses goes largely unrecognized, and when it is acknowledged, it tends to spark conflict and embarrassment rather than creativity and innovation, let alone mutual respect. This is a sad state of affairs for a profession that purportedly values dialogue, certainly more than other sectors of our society seem to do. I want to wind down my book by sounding the depths of one particular gap in understanding created by the assumptions that different Americanists tend to make about the object of their study: is it America or *América?*

AMERICAN STUDIES, LATIN AMERICAN STUDIES, AND THE AMERICAS

The all-too-familiar narrative that equates America with the United States of America and with whiteness is the centerpiece of the dominant discourse that Langston Hughes challenges most consistently throughout his writings. His work reminds us of what we already know but seem at times slow or reluctant to translate into our own writing: "that the polite fictions rendering [US]American culture as a series of neighboring cultures hiding behind masks of legalized racism and racial identification are, in the end, fictions that in the name of domination have hidden our culture from ourselves."[21] Because of the extent to which that same narrative and the same polite fictions pervade academia, especially in the USA, they have been a recurring concern in this book and throughout my scholarship. The geocultural space I have privileged here is that of *the Americas,* or what used to be called America before that appellation defaulted to the USA. At the same time, I have also found it necessary—indeed, inevitable—to attend to locations outside this space, such as Spain and the former Soviet Union, to acknowledge the global connectedness of what would otherwise appear as an isolated continental or bicontinental space. My foregoing arguments have wide-ranging theoretical and methodological implications for the study of a cultural and political geography that has been invented and reinvented as an uneasily shared space ever since that initial moment of Columbus's misrecognition we still dub its discovery.

From the very start, America has been the result of translational displacements. Both the name and what it may signify has been disputed for such a long time that, perhaps like El Dorado, America has yet to be found. The adjective "hemispheric," about which I will have more to say below, encapsulates my understanding of the basic geography of the Americas as being composed of South, Central, and North America as well as the Caribbean archipelago, steering clear of more popular ideological divisions between America and Latin America—that *other* America or *nuestra América*[22]— or even North and South America. That both binary pairs conspicuously exclude the Caribbean and always Canada and that not a few citizens of the USA now believe South America to be inhabited by Mexicans—even though Mexico, the *United States* of Mexico, is actually part of North America—suffices to illustrate just how tricky accepted distinctions are. To conceptualize the Americas as a singular space does, of course, have it its problems, even when done heuristically. In no way do I mean to insinuate some sort of overarching cultural unity, which exists in this hemisphere no more than political accord does. Nor does such consensus exist within individual countries, least of all perhaps in the USA. Yet there are surely compelling historical reasons for regarding the whole of the postcolonial Americas, including the USA, as a dynamic network of cultural, political, and economic forces. Ironically, however, even New Americanists who have duly scrutinized and criticized the less than admirable part that the USA has played on this particular stage since the Monroe Doctrine still hold fast to some version of "American exceptionalism," the "discourse of incomparability" that accompanied the institutional debut of this area of study during the Cold War.[23] The doctrine of exceptionalism that the field of so-called American studies has espoused since then is, in the end, little more than a myth, possibly a mirage. Even as a former colony turned empire, the USA is hardly any more exceptional than its neighbors.

From my dual perspective as a comparatist and an (African) Americanist, I see a widening gap between theory and practice in debates about how American studies—really studies of the USA—might be reshaped, or "worlded," in the increasingly ineluctable contexts of globalization.[24] In my estimation, this gap is the result of terminological slippages and conceptual tautologies that hide a host of assumptions about the role political geography plays in framing ideas about culture and community. Designations such as "American studies," which Djelal Kadir has relabeled "American American studies" to align it with "Latin American studies," are part of the problem.[25] If it were not for the fact that certain groups of academic specialists strongly identify with them, I would not use such labels at all, and I apply them only provisionally.

The notion of a "hemispheric *turn*" in American studies is a symptom of the larger problem it seeks to redress.[26] USAmerican studies have turned far too many times in the last few years. There was the linguistic turn, the cultural turn, and the transnational turn, and since there is a turn for every season, it is now apparently time for the hemispheric turn. The assumption is, of course, that "hemispheric" signifies the Western Hemisphere, also known as the American Hemisphere, which somehow excludes the parts of North and West Africa, the Iberian Peninsula, the British Isles, Ireland, and Antarctica that also lie *west* of the prime meridian. These turns, which are typically announced by each incoming president of the American Studies Association (ASA), do not portend any lasting changes. They are like hanging one's flag with the wind, from whichever direction the breeze happens to blow. The direction from which the wind has more recently blown—indeed gusted—in USAcademia is that of globalization and fearful attempts at internationalization in the wake of 9/11. Unspoken contradictions within the very fabric of USAmerican studies have reduced attempts at the field's meaningful reconceptualization to mere turns. After all, reshaping it would have to begin with a critical assessment of some key assumptions and further theorization on the basis of such questioning. The following passage from a 2007 article by Diana Taylor, director of the Hemispheric Institute for Performance and Politics at New York University, encapsulates the issues with which Hughes grappled in his time and illustrates the extent to which they continue to vex USAmericanists today.

> Although scholars throughout the Americas may share certain objects of study, they seldom share basic assumptions, a common vocabulary, or theoretical readings.... There are problems, always problems, when scholars discuss *America:* the topic is huge, much of the terrain well traveled.... Worse still, everyone is sick of this discussion. Many agree theoretically that *America* is a misnomer yet continue to use it because there is nothing to be done. *America,* however, is more than a misnomer. To colleagues in the south, it is an act of aggression, an appropriation by people in the United States that excludes other inhabitants of the landmass. This critique necessarily gets cast as repetitive whining rather than critical intervention—"necessarily" because if scholars took the critique seriously, they would have to change their practice.[27]

In 1994 Carolyn Porter remarked on the very same issue in her programmatic essay, "What We Know That We Don't Know: Remapping American Literary Studies," in which she rightly lamented the "lip service paid to the severance of the US[A] from its claim of title to America." According to Porter, this lip service is not merely a sign of "bad faith" but of nation-based USAmericanists' collective "failure" to take seriously the need to transform their field in word *and* in deed: "the failure of too many of us to 'rethink' what we thought we already knew in the context of what we all know that we don't know."[28] Why, then, have scholars, presumably those to the north, resisted changing practices that perpetuate an awkwardness that Alexander von Humboldt had pinpointed as early as the 1820s? Why are they so unwilling to inquire into the field's protocols? Taylor doesn't say; neither does Porter. Djelal Kadir, however, is less coy, but his perspective is that of a literary comparatist. The problem, as he diagnoses it, is that "[t]he America of American Studies...becomes the objective correlative of a theory strong enough to have functioned as an unimpeachable determinate ideology. When theory hardens into ideology, and ideology becomes realized as pragmatic embodiment, there is no longer any allowable space for further theorization."[29]

Before offering a brief example of how this hardening can play out and illuminate the practical side of Kadir's point, I want to clarify that while the word "America" does have a range of affective connotations for different users, including academics, it is *not* the object of study for all scholars in the Americas but mainly for those who also have a professional investment in the word itself: that is, those who work in fields whose names include the adjective "American" in some way. Nor are all those who identify as either Americanists or Latin Americanists even located in the Americas. In my experience, the academics with the most deeply held investments in the word "America" are Americanists at universities located in the USA. One major reason for this is a conflation of nationality with professional identity. One becomes quite literally unthinkable without the other, and the very idea of renaming American studies programs to reflect a more hemispheric scope—or what some USAmericanists see as the Latin Americanization of their field—seems downright intolerable.[30] Unsurprisingly, there are no such gripes about Canada and the Caribbean, mainly, I suspect, because there are fewer language differences at issue, or so it seems on the surface. That USAmericanists' worries are cast in the language of conquest and colonization, or of colonization in reverse, speaks volumes to the apparent unavailability of other models for how these fields might relate.

The ground for a hemispheric orientation in the New American Studies, a term coined by Phil Fisher, was prepared in 1990.[31] The New Americanists charted a path away from apprehending the putative "uniqueness of the American experience" (in Perry Miller's phrasing) and toward studying the "cultures of United States imperialism." Yet the contributions to Kaplan and Pease's 1993 signature anthology barely even touched on Mexico and the Caribbean, let alone the rest of the Americas.[32] Later publications in this vein followed and extended the practice of safeguarding the exceptionalism of the USA by domesticating the issue of empire. Despite claims to different perspectives and "hemispheric engagement," essay collections with a hemispheric emphasis, such as the 2007 volume *Hemispheric American Studies* edited by Caroline Levander and Robert Levine, have ended up in a similar place: that is, "chart[ing] new literary and cultural geographies" results merely in a "broader definition of what the US[A] includes."[33] "Carefully partitioned relations between territory and power," as Paul Giles has termed them, remain entirely undisturbed in this scenario.[34]

While it may be true, at least in part, that the idea of hemispheric American studies threatens to disrupt such carefully partitioned relations, as Giles has claimed, the reality is also that the majority of USAmericanists today are rather ill prepared for scholarly work on the Hispanic Americas, as I have preferred to call Latin America to signal at least a partial cultural overlap with the USA.[35] I mean this quite literally: although, regular congressional attempts notwithstanding, English is not now and has never been the official language of the United States of America, a surprising number of USAmericanists are monolingual. This situation is reinforced either by the absence of language requirements as part of graduate training or by not taking existing requirements seriously enough.[36] That this English-only monolingualism extends to many who advocate in favor of broadening American studies puts in perspective the aversion that specialists on the Hispanic Americas typically have to the very idea. In theory, they defend their professional domain against encroachments that they regard as yet another form of academic imperialism. In practice, however, many so-called Latin Americanists see hemispheric American studies as opening the doors to interlopers who have none of the requisite linguistic skills to do what they theoretically propose. In this light, the much-debated question of whether American studies *should* become hemispheric American studies may be moot, for it is not clear at all that it can—except perhaps in theory. But it would be an odd kind of theory, one that precedes and then substitutes for critical practice.

Of course, language acquisition in and of itself is not a method, though area studies have often made it seem that way. For instance, being able to read literary texts in their original languages does not automatically turn one into a comparatist, and one should not overvalue linguistic skill at the expense of scholarly-scientific method. Yet a modicum of linguistic competency in Spanish, Portuguese, and French, which by no means exhaust the possibilities even for the Americas, is an indispensable prerequisite for any scholar in any discipline who wants to approach the hemispheric dimensions of America meaningfully. It even holds true for those who want to focus largely on the USA, a country whose realities are hardly monolingual. Michael Kowalewski has noted that "there has been a healthy and long overdue recognition that every region of the United States is criss-crossed by migratory vectors of in and out-migration. Every area of the country teems with the historical and cultural footprints of multiple populations (some recent, many long-established over generations)"—some forgotten, one might add—so that "culture shock can be experienced at home as well as abroad."[37] Even if it is nearly impossible for midcareer Americanists to learn the languages they would need to practice hemispheric American studies in good faith, they can at least ensure that their students find themselves better positioned. The next generation of USAmericanists—if indeed they will even be called Americanists—will no longer be able to sidestep the issue of linguistic competency, and their training must be responsive to this.[38]

Debates about hemispheric American studies, almost another dispute about the New World,[39] almost invariably frame the contest over America in terms of a familiar geographical binarism: north and south. Even commentators such as Diana Taylor are not immune to the lure of this reductive logic. Attributing misgivings about the misnomer "America" to "colleagues in the south," Taylor makes the "south" the inevitable symbolic location of resistance to the hegemony of a north that, just as inevitably, defaults to the USA, which is only implied in the above excerpt from her article. Taylor's surprisingly unreflective use of geospatial stereotypes is the rule rather than the exception among USAmericanists, regardless of whether they regard their territory as the USA or the Hispanic Americas. Canada and the Caribbean would further complicate matters, both theoretically and practically. Historically, the north-south binary has provided the impetus for studying foreign and remote cultures—as a form of ethnography—which, during the early years of the Cold War, spawned area studies at universities in Europe and the USA. From a USA perspective, area studies proper do not include American studies, though they do so everywhere else. Area studies grafted Cold War political divisions onto the nineteenth-century colonial map of the Western Hemisphere. Among other things, these divisions solidified the cultural separation of the USA (as America) from a Latin America invented by the French to serve its colonial interests. (There were no Romans in the Americas but certainly descendants of the Gauls.)

Literary canons are among the intellectual constructs that have traditionally sustained hemispheric fictions of national or regional impermeability. Americanists, mainly historians and literary scholars at the outset, expounded national exceptionalism in ways consistent with the aspirations of a global superpower at midcentury. Latin Americanists—many of whom initially hailed from the USA's military, where they had worked as interrogators, interpreters, and translators during World War II—contributed heartily to the same goal by providing information about neighboring areas perceived as potential political trouble spots. The implicit goal of both fields was to shore up the idea of the nation, or the region, as a distinct linguistic and, it was assumed, cultural entity.[40] As Harry Harootunian maintains, "regions and areas were simply seen as singularly spatial and often timeless entities that were in the world but were not treated as if they belonged to it."[41] The disregard for temporality in both fields enabled geographical areas and the fields of study identified with them to *perform* as exceptional.

Even though the politics of area studies have changed since the early years of the Cold War—especially in Latin American studies, which has become much more critical of the USA's involvement in other parts of the Americas—the conceptual attachment to holistic cultural communities identifiable with geographic locations has remained largely intact. This attachment echoes, as Harootunian reminds us, "the older obsession with extracting an unchanging and essential national character promised by the study of national literatures and histories."[42] Much like national literature departments, both USAmerican studies and Latin American studies have produced their respective exceptionalist narratives and counternarratives over time, and these narratives tend to reproduce the distinctive ideological dispositions of their respective objects of study.[43] In this scenario, scholarly work is a matter of defending a priori assumptions about cultural and political uniqueness and thereby rendering one's object of study and one's own discourse incomparable. This is also one of the paradoxes of comparative literature, which complicates the role of the truth teller that it has on occasion adopted vis-à-vis American studies.[44]

Sheila Hones and Julia Leyda, two Americanists working at Japanese universities, pinpoint the issue as "a form of spatial fetishism in which people are reductively identified with particular locations, and the relations between people are articulated as relations between places."[45] Hones and Leyda's challenge is specifically to the "nationally oriented geography" that supports the idea of a *transnational* turn in USAmerican studies, which has meant little else, it seems, than including Americanists based in other countries in the field's conversations and forming a separate professional organization, the International American Studies Association (IASA).[46] Once again, theory and practice diverge sharply. Hones and Leyda argue that notwithstanding all the talk about transnational academic networks and circuits, the persistent conflation of scholarly with national identity that I noted earlier "works to *naturalize* the idea that the US[A]-based Americanist position is simultaneously domestic and universal while American studies as practiced elsewhere is by contrast foreign and located."[47] "Naturalization," then, is an effect of the USA and its studies being unlocated and unlocatable, that is, of being a tacit default. As a discursive strategy, this naturalization contains exogamous perspectives that might undermine the appearance of holism and transparency in either nationally or regionally defined areas. Such containment of "foreign" perspectives—that is, rhetorical inclusion, practical exclusion—also accounts for the fact that debates about hemispheric American studies as practiced by scholars located in the USA have tended to downplay the importance of a dialogue not only with Latin Americanists but also with scholars who work on the Americas but in other parts of the world, including those who do not self-identify as Americanists. It is conspicuous, and consistent with Hones and Leyda's argument, that scholarship on the Americas from *elsewhere* in the Americas and the world is often ignored in the USA, especially when it is written in languages other than English.

Good intentions notwithstanding, Porter's above article is not a solution but symptomatic of the same difficulty. For Porter, reshaping USAmerican studies would mean to "confront (at the least) a quadruple set of relations between (1) Europe and Latin America; (2) Latin America and North America; (3) North America and Europe; and (4) Africa and both Americas." "The aim here," she clarifies, "would not be to expand American Studies so as to incorporate the larger territory of the hemisphere, but rather to grasp how the cultural, political, and economic relations between and within the Americas might work to constellate the field itself, reinflecting its questions in accord with a larger frame. Theoretically speaking, 'America,' both geopolitically and historically, would become at once internally fissured and externally relativized."[48] Compared with what Porter has in mind here, the hemispheric turn in USAmerican studies constitutes a significant narrowing of the aperture, with a focus on internal fissuring through "regionalizing" (Phil Fisher's term) subspecialties such as African American studies, Latino studies, Asian American studies, and so forth, as well as privileging special regions known as contact zones (Mary Louise Pratt) or borderlands (Gloria Anzaldúa).[49] External relativizing, too, has produced its own ruptures, making hemispheric studies distinct from other transnational studies in which earlier transoceanic relations focused on USA expatriates and the Lost Generation have been refigured into trans-Atlantic and, more recently, trans-Pacific networks.[50]

Note also that *nobody* constellates the field. In Porter's article, the field somehow creates itself. The same is the case with what Paul Giles calls "hemispheric knowledge." "Hemispheric knowledge," Giles proposes, "might be said to emerge from a jagged conceptual space where the map of homeland security is traversed by unfamiliar cartographies."[51] He uses the metaphorical map of homeland security to refer a larger conceptual problem to a narrow political context: not only the USA but the USA after 9/11. Giles's context is limited by place and by being located in the present. It is unclear, at least to me, why the cartographies that cross-sect this presumably familiar map are unfamiliar and to whom. If we take these foreign cartographies to represent the perspectives of multiple pasts, presents, and futures, it becomes evident that what creates the conceptual space's jaggedness is *movement*. Movement in turn introduces the human dimensions that Giles's own map lacks, that he elides in the figure of maps traversing each other. People move; maps do not, certainly not by themselves. People move in time across geographies and rarely in orderly and predictable fashion. If it is to be anything, hemispheric knowledge would have to be the knowledge of such precise movements. Hemispheric American studies cannot produce such knowledge as long as it merely reproduces and theoretically reenacts "internal fissures and external relations." The slippage between hemispheric *studies* and hemispheric *knowledge* avoids the question of how one can *become* the other. What remains unaddressed, and chronically so, is scholarship's and scholars' own forms of movement—what I would call *method*. Giles's stated preference for "an intriguing partiality of perspectives" over what he calls "new scientific method" makes this evasion surprisingly explicit.[52]

What, then, about a *method* for hemispheric American studies? To my mind, what compromises the field at the level of methodology is that it purports to combine comparative with interdisciplinary approaches.[53] I have found this virtually impossible to do in my own work, and I have found it equally unfeasible as part of research groups that form around either comparative or interdisciplinary agendas, rarely both. Much of the work being produced under the umbrella of hemispheric American studies falls in the category of literary studies. So, hemispheric American studies is really hemispheric American *literary* studies. Porter acknowledges this; Giles and many others do not. The debate about America, then, comes into view as largely a debate among literary scholars without being acknowledged as such.[54] More often than not, "American literary studies" simply slips into "American studies," yet another default. One reason for this may be that, in the USA, unlike in the UK, for instance, literary studies have become virtually indistinguishable from *cultural* studies by virtue of the fact that those who practice cultural studies in the USA do so typically from the institutional location of English departments. Why? Because there are precious few American studies programs in the USA that can hire their own faculty. This fact is often repressed, but it returns in the now more frequent descriptions of American studies as a "discipline."[55]

To be clear: an area study is not a discipline. If anything, area studies are well known for their claims to interdisciplinarity. In fact, interdisciplinarity used to be a major point of distinction between area studies and the core humanities and social science departments from which they had sprung: the national language and literature departments of English and Spanish, as well as history, political science, and sociology. Once interdisciplinarity-as-cultural-studies became an accepted practice in core departments, these distinctions began to blur. Today it is de rigueur, and almost tacitly assumed, that everyone's work is interdisciplinary, which makes one wonder what is so bad about literary scholarship and why it has become so unfashionable in the humanities to admit to working in a single discipline. As Harootunian again reminds us, such claims should be taken with the proverbial grain of salt: "Instead of envisaging genuinely interdisciplinary agendas capable of integrating different disciplines, area studies often settled for the regime of a simple multidisciplinarism as the sign of a comparative method that masquerades coverage for the work of comparison, language acquisition for method, the totality of the nation state for theory."[56] In short, both USAmerican and Latin American studies have yet to develop coherent interdisciplinary methods.

One might argue that herein lies precisely an opportunity for doing so jointly in the context of the Americas. In USAmerican studies at least, the insistence on interdisciplinarity as an incontrovertible reality, rather than as something to be achieved or even as an ongoing process, has resulted in the suppression of disciplinary origins as starting points for developing a practice that crosses disciplinary lines, call it interdisciplinarity or multidisciplinarity.[57] Avoiding this issue has led some hemispheric Americanists to emphasize comparative work but without sufficiently considering that comparability is not inevitably, and certainly not exclusively, tied to geopolitical space, be it national or regional.[58] The idea of hemispheric American studies lacks conceptual coherence precisely because it tries to integrate too many variables without regard to scholarly practice. What might at length produce an integrative methodology—and I am thinking of it not as unified but as systematic—are intellectual reciprocity and collaboration, practices that very much tended *not* to be part of how academics like me have traditionally understood their interdisciplinary practice. The chief deficit of what we consider interdisciplinary work from the vantage point of the humanities is that it may change the way in which a literary scholar thinks about and applies her own analytical methods, but it does not affect anyone or anything in, say, anthropology or history. It is a one-way street and as such is vulnerable to charges of appropriation. Real interdisciplinary practice requires more than just metaphoric dialogue. Dialogue is the point at which interdisciplinarity moves from being a mere discursive effect in a single discipline to becoming an actual scholarly practice. I can easily imagine similar collaborations for comparative work, especially in literary studies, that would be, among many others things, effective ways of dealing with the linguistic gaps that divide Americanists from Latin Americanists.[59] Translation should play a more respected and productive role in such situations.

None of this, however, is likely to happen as long as we self-identify in territorial ways as either Americanists or Latin Americanists or allow ourselves to be categorized along these lines.[60] Unless we accept that the knowledges our respective fields produce are partial formations and that they can be brought together to work against reductions of difference, even our debates will remain mired in the allegorical rhetoric of colonization and imperialism. This rhetoric generates self-fulfilling prophecies that tell us nothing about what other possible frames may be obscured by all-too-familiar representations of political contests within the hemisphere. Politically inspired allegory offers no possibility for perceiving that vast and diverse area known as the USA as anything other than the unchanging center of imperial power, be that power applied for the purposes of internal or external colonization. By contrast, all other countries in the Americas are then relegated to resisting that superpower, and that resistance becomes their sole cultural project.

It bears pointing out at this juncture that there are more than just two Americas. Treating all the different areas, languages, and cultures in what is best described as a heterotopia as *equally limited* would go a long way toward recovering all the diversities tucked away in scholarly abstractions and their popular applications. I have tried in this book to open up an analytical space that is not reducible to the terms and positions of political or cultural allegory. Nor does it treat literature "as evidentiary symptom of American reality."[61] In keeping with this, I want to propose that we reimagine America as an *area* that is not beholden to a single, national or regional, set of values. In analytical terms, hemispheric America itself might be reframed as a "thirdspace" (Soja) or a TransArea (Ette), a hetero-topos constituted by all sorts of simultaneous movements that converge and diverge over time.[62] TransArea studies, to adapt Ette's ideas, would bring together the different patterns and rhythms produced by the infinitely varied human interactions in the hemispheric Americas and connect them with other parts of the globe. By contrast to transnational studies which retains the concept of the national even while interrogating it, TransArea studies makes accessible for critical scrutiny different layers of intra- and intercultural movement for which the two-dimensional metaphor of border crossing is inadequate.[63] We can analyze how these movements converge with and diverge from linguistic and other cultural differences at particular moments in space-time. The knowledge of these sorts of multilayered, motile interactions advances our collective understanding of how the lingering construct of the nation-state, along with definitions of "area" solely predicated on geography, distorts our perceptions of what appear to be static delimiters and guarantors of individual and collective identities. That such delimiters can and do shift, however subtly, is precisely what makes translation so immensely valuable for hemispheric American literary and cultural studies.

TRANSLATION AND DIASPORA

My goal throughout this book has been to work against theoretical reductions of cultural differences by presenting historical and textual evidence in place of the "imagined ahistorical otherness" through which, George Handley reminds us, academics tend to "fantasize" both national and international communities.[64] We cannot cross borders in theory and yet retain as safety nets ideas about linguistic and cultural groups based on the nineteenth-century nation-state, however strategic those idea may be under certain post- and neocolonial circumstances. Regardless of when and where they occur, or from which disciplinary perspective they are theorized, concepts such as border crossing and contact zones must in the end give way to critical practices through which hypotheses about how cultural spaces are shared and disputed on a hemispheric and global scale can be tested rather than merely applied. Testing theories can and will yield new metaphors, and there is a dire need for those in any language. Peter Hulme, for instance, urges "imaginative mass trespass over the established boundaries of literary history."[65] Ottmar Ette offers *Konvivenz*, a Latinate neologism in German that, to me at least, loses its compelling gravitas in the giddiness of the English "conviviality" that Paul Gilroy proposes.[66] Brent Edwards suggests the French *décalage* (a difference or gap in either time or space) to underwrite

"a subtly innovative model with which to read the structure of such uneven-
ness in the African diaspora."[67]

African diaspora studies, more recently called black internationalism, remains an important framework for Hughes and his Afro-Hispanic American
interlocutors. The constitutive multilingualism of black internationalism notwithstanding, the transatlantic theorizing that has been so vital to critiques
of modernity in Europe and the USA is, however, still based almost exclusively on materials written in English. An unfortunate effect of the privileging of *North* Atlantic configurations in Paul Gilroy's influential *The Black
Atlantic* (1993) and much of the work that has followed in its footsteps has
been to eclipse the entire southern part of the Western Hemisphere, including, of course, the Hispanic parts of the Caribbean.[68] That English-speaking
Guyana, the former home of Wilson Harris, has been the sole South American exception to the rule shows just how major a role linguistic factors have
played in the formation of late-twentieth-century diasporic theories that
have relegated Afro- and Asian-Hispanic American cultures to a position of
virtual insignificance. Recent scholarship on black internationalism in other
languages, notably French, has started to challenge the unifying generaliza-
tion about shared literary (and cultural) experience derived from trans- and
circum-Atlantic theories.[69] Brent Edwards deserves much credit for attending closely to the potentially "adversarial" varieties of "black expression"
across languages.[70] So do David Chioni Moore and Kate Baldwin, who, in
their work on Langston Hughes in the former Soviet Union, have also contributed to moving Atlanticism "beyond anglophone archipelagoes and [re-
sisting] the continental confines of a Europe-Africa-US[A] triangulation."[71]
Their work and that of others shows the vital role that translation has played
in mediating the specific relations among the writers of the African diaspora.

TRANSLATION AND LITERARY INFLUENCE

Translation studies also has broad ramifications for literary and cultural
studies, especially when we think of translation as a vehicle for so-called
literary influence on a global scale. All the major models of literary influence we use today, in diaspora studies and elsewhere, are still of a piece
with the theoretical concepts Harold Bloom developed in *The Anxiety of
Influence* (1973) through his readings of British Romantic poetry, which
he extended in subsequent studies to the work of other poets, all of whom
wrote in English. Translation has had no place in such models, except as a
metaphor for intertextuality. Literary translation studies have not helped
matters by privileging those cases in which both "primary" and "secondary" aesthetic functions converge in the same person, that of writer-transla-
tor. For modernist studies, this figure has most frequently, and most ideally,
been embodied in Ezra Pound.[72] Outside such felicitous convergences,

translation as a literary practice is typically ignored. To wit, the figure of the literary translator has only recently begun to recover from her prolonged condition of invisibility and to be grudgingly released from long-standing charges of treason.[73] The question of what claims to authorship, and thus to a special form of cultural authority, a translator might have is, however, far from resolved.

Poets and novelists are rarely also translators; nor is the mere fact of translation tantamount to literary influence. In the case of Hughes, there is virtually no overlap between the writers whom Hughes's poems may have influenced—among them Nicolás Guillén, Pilar Barrios, and Manuel Zapata Olivella—and those who actually translated his poems for publication. Regardless of similar divergences in other cases, countless studies have, for instance, belabored Gabriel García Márquez's influence on Toni Morrison and Faulkner's influence on García Márquez, Juan Rulfo, and other "Boom" novelists, without adding into the equation the fact that these writers most likely read each other in translations by, among others, Gregory Rabassa, Margaret Sayers Peden, and in Faulkner's case Jorge Luis Borges. Even in the occasional grumblings about "bad" translations that come from specialists in Hispanic American literatures who find their academic territory invaded by comparatists, the fact that literary influence often occurs as the result of a specific translation, be it "good" or "bad," is rarely addressed. Nor does a writer's level of linguistic competence ever enter into such discussions, any more than does a translator's role as a cultural mediator who often plays more than just second fiddle.

Literary influence also does not work in exactly the same way in multilingual situations as it is believed to function in monolingual ones. Although the Bloomian model of creative misprision has been applied to other literary contexts both national and comparative,[74] it has not been sufficiently rethought for situations in which writers depend on translations to access texts written in other languages. The workings of influence across languages are messy because the texts that are subject to misprision are rarely so-called originals. This means that any comparison of texts by writers who neither work in nor read shared languages has to take account of translation as a complicating theoretical factor. While I agree that translations "are not a reliable index of cultural difference," any more than they are an unfailing guide to cultural similarities,[75] studying literature in translation points us to important cultural differences within superficial sameness. Being attentive to such differences, however minute they may be, is especially important for comparatists who work with international settings already inscribed with a host of assumptions about, and indeed expectations of, cultural or ideological unity, even in the midst of glaring local differences. This is as true of African diaspora studies as it is of modernist studies. We have to be wary of those assumptions and the simplifications that follow all too readily in their wake, lest we let the mere *appearance* of sameness get in the way of evidence that would suggest otherwise.

SURVIVAL AND THE HUMANITIES

Using translation studies and reception history as a vehicle for literary history, I have shown that the English and Spanish versions of Hughes's work are as much a part of the loosely spun fabric of global modernisms as the writings of both more and less canonical figures in the Western Hemisphere. Most importantly, a literary history that focuses on translation as "the most creative form of active reception"[76] changes the composition and texture of that fabric, bringing into relief previously unnoticed patterns and dimensions. Such patterns emerge when one connects points in time and space where the trajectories of literary vanguards intersect and overlap with the entangled routes of black internationalism, global socialism, and postcolonialism. This book should not, however, be understood as merely another call for greater inclusivity. To be sure, including Langston Hughes and other as yet unrecognized writers from the Americas in the modernist canon that the New Critics and their disciples constructed to wall literature off from the sociopolitical pressures of the Cold War might close certain gaps in modernism's literary history. Greater inclusivity alone does not alter basic conceptual and emotional templates, let alone shift intellectual paradigms with deep ideological roots in the plantation tradition.[77]

Adding another name to a roster changes nothing about the hierarchies of selves and others that most of us still wear like a pair of comfortable shoes. My point in calling Hughes a fringe modernist is to stress, as I have done throughout, that the cultural authority of the so-called margins has been profoundly underestimated and that existing narratives of marginalization may actually prevent us from appreciating this fact.[78] What is so valuable about Hughes's work is the dogged elegance with which his words refuse to let his readers tread easily in their well-worn habits, be those racist, classist, or sexist. Thinking about the margin as disenfranchised and about African American writers as victims is one of those habits, and it seems rather urgent that we in the academies of the world think long and hard about why it is comfortable to think so. Hughes is fundamentally a writer who keeps us on our toes, perpetually pushing the limits of our own culturally bounded assumptions, expectations, and academic master narratives.

Langston Hughes is an African American writer from the USA, a black internationalist, *and* an international modernist. When a writer occupies all three of these positions at once—and many writers do—it becomes difficult to justify why one would conceptually, historically, or methodologically privilege any one position in analyzing his or her writings. As I hope I have shown in this book, what is needed to describe the spatiotemporal crossroads at which these discursive formations, along with the writers themselves, meet is a carefully calibrated comparative approach that can test out critical theories and scrutinize the abstractions that articulate them. Such an approach helps us see the separation of high modernism and black or ethnic literature in the Americas for what it is: a simple mechanism of segregation.

Among the academic segregationists are not just the New Critics and their heirs but also African Americanists who claim that modernism, be it Euro-American or Hispanic American, has no significance for or connection with African American literatures, presumably because those literatures lack "the depersonalizing/hyperpersonal contradiction at the core of modernism."[79]

Ultimately this book is about rejecting segregation in all its manifestations, inside and outside academia, which strikes me as especially vital at a time when it is altogether unclear whether and how the humanities will survive at universities. We as humanities scholars need to drawn on the work of the writers whom we profess to admire as resources for shaping and articulating our own survival strategies. Part of my own tactic is to challenge concepts that are inherently divisive, in my scholarship and in the way I live. If reading Langston Hughes has taught me anything, it is that differences need not divide—either in literature or in life.

Appendix

Hughes's title	First pub.	Translator	Title in Spanish	Date	Where	Page(s)	Country
Advertisement for the Waldorf-Astoria	1931	Alejandro	Un aviso para el Waldorf Astoria (Fragmento)	1936	Nueva Cultura	154–57	Spain
Advertisement…	1931	Rivaud	Un aviso para el Waldorf Astoria	1944	IM 1967	331–34	Argentina; Cuba
Advertisement…	1931	Gáler	Un aviso para el Waldorf Astoria (Fragmento)	1952	Poemas	128–33	Argentina
Advertisement…	1931	Rivaud	Un aviso para el Waldorf Astoria	1971	Renacimiento	91–94	Argentina
Advice	1946	Gáler	Consejo	1952	Poemas	116	Argentina
Afraid	1924	Fernandez de Castro	Miedo	1930	Rev. de la Hab.	186	Cuba
Afraid	1924	Bansart	Tener miedo	1971	Poesía negra	42–43	Chile
Air Raid: Barcelona	1938	Fraile Marcos	Ataque Aereo: Barcelona	1998	Oscuridad	64–	Spain
Always the Same	1932	Pereda Valdés	Siempre lo mismo	1936	Antología (PV)	39–40	Chile; Uruguay
April Rain Song	1921	Gáler	Canción de la lluvia abrileña	1943	Tiempo Vivo	17	Argentina
April Rain Song	1921	Gáler	Canción de la lluvia abrileña	1952	Poemas	71	Argentina
Ardella	1926	Lozano	Ardella	1931	Crisol	230	Mexico
Ardella	1926	Lozano	Ardella	1931	Reportorio Amer.	226	Costa Rica
Ardella	1926	Lozano	Ardella	1936	Antología (PV)	36	Chile; Uruguay
Ardella	1926	Ahumada	Niña silenciosa	1968	YT	21	Mexico
As I Grew Older	1926	Ahumada	Cuando fui mayor	1968	YT	77	Mexico
As I Grew Older	1926	Zardoya	Llegada de la vejez	1951	Alcándara	10	Spain
As I Grew Older	1926	Zardoya	Llegada de la vejez	1967	Ínsula	24	Spain
As I Grew Older	1926	Gáler	Cuando fui creciendo	1952	Poemas	30–31	Argentina

(Continued)

APPENDIX (*Continued*)

Hughes's title	First pub.	Translator	Title in Spanish	Date	Where	Page(s)	Country
Ballad of Harry Moore	1952	González Flores	La balada de Harry Moore	1953	*El Nacional*	5	Mexico
Ballad of Harry M.	1952	González Flores	La balada de Harry Moore	1961	*Nivel*	xv	Mexico
Ballad of Harry M.	1952	Latino	La balada de Harry Moore	1963	*Reportorio Amer.*	2–3	Costa Rica
Ballad of the Landlord	1940	González Flores	Balada del casero	1953	*Poesía de Amer.*	77–78	Mexico
Ballad of the Landlord	1940	González Flores	Balada del casero	1961	*Nivel*		Mexico
Beale Street	1926	Gáler	Calle Beal	1952	*Poemas*	76	Argentina
Beggar Boy	1922	Ahumada	Nino pordiosero	1968	*YT*	27	Mexico
Birth	1947	Gáler	Alumbramiento	1952	*Poemas*	75	Argentina
Blues at Dawn	1951	Ahumada	Blues de la madrugada	1968	*YT*	61	Mexico
Brass Spittoons	1926	Escalante	Escupideras de cobre	1947	*Breve informe*	102–3	Venezuela
Brass Spittoons	1926	Gáler	Salivaderas de bronce	1952	*Poemas*	59–60	Argentina
Brass Spittoons	1926	Ruiz del Vizo	Escupideras de cobre	1972	*Black Poetry*	163	Miami, USA
Brass Spittoons	1926	González, J. L.	Escupideras de cobre	1976	*Poesía negra*	242ff.	Mexico
Brass Spittoons	1926	Anon.	Escupideras de latón	1964	*Ínsula*	15	Spain
Brass Spittoons	1926	Parsons	Escupideras de metal	1930	*Social*	19	Cuba
Breath of a Rose	1940	López Narváez	Canción de la Rosa	1952	*El cielo*	140	Colombia
Cabaret	1923	Cruzado	Cabaret	2004	*Blues*	91	Spain
Caribbean Sunset	1926	Gáler	Atardecer Caribe	1952	*Poemas*	49	Argentina
Cat and the Saxophone, The	1926	Gáler	El gato y el saxofón (dos de la mañana)	1952	*Poemas*	43–44	Argentina
Chant for May Day	1938	Ahumada	Canto al Día de Mayo	1968	*YT*	99	Mexico
Chant for Tom Mooney	1932	Ahumada	Canto a Tom Mooney	1968	*YT*	97	Mexico
Christ in Alabama	1931	González Flores	Cristo es un negro	1948	*El Nacional*	13	Mexico

Christ in Alabama	1931	González Flores	Cristo es un negro	1950	*Pareja*	248–49	Mexico
Christ in Alabama	1931	Gáler	Cristo en Alabama	1952	*Poemas*	127	Argentina
Closing Time	1927	Cardenal	Hora de cierre	1962	*Antología*	335	Spain
Could Be	1949	Ahumada	Pudo ser	1968	*YT*	71	Mexico
Cross	1925	Lozano	Cruz	1931	*Crisol*	229	Mexico
Cross	1925	Lozano	Cruz	1931	*Repertorio Amer.*	226	Costa Rica
Cross	1925	Lozano	Cruz	1936	*Antología* (PV)	35–36	Chile; Uruguay
Cross	1925	Magdaleno	Cruz	1938	*Nueva Democra.*	15	Uruguay
Cross	1925	Gáler	Mulato	1952	*Poemas*	67–69	Argentina
Cross	1925	González, J.L.	Mestizaje	1967	*Siempre*	34–35	Mexico
Cross	1925	Ruiz del Vizo	Cruz	1972	*Black Poetry*	164	Miami, USA
Cross	1925	González, J.L.	Mestizaje	1976	*Poesía negra*	242ff.	Mexico
Cross	1925	Cruzado	Cruce	2004	*Blues*	111	Spain
Dancers	1947	Gáler	Bailarines	1952	*Poemas*	85	Argentina
Danse Africaine	1922	Ahumada	Danza africana	1968	*YT*	35	Mexico
Danse Africaine	1922	Cruzado	Danza africana	2004	*Blues*	83	Spain
Daybreak in Alabama	1940	Ahumada	Aurora en Alabama	1968	*YT*	69	Mexico
Dear Lovely Death	1930	González Flores	Amada muerte encantadora	1948	*El Nacional*	13	Mexico
Dear Lovely Death	1930	González Flores	Amada muerte encantadora	1950	*Pareja*	250	Mexico
Dear Lovely Death	1930	Gáler	Muerte	1952	*Poemas*	86	Argentina
Desire	1927	Gáler	Deseo	1952	*Poemas*	83	Argentina
Dove, The	1962	Cruzado	La paloma	2004	*Blues*	168	Spain
Dream Keeper, The	1925	Gáler	El guarda sueños	1952	*Poemas*	70	Argentina
Dream Keeper, The	1925	Ahumada	El guarda sueños	1968	*YT*	13	Mexico
Dream Keeper, The	1925	Cruzado	El guardian de sueños	2004	*Blues*	99	Spain
Dreams	1933	Ahumada	Sueños	1968	*YT*	11	Mexico
Drum	1931	Gáler	Tambor	1952	*Poemas*	90	Argentina
Early Evening Quarrel	1941	Ahumada	Disputa	1968	*YT*	59	Mexico

(Continued)

APPENDIX *(Continued)*

Hughes's title	First pub.	Translator	Title in Spanish	Date	Where	Page(s)	Country
Early Evening Quarrel	1941	Cruzado	Riña verspertina	2004	*Blues*	141	Spain
Elevator Boy	1926	Parsons	Muchacho de elevador	1930	*Social*	19	Cuba
Fantasy in Purple	1925	Gáler	Fantasia en purpúrea	1952	*Poemas*	48	Argentina
Feet O' Jesus	1926	Ahumada	Pies de Jesús	1968	*Poemas*	41	Mexico
Final Curve	1949	Gáler	Curva final	1952	*Poemas*	110	Argentina
Florida Road Workers	1949	Alberti	Estoy haciendo un camino	1937	*El Mono Azul*	1	Spain
Florida Road Workers	1930	Gáler	Obreros camineros de Florida	1952	*Poemas*	106	Argentina
Florida Road Workers	1949	Ahumada	Trabajadores en un camino de Florida	1968	*YT*	89	Mexico
Florida Road Workers	1949	Ahumada	Trabajadores en un camino de Florida	1976	*Nivel*	6	Mexico
Flotsam	1968	Cruzado	Los restos del naufrágio	2004	*Blues*	170	Spain
Free Man	1942	Figueira	Hombre Libre	1942	*Nueva Democra.*	264	Argentina
Free Man	1942	Figueira	Free Man	1943	*Nueva Democra.*	23	Argentina
Freedom [1]	1943	Gáler	Democracia	1952	*Poemas*	87	Argentina
Freedom [1]	1942	Ahumada	Democracia	1968	*YT*	103–104	Mexico
Freedom Train	1947	Gáler	El tren de la libertad	1948	*Orientación*	14	Argentina
Freedom Train	1947	González Flores	Abordando el tren de la libertad	1950	*Pareja*	4	Mexico
Freedom Train	1947	Gáler	El tren de la libertad	1952	*Poemas*	121–25	Argentina
Freedom Train	1947	González Flores	Abordando el tren de la libertad	1961	*Nivel*	xv	Mexico
Freedom's Plow	1943	González Flores	El arado de la libertad	1946	*America*	63–70	Mexico
Freedom's Plow	1943	González Flores	El arado de la libertad	1948	*El Nacional*	13	Mexico
Freedom's Plow	1943	González Flores	El arado de la libertad	1950	*Pareja*	246	Mexico

From Selma	1941	Gáler	Desde Selma	1952	*Poemas*	136	Argentina
Genius Child	1937	Ahumada	Niño pordiosero	1968	*YT*	27	Mexico
God to Hungry Child	1925	Cruzado	Palabras de Dios a un niño hambriento	2004	*Blues*	103	Spain
Good Morning, Revolution	1932	Alejandro	¡Buenos días, Revolución!	1936	*Nueva Cultura*	154–57	Spain
Grief	1947	Gáler	Pena	1952	*Poemas*	89	Argentina
Harlem [1]	1949	Gáler	Intrigado	1952	*Poemas*	99–100	Argentina
Harlem [1]	1947	Cruzado	Harlem (1)	2004	*Blues*	159	Spain
Harlem [2]	1949	Cruzado	Harlem (2)	2004	*Blues*	167	Spain
Harlem Dance Hall	1947	Magdaleno	La Fiesta de Harlem	1938	*Nueva Democra.*	14	Argentina
Harlem Dance Hall	1947	Blanco	Salón de baile in Harlem	1949	*Asomante*	29	Puerto Rico
Harlem Dance Hall	1947	Cruzado	Salón de baile de Harlem	2004	*Blues*	151	Spain
Harlem Night Club	1926	Ahumada	Centro nocturno en Harlem	1968	*YT*	67	Mexico
Harlem Night Song	1926	Gáler	Canción nocturna de Harlem	1952	*Poemas*	39	Argentina
Harlem Night Song	1926	Cruzado	Canción nocturna de Harlem	2004	*Blues*	125	Spain
Hero-International Brigade	1952	Fraile Marcos	Héroe—Brigada Internacional	1998	*Oscuridad*	70–73	Spain
Hey	1927	Gáler	¡Hey!	1952	*Poemas*	54	Argentina
History	1934	Ahumada	Historia	1968	*YT*	Epigraph	Mexico
Homesick Blues	1926	Gáler	El blues de la añoranza	1952	*Poemas*	57–58	Argentina
Homesick Blues	1926	Cruzado	Blues de la añoranza	2004	*Blues*	119	Spain
House in Taos, A	1926	Gáler	Una casa en Taos	1952	*Poemas*	91–92	Argentina
I, Too	1925	Fernández de Castro	Yo, también	1928	*Social*	30	Cuba
I, Too	1925	Fernández de Castro	Yo, también	1930	*Diario de la Mar.*		Cuba
I, Too	1925	Fernández de Castro	Yo, también	1930	*Rev. de la Haba.*	311–12	Cuba
I, Too	1925	Borges	Yo también	1931	*Sur*	165	Argentina

(Continued)

APPENDIX (Continued)

Hughes's title	First pub.	Translator	Title in Spanish	Date	Where	Page(s)	Country
I, Too	1925	Lozano	Yo también canto a América	1931	*Crisol*	232	Mexico
I, Too	1925	Lozano	Yo también canto a América	1931	*Reportorio Amer.*	226	Costa Rica
I, Too	1925	Villaurrutia	Yo también	1931	*Contemporáneos*	157	Mexico
I, Too	1925	Pereda Valdés	Yo, también, soy America	1936	*Antología* (PV)	35	Chile; Uruguay
I, Too	1925	Borges	Yo también	1937	*El Hogar*		Argentina
I, Too	1925	Alberti	Yo, también	1937	*El Mono Azul*	1	Spain
I, Too	1925	Lozano	Yo, también, canto	1938	*Nueva Democra.*	15	Uruguay
I, Too	1925	Figueira	Yo, también	1942	*Sustancia*	261	Argentina
I, Too	1925	Figueira	Yo, también	1943	*Aurora*	387–88	Argentina
I, Too	1925	Ballagas	Yo, también	1946	*Mapa*	48–49	Argentina
I, Too	1925	Gáler	Yo también	1952	*Poemas*	52–53	Argentina
I, Too	1925	Toruño	Yo también	1953	*Poesía negra*	151	Mexico
I, Too	1925	Florit	Yo también	1955	*Antología*	111	Mexico
I, Too	1925	Gáler	Yo también	1959	*Yo viajo*		Argentina
I, Too	1925	Villaurrutia	Yo también	1961	*Nivel*	4	Mexico
I, Too	1925	Latino	Yo, también	1963	*Antología*	3	Argentina
I, Too	1925	Sastre	Yo también	1964	*Mulato*	epigraph	Spain
I, Too	1925	González, J.L.	Yo también canto a América	1967	*Siempre*	34–35	Mexico
I, Too	1925	Ahumada	Yo también	1968	*YT*	79	Mexico
I, Too	1925	Bansart	Yo, también	1971	*Poesía negra*	32–33	Chile
I, Too	1925	Ahumada	Yo también	1976	*Nivel*	6	Mexico
I, Too	1925	Borges	Yo también	1986	*Textos cautivos*	92–93	Argentina
I, Too	1925	Saval	Yo también	1992	*República*		Spain

English Title	Year	Translator	Spanish Title	Year	Source	Page	Country
I, Too	1925	Cruzado	Yo, también	2004	*Blues*	101	Spain
Jam Session	1951	Gáler	Jam Session	1952	*Poemas*	119	Argentina
Jazz Band in a Parisian Cabaret	1925	Escalante	Jazz en un Café de Paris	1947	*Breve Informe*	104	Venezuela
Jazz Band…	1925	Gáler	Jazz Band en un Cabaret de Paris	1952	*Poemas*	63–64	Argentina
Jazz Girl	1927	Cruzado	La chica del Jazz	2004	*Blues*	127	Spain
Jazzonia	1923	Cruzado	Jazzonia	2004	*Blues*	89	Spain
Jester	1925	Gáler	El juglar	1952	*Poemas*	37	Argentina
Joy	1925	Lozano	Alegría	1931	*Crisol*	230–31	Mexico
Joy	1925	Lozano	Alegría	1931	*Reportorio Amer.*	226	Costa Rica
Joy	1925	Lozano	Alegría	1936	*Antología (PV)*	38	Chile; Uruguay
Joy	1925	Gáler	Alegría	1943	*Tiempo Vivo*	16	Argentina
Joy	1925	Gáler	Alegría	1952	*Poemas*	40	Argentina
Joy	1925	Ahumada	Alegría	1968	*YT*	55	Mexico
Judgment Day	1926	Ahumada	Juicio final	1968	*YT*	51	Mexico
Juke Box Love Song	1926	Gáler	Canción de amor del Juke Box	1952	*Poemas*	120	Argentina
Juke Box Love Song	1950	Cruzado	Canción de amor en un Juke Box	2004	*Blues*	163	Spain
Justice	1923	Ahumada	Justicia	1968	*YT*	81	Mexico
Kids Who Die	1938	Ahumada	Niños que mueren	1968	*YT*	109	Mexico
Lament over Love	1926	Cruzado	Lamento amoroso	2004	*Blues*	117	Spain
Laughers	1926	Cruzado	Reídores	2004	*Blues*	79	Spain
Lenox Avenue	1926	Gáler	Avenida Lenox: Medianoche	1952	*Poemas*	41	Argentina
Let America Be	1936	Ahumada	Dejad que América vuelva a ser América	1968	*YT*	121	Mexico
Lincoln Monument	1927	Ahumada	Monumento de Lincoln: Washington	1968	*YT*	63–64	Mexico
Little Song	1947	Gáler	Cancioncilla	1948	*Continente*	9	Argentina
Little Song	1947	Gáler	Cancioncilla	1952	*Poemas*	78	Argentina
Love	1941	Ahumada	Amor	1968	*YT*	23	Mexico

(Continued)

APPENDIX (*Continued*)

Hughes's title	First pub.	Translator	Title in Spanish	Date	Where	Page(s)	Country
Lumumba's Grave	1941	González Flores	El sepulchro de Lumumba	1961	*Magisterio*		Mexico
Madrid 1937	1937	Fraile Marcos	Madrid 1937	1998	*Oscuridad*	51–37	Spain
Man	1947	Gáler	Hombre	1948	*Continente*	9	Argentina
Man	1947	Gáler	Hombre	1952	*Poemas*	81	Argentina
Man into Men	1947	Alberti	Hombre convertido en hombres	1937	*El Mono Azul*	1	Spain
March Moon	1926	Fernández de Castro	Luna de marzo	1930	*Rev. de la Hab.*	312	Cuba
March Moon	1926	Gáler	Luna del marzo	1952	*Poemas*	47	Argentina
Me and the Mule	1941	Gáler	Yo y mi mula	1952	*Poemas*	95	Argentina
Merry-Go-Round	1942	Gáler	Carroussel (Nino negro en la Feria)	1952	*Poemas*	94	Argentina
Merry-Go-Round	1942	González, J.L.	Tiovivo (Niño negro en el carnaval)	1967	*Siempre*	34–35	Mexico
Merry-Go-Round	1942	González, J.L.	Tiovivo (Niño negro en el carnaval)	1976	*Poesía negra*	242ff.	Mexico
Mexican Market Woman	1922	Lozano	Placera	1931	*Crísol*	231	Mexico
Mexican Market W.	1922	Lozano	Placera	1931	*Reportorio Amer.*	226	Costa Rica
Midnight Dancer	1926	Cruzado	Bailarina de medinoche	2004	*Blues*	123	Spain
Migration [Little Frightened Child]	1923	Cruzado	Migración	2004	*Blues*	97	Spain
Militant [Pride, 1930]	1930	Ahumada	Orgullo	1968	*Poemas*	93	Argentina
Minstrel Man	1925	Gáler	El bufón	1952	*Poemas*	74	Argentina
Minstrel Man	1925	Ahumada	Trovador	1968	*YT*	15	Mexico

Minstrel Man	1925	Cruzado	Minstrel Man	2004	*Blues*	113	Spain
Misery	1926	Cruzado	Desdicha	2004	*Blues*	121	Spain
Moonlight in Valencia: Civil War	1944	Fraile Marcos	Luz de luna en el Valencia: Guerra Civil	1998	*Oscuridad*	66–69	Spain
Mother to Son	1922	Gáler	De madre a hijo	1952	*Poemas*	34–35	Argentina
Mother to Son	1922	Cruzado	De madre a hijo	2004	*Blues*	85	Spain
Movies	1950	Cruzado	Películas	2004	*Blues*	165	Spain
Mulatto	1927	Pereda Valdés	Mulato	1936	*Antología* (PV)	41–43	Chile; Uruguay
Mulatto	1927	Gáler	Mulato	1952	*Poemas*	67–69	Argentina
Mulatto	1927	Cardenal	Mulato	1962	*Antología*	335–37	Spain
My People	1922	Gáler	Mi pueblo	1952	*Poemas*	36	Argentina
My People	1922	Ahumada	Mi gente	1968	*YT*	19	Mexico
My People	1922	Cruzado	Mi gente	2004	*Blues*	95	Spain
Mystery	1951	Ahumada	Misterio	1968	*YT*	49	Mexico
Negro [Proem]	1922	Lozano	Soy un Negro	1931	*Crisol*	228	Mexico
Negro [Proem]	1922	Lozano	Soy un Negro	1931	*Reportorio Amer.*	226	Costa Rica
Negro [Proem]	1922	Lozano	Soy un Negro	1936	*Antología* (PV)	34	Chile; Uruguay
Negro [Proem]	1922	Alberti	Yo soy Negro	1937	*El Mono Azul*	1	Spain
Negro [Proem]	1922	Ballagas	Preludio a Weary Blues	1946	*Mapa*	45–47	Argentina
Negro [Proem]	1922	Zardoya	El Negro	1951	*Alcándara*	10	Spain
Negro [Proem]	1922	Gáler	El Negro	1952	*Poemas*	25–26	Argentina
Negro [Proem]	1922	Florit	El Negro	1955	*Antología*	110	Mexico
Negro [Proem]	1922	Latino	Soy un Negro	1963	*Antología*	2	?
Negro [Proem]	1922	Zardoya	El Negro	1967	*Ínsula*	24	Spain
Negro [Proem]	1922	Ahumada	El negro	1968	*YT*	75	Mexico
Negro [Proem]	1922	Cruzado	Negro	2004	*Blues*	75	Spain
Negro Dancers	1925	Gáler	Bailarines negros	1952	*Poemas*	42	Argentina
Negro Servant	1930	Blanco	Sirviente negro	1949	*Asomante*	29	Puerto Rico

(*Continued*)

APPENDIX (*Continued*)

Hughes's title	First pub.	Translator	Title in Spanish	Date	Where	Page(s)	Country
Negro Servant	1930	Gáler	Sirviente negro	1952	*Poemas*	107–108	Argentina
Negro Speaks of Rivers	1921	Cruzado	El negro habla de los ríos	2004	*Blues*	73	Spain
Negro Speaks…	1921	Lozano	El negro habla de los ríos	1931	*Crisol*	229	Mexico
Negro Speaks…	1921	López Narváez	El negro habla de los ríos	1952	*El cielo*	139	Colombia
Negro Speaks…	1921	López Narváez	El negro habla de los ríos	1948	*El Tiempo*	3	Colombia
Negro Speaks…	1921	Villaurrutia	El negro habla de los ríos	1961	*Nivel*	4 to 5	Mexico
Negro Speaks…	1921	Lozano	El negro habla de los ríos	1936	*Antología* (PV)	36–37	Chile; Uruguay
Negro Speaks…	1921	González, J.L.	El negro habla de los ríos	1976	*Poesía negra*	242ff.	Mexico
Negro Speaks…	1921	Gáler	El negro habla de los ríos	1952	*Poemas*	29	Argentina
Negro Speaks…	1921	Lozano	El negro habla de los ríos	1931	*Reportorio Amer.*	226	Costa Rica
Negro Speaks…	1921	Villaurrutia	El negro habla de los ríos	1967	*Siempre*	viii	Mexico
Negro Speaks…	1921	Iznaga	El negro habla de los ríos	1954	*Signo*	2	?
Negro Speaks.	1921	Borges	El negro habla de los ríos	1931	*Sur*	169	Argentina
New Moon	1922	Gáler	Nueva luna	1948	*Continente*	9	Argentina
New Moon	1922	Gáler	Nueva luna	1952	*Poemas*	84	Argentina
New Song, A	1933	Ahumada	Una nueva canción	1968	YT	113–15	Mexico
New Song, A	1933	Ahumada	Una nueva canción	1976	*Nivel*		Mexico
New Yorkers	1950	Ahumada	Neoyorquinos	1968	YT	57	Mexico
Nude Young Dancer	1925	Gáler	La joven balarina desnuda	1952	*Poemas*	45	Argentina
Nude Young Dancer	1925	Ahumada	Joven bailarina desnuda	1968	YT	37	Mexico
Nude Young Dancer	1925	Cruzado	Joven bailarina desnuda	2004	*Blues*	115	Spain
One	1941	Gáler	Uno	1948	*Continente*	9	Argentina
One	1941	Gáler	Uno	1952	*Poemas*	77	Argentina

One-Way Ticket	1949	Gáler	Boleto de ida sola	1952	*Poemas*	97–98	Argentina
One-Way Ticket	1949	Cruzado	Billete de ida	2004	*Blues*	155	Spain
Only Woman Blues	1942	Ahumada	Blues de la mujer única	1968	*YT*	65	Mexico
Open Letter to the South	1932	Ahumada	Carta abierta al Sur	1968	*YT*	105	Mexico
Our Land	1923	Borges	Nuestra tierra	1931	*Sur*	167	Argentina
Our Land	1932	Ahumada	Nuestra tierra	1968	*YT*	91	Mexico
Our Land	1923	Bansart	Nuestra tierra	1971	*Poesía*	42–43	Chile
Parisian Beggar Woman	1927	Gáler	Mendiga de París	1952	*Poemas*	72	Argentina
Park Bench	1933	Gáler	Banco de plaza	1952	*Poemas*	126	Argentina
Park Bench	1927	Ahumada	Banca del parque	1968	*YT*	95	Mexico
Passing	1950	Gáler	Los que pasaron	1952	*Poemas*	118	Argentina
Passing Love	1927	Gáler	Amor que pasa	1943	*Tiempo Vivo*	16–17	Argentina
Passing Love	1927	Gáler	Amor que pasa	1952	*Poemas*	73	Argentina
Passing Love	1927	Ahumada	Amor pasajero	1968	*YT*	33	Mexico
PH.D.	1932	Cruzado	Doctor en Philosophía (PH.D.)	2004	*Blues*	129	Spain
Po' Boy Blues	1926	Figueira	Blues del pobre muchacho	1942	*Sustancia*	262–63	Argentina
Po' Boy Blues	1926	Figueira	Blues del pobre muchacho	1943	*Aurora*	387–88	Argentina
Po' Boy Blues	1926	Gáler	Blues del pobre muchacho	1952	*Poemas*	55–56	Argentina
Po' Boy Blues	1926	Ahumada	Blues del pobrecito	1968	*YT*	17	Mexico
Poem (1)	1923	Fernández de Castro	Poema	1930	*Rev. de la Hab.*	186	Cuba
Poem (1)	1923	Bansart	Poema	1971	*Poesía negra*	32–33	Chile
Poem (2)	1925	Villaurrutia	Poema	1931	*Contemporáneos*	158	Mexico
Poem (2)	1925	Ballagas	Poema	1946	*Mapa*	52–53	Argentina
Poem (2)	1925	Villaurrutia	Poema	1961	*Nivel*		Mexico
Poem (2)	1925	Ahumada	Poema	1968	*YT*	29	Mexico

(*Continued*)

APPENDIX *(Continued)*

Hughes's title	First pub.	Translator	Title in Spanish	Date	Where	Page(s)	Country
Poem (2)	1925	Cruzado	Poema (2)	2004	*Blues*	109	Spain
Poem (4)	1925	Ahumada	A la negra amada	1968	*YT*	125	Mexico
Poem for an Intellectual on the Way to Submit to His Lady	1944	Cruzado	Poema a un intelectual a punto de someterse a su amada	2004	*Blues*	145	Spain
Port Town	1926	Lozano	Puerto	1931	*Crisol*	230	Mexico
Port Town	1926	Lozano	Puerto	1931	*Reportorio Amer.*	226	Costa Rica
Port Town	1926	Lozano	Puerto	1936	*Antología* (PV)	37	Chile; Uruguay
Porter	1927	Cardenal	Portero	1962	*Antología*	334–35	Spain
Porter	1927	Parsons	Portero de Pullman	1930	*Social*	19	Cuba
Porter	1927	Parsons	Portero de Pullmann	1930	*Diario de la Mar.*	?	Cuba
Porter	1927	Gáler	Sirviente	1952	*Poemas*	65	Argentina
Postcard from Spain	1938	Cruzado	Una postal de España	2004	*Blues*	139	Spain
Prayer [1]	1925	Villaurrutia	Plegaria	1931	*Contemporáneos*	158	Mexico
Prayer [1]	1925	Gáler	Oración	1952	*Poemas*	66	Argentina
Question [1]	1922	Gáler	Pregunta	1952	*Poemas*	88	Argentina
Prayer [1]	1925	Villaurrutia	Plegaria	1961	*Nivel*	4 to 5	Mexico
Prayer [1]	1925	Ahumada	Oración	1968	*YT*	43	Mexico
Quiet Girl. *See* Ardella.							
Reverie on the Harlem River	1942	Figueira	Reverie en el río de Harlem	1942	*Sustancia*	264	Argentina
Reverie...	1942	Figueira	Reverie on the Harlem River	1943	*Nueva Democra.*	23	Argentina
Roar China	1938	Novas Calvo	Ruge China	1937	*Ayuda*	3–47	?
Roar China	1938	Novas Calvo	Ruge China	1937	*Reportorio Amer.*	260	Costa Rica

Ruby Brown	1926	Gáler	Ruby Brown	1952	*Poemas*	61–62	Argentina
Sea Calm	1926	Fernández de Castro	Calma en el mar	1930	*Rev. de la Hab.*	186	Cuba
Shakespeare in Harlem (stanza)	1942	Florit	Domingo	1955	*Antología*	112	Mexico
Share Croppers	1933	Gáler	Peones	1952	*Poemas*	96	Argentina
Silence	1941	Gáler	Silencio	1952	*Poemas*	79	Argentina
Sister Johnson	1937	Ahumada	La Hermana Johnson Marcha	1968	*YT*	119	Mexico
Six-Bit Blues	1939	Gáler	Un Peso de Blues	1952	*Poemas*	93	Argentina
Slave Song	1949	Gáler	Canción del esclavo	1952	*Poemas*	134	Argentina
Sleep	1923	Gáler	Sueño	1952	*Poemas*	80	Argentina
Sliver of Sermon	1951	Ahumada	Plata de sermón	1968	*YT*	47	Mexico
So Tired Blues	1941	Cruzado	Estar harto, en blues	2004	*Blues*	143	Spain
Soledad: A Cuban Portrait	1925	Fernández de Castro	Soledad (Retrato de una Cubana).	1930	*Revista*	186	Cuba
Soledad: A Cuban Portrait	1925	Lozano	Soledad. Retrato de Cubana	1931	*Crisol*	231	Mexico
Soledad	1925	Lozano	Soledad. Retrato de Cubana	1931	*Reportorio Amer.*	226	Costa Rica
Soledad	1925	Gáler	Soledad (Un retrato cubano)	1952	*Poemas*	50	Argentina
Song	1925	Ahumada	Canción	1968	*YT*	31	Mexico
Song for a Dark Girl	1927	Caparicio	Canto a una muchacha negra	1936	*Antología (PV)*	38	Chile; Uruguay
Song for a Dark Girl	1927	Figueira	Canto a una muchacha negra	1942	*Sustancia*	263	Argentina
Song for a Dark Girl	1927	Figueira	Canto a una muchacha negra	1943	*Aurora*	387–88	Argentina
Song for a Dark Girl	1927	Ballagas	Canto a una muchacha negra	1946	*Mapa*	50–51	Argentina
Song for a Dark Girl	1927	Revueltas	Canto a una muchacha negra	1948	*Cont. LA Comp.*		USA
Song for Billie Holiday	1949	Martínez Inglés	Canción para Billie Holiday	2001	*Litoral*		Spain
Song…	1949	Cruzado	Canción para Billie Holiday	2004	*Blues*	153	Spain
Song of Spain	1937	Ahumada	El Canto de España	1968	*YT*	101–104	Mexico
Song of Spain	1937	Ahumada	El Canto de España	1976	*Nivel*	6	Mexico

(Continued)

APPENDIX (Continued)

Hughes's title	First pub.	Translator	Title in Spanish	Date	Where	Page(s)	Country
Song of Spain	1937	Cruzado	La canción de España	2004	*Blues*	131	Spain
Song to a Negro Washer Woman	1925	Gáler	Canción a una lavandera	1952	*Poemas*	137–39	Argentina
Songs	1947	Gáler	Canciones	1952	*Poemas*	82	Argentina
South, The	1922	Gáler	El Sur	1952	*Poemas*	32–33	Argentina
South, The	1922	Cruzado	El Sur	2004	*Blues*	77	Spain
Stalingrad 1942	1943	Gáler	Stalingrado 1942	1952	*Poemas*	140–45	Argentina
Stars	1926	Blanco	Estrellas	1949	*Asomante*	29	Puerto Rico
Stars	1926	Cazani	no title	1963	*Poesía?*	1	Argentina
Subway Rush Hour	1951	Gáler	Mediodía en el subte	1952	*Poemas*	117	Argentina
Subway Rush Hour	1951	Cruzado	Hora punta en el metro	2004	*Blues*	161	Spain
Suicide's Note	1925	Fernández de Castro	Nota de una suicida	1930	*Rev. de la Hab.*	186	Cuba
Suicide's Note	1925	Villaurrutia	Nota de un suicido	1931	*Contemporáneos*	159	Mexico
Suicide's Note	1925	Villaurrutia	Nota de un suicido	1961	*Nivel*		Mexico
Suicide's Note	1925	Gáler	La nota del suicido	1952	*Poemas*	46	Argentina
Sunday Morning Prophecy	1942	Gáler	Profecía del domingo a la mañana	1952	*Poemas*	111–13	Argentina
Tell Me	1951	Gáler	Dime	1952	*Poemas*	114	Argentina
Testimonial	1951	Ahumada	Testimonio	1968	*YT*	45	Mexico
Tomorrow's Seed	1952	Fraile Marcos	La semilla del mañana	1998	*Oscuridad*	68–71	Spain
Tree?	?	Gáler	Arbol	1952	*Poemas*	135	Argentina
Trumpet Player	1949	Cruzado	Él trompetista	2004	*Blues*	147	Spain
Union	1931	Pereda Valdés	Unión	1936	*Antología (PV)*	41	Chile; Uruguay

Union	1931	Ahumada	Unión	1968	*YT*	117	Mexico
Vagabonds	1941	Gáler	Vagabundos	1952	*Poemas*	87	Argentina
Visitors to Black Belt	1940	Gáler	Visitados en el barrio negro	1952	*Poemas*	101–102	Argentina
Warning	1949	Ahumada	Roland Hayes golpeado	1968	*YT*	85	Mexico
Weary Blues, The	1925	Alejandro	Veary [sic] Blues	1936	*Nueva Cultura*	155	Spain
Weary Blues, The	1925	Gáler	Los blues tristes	1952	*Poemas*	27–28	Argentina
Weary Blues, The	1925	Matz and Jordá	Los cansados blues	2001	*Litoral*		Spain
Weary Blues, The	1925	Cruzado	Los cansados blues	2004	*Blues*	105	Spain
When Sue Wears Red	1923	Gáler	Cuando Susana Jones viste de rojo	1952	*Poemas*	38	Argentina
When Sue Wears Red	1923	Ahumada	Cuando Susan se viste de rojo	1968	*YT*	53	Mexico
White Ones, The	1924	Fernández de Castro	Los blancos	1930	*Revista de la Habana*		Cuba
Who but the Lord	1947	Gáler	¿Quien, si no el Señor?	1952	*Poemas*	105–106	Argentina
Who but the Lord	1947	Ahumada	¿Quien si no el Señor?	1968	*YT*	83	Mexico
Winter Sweetness	1921	Ahumada	Dulzura invernal	1968	*YT*	25	Mexico
Yesterday and Today	1947	Ahumada	Ayer y hoy	1968	*YT*	73	Mexico
Young Prostitute	1923	Cruzado	Joven prostituta	2004	*Blues*	87	Spain
Young Singer	1923	Lozano	Cancionera	1931	*Crísol*	232	Mexico
Young Singer	1923	Lozano	Cancionera	1931	*Reportorio Amer.*	226	Costa Rica
Young Singer	1923	Cruzado	Joven cantante	2004	*Blues*	93	Spain
Youth	1924	Gáler	Juventud	1952	*Poemas*	51	Argentina
Youth	1924	Ahumada	Juventud	1968	*YT*	39	Mexico

NOTES

1. See, for instance, John Kerry's preface to the 2004 edition of *Let America Be America Again and Other Poems* (New York: Vintage). The stamp is from the Black Heritage series, 2002. For a complete list of African American subjects on USA postage stamps, see http://www.asalh.org/files/USPS_AfricanAmericanStampSubjects.pdf. Few recall—even after watching this movie—that Tolson was also a poet of some note. See LeRoi Jones, "Langston Hughes's *Tambourines to Glory*," *CR*, 598.

2. In 2001, the *New York Times* ran a fairly elaborate web-only special feature on Hughes. See http://www.nytimes.com/books/01/04/22/specials/hughes.htm.

3. There are four more recent biographies of Hughes: Jodie Shull, *Langston Hughes: "Life Makes Poems"* (Berkeley Heights, NJ: Enslow, 2006); Brenda Haugen, *Langston Hughes: The Voice of Harlem* (Minneapolis: Compass Point Books, 2006); Veda Boyd Jones, *Jazz Age Poet: A Story about Langston Hughes* (Minneapolis: Millbrook Press, 2006); and Bonnie Greer, *Langston Hughes: The Value of Contradiction* (London: Arcadia Books, 2011).

4. I have not, for the most part, included in my analyses the travel writing Hughes did other than in his autobiographies. For excellent work on Hughes's essays on the Caribbean, see Jeff Karem, *The Purloined Islands: Caribbean-U.S. Crosscurrents in Literature and Culture, 1880–1959* (Charlottesville: University of Virginia Press, 2011), 226–32; on his Russian travel writings, see Kate Baldwin, *Beyond the Color Line and the Iron Curtain: Reading Encounters between Black and Red, 1922–1963* (Durham, NC: Duke University Press, 2002); on his work as war correspondent in Spain, see Michael Thurston, *Making Something Happen: American Political Poetry between the World Wars* (Chapel Hill: University of North Carolina Press, 2001).

5. Unlike the Romance languages, English retains both connotations. In Spanish, for instance, these activities were separated during the Renaissance into *traducir* and *transladar(se)*. See Stephanos Stephanides, "The Translation of Heritage: Multiculturalism in the 'New' Europe," in *Rethinking Heritage: Cultures and Politics in Europe*, ed. Robert Shannan Peckham (London: I.B. Tauris, 2003), 46; Karlheinz Stierle, "Translatio Studii and Renaissance: From Vertical to Horizontal Translation," in *The Translatability of Cultures: Figurations of the Space Between*, ed. Sanford Budick et al. (Stanford, CA: Stanford University Press, 1996), 55–56; Christopher L. Miller, *The French Atlantic Triangle: Literature and Culture of the Slave Trade* (Durham, NC: Duke University Press, 2008), 101.

6. See Martin Heidegger, *Poetry, Language, Thought* (New York: Harper & Row), 152. Barbara Johnson contends that translation is "a bridge that creates out of itself the two fields of battle it separates." "Taking Fidelity Philosophically," in *Difference—In Translation*, ed. Joseph F. Graham (Ithaca: Cornell University Press, 1985), 147. The bridge metaphor also has another significant shortfall: it limits our imagination to *two* banks or mainlands, when in fact literary translation connects multiple linguistic and cultural fields. Most translation theorists do not sufficiently question this metaphor. See also Bill Ashcroft's useful comments

on translation and transformation in *Caliban's Voice: The Transformation of English in Post-Colonial Literatures* (Milton Park, UK: Routledge, 2009), 159–82.

7. Steven Ungar, "Writing in Tongues: Thoughts on the Work of Translation," in *Comparative Literature in an Age of Globalizaton*, ed. Haun Saussy (Baltimore: Johns Hopkins University Press, 2006), 132.

8. Jeff Westover, "Africa/America: Fragmentation and Diaspora in the Work of Langston Hughes," *Callaloo* 25, no. 4 (2002): 1209; Daniel C. Turner, "Montage of Simplicity Deferred: Langston Hughes's Art of Sophistication and Racial Intersubjectivity in *Montage of a Dream Deferred*," *Langston Hughes Review* 17 (2002): 23; Larry Scanlon, "Poets Laureate and the Language of Slaves: Petrarch, Chaucer, and Langston Hughes," in *The Vulgar Tongue: Medieval and Postmedieval Vernacularity*, ed. Fiona Somerset and Nicholas Watson (University Park: Pennsylvania State University Press, 2003), 225.

9. On the latter two, see Kirsten Silva Gruesz, *Ambassadors of Culture: The Transamerican Origins of Latino Writing* (Princeton: Princeton University Press, 2002).

10. See George Reid Andrews, *The Afro-Argentines of Buenos Aires, 1800–1900* (Madison: University of Wisconsin Press, 1980), 62–63. Andrews's population data, a combination of census data for 2000 and estimates (see 156), do not even include Argentina.

11. I refer to this geography as "the Americas" because it significantly includes the USA, the Caribbean, and what I prefer to call the Hispanic Americas. I find the term "Hispanic Americas" more congenial than the more popular "Latin America," whose singular appeals to a cultural unity that does not exist. Consequently, I call the people who inhabit the Hispanic Americas "Hispanic Americans." This is not to confuse them with the Latino populations in the USA, an abbreviation that also acknowledges, in a way that simply US does not, the existence of another United States, that of Mexico. I thus follow Djelal Kadir in using the adjective "USAmerican." See "Concentric Hemispheres: American Studies and Comparative Literature," in *Trans/American, Trans/Oceanic, Trans/lation: Issues in International American Studies*, ed. Susana Araújo et al. (Newcastle, UK: Cambridge Scholars, 2010): 27–37. While I am concerned about distinctions among the different parts of the Americas that that are otherwise elided, I also wish to signal in my nomenclature important historical and contemporary linkages between the Hispanic Americas and USA. That no geography is an island without ties to the rest of the world almost goes without saying. The Americas are clearly no exception. See also afterword.

12. Jahan Ramazani's *Poetry of Mourning: The Modern Elegy from Hardy to Heany* (Chicago: University of Chicago Press, 1994) can be said to mark this change. Ian Peddie calls the label "social protest" a "dubious misnomer," pointing out that "Hughes's range was always wider than that description might suggest." " 'There's No Way Not To Lose': Langston Hughes and Intraracial Class Antagonism," *Langston Hughes Review* 18 (Spring 2004): 40.

13. See Larry Scanlon, "News from Heaven: Vernacular Time in Langston Hughes's *Ask Your Mama*," *Callaloo* 25, no. 1 (Winter 2002): 45–65, and "Poets Laureate"; Michael Borshuk, *Swinging the Vernacular: Jazz and African American Modernist Literature* (New York: Routledge, 2006); Edward Brunner, *Cold War Poetry* (Urbana: University of Illinois Press, 2000), 132–42; Eluned Summers-Bremner, "Unreal City and Dream Deferred: Psychogeographies of Modernism in T.S. Eliot and Langston Hughes," in *Geomodernisms: Race, Modernism, Modernity*, ed. Laura Winkiel and Laura Doyle (Bloomington: Indiana University Press, 2005), 262–80; and Turner, "Montage of Simplicity."

14. "There are still many scholars who approach 'emerging' literatures (and which literature really is not 'emerging'?) as if they themselves were ethnographers doing fieldwork." Guido Podestá, "Cultural Liaisons in American Literatures," in *Modernism and Its Margins*, ed. Anthony L. Geist and José B. Monleón (New York: Garland, 1999), 181. The status of literary translation has been complicated by anthropological debates about access to other cultures: the "idea of translation…as a crossing of borders is closely connected to the interpretive

procedures of anthropology and of ethnography as a practice, which, like literary translation, is predicated upon the representation of a fundamental otherness." Stephanides, "Translation of Heritage," 50. There are, however, significant differences between anthropological ethnography and literature. Literature does not assume the translatability of others' cultural codes, and anthropological texts tend not to foreground translational processes in their own linguistic fabric. See also Tejaswini Niranjana, *Siting Translation: History, Post-Structuralism, and the Colonial Context* (Berkeley: University of California Press, 1992), chap. 2; Stephanos Stephanides, "Translation and Ethnography in Literary Translation," in *Studying Transcultural Literary History*, ed. Gunilla Lindberg-Wada (Berlin: de Gruyter, 2006), 300–309; Scanlon, "Poets Laureate," 251; and James Clifford, *Routes: Travel and Translation in the Late-Twentieth Century* (Cambridge, MA: Harvard University Press, 1997).

15. Kadir has wisely noted that fictionalizing—that is, creating reality effects—can be a "deliberate and calculated intervention against the impunity of recalcitrant realities that deem themselves unassailable." "Concentric Hemispheres," 35.

16. Edward Mullen, for one, contends that "the case of Hughes serves not only as a paradigm of the African American literary experience, which has been deeply shaped by influences outside of the USA (one recalls the cases of Richard Wright, James Baldwin, and Chester Himes, all of whom flourished in Paris), but also demonstrates the deeply rooted interconnections among writers of the black diaspora." "Langston Hughes in Mexico and Cuba," *Review: Latin American Literature and Arts* 47 (1993): 24). See also Alice Deck and Marvin Lewis's special issue, "Langston Hughes and the African Diaspora," *Langston Hughes Review* 5, no. 1 (1986); Richard Jackson, *Black Writers in Latin America* (Albuquerque: University of New Mexico Press, 1979), and *Black Writers and Latin America: Cross-Cultural Affinities* (Washington, DC: Howard University Press, 1998).

17. See Brent Edwards, "The Uses of 'Diaspora,'" in *African Diasporas in the New and Old Worlds: Consciousness and Imagination,* ed. Geneviève Fabre and Klaus Benesch (Amsterdam: Rodopi, 2004), 3–38, and his *The Practice of Diaspora: Literature, Translation, and the Rise of Black Internationalism* (Cambridge, MA: Harvard University Press, 2003); Anita Patterson, *Race, American Literature and Transnational Modernisms* (Cambridge: Cambridge University Press, 2008); Edward Pavlić, *Crossroads Modernism: Descent and Emergence in African-American Literary Culture* (Minneapolis: University of Minnesota Press, 2002). Also Stuart Hall, "Cultural Identity and Diaspora," in *Identity: Community, Culture, Difference,* ed. Jonathan Rutherford (London: Lawrence & Wishart, 1990), 222–37.

18. Edwards, *Practice of Diaspora,* 59. See also Alfred Guillaume, Jr., "And Bid Him Translate: Langston Hughes's Translations of Poetry from French," *Langston Hughes Review* 4, no. 2 (1985): 1–23.

19. See Baldwin, *Beyond the Color Line.* Five Hughes poems in the 1934 Uzbek collection *Langston Hyus She'rlari* have no extant English equivalent. See David Chioni Moore on the difficulty of restoring these poems to English as well as the actual restorations. "Colored Dispatches from the Uzbek Border: Langston Hughes' Relevance, 1933–2002," *Callaloo* 25, no. 4 (2002), 1124. On nomadism, see Gilles Deleuze and Félix Guattari, *A Thousand Plateaus: Capitalism and Schizophrenia* (London: Continuum, 2004), 23–24, and Karl Schlögel, *Planet der Nomaden* (Pilsen, Czech Rep.: Oldenbourg, 2006). Hughes mentions in passing that "the [Japanese] translations of my Harlem blues poems, so I was told, were quite well done and attracted considerable attention in Tokyo." *IW,* 242. Since *The Weary Blues* was not published in Japanese translation until 1958—as *Shishu, Niguro to Kawa* by Todatoshi Saito—Hughes's reference might be to earlier journal publications of those poems. The only earlier book-length translation was of *Not Without Laughter*: Yae Yokemura's *Wara Wa Nu Demo Nashi* from 1940. Hughes also briefly remarks on translation of his poems into Spanish and French, *IW,* 295 and 400.

20. Hughes's alternate titles for the play were *Fate at the Wedding* and *Tragic Wedding*. Melia Bensussen published an adapted translation under the title *Blood Wedding* in 1994; see Dellita Martin-Ogunsola, introduction to *The Collected Works of Langston Hughes*, vol. 16, *The Translations*, ed. Arnold Rampersad (Columbia: University of Missouri Press, 2003), 4. Hughes is not even mentioned as the play's translator in Christopher Maurer's introduction to his *García Lorca, Federico: Poet in New York* (New York: Farrar Straus Giroux, 1988). Hughes had published a limited edition folio of the poem "San Gabriel" in 1938. The 1951 *Gypsy Ballads* are available online at http://www.bpj.org/index/Vo2N1.html.

21. Notable exceptions are William Scott's "Motivos of Translation: Nicolás Guillén and Langston Hughes," *CR: The New Centennial Review* 5, no. 2 (Fall 2005), and Edwards's *Practice of Diaspora*, 59–68.

22. Most of the materials I consulted are part of the Langston Hughes Papers housed in the James Weldon Johnson Collection at the Beinecke Rare Book and Manuscript Library at Yale University.

23. It bears pointing out that "Negro dialect" is not the same as "Black English" or as black vernacular. For more details, see chapter 4. See also Joshua Miller, *Accented America: The Cultural Politics of Multilingual Modernism* (New York: Oxford University Press, 2011). An example I do not pursue in this book is Hughes's translation of Jacques Roumain's *Gouverneurs de la rosée*. In *Masters of the Dew*, Hughes and his collaborator, Mercer Cook, consistently translate "nègre" as "Negro." In Haitian Kreyòl, however, and in Roumain's narrative, "nègre" is almost deracialized, being used as a synonym for "man" or "person." I thank J. Ryan Poynter for calling my attention to this.

24. I am very much in agreement with José María Rodríguez García, who urges that "great attention needs to be bestowed upon the shifting locations and historicization of origins in translation, particularly those founding moments which have been transmitted to us in an unexamined way." "Literary into Cultural Translation," *Diacritics* 34, nos. 3–4 (2004): 27.

25. It is astonishing how few scholars seem to have noticed the release of the transcripts of Hughes's secret testimony in 2003. Greer, for instance, recounts the story of Hughes's public testimony as if this is all we knew. See *Langston Hughes*, chap. 1.

26. The eighteen essays in Roseanna Warren's *Art of Translation: Voices from the Field*. (Boston: Northeastern University Press, 1989) include but a single one on translations into Spanish. This is but one example among many.

27. Probably the earliest occurrence of the now popular term "domestication" is in Lawrence Venuti's 1973 essay, "Translation as Cultural Politics: Regimes of Domestication in English," *Textual Practice* 7, no. 2 (1993): 208–23.

28. Edwin Genzler's *Translation and Identity in the Americas: New Directions in Translation Theory* (New York: Routledge, 2008) is one of few studies that takes this into account. Relevant here is also the polysystems theory of translation pioneered by Itamar Even-Zohar and Gideon Toury, whose work is the basis for the more recent work of Lawrence Venuti and others; see Even-Zohar and Toury, *Translation Theory and Intercultural Relations* (Tel Aviv: Porter Institute for Poetics and Semantics, 1981), and Even Zohar, *Polysystem Studies* (Durham, NC: Duke University Press, 1990). Although Even-Zohar's interest is in "locating" translational texts, his polysystems are still based on a hierarchical center-periphery model; see Rodríguez García, "Literary into Cultural Translation," 23–25.

29. See Gayatri Chakravorty Spivak, *Outside the Teaching Machine* (New York: Routledge, 1993), 179–200; Ian Chambers, *Mediterranean Crossings: The Politics of an Interrupted Modernity* (Durham, NC: Duke University Press, 2008); Chana Kronfeld, *On the Margins of Modernism: Decentering Literary Dynamics* (Berkeley: University of California Press, 1996); Beatriz Sarlo, *Una modernidad periférica: Buenos Aires 1920 y 1930* (Buenos Aires: Ediciones Nueva Visión, 1988).

30. See Zora Neale Hurston, *Mules and Men* (New York: Harper Perennial, 1995), 1.

31. I borrow the phrase "lexical shock" from Willis Barnstone, *Poetics of Translation: History, Theory, Practice* (New Haven, CT: Yale University Press, 1993), 266. Siobhan Somerville is quite right in pointing out that "the formation of notions of heterosexuality and homosexuality emerged in the United States through (and not merely parallel to) a discourse saturated with assumptions about the racialization of bodies"; thus the "challenge is to recognize the instability of multiple categories of difference *simultaneously.*" *Queering the Color Line: Race and the Invention of Homosexuality in American Culture* (Durham, NC: Duke University Press, 2003), 4, 5 (my emphasis).

32. Gustavo Pérez Firmat, *The Cuban Condition: Translation and Identity in Modern Cuban Literature* (Cambridge: Cambridge University Press, 1989), 4.

33. Being finally able to grasp "the beauty and the meaning of the words" in Maupassant's stories, which Hughes had read in high school in Cleveland, made him "really want to be a writer and write stories about Negroes so true that people in faraway lands would read them—even after I was dead." *BS*, 34. See Isabel Soto, " 'To Hear Another Language': Lifting the Veil between Langston Hughes and Federico García Lorca," in *Border Transits: Literature and Culture across the Line*, ed. Ana María Manzanas (Amsterdam: Rodopi, 2007), 102.

34. Hughes's writings may be seen as a confrontation with hegemony "in the fibres of the self." Raymond Williams, *Marxism and Literature* (Oxford: Oxford University Press, 1977), 212. Nicolás Guillén recounts that Hughes, during his visit to Cuba in 1930, expressed the desire for being "negro de verdad," really, truly black. "Conversación con Langston Hughes," *El Diario de la Marina* XCVIII (March 9, 1930), 6. Some years later, the Soviet critic Lydia Filatova, who had helped Hughes translate "for American readers some of the poems about Negroes by the great Vladimir Mayakowsky" (*IW*, 198), criticized "Hughes for not being 'black enough,' for failing to incorporate in his poetry the Comintern's Black Nation Thesis." Anthony Dawahare, *Nationalism, Marxism, and African American Literature between the Wars* (Jackson: University Press of Mississippi, 2002), 108.

35. See, for instance, Isaac Julien, *Looking for Langston* (London: British Film Institute, 1989); Brian Loftus, "In/verse Autobiography: Sexual (In)Difference and the Textual Backside of Langston Hughes's *The Big Sea*," *Auto/Biography Studies* 15, no. 1 (2000): 141–61; Martin Ponce, "Langston Hughes's Queer Blues," *Modern Language Quarterly* 66, no. 4 (December 2005): 505–37; Sam See, " 'Spectacles of Color': The Primitive Drag of Langston Hughes," *PMLA* 124, no. 3 (2009): 798–816; and Gregory Woods, "Gay Re-Readings of the Harlem Renaissance Poets," *Journal of Homosexuality* 26, nos. 2–3 (1993): 127–42.

36. Emily Apter, *The Translation Zone: A New Comparative Literature* (Princeton: Princeton University Press, 2006), 6. Edward Said describes exile as a "discontinuous state of being." "Reflections on Exile," in *Out There: Marginalization and Contemporary Cultures*, ed. Russell Ferguson et al. (Cambridge, MA: MIT Press, 1990), 363.

37. See Kenneth Warren on the "comedy of misrecognition" in the context of the black diaspora. "Appeals for (Mis)recognition: Theorizing the Diaspora," in *Cultures of United States Imperialism*, ed. Amy Kaplan and Donald Pease. Durham, NC: Duke University Press, 1993), 400.

38. In Judith Butler's paraphrase of Monique Wittig, "Discourse becomes oppressive when it requires that the speaking subject, in order to speak, participate in the very terms of that oppression—that is, take for granted the speaking subject's own impossibility or unintelligibility." *Gender Trouble: Feminism and the Subversion of Identity* (New York: Routledge, 1999), 147.

39. Stephanides, "Translation of Heritage," 48. His reference point here is Benjamin, who talks about the need to (re)claim source texts for present generations so that translation becomes an allegory of the past's resurrection.

40. On this point, compare Alain Locke's *New Negro* (1925; repr., New York: Atheneum, 1977) with Edwards's *Practice of Diaspora*.

41. Especially notable for work on Hughes in Russia is Baldwin's *Beyond the Color Line*. See also Edward Mullen, *Langston Hughes in the Hispanic World and Haiti* (Hamden, CT: Archon Books, 1977); "Langston Hughes in Mexico and Cuba"; and "Presencia y evaluación de Langston Hughes en Hispanoamérica," *Revista de Latinoamericana de Escritores* 15 (1974): 16–21. Patterson's focus in *Race* is on the French Caribbean (see 93–129).

42. Walter Benjamin, *Illuminations* (New York: Schocken Books, 1969), 75. Stephanides rightly argues that such coming to terms is the basis of creolization. "Translation and Ethnography," 308.

43. Scott, "Motivos of Translation," 47; Iain Chambers, *Migrancy, Culture, Identity* (New York: Routledge, 1994), 13.

44. See Loredana Polezzi, *Translating Travel: Contemporary Italian Travel Writing in English Translation* (Aldershot, UK: Ashgate, 2001), 213.

45. Scott, "Motivos of Translation," 50–51; Chambers, *Migrancy*, 24.

46. Chambers, *Migrancy*, 24.

47. Ibid., 32.

48. Notable exceptions are Edwards, *Practice of Diaspora*, and Patterson, *Race*. See also Isabel Soto, "Translation as Understanding: Alfonso Sastre's Adaptation of 'Mulatto,'" *Langston Hughes Review* 15, no. 1 (1997): 13–23, and "Crossing Over: Langston Hughes and Lorca," in *A Place That Is Not a Place: Essays in Liminality and Text*, ed. Isabel Soto (Madrid: Gateway Press, 2000), 115–32. Also Scott, "Motivos of Translation."

49. Literary translation, a form of cultural mediation that is not as easily consumable as most of the hybridized information with which the media envelop us, has fared no better in this respect.

50. There are relatively few literary and scholarly translations into USAmerican English. In the April 15, 2007 issue of *The New York Times Book Review*, which was devoted to translations, Jascha Hoffman offered a collage of statistical information, culled from a variety of sources, about the state of translation, in the USA and elsewhere, in the twenty-first century. In 2004, for instance, only 2.6 percent of the total number of new books published in the USA in 2004 were translations, compared with 29 percent in the Czech Republic and South Korea; China is low with 4 percent but still better than the USA. The percentages would, of course, depend on the total numbers of new books published in each country, which this collage does not provide. But if we consider that in 2005, about 1.5 million new books were published worldwide and that 30 percent of those were in English, it is a pretty good guess that we are talking about something in the vicinity of eight thousand books out of roughly three hundred thousand. That leaves us with 70 percent distributed unevenly among the remaining 6,912 languages of the rest of the world. We also read here that the National Endowment for the Arts' funding for literary translation into English for 2006 was a whopping $200,000 (compared with the $13.3 million the French Ministry for Culture expended for translation of French literature into other languages in the same year).

51. Lawrence Venuti has argued that "[m]odernism seeks to establish the cultural autonomy of the translated text by effacing its manifold conditions and exclusions, especially the process of domestication by which the foreign text is rewritten to serve modernist cultural agendas." *The Translator's Invisibility: History of Translation* (London: Routledge, 1995), 188. He also calls for "historicizing various forms of receiving the foreign." *The Scandals of Translation: Towards an Ethics of Difference* (London: Routledge, 1998), 94. But his default for "foreign" is nondominant or marginalized.

52. David Damrosch, "Where Is World Literature?," in Lindberg-Wada, *Studying Transcultural Literary History*, 212.

53. Chris Prentice uses the biological term "translocation," which is typically applied to chromosomes, in the subtitle to *Cultural Transformations: Perspectives on Translocation in a Global Age* (Amsterdam: Rodopi, 2010).

54. Ottmar Ette uses the term "Vektorisierung" (vectorization) in *ZwischenWelten-Schreiben: Literaturen ohne festen Wohnsitz* (Berlin: Kulturverlag Kadmos, 2005), 11.

55. David Johnston, "Mapping the Geographies of Translation," in *Betwixt and Between: Place and Cultural Translation*, ed. Stephen Kelly and David Johnston (Newcastle, UK: Cambridge Scholars, 2007), 255.

56. Stephanides has proposed that "the foregrounding of a translation poetics in the act of writing and in the defining of the literary" is a distinguishing feature of literary writing from the Americas. "Translation and Ethnography," 301. Although his point is compelling, its hemispheric exceptionalism might be hard to sustain in a more global context. See, for instance, Ette, *ZwischenWeltenSchreiben*, on so-called New German writers such as Yoko Tawada, Emine Sevgi Özdamar, and José Oliver.

57. Johnston, "Mapping the Geographies," 258. For a similar framework, see also Pavlić, *Crossroads Modernism*. Also see Michael Soto, who asks, "What impact do Berlin and Paris and Mexico City have on the African American literary imagination as opposed to, say, Harlem or rural Georgia?" *The Modernist Nation: Generation, Renaissance, and Twentieth-Century American Literature* (Tuscaloosa: University of Alabama Press, 2004), 90.

58. Chambers, *Mediterranean Crossings*, 144; see also Astradur Eysteinsson, *The Concept of Modernism* (Ithaca: Cornell University Press, 1990), and Ette on the "unabschliessbarer Prozess ständiger Sprachenquerung" (endless process of continuous linguistic crossings), *ZwischenWeltenSchreiben*, 21.

1. NOMAD HEART

1. See Robert B. Stepto, *From Behind the Veil: A Study of Afro-American Narrative* (Urbana: University of Illinois Press, 1979).

2. Naoki Sakai, *Translation and Subjectivity: On "Japan" and Cultural Nationalism* (Minneapolis: University of Minnesota Press, 1997), 2ff.

3. Meshrabpom, or Meshrabpom-Rus, was a German-Russian collaboration with headquarters in Berlin and production facilities in Moscow. It was founded in 1924 and was actually quite successful. The fiasco Hughes describes appears not to have been a representative episode in the studio's history. Film historians are now beginning to rediscover this company.

4. Some reviewers damned *The Big Sea* with faint praise: "a string of good stories" or "a strange commentary on twentieth-century America"; "some three-hundred odd pages of charming conversational reminiscence" (*CR*, 249, 258). There are many charges that Hughes wrote autobiographies without "revealing himself," as George Kent still claimed in 1972. Quoted in R. Baxter Miller, " 'Even After I Was Dead': *The Big Sea*—Paradox, Preservation, and Holistic Time," *Black American Literature Forum* 11, no. 2 (1977): 42. Miller disagrees but offers no evidence to the contrary. More recently, Hughes has been accused of being "shallow" for not revealing the intimate details about his personal life that would enable scholars to make the kinds of incontrovertible pronouncements about his sexuality that Rampersad resists in his biography.

5. Craig Werner rather unconvincingly singles out Toomer, Hurston, and Hughes as writers "whose explicit modernist awareness contrasts sharply with their conventional autobiographical voice." According to him, "neither *I Wonder As I Wander* or *The Big Sea* would alert a reader to the modernist complexities beneath the tactful surfaces of Hughes's Simple stories." *Playing the Changes: From Afro-Modernism to the Jazz Impulse* (Urbana: University of Illinois Press, 1994), 89.

6. Robert Hemenway, *Zora Neale Hurston: A Literary Biography* (Urbana: University of Illinois Press, 1978), 276. For an assessment of reviews see 277ff. According to Hemenway's still unsurpassed literary biography, the manuscript version of *Dust Tracks* "displays a more self-assured, irreverent, and politically astute figure than the Hurston of the published book" (287).

7. John Lowney, "Langston Hughes and the 'Nonesense' of Bebop," *American Literature* 72, no. 2 (June 2000): 376–77. Hughes's oft-quoted lines from "The Negro Artist and the Racial Mountain" are the following: "We younger Negro artists who create now intend to express our individual dark-skinned selves without fear or shame. If white people are pleased we are glad. If they are not, it doesn't matter. We know we are beautiful. And ugly too....If colored people are pleased we are glad. If they are not, their displeasure doesn't matter either" (*Essays*, 36). See also James Weldon Johnson's "The Dilemma of the Negro Author" in *The Essential Writings of James Weldon Johnson*, ed. Rudolph P. Byrd (New York: Modern Library, 2008), 201–9.

8. Lucy Angulo, "Life of Adventure" (*CR*, 271); Luther Jackson, "Globe-Trotting Bard" (*CR*, 507); and Ted Robinson, "Fugitive Otto Strasser, Fate Unknown, Tells How Ex-Friend 'Missed the Bus'" (*CR*, 240).

9. For Hughes's decision to omit pieces on central Russia from *I Wonder As I Wander*, see Baldwin, *Beyond the Color Line*, 87.

10. I do not agree with Paul Gardullo that "[b]y describing his radical years as 'wanderings,' Hughes downplays their importance. "Heading Out for the Big Sea: Hughes, Haiti and Constructions of Diaspora in Cold War America," *Langston Hughes Review* 18 (2004): 64. The word itself may downplay strategy, but it also opens a space for critique as Hughes navigates an increasingly perilous domestic climate.

11. On Hurston's unwillingness to fix the autobiographical subject in *Dust Tracks*, see Sidonie Smith, *Subjectivity, Identity, and the Body: Women's Autobiographical Practices in the Twentieth Century* (Bloomington: Indiana University Press, 1993), 103–25.

12. Baxter Miller quotes Du Bois's *A Soliloquy on Viewing My Life from the Last Decade of Its First Century* (1968) to make the point that "[a]utobiographies do not form indisputable authorities. They are always incomplete, and often unreliable....What I think of myself, now and in the past, furnishes no certain document proving what I really am." "'For a Moment I Wondered': Theory and Symbolic Form in the Autobiographies of Langston Hughes," *Langston Hughes Review* 3, no. 2 (1984): 1. Miller does not connect this point with an analysis of Hughes's autobiographical writing.

13. John Paul Eakin, *Fictions in Autobiography: Studies in the Art of Self-Invention* (Princeton: Princeton University Press, 1985), 226. See also Bart Moore-Gilbert, *Postcolonial Life-Writing: Culture, Politics, and Self-Representation* (London: Routledge, 2009), 1–2.

14. Loftus, "In/verse Autobiography," 144. Relevant here also are Georgia Johnston's comments on modernist lesbian autobiography as a "fluctuating genre." *The Formation of 20th-Century Queer Autobiography: Reading Vita Sackville-West, Virginia Woolf, Hilda Doolittle, and Gertrude Stein* (New York: Palgrave Macmillan, 2007), 10. See also Karen Caplan, "Resisting Autobiography: Out-Law Genres and Transnational Feminist Subjects," in *Women, Autobiography, Theory: A Reader*, ed. Sidonie Smith and Julia Watson (Madison: University of Wisconsin Press, 1998), 208–21.

15. See Chambers: "The figure of the author is not dead but displaced. It is a point of departure not of arrival." *Migrancy*, 129.

16. Ralph Ellison, "Stormy Weather," *CR*, 260.

17. See Michael Borshuk, "'Noise Modernism': The Cultural Politics of Langston Hughes's Early Jazz Poetry," *Langston Hughes Review* 17, nos. 1–2 (2002): 18.

18. Chambers, *Mediterranean Crossings*, 32 (my emphasis).

19. See Amiri Baraka, "The Changing Same (R&B and New Black Music)," in *The LeRoi Jones / Amiri Baraka Reader*, ed. William J. Harris (New York: Thunder's Mouth Press, 1991), 186–209. See also Kimberly Benston, *Performing Blackness: Enactments of African-American Modernism* (London: Routledge, 2000), chap. 5.

20. Langston Hughes, *The Langston Hughes Reader* (New York: G. Braziller, 1958), 493.

21. Patterson, *Race*, 109.

22. On jazz, see also Hughes's "The Negro Artist and the Racial Mountain," *Essays* 35–36. Borshuk, who locates Hughes as a "hybrid modernist," places his "unique jazz-inspired innovations within the Signifyin(g) tradition" of African American literature. *Swinging the Vernacular*, 32, 50. See also Brent Edwards's readings of jazz in Hughes's poetry, *Practice of Diaspora*, 65ff, and Scanlon on the differences between Hughes and white vanguardists, "Poets Laureate".

23. Scanlon, "Poets Laureate," 236 (my emphasis).

24. Much valuable work has been done on Hughes and the blues. See, for instance, Steven Tracy, *Langston Hughes and the Blues* (Urbana: University of Illinois Press, 1988); Werner, *Playing the Changes*; Jürgen Grandt, *Shaping Words to Fit the Soul* (Columbus: Ohio State University Press, 2009).

25. William C. Handy, *Father of the Blues: An Autobiography* (New York: Da Capo Press, 1991),137, 139; see also Grandt, *Shaping Words*, 78

26. Grandt, 79.

27. Pavlić, *Crossroads Modernism*, 22. The term is derived from the Greek συν-syn+ δέσις-desis, "binding together" (OED), and is used in the study of chromosomes; its first documented use was in 1904 (in zoology).

28. Ibid., 58.

29. The preeminent symbolic spaces in relation to African American literature from the USA are the North and the South. Stepto has aptly called them "ritual grounds" (see his *From Behind the Veil*). Unlike Stepto, who limits himself to narrative, Pavlić analyzes both fiction and poetry. Surprisingly, to my mind, he does not have much to say about Hughes; he does, however, include Hurston's autobiography in his excellent discussion of asymmetries and angles in her writing. See *Crossroads Modernism*, chapter 3.

30. Chambers, *Migrancy*, 12.

31. Apter defines what she calls Being "in-translation" as "belonging to no single, discrete language or single medium of communication." *Translation Zone*, 6.

32. Loftus poignantly notes that "Rampersad misses the irony and inversions that saturate the text." "In/verse Autobiography," 147.

33. An exception here is Edwards's *Practice of Diaspora*.

34. Pavlić, *Crossroads Modernism*, 22.

35. Carl Van Vechten, introduction to *TWB*, 9 (my emphasis).

36. *La vida de Lazarillo de Tormes y de sus fortunas y adversidades* was first published in 1554 and 1555. Translated widely in Europe, it was considered heretical in Spain and banned by the Inquisition. See also Patterson on Hughes and Laforgue's Pierrot in *Race*, 100–101.

37. See Henry Louis Gates, Jr., *The Signifying Monkey: A Theory of African American Literary Criticism* (New York: Oxford University Press, 1988).

38. In his Spanish translation of *I Wonder*, Gáler leaves the lyrics in English and adds explanatory notes. See *Yo viajo*, 89.

39. Hughes recounts that he began reading *Don Quixote* with a tutor in Mexico and mentions his Simple stories in connection with this. IW, 291.

40. Baldwin, *Beyond the Color Line*, 116–17.

41. Zora Neale Hurston, "How It Feels to Be Colored Me," *World Tomorrow* 11 (May 1928): 215–16. See also Hemenway, *Zora Neale Hurston*, 11.

42. Baldwin shows how Hughes rewrote Du Bois's Hegelian-inspired trope of the veil, especially its heteronormative bias. *Beyond the Color Line*, 90, 108.

43. Chambers, *Migrancy*, 16. For a different argument, see Anita Patterson, "Jazz, Realism, and the Modernist Lyric: The Poetry of Langston Hughes," *Modern Language Quarterly* 61, no. 4 (December 2000): 651–82.

44. Koestler's book was published in an expurgated German version in Kharkov, Ukraine. Unlike Hughes, Koestler had become disaffected with communism by 1940, the year he published the influential anti-Soviet novel *Darkness at Noon*.

45. Hall, "Cultural Identity and Diaspora," 235.

46. Borshuk usefully compares Hughes's "The Weary Blues" to Louis Armstrong's "West End Blues." *Swinging the Vernacular*, 41ff.

47. See, for instance, Nick Aaron Ford, "Literature of Race and Culture," *CR*, 501, and Webster Gault, "Days of Travel," *CR*, 491. Faith Berry argues that Hughes's heterosexual persona may have been a way of protecting Zell Ingram, "whose interest in men was greater than his interest in women." *Langston Hughes: Before and Beyond Harlem* (Westport, CT: Lawrence Hill, 1983), 123. Gardullo also notes that this autobiographical persona might have been a way for Hughes to protect himself, since homosexuals were persecuted by McCarthy almost as much as supposed Communists were. It is quite possible that Hughes chose to "perform heterosexuality as well as conservatism to protect himself from several vectors of McCarthyist attack." "Heading Out," 63. See also chapter 5.

48. Johan Huizinga, *Homo Ludens: A Study of the Play Element in Culture* (Boston: Beacon Press, 1955), 8–10. Note Huizinga's definition of play as "a voluntary activity or occupation executed within certain fixed limits of time and place, according to rules freely accepted and absolutely binding, having its aim in itself and accompanied by a feeling of tension, joy and the consciousness that it is 'different' from 'ordinary' life" (28).

49. Gilroy, *The Black Atlantic: Modernity and Double Consciousness* (Cambridge, MA: Harvard University Press, 1993), 6.

50. Based on the short story "Father and Son" that closes *The Ways of White Folks* (1934), *Mulatto* ran at the Vanderbilt Theater on Broadway for more than a year and then toured for two seasons. On Hughes's clash with the producer, who changed the play to include a rape scene, see Nancy Johnston and Leslie Sanders, eds., *Langston Hughes: The Plays to 1942* (ebrary, Inc, 2002), 17; Annmarie Bean, "Playwrights and Plays of the Harlem Renaissance," in *A Companion to Twentieth-Century American Drama*, ed. David Krasner (Malden, MA: Blackwell, 2006), 91–105; and *Life*, 1:131–15.

51. Hughes was not only a playwright but also a producer and director. He helped found the Karamu Theater and the Harlem Suitcase Theater. See David Krasner, "Negro Drama and the Harlem Renaissance," in *The Cambridge Companion to the Harlem Renaissance*, ed. George B. Hutchinson (Cambridge: Cambridge University Press, 2007), 68.

52. These conventions were first analyzed by Stepto in *From Behind the Veil* (1979).

53. Almost without exception the label "postcolonial" is seen as excluding African American writers from the USA by definition, which implicitly creates yet another American exceptionalism. See, for instance, Moore-Gilbert, *Postcolonial Life-Writing*.

54. The "dark moving waters" (*las oscuras aguas movedizas*) in the Spanish translation makes the connection to the Middle Passage more readily available than Hughes's own phrasing, IM, 17. See also the "[t]all, black, sinister ships" off the Nigerian coast, *BS*, 120, which evoke Robert Hayden's poem "Middle Passage." See also Miller, "For a Moment."

55. Loftus prefers to cast this mixture in terms of hybridity, which I find too limiting: "The text [*The Big Sea*] is populated by hybrid figures that...are figures for the text and its performance; the text simplifies subject matter so that the content remains benign, yet it functions simultaneously to signify the return of the suppressed term(s)." With reference to Loftus's

earlier point, I should note that in order "to destabilize the categories of race, class, and sex that attempt to define them," hybrids do not just invert available categories of identity. "In/verse Autobiography," 144, 146.

56. Ashcroft, *Caliban's Voice*, 159. On translation as transcreation, see Else Ribeiro Pires Vieira, "Liberating Calibans: *Antropofagia* and Haroldo de Campos' Poetics of Transcreation," in *Post-Colonial Translation: Theory and Practice*, ed. Susan Bassnet and Harish Trivedi (New York: Routledge, 1999), 95–113.

57. See Lamming's *Water with Berries* (1971) and *The Pleasures of Exile* (1960), Césaire's *Un tempête* (1969), and James's *Toussaint L'Ouverture* (1936). USAmerican-born African American writers have not usually embraced an affinity with this figure and its linguistic dualities. On second-language acquisition in the play, see also Rodríguez García, "Literary into Cultural Translation," 7.

58. Lamming, *The Pleasures of Exile* (Ann Arbor: University of Michigan Press, 1992), 15.

59. On the falling out Hughes had with Hurston over the play *Mule Bone*, see Hemenway, *Zora Neale Hurston*, 136–48; also *Life*, 1:195–200.

60. Wilson Harris, *Carnival* (London: Faber, 1985), 31.

61. Florian Niedlich takes identity as "something that is always already constructed and which privileges play, performativity, and plurality." "Travel as Transgression: Claude McKay's *Banana Bottom*, J.M. Coetzee's *Life and Times of Michael K.*, and Hanif Kureishi's *The Black Album*," in *Local Natures, Global Responsibilities: Ecocritical Perspectives on the New English Literatures*, ed. Laurenz Volkmann (Amsterdam: Rodopi, 2010), 349.

62. There are other strategic omissions in *The Big Sea*: for instance, Hughes leaves his father out in his recitation of his family's genealogy.

63. See Harry Sieber, *The Picaresque* (London: Methuen, 1977).

64. The episode entitled "Salvation" must also be read in this context. *BS*, 18–21.

65. Loftus claims that "this repetition is a literal inversion." "In/verse Autobiography," 160. I disagree.

66. Chambers, *Mediterranean Crossings*, 32; Homi Bhabha, "The Third Space: Interview with Homi Bhabha," in Rutherford, *Identity*, 211. Bhabha regards "all forms of culture [as] continually in a process of hybridity" and defines hybridity as the "third space" that enables other positions to emerge.

67. Chambers, *Migrancy*, 11; see also 25.

68. Hughes's *S.S. Malone* was the freighter *West Hesseltine. Life*, 1:71.

69. Gardullo, "Heading Out, "62. Gardullo also rightly notes that this scene brings to mind Gilroy's metaphor of the ship as a chronotope.

70. Pavlić, *Crossroads Modernism*, 24 (my emphasis). See also Benston, *Performing Blackness*, chap. 8.

71. George is only implicitly racialized by the reference to his Harlem landlady.

72. Loftus, "In/verse Autobiography," 148.

73. Hughes mentions *Arabian Nights* in *IW*, 123.

74. If translation is a hybrid form, then, as Eileen Julien suggests, we also need to "query the appropriateness of the terms 'target' and 'source.'...[T]he term 'target literature' seems a misnomer, for the fusion of two (or more) sources produces a literature which—in linguistic terms—is neither the superstrate nor substrate but a creole. The *creole* (rather than 'target') literature is the product of the *contact* (rather than 'interference') of metropolitan culture and literature and that of the periphery." "Arguments, and Further Conjectures on World Literature," in Lindberg-Wada, *Studying Transcultural Literary History*, 127. Wai-Chee Dimock has pointed out is that literature "is a creole tongue not only in the commingling of languages, but equally in the commingling of expressive media....[S]cripts made with words and scripts not made with words are also gathered together." *Through Other Continents: American Literature across Deep Time* (Princeton: Princeton University Press, 2008), 158–59.

75. See also Loftus, "In/verse Autobiography," 149: "While the body is the signifier of race, in this anecdote Hughes makes the body signify contradictory races and defy the language that confirms the difference between them."

76. On Seki Sano's work in Mexico, see Philip Kolin, "The Mexican Premiere of Tennessee Williams's *A Streetcar Named Desire*," *Mexican Studies/Estudios Mexicanos* 10, no. 2 (Summer 1994): 315–40.

77. Compare this with Charles Wilder's snide remark that "[o]ne would like to know quite a bit more about just what Langston Hughes did wonder as he wandered." "A Poet Retraces the '30s," *CR*, 488.

78. Chambers, *Migrancy*, 5. See also Ette, *ZwischenWeltenSchreiben*, 27–60.

79. I will elaborate on this in connection with Waldo Frank in chapter 3.

80. See Edwards, "Translating the Word Nègre," in *Practice of Diaspora*, 25–38, which includes a brief commentary on this passage.

81. Huizinga, *Homo Ludens*, 9.

82. See Hughes, *Little Ham*, in Johnston and Sanders, *Langston Hughes*, 219–22; Scanlon, "News from Heaven," 61–62.

83. Chambers, *Migrancy*, 10.

84. See especially *Little Ham*, in Johnston and Sanders, *Langston Hughes*, 217. See also Anne Borden, "Heroic 'Hussies' and 'Brilliant Queers': Genderracial Resistance in the Works of Langston Hughes," *African-American Review* 28, no. 3 (1994): 333–45.

85. See chapter 3. Isabel Soto, Brent Edwards, and Michael Thurston, among others, have written about Hughes's stay in Spain. See also Ana María Fraile Marcos, *Langston Hughes: Oscuridad en España/Darkness in Spain (Texto bilingüe)* (León, Sp.: Universidad, Secretario de Publicaciones, 1998).

86. For details on Gáler and Rivaud, whom Mullen mistakenly turns into Luis Rivand, see chapter 3. For a review of Rivaud's translation, see Antonio Aparicio, "Langston Hughes: *El immenso mar*," *Nuestra Raza* 14, no. 165 (May 1947): 5. *The Big Sea* also appeared in Portuguese in a translation by Francisco Burkinski as *O imenso mar* (Rio de Janeiro: Editorial Vitória, 1944).

87. Hughes did write Spanish dialogue in his first play, *Harvest* (1934), whose characters include Mexican farm workers in California.

88. Much more could be said on this subject, but doing so is beyond the scope of this book. Suffice it to note that Claude McKay's untranslated autobiography, *A Long Way from Home* (1937), is a notable contrast to Hughes's *I Wonder*. Like Hughes, McKay had spent some time in the Soviet Union, being "the first Negro to arrive in Russia since the revolution." McKay, *A Long Way from Home: An Autobiography* (New York: Harcourt, Brace and World, 1970), 168. If translation is any indication, the Jamaican-born McKay was more of an internationally recognized figure than either Johnson or Locke, at least in the early 1930s. Louis Guilloux translated McKay's *Home to Harlem* as *Quartier noir* (1932); an Italian version, *Ritorno ad Harlem*, by Alessandra Scalero had appeared in Milan in 1930. A Spanish version by A. Rodríguez de Léon and R. R. Fernández-Andes was issued in Madrid in 1931 under the title *Cock-tail negro*. Hughes mentions McKay once, *BS*, 165. In the eighty-some pages McKay devotes to chronicling this journey, he spends much time glorying in his "personal triumph" and the special treatment he received for having been "a typical Negro" who had "mobilized [his] African features and won the masses of the people." *A Long Way from Home*, 153, 173. When McKay recounts being invited to speak about and for "American Negro workers" at the Congress of the Communist International at the Bolshoi Theater in Moscow in place of the "official mulatto delegate," he declares, "I was like a black ikon in the flesh." Ibid., 168, 173.

89. Consequently, diaspora, for Edwards, "is a term that marks the ways that internationalism is pursued by translation." *Practice of Diaspora*, 7, 11.

90. See Manuel Zapata Olivella, *Pasión vagabunda* (Colombia: Ministerio de Cultura, 2000), 351; also Antonio Tillis, *Manuel Zapata Olivella and the "Darkening" of Latin American Literature* (Columbia: University of Missouri Press, 2005), 6–7.

91. Manuel Zapata Olivella, *Changó el Gran Putas* (Santafé de Bogotá, Col.: Rei Andes Ltda., 1992), 571–72; Zapata Olivella, *Changó, the Biggest Badass*, trans. Jonathan Tittler (Lubbock: Texas Tech University Press, 2010), 347. I have made changes in Tittler's translation. Unless otherwise noted, all translations are my own.

92. Zapata Olivella's visit to Harlem led to occasional correspondence between the two writers. See also Jackson, *Black Writers in Latin America*, 90–91, and Lawrence Prescott, "Brother to Brother: The Friendship and Literary Correspondence of Manual Zapata Olivella and Langston Hughes," *Afro-Hispanic Review* 25, no. 1 (Spring 2006): 87–103.

93. Huizinga noted that the ludic character of poiesis as play is not necessarily or always "outwardly preserved." He argues that this is true of epic and lyric poetry alike, and that of all literary genres, only drama retains a connection to play. See *Homo Ludens*, 143–44. He never mentions the novel or any form of literary narrative and would likely have been surprised by the extent to which the playfulness in *Changó* proves him wrong. It is also worth noting that the work of Mikhail Bakhtin on the theory of the novel roughly coincides with Huizinga's *Homo Ludens* but did not become known in Russia or elsewhere until the 1970s.

94. Zapata Olivella, *Changó el Gran Putas*, 572; Zapata Olivella, *Changó, the Biggest Badass*, 348. Tittler misses this allusion by translating the journal's title as *The New Black*.

95. On February 19, 1954, Hughes wrote to Zapata Olivella that he was "most pleased that you have used a portion of my poems, THE NEGRO SPEAKS OF RIVERS, in the front of your book" (LHP, 176:79). The book in question is *He visto la noche* (1949).

96. Zapata Olivella took the first stanza of this poem from Carlos López Narvaez's collection, which also includes "Canción de la rosa," a translation of "Breath of a Rose," which had first been published in *BS*, 170–71. *El cielo en el río* (Bogotá: Ediciones Espiral Colombia, 1952), 139–40. In a letter from Bogotá, Colombia, dated August 29, 1947, Zapata Olivella, founder of the Centro de Estudios Afrocolombianos, mentions to Hughes that the Bogoteño poet Aurelio Arturo planned to translate a series of Hughes poems for the literary page of *El Tiempo* (LHP, 176:3229). But it was López Narváez who published "El negro habla de los ríos" in the literary supplement of *El Tiempo* on June 6, 1948. Some of Hughes's poems also appear to be included in another Colombian publication, José Ratto Ciarlos's *Defensa y apología de las razas de color* (Caracas: Editorial Bolívar, 1937). I have not yet been able to locate this volume.

97. See Deck and Lewis, "Langston Hughes and the African Diaspora."

98. Jessica Berman uses the example of Gertrude Stein and others to argue that modernist fiction "gestures toward a new and profound cosmopolitan geography" that resists "an oversimplified biological determinism" and "static national or racial categories." "Modernism's Possible Geographies," in Winkiel and Doyle, *Geomodernisms*, 296. Hughes's geography, though it resists the same assignations, is quite different from Stein's.

99. Wright, *Dimensions of History* (Santa Cruz, CA: Kayak, 1976), 90. See also Edwards's comments on "articulated structure" in "Uses of Diaspora," 24ff.

2. SOUTHERN EXPOSURES

1. See also Rodríguez García, "Literary into Cultural Translation," 4.

2. See Heriberto Dixon, "Who Ever Heard of a Black Cuban?" *Afro-Hispanic Review*, September 1982, 10–12.

3. Nicolás Guillén, *Prosa de prisa: Crónicas* (Buenos Aires: Editorial Hernandez, 1968), 157–58. See Ben Carruthers's introduction to *Cuba Libre:* "Nicolás Guillén, without knowing it, started a movement known as Afro-Cuban poetry." *CL,* ix.

4. Maribel Cruzado and Mary Hricko, eds. and trans., *Langston Hughes. Blues* (Valencia, Sp.: Colección La Cruz de Sur, 2004), 9.

5. Mullen rightly calls 1931 a "key year" for Hughes's evolving reputation in the Hispanic world. "Presencia y evaluación," 18. Fourteen poems were translated and put into circulation during this one year alone.

6. Salvador Novo, "Notas sobre la poesía de los negros en los Estados Unidos," *Contemporáneos* 4, nos. 40–41 (September–October 1931), 199; Hildamar Escalante, ed., *Breve informe de poesía norteamericana (Versión del inglés)* (Caracas: Tipografía La Nación, 1947), 101.

7. See Nicolás Guillén, "Recuerdo a Langston Hughes," in *IM;* Andrés Henestrosa, "Un poeta negro, amigo de México," *Novedades* 1 (June 1967): 4; Francisco Hernández Urbina, "Vida y muerte del poeta Langston Hughes," *Universidad Central* 5, no. 118 (April 13, 1961), 4; Germán Pardo García, "Honrando la memoria de Langston Hughes," *Nivel* 55 (February 15, 1963), 1; and Jean Wagner, "Langston Hughes. El gran poeta norteamericano," *Nivel* 31 (July 25, 1961), 6.

8. See Cruzado and Hricko, *Langston Hughes,* 9.

9. See Francine Masiello, "Joyce in Buenos Aires (Talking Sexuality through Translation)," *Diacritics* 34, nos. 3–4 (Fall–Winter 2004): 55–72, and Sergio Waisman, "Jorge Luis Borges's Partial Argentine *Ulysses:* A Foundational (Mis-)Translation," in *Traduire les Amériques/ Translating the Americas,* ed. Marc Charron and Clara Foz, special issue of *Études sur le texte et ses transformations* 19, no. 2 (2006): 37–51.

10. The basis for the total of poems Hughes published is Rampersad and Roessel's *Collected Poems of Langston Hughes* (New York: Random House, 1994). Portuguese translations of three Hughes poems were included in two Brazilian anthologies in the 1950s: Oswaldino Marques, ed. *Videntes e sonâmbulos: Coletânea de poemas norte-americanos* (Rio de Janeiro: Minstério da Educação e Cultura, Servico de Documentação, 1955), and Helena R. Gandelman and Maria Helena Muus, eds., *Negros famosos a America do Norte* (Sao Paulo: Editorial Classico-Cientifica, 1957). So far, I have found twenty-five Portuguese versions of Hughes's poems, the majority of them in Eduardo Martins's *Poemas de Langston Hughes* (João Pessoa: Impresso an Gráfica "A Imprensa," 1970).

11. See Mullen, *Langston Hughes,* 47–65. Without this bibliography, any work on Hughes translations in the Hispanic Americas and Spain would have been nearly impossible. But Mullen's information is neither entirely reliable nor complete. I have found it necessary to go back to the original sources and to supplement the information he provides. Mullen also did not have the benefit of Rampersad and Roessel's *Collected Poems,* without which it would be have been exceedingly difficult to trace any given translation back to an original and make any reliable pronouncements about the version of a poem that a given translator used. Helpful in this respect is also Peer Mandelik and Stanley Schatt's earlier *Concordance to the Poetry of Langston Hughes* (Detroit: Gale Research Co., 1975). There are also three poems that I have been unable to trace back to any of Hughes's published texts (more on this in chapter 3). Future research will likely add to the information in the appendix.

12. Using as landmarks the three book-length collections, these numbers can be broken down to show how many poems were added to the archive at what time. In 1952, Gáler added eighty-two translations of Hughes's poems to the seventy-six that had already been circulated in anthologies and periodicals. In 1968, the year after Hughes's death, Ahumada offered yet another fifty-two translations in *YT,* thirty-three of poems not previously rendered in Spanish. In 2004, Cruzado and Hricko's *Blues* contributed forty more new translations of Hughes poems, among them their versions of eighteen previously untranslated early lyrics.

13. The abiding interest of literary comparatists has been in assessing Hughes's influence on Hispanic American writers through close-ups on the relationship between Hughes and Guillén as represented in the early poetry of each. I show in chapter 3 that most of these scholarly assessments, carried out mainly under the auspices of African American/Afro-Hispanic Studies, are based on assumptions grounded in precious little historical and textual evidence.

14. One could of course take my initial quantitative analysis further. To estimate how many Hispanic American readers may have read a translation of a particular Hughes poem at a particular time, one might cross-reference the source of the above data with the print runs, subscription data, and sales figures for all relevant publications (assuming those are available for the relevant dates). But that work will have to wait for another day. Whatever data one might derive in this fashion, they could not include library readers or casual readers of the books or journals of family, friends, and acquaintances. They would also not include readers of Hughes's autobiographical and fictional prose.

15. See my introduction; also Richard L. Jackson, "Langston Hughes and the African Diaspora in South America," *Langston Hughes Review* 5, no. 5 (1986): 28–31.

16. I disagree with Mullen's view that some of Hughes's Hispanic American audiences (notably Mexicans), "while almost always appreciative, often misread him." "Langston Hughes in Mexico and Cuba," 25.

17. Edwards, "Uses of Diaspora," 30 (my emphasis).

18. Many Hispanic Americans regarded racial prejudice as an entirely USAmerican import. On the Caribbean, see also Suzanne Bost, *Mulatas and Mestizas: Representing Mixed Identities in the Americas, 1850–2000* (Athens: University of Georgia Press, 2003), 92–93.

19. Richard Wright applied the term "ambassador" to Hughes in 1940. See "Forerunner and Ambassador," *CR*, 268–69.

20. Podestá, "Cultural Liaisons," 175. The north-south traffic in literary texts that the translations of Hughes's poems embody is, in many ways, a continuation of the nineteenth-century cultural exchanges between the USAmerican and Hispanic Americas that Gruesz has delineated in her *Ambassadors of Culture.*

21. Podestá, "Cultural Liaisons," 175.

22. See Vera M. Kutzinski, *Sugar's Secrets: Race and the Erotics of Cuban Nationalism* (Charlottesville: University Press of Virginia, 1993), chap. 5, and "Afro-Hispanic American Literature," in *The Cambridge History of Latin American Literature,* ed. Roberto González Echevarría and Enrique Pupo-Walker (Cambridge: Cambridge University Press, 1996), 2:164–94; also Marvin A. Lewis, *Afro-Uruguayan Literature: Post-Colonial Perspectives* (Danvers, MA: Rosemont Publishing and Printing Corp., 2003).

23. One example here is the "Ideales de una Raza" page, which became part of the Sunday supplement of Havana's *Diario de la Marina* in 1928. For details, see Kutzinski, *Sugar's Secrets,* 146–49. Also relevant here is the attraction of Mexican artists to Harlem. See Deborah Cullen, "Allure of Harlem: Correlations between Mexicanidad and the New Negro Movements," in *Nexus New York: Latin American Artists in the Modern Metropolis,* ed. Deborah Cullen (New York: El Museo del Barrio in association with Yale University Press, 2009), 126–49.

24. Jackson speculates that Hughes's criticisms of the USA were similar to those that many Hispanic American intellectuals advanced at the time. See "Langston Hughes," 28. See also the editor's preface from the inaugural issue of the *Revista de la Havana,* which is reprinted in Berta G. Montalvo, *Índice bibliográfico de la Revista de la Habana* (Miami: Ediciones Universal, 2001), 33.

25. See Martí's "Letter to Manuel Mercado" (1895), in *José Martí: Selected Writings,* ed. Esther Louise Allen (New York: Penguin, 2002), 347.

26. In Pereda Valdés's anthology, *Antologia de la poesía negra americana* (Santiago de Chile: Ediciones Ercilla, 1936; repr., Montevideo, Biblioteca Uruguaya de Autores, 1953), Hughes finds himself in the company of Phyllis Wheatley, James Corrothers, Albert Whitman,

Carrie Williams Clifford, James Weldon Johnson, Lewis Alexander, Sterling Brown, William Stanley Braithwaite, Angelina Weld Grimké, Gwendolyn Bennet, Paul Laurence Dunbar, Countee Cullen, Fenton Johnson, and Claude McKay. While most contributions to the volume are limited to one or two poems, Hughes's work is represented by eleven, with Nicolás Guillén's nine poems the only close second. Ballagas's section on the USA also includes Whitman, Longfellow, Johnson, and Cullen. *Mapa de la poesía negra americana* (Buenos Aires: Editorial Pleamar, 1946).

27. See Karem, *Purloined Islands,* esp. chap. 3.

28. Novo, "Notas," 198.

29. Eugenio Florit, *Antología de la poesía norteamericana contemporánea* (Mexico: Unión Panamericana, 1955), xxiii.

30. Ibid., xxiv (my emphasis).

31. Gastón Figueira, "Dos poetas norteamericanos: I. Sinclair Lewis; II. Langston Hughes," *Revista Iberoamericana* 18 (January–September 1953): 404. There are twenty different Spanish versions of this poem (see appendix).

32. Cruzado and Hricko are mistaken in their claim that "The Negro Speaks of Rivers" was the most anthologized of Hughes's poems in translation. *Blues,* 13.

33. To the eight poems Fernández de Castro had translated earlier, Lozano added "Ardella" ("Ardella"), "Cross" ("Cruz"), "Negro" ("Soy un negro"), "The Negro Speaks of Rivers" ("El negro habla de los ríos"), "Port Town" ("Puerto"), "Joy" ("Alegría"), "Little Song" ("Cancionera"), and "Mexican Market Woman" ("Placera"). Villaurrutia added two more new ones, "Poem [2]" ("Poema"), and "Prayer" ("Plegaria"). Borges further expanded the available repertoire (to nineteen) by offering "Nuestra tierra" ("Our Land") and another version of "The Negro Speaks of Rivers." Ivan Parsons also published translations of three Hughes poems in 1930. See " 'Escupideras de metal,' 'Muchacho de elevador,' 'Portero de Pullman,' " *Social* 15, no. 5 (May 1930): 19. "Portero de Pullman" was reprinted in *El Diario de l Marina* 98 (June 8, 1930): n.p.

34. Cruzado and Hricko's volume consists almost exclusively of poems from *The Weary Blues* and *Fine Clothes*—precisely the poems that had rarely, if ever, been translated (see below).

35. Edward Mullen, "European and North American Writers in *Contemporáneos,*" *Comparative Literature Studies* 8 (December 1971): 342.

36. See my comments on Silvia Ocampo and *Sur* in chapter 3.

37. See Bost, *Mulatas and Mestizas,* 102.

38. See Kutzinski *Sugar's Secrets,* 144, 152–62; also Michael North, *The Dialect of Modernism: Race, Language, and Twentieth-Century Literature* (New York: Oxford University Press, 1994).

39. See Kutzinski, "Afro-Hispanic American Literature," 169, 179.

40. Rafael Lozano, "Langston Hughes, El poeta afroestadounidense," *Crísol* 5 (1931): 227; see also Mullen, "Langston Hughes in Mexico and Cuba," 25.

41. Rafael Alberti, trans., "Yo soy Negro," *El Mono Azul* 11, no. 29 (August 19, 1937): 1; this translation was published on the occasion of Hughes's visit to Madrid during the Spanish Civil War (see chapter 3). Alberti was also loosely affiliated with the vanguardist Mexican group Contemporáneos and their journal. See Mullen, "European and North American Writers," 339.

42. Andrés Bansart, Amelia Jiménez, and Diego Santa Cruz, eds., *Poesía negra-africana* (Santiago de Chile: Universidad Católica de Chile, Ediciones Nueva Universidad de la Vicerrectoría de Comunicación, 1971), 41; Juan Felipe Toruño, ed., *Poesía negra: Ensayo y antología* (Mexico: Colección obsidiana, 1953), 46. See also José Luis González and Mónica Mansour, eds., *Poesía negra de América* (Mexico City: Ediciones Era, 1976), 39. One of the founders of *Ultraísmo* was Borges, whose Hughes translations I analyze in the following chapter.

Lozano also regarded Hughes as "un cantor primitivo" (a primitive singer) whose verse was "no suprarealista, ni mallarmeño" (neither suprarealist nor Mallarménean). Lozano, "Langston Hughes," 227.

43. Ernesto Mejía Sánchez, review of "Yo también soy América," *Amaru: Revista de Artes y Ciencias* (April–June 1968): 95.

44. Pereda Valdés, *Antología*, 7–8.

45. See also his *Línea de color (ensayos afro-americanos)* (Santiago de Chile: Ediciones Ercilla, 1938); *El negro rioplatense y otros ensayos* (Montevideo: C. García & Cía, 1937); *Negros esclavos y negros libres: Esquema de una sociedad esclavista y aporte del negro en nuestra formación nacional* (Montevideo: Imprenta "Gaceta comercial," 1941); and the compilation *Toda la poesía negra de Ildefonso Pereda Valdés* (Montevideo: Índice Mimeografía, 1979).

46. Pereda Valdés, *Antología*, 42.

47. Pereda Valdés writes in the foreword to his anthology that the *poesía negra* written in the rest of the Americas, with the exception of Cuba and Brazil, pales (*resulta pálida*) by comparison with Negro poetry from the USA. *Antología*, 10.

48. Florit, *Antología*, xxiv.

49. Pereda Valdés, *Antología*, 30.

50. Ibid., 9 (my emphasis).

51. Neither poem enjoyed much popularity in the Hispanic Americas. There are only two Spanish versions of the former, Pereda Valdés's and Ahumada's. The latter has been neither reprinted nor translated since.

52. Alejandro's Spanish titles are "Buenos días, revolución" and "El Waldorf-Astoria."

53. Jackson, "Langston Hughes and the African Diaspora," 24. Such sympathies did not prompt the poem's translation into Spanish, neither in the 1930s nor at any later point.

54. "Unión" in Pereda Valdés, *Antología*, 39. For a reading of Hughes's "Union," see Thurston, *Making Something Happen*, 90–91.

55. In Gáler, see, for instance, "Los blues tristes" (27–28) ("The Weary Blues," *CP,* 50), "Blues del pobre muchacho" (55–56) ("Po' Boy Blues," *CP,* 83), and "Blues de la añoranza" (57–58) ("Homesick Blues," *CP,* 72).

56. Caparicio also translated the poems by Cullen and McKay in this volume.

57. Emilio Ballagas also includes in his section on the USA in *Mapa* a clunky version of "I, Too," along with translations of two other poems, "Negro" ("Preludio a Weary Blues"), "Poem [1]" ("Poema").

58. Ballagas, *Mapa,* 51.

59. Jackson, "Langston Hughes," 26.

60. Mullen's *Langston Hughes in the Hispanic World* offers a useful summary of Hughes's connections with Hispanic writers. But Mullen focuses much more on Hughes in Spain than on Hughes in the Hispanic Americas. Mullen also does not appear to have consulted any of Hughes's correspondence. See also Mullen's earlier articles, "European and North American Writers in *Contemporáneos*" and "Presencia y evaluación." See also Drewey Wayne Gunn, *American and British Writers in Mexico, 1556–1973* (Austin: University of Texas Press, 1974), 82–86. It is somewhat difficult to believe that Hughes's Hispanic American connections—he had cultivated countless contacts there since his initial stays in Mexico as a young man—did not at all impact McCarthy's decision to subpoena him in 1953 (see chapter 5).

61. Only two "revolutionary" poems are included in either the 1936 or the 1953 edition of *Antología de la poesía negra americana:* "Siempre lo mismo" ("Always the Same," from *Negro Worker,* 1932) and "Unión" ("Union," from *New Masses,* 1931). Hughes included only "Union" in *A New Song* (1938); "Always the Same" was not reprinted.

62. Cruzado and Hricko's volume still reflects this tendency to exclude Hughes's socialist poetry. They note that they gave special emphasis to "los elementos más importantes de su

[Hughes's] obra: la música, la afirmación de la negritude, el deseo de integración social y racial y el problema de la identidad." *Blues,* 68 (the most important elements of Hughes's work: music, affirmation of blackness, the desire for social and racial integration, and the problem of identity).

63. Bansart, Jiménez, and Santa Cruz, *Poesía negra-africana,* 9.

64. Both editors, neither of African descent as far as I know, were themselves poets who wrote their own *poesía negra.*

65. Escalante included "Brass Spittoons" ("Escupideras de cobre") and "Jazz Band in a Parisian Cabaret" ("Jazz en un café de Paris") in their first Spanish translations. Ruiz de Vizo included another version of "Brass Spittoons" and a translation of "Cross" ("Cruz"). *Black Poetry of the Americas: A Bilingual Anthology* (Miami: Ediciones Universal, 1972), 162–64.

66. González's translation, "Yo también canto a América," was reprinted from *Siempre! Presencia de México* 278 (June 14, 1967), 34–35, where it had appeared along with two other Hughes poems, "Tiovivo: Niño negro en el carnaval" ("Merry-Go-Round: Colored Child at Carnival") and "Mestizaje" ("Cross").

67. Marques's *Videntes e sonâmbulos,* which ranges broadly from Longfellow and Dickinson to the Anglo-USAmerican modernists and features Cullen and Hughes as the only Negro poets, includes "Eu também canto a América" by Orígenes Lessa (235) and "Jazzonia" by Guilherme de Almeida (239).

68. Borges, whose other translations I analyze in the following chapter, was one of the founders of *ultraísmo,* one of the "tendencias modernas o ultramodernas" (modern or ultramodern tendencies) to which others liked to juxtapose black poetry in general and Hughes's poems in particular. Toruño, *Poesía negra,* 46. See also note 42. The Sunday supplement of *El Diario de la Marina* was a bit of an oddity in what was otherwise a politically conservative paper. For details see Kutzinski, *Sugar's Secrets,* 146–47. The George A. Smathers Libraries at the University of Florida, Gainesville, is in the process of digitizing the entire run of the *Diario de la Marina.* For available volumes see http://dloc.com/UF00001565/05607/allvolumes. The Sunday supplement was a bit of an oddity in what was otherwise a politically conservative paper. For details see Kutzinski, *Sugar's Secrets,* 146–47.

69. See *Life,*1:177. In a letter to Hughes dated May 1,1930, Gustavo E. Urrutia called Fernández de Castro a leader of "the white 'intelectuales' [who] wrote an energetic letter of solidarity with the negroes" on the occasion of an incident of racial discrimination at the Havana Yacht Club. "This is the first time," Urrutia continues, "that the white people take our defence in cases like this, whenever we had some trouble of this character we fighted [sic] alone against bigotry, while our best white friends kept silence" (LHP, 158:2926). For Fernández de Castro's continued interest in African American literatures, see his "La literatura negra actual de Cuba," *Estudios Afrocubanos* 4, nos.1–4 (1940): 9, 11, 17, 22; his prologue to Raúl C. Vianello 's *Versos negros* (Mexico City: Librería Urbe, 1942, 5–9); and his *Tema negro en las letras de Cuba (1608–1935)* (Havana: Mirador, 1943).

70. The poem was reprinted in both *The Weary Blues* and *The Dream Keeper* (1932). Its title in *The Weary Blues* was "Epilogue" (see *CP,* 625).

71. There are some variations on these three lines as well, but they do not rise to the same level of importance as the others. Most translators, unlike Fernández de Castro and also Lozano, do not omit Hughes's rhythmically and insistently repeated "And." Other phrases used to translate "I grow strong" range from Fernández de Castro's "fortalezco" (also used by Alberti) to "me pongo fuerte" (Borges and Toruño), "me hago fuerte" (Florit) to "crezco fuerte," which is the most common (in Villaurrutia, Lozano, Ballagas, Gáler, González, and Ahumada, as well as Sastre and Cruzado). Bansart uses "tomo fuerzas" to rhyme more resonantly with "como," something that "fortalezco" does as well and "pongo" does more subtly, whereas most of the others seem to prefer the simpler alliteration of "crezco" with "como."

72. Xavier Villaurrutia, trans., "Yo también," *Contemporáneos* 11 (September–October 1931): 157–58.

73. Borges, "Tres poemas de Langston Hughes," *Sur* 1, no. 2 (1931): 165.

74. Compare this with Ahumada's version of "Song" ("Canción") in which he translates "Lovely, dark, and lonely one" as "amada obscura y solitaria." By contrast, Ahumada renders "dark closed gate" as "verja negra y cerrada" (*YT*, 31; *CP*, 45, 31).

75. Hughes translated several pieces by Urrutia for *Opportunity* and *Crisis* in 1931. Urrutia was the one who wrote a letter to the secretary of state in Havana on March 5, 1930, to get permission for Hughes to enter the country. In his correspondence with Hughes from the same year, he mentions receiving these and other USAmerican publications regularly. He also acknowledges receipt of several books that Hughes sent him, including *The Weary Blues* and *The New Negro*. See LHP, 158:2926, and 434:9959 for details.

76. In 1926, Fernández de Castro, together with Félix Lizaso, published *La poesía moderna en Cuba (1882–1925)* (Madrid: Librería y Casa Editorial Hernando). See also Fernández de Castro's prologue to the Mexican poet Raúl C. Vianello's *Versos negros* (Mexico City: Librería Urbe, 1942).

77. It is unclear whether the translation that appeared in *El Diario* in April 1930 is a reprint from *La Revista de la Habana*, a small literary and cultural journal edited by Gustavo Gutiérrez y Sánchez, of which only twelve issues, in four volumes, appeared between January and October 1930. For an index and details on the journal, most of which appears to have been lost, see Montalvo, *Índice bibliográfico*, 18–19.

78. It has been generally assumed that the 1930 version in *El Diario de la Marina* is a reprint of the 1928 translation from *Social*, which is not the case. Borges also translated the poem twice (see chapter 4).

79. José Antonio Fernández de Castro, "Presentación de Langston Hughes," *Revista de La Habana* 1, no. 3 (March 1930): 367. See also Mullen, *Langston Hughes*, 171.

80. On Mexico see Jackson, "Langston Hughes," 27, and Gunn, *American and British Writers*, 83–86.

81. "¡Oh! blancos poderosos! / ¿Por qué me torturáis, oh blancos poderosos?"; "tan profundamente señalada, con tantos gritos silenciosos." *Diario de la Marina* 98, no. 116 (April 27, 1930): 36.

82. Fernández de Castro, "Langston Hughes, poeta militante negro," *El Nacional* (March 3, 1935), 1.

83. Review in the *Chicago Whip*, February 16, 1927 (*CR*, 100).

84. *Social* 13, no. 9 (September 1928), 30.

85. *Diario de la Marina* 98, no. 116 (April 27, 1930): 36. Full page at http://dloc.com/UF00001565/05632/36j.

86. Martí's "Nuestra América" was first published in 1891 in New York City. See Juan de Onís, trans., *The America of José Martí. Selected Writings* (1954, repr. New York: Minerva Press, 1968).

87. This would not have worked in the case of another Hughes poem from 1925, entitled "America," *CP*, 52–53. Retaining the poem's specific USAmerican references while turning the title and its many recurrences into "América" would have had precisely the opposite effect. In such a translation, the title would have suggested a familiarity confounded by the very inaccessibility of local references and allusions to a non-USAmerican reader. "America" has never been translated into Spanish.

88. Bansart makes the first and last lines of his translation identical; they both read "Yo también soy América."

89. Sixteen of the poem's eighteen translators rendered the line in the exactly same way. Lozano prefers "Me sentarán a la mesa" (they will invite me to the table), Bansart, "Yo me quedaré en la mesa" (I will stay at the table).

90. Among the later translators, only Gáler, Toruño, and Bansart avoid the comparative "darker." Florit (in 1955) is the first one to pick it up in Spanish as "el hermano más oscuro." Later translators, including González, Ahumada, and Cruzado, seem to have adopted this phrasing from Florit. There are only very minor differences between their translations and Florit's earlier version.

91. Lozano, Gáler, and Toruño use "negro" as well, but they do not repeat it later in the poem.

92. *Negro,* in a lowercase spelling, was not infrequently used to translate "nigger." See, for instance, Pereda Valdés's lines from "Mulato": "negros, no sois mis hermanos. / No. Nunca, / negros, series mis hermanos" (*Antologia,* 41), which in Hughes's "Mulatto" read: "Niggers ain't my brother. /Not ever. / Niggers ain't my brother" (*CP,* 100).

93. See Edwards, *Practice of Diaspora,* 35. Hughes does this in other poems, however, most notably in "The Negro Speaks of Rivers" and "The Negro," where the translators usually retained the noun, mostly in lowercase. See, for instance, Lozano's version of the opening stanza "I am a Negro: / Black as the night is black, / Black like the depths of my Africa" (*CP,* 24): "Soy un negro: / Negro, como la noche es oscura, / Negro, como el corazón de mi Africa" ("Langston Hughes," 228). Alberti was the only translator to capitalize "Negro" in "Yo soy Negro." Cruzado and Hricko are the only ones thus far to use "oscuro" in these lines: "Soy negro: / Oscuro como oscura es la noche, / Oscuro como mi África profunda." *Blues,* 75.

94. Guillén, "Conversación con Langston Hughes," *El Diario de la Marina* 98 (March 9, 1930): 6.

95. See, for example, *Life,* 1:178–81. Also chapter 4.

96. Cruzado and Hricko, *Blues,* 9. On Guillén's knowledge of English, see chapter 5.

97. Fernández de Castro, "Presentación," 368. See also Mullen, *Langston Hughes,* 170 (my emphasis).

98. With the exception of Claude McKay, the other African American writers from the USA mentioned in Fernández de Castro's article—Countee Cullen, Jessie Fauset, and Walter White—do not exemplify the activist outspokenness on racial issues that the Cuban imputes to Hughes.

99. See also "Dinner Guest: Me" from 1965, which can be read as an updated revision of the much earlier "I, Too": "I know I am / The Negro Problem / Being wined and dined." *CP,* 547.

100. See Ifeoma C. K. Nwankwo, "Langston Hughes and the Translation of Nicolás Guillén's Afro-Cuban Culture and Language," *Langston Hughes Review* 16, nos. 1–2 (1999–2001): 56–60.

101. Podestá rightly complaints about this "obsessive pursuit of analogies" among literary comparatists. "Cultural Liaisons," 173. Radhakrishnan, writing about postcolonial theories, points out that "[a]ll hybridities are not equal, and furthermore hybridity does carry with it an ideologically tacit nominal qualifier, such as in western or European hybridity. Though, theoretically speaking, it would seem that hybridity functions as the ultimate decentering of all identity, in fact and in history hybridity is valorized on the basis of a stable identity, such as European hybridity, French hybridity, American hybridity, etc.... Metropolitan hybridity is underwritten by the stable regime of western secular identity and the authenticity that goes with it, whereas postcolonial hybridity has no such guarantees: neither identity nor authenticity." "Postcolonialities and the Boundaries of Identity," *Callaloo* 16, no. 4 (1993): 753–55.

102. Venuti, *Scandals,* 158. I am taking my cue here from Benjamin's comments on "the kinship of languages," which he then generalizes: "Wie es denn überhaupt einleuchtet, daß Ähnlichkeit nicht notwendig bei Verwandtschaft sich einfinden muß." *Gesammelte Schriften IV.i.,* ed. Tillman Rexroth (Frankfurt-Main: Suhrkamp, 1972), 13(It makes sense that likeness

need not accompany kinship). See also Monica Kaup, "Our America That Is Not One: Transnational Black Atlantic Disclosures in Nicolás Guillén and Langston Hughes," *Discourse* 22, no. 3 (2000): 107.

103. Venuti, *Scandals* 10.

104. Radhakrishnan, "Postcolonialities," 757.

105. Melvin Dixon, "Rivers Remembering Their Source: Comparative Studies in Black Literary History—Langston Hughes, Jacques Roumain, and Negritude," in *Afro-American Literature: The Reconstruction of Instruction,* ed. Dexter Fisher and Robert B. Stepto (New York: MLA, 1979), 41; see also, for instance, Jackson, *Black Writers in Latin America* and *Black Writers and Latin America.*

106. Notable exceptions are Marilyn Miller, "(Gypsy) Rhythm and (Cuban) Blues: The Neo-American Dream in Guillén and Hughes," *Comparative Literature* 51, no. 4 (1999): 324–44, and Scott, "Motivos of Translation."

107. Mullen, "Langston Hughes in Mexico and Cuba," 24 (my emphasis).

3. BUENOS AIRES BLUES

1. Robin Kelley, "This Ain't Ethiopia but It'll Do,'" in *African-Americans in the Spanish Civil War,* ed. Collum Danny Duncan (New York: G.K. Hall, 1992), 121.

2. See also Joan Oleza, "Rafael Alberti, Max Aub, Pablo Picasso: Urdimbres," *El Correo de Euclides, Anuario científico de la Fundación Max Aub (Segorbe)* 1 (2006): 188–205, and Barbara May, "Poetry and Political Commitment: Alberti, Guillén, and Hughes," *Studies in Afro-Hispanic Literature* 2–3 (1978–79): 14–27.

3. See Brian Bethune, "Langston Hughes' Lost Translation of Federico García Lorca's 'Blood Wedding,'" *Langston Hughes Review* 15, no. 1 (1997): 24–36.

4. Gustav, Regler, ed., *Romancero de los Voluntarios de la Libertad* (Madrid: Ediciones del Comisario de Las Brigadas Internacionales, 1937). I thank the Rare Book, Manuscript, and Special Collections Library at Duke University for providing me with a copy of this pamphlet.

5. On Hughes and Rolfe, see Cary Nelson, "Lyric Politics: The Poetry of Edwin Rolfe," in *Edwin Rolfe: Collected Poems,* ed. Cary Nelson and Jefferson Hendricks (Urbana: University of Illinois Press, 1996), 51, 55; Thurston, *Making Something Happen,* 116–18, 132. Rolfe had been a member of the CPUSA since 1925. While in Spain, he edited *Volunteer for Liberty,* the English-language publication of the International Brigades, to which Hughes also contributed.

6. Isabel Soto, "Crossing Over: Langston Hughes and Lorca," in Soto, *A Place That Is Not a Place,* 115–32, and Brent Edwards, "Langston Hughes and the Futures of Diaspora," *American Literary History* 19, no. 3 (2007): 689–711. Thurston is the only one to read Hughes's journalistic writing in tandem with his poetry about Spain. *Making Something Happen,* 115–34.

7. *La rosa blindada* might be rendered in English as "the armored, or bullet-proof, rose."

8. Nicolás Guillén, "González Tuñón," in *Recordando a Tuñón. Testimonios, Ensayos y Poemas,* ed. Pedro Orgambide (Buenos Aires: Desde la Gente. Ediciones Instituto Movilizador de Fonos Cooperativos C.I., 1997), 117; Orgambide, *El hombre de la rosa blindada: Vida y poesía de Raúl González Tuñón* (Buenos Aires: AMEGHINO Editora, 1998), 143. Hughes and Tuñón also attended the Second Congreso Internacional de Escritores para la Defensa de la Cultura held in Valencia on July 4, 1937. See Antonio Merino, ed., *Nicolás Guillén. En la guerra de España: crónicas y enunciados* (Madrid: Ediciones de la Torre, 1988), 17–19, 84–86.

9. Patterson, "Jazz," 652.

10. Patterson limitedly takes into account trans-American contexts, such as Hughes's links to some parts of the Caribbean, mainly the francophone ones.

11. John Timberman Newcomb, *Would Poetry Disappear? American Verse and the Crisis of Modernity* (Columbus: Ohio State University Press, 2004), xix.

12. Guillén, "Recuerdo de Langston Hughes," 10–11.

13. See Friedrich Nietzsche, "On the Uses and Disadvantages of History for Life," in *Untimely Meditations,* ed. Daniel Breazeale and Reginald John Hollingdale (Cambridge: Cambridge University Press, 2004).

14. See, for instance, Fernando Ortiz, *Los negros brujos: Hampa afrocubana. Apuntes para un estudio de etnología criminal* (Miami: Universal, 1973), and Raúl González Tuñón, "Blues de los baldíos," which I discuss below; also See, "Spectacles of Color" on the related phrase "down-low." Hughes used the term "low-down" in "Hard Luck," "Fire," "Evil Woman," and "The Black Clown" (*CP,* 82, 117, 120, 150).

15. An example is Hughes's reading tour through the southern states of the USA (*IW,* 40ff).

16. Sarlo, *Una modernidad periférica,* 176.

17. The same holds true for writers such as Richard Wright who were part of the Chicago Renaissance of which Hughes is also sometimes considered a part. See Mary Hricko, *Genesis of the Chicago Renaissance: Theodore Dreiser, Langston Hughes, Richard Wright, and James T. Farrell* (New York: Routledge, 2009).

18. Gruesz's *Ambassadors of Culture* is among the few studies that explore nineteenth-century intellectual crossovers between the Hispanic Americas and the USA in the varied print culture of the time.

19. George Hutchinson, *Harlem Renaissance in Black and White* (Cambridge, MA: Belknap Press, 1995), 14, 30. Mark Sanders follows Hutchinson in categorically rejecting "the dichotomy dividing hegemonic modernism and New Negroism." Sanders sees Brown's dialect poetry as an "artistic and aesthetic project that fundamentally reconceives black modernity" by "appropriating modernist notions concerning subjectivity and process." *Afro-Modernist Aesthetics and the Poetry of Sterling Brown* (Athens: University of Georgia Press, 1999), 16, 9.

20. Examples of such studies are Guido Podestá, George Handley, and, to some extent, Joshua Miller, James DeJongh, Anita Patterson, and Jeff Karem. By contrast, the *Cambridge History of Latin American Literature* has a separate chapter on Afro-Hispanic American literature.

21. González Echevarría and Pupo-Walker, *Cambridge History,* 7, 69. Patterson points out that theoretical categories such as "postmodernism" and "postcolonialism," which also have different valences in different parts of the world, have done their share to exacerbate the confusion. *Race,* xx. See also Ned Davidson, *The Concept of Modernism in Hispanic American Criticism* (Boulder, CO: Pruett Press, 1966).

22. For a more complete list see Cathy Jrade, "Modernist Poetry," in González Echevarría and Pupo-Walker, *Cambridge History,* 2:22. See also Gwen Kirkpatrick, *The Dissonant Legacy of Modernismo: Lugones, Herrera y Reissig, and the Voices of Modern Spanish American Poetry* (Berkeley: University of California Press, 1989).

23. See Hugo Verani, "The Vanguardia and Its Implications," in González Echevarría and Pupo-Walker, *Cambridge History,* 2:114. Important to Hutchinson is that "*Modernismo* was the movement through which Latin American writers in Spanish broke from their Spanish literary tradition and established the basic vectors of their own indigenous bearings. To North American eyes, their 'modernisms' look much like realist localism." *Harlem Renaissance,* 220. The political geography of North America, however, also includes Mexico, a fact that is often elided.

24. Podestá, "Cultural Liaisons," 181. On Huidobro compared with Pound, see Justin Read, *Modern Poetics and Hemispheric American Cultural Studies* (New York: Palgrave Macmillan, 2009).

25. Verani, "Vanguardia," 131.

26. See Tace Hedrick, *Mestizo Modernism: Race, Nation and Identity in Latin American Culture, 1900–1940* (New Brunswick, NJ: Rutgers University Press, 2003). Her examples are Peru's César Vallejo (1892–1938), the Chilean expatriate Gabriela Mistral (1889–1957), and the Guatemalan Miguel Angel Asturias (1899–1974).

27. As a field, Afro-Hispanic studies developed in the USA largely around the journal *Afro-Hispanic Review.* See also Kutzinski, "Afro-Hispanic American Literature."

28. The work of non-black writers with an interest in African American culture has typically been dismissed as inauthentic and exoticist—the poetic (and political) equivalent of blackface minstrelsy. Their counterparts during the Harlem Renaissance would be Carl Van Vechten and Waldo Frank, among others.

29. See Dixon, "Rivers," 30.

30. *Contemporáneos* was launched in 1928. See also Lozano's *Euterpe. Poesías sobre motivos musicales* (Mexico City: Ediciones del Bloque de Obreros Intelectuales de Mexico, 1930), which includes poems such as "Minstrels" (37–39), "Danzón Cubano" (115–16), "Canciones Criollas" (125–26), and "Blues Medley" (155–57). Mullen notes that by 1934, "Hughes had become a familiar figure among the Mexican litterati," to whom he had first been introduced by the poet Carlos Pellicer, who introduced Hughes to Novo and Villaurrutia. According to Mullen, they "were fascinated with both the content and form of [Hughes's] poetry and had begun to view him as a genuine spokesman for the black proletariat." Mullen also contends that Hughes's Mexican audience, while almost always appreciative, often misread him. "Langston Hughes in Mexico and Cuba,"25.

31. See Stanley Cyrus, "Ethnic Ambivalence and Afro-Hispanic Novelists," *Afro-Hispanic Review* 21, nos. 1–2 (Spring–Fall 2002): 185–89; Houston Baker, *Modernism and the Harlem Renaissance* (Chicago: University of Chicago Press, 2003), and Pavlić's criticisms of Baker in *Crossroads Modernism,* 51.

32. See Alfred A. Knopf, *Publishing Then and Now, 1912–1964* (New York: New York Public Library, 1964), 119. See also Maria Eugenia Mudrovcic, "Reading Latin American Literature Abroad: Agency and Canon Formation in the Sixties and Seventies," in *Voice-Overs: Translation and Latin American literature,* ed. Daniel Balderston and Marcy Schwartz (Albany: State University of New York Press, 2002),131ff.; Irene Rostagno, *Searching for Recognition: The Promotion of Latin American Literature in the United States* (Westport, CT: Greenwood Press, 1997), and Margaret Sayers Peden, "Knopf, Knopf, Who's There?" *Translation Review* 50 (1996): 27–30.

33. See Knopf's letter to Hughes from June 19, 1942, in which she mentions that she is about to leave for South America. Also Hughes to Blanche Knopf, November 30, 1950, LHP, 176:1828 and 1830.

34. Knopf issued Clarice Lispector's *The Apple in the Dark* in 1957; Arturo Uslar Pietri's *The Red Lances* in 1963; José Donoso's *This Sunday* in 1967, followed by *The Obscene Bird of Night;* Gilberto Freyre's *Mother and Son: A Brazilian Tale* in 1967; João Guimarães Rosa's *The Third Bank of the River, and Other Stories* in 1968; Autran Dourado's *A Hidden Life* in 1969; José María Gironella's *Peace after War* in 1969; Jorge Amado's *Dona Flor and Her Two Husbands* in 1969; and Jose J. Veiga's *The Misplaced Machine and Other Stories* and Alejo Carpentier's *War of Time* in 1970. These were followed by Manuel Puig's *Kiss of the Spider Woman* in 1979, Julio Cortázar's *Change of Light and Other Stories* in 1980, *We Love Glenda so Much* in 1983, and in 1990 García Márquez's *The General in His Labyrinth.*

35. See Lucía Dominga Molina and Mario Luis López, "Afro-Argentineans: "Forgotten" and "Disappeared"—Yet Still Present," in *African Roots/American Cultures: Africa in the Creation of the Americas,* ed. Sheila S. Walker (Lanham, MD: Rowman & Littlefield, 2001), 337. Also George Andrews, *Afro-Latin America, 1800–2000* (Oxford: Oxford University Press, 2004), 57–66, and *Afro-Argentines of Buenos Aires;* Alberto Britos Serrat, *Antologiʹa de poetas*

negros uruguayos (Montevideo, Uru.: Ediciones Mundo Afro, 1990). John King comments that "Hughes could reach few people in Argentina—the black population had largely disappeared by now, having once formed a high percentage of the inhabitants of Buenos Aires." *Sur: A Study of the Argentine Literary Journal and Its Role in the Development of a Culture, 1931–1970* (Cambridge: Cambridge University Press, 1986), 51. *Poesía negra* appears to have been written later in Argentina than in most other Hispanic American countries. See Alejandro Solomianski, *Identidades secretas: La negritud argentina* (Rosario, Arg.: Beatriz Viterbo Editora, 2003), 247ff. Also Manuel Antonio Zuloaga, *Nuestra raza y los problemas de posguerra en la Argentina* (Buenos Aires: Editorial "La Facultad," 1943); Jorge Emilio Gallardo, *Bibliografía afroargentina* (Buenos Aires: Idea Viva, 2002); and Sylvia G. Carullo, "Una aproximación a la poesía federal afro-argentina de la época de Juan Manuel Rosas," *Afro-Hispanic Review* 4, no. 1 (1985): 15–22.

36. Sergio Waisman, "Foundational Scenes of Translation," *Estudios Interdisciplinarios de América Latina y el Caribe* 21, no. 1 (January–June 2010): 53–77.

37. See José Quiroga, "Spanish American Poetry from 1922 to 1975," in González Echevarría and Pupo-Walker, *Cambridge History*, 2:316–17. Raúl González Tuñón recalls, "Yo tengo dos imágenes de Borges: el que yo conocí, el de los grandes libros de su juventud—*Fervor de Buenos Aires, Luna de enfrente, Cuaderno San Martín*—, el Borges yrigoyenista acérrimo" (I had two images of Borges: the one I knew, the one of the great books of his youth...and the staunch defender of Yrigoyen). "Autoretrato," in Orgambide, *Recordando a Tuñón*, 35. In 1930 Borges had founded a committee to support the reelection of Hipólito Yrigoyen, two-time president of Argentina (1916–22, and 1928–30). In this he turned against the oligarchy and imperialism, something, Tuñón remarks, Borges had absorbed from his father and his circle of socialist and anarchist friends. Yrigoyen was deposed in September of 1930 by José Felix Uriburu, whose military regime opened what was known as the Infamous Decade; it ended with another coup in 1943.

38. Frank's *Dawn in Russia* was published in the same year as Hughes's *The Big Sea*. Also like Hughes, he did not join the Communist Party. See Michael Ogorzaly, *Waldo Frank: Prophet of Hispanic Regeneration* (Lewisburg, PA: Bucknell University Press, 1994), 36, 73–75.

39. Frank's Buenos Aires speech is quoted in Ogorzaly, *Waldo Frank*, 80. On Mallea, whom Frank considered a major Argentine writer, see Gloria Majstorovic, "An American Place: Victoria Ocampo's, the Foundation of *Sur*, and Hemispheric Alliances," *Arizona Journal of Hispanic Cultural Studies* 9 (2005), 175.

40. Beatriz Sarlo, *La máquina cultural: Maestras, traductores, y vanguardistas* (Buenos Aires: Editorial Planeta Rgentina S.A.I.C., 1998), 117. The second part of Sarlo's book is a fascinating meditation on Ocampo, language, and translation. Many of Ocampo's own translations were published in *Sur*. Majstorovic notes that "[t]he American images in Ocampo are... first born in a foreign language: French." "An American Place," 177.

41. Ogorzaly, *Waldo Frank*, 79.

42. King, *Sur*, 42.

43. Victoria Ocampo, "Carta a Waldo Frank," *Sur* 1, no. 1 (1931): 16, 17. *Sur* ran from 1931 to 1970; see also Héctor René Lafleur et al., eds., *Las revistas literarias argentinas (1893–1967)* (Buenos Aires: El 8vo. Loco Ed., 2006), 142–44.

44. King, *Sur*, 43. Sarlo argues that Ocampo saw *Sur* "como instrumento del purificación del gusto, indispensable, a juicio de Ocampo, en una ciudad donde la inmigración ha ido dejando marcas materiales que producen una anarquía estilística con diversos orígenes nacionales" (as an instrument for purifying taste, which, in Ocampo's estimation, was indispensable in a city where immigration had left palpable marks, producing a stylistic anarchy with diverse national origins). *Borges, un escritor en las orillas* (Buenos Aires: Ariel, 1995), 34.

45. Ocampo, "Carta," 11, 14, 17. See also Elizabeth Horan and Doris Mayer, eds., *This America of Ours: The Letters of Gabriela Mistral and Victoria Ocampo* (Austin: University of Texas Press, 2003), 10–11, 27.

46. See Frank, *Memoirs of Waldo Frank,* ed. Alan Trachtenberg (Amherst: University of Massachusetts Press, 1973), 163–64, 170–71; also Ogorzaly, *Waldo Frank,* 77. King emphasizes more than others have the role Glusberg, who organized Frank's speaking tour, played in the discussions that led to the founding of Sur. *Sur,* 41–43.

47. Frank, *Memoirs,* 171. On the inaugural issue of *Sur,* see Majstorovic, "An American Place," 174.

48. Ogorzaly, *Waldo Frank,* 79.

49. See Sergio Waisman, *Borges and Translation: The Irreverence of the Periphery* (Lewisburg, PA: Bucknell University Press, 2005), 35; on Ocampo and translation, see Sarlo, *La máquina cultural,* 127.

50. Waldo Frank, *South American Journey* (New York: Duell, Sloan, and Pearce, 1943), 72.

51. Majstorovic, "An American Place," 175.

52. It is not surprising that the epigraph to Frank's *Our America* is from Whitman. Toomer chided Frank for "not including the Negro" in *Our America,* an omission that Frank promised to remedy in a later edition of that book. See Kathleen Pfeiffer, ed., *Brother Mine: The Correspondence of Jean Toomer and Waldo Frank* (Urbana: University of Illinois Press, 2010), 28, 47. He never did.

53. Pfeiffer, *Brother Mine,* 169.

54. See Sarlo, *Borges,* and *Una modernidad periférica,* 180.

55. Pfeiffer, *Brother Mine,* 169.

56. Jorge Luis Borges, "Langston Hughes," in *Textos cautivos. Ensayos y renseñas en "El Hogar"* (Barcelona: Tusquets Editores, 1986), 92.

57. Pfeiffer, *Brother Mine,* 170.

58. Some of Hughes's more starkly modernist lyrics, such as "The Cat and the Saxophone," rather vexed Cullen.

59. See Walt Whitman, *Hojas de hierba,* trans. Jorge Luis Borges (Buenos Aires: Juárez, 1969).

60. Lozano, "Langston Hughes," 226; Toruño, *Poesía negra,* 99, 46.

61. Waisman, *Borges and Translation,* 29, 80–81; see also Edwin Gentzler, *Translation and Identity in the Americas: New Directions in Translation Theory* (London: Routledge, 2008), 111–19.

62. See, for instance, Franz Kafka, *La metamorfosis,* trans. Jorge Luis Borges (Buenos Aires: Losada, 1943). See also Waisman, *Borges and Translation,* 37.

63. On Borges's translations of the last page of *Ulysses* in 1925 see Waisman, *Borges and Translation,* 157–201; on Borges and Eliot, 146–48; on Cummings, 76–78; see also his "Jorge Luis Borges's Partial Argentine *Ulysses*" and Masiello, "Joyce in Buenos Aires." On Borges and Faulkner see María Elena Bravo, "Borges traductor: El caso de *Wild Palms* de William Faulkner," *Ínsula* 40, no. 462 (1985): 11–12.

64. Waisman, *Borges and Translation,* 42. See Rodríguez García's excellent commentary on this essay in "Literary into Cultural Translation," 11–12.

65. Ibid. See also Roberto González Echevarría's *Myth and Archive: A Theory of Latin American Narrative* (Cambridge: Cambridge University Press, 1990) on the Latin American novel's mediating discourses. `·`

66. See Rodríguez García, "Literary into Cultural Translation," 4.

67. In this, Borges anticipated the reader-response theories that have been promulgated by Wolfgang Iser and others since the 1970s. Borges's concept of infidelity resonates with Ette's

notion of the translator as *wahrer Lügner* (true liar), though Ette does not place it in the context of (post)colonialism. See *ZwischenWeltenSchreiben*, 107ff.

68. Waisman, *Borges and Translation*, 46.

69. Waldo Frank to Jean Toomer, 1923, in Pfeiffer, *Brother Mine*, 121. The occasion was Frank's reaction to the negative reviews of his novel *Holiday*.

70. King, *Sur*, 51.

71. Patterson, "Jazz," 652.

72. Van Vechten, introduction to *TWB*, 12.

73. Patterson "Jazz," 660.

74. Compare the end first stanza of "Po' Boy Blues": "Since I come up North de / Whole damn world 's turned cold" (*CP*, 83). Gáler translates this very freely and without consideration of the vernacular: "Desde que me vine al Norte / Hasta la luz se me ha enfriado" (Ever since I came to the North, / the light gave me chills). *Poemas*, 55. In colloquial use, the Spanish verb *enfriarse* can also mean "to die." Ahumada's later translation, which is entitled "Blues del Pobrecito," stays closer to Hughes: "Desde que vine al Norte / el mundo todo se ha vuelto frío." *YT*, 17.

75. Nicholas Evans, "Wandering Aesthetic, Wandering Consciousness: Diasporic Impulses and 'Vagrant' Desires in Langston Hughes's Early Poetry," in *New Voices on the Harlem Renaissance: Essays on Race, Gender, and Literary Discourse*, ed. Australia Tarver and Paula C. Barnes (Madison, NJ: Fairleigh Dickinson University Press, 2006), 177, 178.

76. It was reprinted in *Opportunity* (1924) and *Survey Graphic* (1925).

77. The journal Frank had first discussed with Glusberg and then proposed to Ocampo was to have been entitled *Nuestra América*, not *Sur*.

78. Jorge Luis Borges, trans., "Tres poemas de Langston Hughes," *Sur* 1, no. 2 (1931): 167.

79. In his review of the book, Mejía Sánchez calls Ahumada's book "una vehemente elegía" for King. *YT*, 95.

80. Gáler translates these lines rather differently: "Seguro, / El camino es para todos, / Los blancos pasan en autos / Y el negro los ve pasar" (Sure, / the road is for everyone, / the whites pass by in cars / And the negro seen them pass). *Poemas*, 109.

81. "Espléndido sol" in Ahumada, *YT*, 91.

82. Patterson has convincingly argued that "the deceptive simplicity of Hughes's early lyrics obscures a concern with craft and stylistic innovation he shared with his modernist contemporaries, and his engagement with the European avant-gardes, and poets such as Laforgue and especially Baudelaire, was deeper and more extensive than has previously been shown." *Race*, 93, also 103–9.

83. Compare this with Gáler's version, which puts an emphasis on the "I" (*yo*) that is unusual in Spanish: "Yo he conocido ríos viejos como el mundo, y / Más viejos que el fluir de sangre humana por humanas venas. / Mi alma se ha tornado profundo como los ríos." Lozano puts the poem in the present tense: "Conozco algunos ríos: / Conozco algunos ríos tan antiguos como el mundo y más viejo que la / Corriente de sangre humana en las venas de la humanidad."

84. Gáler: "Yo me bañe en el Éufrates cuando las albas eran jóvenes. / Alce mi choza junto al Congo y al me arrullo en mi sueño. / Mis ojos se miraron en el Nilo y erigí la Pirámide a su vera. / Oí cantar el Mississippi cuando Abraham Lincoln bajo hasta Nueva Orleans, y he visto / Su barroso pecho volverse dorado en el atardecer." Lozano: "Me bañe en el Éufrates cuando las auroras eran jóvenes. / Construí mi choza cerca del Congo, el cual me arrullo a mi sueño. / Contemple el Nilo y construí las pirámides sobre de él. / Oí la canción del Mississippi cuando Abraham Lincoln fue a Nueva Orleans, / Y vi su corriente lodosa volverse aurea con el crepúsculo."

85. Borges, "Tres poemas," 169; "Langston Hughes," 93. Gáler: "Yo he conocido ríos, / Viejos, crepusculares ríos. / Mi alma se ha vuelto profunda como los ríos." Lozano: "Conozco algunos ríos: / Ríos antiguos y sombríos. / Mi alma se ha hecho tan profunda como los ríos."

86. We might say that he updates the poem when he writes "Mississippi" in 1955. See *CP,* 452.

87. Emphasizing the "link between *traduzione* (traducement) and *tradizione* (tradition)," Stephanides comments that "[t]ranslation might be infidelity but it is also an agent for reshaping tradition." "Translation of Heritage," 45.

88. In his brief reading of the poem's "routes," Jahan Ramazani comments on the "remarkable freedom of movement and affiliative connection." *A Transnational Poetics* (Chicago: University of Chicago Press, 2009), 62–63.

89. For the song's lyrics and music, see W. C. Handy, ed. *Blues: An Anthology* (New York: Albert and Charles Boni, 1926), 71–74.

90. Jason Miller, who contends that this poem "needs to be read within the context of a United States lynching culture that grew more and more intimidating after the Red Summer of 1919," argues that "The Negro Speaks of Rivers" "reserves Hughes's need to contemplate the way in which African Americans have previously survived and flourished near riverscapes. The meditation implies that because others have survived, he and his readers can survive too. Hughes must have attached much personal significance to a poem that serves as a reminder that passing through the South can be a survivable act." "Justice, Lynching, and American Riverscapes: Finding Reassurance in Langston Hughes's 'The Negro Speaks of Rivers,'" *Langston Hughes Review* 18, no. 1 (Spring 2004): 25, 31.

91. The Spanish version is from Borges, *Obras completas* (Buenos Aires: Emece 1974), 1:295; the English translation is in Borges, *A Universal History of Infamy,* trans. Borges and Norman Thomas di Giovanni (New York: Dutton, 1970), 19. Borges collaborated with di Giovanni on this and many other translations of his own work. For additional details on their collaborations, see http://www.digiovanni.co.uk; also Kimberly Brown, "In Borges' Shadow: Review of *The Lesson of the Master* by Norman Thomas di Giovanni," *Janus Head* 1, no. 8 (Summer 2005): 349–51, http://www.janushead.org/8-1/index.cfm. I have flagged all additions the English translation makes to the Spanish text by putting them in boldface. They were clearly designed to make certain historical references more easily accessible to English-speaking readers.

92. See Grandt, *Shaping Words to Fit the Soul,* 79, which I quoted in chapter 1. There is also a very interesting possible connection here to another blues that Handy both performed and included in his anthology with words both in English and Spanish: "Deep River Blues" (1925; *Blues,* 106–108).

93. Borges, *Obras completas,* 1:295–96; Borges and di Giovanni, *Universal History,* 20 (my emphases).

94. Tuñón explains that "no dice al otro poeta de Buenos Aires, que sería una cosa ambiciosa, como diciendo en Buenos Aires hay solamente dos poetas" (he did not say 'to the other poet of Buenos Aires,' which would have been an ambitious thing, like saying that there are only two poets in Buenos Aires). Horacio Salas, *Conversaciones con* Raúl González Tuñón (Buenos Aires: Ediciones La Bastilla, 1975), 41. See also Héctor Yanover, who does not get this story quite right. "Raúl González Tuñón," in Orgambide, *Recordando a Tuñón,* 51.

95. Raúl González Tuñón, *Todos bailan. Los poemas de Juancito Camindor* (Buenos Aires: Libros de Tierra Firme, 1987), 50.

96. Jorge Luis Borges, "Arrabal," in *Fervor de Buenos Aires* (Buenos Aires: Emecé, 1970), 71.

97. See Sarlo, *Una modernidad periférica,* 180–81. Also important, as James Smethurst explains, is that "bohemia is a place or a quarter, but one of shifting, mobile, and unusually permeable boundaries" of class, gender, race, ethnicity, and nationality." *The African American Roots of Modernism: From Reconstruction to the Harlem Renaissance* (Chapel Hill: University of North Carolina Press, 2011), 125.

98. On *Martín Fierro,* see Lafleur et al., *Las revistas literarias,* 91–112.

99. Borges, "Arrabal," in *Fervor,* 71.

100. See James DeJongh, *Vicious Modernism: Black Harlem and the Literary Imagination* (Cambridge: Cambridge University Press, 1990), 173ff.

101. Ibid., 24–25; also Smethurst, *African American Roots,* chap. 3.

102. "¿Y qué dirá la muerte cuando vaya / y nadie sepa dónde vive / la persona que busca en esa calle, / la oscura, la cortada, / la ignorada del censo municipal, sin nombre, /sin ayer, sin mañana? // Perdida entre los yugos y la siesta, / La soledad y la desesperanza." (And what will death say when it comes / and no one knows where lives / the person she looks for in that street / the dark, the dead end / ignored by the local census, nameless, / without a yesterday, without a tomorrow? // Lost between the grindstone and the siesta, / solitude and hopelessness.) "Calles sin nombre" from *Poemas para el atril de una pianola* (Poems for the Music Stand of a Player Piano) (1971), in *Raúl González Tuñón: Poemas de Buenos Aires. Antología,* ed. Luis Osvaldo Tedesco (Buenos Aires: Torres Aguero, 1983), 80.

103. González Tuñón, *Todos bailan,* 20.

104. Ibid., 36–37.

105. DeJongh devotes the fourth chapter in *Vicious Modernism* to Harlem as a literary topic/topos in the work of select writers from the Caribbean, Africa, and some parts of South America. He includes many poems written in homage to Hughes (see 48–70). See also his very helpful Checklist of Black Harlem in Poetry, app. 1, 218–43.

106. Chambers, *Mediterranean Crossings,* 43.

107. Patrick Chamoiseau, *Texaco. Roman* (Paris: Gallimard, 2004), 243.

108. "Canción que compuso Juancito Camindor para la supuesta muerte de Juancito Caminador" (Song that JC composed about the supposed death of JC), from *Nuevos poemas de Juancito Caminador* (1941) in *Raúl González Tuñón. Antología poética,* ed. Héctor Yanover (Madrid: Visor Libros, 1986), 100.

109. In 1958, Tuñón traveled to Tashkent for the First Congress of the Writers of Asia and Africa; he had been invited as a special guest. See Orgambide, *El hombre,* 60, 233.

110. See Jonathan Gill, "Ezra Pound and Langston Hughes, The ABC of Po'try" in *Ezra Pound and African American Modernism,* ed. Michael Coyle (Orono, ME: National Poetry Foundation, 2001), 86.

111. Yanover, *Raúl González Tuñón. Antología,* 101.

112. Enrique González Tuñón, Raúl's older brother and also a poet, published the volume *Tangos* in 1926, the same year as *The Weary Blues.* Sarlo argues that, for Raúl González Tuñón, the tango did not have the popular dimension that interested him. Instead, what attracted him was "[l]a música de feria y de barraca, la chanson, los sonidos y los instrumentos de jazz o de las orquestas de circo, las cajas de música y las canciones de guignol" (the music of the fairs and the barracks, the chanson, the sounds and instruments of jazz and of the circus orchestras, the juke boxes and the songs of the guignol). *Una modernidad periférica,* 165.

113. See Arile Bignami and Arturo M. Lozza, "Pablo Neruda y Raúl González Tuñón: El resplandor de las palabras," *Suplemento cultural de Nuestra Propuesta. Semanario del Comité Central del Partido Comunista* (n.d.), 8, http://www.elortiba.org/pdf/Neruda_y_Tunon.pdf.

114. See James Weldon Johnson, *Black Manhattan* (New York: Arno Press, 1968), 169, 179, 217. Similar blues characters also appeared in the now little-known work of Fenton Johnson. See Smethurst, *African American Roots,* 144. On Hughes's later poetry about drug addicts, see Margaret Reid, "Langston Hughes: Rhetoric and Protest," *Langston Hughes Review* 3, no. 1 (1984): 18–20.

115. Sarlo, *Una modernidad,* 155.

116. Ibid., 157. *Costumbrismo* is, in many ways, the equivalent of nineteenth-century regionalism in the USA.

117. Venuti, *Scandals*, 27.

118. Ibid., 98.

119. In blues terminology, eagle rock, which typically refers to a 1920 dance first developed by rural slaves, can also function as a sexual metaphor.

120. Scanlon has commented at some length on the significance of the mother tongue's institutional location in the domestic sphere (the nursery, the household, set against the authority of the church). He argues that Hughes "presents motherhood as the crucial mediating category between the public and the private, and the vernacular and the poetic. This enables him to insist that race relations are not only more urgent but also more intimate than commonly imagined." An example is "Mother to Son," a poem in which the vernacular form is transmitted from mother to child "to include the whole of culture, not just language." Scanlon, "Poets Laureate," 246–48, 250.

121. Sarlo, *Una modernidad*, 158–68.

122. Ibid., 179–80.

123. See also Scanlon, "Poets Laureate," 234.

124. From *El violín del diablo*, quoted in Sarlo, *Una modernidad*, 161. See also Antonio Vallejo, "*El violín del diablo* de Raúl González Tuñón," *Martín Fierro* (1993), http://www.elortiba.org/pdf/Raul-Gonzalez-Tunon.pdf.

125. González Tuñón, *Las brigadas de choque*, http://eltrenliterario.blogspot.com/2008/12/las-brigadas-de-choque-de-la-poesa.html. See also Orgambide, *El hombre*, 83ff. Tuñón did not include this poem in *Todos bailan* so as not to delay the book's publication, and the book itself opens with a note to this effect.

126. See Rosana Gutiérrez, *Raúl González Tuñón: Prestidigitador de poemas y revoluciones* (Babab Biblioteca, 2001), http://www.babab.com/no07/gonzalez_tunon.htm. "Juratory caution" is a special kind of bail under judicial discretion, in which a defendant who lacks financial resources is released on his own good word. Guillén suffered a similar fate under Batista, whose government exiled him in 1957. Guillén spend two years in Buenos Aires, where he apparently saw much of Tuñón.

127. See Orgambide, *El hombre*, 115.

128. See González Tuñón, *Todos bailan*, 70–71.

129. See Hilton Als, "Driver's License: Broadway Transforms 'Driving Miss Daisy' and 'The Scottsboro Boys,'" *New Yorker Magazine*, November 8, 2010, 90.

130. "A New Song" was never translated. Pereda Valdes translated "Always the Same" as "Siempre lo mismo" in 1936. "Canto a Tom Mooney" was included in *YT.*

131. "El mercado de las pulgas" (Flea Market) from Tuñón, *Todos bailan*, 57.

132. Borges had family connections to publishing. His brother-in-law, Guillermo de Torre, who had married Borges's sister Norah in 1928, was involved in the founding of Losada, which soon became a major press.

133. See King, *Sur*, 104–5; Sarlo on the emergence of "periodismo profesional," *Una modernidad*, 155; Lafleur et al., *Las revistas*, 75–169.

134. Lautaro is renowned for publishing Spanish translations of six volumes of Antonio Gramsci's writings between 1950 and 1962.

135. Blanche Knopf wrote to Hughes on September 16, 1941, "We have been in correspondence with him [Pereda Valdés] and maybe something will come of it as far as THE BIG SEA is concerned." LHP, 176:1826 and 1939. Part 3 of *The Big Sea* was printed as a separate book entitled *Renacimiento negro* (1971). This part had been included in the 1940 Knopf edition only at Carl Van Vechten's insistence.

136. In 1964, the Spaniard Alfonso Sastre wrote an adaptation of Hughes's play *Mulatto* (1929); it was reprinted in 1993. In 1998, Fraile Marcos published a bilingual edition of section 8 of *I Wonder As I Wander,* entitled *Oscuridad en España.*

137. Dorothy L. Shereff (at Knopf) to Hughes, July 13, 1945. The contract states that the Spanish edition was to be published by June 31, 1945. In December Hughes received three copies from Lautaro. That same month he also found in his mail a copy of the Brazilian translation of *The Big Sea (O imenso mar,* 1944) from Editorial Vitória in Rio de Janeiro, commenting that he had not known about this one. See LHP 176:75.

138. See Ana Julieta Núñez, *Raúl Larra: Payró y el recorrido de una lectura,* 2009, www.jornadashumha.com.ar.

139. Hughes to Editorial Lautaro, January 29, 1949, LHP 58:1101.

140. Hughes to Margarete A. Rente (at Knopf), June 16, 1948, LHP 4:79. The letter includes a list of the books sent to Gáler.

141. See reviews by Peloso, Woodson, and Watkins the *Journal of Negro History* 30 (1945). *Phylon* 13 (1952). It was not until the 1970s, however, that Ortíz Oderigo turned to the study of Afro-Argentine culture in *Aspectos de la cultural africana en el Río de la Plata* (1974). See also Alicia Dujovne Ortíz, "Un pequeño triunfo negro," *La Nación.* http://www.lacion.com.ar/nota.sp?nota_id = 735432.

142. See Orgambide, *Recordando a Tuñón,* 56–57.

143. When he was in the process of translating *I Wonder,* to which Muchnik refers as "la hermosa autobiografía de Langston Hughes" (Langston Hughes's beautiful autobiography), Gáler went to Muchnik for a job. He started working for Jacobo Muchnik Editor right after it was launched in 1955 and then continued at Fabril. Muchnik, who effectively ran Fabril, describes Gáler as "mi alter ego." Jacobo Muchnik, *Editing: Arte de poner los puntos sobres las íes—y difundirlas* (Madrid: del Taller de Mario Muchnik, 2004), 121–23.

144. See Joaquín Marco, *La llegada del los barbaros: La recepción de la narrativa hispanoamericana en España, 1960–1981* (Barcelona: Edhasa, 2004); Washington Luis Pereyra, ed., *La prensa literaria Argentina 1890–1974,* vol. 4, *Los años de compromiso, 1940–1949* (Buenos Aires: Fundación Bartolomé Hidalgo, 2008), 283; María Angélica Bosco, *Memorias de las casas* (Buenos Aires: Colecciones Testimonios del Fin del Milenio, Editorial Vinciguerra, 1998), 59, 70. Muchnik and Gáler collaborated in translating Arthur Miller's play *A Memory of Two Mondays* as *Recuerdo de dos lunes* (1958). See Muchnik, *Editing,* 194ff.

145. After he retired from the ILO in 1987, he worked for the government of Argentina as part of the Ministry of Labor and International Relations. Gáler died in 2006.

146. See Fernando Sabsay, *Sin telón: Losange Teatro. Una experiencia de teatro impreso en Buenos Aires, 1952–1960* (Buenos Aires: Ediciones Ciudad Argentina, 1997), 95. In academic scholarship, Rivaud is frequently misspelled Rivaudi or Rivand.

147. See Lucie Lipschutz Gabriel, *El siglo de la siglas* (Madrid: Hebraica Ediciones, 2005), 159ff. She may very well have heard of Hughes while she was still in Spain.

148. She returned to Madrid in 1974 with her husband and has since collaborated on several films and television series with her son, the Spanish director Enrique Gabriel.

149. Guillén's main publisher in Buenos Aires was Losada.

150. Gáler, "Homenaje," in *Del tiempo y des las ideas: Textos en honor de Gregorio Weinberg,* ed. Agustín Mendoza (Buenos Aires: Carlos A. Firpo S.R.L., 2000), 37.

151. Gáler to Hughes, May 14, 1948, LHP 443:10,372 and 10,373.

152. Hughes asked that fifty copies be sent to him. The inscribed copy in LHP is dated September 3, 1952.

153. Gáler calls Dunbar the first to use the blues form *(el blue)* in his poetry.

154. Ahumada includes translations of fifty-five poems, twenty-seven of which were published between 1921 and 1927. Of the eighty-three poems in Gáler's volume, forty-five are from the same time period.

155. The two other translations appeared in Spain more than half a century later. See Cruzado and Hricko, *Blues;* Charles Matz and Ana Jordá, "Los cansados Blues," *Litoral* (2001): 227–28; and Txema Martínez Inglés, "Canción para Billie Holiday," *Litoral* (2001): 227–28.

156. Gáler was the first and only translator of a total of thirty-eight Hughes poems.

157. Ramazani, *Poetry of Mourning,* 163.

158. Hughes, *The Ways of White Folks* (New York: Knopf, 1934), 49 (my emphasis).

159. From "Lenox Avenue: Midnight," *CP,* 92).

160. Gáler: "El calmo, / Frío rostro del torrente / Me pidió un beso" (The calm, / freezing face of the stream / asked me for a kiss), *Poemas,* 46. See also Villaurrutia: "La serena, / fría cara del río / me pidió un beso" (The serene, / cold countenance of the river / asked me for a kiss), *Contemporáneos,* 159.

161. The others are "The South" ("El Sur"), "Song to a Negro Washerwoman" ("Canción a una lavandera negra"), "Negro Dancers" ("Bailarines negros"), "Ruby Brown," and "The Cat and the Saxophone" ("El gato y el saxofón"). Other poems that fall into this category are "April Rain Song" ("Canción de la lluvia abrileña"), "Question" ("Pregunta"), "The Jester" ("El juglar"), "Parisian Beggar Woman" ("Mendiga de Paris"), and "Lenox Avenue" ("Avenida Lenox: Medianoche").

162. See chapter 1. Also Scanlon, "Poets Laureate," 251.

163. See also Bansart, "Tener miedo," in Bansart, Jiménez, and Santa Cruz, *Poesía negra-africana.*

164. George Steiner's comment on the "heightening of a work's existence when it is confronted and reenacted by alternate versions of itself" applies well here. *After Babel: Aspects of Language and Translation* (Oxford: Oxford University Press, 1998), 453.

4. HAVANA VERNACULARS

1. The complete text of *Cuba Libre,* unfortunately minus the line drawings from the original edition, is reprinted in volume 16 of Rampersad's *The Collected Works of Langston Hughes.* There are no notes on textual variations. Translations of a handful of Guillén's poems had been published earlier in USAmerican journals, magazines, and anthologies.

2. Hughes believed that, with library sales, they could sell at least 500 copies. Hughes to Caroline Anderson, July 8, 1948, LHP, 7:160. Later sales figures indicate that more than 250 copies must have been printed.

3. Hughes kept carbon copies of most of his letters. Additional letters from Hughes can be found in Ángel Augier, "Epistolario Nicolás Guillén — Langston Hughes," *Revista de Literatura Cubana* 13, nos. 24–26 (1995–96): 145–61, and Alexander Pérez Heredia, ed., *Epistolario de Nicolás Guillén* (Havana: Letras Cubanas, 2002).

4. That contested ground has been amply covered. See, for example, Martha Cobb, *Harlem, Haiti, and Havana: A Comparative Critical Study of Langston Hughes, Jacques Roumain, Nicolás Guillén* (Washington, DC: Three Continents Press, 1979); Keith Ellis, "Nicolás Guillén and Langston Hughes: Convergences and Divergences," in *Between Race and Empire: African-Americans and Cubans before the Cuban Revolution,* ed. Lisa Brock and Digna Castaneda Fuertes (Philadelphia: Temple University Press, 1998), 129–67; Leslie Feracho, "The Legacy of Negrismo/Negritude: Inter-American Dialogues," *Langston Hughes Review* 16, nos. 1–2 (1999–2001): 1–7; Jackson, "Langston Hughes;" David Arthur McMurray, "Dos negros en el Nuevo Mundo: Notas sobre el 'americanismo' de Langston Hughes y la cubanía de Nicolás Guillén," *Casa de las Américas* 14 (1974), 122–28; Edward Mullen, *Langston Hughes;* Enrique Noble, "Nicolás Guillén y Langston Hughes," *Nueva Revista Cubana* (1961–62): 41–85; Belén Rodríguez-Mourelo, "The Search for Identity in the Poetry of Langston Hughes and Nicolás Guillén," *Langston Hughes Review* 16, nos. 1–2 (Fall–Spring 1999–2001): 39–54; Gerardo Sáenz, "Nicolás Guillén, Langston Hughes y Luis Palés Matos: África en tres tonos," in *Homenaje a Lydia Cabrera,* ed. Reinaldo Sánchez, José Antonio Madrigal, and José

Sánchez-Boudy (Miami: Ediciones Universal, 1978), 183–88; and Eloise Spicer, "The Blues and the Son: Reflections of Black Self-Assertion in the Poetry of Langston Hughes and Nicolás Guillén," *Langston Hughes Review* 3, no. 1 (1984): 1–12. Monica Kaup helpfully suggests that "transnational and interdisciplinary research in comparative studies of the Americas needs to delve deeper into translation theory when studying the trans-national traffic of parallel expressive forms like 'blues' and *son*" ("'Our America,'"107).

5. Hughes to Guillén, August 27, 1948, LHP, 70:1366). Ironically, Hughes specifically asked Ben Carruthers, who was traveling in South America at the time, to look for work by "poets having Negro blood." Hughes to Carruthers, June 13, 1947, LHP, 42:726.

6. When Doubleday issued a revised and expanded version in 1970, not a trace of the Caribbean section remained. See Langston Hughes and Arna Bontemps, eds., *The Poetry of the Negro, 1746–1970* (Garden City, NY: Doubleday, 1970). The entire section was scrapped to make room for new black poets from the USA; it was as if it had never existed. In the first edition, *The Poetry of the Negro, 1746–1949* (Garden City, NY: Doubleday, 1949), the francophone and Hispanic Caribbean are represented by Oswald Durand, Isaac Toussaint-Louverture, Louis Morpeau, Ignace Nau, Luc Grimard, Philippe Thoby-Marcelin, Christian Werleigh, Normil Sylvain, Duracine Vaval, Emile Roumer, Charles F. Pressoir, Jacques Roumain, Roussau Camille, Jean Brierre, Aquah Laluah (all from Haiti), Martinique's Aimé Césaire, French Guiana's Léon Damas, and Cuba's Regino Pedrozo and Guillén. LHP, 333:5419 has the actual poems, 5420 the material on the Caribbean plus the notes on contributors. For this first edition of *The Poetry of the Negro*, Hughes also translated poems by Regino Pedrozo ("Opinions of the New Chinese Student"), as well as Léon Damas, and Jacques Roumain ("When the Tom-Tom Beats" and "Guinea" are both reprinted from Dudley's Fitts's *Anthology of Contemporary Latin-American Poetry/Antologia de la poesía americana contemporánea* (Norfolk, CT: New Directions, 1942). For a discussion of the mixed reviews of *The Poetry of the Negro*, see *Life*, 2:159–60, 397–98.

7. See, for instance, Guillén's "Conversación con Langston Hughes," which is translated in Mullen, *Langston Hughes*, 27–29. Hughes would visit Cuba for a third time in 1931.

8. "La última vez que vi a Langston Hughes fue en Nueva York, en 1949, en un congreso por la paz" (The last time I saw Langston Hughes was in New York in 1949, at a peace conference), Guillén wrote in "Recuerdo de Langston Hughes," in Guillén, *Prosa de Prisa (1929–1972, ed. Ángel Augier (Havana: Editorial Arte y Literatura, 1975),* 3:315.

9. Guillén to Hughes, July 11, 1930. What Guillén also meant had less to do with Hughes's abilities as a translator, however, than it did with Guillén's sense of Hughes as someone with potentially lucrative connections to USAmerican editors, publishers, and foundations. On November 3, 1938, as he was working on "España," Guillén expressed his desire to live in New York City for a while, and he asked Hughes about the possibility of getting a Guggenheim Fellowship. There is pencil-written note from Hughes on the letter indicating that he sent Guillén the Guggenheim announcement. Guillén returned to the topic in a letter dated December 31, 1939, in which he hoped that Hughes would support his application for the fellowship. Guillén seemed unusually insistent, even a bit desperate. He did spend two weeks in New York in March of 1949. He had been invited to the Fourth American Writers Congress to be held in New York City in early June 1942 but was denied a visa, which incensed him: "En los Estados Unidos entran todos los días escritores *fascistas* y no son molestados en lo absoluto." Guillén to Hughes, May 15, 1941; both in LHP, 70:1366.

10. On September 30, 1930, Guillen asks Hughes (again) for a copy of the number of *Opportunity* in which "Mujer Negra" appeared.

11. Hughes to Caroline Anderson, August 23, 1948, LHP 7:160.

12. Scanlon calls Hughes, for whom the relation between the African American "vernacular and poetic tradition was one of the defining concerns of his entire career," a "crucial authority in the vernacular in Anglophone culture generally." "Poets Laureate," 225–26.

13. Fernández de Castro to Hughes, February 2, 1931, LHP 61:1180; Urrutia to Hughes, March 5, 1930, LHP, 158:2926. These letters are written in English. See also Kaup, who points out that Guillén himself never mentioned any "direct influence by Hughes." She adds parenthetically, "Given the enormous affinities between Guillén and Hughes, I do not think that the controversy that has developed between Guillén and Hughes scholars over the 'Hughes prompt' theory matters much at all" ("'Our America,'" 92). I agree that the question of who had been there first matters little when it comes to an assessment of their work's quality. But it does have considerable relevance in light of the perpetually strained relations between Cuba and the USA ever since Cuba's so-called liberation in 1898 and the assumed unidirectionality of literary exchanges that persists even in diasporic theories.

14. For a fascinating history of the different usages of these terms in the colonial Americas, see Jack Forbes, *Black Africans and Native Americans: Color, Race, and Caste in the Evolution of Red-Black Peoples* (Oxford: Blackwell, 1988), chap. 3.

15. On Fitts's reputation as translator, see Venuti, *Translator's Invisibility*, 208–14.

16. Volume 16 of *The Collected Work of Langston Hughes* includes only the former three translations. It appears that the executor of Gabriela Mistral's estate did not care for Hughes's translations of Mistral's poetry and refused permission to have them reprinted in any form. This is why I decided not to write a chapter on Hughes's Mistral translations. The above volume also does not include the *Gypsy Ballads*.

17. Compare this with the story of Knopf's marketing of translations of Thomas Mann. Catherine Turner, *Marketing Modernism between the Two World Wars* (Amherst: University of Massachusetts Press, 2003), chap. 3. See also *IW*, 288.

18. Hughes wrote to Blanche Knopf on September 25, 1946: "For a while, as you probably know, you were considering publication of my translation of García Lorca's Romancero Gitano, with illustrations by Miguel Covarrubias, but that manuscript was returned to me not long ago." In a letter to Hughes from June 28 of that same year, Herbert Weinstock, then executive editor at Knopf, mentions a García Lorca project for which Knopf had no enthusiasm. LHP, 97:1828.

19. Hughes to Blanche Knopf, June 2, 1947, LHP, 97:1828.

20. Weinstock to Hughes, September 1952. On September 3 Hughes had sent Weinstock the shorter version, for non-Cuban readers, of Manuel Horrego Estuch's *Maceo, héroe y cáracter*, titled *El titán de bronce*. A note on the carbon of the rejection letter indicates that Hughes intended to offer the manuscript to Putnam next. LHP, 5:84. Although things did change in the 1960s, Maarten Steenmeijer's analyses show that the USA was rather behind European countries such as Italy and Germany when it came to introducing Hispanic American fiction. "How the West Was Won: Translations of Spanish American Fiction in Europe and the United States," in Balderston and Schwartz, *Voice-Overs*, 150.

21. See Susan Jill Levine, *Latin America: Fiction and Poetry in Translation* (New York: Center for Inter-American Relations, 1970).

22. Pierre Bourdieu, *The Field of Cultural Production: Essays on Art and Literatures* (New York: Columbia University Press, 1993), 119,164, and 79.

23. *Cuba Libre* was a pro bono project. Anderson called it "one of [their] own non-profit, cooperative projects." Anderson to Hughes, June 30, 1948, LHP, 7:160. The book won a prize for graphic design from the American Institute of Graphic Arts, but it received little other attention and did not sell well. For commentary on reviews, see *Life*, 2:159. Anderson still had copies on hand in early 1960. Anderson to Hughes, February 6, 1960. For details about marketing, expectations, and actual sales figures see the correspondence between Hughes and Caroline Anderson, head of the Ward Ritchie Press, LHP, 7:60–61.

24. Karen Jackson Ford, "Making Poetry Pay: The Commodification of Langston Hughes," in *Marketing Modernisms: Self-Promotion, Canonization, Rereading*, ed. Kevin J. H. Dettmar and Stephen Watt (Ann Arbor: University of Michigan Press, 1996), 276.

25. On August 28, 1948, Hughes mentions that he sent Anderson an address list for the book's promotion, for which he himself wrote the flyer. He adds, "You probably have thought of this, too that we send announcements to all LIBRARIES, and to the heads of Romance language, Spanish, and English Departments at all COLLEGES. Also, of course, all COLLEGE LIBRARIES." Hughes also organized an evening of readings and performances of Guillén's poetry at the Schomburg Library: "After the program I was able to dispose of every single copy of CUBA LIBRE which I had, and I would have been able to sell more had I had them on hand at the time." Hughes to Anderson, January 10, 1949, LHP, 7:161.

26. For the full text of this amendment, which became part of Cuba's Constitution in 1902, see http://www.fordham.edu/halsall/mod/1901platt.asp.

27. Guillén, *Prosa de Prisa*, 1:21.

28. A prominent example at the time was Dudley Fitts, whose massive bilingual anthology from 1942 does not include a single vernacular poem. Nor does Ortíz-Carboneres's also bilingual edition of Guillén's poems, *Yoruba from Cuba: Selected Poems/Poesías Escogidas de Nicolás Guillén* (Leeds: Peepal Tree, 2005). See Fitts's introduction for details on his approach to translating the poems he chose to include. *Anthology*, xiv–xv. See also Macha Rosenthal, "Notes on Some Afro-Cuban Translations," *Phylon* 6, no. 3 (1945): 267–72.

29. "Tuve el gusto de enviarle un pequeño folleto con mis motivos de son. Supongo también que habrá recibido un número de 'La Semana' con la entrevista que me hizo José Antonio [Fernández de Castro], y el cual le envió [Gustavo E.] Urrutia" (It is my pleasure to send you a little booklet with my Motivos de son. I also assume that you will have received an issue of *La Semana* with the interview José Antonio did with me and which Urrutia sent you). Guillén to Hughes, May 19, 1930 in Pérez Heredia, *Epistolario*, 35. In the same letter, Guillén tells Hughes, "Creo que Urrutia le envía a usted regularmente la Página Negra todos los domingos" (I believe that Urrutia is sending you the "Black Page" every Sunday). Mullen quotes (and translates) this letter from Hughes from Augier's *Nicolás Guillén: Notas para un estudio biográfico crítico* (Santa Clara, Cuba: Universidad Central de las Villas, 1964), 139–40. See Mullen, *Langston Hughes*, 30. See Guillén to Hughes, May 19, 1930. Pérez Heredia, *Epistolario*, 35. The "Página Negra" is "Ideales de una Raza," part of the Sunday Literary Supplement of *El Diario de la Marina*, which Urrutia edited.

30. "'Ayé me dijeron negro' es precioso!" Hughes wrote to Guillén on July 17, 1930. Augier, "Epistolario," 150; Pérez Heredia, *Epistolario*, 41. The poem is omitted from all later collections of Guillén's poems, including his *Obra poética, 1920–1972* (Havana: Editorial Arte y Literatura, 1975), where it is reproduced only in the notes (1:482) without any reason for its disappearance. In its place appears "Hay que tené boluntá" ("One Must Have Willpower"), another 1930 poem that was not part of the original "Motivos." *Poema-son* is Guillén's own term. It refers to a poem structurally modeled on the popular musical form of the Cuban *son*.

31. Podestá, "Cultural Liaisons," 178.

32. Rodríguez García, "Literary into Cultural Translation," 6.

33. In an argument that might be extended to ethnic texts, Astradur Eysteinsson presents the condition of marginality almost as a guarantee that certain texts, precisely because of their noninstitutionalized status, would better retain their ability to be subversive of the high-modernist mainstream. The basis for Eysteinsson's argument is his claim that "as soon as writers become more prominent members of the canon...there is clearly much less tendency to emphasize the experimental character of their works." He contends that literary experimentation "is not assumed to accord with respectability" because "[e]xperiments with language or other aesthetic media relate to a certain paranoia concerning 'authenticity.'" *Concept of Modernism*, 154. Hutchinson argues that "the very voicing of formerly suppressed speech could be an intervention in the very settled language of literature no less 'new' and disruptive than the

experiments of the avant-garde." *Harlem Renaissance*, 119. See also Sanders, *Afro-Modernist Aesthetics*.

34. Podestá, "Cultural Liaisons," 177.

35. Jonathan Gill argues that "Hughes's most significant contribution to the poetry of the Harlem Renaissance—the use of black English instead of the stilted dialect voices that had dominated Negro poetry thus far—may be seen as a typically modernist rejection of the artificial in favor of the natural." "Ezra Pound and Langston Hughes,"82.

36. Guillén, *Prosa de prisa*, 1:21.

37. Anderson to Hughes, June 30, 1948. On September 29, 1948, just as *Cuba Libre* had finally gone to press, Hughes wrote to Carruthers that *The Crisis* "is taking a double page spread of Guillén's poems (mostly your translations) with his picture and a note about him. Your Introduction (minus the last paragraph) I'm trying to place as an article somewhere, as it will help publicize the book. Maybe we can get it into the SATURDAY REVIEW." LHP, 42:726.

38. Carruthers had ended with a fawning paragraph that Hughes, to his credit, crossed out: "The justly celebrated poet, Langston Hughes, is the co-creator of this volume of translations. His was the original suggestion which led to the publication of CUBA LIBRE and it is to him that I am indebted for innumerable suggestions and valuable assistance in the selection and revision of my part of this work." Dated August 1945, received August 8, 1948, LHP, 424:9438.

39. This is the final sentence in the draft of a promotional flyer that Hughes sent to Anderson on September 20, 1948. LHP, 7:160.

40. See Hutchinson, *Harlem Renaissance*, 10.

41. Hughes to Anderson, September 20, 1948, LHP 7:160.

42. In fact, Hughes compared Guillén to Whitman when he likened the Cuban's proclivity for revising to Whitman's: "[Guillén] has made quite a few little revisions and changes—a la Walt Whitman who revised until he died." Hughes to Anderson, August 9, 1948, LHP 7:160.

43. Ramón Guirao, *Órbita de la poesía afrocubana, 1928–1937 (antología)* (Havana: Talleres de Ucar, 1938), 85. Carruthers translated "Me bendo caro" as "High-Priced Now." The eight original "Motivos" were "Negro bembón" ("Thick-Lipped Cullud Boy"), "Mi chiquita" ("My Gal"), "Búcate plata" ("No, Sirrie!"), "Sigue" ("Pass on By"), "Ayé me dijeron negro" ("Last Night Someone Called Me Darky"), "Tú no sabe inglé" ("Don't Know No English"), "Si tú supiera" (omitted), and "Mulata" ("High Brown"). The translations in parentheses are Carruthers's versions of the poems' titles. Guillén retitled "Si tú supiera" (If only you knew) "Sóngoro consongo" when he included it in *Sóngoro cosongo: Poemas mulatos* (Havana, 1931), his first collection of poems to appear in book form. It may have been omitted from *Cuba Libre* because the repeated phrase *sóngoro cosongo* and its variations, usually read as *jitanjáfora*, made it particularly resistant to translation. But this would have been equally true of "Sensemayá," which Carruthers did translate for *Cuba Libre*. For a reading of "Sóngoro cosongo," see Roberto González Echevarría, "Guillén as Baroque: Meaning in *Motivos de Son*," *Callaloo* 10, no. 2 (1987): 312ff.

44. Blanche Knopf wrote to Hughes on October 2, 1946, "I do not believe, also, there is anything in the poems by Nicolás Guillén for us." LHP, 97:1830). John Farrar returned the manuscript on April 21, 1947, commenting, "I am afraid, alas, that it does not seem to make sense from a broad publishing point of view and I am sorry." LHP, 61:1158. See Hughes's remark to Anderson from September 29, 1948. "We were originally thinking of a university press as a possible publishers [*sic*]." LHP, 7:160.

45. Carruthers had written a thesis on the Cuban mulatto poet Plácido (Gabriel de la Concepción Valdés) in 1941. He taught Spanish at Atlanta University and Howard and later worked in public relations for the Venezuelan government. Hughes had envisioned a primarily

academic audience for *Cuba Libre* at an earlier stage of the project, when he had hoped to do this book with a university press.

46. Urrutia to Hughes, March 5, 1930, LHP, 158:2926. Urrutia's letters to Hughes were mostly written in English.

47. Guillén to Hughes, April 21, 1930, LHP, 70:1366.

48. Rampersad seems to be under the impression that Guillén asserted a direct link between his own poetry and that of Hughes in this brief article. What Guillén actually wrote, however, is less unequivocal: "[S]in ser el son igual al *blues* ni no existir semejanza entre Cuba y el Sur de los Estados Unidos, es a mi juicio una forma adecuada para lograr poemas vernáculos, acaso porque ésa sea también actualmente nuestra música representativa" ([W]ithout either the *son* being equal to the blues, or even Cuba and the South of the United States being similar places, the *son*, in my view, is an appropriate form in which to write vernacular poems, perhaps because it is also, in fact, our most representative music). Guillén, *Prosa de prisa*, 1:20).

49. See the respective introductions in James Weldon Johnson, ed., *The Book of American Negro Poetry* (1922; repr., New York: Harcourt Brace Jovanovich, 1969), and Countee Cullen, ed., *Caroling Dusk: An Anthology of Verse by Negro Poets* (New York, Harper and Brothers, 1927). *Southern Road* is in many respects a better point of comparison for Guillén's *Motivos* than is Hughes's verse. See also Hutchinson, *Harlem Renaissance*, 111ff. On differences between Hughes and Brown (that is, vaudeville blues vs. country blues, work songs, and folk ballads), see Sanders, *Afro-Modernist Aesthetics*, 32–33.

50. Johnson, "Negro with a Big N," quoted in Miriam Thaggert, *Images of Black Modernism: Verbal and Visual Strategies of the Harlem Renaissance* (Amherst: University of Massachusetts Press, 2010), 46. Thaggert analyzes Johnson's positions on Negro dialect in his prefaces to *The Book of American Negro Poetry* and *The Book of American Negro Spirituals* (1923). See 31–51. For an argument about Dunbar's dialect poetry as part of the genealogy of modernism, see Geoffrey Jacques, *A Change in the Weather* (Amherst: University of Massachusetts Press, 2009), 83.

51. See North, *Dialect of Modernism*.

52. Miller, "Gypsy Rhythm," 331–32, attributes to both a poem, "Song of the Cuban Drum," that was actually translated entirely by Carruthers but with a different title: "Song of the Bongo." See LHP, 424:9431.

53. Carruthers contacted Hughes on October 4, 1941, including his thesis abstract with the letter. He also sent Hughes "a few translations from Cuban Negro poets and from two white poets, Estenguer and Portuondo writing in the Afro-Cuban idiom." He also mentions that he had translated Regino Pedrozo's "Hermano negro." At the time, he was likely back at Howard. LHP, 42:726.

54. Letter from Ben Carruthers quoted in John F. Matheus, "Langston Hughes as Translator," in *Langston Hughes, Black Genius: A Critical Evaluation*, ed. Therman B. O'Daniel (New York: William Morrow, 1971), 165.

55. Carruthers to Hughes, October 4, 1941, LHP, 42:726.

56. Anderson to Hughes, June 17, 1948. Hughes replied to Anderson on July 8, 1948, "I've...seen a couple of big articles about [Guillén's] work in Latin magazines recently. Certainly I feel that he is a poet whom we should know better in the U.S.A." LHP, 7:160.

57. "The Poetry Bulletin: Review of *Cuba Libre*," *Tiger's Eye*, March 1, 1949, 116.

58. LHP, 424:9430 (my emphases). The original lines are "poqque tu boca e bien grande / y tu pasa, colorá."

59. Matheus, "Langston Hughes as Translator," 165.

60. The draft manuscripts of *Cuba Libre* show that Carruthers was the one who worked on the "Motivos de son" and other *poemas-son*. In the manuscript versions of *Cuba Libre*, each poem is signed with the translator's initials, either L.H. or B.C.

61. Spicer, for instance, simply places Guillén's poems side by side with her own English translations instead of offering literary analysis. See "The Blues and the Son."

62. Venuti, *Scandals*, 98.

63. This would be true in reverse as well, and the demand for a nonstandard version of Hispanic American Spanish in translations of USAmerican Negro dialect is as problematic. See Soto, "Translation as Understanding," 15–16.

64. Hughes's own books, all in hardcover editions since there was little paperback publishing as the time, retailed for $2.00 to $2.50 (*The Weary Blues*, for instance, retailed for $2.00 in 1945 and *One-Way Ticket* for $2.50 in 1949). Hughes to Joseph Levin, Knopf Order Department, March 25, 1945, and January 25, 1949, LHP, 4:77.

65. Anderson to Hughes, June 30, 1948, LHP, 7:160–61. For information about New Directions, see Morris, "A Taste of Fortune: *In the Money* and Williams's New Directions Phase," in Dettmar and Watt, *Marketing Modernisms*, 161–87.

66. The poem is reprinted in the notes to Guillén, *Obra poética*, 1:482.

67. See González Echevarría, "Guillén as Baroque," 311. The poem can also be read as a descendant of the popular "¿De dónde son los cantantes?," a *son* about the origins of the *son* and of those who sing it. In a sense, all *sones* are about origins, including that mother of all *sones*, "El son de la Ma Teodora."

68. Charles Johnson, *Oxherding Tale* (Bloomington: Indiana University Press, 1982), 152.

69. Sere Kutzinski, *Sugar's Secrets*, 163–64.

70. Ramón Guirao, ed., *Órbita de la poesía afrocubana, 1928–1937 (antología)* (Havana: Talleres de Ucar, 1938), 9–10.

71. Guillén, *Obra poética*, 1:114.

72. *Choteo* means playful mockery or jest, a form of trickery that might be traced back to the picaresque. Its ritual character also makes it comparable to the USAfrican American play of the dozens. The classic work on the Cuban *choteo* is Jorge Mañach's *Indagación del choteo* from 1928 (rev. ed. Havana: Editorial Libro Cubano, 1955). See also Gustavo Pérez Firmat, "Riddles of the Sphincter: Another Look at the Cuban *Choteo*," *Diacritics* 14, no. 4 (1984): 67–77.

73. Clayton Eshleman and Annette Smith were among the few who dared render Aimé Césaire's "nègre," in his *Cahier d'un retour au pays natal*, as "nigger." *Aimé Césaire: The Collected Poetry* (Berkeley: University of California Press, 1983), 27. See also Edwards, *Practice of Diaspora*, 25–43. Nella Larsen's novel *Passing* (1929; repr., New York: Penguin, 1997), 39–40, features a comparable, though much more highly charged, use of the epithet "nig."

74. N.d., LHP, 425:9434. In José Juan Arrom's introduction to Lloyd Mallan's "Little Anthology of Afro-Cuban Poetry," "negro bembón" is rendered as "niggah-lips." "Afro-Cuban Poetry," in Mallan, "A Little Anthology of Afro-Cuban Poetry," *New Directions 1944, Number 8*, edited by James McLaughlin (Norfolk, CT: New Directions, 1944), 270. The translation appears to be Mallan's.

75. McLaughlin, ed., *New Directions 1944*, xvi.

76. Mallan, "A Little Anthology," 287–92.

77. I am using boldface and strikethroughs to represent Hughes's handwritten revisions to the typed manuscript.

78. Anderson to Hughes, n.d., "Saturday" (1948), LHP, 7:160.

79. Hughes to Anderson, September 29, 1948, LHP, 7:160.

80. See also Carruthers's "adaptation" of Rafael Estenguer's poem "Colloquio" ("Conversation") in McLaughlin, *New Directions 1944*, 293.

81. Mallan, "Little Anthology," 270.

82. Only the plural *nietos* can encompass both genders.

83. See Kutzinski, *Sugar's Secrets*.

84. In the obituary he published in *Granma* shortly after Hughes's death in 1967, Guillén wrote: "¿Hablaba él [Hughes] español? Pues sí, pero como hablan sus numerosos idiomas los marineros (y él lo había sido). Lo conocía mejor de lectura, y podía traducirlo sin dificultad." *Prosa de prisa*, 3:314. (Did he speak Spanish? Of course, but like a sailor speaks it (and he had been a sailor). His reading abilities were better, and he could translate without any problems).

85. Urrutia to Hughes, April 20, 1930, LHP, 158:2926.

86. Guillén to Hughes, April 21, 1930, LHP, 17:1366; Augier, "Epistolario," 148; Pérez Heredia, *Epistolario*, 27. Augier published thirteen Guillén-Hughes letters in 1995–96, six of which are reprinted in Pérez Heredia's edition. Language is an issue to which Guillén returns again on May 19, 1930, when he asks if Hughes liked the "Motivos" and again expresses concerns about his ability to understand them since they are "escritos en el lenguaje popular de Cuba" (written in Cuba's popular idiom). See also *Life*, 1:180–81, and Guillén, *Páginas vueltas. Memorias* (Havana: Ediciones Unión, 1982), 105.

87. Hughes to Guillén, July 17, 1930. Augier, "Epistolario," 150; Pérez Heredia, *Epistolario*, 41.

88. Anderson to Hughes, n.d. "Thursday," 1948; Hughes to Anderson, August 30, 1948, LHP, 7:160.

89. Guillén to Hughes, July 11, 1930, LHP, 70:1366.

90. Guillén to Hughes, September 30, 1930. In an earlier letter to Hughes, from July 11, 1930, Guillén alludes to Fernández de Castro's "Oye muchacho," a translation of a chapter from the novel *Not Without Laughter*, which was published in the *Revista de La Habana* 3, nos. 1–2 (July–August 1930): 77–84.

91. Guillén to Hughes, September 30, 1930, LHP, 70:1366.

92. Fernández de Castro to Hughes, February 2, 1930, LHP, 61:1179; Urrutia to Hughes, LHP 158:2926.

93. Guillén to Hughes, January 28, 1949, LHP, 70:1366.

94. He did write one for Roumain, however: "Elegía a Jacques Roumain" (1948). Guillén, *Obra poética*, 1:403). See also Cobb, *Harlem*, 139. On Hughes and Roumain, see De-Jongh, *Vicious Modernism*, 65–66.

95. *Diario de la Marina*, April 27, 1930.

96. Jean-Jacques Lecercle, *The Violence of Language* (London: Routledge, 1990), 229. Stephanides has remarked that translation calls attention to the fact that "[n]ationalism suppresses the process of creolization or syncretization in the construction of the nations, and naturalizes what it has invented to give purity and homogeneity to its narrative." "Translation and Ethnography," 301.

97. According to Roman Jakobson, a verbal sign "may be translated into other signs of the same language, into another language, or into another, non-verbal system of symbols." "On Linguistic Aspects of Translation," in *Language in Literature*, ed. Krystyna Pomorska and Stephen Rudy (Cambridge, MA: Harvard University Press, 1987), 114.

98. So was Carl Van Vechten; see his introduction to *The Weary Blues*.

99. This may well be the reason why Scanlon speculates that it is "difficult to find a systematic account of the term in any field; nor does there seem much awareness of interest in a particular field in the term's functioning in others. Instead, 'vernacular' seems to mark a place where disciplines allow themselves to become a bit less than systematic, less than disciplined, where they aspire to speak of what lies beyond them, the unlearned, the prediscipinary, the nondisciplinary, or antidisciplinary, to get beyond their own learned boundaries and speak from it and with it." "Poets Laureate," 200.

100. Fiona Somerset and Nicholas Watson, eds., *The Vulgar Tongue: Medieval and Postmedieval Vernacularity* (University Park: Pennsylvania State University Press, 2003), x (my emphasis).

101. Ibid., ix. Scanlon has pointed out that "the African-American literary tradition is the first Anglophone tradition to originate in a condition of enslavement," so "(b)y a weird and sobering irony, applying 'vernacular' to that tradition [as Houston Baker has done] literally returns the term to its original Latin roots." "Poets Laureate," 226.

102. Somerset and Watson, *Vulgar Tongue*, ix.

103. See Coco Fusco, *English Is Broken Here: Notes on Cultural Fusion in the Americas* (New York: New Press, 1995).

104. See Fernando Ortiz, *Los negros brujos: Hampa afro-cubana.*

105. Ette, *ZwischenWeltenSchreiben*, 109.

106. The result is a misrepresentation of how Bito Manué would have pronounced "strike one, and one, two, three"—which might have been better represented as "estraike uan and uan, tu, tree" to capture the suggestion that what is being spoken here is not English, and certainly not any standard English, but what might be represented as "Inglish," something in between English and Spanish.

107. Roberto González Echevarría, *The Pride of Havana: A History of Cuban Baseball* (New York: Oxford University Press, 2001), 258, 288–89.

108. See *Loving v. Virginia*, 388 U.S. 1 (1967). In 1967, Virginia and fifteen other states still had statutes that outlawed interracial marriage: Alabama, Arkansas, Delaware, Florida, Georgia, Kentucky, Louisiana, Mississippi, Missouri, North Carolina, Oklahoma, South Carolina, Tennessee, Texas, and West Virginia. The first state that had recognized that the miscegenation statutes violated the Equal Protection Clause was the Supreme Court of California in *Perez v. Sharp*, 32 Cal. 2d 711, 198 P.2d 17 (1948).

109. Lisa Brock and Digna Castaneda Fuertes, eds., *Between Race and Empire: African-Americans and Cubans before the Cuban Revolution* (Philadelphia: Temple University Press, 1998), 9–10.

110. Lisa Brock and Bijan Bayne write, "But there were before 1959, and still are today, Afro-Cubans who, while recognizing USAmerican racism to be blunt and brutish, find the island's more subtle forms of racism equally if not more distressing. For these Cubans, the assertiveness of American blacks, provoked by an overt and unabashed USAmerican racism, is preferable to the undermined sense of self created by the more hidden Cuban racism." "Not Just Black: African-Americans, Cubans, and Baseball," in Brock and Castaneda Fuertes, *Between Race and Empire*, 168.

111. Louis Pérez, "Between Baseball and Bullfighting: The Quest for Nationality in Cuba, 1888–1898," *Journal of American History* 81 (September 1994): 494.

112. Brock and Bayne, "Not Just Black," 169.

113. Both are quoted in Brock and Bayne, "Not just Black," 185–86. The occasion was Gómez's joining the Washington Senators in 1944.

114. Brock and Bayne, "Not Just Black," 184.

115. See *Sugar* (Sony Classics, 2008) directed by Anna Boden and Ryan Fleck, http://www.sonyclassics.com/sugar/. "For most North Americans," Brock and Bayne comment, "Cubans were feminized colonial subjects, and as long as the island remained tightly under US(American) control and their 'racial mixing' was contained there, white Americans felt little to fear from an occasional Cuban playing in a white team." "Not Just Black," 191.

116. See Eric Rise, *The Martinsville Seven: Race Rape and Capital Punishment* (Charlottesville: University Press of Virginia, 1995). Guillén mentions the Martinsville Seven in his "Elegía a Jesús Menéndez," *Obra poética*, 1:432–33.

117. See Bhabha, "The Third Space," 307.

118. Max Hecker, ed., *Goethe: Maximen und Reflexionen* (Weimar: Verlag der Goethe-Gesellschaft, 1907), 56.

119. Roberto Márquez's English version of Guillén's poem, entitled "Yu Don't Know No English," adds yet another variation with its distinctly anglophone Caribbean tone and inflections: "The American's looking for yu, / An' yu gots to hide from she." *My Last Name and Other Poems / El apellido y otros poemas y/ de Nicolás Guillén* (London: Mango Publishing, 2002), 49. While Carruthers's cultural and historical context demands a warning about race relations in the USA, the context in Márquez's translation more plausibly speaks to the inherent uncertainties in romances such as the one between a USAmerican tourist and the Jamaican bellboy depicted in Terry McMillan popular novel *How Stella Got Her Groove Back* (1996). See also Hughes's "Brothers" (1924): "You're related—you and I, / You're from the West Indies, / I from Kentucky."*CP*, 424.

120. Venuti, *Translator's Invisibility,* 203.

121. Venuti, *Scandals,* 11.

122. Benjamin, *Gesammelte Schriften* IV, 20; Venuti, *Scandals,* 189.

123. Spengler's *Der Untergang des Abendlandes* is surely behind phrasings such as "morsche Schranken der eigenen Sprache" (decaying barriers of his own language), quoted in Benjamin, *Gesammelte Schriften* IV, 19.

124. Venuti ends *The Translator's Invisibility* with the laudable statement that "translation strategies can be defined as 'foreignizing' or 'domesticating' only in relation to specific cultural situations, specific moments in the changing reception of a foreign literature, or in the changing hierarchy of domestic values" (272). In later work he does not seem to heed his own advice as much as one would have hoped.

125. See note 50 in the introduction. See also Stephen Kinzer, "America Yawns at Foreign Fiction," *New York Times,* July 16, 2003.

126. The phrase is Michel de Certeau's, or more accurately, that of his translator, Steven Rendall, in *The Practice of Everyday Life* (Berkeley: University of California Press, 1988), 32.

127. On cultural pluralism see Hutchinson, *Harlem Renaissance,* 78–93.

128. Dudley Fitts, "The Poetic Nuance" (1958), quoted in Venuti, *Translator's Invisibility,* 211. Venuti comments that "Fitts's work as a translator and as an editor and reviewer makes quite clear that the innovations of modernist translation were the casualty of the transparent discourse that dominated Anglo-American literary culture" (214).

129. Several translations appear in both collections: "Cane" ("Caña"), "Dead Soldier" ("Soldado muerto"), "Two Weeks" ("Dos semanas"), "Proposition" (?), "Barren Stone" ("Piedra púlida"), "Federico," "Wake for Papa Montero" ("Velorio de Papá Montero"), and "Sightseers in a Courtyard." The latter is Hughes's version of Guillén's "Visita a un solar," which Fitts translates as "Visit to a Tenement." *Anthology,* 255. The versions of the translations in these two volumes are identical, except for an omitted line in "Barren Stone" as it appears in *Cuba Libre* (97). The line was probably omitted because it would have made the poem just slightly too long for one page.

130. Fitts, *Anthology,* 251; *CL,* 37.

131. Fitts, *Anthology,* 261.

132. Ibid., 260. The version of this stanza reprinted in Guillén's *Obra poética,* 1:125, no longer includes the exclamation marks.

133. There are four drafts of this translation in LHP, 424:9430, each with significant changes.

134. Mallan, "Little Anthology," 274.

135. Venuti, *Scandals,* 12.

136. Fitts, *Anthology,* 253.

137. Guillén, *Obra poética,* 1:201.

138. See Lecercle, *Violence of Language,* esp. 182ff.

139. Hughes had met first Mistral in Madrid during the 1930s.

140. According to Nwankwo, Hughes's translations in *Cuba Libre* show that he "was absolutely committed to conceptualizing and actualizing a transnational Black collectivism." "Langston Hughes," 60. She musters no evidence to support this claim.

141. These drawings are not, as Nwankwo argues in "Langston Hughes," 67–68, replacements for Guillén's own hand-drawn illustrations in the first volume of *Obra poética* for the simple reason that that volume was not published until 1974, seven years after Hughes's death.

142. On Vallejo's often vexing orthographical, syntactic, and typographical inventions, see Jean Franco, *César Vallejo: The Dialectics of Poetry and Silence* (Cambridge: Cambridge University Press, 1976), 96ff.

143. In his New York Public Library lecture of 1964, Alfred Knopf does not even mention Hughes as a Knopf author. But he does mention Van Vechten, who clearly brought Hughes into the fold. *Publishing Then and Now*, 14.

144. Anderson (Mrs. Trench R. Fogle) to Hughes, February 6, 1960, LHP 7:160.

145. Bernard Smith to Hughes, February 15, 1938, LHP 4:72.

146. Western Union night letter to Anderson, December 16, 1948, LHP 7:160.

147. On January 27, 1949, Hughes reported to the good news to Carruthers. LHP 7:160.

148. Hughes to Guillén, January 31, 1949. Guillén's *El son entero* had just been published in Buenos Aires in what Hughes called a "de luxe edition." Hughes to Anderson, August 9, 1948, LHP, 70:1366.

149. Hughes to Anderson, January 27, 1949, LHP 7:160.

150. Guillén to Hughes, August 7, 1931, LHP 70:1366.

151. In a letter dated July 19, 1952, to Lautaro concerning payment for the fifty copies of *Poemas de Langston Hughes* they had sent him, Hughes complains that his bank seems unable to translate the amount of pesos on the invoice into dollars. LHP, 58:1101.

152. Hughes to Guillén, May 5, 1951, details the breakdown. The money is sent to Guillén on May 7, and he acknowledges receipt of it on June 6. Guillén and Regino Pedrozo also received royalties ($2.50 per poem) from Doubleday for the poems in translation published in Hughes and Bontemps's anthology. See Hughes to Guillén, September 12, 1948, LHP 70:1366.

153. Joseph C. Lesser to Hughes, April 30, 1937, LHP, 5:72, and statement of January 31, 1950, LHP, 5:82.

154. Anderson to Hughes, July 27, 1948, LHP, 7:160.

155. Hughes to Anderson, August 9, 1948. "We have a beautiful gold stamped red-sealed Cuban government approved agreement with Guillén for the publication of his poems in this country under which royalties are shared with him." Hughes to Anderson, July 8, 1948, LHP, 7:160. Apparently Hughes did not keep the original document, only a carbon.

156. See Ford, "Making Poetry Pay," 275; also *Life* II, 133.

157. Ford, "Making Poetry Pay"; see also Elizabeth Davey, "Building a Black Audience in the 1930s: Langston Hughes, Poetry Readings, and the Golden Stair Press," in *Print Culture in a Diverse America*, ed. James Philip Danky and Wayne A. Wiegand (Urbana: University of Illinois Press, 1998), 223–43.

158. Hughes quoted in Davey, "Building a Black Audience," 224.

5. BACK IN THE USSA

1. James Smethurst, *The New Red Negro: The Literary Left and African American Poetry, 1930–1946* (New York: Oxford University Press, 1999), 93.

2. Noteworthy exceptions are Robert Young, "Langston Hughes's Red Poetics and the Practice of 'Disalienation,'" in *Montage of a Dream: The Art and Life of Langston Hughes*, ed. John Edgar Tidwell and Cheryl R. Ragar (Columbia: University of Missouri Press, 2007),

135–46; Smethurst, *New Red Negro;* Dawahare, *Nationalism, Marxism, and African American Literature;* Michael Denning, *The Cultural Front: The Laboring of American Culture in the Twentieth Century* (London: Verso, 1996); Cary Nelson, *Revolutionary Memory: Recovering the Poetry of the American Left* (London: Routledge, 2001); Robert Shulman, *The Power of Political Art: The 1930s Literary Left Reconsidered* (Chapel Hill: University of North Carolina Press, 2000); and Alan Wald, ed., *Writing from the Left: New Essays on Radical Culture and Politics* (London: Verso, 1994).

3. See Nelson, *Revolutionary Memory.* Chapter 1 is entitled, "Modern Poems We Have Wanted to Forget." Faith Berry's *Good Morning Revolution: Uncollected Writings of Social Protest* (Secaucus, NJ: Carol Pub. Group, 1992), first published in1973, is an exception, but it does not, for instance, include "One More 'S' in the U.S.A." Breaking open the USAmerican canon seems not to have extended yet to Communist writers. See Wald, *Writing from the Left,* 69.

4. The McCarthy Committee had nothing to worry about when it came to the image of the USA that Hughes's poems in translation represented to Latin Americans. Only one of the poems to which the committee objected, "Good Morning, Revolution," was ever translated; it was printed once in the journal *Nueva Cultura* in 1936, never to surface again. See Miguel Alejandro, "Buenos días, revolución," *Nueva Cultura* 2 (January 1936): 154–57.

5. Although Joseph McCarthy became chair of this particular Senate subcommittee only in 1953, to be followed by John McClellan in 1955, McCarthyism, as the term is popularly used, dates back to McCarthy's announcement in the early 1950s that he had a list of Communist subversives who were working in the State Department. The House Committee on Un-American Activities (HUAC), which came to target the entertainment industry in 1947, was formed in 1938 under the leadership of Texas Democrat Martin Dies, Jr. as the Dies Committee. See Ted Morgan, *Reds: McCarthyism in Twentieth-Century America* (New York: Random House, 2004), chap. 8, for further details. The first permanent congressional committee established to investigate subversive activities in 1945, HUAC remained in existence until 1975. It is ironic that McCarthy acquired his Senate seat with the help of Communist organizations in Wisconsin. See David Oshinsky, *A Conspiracy So Immense: The World of Joe McCarthy* (New York: Oxford University Press, 2005), 47.

6. Nelson, *Revolutionary Memory,* 67, 68.

7. See, for instance, Morgan, *Reds;* Thomas C. Reeves, *McCarthyism* (Hinsdale, IL: Dryden Press, 1973); and Ellen Schrecker, *Many Are the Crimes: McCarthyism in America* (Princeton: Princeton University Press, 1998). For a different perspective, see William F. Buckley and L. Brent Bozell, *McCarthy and His Enemies: The Record and Its Meaning* (Chicago: H. Regnery Co., 1954).

8. Nicholas von Hoffman, *Citizen Cohn* (New York: Doubleday, 1988), 164; Morgan, *Reds,* xiv. For the version of McCarthy's incendiary speech in Wheeling, West Virginia, on February 9, 1950, see Albert Fried, ed., *McCarthyism: The Great American Red Scare: A Documentary History* (New York: Oxford University Press, 1997), 78–80. The text of the speech is available at http://us.history.wisc.edu/hist102/pdocs/mccarthy_wheeling.pdf. For an early study that challenges the idea that McCarthyism came from "agrarian radical roots," see Michael Paul Rogin, *The Intellectuals and McCarthy* (Cambridge, MA: M.I.T. Press, 1967).

9. See Morgan, *Reds,* 431ff.; Martin H. Redish, *The Logic of Persecution: Free Expression and the McCarthy Era* (Stanford, CA: Stanford University Press, 2005), 24ff.

10. Redish, *Logic,* 4; also 72ff.

11. Ibid., 25; also 99.

12. United States Senate, *Executive Sessions of the Senate Permanent Subcommittee on Investigations of the Committee on Government Operations, 83rd Congress, First Session, 1953,* ed. Donald A. Ritchie, 5 vols. (Washington, DC: U.S. Government Printing Office, 1953–54).

The complete set is available at http://www.access.gpo.gov/congress/senate/senate12cp107. html. Hughes's complete testimony is in 2: 973–98. The records of the closed-door hearings of HUAC are still sealed.

13. Morgan, *Reds*, 430.

14. See Redish, *Logic*, 37–44.

15. On the investigation of the so-called Hollywood Ten, see Redish, *Logic*, 137ff. See also Victor S. Navasky, *Naming Names* (New York: Penguin, 1980), pt. 1.

16. There is a passing reference to the secret testimony in "Simple Speaks His Mind before the McCarthy Committee," a one-page commentary Hughes wrote in 1954 and sent to Arthur P. Davis and Charles S. Johnson, among others. See LHP, 365:5863). See also Donna Harper, *Not So Simple: The "Simple" Stories by Langston Hughes* (Columbia: University of Missouri Press, 1995), 158. There seems to be some persistent confusion among scholars about which committee actually subpoenaed Hughes. See, for example, Dawahare, *Nationalism*, 92, and Peddie, "There's No Way," 41. Hughes never appeared before HUAC.

17. Hughes sent a wire to McCarthy on March 22, 1953: "The space apparently provided in the subpoena to inform me why my presence is required is entirely blank. I therefore do not know and have not been informed why or what you wish to question me about." Carbon and actual wire in LHP, 109:2030.

18. Jim Tuck claims that the committee's aim was "to enlist the poet as a guide on how to expunge the works of 'subversive' Hughes and replace them with those of the 'patriotic' Hughes." *McCarthyism and New York's Hearst Press: A Study of Roles in the Witch Hunt* (Lanham, MD: University Press of America, 1995), 190.

19. This series, which began on March 6, 1943, is reproduced in its entirety in Christopher de Santis, *Langston Hughes and the Chicago Defender: Essays on Race, Politics, and Culture, 1942–62* (Urbana: University of Illinois Press, 1995), 161–90.

20. See William Beyer, "Langston Hughes and Common Ground in the 1940s," *American Studies in Scandinavia* 23 (1991): 41.

21. Hughes, "Are You a Communist?" in de Santis, *Langston Hughes and the Chicago Defender*, 181.

22. LHP, 365:5861 includes two pages of typewritten notes that describe the origin of the charges of Communism against Hughes. See also *Life*, 2:140–43.

23. LHP, 365:5861 has an excerpt from the *Capitol City News*, dated March 6, 1948, that reads, "A letter was sent even to Congressman Richard Vail, a member of the committee on Un-American Activities, who wrote from Washington, D.C., 'The House Committee on Un-American Activities has never arrived at the conclusion that Langston Hughes is a self-confessed Communist.'" The committee had earlier accused Hughes of being a member of the Communist Party, at which point Hughes suggested that "they check with the F.B.I.," which did not share this belief. De Santis, *Langston Hughes and the Chicago Defender*, 181).

24. Smethurst, *New Red Negro*, 163.

25. In a letter to Caroline Anderson from August 9, 1948, Hughes mentions a bit coyly that he, like Guillén, does not expect to make a living from writing poetry. LHP 7:160. In fact, however, Hughes was one of the few African American poets who did succeed in doing precisely that. See Ford, "Making Poetry Pay," 275. See also *Life*, 2:133.

26. For accounts of Hughes's public hearing, see Berry, *Langston Hughes*, 315ff.; *Life*, 2:213–19; also Hoffmann, *Citizen Cohn*, 155–59; Morgan, *Reds*, 442.

27. At the public hearing, Cohn explained to McCarthy that "we went into them [a number of writings] with Mr. Hughes in executive session." PT, 79.

28. Jeff Woods, *Black Struggle, Red Scare: Segregation and Anti-Communisms in the South, 1948–1968* (Baton Rouge: LSU Press, 2004), 25. The records indicate that three Democratic members of this bipartisan subcommittee—McClellan, Henry M. Jackson (Washington),

and Stuart Symington (Missouri)—were typically absent from its closed proceedings, but they were clearly present during at least some of its public hearings.

29. Roumain was imprisoned for his Communist activities in 1934. Hughes protested and demanded his release in the *New Republic*. See Gardullo, "Heading Out," 62.

30. Hughes stated earlier in the hearing that he "completely broke with the Soviet ideology" "roughly 4 or 5 years ago." When questioned further by Cohn about statements he had made in 1949, Hughes acceded to the suggestion that "your complete change in ideology came about 1950": "I would say certainly by 1950: yes." PT, 74–75.

31. *Life*, 2:218. See also Tuck, who sees Hughes as "a fondly welcomed prodigal son." *McCarthyism*, 190.

32. Berry, *Langston Hughes*, 318.

33. From the public testimony: McCarthy agreed with Cohn that "in deference to Mr. Hughes, there are a number of writings of his written during this period of time...which I frankly think should not be read to the public" because "some of them use words and terms that would not be too good" and because "we went into them with Mr. Hughes in executive session." PT, 79. The deal with McCarthy apparently involved an agreement that "Hughes' most inflammatory poems would not be read aloud—unlike the work of other authors who dared to resist the subcommittee." *Life*, 2:213.

34. Berry, *Langston Hughes*, 318.

35. One of them was the Mississippi Democrat James Oliver Eastland, "the quintessential southern red- and black-baiter" who would become chairman of the Senate Judiciary Committee in 1956. " 'Just as Joseph McCarthy saw a Red behind every government door,' one witness called before SISS commented, 'Eastland saw a Red behind every Black.' " Woods, *Black Struggle*, 43. See also Griffin Fariello, *Red Scare: Memories of the American Inquisition: An Oral History* (New York: Norton, 1995), 469ff., and Brandon Toropov, *Encyclopedia of Cold War Politics* (New York: Facts on File, 2000), 53.

36. Cohn was likely referring to a HUAC hearing. Supposedly, the professional government witnesses Manning Johnson and Louis Budenz, who also testified at the *Dennis* trial, had named Hughes in 1953. Navasky, *Naming Names*, 191–92. LHP, 365:5861, includes a four-page rebuttal from one Dr. Watson to an American Legion pamphlet denouncing Watson and, implicitly, Hughes. Of particular interest is the following sentence from the pamphlet: "*At the time, Dr. Watson knew that Hughes was a Communist, for he had so testified under oath before HSC on April 1, 1943.*" In the *Report of the Joint Fact-Finding Committee to the 1948 Regular California Legislature, Sacramento*, Hughes is named—"together with such well-known Communists" as Mary McLeod Bethune, J. R. Brodsky, and Theodore Dreiser, among others—as a signatory of the January 1943 Message to the House of Representatives opposing the Dies Committee investigating un-American activities in the USA. LHP, 365:5862 includes "Material refuting charges of Langston Hughes as a member if the Communist Party." Most of the documents collected here are from 1947 and early 1948, but some go back to 1945.

37. *Daily Worker*, April 2, 1934; not reprinted until *CP*. Berry notes that this poem "would later be 'sung' into the Senate Record by Senator Albert Hawkes as proof of Hughes's Communist sympathies." Berry, *Langston Hughes*, 316; see also Dawahare, *Nationalism*, 107–8.

38. First published in *New Masses* (1932); also mentioned in Hughes's public testimony.

39. First published in *Anvil* (1933) and later included in *A New Song* (1938).

40. First published in *Poetry* (1926) and later included in *Fine Clothes*. This poem was mentioned to accuse Hughes of disrespect for Jews. ST, 993.

41. At the public hearing, Cohn informed Hughes that this book was in libraries in Tel-Aviv, Singapore, Hong Kong, and Kuala-Lumpur at that time. PT, 76. McCarthy viewed libraries abroad largely as tools for pro-USAmerican propaganda. Oshinsky, *Conspiracy*, 278. Cohn's ideas on censorship are worth quoting:

Were we book burners? In a way, I guess we were. Confronted with more than thirty thousand works by Communists, fellow-travelers and unwitting promoters of the Soviet cause on the shelves of America's overseas libraries, we decided to do something about it. The whole purpose of these libraries and reading rooms was to sell America to Western Europe, that's what we were paying for. One could argue—but how many liberals did?—that this in itself was wrong, was jingoistic, was playing the Ugly American. But having made the decision to fight for the minds of men during the Cold War, why lead with our chin? Why beat up on America and extol totalitarianism? This wasn't the New York Public Library we were talking about, where free circulation of ideas is the reigning virtue. Our job, on behalf of the McCarthy committee, was to see that the taxpayers weren't footing the bill for anti-American propaganda. The issue was salesmanship, not censorship. (Cohn and Sidney Zion, *The Autobiography of Roy Cohn* [Secaucus, NJ: Lyle Stuart, 1988], 95)

For an account of Cohn and Schine's trip to inspect libraries in Europe in April 1953, see Roy Cohn, *McCarthy* (New York: New American Library, 1968), 76–78; Richard Rovere, *Senator Joe McCarthy* (New York: Harper & Row, 1973), 199–205; and Oshinsky, *Conspiracy*, 279.

42. Smethurst notes that Cohn did not discuss anything from *Montage of A Dream Deferred* (1951), even though *Montage* was hardly the portrait of the steadily improving race relations in which Hughes claimed to believe under Cohn's questioning. See *New Red Negro*, 226.

43. The flyer is reproduced in Nelson, *Revolutionary Memory*, 67 (figure 19).

44. I am quoting the poem from the transcript, here and below, in which it differs from the version in *CP* 166.

45. Hughes's reply is consistent with what he had written in 1941 in "Concerning 'Goodbye, Christ,'" a response to the poem's unauthorized reprints and the flyer mentioned above: "The I which I pictured was the newly liberated peasant of the state collectives I had seen in Russia merged with those American Negro workers of the depression period who believed in the Soviet dream and the hope it held out for a solution of their racial and economic difficulties. (Just as the *I* pictured in many of my blues poems is the poor and uneducated Negro of the South—and not myself who grew up in Kansas)." *Essays*, 208.

46. Hughes had ended his 1941 essay on the poem with the following statement: "Goodbye, Christ" does not represent my personal viewpoint. It was long ago withdrawn from circulation and has been reprinted recently without my knowledge or consent. I would not now use such a technique of approach since I feel that a mere poem is quite unable to compete in power to shock with the current horrors of war and oppression abroad in the greater part of the world. I have never been a member of the Communist party." *Essays*, 209. See also LHP, 291:4754, which has several versions of "Concerning Goodbye Christ," and Thurston's reading of "Christ in Alabama" in *Making Things Happen*, 95–101.

47. Lowney notes that "[a]s the McCarthyist hysteria about social deviance intensified during these early years of the Cold War bebop musicians were increasingly targeted as symbolic figures of racial and generational rebellion. And as jazz became increasingly associated by police and police authorities with illegal drug use, jazz musicians were identified with Communists as agents of moral decays and threats to national unity." "Langston Hughes," 367.

48. See Woods, *Black Struggle*, 38ff. HUAC would not be abolished until 1975. On the effects on black federal workers and the NAACP, see Hoffman, *Citizen Cohn*, 136–37.

49. See Stephen J. Whitfield, *The Culture of the Cold War* (Baltimore: Johns Hopkins University Press, 1991), 192–96.

50. Robeson's wife, Eslanda, testified publicly before McCarthy in July 1953; like Hughes, she was deposed in closed session first. See ST, 1223–27. See Tuck, *McCarthyism,* 192–95.

51. Woods, *Black Struggle,* 48; see also 5.

52. Hoffman, *Citizen Cohn,* 140.

53. Schine became an unpaid "consultant" to the committee after his pamphlet *Definition of Communism* in 1952 attracted Cohn's attention. After he was drafted into the army in late 1953, Cohn obtained special privileges for him. During the Army-McCarthy Hearings in 1954, Schine's preferential treatment became an occasion for charges that McCarthy and Cohn had unduly influenced the Army on behalf of a member of his staff. There were also insinuations that Cohn and Schine had a homosexual relationship, which have never been proven. Nonetheless, many historians have called Schine Cohn's "dumb blonde." Morgan, *Reds,* 429. The fact that the Army-McCarthy Hearings were televised live exposed the public to the committee's methods of interrogation and precipitated McCarthy's demise in 1954. A particular concern among Europeans was "that McCarthy would trigger a revival of the American isolationism of the thirties. They castigated Schine and Cohn as witch-hunters and 'book burners.'... The image of book burner stuck." Arthur Herman, *Joseph McCarthy: Reexamining the Life and Legacy of America's Most Hated Senator* (New York: Free Press, 2000), 229.

54. Oshinsky, *Conspiracy,* 29.

55. The attendance list in the record for Tuesday, March 24, 1953 is as follows: "Senator Karl E. Mundt, Republican, South Dakota; Senator Everett M. Dirksen, Republican, Illinois; Senator John L. McClellan, Democrat, Arkansas; and Senator Stuart Symington, Democrat, Missouri. Present also: Roy Cohn, chief counsel; David Schine, chief consultant; Daniel Buckley, assistant counsel; Henry Hawkins, investigator; and Ruth Young Watt, chief clerk." United States Senate, *Executive Sessions,* 2:945.

56. After again consulting with Frank Reeves, Hughes finally concedes: "If that statement is from a column of mine, as I presume it probably is, I would say that I believed the entire context of the article in which it is included." ST, 985.

57. De Santis, *Langston Hughes and the Chicago Defender,* 184.

58. For an excellent account of the trial, see Peter L. Steinberg, *The Great "Red Menace": United States Prosecution of American Communists, 1947–1952* (Westport, CT: Greenwood Press, 1984), chap 8.

59. *Dennis et al. v. United States* began in as a trial in the U.S. District Court for Southern New York in 1949: *United States v. Foster et al.,* 83 F. Supp. 197. The named defendant in that case was William Z. Foster, the then chairman of the Communist Party, who later fell ill and was replaced in the appeal by the party's general secretary, Eugene Dennis, the assumed name of Frankie Waldron. Judge Medina overruled the defendants' motion to quash and dismiss the entire panel, venue, and jury list and to dismiss the indictments against them on the grounds that there had been a willful, deliberate, and systematic exclusion of jurors based on their economic, racial, and political status and affiliation. The case subsequently went to the U.S. Court of Appeals, Second Circuit, where Medina's decision was upheld by Judge Learned Hand on August 1, 1950. See *United States v. Dennis et al.,* 183 F.2d 201, 205–9 (2d Cir. 1950). From there the case went to the U.S. Supreme Court. *Dennis* has never been overruled. See J. Woodford Howard and John Maltese, "Revisiting Judge Harold R. Medina's Charge to the Jury in United States v. Dennis: Notes on Freedom of Speech" (paper prepared for presentation at the Annual Meeting of the American Political Science Association, Washington, DC, September 2005), 2.

60. The Sedition Act, one of four Alien and Sedition Acts, was known as "An Act for the Punishment of Certain Crimes against the United States." Enacted on July 14, 1798, with an expiration date of March 3, 1801, it can be regarded as a precedent, though not a legal one, for the sentiments of the Smith Act. See United States, *Statutes at Large,* 5th Cong., 2nd Sess. (1798), ch. 73–74, 1 Stat. 596.

61. Alien Registration Act, 18 U.S.C. § 2385 (1940). This act was last amended in 1994; for a history of the revisions see http://pir.pnl.gov/FileStream.ashx?DriverDocID=838. I am quoting from the United States Code, 2009 ed. See also Howard Ball, *The USA Patriot Act of 2001: Balancing Civil Liberties and National Security: A Reference Handbook* (Santa Barbara, CA: ABC-CLIO, 2004), 144. On other post-World War II legislation, such as the Internal Security Act (the McCarran Act) of 1950 and the Communist Control Act of 1954, see Redish, *Logic,* 36ff.

62. See *Yates v. United States,* 354 U.S. 298, 300–338 (1957). The Court's opinion delivered by Justice Harlan reversed the convictions of the fourteen convicted petitioners and remanded the case with directions to enter judgments of acquittal in five cases where the evidence was insufficient. The remaining members of the Communist Party were granted a new trial.

63. Redish, *Logic,* 7 (my emphasis).

64. This was in part because the Court "refused to examine the evidentiary sufficiency of the conviction." Redish, *Logic,* 90; see also 97 and, for a detailed legal reading of *Dennis* and its implications, 81–106).

65. *Dennis et al. v. United States,* 341 U.S. 494, 583, 584 (1951).

66. Ibid., 587–88 (my emphases). Teaching was an issue in this trial because several of the defendants were academics. See Ellen Schrecker, *No Ivory Tower: McCarthyism and the Universities* (New York: Oxford University Press, 1986).

67. "Clear and present danger" are the words Justice Oliver Wendell Holmes used in his 1919 opinion in *Schenck v. United States,* 249 U.S. 47, 52 (1919), which confirmed the convictions of a lower court: "The question in every case is whether the words used are used in such circumstances and are of such a nature as to create a clear and present danger that they will bring about the substantive evils that Congress has a right to prevent.... If the act, (speaking, or circulating a paper), its tendency and the intent with which it is done are the same, we perceive no ground for saying that success alone warrants making the act a crime."

68. Alan Filreis, "Words with 'All the Effects of Force': Cold-War Interpretation," *American Quarterly* 39, no. 2 (1987): 306–7. As Howard and Maltese point out, the eleven leaders of CPUSA were convicted "for knowing conspiracy (1) to advocate and teach Marxist-Leninist doctrines of violent overthrow of the federal government as principles or rules of action, and (2) to organize secret programs of revolutionary indoctrination and infiltration, preparatory to action. Party membership charges, probably the strongest, were dropped during pretrial. No charges were brought for publishing, the only statutory offense requiring 'with intent.'" "Revisiting."

69. Richard J. Bonnie et al., *Criminal Law,* 3rd ed. (New York: Thomson Reuters/Foundation Press, 2010), 175.

70. Ibid., 163.

71. Filreis, "Words," 309.

72. See Hoffman, *Citizen Cohn,* 329.

73. Redish, *Logic,* 92.

74. See the full text of Sidney's essay at http://etext.lib.virginia.edu/etcbin/toccer-new2?id=SidDefe.sgm&images=images/modeng&data=/texts/english/modeng/parsed&tag=public&part=1&division=div1.

75. Filreis, "Words," 308.

76. Nelson, *Revolutionary Memory,* 144, 157. For an earlier argument against the monologic nature of poetry, see Vera M. Kutzinski, *Against the American Grain: Myth and History in William Carlos Williams, Jay Wright, and Nicolás Guillén* (Baltimore: Johns Hopkins University Press, 1987), 168–69.

77. No one has been convicted under the Smith Act since *Scales v. United States,* 367 U.S. 203 (1961); at least no conviction appears to have been upheld since then. It seems that federal

law enforcement and jurisprudence's attention has now solidly shifted toward the (apparently) less thorny question of terrorism, including what it might mean to provide "material support" to a U.S.-government-designated "foreign terrorist organization." For better or for worse, a 2010 U.S. Supreme Court decision (*Holder v. Humanitarian Law Project,* 130 S. Ct. 2705) briefly used the Smith Act, via the Scales case, as a point of comparison to a post 9/11 criminal statute (18 USCS §2339B) that controls the question of criminal aid or support to a designated foreign terrorist organization. The 2010 U.S. Supreme Court, in a 6-3 decision authored by Chief Justice Roberts, determined that compared with the Smith Act, 18 USCS §2339B was better defined by Congress and less problematic in its scope than the Smith Act. It was deemed less problematic in part because "material support and resources" can be more easily defined than "intent." With respect to the question of the constitutionality of the Smith Act, this decision left us right where we were before.

78. For another reading, see Robert Shulman, *The Power of Political Art: The 1930s Literary Left Reconsidered* (Chapel Hill: University of North Carolina Press, 2000), 282–83.

79. Brunner, *Cold War Poetry,* 141. See also his "Langston Hughes: *Fine Clothes to the Jew,*" in *A Companion to Modernist Literature and Culture,* ed. David Bradshaw and Kevin H. Dettmar (Blackwell Publishing, 2005), Blackwell Reference Online.

80. Smethurst aptly notes that "[a]s would be the case with much of Hughes's most successful later poetry, Hughes...drew on a complex of discourses that often contradicted each other, allowing many of the contradictions to remain within the poems." *New Red Negro,* 97.

81. Shulman, *The Power,* 281. See also Smethurst, *New Red Negro,* 226.

82. Smethurst, *New Red Negro,* 102.

83. On "Scottsboro" and *Scottsboro Limited,* see also Thurston, *Making Something Happen,* 107–13.

84. For a reading of this poem, see Shulman, *The Power,* 272–75.

85. Nelson, *Revolutionary Memory,* 155–56.

86. Dawahare, *Nationalism,* 106. See also *Life,* 1:285–86.

87. Dawahare regards Hughes's radical poetry as "truly an accomplishment of modern poetry" because, "unlike most other twentieth-century poetry," it is not "marred by spurious nationalism." *Nationalism,* 109–10.

88. De Santis, *Langston Hughes and the Chicago Defender,* 26–27.

89. Hughes's autobiographical "digression" was printed in *Harper's* (December 2003). Virtually no context is provided for these remarks.

90. This is at variance with what Hughes said elsewhere about how he wrote poetry. See especially his remarks on "The Negro Speaks of Rivers" in *BS.*

91. James Baldwin, "Envoi," in *A Quarter Century of Un-Americana,* ed. Charlotte Pomerantz (New York: Marzani & Munsell, 1963), 127.

92. Indicted as "an agent of a foreign principal," Du Bois was later acquitted. He wrote in his 1968 *Autobiography:* "[N]othing has so cowed me as that day, November 8, 1951, when I took my seat in a Washington courtroom as an indicted criminal." *The Autobiography of W. E. B. Du Bois: A Soliloquy on Viewing My Life from the Last Decade of Its First Century* (New York: International Publishers, 1968), 379. See also Hughes, "The Accusers' Names Nobody Will Remember, but History Records Du Bois," *Chicago Defender,* October 6, 1951, in de Santis, *Langston Hughes and the Chicago Defender,* 187–88.

93. On the Hollywood and other blacklists in the media and the entertainment industry, see Fariello, *Red Scare,* 255–374.

94. See Wald, *Writing from the Left,* 67–68.

95. See Hoffman, *Citizen Cohn,* 127–33; Morgan, *Reds,* 428; see Tuck, *McCarthyism,* 147. Cohn died of AIDS-related complications in 1986. Tony Kushner's acclaimed play *Angels in America: A Gay Fantasia on National Themes* (1993) grimly portrays an unrepentant Cohn

who, though disbarred, proudly reprises his role in the Rosenberg trial on his deathbed, all the while pretending that he has not AIDS but liver cancer (a bit like McCarthy's cirrhosis of the liver!). The play became the basis for an HBO miniseries in 2003, in which Al Pacino played Cohn, and an opera in 2004.

96. See also the construction of Charlie Chaplin's image as a subversive, which led to attacks not only on his political views but also on his sex life and his alien status. John Sbardellati and Tony Shaw, "Booting a Tramp: Charlie Chaplin, the FBI, and the Construction of the Subversive Image in Red Scare America," *Pacific Historical Review* 72, no. 4 (November 2003), 514.

97. A copy of Hughes's transcript (80–83 of the official transcript), can be found in LHP, 365:5863. LHP, 365:5862, has a list of those who received a transcript of portions of the testimony's radio broadcast. Rampersad claims that Hughes's prepared statement, which he quotes at *Life*, 2:213–15, was formally accepted at his March 26 hearing, but there is no record of it in any of the government documents. See PT, 73. It was certainly not part of what Hughes sent out.

98. On McCarthyism as a waning intellectual force in the late 1950s and early 1960s, see Wald, *Writing from the Left*, 17ff. The one book that Wald particularly emphasizes as an indicator of the return to political tolerance is Daniel Aaron's *Writers on the Left: Episodes in American Literary Communism* (1961).

99. This voice, Smethurst explains, "usually means what it says, but never quite says all that it means in a straightforward way. Instead it remains elusive through a skillful use of syntactic manipulation, rhythm, and other formal devices, conveying multiple meanings to multiple audiences." *New Red Negro*, 103.

100. De Santis, *Langston Hughes and the Chicago Defender*, 7.

101. Smethurst reads Hughes's treatment of concealment in "Dream Boogie," the opening poem in *Montage of a Dream Deferred* (1951) as a prophetic commentary on the McCarthy hearings. *New Red Negro*, 162–63.

102. See Whitfield, *Culture of the Cold War*, 16.

103. Ibid., 195.

104. Hughes to Frank Reeves, March 30, 1959, LHP, 136:2525.

105. "Unfortunately for the peace of mind of the artist, art has a political value, that is why, in times of stress, the politicians set up various open or covert censorships to try for their own ends to control art. In order to play safe, the bad artist often conforms to the political needs of the moment and creates a saleable tissue of conscious lies in order to keep his cupboard full." Hughes, "Art and Integrity," *Chicago Defender*, October 20, 1945, in de Santis, *Langston Hughes and the Chicago Defender*, 201.

106. "Diplomacy: Flight to Harlem," *Time*, October 3, 1960, 16. See also Edward Field's poem "Ode to Fidel Castro" in *After the Fall: Poems Old and New* (Pittsburgh, PA: University of Pittsburgh Press, 2007), 73–80.

107. Unsigned carbon copy. A handwritten note in green ink at the bottom of the letter reads, " 'Time' published the above retraction. L.H." LHP, 291:4754.

108. Rampersad mentions the telegram in his biography of Hughes. *Life*, 2:330–31).

Afterword

1. William Carlos Williams, *In the American Grain* (New York: New Directions, 1993), 109. See also Ette, *ZwischenWeltenSchreiben*.

2. Lawrence Jackson rightly points out that "[o]nly recently have we begun to reckon fully with the import and prominence of the American Communist Party as an engine of

intellectual and artistic development for black Americans who were committed to issues of social and economic justice." *The Indignant Generation: A Narrative History of African American Writers and Critics, 1934–1960* (Princeton: Princeton University Press, 2010), 12.

3. Hughes's blues poems may well be elegies of sorts, as Ramazani has argued in *Poetry of Mourning*. But they are ultimately about life and especially survival. Singing is a survival mechanism; so is writing poetry.

4. Andrew J. M. Bundy, ed., *Selected Essays of Wilson Harris: The Unfinished Genesis of the Imagination* (London: Routledge, 1999), 65.

5. Damrosch, "Where is World Literature?" 213.

6. See Apter, *Translation Zone*, 6.

7. For the purposes of my discussion, I have defined "nation" as a provisional political construct that proffers, and restricts, cultural affiliation or extended kinship.

8. Ette, *ZwischenWeltenSchreiben*, 14.

9. See also Damrosch: "All works cease to be the exclusive products of their original culture once they are translated; all become works that only 'began' in their original language." *What Is World Literature?* (Princeton: Princeton University Press, 2003), 22. What if they did not begin in just one originary language? For critical perspectives on hybridity, see Gerry Smyth, "The Politics of Hybridity: Some Problems with Crossing the Border," in *Comparing Postcolonial Literatures: Dislocations,* ed. Ashok Bery (Basingstoke, UK: Macmillan, 2000), 43–55; and Cyrus Patell, "Comparative American Studies: Hybridity and beyond," *American Literary History* 11, no. 1 (1999): 166–86.

10. Ette, *ZwischenWeltenSchreiben*, 18 (my emphasis). Ette suggests terms such as "translocal," "transregional," "transareal," "transnational," and "transcontinental," which would articulate five different layers of relations that would then have to be combined with temporal movements. Ibid., 23). For a narrower focus, see also Damrosch, "Global Regionalism," *European Review* 15, no. 1 (2007): 135–43.

11. It is ironic because Ette's theories are, in many respects, self-conscious extensions of Wolfgang Iser's phenomenology of reading. See, for instance, "The Reading Process: A Phenomenological Approach," *New Directions in Literary History,* ed. Ralph Cohen (Baltimore: Johns Hopkins University Press, 1974), 125–45; and *The Act of Reading: A Theory of Aesthetic Response* (Baltimore: Johns Hopkins University Press, 1978).

12. Ette, *ZwischenWeltenSchreiben*, 105.

13. Octavio Paz, "Translation, Literature and Letters," in *Theories of Translation: An Anthology of Essays from Dryden to Derrida,* ed. Rainer Schulte and John Bignenet (Chicago: University of Chicago Press, 1992), 154.

14. Natalie Melas, *All the Difference: Postcoloniality and the Ends of Comparison* (Stanford, CA: Stanford University Press, 2007), 31.

15. Karl Marx, *Capital: A Critique of Political Economy,* trans. Samuel Moore and Edward Aveling (New York: Random House, 1906), 1:66 (my emphasis). According to Marx, "[i]t is the expression of equivalence between different sorts of commodities that alone bring into bring into relief the specific character of value-creating labour, and this it does by actually reducing the different varieties of labor embodied in the different kinds of commodities to their common quality of labour in the abstract." Ibid., 1:59. For details see "The Equivalent Form of Value," ibid., 1:64ff. See also Melas, *All the Difference,* 42.

16. See Moretti, "Conjectures on World Literature," in *Debating World Literature,* ed. Christopher Prendergast (London: Verso, 2004), 148–62, and Dimock, *Through Other Continents.*

17. Moretti, "Conjectures," 151. Dimock, *Through Other Continents,* which is heavily indebted to Moretti's ideas, offers a good demonstration of what happens when textual and historical details disappear.

18. Cultural anthropology and sociology are disciplines in which translation has been assumed to be wholly transparent. See Scanlon on the limits of ethnography in relation to literature. "Poets Laureate," 251–52.

19. The gaps of which I speak are analogous to the loci of indeterminacy that Wolfgang Iser has identified in modern literature (specifically narrative) as spaces where readers most actively interact with texts.

20. See Joshua Miller's comments on the *Vox Americana* in his *Accented America*, chap. 1. On whiteness studies, see, for instance, Vron Ware and Les Back, *Out of Whiteness: Color, Politics, and Culture* (Chicago: University of Chicago Press, 2002); David Roediger, *The Wages of Whiteness: Race and the Making of the American Working Class* (London: Verso, rev. ed. 2007); and *What White Looks Like: African-American Philosophers on the Whiteness Question*, ed. George Yancy (New York: Routledge, 2004), among many others.

21. Jacques, *Change in the Weather*, 150–51.

22. Gentzler avers that "the name Latin America is already a translation," adding, no doubt with a chuckle, that "[t]here were no Romans in South America." *Translation and Identity*, 174. See also Aims McGuinness, "Search for "Latin America": Race and Sovereignty in the America in the 1850s," in *Race and Nation in Modern Latin America*, ed. Nancy P. Appelbaum, Anne S. Macpherson, and Karin Alejandra Rosemblatt (Chapel Hill: University of North Carolina Press, 2003), 87–107; Martin Hopenhayn, "Essential Histories, Contingent Outcomes: Latin Americanists in Search of a Discourse," in *Our Americas: Political and Cultural Imaginings*, ed. Sandhya Shukla and Heidi Tinsman (Durham, NC: Duke University Press, 2004), 25–35.

23. Kadir, "Concentric Hemispheres," 31. See also Michael Berubé, "American Studies without Exceptions," *PMLA* 118, no. 1 (2003): 103–13. For perspectives on the politically radical roots of American studies, see Günter Lenz, "American Studies and the Radical Tradition: From the 1930s to the 1960s," *Prospects* 12 (1987): 21–58, and Denning, *The Cultural Front*.

24. See Susan Gillman, Kirsten Silva Gruesz, and Rob Wilson, "Worlding American Studies," special issue of *Comparative American Studies* 2, no. 3 (2004).

25. See Kadir, "Introduction: America and Its Studies," *PMLA* 118, no. 1 (2003): 10.

26. See Ralph Bauer, "Hemispheric American Studies," *PMLA* 124, no. 1 (2009): 234–50, and "Early American Literature and American Literary History at the 'Hemispheric Turn,'" *American Literary History* 22, no. 2 (2010): 250–65; Justin Read, *Modern Poetics and Hemispheric American Cultural Studies*, xvii–xxi; also Peter Birle et al., eds., *Hemisphärische Konstruktionen der Amerikas*, (Frankfurt am Main: Vervuert, 2006); and Marianne Braig and Ottmar Ette, "Construcciones hemisféricas," special issue of *Iberoaméricana* 5, no. 20 (2005).

27. Diana Taylor, "Remapping Genre through Performance: From 'American' to 'Hemispheric' Studies," *PMLA* 122, no. 5 (2007): 1418.

28. Carolyn Porter, "What We Know That We Don't Know: Remapping American Literary Studies," *American Literary History* 6, no. 3 (1994): 471.

29. Kadir, "Concentric Hemispheres," 28.

30. Kadir puts it well: "Traditionally..., American Studies has been engaged not in a discourse of differentiation, but enmeshed in a conjunctive logic of rationalization that incorporates the scientific enterprise to the object of its science. When the contradictions of field object and of disciplinary practice fuse, contradiction is not transcended but compounded." "Concentric Hemispheres," 33. See also Jennifer Gurley, "How U.S.A. Transnational Studies Reinforce American Exceptionalism," in *Trans/American, Trans/Oceanic, Trans/lation: Issues in International American Studies*, ed. Susana Araújo, João F. Duarte, and Marta Pacheco Pinto (Newcastle, UK: Cambridge Scholars, 2010), 39–49.

31. See Phil Fisher, ed., *The New American Studies: Essays from Representations* (Berkeley: University of California Press, 1991), and John Carlos Rowe, "Postnationalism, Globalism, and the New American Studies," in *The Futures of American Studies*, ed. Donald E. Pease and Robyn Wiegman (Durham, NC: Duke University Press, 2002), 167–82.

32. Perry Miller, *Errand into the Wilderness* (1956. Cambridge, MA: Belknap Press of Harvard University Press, 1984), ix. See Amy Kaplan and Donald Pease, eds. Cultures of United States Imperialism (Durham, NC: Duke University Press, 1993). See also Rowe, *Literary Culture and U.S. Imperialism: From the Revolution to World War II* (New York: Oxford University Press, 2000).

33. Caroline Levander and Robert S. Levin, *Hemispheric American Studies* (New Brunswick, NJ: Rutgers University Press, 2008), 3, 7.

34. Paul Giles, "Hemispheric Partiality," *American Literary History* 18, no. 3 (Fall 2006): 653.

35. There have, of course, always been exceptions to this rule. More significant than such exceptions, however, is the significant generational shift among USAmericanists during the past two decades, exemplified by the work of Anna Brickhouse, Suzanne Bost, Robert Irwin, Kirsten Gruesz, Justin Read, and Jeff Karem, among others.

36. Gurley diagnoses "an antipathy for foreign languages" among USAmericanists "that at times limits their ability to be precise when revealing the internationality of national literatures." "How U.S.A. Transnational Studies," 39.

37. Kowalewski, "Contemporary Regionalism," in *A Companion to the Regional Literatures of America*, ed. Charles L. Crow (Malden, MA: Blackwell, 2003), 18–19. See also Miller, *Accented America*.

38. In her ASA presidential address, Jan Radway emphasized multilingualism but largely from a utilitarian point of view (64–65). Her methodological preferences for analyzing "the complexity of social relations that produce the cultural flows, transactions, and exchanges" are social scientific. "What's in a Name?," in Pease and Wiegman, *The Futures of American Studies*, 64–66. Jing Tsu points us in a more fruitful direction by arguing that "[a]s nationalization now shows signs of giving way to the unraveling of standardization histories and their polymorphous strands of origin and diffusion, language returns us to multiplicity as a starting norm... the once limiting, naturalizing linguistic mandate of area studies moves to center stage as a valuable source of pluralism." "New Area Studies and Languages on the Move," *PMLA* 126, no. 3 (May 2011), 698–99.

39. The so-called Berlin Debate on the New World had reached its first culmination point after the publication of the initial volume of Cornelius de Pauw's *Réflections philosophiques sur les Américains (Philosophical Reflections about the Americans)* in 1768.

40. For a useful commentary on the foundations of what became Latin American studies during the age of Pan-Americanism (1890–1940), see Ricardo D. Salvatore, "Library Accumulation and the Emergence of Latin American Studies," *Comparative American Studies* 3, no. 4 (2005): 415–36.

41. Harry Harootunian, "Some Thoughts on Comparability and the Space-Time Problem," *boundary 2* 32, no. 2 (2005): 28.

42. Ibid.

43. A recent example of this on the Latin Americanist side is Walter Mignolo's *Idea of Latin America* (Malden, MA: Blackwell, 2005).

44. See Kadir, "Concentric Hemispheres," 32.

45. Sheila Hones and Julia Leyda, "Geographies of American Studies," *American Quarterly* 57, no. 4 (2005): 1025.

46. See Theo d'Haen et al, *How Far Is America from Here? Selected Proceedings of the First World Congress of the International American Studies Association 22–24 May 2003*

(Amsterdam: Rodopi, 2005). For USAmericanists to embrace the concept of transnationalism has been far less risky because the transnational leaves untouched the shape of the nation, complete with political, cultural, and psychological borders that may then be crossed in orderly fashion and by the light of day. What applies here is Stuart Hall's insight that "a transgressive politics in one domain is constantly sutured and stabilized by reactionary or unexamined politics in another." "What Is This 'Black' in Black Popular Culture?" in *Black Popular Culture,* ed. Michelle Wallace and Gina Dent (Seattle: Bay Press, 1992), 31.

47. Sheila Hones and Julia Leyda, "Towards a Critical Geography of American Studies," *Comparative American Studies* 2, no. 2 (2004): 185–203 (my emphasis).

48. Porter, "What We Know," 510.

49. See Mary Louise Pratt, *Imperial Eyes: Travel Writing and Transculturation* (New York: Routledge, 1992), and Gloria Anzaldúa, *Borderlands / La Frontera* (San Francisco: Aunt Lute Books, 1987).

50. See the journal *Atlantic Studies,* Gilroy, *Black Atlantic,* Christopher Miller, *The French Atlantic Triangle,* and *AfroAsian Encounters: Culture, History, Politics,* ed. Heike Raphael-Hernandez and Shannon Steen (ebrary, Inc, 2006), which makes a case for a "Black Pacific."

51. Giles, "Hemispheric Partiality," 654.

52. Ibid., 655.

53. Translation, in my view, it not a form of interdisciplinarity. See Marguerite Suárez-Murias, "Interdisciplinary Credit in the Humanities: Black Literature in Latin America in Translation," *Latin American Literary Review* 4, no. 7 (Fall–Winter 1975): 49–56, for a different perspective.

54. By contrast, see Gustavo Pérez Firmat, ed., *Do the Americas Have a Common Literature?* (Durham, NC: Duke University Press, 1990).

55. Kadir argues the same point differently, chiding practitioners of American studies for denying "that theirs is even a discipline." He argues that "there is a strong form of disciplinarity at work in this denial and, in the context of interdisciplinary transaction, it has often fallen to disciplines such as Comparative Literature, as one of the front-lines of theoretical discourse and cultural critique, to point out this fact to American Studies, something which has not always gone down well with a good number of more traditional Americanists." "Concentric Hemispheres," 32. See also Amy Kaplan, "Violent Belongings and the Question of Empire Today: Presidential Address to the American Studies Association, Hartford, Connecticut, October 17, 2003," *American Quarterly* 56, no. 1 (2004): 1–18.

56. Harootunian, "Some Thoughts," 29.

57. For distinctions between these and related terms, see Ette, *ZwischenWeltenSchreiben,* 20. See also Lisa R. Lattuca, *Creating Interdisciplinarity: Interdisciplinary Research and Teaching among College and University Faculty* (Nashville: Vanderbilt University Press, 2001); Julie Thompson Klein, *Crossing Boundaries: Knowledge, Disciplinarities, and Interdisciplinarities* (Charlottesville: University Press of Virginia, 1996); and Lewis Pyenson, ed., *Disciplines and Interdisciplinarity in the New Century* (Lafayette: Center for Louisiana Studies, 1997).

58. Examples of this are Charles W. Pollard's *New World Modernisms: T.S. Eliot, Derek Walcott, and Kamau Brathwaite* (Charlottesville: University Press of Virginia, 2004) and Karem, *The Purloined Islands.*

59. See Robert Irwin, "¿Qué hacen los nuevos americanistas? Collaborative Strategies for a Postnationalist American Studies," in Gillman, Gruesz, and Wilson, eds., "Worlding American Studies," 303–23. On interdisciplinary collaboration, see Marilyn J. Amey and Dennis F. Brown, eds. *Breaking Out of the Box: Interdisciplinary Collaboration and Faculty Work* (Greenwich, CT: Information Age Publishing, 2004); Merle Richards et al., *Collaboration Uncovered: The Forgotten, the Assumed, and the Unexamined in Collaborative Education* (Westport, CT: Bergin & Garvey, 2001). See also Moretti on collaboration in comparative literary studies. "Conjectures, 161.

60. To put the affective and professional value of these identifications in perspective, it is worth remembering that these and similar geopolitical labels are quite meaningless, indeed perplexing, outside the humanities and the social sciences.

61. Kadir, "Concentric Hemispheres," 34.

62. See Edward Soja, *Thirdspace: Journeys to Los Angeles and Other Real-and-Imagined Places* (Cambridge, MA: Blackwell, 1996), and Ette, *ZwischenWeltenSchreiben*, 23–26. Also Smyth insists that this space "has to remain a *potential* rather than a *programme* if it is to avoid being re-absorbed into disabling neo-colonialist narratives." "Politics of Hybridity," 52.

63. See Giles on nation and transnationalism in *Virtual Americas: Transnational Fictions and the Transatlantic Imaginary* (Durham, NC: Duke University Press, 2002), 5, 17. Smyth rightly cautions that rather than "bringing about a re-distribution of power relations," destabilizing the border "could instead feed into the stereotypical assumptions which helped to create the border in the first place." "Politics of Hybridity," 51.

64. George Handley, "A New World Poetics of Oblivion," in *Look Away! The US South in New World Studies,* ed. Jon Smith and Deborah Cohn (Durham, NC: Duke University Press, 2004), 46–47.

65. Peter Hulme, "Expanding the Caribbean," in *Perspectives on the 'Other America': Comparative Approaches to Caribbean and Latin American Culture,* ed. Michael Niblett and Kerstin Oloff (Amsterdam: Rodopi, 2009), 45.

66. See Ette, *Konvivenz. Leben und Schreiben nach dem Paradies* (Berlin: Kulturverlag Kadmos, 2012). Gilroy uses the adjectival version in the subtitle of *After Empire: Melancholia or Convivial Culture?* (Abingdon, UK: Routledge, 2004). On Gilroy, see David Palumbo-Liu, "Against Race. Yes, But at What Cost?," in Fabre and Benesch, *African Diasporas,* 39–58.

67. Edwards, "Uses of Diaspora," 31–32.

68. Former Dutch and Danish colonies in the greater Caribbean have suffered a similar fate.

69. The field of Afro-Hispanic studies, by contrast, has rarely presented challenges to the paradigms of African diaspora studies.

70. See Edwards, *The Practice of Diaspora,* 7.

71. Baldwin, *Beyond the Color Line,* 10; Moore, "Colored Dispatches."

72. See, for instance, Coyle, *Ezra Pound and African American Modernism;* Daniel Katz, *American Modernism's Expatriate Scene: The Labour of Translation* (Edinburgh: Edinburgh University Press, 2007); also Venuti on Pound. *Translator's Invisibility,* 202ff.

73. In the English-speaking world, the work of Lawrence Venuti has probably contributed most to rehabilitating the figure of the translator.

74. See Lois Parkinson Zamora, *The Usable Past: The Imagination of History in Recent Fiction of the Americas* (Cambridge: Cambridge University Press, 1997), 5.

75. Riffaterre, "On the Complementarity of Comparative Literature and Cultural Studies," in *Comparative Literature in the Age of Multiculturalism,* ed. Charles Bernheimer (Baltimore: Johns Hopkins University Press, 1995), 68.

76. Ette, *ZwischenWeltenSchreiben,* 102.

77. On the politics of the New Critics and the failure of progressive northerners to question "the fundamental assumptions and images of the plantation tradition," see Pavlić, *Crossroads Modernism,* 55.

78. On the "marginality" narrative as a significant obstacle to a deeper understanding of the interrelation between black writers and their societies, see Jacques, *Change in the Weather,* 151.

79. See, for example, Baker, *Modernism and the Harlem Renaissance.* See also Pavlić's excellent survey of (black) modernist scholarship, or the lack thereof, in his preface to *Crossroads Modernism.*

BIBLIOGRAPHY

Ahumada, Herminio, ed. and trans. *Yo también soy América. Poemas de Langston Hughes: En memoria de Martin Luther King*. Mexico: Editorial Novaro, 1968.

Alberti, Rafael, trans. "'Yo Soy Negro,' 'Estoy Haciendo un Camino,' 'Hombre Convertido en Hombres,' 'Yo También.'" By Langston Hughes. *El Mono Azul* 11, no. 29 (August 19, 1937): 1.

Alegría, Carmen. "Langston Hughes: Six Letters to Nicolás Guillén." *Black Scholar*, July–August 1985, 54–60.

Alejandro, Miguel. "Langston Hughes." *Nueva Cultura* 2 (January 1936): 154–57.

Alemán, Matilde, trans. *El ghetto negro: Harlem, una ciudad dentro de una ciudad. Harlem USA*. By Langston Hughes. Buenos Aires: Sílaba, 1966.

Allen, Esther Louise, ed. *José Martí: Selected Writings*. New York: Penguin, 2002.

Als, Hilton. "Driver's License: Broadway Transforms "'Driving Miss Daisy' and 'The Scottsboro Boys.'" *New Yorker*, November 8, 2010, 90.

Amey, Marilyn J., and Dennis F. Brown, eds. *Breaking Out of the Box: Interdisciplinary Collaboration and Faculty Work*. Greenwich, CT: Information Age Publishing, 2004.

Andrews, George Reid. *The Afro-Argentines of Buenos Aires, 1800–1900*. Madison: University of Wisconsin Press, 1980.

——. *Afro-Latin America, 1800–2000*. Oxford: Oxford University Press, 2004.

Anon., trans. "Escupideras de latón." By Langston Hughes. *Ínsula* XIX, no. 215 (October 1964): 15.

Anzaldúa, Gloria. *Borderlands/La Frontera*. San Francisco: Aunt Lute Books, 1987.

Aparicio, Antonio. "Langston Hughes: *El inmenso mar.*" *Nuestra Raza* 14, no. 165 (1947): 5.

Appelbaum, Nancy P., Anne S. Macpherson, and Karin Alejandra Rosemblatt, eds. *Race and Nation in Modern Latin America*. Chapel Hill: University of North Carolina Press, 2003.

Apter, Emily S. *The Translation Zone: A New Comparative Literature*. Princeton: Princeton University Press, 2006.

Araújo, Susana, João F. Duarte, and Marta Pacheco Pinto. eds. *Trans/American, Trans/Oceanic, Trans/lation: Issues in International American Studies*. Newcastle, UK: Cambridge Scholars, 2010.

Ashcroft, Bill. *Caliban's Voice: The Transformation of English in Post-Colonial Literatures*. Milton Park, UK: Routledge, 2009.

Augier, Ángel. "Epistolario Nicolás Guillén—Langston Hughes." *Revista de Literatura Cubana* 13, nos. 24–26 (1995–1996): 145–61.

——. *Nicolás Guillén: Notas para un estudio biográfico crítico*. Santa Clara, Cuba: Universidad Central de las Villas, 1964.

B[erry], A[bner] W. "'Cuba Libre' by Nicolás Guillén, Cuba's Greatest Poet." *Daily Worker,* February 13, 1949, 13.

Baker, Houston A. *Modernism and the Harlem Renaissance.* Chicago: University of Chicago Press, 2003.

Balderston, Daniel, and Marcy Schwartz, eds. *Voice-Overs: Translation and Latin American Literature.* Albany: State University of New York Press, 2002.

Baldwin, Kate A. *Beyond the Color Line and the Iron Curtain: Reading Encounters between Black and Red, 1922–1963.* Durham, NC: Duke University Press, 2002.

Ball, Howard. *The USA Patriot Act of 2001: Balancing Civil Liberties and National Security: A Reference Handbook.* Santa Barbara, CA: ABC-CLIO, 2004.

Ballagas, Emilio, ed. *Mapa de la poesía negra americana.* Buenos Aires: Editorial Pleamar, 1946.

Bansart, Andrés, Amelia Jiménez, and Diego Santa Cruz, eds. *Poesía negra-africana.* Santiago de Chile: Universidad Católica de Chile, Ediciones Nueva Universidad de la Vicerrectoría de Comunicación, 1971.

Barnstone, Willis. *The Poetics of Translation: History, Theory, Practice.* New Haven, CT: Yale University Press, 1993.

Barrios, Pilar E. *Piel Negra. Poesía 1917–1947.* Montevideo: Nuestra Raza, 1947.

Bassnet, Susan, and Harish Trivedi, eds. *Post-Colonial Translation: Theory and Practice.* New York: Routledge, 1999.

Bauer, Ralph. "Early American Literature and American Literary History at the 'Hemispheric Turn.'" *American Literary History* 22, no. 2 (2010): 250–65.

——. "Hemispheric American Studies." *PMLA* 124, no. 1 (2009): 234–50.

Bayley, Edwin R. *Joe McCarthy and the Press.* Madison: University of Wisconsin Press, 1981.

Bean, Annmarie. "Playwrights and Plays of the Harlem Renaissance." In *A Companion to Twentieth-Century American Drama,* edited by David Krasner, 91–105. Malden, MA: Blackwell, 2006.

Benjamin, Walter. *Gesammelte Schriften IV.i.* Edited by Tillman Rexroth. Frankfurt-Main: Suhrkamp, 1972.

——. *Illuminations.* Edited by Hannah Arendt. New York: Schocken Books, 1969.

Benston, Kimberly W. *Performing Blackness: Enactments of African-American Modernism.* London: Routledge, 2000.

Berman, Jessica Schiff. *Modernist Fiction, Cosmopolitanism and the Politics of Community.* Cambridge, UK: Cambridge University Press, 2001.

Bernheimer, Charles, ed. *Comparative Literature in the Age of Multiculturalism.* Baltimore: Johns Hopkins University Press, 1995.

Berry, Faith, ed. *Good Morning Revolution: Uncollected Writings of Social Protest.* By Langston Hughes. Secaucus, NJ: Carol Pub. Group, 1992.

——. *Langston Hughes: Before and Beyond Harlem.* Westport, CT: Lawrence Hill & Co., 1983.

Berubé, Michael. "American Studies without Exceptions." *PMLA* 118, no. 1 (2003): 103–13.

Bery, Ashok, ed. *Comparing Postcolonial Literatures: Dislocations.* Basingstoke, UK: Macmillan, 2000.

Bethell, Leslie, and Ian Roxborough, eds. *Latin American between the Second War World and the Cold War, 1944–1948.* Cambridge: Cambridge University Press, 1992.

Bethune, Brian D. "Langston Hughes' Lost Translation of Federico García Lorca's 'Blood Wedding.'" *Langston Hughes Review* 15, no. 1 (1997): 24–36.

Beyer, William. "Langston Hughes and Common Ground in the 1940s." *American Studies in Scandinavia* 23 (1991): 29–42.

Bignami, Arile, and Arturo M. Lozza. "Pablo Neruda y Raúl González Tuñón: El resplandor de las palabras." *Suplemento cultural de Nuestra Propuesta. Semanario del Comité Central del Partido Comunista* (n.d.). http://www.elortiba.org/pdf/Neruda_y_Tunion.pdf.

Birle, Peter et al, eds. *Hemisphärische Konstruktionen der Amerikas.* Frankfurt am Main: Vervuert, 2006.

Blanco, Tomás. "'Salón de Baile in Harlem,' 'Sirviente negro,' 'Estrellas.'" *Asomante* 5, no. 2 (1949): 28–31.

Bonnie, Richard J. et al. *Criminal Law.* 3rd ed. New York: Thomson Reuters/Foundation Press, 2010.

Borden, Anne. "Heroic 'Hussies' and 'Brilliant Queers': Genderracial Resistance in the Works of Langston Hughes." *African-American Review* 28, no. 3 (1994): 333–45.

Borges, Jorge Luis. *Fervor de Buenos Aires.* 1923. Reprint, Buenos Aires: Emecé, 1970.

—, trans. *Hojas de hierba.* By Walt Whitman. Buenos Aires: Juárez, 1969.

—, trans. *La metamorfósis.* By Franz Kafka. Buenos Aires: Losada, 1943.

—, trans. "Langston Hughes ['I, Too,' 'Our Land,' 'The Negro Speaks of Rivers']." *El Hogar,* February 19, 1937. Reprinted in *Textos cautivos. Ensayos y reseñas en "El Hogar."* Barcelona: Tusquets Editores, 1986, 92–93.

—. *Luna de enfrente y Cuaderno San Martín.* 1925; 1929. Buenos Aires: Emecé, 1969.

—. *Obras completas.* 2 vols. Buenos Aires: Emecé, 1974.

—, trans. "Tres poemas de Langston Hughes." *Sur* 1, no. 2 (1931): 164–69.

—, trans. "Tres Poemas (Edgar Lee Masters)." *Sur* 1, no. 3 (1931): 132–37.

—. *A Universal History of Infamy.* Translated by Norman Thomas di Giovanni and Jorge Luis Borges. New York: E.P. Dutton, 1970.

Borshuk, Michael. "'Noise Modernism': The Cultural Politics of Langston Hughes's Early Jazz Poetry." *Langston Hughes Review* 17, nos. 1–2 (2002): 4–21.

—. *Swinging the Vernacular: Jazz and African American Modernist Literature.* New York: Routledge, 2006.

Bosco, María Angelica. *Memorias de las casas.* Buenos Aires: Vinciguerra, 1998.

Bost, Suzanne. *Mulatas and Mestizas: Representing Mixed Identities in the Americas, 1850–2000.* Athens: University of Georgia Press, 2003.

Bourdieu, Pierre. *The Field of Cultural Production: Essays on Art and Literatures.* New York: Columbia University Press, 1993.

Bradshaw, David, and Kevin H. Dettmar, eds. *A Companion to Modernist Literature and Culture.* Blackwell Publishing, 2005. Blackwell Reference Online. http://www.blackwellreference.com.

Braig, Marianne, and Ottmar Ette, eds. "Construcciones hemisféricas." Special issue of *Iberoaméricana* 5, no. 20 (2005).

Bravo, María Elena. "Borges traductor: El caso de *Wild Palms* de William Faulkner." *Ínsula* 40, no. 462 (1985): 11–12.

Britos Serrat, Alberto. *Antología de poetas negros uruguayos.* Montevideo, Uruguay: Mundo Afro, 1990.

Brock, Lisa, and Digna Castaneda Fuertes, eds. *Between Race and Empire: African-Americans and Cubans before the Cuban Revolution.* Philadelphia: Temple University Press, 1998.

Brown, Kimberly. "In Borges' Shadow: Review of *The Lesson of the Master* by Norman Thomas di Giovanni." *Janus Head* 1, no. 8 (Summer 2005): 349–51. http://www.janushead.org/8-1/index.cfm.

Brunner, Edward. *Cold War Poetry.* Urbana: University of Illinois Press, 2000.

Buckley, William F., and L. Brent Bozell. *McCarthy and His Enemies: The Record and Its Meaning.* Chicago: H. Regnery, 1954.

Budick, Sanford, and Wolfgang Iser, eds. *The Translatability of Cultures: Figurations of the Space Between.* Stanford, CA: Stanford University Press, 1996.

Buescu, Helena Carvalhão, and Manuela Robeiro Sances, eds. *Literature y Viagens pós-coloniais.* Lisbon: Colibri, 2002.

Bundy, Andrew J. M., ed. *Selected Essays of Wilson Harris: The Unfinished Genesis of the Imagination.* London: Routledge, 1999.

Burkinski, Francisco, trans. *O imenso mar.* By Langston Hughes. Rio de Janeiro: Editorial Vitória, 1944.

Butler, Judith. *Gender Trouble: Feminism and the Subversion of Identity.* New York: Routledge, 1999.

Calvo, Lino Novas. "El que canto Harlem, canta China y España ['Roar China']." *Ayuda* September 18, 1937: 3–4.

Cardenal, Ernesto, trans. "'Portero,' 'Hora de Cierre,' 'Mulato.'" By Langston Hughes. In *Antología de la poesía norteamericana,* edited by Ernesto Cardenal and José Coronel Urtecho, 334–37. Madrid: Aguilar, 1962.

Cardoza y Aragón, Luis. "Langston Hughes, el poeta de los negros." *El Nacional,* March 17, 1935, 6.

Carullo, Sylvia G. "Una aproximación a la poesía federal afro-argentina de la época de Juan Manuel Rosas." *Afro-Hispanic Review* 4, no. 1 (1985): 15–22.

Certeau, Michel de, *The Practice of Everyday Life.* Translated by Steven Randall. 1984. Reprint, Berkeley: University of California Press, 1988.

Chambers, Iain. *Mediterranean Crossings: The Politics of an Interrupted Modernity.* Durham, NC: Duke University Press, 2008.

——. *Migrancy, Culture, Identity.* New York: Routledge, 1994.

Chamoiseau, Patrick. *Texaco: Roman.* Paris: Gallimard, 2004. Translated by Rose-Myriam Réjouis and Val Vinokur. New York: Vintage International, 1997.

Chanady, Amaryll Beatrice, George B. Handley, and Patrick Imbert. *Americas' Worlds and the World's Americas = Les mondes des Amériques et les Amériques du monde.* Ottawa: Legas, 2006.

Chrisman, Robert. "Langston Hughes: Six Letters to Nicolás Guillén." *Black Scholar* 16, no. 4 (1985): 54–60.

Clementi, Hebe. *Lautaro: Historia de una editora.* Buenos Aires: Leviatán, 2004.

Clifford, James. *Routes: Travel and Translation in the Late-Twentieth Century.* Cambridge, MA: Harvard University Press, 1997.

Cobb, Martha. *Harlem, Haiti, and Havana: A Comparative Critical Study of Langston Hughes, Jacques Roumain, Nicolás Guillén.* Washington, D.C.: Three Continents Press, 1979.

Cohn, Roy M. *McCarthy.* New York: New American Library, 1968.

Cohn, Roy M., and Sidney Zion. *The Autobiography of Roy Cohn*. Secaucus, NJ: Lyle Stuart, 1988.

Cruzado, Maribel, and Mary Hricko, eds. and trans. *Langston Hughes. Blues*. Valencia, Spain: Colección La Cruz de Sur, 2004.

Cullen, Countee. *Caroling Dusk: An Anthology of Verse by Negro Poets*. New York: Harper and Brothers, 1927.

Cullen, Deborah, ed. *Nexus New York: Latin American Artists in the Modern Metropolis*. New York: El Museo del Barrio in association with Yale University Press, 2009.

Cyrus, Stanley A. "Ethnic Ambivalence and Afro-Hispanic Novelists." *Afro-Hispanic Review* 21, nos. 1–2 (Spring–Fall 2002): 185–89.

Dace, Letitia, ed. *Langston Hughes: The Contemporary Reviews*. Cambridge: Cambridge University Press, 1997.

Damrosch, David. "Global Regionalism." *European Review* 15, no. 1 (2007): 135–43.

——. *What Is World Literature?* Princeton: Princeton University Press, 2003.

Danky, James Philip, and Wayne A. Wiegand, eds. *Print Culture in a Diverse America*. Urbana: University of Illinois Press, 1998.

Davidson, Ned J. *The Concept of Modernism in Hispanic American Criticism*. Boulder, CO: Pruett Press, 1966.

Dawahare, Anthony. *Nationalism, Marxism, and African American Literature between the Wars*. Jackson: University Press of Mississippi, 2002.

"The Day Langston Hughes Instructed Joe McCarthy about Going to School in a Racially Segregated America." *Journal of Blacks in Higher Education* 44 (Summer 2004): 38–40.

Deck, Alice A., and Marvin A. Lewis. "Langston Hughes and the African Diaspora." Special issues of *Langston Hughes Review* 5, no. 1 (1986).

DeJongh, James. *Vicious Modernism: Black Harlem and the Literary Imagination*. Cambridge: Cambridge University Press, 1990.

Deleuze, Gilles, and Félix Guattari. *A Thousand Plateaus: Capitalism and Schizophrenia*. Translated by Brian Massumi. 1986. Reprint, London: Continuum, 2004.

Denning, Michael. *The Cultural Front: The Laboring of American Culture in the Twentieth Century*. London: Verso, 1996.

Derrida, Jacques. "Living on / Border Lines." Translated by James Hulbert. In *Deconstruction and Criticism*, edited by Harold Bloom, 75–176. New York: Continuum, 1999.

d'Haen, Theo et al., eds. *How Far Is America from Here? Selected Proceedings of the First World Congress of the International American Studies Association 22–24 May 2003*. Amsterdam: Rodopi, 2005.

de Santis, Christopher C., *Essays on Art, Race, Politics, and World Affairs*. Lincoln: University of Missouri Press, 2002.

——. *Langston Hughes: A Documentary Volume*. Detroit: Thomson Gale, 2005.

——, ed. *Langston Hughes and the Chicago Defender: Essays on Race, Politics, and Culture, 1942–62*. Urbana: University of Illinois Press, 1995.

Dettmar, Kevin J. H., and Stephen Watt, eds. *Marketing Modernisms: Self-Promotion, Canonization, Rereading*. Ann Arbor: University of Michigan Press, 1996.

Dimock, Wai Chee. *Through Other Continents: American Literature across Deep Time*. Princeton: Princeton University Press, 2008.

"Diplomacy: Flight to Harlem." *Time,* October 3, 1960, 16. http://www.time.com/time/magazine/article/0,9171,894930–1,00.html.

Dixon, Heriberto. "Who Ever Heard of a Black Cuban?" *Afro-Hispanic Review,* September 1982, 10–12.

Dixon, Melvin. "Rivers Remembering Their Source: Comparative Studies in Black Literary History—Langston Hughes, Jacques Roumain, and Negritude." In *Afro-American Literature: The Reconstruction of Instruction,* edited by Dexter Fisher and Robert B. Stepto, 25–43. New York: MLA, 1979.

Doyle, Don Harrison, and Marco Antonio Villela Pamplona, eds. *Nationalism in the New World.* Athens: University of Georgia Press, 2006.

Du Bois, W. E. B. *The Autobiography of W. E. B. Du Bois: A Soliloquy on Viewing My Life from the Last Decade of Its First Century.* New York: International Publishers, 1968.

Dujovne Ortiz, Alicia. "Un pequeño triunfo negro." *La Nación.* http://www.lacion.com.ar/nota.sp?nota_id = 735432.

Eakin, John Paul. *Fictions in Autobiography: Studies in the Art of Self-Invention.* Princeton: Princeton University Press, 1985.

Edwards, Brent Hayes. "Langston Hughes and the Futures of Diaspora." *American Literary History* 19, no. 3 (2007): 689–711.

——. *The Practice of Diaspora: Literature, Translation, and the Rise of Black Internationalism.* Cambridge, MA: Harvard University Press, 2003.

Escalante, Hildamar, ed. *Breve informe de poesía norteamericana (Versión del inglés).* Caracas: Tipografía La Nación, 1947.

Eshleman, Clayton, and Annette Smith, eds. *Aimé Césaire: The Collected Poetry.* Berkeley: University of California Press, 1983.

Ette, Ottmar. *ÜberLebensWissen: Die Aufgabe der Philologie.* Berlin: Kadmos, 2004.

——. *ZwischenWeltenSchreiben: Literaturen ohne festen Wohnsitz.* Berlin: Kulturverlag Kadmos, 2005.

——. *Konvivenz. Leben und Schreiben nach dem Paradies.* Berlin: Kulturverlag Kadmos, 2012.

Even-Zohar, Itamar. *Polysystem Studies.* Durham, NC: Duke University Press, 1990.

Even-Zohar, Itamar, and Gideon Toury, eds. *Translation Theory and Intercultural Relations.* Tel Aviv: Porter Institute for Poetics and Semantics, 1981.

Eysteinsson, Astradur. *The Concept of Modernism.* Ithaca: Cornell University Press, 1990.

Fabre, Geneviève, and Klaus Benesch, eds. *African Diasporas in the New and Old Worlds: Consciousness and Imagination.* Amsterdam: Rodopi, 2004.

Fariello, Griffin. *Red Scare: Memories of the American Inquisition: An Oral History.* New York: Norton, 1995.

Farley, David G. *Modernist Travel Writing: Intellectuals Abroad.* Columbia: University of Missouri Press, 2010.

Feracho, Leslie. "The Legacy of Negrismo/Negritude: Inter-American Dialogues." *Langston Hughes Review* 16, nos. 1–2 (1999–2001): 1–7.

Fernández de Castro, José Antonio. "A manera de Prologo." In *Versos negros,* Raúl C. Vianello, 5–9. Mexico City: Librería Urbe, 1942. 5–9.

——. "Ha surgido el poeta del son: Nicolás Guillén [entrevista con el seudónimo de Juan del Pueblo]." *La Semana,* May 6, 1930.

——. "La literatura negra actual de Cuba." *Estudios Afrocubanos* 4, nos. 1–4 (1940): 9, 11, 17, 22.

——. "Langston Hughes, poeta militante negro." *El Nacional,* March 3, 1935, 1.

——, trans. "Oye muchacho." By Langston Hughes. *Revista de La Habana* 3, nos. 1–2 (July–August 1930): 77–84.

——, trans. "'Poema,' 'Calma en el mar,' 'Nota de una suicida,' 'Miedo.'" By Langston Hughes. *Revista de La Habana* 2, no. 2 (May 1930): 186.

——. "Presentación de Langston Hughes." *Revista de La Habana* 1, no. 3 (March 1930): 367–69.

——. *Tema negro en las letras de Cuba (1608–1935).* Havana: Mirador, 1943.

——, trans. "Yo, también." By Langston Hughes. *Social* 13, no. 9 (September 1928): 30.

——, trans. "'Yo, También,' 'Los Blancos,' 'Luna de marzo,' 'Soledad (Retrato de una cubana).'" By Langston Hughes. *Revista de La Habana* 1, no. 3 (March 1930): 311–12.

——, trans. "'Yo, también,' 'Los blancos,' 'Soledad (Retrato de una cubana).'" By Langston Hughes. *Diario de la Marina* XCVIII, no. 116 (April 27, 1930), 36. http://dloc.com/UF00001565/05632/36j.

Fernández de Castro, José Antonio, and Félix Lizaso, eds., *La poesía moderna en Cuba (1882–1925).* Madrid: Librería y Casa Editorial Hernando.

Ferrer, José. "Langston Hughes: El cantor de la pena de la raza de color ha tenido contacto con la cultura hispánica." *Reportorio Americano* 49 (1955): 104–06.

Field, Edward. *After the Fall: Poems Old and New.* Pittsburgh: University of Pittsburgh Press, 2007.

Figueira, Gastón. "Dos poetas norteamericanos: I. Sinclair Lewis; II. Langston Hughes." *Revista Iberoamericana* 18 (January–September 1953): 401–04.

——. "Langston Hughes, voz de una raza." *Sustancia: Revista de Cultura Superior* 12 (July 1942): 260–65.

——, trans. "Poemas de Langston Hughes: 'Reverie on the Harlem River,' 'Free Man.'" *Nueva Democracia* 24 (February 1943): 23.

——, trans. "Yo también." By Langston Hughes. *Sustancia: Revista de Cultura Superior* 12 (July 1942): 261.

——, trans. "'Yo también,' 'Blues del pobre muchacho,' 'Canción de una muchacha negra.'" By Langston Hughes. *Aurora,* September 1943, 387–88.

Filreis, Alan. "Words with 'All the Effects of Force': Cold-War Interpretation." *American Quarterly* 39, no. 2 (1987): 306–12, http://works.bepress.com/afilreis/15.

Fisher, Phil, ed. *The New American Studies: Essays from Representations.* Berkeley: University of California Press, 1991.

Fitts, Dudley, ed. *Anthology of Contemporary Latin-American Poetry. Antología de la poesía americana contemporánea.* Norfolk, CT: New Directions, 1942.

Florit, Eugenio, ed. *Antología de la poesía norteamericana contemporánea.* Mexico: Unión Panamericana, 1955.

Forbes, Jack D. *Black Africans and Native Americans: Color, Race, and Caste in the Evolution of Red-Black Peoples.* Oxford: Blackwell, 1988.

Ford, Karen Jackson. "Do Right to Write Right: Langston Hughes's Aesthetics of Simplicity." *Twentieth Century Literature* 38, no. 4 (Winter 1992): 436–56.

Fraile Marcos, Ana María, trans. *Langston Hughes: Oscuridad en España/ Darkness in Spain (Texto bilingüe).* León, Sp.: Universidad, Secretario de Publicaciones, 1998.

Franco, Jean. *César Vallejo: The Dialectics of Poetry and Silence.* Cambridge: Cambridge University Press, 1976.

Frank, Waldo. *América Hispana. Un retrato y una perspectiva.* Translated by León Felipe. Santiago de Chile: Ediciones Ercilla, 1937.

——. *Dawn in Russia: The Record of a Journey.* New York: Charles Scribner's Sons, 1932.

——. *Our America.* New York: Boni and Liveright, 1919.

——. *South American Journey.* New York: Duell, Sloan, and Pearce, 1943.

Franulic, Lenka, trans. "'Los blues que estoy tocando.'" By Langston Hughes. In *Antología del cuento norteamericano.* Santiago de Chile: Ercilla, 1943.

Fried, Albert, ed. *McCarthyism: The Great American Red Scare: A Documentary History.* New York: Oxford University Press, 1997.

Fusco, Coco. *English Is Broken Here: Notes on Cultural Fusion in the Americas.* New York: New Press, 1995.

Gáler, Julio, trans. "'Amor que pasa,' 'Alegría,' 'Canción de la lluvia abrileña.'" By Langston Hughes. *Tiempo Vivo. Revista de Literatura y Arte* 2, no. 708 (July–December 1948): 16–17.

——, trans. "'Hombre,' 'Cancionillo,' 'Uno,' and 'Luna Nueva.'" By Langston Hughes. *Continente,* July 15, 1948, 9.

——, trans. *Langston Hughes. Poemas.* Buenos Aires: Lautaro, 1952.

——, trans. *Mulato: Drama en dos actos (El segundo en dos escenas).* By Langston Hughes. Buenos Aires: Quetzal, 1954.

——, trans. *Riendo por no llorar.* By Langston Hughes. Buenos Aires: Siglo Veinte, 1955.

——, trans. "'Yo fui a buscar la alegría,' 'Amor que pasa.'" By Langston Hughes. *Tiempo Vivo. Revista de Literatura y Arte,* July–December 1943, 16–17.

——, trans. *Yo viajo por un mundo encantado.* By Langston Hughes. Buenos Aires: Fabril, 1959.

Gallardo, Jorge Emilio. *Bibliografía afroargentina.* Buenos Aires: Idea Viva, 2002.

Gandelman, Helena R., and Maria Helena Muus, eds. *Negros famosos a America do Norte.* Sao Paulo: Editorial Classico-Cientifica, 1957.

Gannet, Lewis. "Review of *The Big Sea.*" *Boston Evening Transcript,* August 29, 1940, 11.

García Lorca, Federico. "Gypsy Ballads." Translated by Langston Hughes. *Benoit Poetry Journal,* 1951. http://www.bpj.org/index/Vo2N1.html.

Gardullo, Paul. "Heading Out for the Big Sea: Hughes, Haiti and Constructions of Diaspora in Cold War America." *Langston Hughes Review* 18 (Spring 2004): 56–67.

Gary Bartz and NTU Troop. *I've Known Rivers and Other Bodies.* Prestige PRCD-66001-2. Compact disc released in 2003. Originally recorded in 1973.

Gates, Henry Louis, Jr. *The Signifying Monkey: A Theory of African American Literary Criticism.* New York: Oxford University Press, 1988.

Gates, Henry Louis, and K. A. Appiah, eds. *Langston Hughes: Critical Perspectives Past and Present.* New York: Amistad, 1993.

Gentzler, Edwin. *Translation and Identity in the Americas: New Directions in Translation Theory.* London: Routledge, 2008.

Gibson, Karen Bush. *Langston Hughes.* Hockessin, DE: Mitchell Lane Publishers, 2007.

Giles, Paul. "Hemispheric Partiality." *American Literary History* 18, no. 3 (Fall 2006): 648–55.

——. *Virtual Americas: Transnational Fictions and the Transatlantic Imaginary.* Durham, NC: Duke University Press, 2002.

Gillman, Susan, Kirsten Silva Gruesz, and Rob Wilson, eds. "Worlding American Studies." Special issue of *Comparative American Studies* 2, no. 3 (2004).

Gilroy, Paul. *After Empire: Melancholia or Convivial Culture?* Abingdon, UK: Routledge, 2004.

——. *The Black Atlantic: Modernity and Double Consciousness.* Cambridge, MA: Harvard University Press, 1993.

Goddard, Jean Luc, and Manohla Dargis. "Goddard's Metaphysics of the Movies: An Interview with Jean Luc Goddard." *New York Times,* November 21, 2004, Arts and Leisure, 22.

González, José Luis. "La muerte de dos grandes escritores norteamericanos." *Siempre! Presencia de México,* June 14, 1967, v–ix, 34–35.

González, José Luis, trans. "'Yo también canto América,' 'Tiovivo (Niño negro en el carnaval),' 'Mestizaje.'" By Langston Hughes. *Siempre! Presencia de México,* June 14, 1967, 34–35.

González, José Luis, and Mónica Mansour, eds. *Poesía negra de América.* Mexico City: Ediciones Era, 1976.

González Echevarría, Roberto. "Guillén as Baroque: Meaning in *Motivos de Son.*" *Callaloo* 10, no. 2 (1987): 302–17.

——. *Myth and Archive: A Theory of Latin American Narrative.* Cambridge: Cambridge University Press, 1990.

——. *The Pride of Havana: A History of Cuban Baseball.* New York: Oxford University Press, 2001.

González Echevarría, Roberto, and Enrique Pupo-Walker, eds. *The Cambridge History of Latin American Literature.* 3 vols. Cambridge: Cambridge University Press, 1996.

González Flores, Manuel, trans. "Abordando el tren de la libertad ['Freeedom Train']." By Langston Hughes, *Nivel* 31 (July 25, 1961): xv.

——, trans. "'Cristo es un negro,' 'Amada muerte encantadora,' 'Cuando sin elementos, sin mas armas.'" By Langston Hughes. *El Nacional,* September 12, 1948, 13.

——, trans. "El arado de la libertad. Por Langston Hughes [Freedom's Plough]." *América. Revista Antología* 52 (1946): 63–70.

——. "El gran poeta negro Langston Hughes regresa a los Estados Unidos." *Nivel* 46 (October 25, 1962): 6.

——. "El gran poeta negro norteamericano Langston Hughes." *Nivel* 31 (July 25, 1961): xv.

——, trans. "El sepulchro de Lumumba." By Langston Hughes. *Magisterio* (Mexico City), November 1961.

——, trans. "La balada de Harry Moore (Asesinado en Mims, Florida, EE.UU.)." *Suplemento de El Nacional,* March 15, 1953, 5.

——, trans. *Una pareja de tantas.* By Langston Hughes. Mexico City: Yolotepec,1950.

González Tuñón, Enrique. *Tangos.* Buenos Aires: Librería Histórica, 2003.

Gonález Tuñón, Raúl. "Autoretrato." In *Recordando a Tuñón. Testimonios, Ensayos y Poemas,* edited by Pedro Orgambide, 27–42. Buenos Aires: Desde la Gente. Ediciones Instituto Movilizador de Fonos Cooperativos C.I., 1997.

——. *Las brigadas de choque.* http://eltrenliterario.blogspot.com/2008/12/las-brigadas -de-choque-de-la-poesa.html.

——. *Todos bailan. Los poemas de Juancito Camindor.* 1935. Reprint, Buenos Aires: Libros de Tierra Firme, 1987.

Grandt, Jürgen E. *Shaping Words to Fit the Soul.* Columbus: Ohio State University Press, 2009.

Greer, Bonnie. *Langston Hughes: The Value of Contradiction.* London: Arcadia Books, 2011.

Gruesz, Kristen Silva. *Ambassadors of Culture: The Transamerican Origins of Latino Writing.* Princeton: Princeton University Press, 2002.

Guillaume, Alfred J., Jr. "And Bid Him Translate: Langston Hughes's Translations of Poetry from French." *Langston Hughes Review* 4, no. 2 (1985): 1–23.

Guillén, Nicolás. "Conversación con Langston Hughes." *Diario de la Marina* XCVIII (March 9, 1930), 6.

——. "Motivos de son." *Diario de la Marina* XCVIII, no. 109 (April 20, 1930), 38. http://dloc.com/UF00001565/05625/38j.

——. *Obra poética, 1920–1972.* 2 vols. Havana: Editorial Arte y Literatura, 1974.

——. *Páginas vueltas. Memorias.* Havana: Ediciones Unión, 1982.

——. *Prosa de Prisa: Crónicas.* Buenos Aires: Editorial Hernandez, 1968.

Guillén, Nicolás. *Prosa de Prisa (1929–1972).* Edited by Ángel Augier, 3 vols. Havana: Editorial Arte y Literatura, 1975.

Guirao, Ramón, ed. *Órbita de la poesía afrocubana, 1928–1937 (antología).* Havana: Talleres de Ucar, 1938.

Gunn, Drewey Wayne. *American and British Writers in Mexico, 1556–1973.* Austin: University of Texas Press, 1974.

Gutiérrez, Rosana. *Raúl González Tuñón: Prestidigitador de poemas y revoluciones.* Babab Biblioteca, 2001. http://www.babab.com/no07/gonzalez_tunon.htm.

Hackett, John T. "Review of *The Weary Blues.*" *Springfield Union,* n.d.

Hall, Stuart. "What Is This 'Black' in Black Popular Culture?" In *Black Popular Culture,* edited by M. Wallace and Gina Dent, 21–36. Seattle: Bay Press, 1992.

Handley, George B. "A New World Poetics of Oblivion." In *Look Away! The US South in New World Studies,* edited by Jon Smith and Deborah Cohn, 25–51. Durham, NC: Duke University Press, 2004.

Handy, William C., ed. *Blues: An Anthology.* New York: Albert and Charles Boni, 1926. Reprint, Bedford, MA: Applewood Books.

Handy, William C., and Arna Bontemps. *Father of the Blues: An Autobiography.* 1941. New York: Da Capo Press, 1991.

Harootunian, Harry. "Some Thoughts on Comparability and the Space-Time Problem." *boundary* 2 32, no 2 (2005): 23–52.

Harper, Donna Sullivan. *Not So Simple: The "Simple" Stories by Langston Hughes.* Columbia: University of Missouri Press, 1995.

Harris, William J., ed. *The LeRoi Jones/Amiri Baraka Reader.* New York: Thunder's Mouth Press, 1991.

Harris, Wilson. *Carnival.* London: Faber, 1985.

Harrison, William. "Review of Cuba Libre." *Boston Chronicle,* February 12, 1949.

Hathaway, Heather, Josef Jarab, and Jeffrey Melnick, eds. *Race and the Modern Artist.* New York: Oxford University Press, 2003.

Haugen, Brenda. *Langston Hughes: The Voice of Harlem.* Minneapolis: Compass Point Books, 2006.

Hecker, Max, ed. *Goethe: Maximen und Reflexionen.* Weimar: Verlag der Goethe-Gesellschaft, 1907.

Hedrick, Tace. *Mestizo Modernism: Race, Nation and Identity in Latin American Culture, 1900–1940.* New Brunswick, NJ: Rutgers University Press, 2003.

Heidegger, Martin. *Poetry, Language, Thought.* Translated by Albert Hofstadter. New York: Harper & Row.

Hemenway, Robert E. *Zora Neale Hurston: A Literary Biography.* Urbana: University of Illinois Press, 1978.

Henestrosa, Andrés. "Un extraño suceso." *Novedades,* June 8, 1968, 4, cols. 3–4.

——. "Un poeta negro, amigo de México." *Novedades,* June 1967, 4, cols. 3–4. Reprinted in Ahumada, *Yo también soy América,* 7–9.

Herbrechter, Stefan, ed. *Cultural Studies, Interdisciplinarity, and Translation.* Amsterdam: Rodopi, 2002.

Herman, Arthur. *Joseph McCarthy: Reexamining the Life and Legacy of America's Most Hated Senator.* New York: Free Press, 2000.

Hernández Urbina, Francisco. "Vida y muerte del poeta Langston Hughes." *Universidad Central* (Caracas), April 13, 1961, 16–17.

Hicks, Granville, ed. *Proletarian Literature of the United States: An Anthology.* New York: International Publishers, 1935.

Hoffman, Jascha. "DATA; COMPARATIVE LITERATURE." *New York Times Book Review.* http://query.nytimes.com/gst/fullpage.html?res=9A06E3D8163FF936A25757C0A9619C8B63&scp=5&sq=jascha+hoffman&st=nyt.

Hoffman, Nicholas von. *Citizen Cohn.* New York: Doubleday, 1988.

Hones, Sheila, and Julia Leyda. "Geographies of American Studies." *American Quarterly* 57, no. 4 (2005): 1019–32.

——. "Towards a Critical Geography of American Studies." *Comparative American Studies* 2, no. 2 (2004): 185–203.

Horan, Elizabeth, and Doris Mayer, eds. *This America of Ours: The Letters of Gabriela Mistral and Victoria Ocampo.* Austin: University of Texas Press, 2003.

Howard, J. Woodford, and John Maltese. "Revisiting Judge Harold R. Medina's Charge to the Jury in United States v. Dennis: Notes on Freedom of Speech." Paper prepared for presentation at the Annual Meeting of the American Political Science Association, Washington, D.C., September 2005.

Hricko, Mary. *Genesis of the Chicago Renaissance: Theodore Dreiser, Langston Hughes, Richard Wright, and James T. Farrell.* New York: Routledge, 2009.

Hughes, Langston. *ASK YOUR MAMA: 12 Moods for Jazz.* New York: Knopf, 1961.

——. *The Big Sea: An Autobiography.* 1940. Reprint, New York: Hill and Wang, 1993.

——. *The Dream Keeper and Other Poems.* New York: Knopf, 1932.

——. *Fine Clothes to the Jew.* New York: Knopf, 1927.

——, ed. *I Hear the People Singing: Selected Poems of Walt Whitman.* New York: International Publishers, 1946.

——. *I Wonder As I Wander: An Autobiographical Journey.* 1956. New York: Hill and Wang, 1995. With an introduction by Arnold Rampersad.

——. The Langston Hughes Papers. James Weldon Johnson Memorial Collection, Beinecke Rare Book and Manuscript Library, Yale University.

——. *The Langston Hughes Reader.* New York: G. Braziller, 1958.

——. *Let America Be America Again and other Poems.* New York: Vintage Books, 2004. With preface by John Kerry.

——. *Montage of a Dream Deferred*. New York: Holt, 1951.

——. "The Negro Artist and the Racial Mountain." *Nation,* June 23, 1926.

——. *The Negro Mother and Other Dramatic Recitations*. New York: Golden Stair Press, 1931.

——. *Scottsboro Limited: Four Poems and a Play in Verse*. New York: Golden Stair Press, 1932.

——, trans. *Selected Poems of Gabriela Mistral* [pseud.]. Bloomington: Indiana University Press, 1957.

——. *Selected Poems of Langston Hughes*. 1959. Reprint, New York: Vintage Books, 1974.

.——. *Shakespeare in Harlem*. New York: Knopf, 1942.

——. "Sobre Guillén." *El Heraldo de Cuba,* November 1948, 336.

——. "Testimony of Langston Hughes (Accompanied by His Counsel, Frank D. Reeves), March 24, 1953." In *Executive Sessions of the Senate Permanent Subcommittee on Investigations of the Committee on Government Operations, 83rd Congress, First Session, 1953,* edited by Donald A. Ritchie. Washington, DC: U.S. Government Printing Office, 1953–54, 2:973–98.

——. "Testimony of Langston Hughes, Accompanied by His Counsel, Frank D. Reeves, March 26, 1953." *Hearings and Reports Published by the Subcommittee on Investigations of the Committee on Government Operations, United States Senate, under the Chairmanship of Joseph R. McCarthy (R-Wisconsin): Part 1, 1953–54.* Washington, D.C.: State Department Information Program— Information Centers, 1953, 73–83.

——. *The Ways of White Folks*. New York: Knopf, 1934.

——. *The Weary Blues*. New York: Knopf, 1926.

——. "When a Man Sees Red." In *Simple Speaks His Mind,* 209–13. Mattituck, NY: Aeonian Press, 1950.

Hughes, Langston, and Arna Bontemps, eds. *The Poetry of the Negro, 1746–1949.* Garden City, NY: Doubleday, 1949.

——, eds. *The Poetry of the Negro, 1746–1970.* Rev. and updated ed. Garden City, NY: Doubleday, 1970.

Hughes, Langston, and Ben Frederic Carruthers, trans. *Cuba Libre: Poems by Nicolás Guillén.* Los Angeles: Ward Ritchie Press, 1948.

Hughes, Langston, and Mercer Cook, trans. *Masters of the Dew.* By Jacques Roumain. 1947. Oxford: Heinemann, 1997.

Hughes, Langston, and W. S Mervin, trans. *Blood Wedding and Yerma [Bodas de Sangre y Yerma].* By Frederico García Lorca. New York: Theatre Communications Group, 1994.

Huizinga, Johan. *Homo Ludens: A Study of the Play Element in Culture.* 1950. Boston: Beacon Press, 1955.

Hulme, Peter. "Expanding the Caribbean." In *Perspectives on the 'Other America': Comparative Approaches to Caribbean and Latin American Culture,* edited by Michael Niblett and Kerstin Oloff, 29–49. Amsterdam: Rodopi, 2009.

Hurston, Zora Neale. "How It Feels to Be Colored Me." *World Tomorrow* 11 (May 1928): 215–16.

——. *Mules and Men*. 1935. Reprint, New York: Harper Perennial, 1995.

Hutchinson, George B. *The Cambridge Companion to the Harlem Renaissance.* Cambridge: Cambridge University Press, 2007.

——. *The Harlem Renaissance in Black and White*. Cambridge, MA: Belknap Press of Harvard University Press, 1995.

——. "'Langston Hughes and the 'Other' Whitman.'" In *The Continuing Presence of Walt Whitman: The Life after the Life,* edited by Robert K. Martin, 16–27. Iowa City: University of Iowa Press, 1992.

Iser, Wolfgang. *The Act of Reading: A Theory of Aesthetic Response*. Baltimore: Johns Hopkins University Press, 1978. 2nd ed., 1980.

——. "The Reading Process: A Phenomenological Approach." *New Directions in Literary History,* edited by Ralph Cohen, 125–45. Baltimore and London: Johns Hopkins University Press, 1974.

Iznaga, Alcides, and Aldo Menéndez, trans. "The Negro Speaks of Rivers (El Negro habla de los ríos)." By Langston Hughes. *Signo* 2 (1954).

Jackson, Lawrence Patrick. *The Indignant Generation: A Narrative History of African American Writers and Critics, 1934–1960*. Princeton: Princeton University Press, 2010.

Jackson, Richard L. *Black Writers and Latin America: Cross-Cultural Affinities*. Washington, DC: Howard University Press, 1998.

——. *Black Writers in Latin America*. Albuquerque: University of New Mexico Press, 1979.

——. "Langston Hughes and the African Diaspora in South America." *Langston Hughes Review* 5, no. 5 (1986): 23–33.

——. "The Shared Vision of Langston Hughes and Black Hispanic Writers." *Black American Literature Forum* 15, no. 3 (Fall 1981): 89–92.

Jacques, Geoffrey. *A Change in the Weather*. Amherst: University of Massachusetts Press, 2009.

Jakobson, Roman. "On Linguistic Aspects of Translation." In *Language in Literature,* Edited by Krystyna Pomorska and Stephen Rudy, 428–35. Cambridge, MA: Harvard University Press, 1987.

Johnson, Barbara. "Taking Fidelity Philosophically." *Difference—In Translation,* edited by Joseph F. Graham, 142–48. Ithaca: Cornell University Press, 1985.

Johnson, Charles R. *Oxherding Tale*. Bloomington: Indiana University Press, 1982.

Johnson, David, ed. *Stages of Translation*. Bath, UK: Absolute Classics, 1996.

Johnson, James Weldon. *Black Manhattan*. 1930. Reprint, New York: Arno Press, 1968.

——, ed. *The Book of American Negro Poetry*. 1922. Reprint, New York: Harcourt Brace Jovanovich, 1969.

——. "The Dilemma of the Negro Author." In *The Essential Writings of James Weldon Johnson,* edited by Rudolph P. Byrd, 201–9. New York: Modern Library, 2008.

Johnston, Georgia. *The Formation of 20th-Century Queer Autobiography: Reading Vita Sackville-West, Virginia Woolf, Hilda Doolittle, and Gertrude Stein*. New York: Palgrave Macmillan, 2007.

Johnston, Nancy, and Leslie Catherine Sanders. *Langston Hughes: The Plays to 1942: Mulatto to The Sun Do Move*. ebrary, Inc., 2002. http://site.ebrary.com/lib/academiccompletetitles/home.action.

Jones, Veda Boyd. *Jazz Age Poet: A Story about Langston Hughes*. Minneapolis: Millbrook Press, 2006.

Jrade, Cathy L. *Modernismo, Modernity, and the Development of Spanish American Literature*. Austin: University of Texas Press, 1998.

Julien, Isaac. *Looking for Langston.* London: British Film Institute, 1989.

Kadir, Djelal. "Introduction: America and Its Studies." *PMLA* 118, no. 1 (2003): 9–24.

Kapchan, Deborah A., and Pauline Turner Strong. "Theorizing the Hybrid." *Journal of American Folklore* 112, no. 445 (Summer, 1999): 239–53.

Kaplan, Amy. "Violent Belongings and the Question of Empire Today: Presidential Address to the American Studies Association, Hartford, Connecticut, October 17, 2003." *American Quarterly* 56, no. 1 (2004): 1–18.

Kaplan, Amy and Donald Pease, eds. *Cultures of United States Imperialism.* Durham, NC: Duke University Press, 1993.

Kaplan, Caren. "Resisting Autobiography: Out-Law Genres and Transnational Feminist Subjects." In *Women, Autobiography, Theory: A Reader,* edited by Sidonie Smith and Julia Watson, 208–21. Madison: University of Wisconsin Press, 1998.

Kaplan, Lewis A. "The House Un-American Activities Committee and Its Opponents: A Study in Congressional Dissonance." *Journal of Politics* 30, no. 3 (1968): 647–71.

Karem, Jeff. *The Purloined Islands: Caribbean-U.S. Crosscurrents in Literature and Culture, 1880–1959.* Charlottesville: University of Virginia Press, 2011.

Katz, Daniel. *American Modernism's Expatriate Scene: The Labour of Translation.* Edinburgh: Edinburgh University Press, 2007.

Kaup, Monica. "'Our America' That Is Not One: Transnational Black Atlantic Disclosures in Nicolás Guillén and Langston Hughes." *Discourse: Journal for Theoretical Studies in Media and Culture* 22, no. 3 (2000): 87–113.

Kelley, Robin D. G. "'This Ain't Ethiopia, but It'll Do.'" In *African-Americans in the Spanish Civil War,* edited by Collum Danny Duncan, 5–60. New York: G. K. Hall, 1992.

Kelly, Stephen, and David Johnston, eds. *Betwixt and Between: Place and Cultural Translation.* Newcastle, UK: Cambridge Scholars, 2007.

Kent, Alicia A. *African, Native, and Jewish American Literature and the Reshaping of Modernism.* New York: Palgrave Macmillan, 2007.

King, John. *Sur: A Study of the Argentine Literary Journal and Its Role in the Development of a Culture, 1931–1970.* Cambridge: Cambridge University Press, 1986.

Kinzer, Stephen. "America Yawns at Foreign Fiction." *New York Times,* July 16, 2003.

Kirkpatrick, Gwen. *The Dissonant Legacy of Modernismo: Lugones, Herrera y Reisseg, and the Voices of Modern Spanish American Poetry.* Berkeley: University of California Press, 1989.

Klein, Julie Thompson. *Crossing Boundaries: Knowledge, Disciplinarities, and Interdisciplinarities.* Charlottesville: University Press of Virginia, 1996.

Knopf, Alfred A. *Publishing Then and Now, 1912–1964.* New York: New York Public Library, 1964.

Kolin, Philip C. "The Mexican Premiere of Tennessee Williams's *A Streetcar Named Desire.*" *Mexican Studies/Estudios Mexicanos* 10, no. 2 (Summer 1994): 315–40.

Kowalewski, Michael. "Contemporary Regionalism." In *A Companion to the Regional Literatures of America,* edited by Charles L. Crow, 7–24. Malden, MA: Blackwell, 2003.

Kronfeld, Chana. *On the Margins of Modernism: Decentering Literary Dynamics.* Berkeley: University of California Press, 1996.

Kushner, Tony. *Angels in America: A Gay Fantasia on National Themes.* New York: Theatre Communications Group, 1993.

Kutzinski, Vera M. *Against the American Grain: Myth and History in William Carlos Williams, Jay Wright, and Nicolás Guillén.* Baltimore: Johns Hopkins University Press, 1987.

——. *Sugar's Secrets: Race and the Erotics of Cuban Nationalism.* Charlottesville: University Press of Virginia, 1993.

Lafleur, Héctor René, Sergio Demetrio Provenzano, Fernando Pedro Alonso, and Marcela Croce, eds. *Las revistas literarias argentinas (1893–1967).* Buenos Aires: El 8vo. Loco Ed., 2006.

Lamming, George. *The Pleasures of Exile.* 1960. Reprint, Ann Arbor: University of Michigan Press, 1992.

Lanero, Juan José, and Secundino Villoria, eds. *Literatura en traducción: Versiones españoles de Franklin, Irving, Cooper, Poe, Hawthorne, Longfellow, Prescott, Emerson y Whitman en el siglo XIX.* León: Universidad de León, 1996.

Larsen, Nella. *Passing.* 1929. Reprint, New York: Penguin, 1997.

Latino, Simon [Carlos Henrique Pareja, pseud.], ed. *Antologia de la poesia negra latinoamericana.* Buenos Aires: Editorial Nuestra América,

Lattuca, Lisa R. *Creating Interdisciplinarity: Interdisciplinary Research and Teaching among College and University Faculty.* Nashville: Vanderbilt University Press, 2001.

Laughlin, James, ed. *New Directions in Prose and Poetry.* Norfolk, CT: New Direction, 1944.

Lecercle, Jean-Jacques. *The Violence of Language.* London: Routledge, 1990.

Lefevre, André. "Literary Theory and Translated Literature." *Dispositio* 7, nos. 19–20: 3–22.

——. *Translation, Rewriting and the Manipulation of the Literary Frame.* New York: Routledge, 1992.

Lemke, Sieglinde. *Primitivist Modernism: Black Culture and the Origins of Transatlantic Modernism.* New York: Oxford University Press, 1998.

Lenz, Günter H. "American Studies and the Radical Tradition: From the 1930s to the 1960s." *Prospects* 12 (1987): 21–58.

Levander, Caroline Field, and Robert S. Levine, eds. *Hemispheric American Studies.* New Brunswick N.J.: Rutgers University Press, 2008.

Levine, Susan Jill. *Latin America. Fiction and Poetry in Translation.* New York: Center for Inter-American Relations, 1970.

Lewis, Marvin A. *Afro-Argentine Discourse: Another Dimension of the Black Diaspora.* Columbia: University of Missouri Press, 1996.

——. *Afro-Uruguyan Literature: Post-Colonial Perspectives.* Danvers: Rosemont Publishing and Printing Corp., 2003.

Lichtman, Robert M. "Addendum to "Louis Budenz, the FBI, and the 'List of 400 Concealed Communists.'" *American Communist History* 5, no. 1 (2006): 145–46.

Lindberg-Wada, Gunilla, ed. *Studying Transcultural Literary History.* Berlin: Walter de Gruyter, 2006.

Lipschutz Gabriel, Lucie. *El siglo de la siglas.* Madrid: Hebraica Ediciones, 2005.

Locke, Alain LeRoy, ed. *The New Negro.* 1925. Reprint, New York: Atheneum, 1977.

Loftus, Brian. "In/verse Autobiography: Sexual (In)Difference and the Textual Backside of Langston Hughes's *The Big Sea.*" *Auto/Biography Studies* 15, no. 1 (2000): 141–61.

López Narváez, Carlos. *El cielo en el río: Versiones de poemas del francés y del inglés.* Bogotá: Ediciones Espiral Colombia, 1952.

López Narváez, Carlos, trans. "El negro habla de los ríos." By Langston Hughes. *El Tiempo,* Suplemento literario, June 6, 1948, 3.

Lowney, John. "Langston Hughes and the 'Nonesense' of Bebop." *American Literature* 72, no. 2 (2000): 357–85.

Lozano, Rafael. *Euterpe: Poesías sobre motivos musicales.* Mexico City: Ediciones del Bloque de Obreros Intelectuales de Mexico, 1930.

——. "Langston Hughes, El poeta afroestadounidense." *Crísol. Revista de Crítica* 5 (1931): 225–27. Reprinted in *Reportorio Americano,* April 22, 1931, 226.

——, trans., "Poemas por Langston Hughes: 'Yo también,' 'Soy un Negro,' 'El Negro habla de los Ríos,' 'Cruz,' 'Ardella,' 'Puerto,' 'Alegría,' 'Soledad,' 'Placera,' 'Cancionera,' ['I, Too,' 'Negro,' 'The Negro Speaks of Rivers,' 'Cross,' 'Ardella,' 'Port Town,' 'Joy,' 'Soledad']." *Crísol, Revista de Crítica* 27 (March 1931): 227–32.

——, trans. "Yo también." By Langston Hughes. *La Nueva Democracia* 19 (August 1938): 15.

Magdaleno, Mauricio. "La Fiesta de Harlem." *La Nueva Democracia* 19 (August 1938): 14–15.

Majstorovic, Gloria. "An American Place: Victoria Ocampo, the Foundation of Sur, and Hemispheric Alliances." *Arizona Journal of Hispanic Cultural Studies* 9 (2005): 171–80.

Mallan, Lloyd, ed. "A Little Anthology of Afro-Cuban Poetry," in *New Directions 1944,* edited by James McLaughlin. Norfolk, CT: New Directions, 1944.

Mañach, Jorge. *Indagación del choteo.* 1928. Rev. ed. Havana: Editorial Libro Cubano, 1955. http://lilt.ilstu.edu/jjpancr/Spanish_305/indagaci%C3%B3n_del_choteo.htm.

Mandelik, Peter, and Stanley Schatt, eds. *Concordance to the Poetry of Langston Hughes.* Detroit: Gale Research Co., 1975.

Manzanas, Ana Maria, ed. *Border Transits: Literature and Culture across the Line.* Amsterdam: Rodopi, 2007.

Marco, Pedro, trans. "Canción de la calle." By Langston Hughes. *Diario de la Marina* XCVIII (March 16, 1930), 6.

Marques, Oswaldino, ed. *Videntes e sonâmbulos: Coletânea de poemas norteamericanos.* Rio de Janeiro: Minstério da Educação e Cultura, Servico de Documentação, 1955.

Márquez, Roberto, ed. *My Last Name and Other Poem /El apellido y otros poemas y/de Nicolás Guillén.* London: Mango Publishing, 2002.

Martínez Inglés, Txema. "Canción para Billie Holiday." *Litoral,* nos. 227–28 (2001), n.p.

Martins, Eduardo, ed. and trans. *Poemas de Langston Hughes.* João Pessoa: Impresso an Gráfica "A Imprensa," 1970.

Marx, Karl. *Capital: A Critique of Political Economy.* Vol. 1. Translated by Samuel Moore and Edward Aveling. New York: Random House, 1906. http://books.google.com/books/about/Capital.html?id = afUtAAAAIAAJ

Masiello, Francine. "Joyce in Buenos Aires (Talking Sexuality through Translation)." *Diacritics* 34, nos. 3–4 (Fall–Winter 2004): 55–72.

——. *Lenguaje e ideología: Las escuelas argentinas de vanguardia.* Buenos Aires: Hachette, 1986.

Matz, Charles, and Ana Jordá. "Los cansados Blues." *Litoral* 227–28 (2001), n.p.

Maurer, Christopher, ed. *García Lorca, Federico: Poet in New York.* New York: Farrar Straus Giroux, 1988.

May, Barbara Dale. "Poetry and Political Commitment: Alberti, Guillén, and Hughes." *Studies in Afro-Hispanic Literature* 2–3 (1978–79): 14–27.

McKay, Claude. *A Long Way from Home: An Autobiography.* 1937. New York: Harcourt, Brace and World, 1970.

McLaughlin, James, ed. *New Directions 1944, Number 8.* Norfolk, CT: New Directions, 1944.

McMurray, David Arthur. "Dos negros en el Nuevo Mundo: Notas sobre el 'americanismo' de Langston Hughes y la cubanía de Nicolás Guillén." *Casa de las Américas* 14 (1974): 122–28.

Mejía Sánchez, Ernesto. Review of "Yo también soy América." *Amaru: Revista de Artes y Ciencias,* April–June 1968, 95.

Melas, Natalie. *All the Difference in the World: Postcoloniality and the Ends of Comparison.* Stanford, CA: Stanford University Press, 2007.

Mendoza, Agustín, ed. *Del tiempo y des las ideas: Textos en honor de Gregorio Weinberg.* Buenos Aires: Carlos A. Firpo S.R.L., 2000.

Merino, Antonio, ed. *Nicolás Guillén. En la guerra de España: Crónicas y enunciados.* Madrid: Ediciones de la Torre, 1988.

Mignolo, Walter. *The Idea of Latin America.* Malden, MA: Blackwell, 2005.

Miller, Christopher L. *The French Atlantic Triangle: Literature and Culture of the Slave Trade.* Durham, NC: Duke University Press, 2008.

Miller, Joshua L. *Accented America: The Cultural Politics of Multilingual Modernism.* New York: Oxford University Press, 2011.

Miller, Marilyn. "(Gypsy) Rhythm and (Cuban) Blues: The Neo-American Dream in Guillén and Hughes." *Comparative Literature* 51, no. 4 (1999): 324–44.

Miller, Perry. *Errand into the Wilderness.* 1956. Reprint, Cambridge, MA: Belknap Press of Harvard University Press, 1984.

Miller, R. Baxter. *The Art and Imagination of Langston Hughes.* Lexington: University Press of Kentucky, 2006.

——. "'Even After I Was Dead': *The Big Sea*—Paradox, Preservation, and Holistic Time." *Black American Literature Forum* 11, no. 2 (1977): 39–45.

——. "'For a Moment I Wondered': Theory and Symbolic Form in the Autobiographies of Langston Hughes." *Langston Hughes Review* 3, no. 2 (Spring 1984): 1–6.

Miller, W. Jason. "Justice, Lynching, and American Riverscapes: Finding Reassurance in Langston Hughes's 'The Negro Speaks of Rivers.'" *Langston Hughes Review* 18, no. 1 (Spring 2004): 24–37.

Molina, Lucía Dominga, and Mario Luis López. "Afro-Argentineans: "Forgotten" and "Disappeared"—Yet Still Present." In *African Roots/American Cultures: Africa in the Creation of the Americas,* edited by Sheila S. Walker, 332–47. Lanham, MD: Rowman & Littlefield, 2001.

Montalvo, Berta G. *Índice bibliográfico de la Revista de la Habana.* Miami: Ediciones Universal, 2001.

Moore, David Chioni. "Colored Dispatches from the Uzbek Border: Langston Hughes' Relevance, 1933–2002." *Callaloo* 25, no. 4 (2002): 1115–35.

Moore-Gilbert, Bart J. *Postcolonial Life-Writing: Culture, Politics, and Self-Representation.* London: Routledge, 2009.

Moretti, Franco. "Conjectures on World Literature." In *Debating World Literature,* edited by Christopher Prendergast, 148–62. London: Verso, 2004.

Morgan, Ted. *Reds: McCarthyism in Twentieth-Century America.* New York: Random House, 2004.

Muchnik, Jacobo. *Editing: Arte de poner los puntos sobres las íes—y difundirlas.* Madrid: del Taller de Mario Muchnik, 2004.

Mullen, Edward J. "European and North America Writers in *Contemporáneos.*" *Comparative Literature Studies* 8 (December 1971): 338–46.

——. "Presencia y evaluación de Langston Hughes en Hispanoamérica." *Revista de Latinoamericana de Escritores* 15 (1974): 16–21. Also in *Memoria del XVII Congreso del Instituto Internacional de Literatura Iberonamericana,* 1395–401. Madrid: Ediciones Cultura Hispánica, 1978.

——. "Langston Hughes in Mexico and Cuba." *Review: Latin American Literature and Arts* 47 (1993): 23–27.

——. *Langston Hughes in the Hispanic World and Haiti.* Hamden, CT: Archon Books, 1977.

Navasky, Victor S. *Naming Names.* New York: Penguin, 1980.

Nelson, Cary. "Lyric Politics: The Poetry of Edwin Rolfe." In *Edwin Rolfe: Collected Poems,* edited by Cary Nelson and Jefferson Hendricks, 1–55. Urbana: University of Illinois Press, 1996.

——. *Revolutionary Memory: Recovering the Poetry of the American Left.* London: Routledge, 2001.

Newcomb, John Timberman. *Would Poetry Disappear? American Verse and the Crisis of Modernity.* Columbus: Ohio State University Press, 2004.

"Nicolás Guillén." *Daily Worker,* June 3, 1941.

Niedlich, Florian. "Travel as Transgression: Claude McKay's *Banana Bottom,* J. M. Coetzee's *Life and Times of Michael K.,* and Hanif Kureishi's *The Black Album.*" In *Local Natures, Global Responsibilities: Ecocritical Perspectives on the New English Literatures,* edited by Laurenz Volkmann, 337–50. Amsterdam: Rodopi, 2010.

Nietzsche, Friedrich. *Untimely Meditations.* Edited by Daniel Breazeale and Reginald John Hollingdale. Cambridge: Cambridge University Press, 2004.

Niranjana, Tejaswini. *Siting Translation: History, Post-Structuralism, and the Colonial Context.* Berkeley: University of California Press, 1992.

Noble, Enrique. "Nicolás Guillén y Langston Hughes." *Nueva Revista Cubana* (1961–62): 41–85.

North, Michael. *The Dialect of Modernism: Race, Language, and Twentieth-Century Literature.* New York: Oxford University Press, 1994.

Novás Calvo, Lino. "El que cantó Harlem, canta China y España." *Ayuda* 18 (1937): 3–47.

Novo, Salvador. "Notas sobre la poesía de los negros en los Estados Unidos." *Contemporáneos* 4, nos. 40–41 (1931): 197–200.

Núñez, Ana Julieta. *Raúl Larra: Payró y el recorrido de una lectura,* 2009. www.jornadashumha.com.ar.

Nwankwo, Ifeoma C. K. "Langston Hughes and the Translation of Nicolás Guillén's Afro-Cuban Culture and Language." *Langston Hughes Review* 16.1–2 (1999–2001): 55–72.

Ocampo, Victoria. *Autobiografía.* Madrid: Alianza Editorial, 1991.

——. "Carta a Waldo Frank." *Sur* 1, no. 1 (1931): 7–18.

O'Daniel, Therman B. *Langston Hughes, Black Genius: A Critical Evaluation.* New York: William Morrow, 1971.

Ogorzaly, Michael A. *Waldo Frank: Prophet of Hispanic Regeneration.* Lewisburg, PA: Bucknell University Press, 1994.

Oleza, Joan. "Rafael Alberti, Max Aub, Pablo Picasso: Urdimbres." *El Correo de Euclides, Anuario científico de la Fundación Max Aub (Segorbe)* 1 (2006): 188–205.

Orgambide, Pedro, ed. *El hombre de la rosa blindada: Vida y poesía de Raúl González Tuñón.* Buenos Aires: AMEGHINO Editora, 1998.

——. *Recordando a Tuñón. Testimonios, Ensayos y Poemas.* Buenos Aires: Desde la Gente. Ediciones Instituto Movilizador de Fonos Cooperativos C.I., 1997.

Ortíz, Fernando. *Los negros brujos: Hampa afro-cubana. Apuntes para un estudio de etnología criminal.* Miami: Universal, 1973.

Ortíz Ávila, Raúl. "El ruiseñor y la prosa." *El Nacional* 20 (April 1952): 12.

Ortíz Oderigo, Nestor R. "El tema del negro en la literatura de América." *Claridad* (Buenos Aires) 19, no. 345 (1940): 550, 554.

——, trans. *Pero con risas…novela.* By Langston Hughes. Buenos Aires: Editorial Futuro, 1945.

Ortíz-Carboneres, Salvador, ed. *Yoruba from Cuba: Selected Poem /Poesías Escogidas de Nicolás Guillén.* Leeds: Peepal Tree, 2005.

Oshinsky, David M. *A Conspiracy So Immense: The World of Joe McCarthy.* New York: Oxford University Press, 2005.

Pardo García, Germán. "Honrando la memoria de Langston Hughes." *Nivel* 55 (February 15, 1963): 1.

Pareja, Carlos Henrique. *Los mejores versos de poesía negra.* Buenos Aires: Editorial Nuestra América, 1958.

Parkinson Zamora, Lois. *The Usable Past: The Imagination of History in Recent Fiction of the Americas.* Cambridge: Cambridge University Press, 1997.

Parsons, Ivan, trans. "'Escupideras de metal,' 'Muchacho de elevador,' 'Portero de Pullman.'" By Langston Hughes. *Social* XV, no. 5 (May 1930), 19.

——. "Portero de Pullman." By Langston Hughes. *Diario de la Marina* XCVIII (June 8, 1930), n.p.

Patell, Cyrus R.K. "Comparative American Studies: Hybridity and beyond." *American Literary History* 11, no. 1 (1999): 166–86.

Patterson, Anita Haya. "Jazz, Realism, and the Modernist Lyric: The Poetry of Langston Hughes." *Modern Language Quarterly* 61, no. 4 (December 2000): 651–82.

——. *Race, American Literature and Transnational Modernisms.* Cambridge: Cambridge University Press, 2008.

Pavlić, Edward Michael. *Crossroads Modernism: Descent and Emergence in African-American Literary Culture.* Minneapolis: University of Minnesota Press, 2002.

Paz, Octavio. *Traducción: Literatura y literalidad.* Barcelona: Tusquets, 1979.

Paz, Octavio, and Irene del Corral. "Translation: Literature and Letters." In *Theories of Translation: An Anthology of Essays from Dryden to Derrida,* Edited by Rainer Schulte and John Bignenet, 152–62. Chicago: University of Chicago Press, 1992

Pease, Donald E., and Robyn Wiegman, eds. *The Futures of American Studies.* Durham, NC: Duke Univ. Press, 2002.

Peddie, Ian. "'There's No Way Not to Lose': Langston Hughes and Intraracial Class Antagonism." *Langston Hughes Review* 18 (Spring 2004): 38–55.

Peloso, Vicente. Review of *Aspectos de la Cultura Africana en el Rio de la Plata* by Nestor Ortiz Oderigo. *Journal of Negro History* 61, no. 2 (1976): 224–25.

Pereda Valdés, Ildefonso, ed. *Antología de la poesía negra americana.* Santiago de Chile: Ediciones Ercilla, 1936. Reprint, Montevideo: Biblioteca Uruguaya de Autores, 1953.

———. *El negro rioplatense y otros ensayos.* Montevideo: C. Garciá & Ciá, 1937.

———, ed. *La guitarra del los negros.* Montevideo: Ricordi, 1926.

———. *Línea de color (ensayos afro-americanos).* Santiago de Chile: Ediciones Ercilla, 1938.

———. *Negros esclavos y negros libres; esquema de una sociedad esclavista y aporte del negro en nuestra formación nacional.* Montevideo: [Imprenta "Gaceta comercial"], 1941.

———. *Raza negra: 1. Poemas de Negros. 2. Cantos Africanos. 3. Cancionero Afro-Monteviedeano.* [Montevideo]: Edición del periódico negro La Vanguardia, 1929.

———. *Toda la poesía negra de Ildefonso Pereda Valdés.* Montevideo: Índice Mimeografía, 1979.

Pereyra, Washington Luis, ed. *La prensa literaria Argentina 1890–1974.* Vol. 4, *Los años de compromiso, 1940–1949.* Buenos Aires: Fundación Bartolomé Hidalgo, 2008.

Pérez, Louis. "Between Baseball and Bullfighting: The Quest for Nationality in Cuba, 1888–1898." *Journal of American History* 81 (September 1994): 493–517.

Pérez Firmat, Gustavo. "Riddles of the Sphincter: Another Look at the Cuban Choteo." *Diacritics* 14, no. 4 (1984): 67–77.

———. *The Cuban Condition: Translation and Identity in Modern Cuban Literature.* Cambridge: Cambridge University Press, 1989.

———, ed. *Do the Americas Have a Common Literature?* Durham, NC: Duke University Press, 1990.

Pérez Heredia, Alexander, ed. *Epistolario de Nicolás Guillén.* Havana: Letras Cubanas, 2002.

Pfeiffer, Kathleen, ed. *Brother Mine: The Correspondence of Jean Toomer and Waldo Frank.* Urbana: University of Illinois Press, 2010.

Podestá, Guido. "Cultural Liaisons in American Literatures." In *Modernism and Its Margins,* edited by Anthony L. Geist and José B. Monleón, 168–85. New York: Garland, 1999.

Podhoretz, Norman. *The Bloody Crossroads: Where Literature and Politics Meet.* New York: Routledge, 1986.

"The Poetry Bulletin: Review of *Cuba Libre.*" *Tiger's Eye* (Westport, CT), March 1, 1949, 116.

Polezzi, Loredana. *Translating Travel: Contemporary Italian Travel Writing in English Translation.* Aldershot, UK: Ashgate, 2001.

Pollard, Charles W. *New World Modernisms: T. S. Eliot, Derek Walcott, and Kamau Brathwaite.* Charlottesville: University of Virginia Press, 2004.

Pomerantz, Charlotte, ed. *A Quarter Century of Un-Americana.* New York: Marzani & Munsell, 1963.

Ponce, Martin Joseph. "Langston Hughes's Queer Blues." *Modern Language Quarterly* 66, no. 4 (2005): 505–37.

Porter, Carolyn. "What We Know That We Don't Know: Remapping American Literary Studies." *American Literary History* 6, no. 3 (1994): 467–526.

Pratt, Mary Louise. *Imperial Eyes: Travel Writing and Transculturation.* New York: Routledge, 1992.

Prentice, Chris. *Cultural Transformations: Perspectives on Translocation in a Global Age.* Amsterdam: Rodopi, 2010.

Prescott, Lawrence. "Brother to Brother: The Friendship and Literary Correspondence of Manuel Zapata Olivella and Langston Hughes." *Afro-Hispanic Review* 25, no. 1 (Spring 2006): 87–103.

Pyenson, Lewis, ed. *Disciplines and Interdisciplinarity in the New Century.* Lafayette: Center for Louisiana Studies, 1997.

Radhakrishnan, R. "Globality Is Not Wordliness." *Gramma: Journal of Theory and Criticism* 13 (2005): 183–98.

——. "Postcoloniality and the Boundaries of Identity." *Callaloo* 16, no. 4 (1993): 750–51.

Ramazani, Jahan. *Poetry of Mourning: The Modern Elegy from Hardy to Heaney.* Chicago: University of Chicago Press, 1994.

——. *A Transnational Poetics.* Chicago: University of Chicago Press, 2009.

Rampersad, Arnold, ed. *The Collected Works of Langston Hughes.* Vol. 16, *The Translations.* Introduction by Dellita Martin-Ogunsola. Columbia: University of Missouri Press, 2003.

——. *The Life of Langston Hughes.* Vol. 1, *1902–1941. I, Too, Sing America.* New York: Oxford University Press, 1986.

——. *The Life of Langston Hughes.* Vol. 2, *I Dream a World.* New York: Oxford University Press, 1988.

Rampersad, Arnold, and David Roessel, eds. *The Collected Poems of Langston Hughes.* New York: Random House, 1994.

Raphael-Hernandez, Heike, and Shannon Steen. *AfroAsian Encounters: Culture, History, Politics.* ebrary, Inc., 2006. http://site.ebrary.com/lib/academiccompletetitles/home.action.

Ratto Ciarlo, José. *Defensa y apología de las razas de color.* Caracas: Editorial Bolívar, 1937.

Read, Justin. *Modern Poetics and Hemispheric American Cultural Studies.* New York: Palgrave Macmillan, 2009.

Redish, Martin H. *The Logic of Persecution: Free Expression and the McCarthy Era.* Stanford, CA: Stanford University Press, 2005.

Reeves, Thomas C. *McCarthyism.* Hinsdale, IL: Dryden Press, 1973.

Regler, Gustav, ed. *Romancero de los Voluntarios de la Libertad.* Madrid: Ediciones del Comisario de Las Brigadas Internacionales, 1937.

Reid, Margaret A. "Langston Hughes: Rhetoric and Protest." *Langston Hughes Review* 3, no. 1 (1984): 13–20.

Revueltas, Silvestre, trans. "Canto de una muchacha negra = Song for a dark girl [by Langston Hughes]. For voice and piano." *Contemporary Latin-American Composers*. New York: Edward B. Marks, 1948.

Richards, Merle et al., eds. *Collaboration Uncovered: The Forgotten, the Assumed, and the Unexamined in Collaborative Education*. Westport, CT: Bergin & Garvey, 2001.

Rise, Eric W. *The Martinsville Seven: Race, Rape, and Capital Punishment*. Charlottesville: University Press of Virginia, 1995.

Rivaud, Luisa, trans. *El inmenso mar: Una autobiografía*. By Langston Hughes. Buenos Aires: Editorial Lautaro, 1944. Reprint, Havana: Editorial Arte y Literatura, 1967.

——, trans. *Renacimiento negro*. By Langston Hughes. Buenos Aires: Centro Editor de América Latina, 1971.

Rodríguez Aycaguer, Miguel. *Visitas misionales: Waldo Frank en Buenos Aires*. Buenos Aires: Impresiones Buenos Aires Editorial, 2007.

Rodríguez García, José María. "Literary into Cultural Translation." *Diacritics* 34, nos. 3–4 (2004): 3–30.

Rodríguez-Mourelo, Belén. "The Search for Identity in the Poetry of Langston Hughes and Nicolás Guillén." *Langston Hughes Review* 16, nos. 1&2 (Fall–Spring 1999–2001): 39–54.

Roediger, David R. *The Wages of Whiteness: Race and the Making of the American Working Class*. Rev. ed. London: Verso, 2007.

Rogin, Michael Paul. *The Intellectuals and McCarthy*. Cambridge, MA: M.I.T. Press, 1967.

Romera-Navarro, Miguel. *Hispanismo en Norte-América: Exposición y crítica de su aspecto literario*. Madrid: Renacimiento, 1917.

Rosenthal, Macha. "Notes on Some Afro-Cuban Translations." *Phylon* 6, no. 3 (1945): 267–72.

Rostagno, Irene. *Searching for Recognition: The Promotion of Latin American Literature in the United States*. Westport, CT: Greenwood Press, 1997.

——. "Waldo Frank's Crusade for Latin American Literature." *Americas* 46, no. 1 (July 1989): 41–69.

Rovere, Richard H. *Senator Joe McCarthy*. 1959. New York: Harper & Row, 1973.

Rowe, John Carlos. *Literary Culture and U.S. Imperialism: From the Revolution to World War II*. New York: Oxford University Press, 2000.

Rubio Martin, María, ed. *Palabras para Nicolás Guillén*. Almagro, Sp.: Universidad de Castilla-La Manchas, 1999.

Rühle, Jürgen, and Jean Steinberg. *Literature and Revolution: A Critical Study of the Writer and Communism in the Twentieth Century*. New York: Frederick A. Praeger, 1969.

Ruiz del Vizo, Hortensia, ed. *Black Poetry of the Americas: A Bilingual Anthology*. Miami: Ediciones Universal, 1972.

Rushmore, Howard. "Leftist Poet Opens Educator Parley." *New York Journal American*, November 1947.

Rutherford, Jonathan, ed. *Identity: Community, Culture, Difference*. London: Lawrence & Wishart, 1990.

Sabsay, Fernando. *Sin telón: Losange Teatro. Una experiencia de teatro impreso en Buenos Aires, 1952–1960.* Buenos Aires: Ediciones Ciudad Argentina, 1997.

Sáenz, Gerardo. "Nicolás Guillén, Langston Hughes y Luis Palés Matos: África en tres tonos." In *Homenaje a Lydia Cabrera,* edited by Reinaldo Sánchez, José Antonio Madrigal, and José Sánchez-Boudy, 183–88. Miami: Ediciones Universal, 1978.

Said, Edward. "Reflections on Exile." In *Out There: Marginalization and Contemporary Cultures,* edited by Russell Ferguson et al., 357–63. Cambridge, MA: MIT Press, 1990.

Sakai, Naoki. *Translation and Subjectivity: On "Japan" and Cultural Nationalism.* Minneapolis: University of Minnesota Press, 1997.

Salas, Horacio. *Conversaciones con Raúl González Tuñón.* Buenos Aires: Ediciones La Bastilla, 1975.

Salvatore, Ricardo D. "Library Accumulation and the Emergence of Latin American Studies." *Comparative American Studies* 3, no. 4 (2005): 415–36.

Sanders, Mark. *Afro-Modernist Aesthetics and the Poetry of Sterling Brown.* Athens: University of Georgia Press, 1999.

Sarlo, Beatriz. *Borges, un escritor en las orillas.* Buenos Aires: Ariel, 1995.

——. *Jorge Luis Borges: A Writer on the Edge.* Translated by John King. London: Verso, 2006.

——. *La máquina cultural: Maestras, traductores, y vanguardistas.* Buenos Aires: Editorial Planeta Rgentina S.A.I.C., 1998.

——. *Una modernidad periférica: Buenos Aires 1920 y 1930.* Buenos Aires: Ediciones Nueva Visión, 1988.

Sastre, Alfonso, trans. *Mulato. Drama de Langston Hughes.* Madrid: Alfíl, 1964. Reprint, Hondarribia: Argitaletxe HIRU, 1992.

Saussy, Haun, ed. *Comparative Literature in an Age of Globalizaton.* Baltimore: Johns Hopkins University Press, 2006.

Saval, Lorenzo, trans. "Yo también." By Langston Hughes. *República de las Letras* (Madrid) 32 (1992).

Sayers Peden, Margaret. "Knopf, Knopf: Who's There?" *Translation Review* 50 (1996): 27–30.

Sbardellati, John, and Tony Shaw. "Booting a Tramp: Charlie Chaplin,the FBI, and the Construction of the Subversive Image in Red Scare America." *Pacific Historical Review* 72, no. 4 (November 2003): 495–530.

Scanlon, Larry. ""Death Is a Drum": Rhythm, Modernity, and the Negro Poet Laureate." In *Music and the Racial Imagination,* edited by Ronald Radano and Philip V. Bohlman, 510–53. Chicago: University of Chicago Press, 2000.

——. "'News from Heaven': Vernacular Time in Langston Hughes's *Ask Your Mama.*" *Callaloo* 25, no. 1 (Winter 2002): 45–65.

——. "Poets Laureate and the Language of Slaves: Petrarch, Chaucer, and Langston Hughes." In *The Vulgar Tongue: Medieval and Postmedieval Vernacularity,* edited by Fiona Somerset and Nicholas Watson, 220–56. University Park, PA: Pennsylvania State University Press, 2003.

Schlögel, Karl. *Planet der Nomaden.* Pilsen, Czech Rep.: Oldenbourg, 2006.

Schrecker, Ellen. *Many Are the Crimes: McCarthyism in America.* Princeton: Princeton University Press, 1998.

——. *No Ivory Tower: McCarthyism and the Universities*. New York: Oxford University Press, 1986.

Scott, Jonathan. *Socialist Joy in the Writing of Langston Hughes*. Columbia: University of Missouri Press, 2006.

Scott, William. "*Motivos* of Translation: Nicolás Guillén and Langston Hughes." *CR: The New Centennial Review* 5, no. 2 (Fall 2005): 35–71.

See, Sam. "'Spectacles of Color': The Primitive Drag of Langston Hughes." *PMLA* 124, no. 3 (2009): 798–816.

Shukla, Sandhya, and Heidi Tinsman, eds. *Our Americas: Political and Cultural Imaginings*. Durham, NC: Duke University Press 2004.

Shull, Jodie A. *Langston Hughes: "Life Makes Poems."* Berkeley Heights, NJ: Enslow Publishers, 2006.

Shulman, Robert. *The Power of Political Art: The 1930s Literary Left Reconsidered*. Chapel Hill: University of North Carolina Press, 2000.

Sieber, Harry Charles. *The Picaresque*. London: Methuen, 1977.

Smethurst, James Edward. *The African American Roots of Modernism: From Reconstruction to the Harlem Renaissance*. Chapel Hill: University of North Carolina Press, 2011.

——. *The New Red Negro: The Literary Left and African American Poetry, 1930–1946*. New York: Oxford University Press, 1999.

Smith, Raymond. "Hughes: Evolution of the Poetic Persona." In *Modern Critical Views: Langston* Hughes, edited by Harold Bloom, 45–60. New York: Chelsea House, 1989.

Smith, Sidonie. *Subjectivity, Identity, and the Body: Women's Autobiographical Practices in the Twentieth Century*. Bloomington: Indiana University Press, 1993.

Solomianski, Alejandro. *Identidades secretas. La negritud argentina*. Rosario, Argentina: Beatriz Viterbo, 2003.

Soja, Edward W. *Thirdspace: Journeys to Los Angeles and Other Real-and-Imagined Places*. Cambridge, MA: Blackwell, 1996.

Somerville, Siobhan B. *Queering the Color Line: Race and the Invention of Homosexuality in American Culture*. Durham, NC: Duke University Press, 2003.

Soto, Isabel, ed. *A Place That Is Not a Place: Essays in Liminality and Text*. Madrid: Gateway Press, 2000.

——. "Translation as Understanding: Alfonso Sastre's Adaptation of 'Mulatto.'" *Langston Hughes Review* 15, no. 1 (1997): 13–23.

Soto, Michael. *The Modernist Nation: Generation, Renaissance, and Twentieth-Century American Literature*. Tuscaloosa: University of Alabama Press, 2004.

Spicer, Eloise. "The Blues and the Son: Reflections of Black Self-Assertion in the Poetry of Langston Hughes and Nicolás Guillén." *Langston Hughes Review* 3, no. 1 (1984): 1–12.

Spivak, Gayatri Chakravorty. *Outside the Teaching Machine*. New York: Routledge, 1993.

Steinberg, Peter L. *The Great "Red Menace": United States Prosecution of American Communists, 1947–1952*. Westport, CT: Greenwood Press, 1984.

Steiner, George. *After Babel: Aspects of Language and Translation*. Oxford: Oxford University Press, 1998.

Stephanides, Stephanos. "Spaces of Translatability in Twentieth-Century Poetry." *Annales du monde anglophone: Revue littéraire semestrielle bilingue* 17 (2003): 141–49.

——. "Translatability of Memory in an Age of Globalization." *Comparative Literature Studies* 41, no. 1 (2004).

——. "The Translation of Heritage: Multiculturalism in the 'New' Europe." In *Rethinking Heritage: Cultures and Politics in Europe,* edited by Robert Shannan Peckham, 45–57. London: I.B. Tauris, 2003.

Stepto, Robert B. *From Behind the Veil: A Study of Afro-American Narrative.* Urbana: University of Illinois Press, 1979.

Stohlberg, Sherlyn Gay. "Transcripts Detail Secret Questioning in 50's by McCarthy." *New York Times,* May 6, 2003.

Suárez-Murias, Marguerite. "Interdisciplinary Credit in the Humanities: Black Literature in Latin America in Translation." *Latin American Literary Review* 4, no. 7 (FallWinter 1975): 49–56.

Tarver, Australia, and Paula C. Barnes, eds. *New Voices on the Harlem Renaissance: Essays on Race, Gender, and Literary Discourse.* Madison, NJ: Fairleigh Dickinson University Press, 2006.

Taylor, Diana. "Remapping Genre through Performance: From 'American' to 'Hemispheric' Studies." *PMLA* 122, no. 5 (2007): 1416–30.

Tedesco, Luis Osvaldo, ed. *Raúl González Tuñón: Poemas de Buenos Aires. Antología.* Buenos Aires: Torres Aguero, 1983.

Tejera, Humberto. "Langston Hughes en Mexico." *El Nacional* 28 (November 1948): 5 and 28.

Thaggert, Miriam. *Images of Black Modernism: Verbal and Visual Strategies of the Harlem Renaissance.* Amherst: University of Massachusetts Press, 2010.

Thurston, Michael. *Making Something Happen: American Political Poetry between the World Wars.* Chapel Hill: University of North Carolina Press, 2001.

Tidwell, John Edgar, and Cheryl R. Ragar, eds. *Montage of a Dream: The Art and Life of Langston Hughes.* Columbia: University of Missouri Press, 2007: 135–46.

Tillis, Antonio D. *Manuel Zapata Olivella and the "Darkening" of Latin American Literature.* Columbia: University of Missouri Press, 2005.

Toropov, Brandon. *Encyclopedia of Cold War Politics.* New York: Facts on File, 2000.

Toruño, Juan Felipe, ed. *Poesía negra: Ensayo y antología.* Mexico City: Colección obsidiana, 1953.

Trachtenberg, Alan, ed. *Memoirs of Waldo Frank.* Amherst: University of Massachusetts Press, 1973.

Tracy, Steven C. *Langston Hughes & the Blues.* Urbana: University of Illinois Press, 1988.

Trotman, C. James, ed. *Langston Hughes: The Man, His Art, and His Continuing Influence.* New York: Garland, 1995.

Tsu, Jing. "New Area Studies and Languages on the Move." *PMLA* 126, no. 3 (2011): 693–700.

Tuck, Jim. *McCarthyism and New York's Hearst Press: A Study of Roles in the Witch Hunt.* Lanham, MD: University Press of America, 1995.

Turner, Catherine. *Marketing Modernism between the Two World Wars.* Amherst: University of Massachusetts Press, 2003.

Turner, Daniel C. "Montage of Simplicity Deferred: Langston Hughes's Art of Sophistication and Racial Intersubjectivity in *Montage of a Dream Deferred.*" *Langston Hughes Review* 17 (2002): 22–34.

United States Congress. *Violations of State Department Regulations and Pro-Castro Propaganda Activities in the United States, Part 1.* Washington, D.C.: U.S. Government Printing Office, May 6, 7, and 23, 1963.

United States Court of Appeals for the Second Circuit. *United States v. Dennis et al.,* 183 F.2d 201 (2d Cir. 1950).

United States District Court for the Southern District of New York. *United States v. Foster et al.,* 83 F. Supp. 197 (S.D.N.Y. 1949).

United States Senate. *Executive Sessions of the Senate Permanent Subcommittee on Investigations of the Committee on Government Operations, 83rd Congress, First Session, 1953.* Edited by Donald A. Ritchie. 5 vols. Washington, DC: U.S. Government Printing Office, 1953–54. Vol. 2. http://www.gpo.gov/congress/senate/mccarthy/83870.pdf.

——. *Hearings and Reports Published by the Subcommittee on Investigations of the Committee on Government Operations, United States Senate, under the Chairmanship of Joseph R. McCarthy (R-Wisconsin): Part 1, 1953–54.* Washington, DC: State Department Information Program—Information Centers, 1953.

United States Statutes. Alien Registration Act (aka Smith Act), 18 U.S.C. § 2385 (1940) (Title 18, Crimes and Criminal Procedure; Section 2385, Advocating Overthrow of Government).

——. *Public Statutes at Large of the United States of America.* http://memory.loc.gov/cgi-bin/ampage?collId=llsl&fileName=001/llsl001.db&recNum=719.

United States Supreme Court. *Dennis et al. v. United States,* 341 U.S. 494 (1951).

——. *Scales v. United States,* 367 U.S. 203 (1961).

——. *Schenck v. United States,* 249 U.S. 47 (1919).

——. *Yates v. United States,* 354 U.S. 298 (1957).

Urrutia, Gustavo F. "Guillén, poeta americano." *Diario de la Marina* XCIX (November 14, 1931), n.p.

Vallejo, Antonio. "El violín del diablo de Raúl González Tuñón." *Martín Fierro* (1993). http://www.elortiba.org/pdf/Raul-Gonzalez-Tunon.pdf.

Venuti, Lawrence, ed. *Rethinking Translation: Discourse, Subjectivity, Ideology.* London: Routledge.

——. *The Scandals of Translation: Towards an Ethics of Difference.* London: Routledge, 1998.

——. "Translation as Cultural Politics: Regimes of Domestication in English." *Textual Practice* 7, no. 2 (1993): 208–23.

——. *The Translator's Invisibility: History of Translation.* London: Routledge, 1995.

Vianello, Raúl C. *Versos negros.* Mexico City: Librería Urbe, 1942.

Vieira, Else Ribeiro Pires. "Liberating Calibans: *Antropofagia* and Haroldo de Campos' Poetics of Transcreation." In *Post-Colonial Translation: Theory and Practice,* edited by Susan Bassnet and Harish Trivedi, 95–113. New York: Routledge, 1999.

Villaurrutia, Xavier, trans. "El Negro Habla de los Ríos." By Langston Hughes. *Nivel* 31 (July 25, 1961): 4–5.

——, trans. "'Yo también,' 'Poema,' 'Plegaria,' 'Nota de un Suicido.'" By Langston Hughes. *Contemporáneos* 11 (September–October 1931): 157–59.

——, trans. "'Yo También'; 'Poema'; 'Plegaria'; 'Nota de un suicida.'" By Langston Hughes. *Nivel* 31 (July 25, 1961): 4–5.

Wagner, Jean. "Langston Hughes. El gran poeta norteamericano." *Nivel* 31 (July 25, 1961): 6.

Waisman, Sergio. *Borges and Translation: The Irreverence of the Periphery.* Lewisburg, PA: Bucknell University Press, 2005.

——. "Foundational Scenes of Translation." *Estudios Interdisciplinarios de América Latina y el Caribe* 21, no. 1 (January–June 2010): 53–77.

——. "Jorge Luis Borges's Partial Argentine *Ulysses*: A Foundational (Mis-)Translation." In *Traduire les Amériques/Translating the Americas,* edited by Marc Charron and Clara Foz. Special issue of *Études sur le texte et ses transformations* 19, no.2 (2006): 37–51.

Wald, Alan M., ed. *Writing from the Left: New Essays on Radical Culture and Politics.* London: Verso, 1994.

Walkowitz, Rebecca L. *Cosmopolitan Style: Modernism beyond the Nation.* New York: Columbia University Press, 2006.

——. "The Location of Literature: The Transnational Book and the Migrant Writer." *Contemporary Literature* 47, no. 4 (Winter 2006): 527–45.

——. "Shakespeare in Harlem: The Norton Anthology, 'Propaganda,' Langston Hughes." *Modern Language Quarterly: A Journal of Literary History* 60, no. 4 (December 1999): 495–519.

Wallace, Maurice O. *Langston Hughes: The Harlem Renaissance.* New York: Marshall Cavendish Benchmark, 2008.

Ware, Vron, and Les Back. *Out of Whiteness: Color, Politics, and Culture.* Chicago: University of Chicago Press, 2002.

Warren, Rosanna, ed. *The Art of Translation: Voices from the Field.* Boston: Northeastern University Press, 1989.

Watkins, Alma T. "Review: The Roots of Jazz. Estética del Jazz by Nestor R. Ortiz Oderigo." *Phylon* 13, no. 2 (1952): 176–77.

Werner, Craig Hansen. *Playing the Changes: From Afro-Modernism to the Jazz Impulse.* Urbana: University of Illinois Press, 1994.

West, Russell, ed. *Rethinking Translation: Discourse, Subjectivity, Ideology.* New York and London: Routledge, 1992.

Westover, Jeff. "Africa/America: Fragmentation and Diaspora in the Work of Langston Hughes." *Callaloo* 25, no. 4 (2002): 1207–23.

Wheeler, Lesley. *Voicing American Poetry: Sound and Performance from the 1920s to the Present.* Ithaca: Cornell University Press, 2008.

"Where Free Speech Ends: From Judge Medina's Charge to the Jury." *Time,* October 24, 1949. http://www.time.com/time/magazine/article/0,9171,805105,00.html.

White, Jeanette S., and Clement A. White. "Two Nations, One Vision: America's Langston Hughes and Cuba's Nicolás Guillén: Poetry of Affirmation, A Revision." *Langston Hughes Review* 12, no. 1 (Spring 1993): 42–50.

Whitfield, Stephen J. *The Culture of the Cold War.* Baltimore: Johns Hopkins University Press, 1991.

William Kerwin, ed. *Brian Friel: A Casebook.* New York: Garland, 1997.

Williams, Raymond. *Marxism and Literature.* Oxford: Oxford University Press, 1977.

——. *Politics of Modernism.* London: Verso, 2007.

Williams, William Carlos. *In the American Grain.* 1925. Reprint, New York: New Directions, 1993.

Winkiel, Laura. *Modernism, Race, and Manifestos.* Cambridge: Cambridge University Press, 2008.

Winkiel, Laura, and Laura Doyle, eds. *Geomodernisms: Race, Modernism, Modernity.* Bloomington: Indiana University Press, 2005.

Wogan-Browne, Jocelyn, Nicholas Watson, Andrew Taylor, and Ruth Evans, eds. *The Idea of the Vernacular: An Anthology of Middle English Literary Theory, 1280–1520.* University Park: Pennsylvania State University Press, 1999.

Woods, Gregory. "Gay Re-Readings of the Harlem Renaissance Poets." *Journal of Homosexuality* 26, nos. 2–3 (1993): 127–42.

Woods, Jeff. *Black Struggle, Red Scare. Segregation and Anti-Communisms in the South, 1948–1968.* Baton Rouge: LSU Press, 2004.

Woodson, Carter J. "Panorama de la música afroamericana. By Nestor R. Ortiz Oderigo." *Journal of Negro History* 30, no. 1 (1945): 99–100.

Wright, Jay. *Dimensions of History.* Santa Cruz, CA: Kayak, 1976.

Yancy, George, ed. *What White Looks Like: African-American Philosophers on the Whiteness Question.* New York: Routledge, 2004.

Yanover, Héctor, ed. *Raúl González Tuñón. Antología.* Buenos Aires: Ediciones Culturales Argentinas, 1962.

——, ed. *Raúl González Tuñón. Antología poética.* Madrid: Visor Libros, 1986.

Zapata Olivella, Manuel. *Changó el Gran Putas.* 1983; Reprint, Santafé de Bogotá, Colombia: Rei Andes Ltda., 1992.

——. *Changó, the Biggest Badass.* Translated by Jonathan Tittler. Lubbock: Texas Tech University Press, 2010.

——. *He visto la noche.* Bogotá: Editorial "Los Andes," 1953.

——. *Pasión vagabunda [and He visto la noche].* 1949. Reprint, Colombia: Ministerio de Cultura, 2000.

Zardoya, Concha, trans. "Dos poemas de Langston Hughes: 'Llegada de la vejez' y 'El Negro.'" *Ínsula* XXII, nos. 248–49 (June-August 1967): 24.

Zuloaga, Manuel Antonio. *Nuestra raza y los problemas de posguerra en la Argentina.* Buenos Aires: Editorial "La Facultad," 1943.

INDEX

Aaron, Daniel, 116
"Advertisement for the Opening of the
  Waldorf-Astoria" (poem), 115, 184–
  85, 209; translations of, 66, 88, 125
Aesthetics: literary, 5, 29, 30, 31, 64,
  78, 99, 109, 119, 139, 150, 157,
  237, 289, 290; blues/jazz, 21; and
  ethics, 173; modernist, 103, 139,
  148, 173, 179, 278n19, 291n35; and
  pleasure, 30, 35, 102; and politics,
  94, 112, 116, 205; of translation, 177
"Afraid" (poem), translations of, 70,
  73, 130–31
African American studies in the USA,
  12, 21, 22, 59, 83–84, 225, 233
African American writers from the
  USA: and postcolonialism, 32–33,
  84, 266n53; in Hispanic American
  anthologies, 61, 70, 276n101; and
  primitivism, 139
Afro-Antillean movement, 64, 94, 139.
  See also Afro-Cubanism
Afro-Cubanism, 56–57
Afro-Hispanic American studies, 60,
  94, 271n13, 279n27, 310n69
Ahumada, Herminio, 58, 70–71,
  103–6, 125, 127, 270, 273, 274–76,
  282, 286
Alberti, Rafael, 64, 88–89, 272n41,
  274n71 276n92, 277n2
Alejandro, Miguel, 66–67, 88, 103,
  105–6, 273n52, 298n4
Alfred A. Knopf (press), 69, 95, 123,
  133, 135–36, 182–83, 215, 279n32,
  n34, 285n135, 286n137, n140,
  289n17, 289n18, 293n64 297n143.
  See also Knopf, Blanche
Almeida, Guilherme de, 274n67

"Always the Same" (poem), 120–21,
  273; translations of, 66, 285n130
America: and América, 4, 43, 75–76,
  221, 226–29; American A., 212; and
  the Americas, 221, 226–27, 230–31,
  233–34, 236, 258n11; feminization
  of, 169, 171
American studies (studies of the USA): as
  area study, 12, 231, 234; and comparative literature, 232; as a discipline,
  234, 309n55; and exceptionalism,
  227; geographies of, 231; hemispheric turn in, 228, 230, 232–34;
  institutional history of, 307n23; and
  language acquisition, 230; and Latin
  American studies, 227, 232, 308n40;
  and/as literary studies, 232–33; and
  methodology, 243–35; renaming of,
  229; transnational turn in, 232
Amey, Marilyn J., 309n59
Anderson, Caroline, 133, 140, 142,
  146, 148, 154, 182–83, 287n2,
  288n11, 289n23, 290n25, 291n37,
  n39, n41, n42, n44, 292n56,
  293n65, n78–79, 294n88, 297n144,
  n146, n148–49, n154–55, 299n25
Anderson, Sherwood, 94
Andrews, George Reid, 258n10, 279n35
Anthropology, cultural, 21, 123,
  258n14, 307n18. See also
  Ethnography
Anti-Semitism, 90, 194
Anzaldúa, Gloria, 122, 233, 309n49
Aparicio, Antonio, 268n86
"April Rain Song" (poem), translations
  of, 125, 130, 287n161
Apter, Emily, 10, 233, 261n36,
  265n31, 306n6

339

Araújo, Susana, 258n11, 307n30
"Árbol" (poem), 130–31
"Ardella" (poem), translations of, 272n33
Armstrong, Louis, 28, 266n46
Arrom, Juan José, 156, 293n74
Artel, Jorge, 94
Arturo, Aurelio, 269n96
Ashcroft, Bill, 33, 257n6, 267n56
ASK YOUR MAMA: 12 Moods for Jazz (poems), 4, 47, 89, 112, 185, 258n13
Atlanticism, 53, 55, 237, 257; Black, 12, 52–53, 237, 266n49, 309n50
Audiences: academic, 291n45; African American, 18, 79, 136, 139, 142–43, 145, 148, 156, 178–79, 216; implied, 29, 150, 154, 157–58; Mexican, 271n16, 279n30; white, 18, 148
Augier, Ángel, 287n3, 288n8, 290n29–n30, 294n86–n87
Authenticity: cultural, 4, 126, 173, 276n101, 290n33; and ethnic effects, 137, 179; racial, 137, 139, 163, 185, 279n28
Autobiography, African American, 15; and the picaresque, 23–24, 34, 39, 265n36, 267n63, 293n72; reader's expectations of, 13, 17; theories of, 19, 40, 264n13–14; tropes of transit in, 20, 35, 42
Avant-gardes, literary: in the Americas, 4, 8, 13, 85, 93–94, 116, 122, 136, 179, 290n33; European, 282n82; journals, 6, 57. See also Modernism

Baker, Houston, 279n31, 295n101, 310n79
Baldwin, James, 215, 259n16, 304n91
Baldwin, Kate, 26, 237, 257n4, 259n19, 262n41, 264n9, 265n40, 266n42, 310n71
Ball, Howard, 303n61
"Ballad of Roosevelt" (poem), 207
"Ballads of Lenin" (poem), 194–95, 198, 204–8

Ballagas, Emilio, 60, 69, 71, 273n57–58, 274n71
Bansart, Andrés, 64, 70–71, 272n42, 274n63, n71, 275n88, n89, 276n90, 287n163
Baraka, Amiri, 20, 90, 265n19
Barnstone, Willis, 261n31
Barrios, Pilar, 56, 70, 94, 238
Baseball: and Cuban nationalism, 168; Cuban players in USAmerica, 167–70, 295n113; in "Don't Know No English," 161–70; integration of major leagues, 168; Sugar (movie), 168–69
Baudelaire, Charles, 106, 282n82
Bauer, Ralph, 307n26
Bayne, Bijan, 295n110, n112–114
Bean, Annmarie, 266n50
Belonging, cultural, 10; alternative spaces of, 35, see also Communities: provisional; crises of, 31, 40; and translation, 13, 55, 265n31
Benjamin, Walter, 11, 56, 100, 172–73, 261n39, 262n42, 276n102, 296n122–23
Benston, Kimberly, 265n19, 267n70
Bensussen, Melia, 260n20
Berman, Jessica, 269n98
Berry, Faith, 1, 191–92, 266n47, 298n3, 229n26, 300n32, n34, n37
Berubé, Michael, 307n23
Bethune, Brian, 277n3
Beyer, William, 299n20
Bhabha, Homi, 42, 267n66, 295n117
Big Sea, The (autobiography), 2, 10, 15, 17–20, 22–23, 34–35, 107–8, 184, 263n5, 264n10, 268n88, 280n38, 304n90; critical reception of, 17, 19, 263n4; fictional uses of, 52–54; hybridity in, 266n55; Maupassant in, 261n33; Middle Passage in, 32, 36, 128, 266n54; and music, 20; narrative interruptions in, 209; omissions in, 34, 213–14, 267n62; and the picaresque, 22, 24; provisional communities in, 30–31; sexual ambivalence in, 38; scenes of translation in, 23–24, 26–27, 31–32,

37–43, 47, 55; survival strategies in, 31; and *The Tempest*, 32–34; translations of, *see* Rivaud, Luisa; travel metaphors in, 32, 34–35
Bignami, Arile, 284n113
"Birth" (poem), translation of, 128
Blackness, 60, 66; academic discourses on, *see* African American studies; and class, 10, 39, 44, 84, 144, 151, 163–64, 266n55; and color hierarchies, 82, 116–17, 149–51; and culture, 84, 151, 165, 178; and the gaze, 156–58; and gender, 39, 48, 82, 171; literary, 84–85, 178; and nationality, 10, 48; and phenotype, 79, 95, 151, 155–56, 169, 268n75; and sexuality, 39, 103, 163–64, 266n55; and universality, 66, 99
Bloom, Harold, 210, 237–38
Blues, 170, 285n119, 292n49, 288n4, 292n48; characters, 114–15; 284n114; formal aspects of, 69; history of, 21, 54, 109–10; and interracial relations, 170; motifs, 39, 42; 112; singers of, 54, 110, 114; and survival, 39. *See also* Handy, W.C.; Jazz
Blues poetry, 4, 10, 21, 39, 49, 54, 69–70, 74, 81, 94, 101, 116–18, 134, 139, 185, 208, 259n19, 301n45, 306n3. *See also* Brown, Sterling; Dunbar, Paul Laurence; González Tuñón, Raúl; Lozano, Rafael
Bontemps, Arna, 125, 133, 288n6, 297n152
Borden, Anne, 268n84
Borges, Jorge Luis, 17, 93–94, 123, 238, 285n132; and Argentine politics, 280n37; *Fervor de Buenos Aires*, 111–12, 116, 280n37, 283n96, 284n99; and Raúl González Tuñón, 111, 114–15, 122, 280n37; *Historia universal de la infamía*, 109–11, 283n91, 283n93; *Luna de enfrente*, 111, 280n37; "Pierre Menard," 101; and *Sur*, 96, 98, 100; and translation, 99–101, 131, 270, 281n49, 281n59, 281n62, 281n63,

281n67, 274n68; as translator of Hughes, 57, 59, 62, 65, 71–72, 76, 94, 97–99, 101, 103, 105–8, 115, 122, 272, 274n68, 274n71, 275n73, 275n78, 281n56, 282n78, 282n85; and Ultraísmo, 272n42
Borshuk, Michael, 258n13, 264n17, 265n22, 266n46
Bosco, María Angélica, 286n144
Bost, Suzanne, 271n18, 272n37, 308n35
Bourdieu, Pierre, 136, 178–79, 289n22
Bourgeoisie, black: in the USA, 42, 114, 145, 169, 179, 189; in Cuba, 79, 144
Braithwaite, William Stanley, 227n26
Bravo, María Elena, 281n63
"Breath of a Rose" (poem), translation of, 269n96
Brickhouse, Anna, 308n35
Brock, Lisa, 287n4, 295n109–115
"Brothers" (poem), 296n119
Brown, Kimberly, 283n91
Brown, Sterling, 151, 179, 182, 272n26, 278n19, 292n49
Brunner, Edward, 258n13, 304n79
Buckley, William F., 298n7
Burkinski, Francisco, 268n86
Butler, Judith, 261n38

"Cane" (poem; Hughes's translation of "Caña"), 296n129
Caparicio, G., 69, 273n56
Caplan, Karen, 264n14
Caribbean, 79, 93, 111, 229, 231, 271n18, 284n105, 288n6, 310n65; anglophone, 83, 296n119; Danish, 310n68; Dutch, 310n68; French, 83, 133, 262n41, 277n10; geography of, 227, 237, 258; Hispanic, 132–33, 143, 150; Hughes's essays on, 257n4; Hughes's travels to, 2, 55, 114; and USAmerican imperialism, 141, 172–73
"Caribbean Sunset" (poem), translations of, 127–29
Carpentier, Alejo, 56, 70, 88–89

Carruthers, Ben Fredric: collaboration with Hughes, 132–33, 145–46, 288n5, 292n53, 292n60, 297n147; introduction to *Cuba Libre*, 140–43, 270n3, 291n37–n38; 291n45; as translator, 134, 146–47, 151–51, 166–76, 178–79, 291n43, 292n52, 293n80, 296n119

Carullo, Sylvia G., 280n35

Castaneda Fuertes, Digna, 287n4, 295n109

Castro, Fidel, 219, 305n106

"The Cat and the Saxophone" (poem), 281n58; translations of, 130, 287n161

Censorship: Hughes on, 305n105; and McCarthyism, 216–17, 306n93; and the New Criticism, 206; in the Soviet Union, 25

Center-margin model, 6–8, 14, 30, 100, 260n28; and narratives of marginalization, 102, 239

Certeau, Michel de, 296n126

Cervantes, Miguel de, 17, 23–24

Césaire, Aimé, 33, 267n57, 288n6, 293n73

Chambers, Iain, 8, 11, 20, 26, 35, 42, 113, 260n29, 262n43, n45, n46, 263n58, 264n15, n18, 265n30, 266n43, 267n66, n67, 268n78, n83, 284n106

Chamoiseau, Patrick, 86, 113, 122, 184n107

"Chant for Tom Mooney" (poem), 120; translation of, 285n130

Chesnutt, Charles Wadell, 25, 145

Choteo, 151, 293n72

"Christ in Alabama" (poem), 301n46; translation of, 125

Ciarlos, José Ratto, 296n96

Class: biases, 42, 239; and the blues, 116–17; and classlessness, 36; crossing the boundaries of, 39, 267n55, 283n97; and language, 111, 145, 164, 151, 163, 167, 210; and race, 44, 84, 105, 163, 167; and skin color, 9, 78–79, 93, 117, 149; socioeconomic, 34, 168; struggle, 59

Clifford, Carrie Williams, 272n26

Clifford, James, 259n14

Cobb, Martha, 287n4, 294n94

Cognates, false, 4, 75, 79, 92, 147, 203, 221

Cohn, Roy, 190–201, 204–8, 210, 213–14, 218, 299n27, 300n30, n33, n36, n41, 301n42, 302n53, n55; and homosexuality, 216; in *Angels in America*, 304n95; and the Rosenberg trial, 201, 305n95. *See also* McCarthy committee

Cold War: and area studies, 231; and bebop musicians, 301n47; politics, 9, 41, 143, 179, 187–89, 227, 239, 301n41

Colonialism, and neo-colonialism, in the Americas, 7, 59, 70, 100, 148, 174–75, 229, 231, 235–36, 282n67, 289n14, 310n62

Colonization: internal, 59–60; in reverse, 229; rhetoric of, 235

Color line: in the Hispanic Americas, 79, 83; in literary and cultural studies, 92; in the USA, 42, 116, 147, 151, 168–69. *See also* Class; Blackness; Whiteness

Communism, Soviet, 92, 98; and African American intellectuals, 189, 222, 305n2; and the Comintern, 87, 187, 261n34; and global socialism, 59, 66, 92, 217, 239; and homosexuality, 192, 216, 266n47; and literature, 93, 122, 195, 201, 211, 298n3; and the Red Scare, 18, 188, 198, 216; and social deviance, 196–97, 301n47. *See also* Communist Party

Communist Party: in Argentina, 123; in Cuba, 182; legal action against in the USA, 199, 201, 302n59, 303n61, n64, *see also* U.S. Supreme Court decisions, Smith Act; in the USA, 189, 192, 194, 197, 199, 211

Communities: and area studies, 231; and belonging, 10, 40; and conviviality, 236, 310n66; cross-racial, 55; diasporic, 84; ludic, 47; and nations, 85, 171, 236; open (differentiated), 14, 42; provisional, 31, 35, 37, 46,

102, 170–71; and translation, 13, 55, 265n31

Conspiracy, 200, 202, 303n68. *See also* Intent

Cook, Mercer, 135, 260n23

Cosmopolitanism, 8, 20, 100–11, 269n98; hemispheric, 44, 98, *see also* Pan-Americanism

Crane, Hart, 60–61, 100, 145

"Cross" (poem), translations of, 62, 119, 272n33, 274n65–66

Cruzado, Maribel, 57, 81, 125, 270n4, n8, n12, 272n32, n34, 273n62, 274n71, 276n90, n93, n96, 286n155

Cuba Libre: 5, 132–83, 189, 191, 297n140; and ethnographic realism, 139; design award for, 182, 298n23; drawings in, 180–81, 287n1, *see also* Gilbert, Gar; Hughes as editor-anthologizer and marketer of, 136–37, 140–41, 143–44, 175, 183, 216; translated poems included in, 296n129, *see also* "Don't Know No English"; "The Grandfather"; "Last Night Somebody Called Me Darky"; "Song in an [sic] Havana Bar"; projected audiences for, 136, 143–44, 154, 160, 291n45; reviews of, 145, 148, 292n57; royalties for, 183; sales of, 136, 148, 182. *See also* Anderson, Caroline; Carruthers, Ben

Cuba-USA relations, 136, 140–41, 143, 220

"Cubes" (poem), 209

Cullen, Countee, 50, 61, 73, 99, 115, 144, 272n26, 273n56, 274n67, 276n98, 281n58, 292n49

Cullen, Deborah, 271n23

Cummings, E.E., 100, 211, 281n63

Cyrus, Stanley, 279n31

Damrosch, David, 12, 222, 262n52, 306n5, n9, n10

Danky, Philip James, 297n157

Davey, Elizabeth, 297n157–158

Davidson, Ned, 278n21

Dawahare, Anthony, 210, 261n34,

298n2, 299n16, 300n37, 304n86–87

"Dead Soldier" (poem; Hughes's translation of "Soldado muerto"), 175, 296n129

Deck, Alice, 259n16, 269n97

DeJongh, James, 112, 278n20, 284n100, n105

Denning, Michael, 298n2, 307n23

Depression, economic: in Argentina, 119; the Great, 189, 206, 211, 301n45

"Desire" (poem), 118; translation of, 125, 130

Diaspora, African, 3, 53, 94; and misrecognition, 261n37; theoretical assumptions about, 5, 10, 55, 56, 59, 83–85, 93, 145, 237–38, 259n16; 310n69; and translation, 5, 51, 237, 268n89. *See also* Migrancy; Slavery

Dies Committee, 189, 298n5, 300n36

Dimock, Wai-Chee, 267n74, 306n16–17

"Dinner Guest: Me" (poem), 276n99

Dirksen, Everett McKinley (U.S. Senator), 190, 192–94, 196–99, 204, 208, 215–16, 218, 302n55

Disciplines: academic, discourses of, 294n99, 297n18, 307n30, 309n55; collaboration among, 309n59; and interdisciplinarity, 12, 92, 185, 226, 230, 234–36, 228n4, 309n53, 309n57

Dixon, Heriberto, 269n2

Dixon, Melvin, 277n105, 279n29

"Don't Know No English" (poem; translation of "Tú no sabe inglé"), 161–70

Douglass, Frederick, 15, 24, 32

Doyle, Laura, 258n13, 269n98

"Dream Boogie" (poem), 305n101

The Dream Keeper (poems), 125, 274n70

"Dreams" (poem), translation of, 125

Du Bois, W.E.B., 51; and autobiography, 264n12, 304n92; and Communism, 215, 218, 304n92; and double-consciousness, 25–26,

Du Bois, W.E.B. *(cont.)*
   112, 266n42; in the Hispanic
   Americas, 60
Dujovne Ortíz, Alicia, 286n141
Dunbar, Paul Laurence, 61, 126, 151,
   272n26; and the blues, 286n153;
   and modernism 292n50; and the
   plantation tradition, 144–45

Eakin, John Paul, 264n13
Edwards, Brent Hayes, 5, 51, 59, 85,
   89, 268n85, 277n6; *The Practice of
   Diaspora*, 236–37, 259n18, 60n21,
   262n40, n48, 265n22, n33, 268n80,
   268n89, 269n99, 293n73; "The
   Uses of Diaspora," 259n17, 271n17,
   310n67, n70
"Elderly Leaders" (poem), 209
Eliot, T.S., 20, 60–61, 90–92, 105,
   111, 210; and anti-Semitism, 90;
   and racial idioms, 145; in transla-
   tion, 100, 281n63
Ellis, Keith, 287n4
Ellison, Ralph, 17, 19, 36, 264n16
Equivalence: cultural, 57, 83; theories
   of, *see* Marx, Karl
Escalante, Hildamar, 270n6, 274n65
Eshleman, Clayton, 293n73
Espinoza, Enrique. *See* Glusberg,
   Samuel
Estenguer, Rafael, 292n53, 293n80
Ethnography: and area studies, 231;
   and ethnopoetry, 139, 174; as
   mediating discourse for literature,
   164; and nonstandard vernaculars,
   179; and translation, 258n14,
   307n18
Ette, Ottmar, 221–25, 236, 268n78,
   306n11, 307n26; *Konvivenz*, 236,
   310n66; *ZwischenWeltenSchreiben*, 263n54, n56, n58, 281n67,
   295n105, 305n1, 306n8, n10, n12,
   309n57, 310n62, n76
Evans, Nicholas, 103, 282n75
Even-Zohar, Itamar, 260n28
Exceptionalism: hemispheric, 263n56;
   USAmerican, 227, 229, 231,
   266n53, 307n30

"Execution" (poem; Hughes's translation of "Fusilamiento"), 175
Exile, 10, 32, 40–41, 76, 123–24,
   223; definition of, 261n36. *See
   also* Homes
Exoticism, in poetry, 99, 102, 141,
   143, 145, 168, 279n28
Eysteinsson, Astradur, 263n58,
   290n33

"Fantasy in Purple" (poem), 128;
   translation of, 127–30
Fariello, Griffin, 300n35, 304n93
Faulkner, William: in translation,
   100, 281n63; influence on Hispanic
   American writers, 238
Fauset, Jessie, 276n98
Feracho, Leslie, 287n4
Fernández de Castro, José Antonio
   de, 130, 132, 275n76; and African
   American cultures, 71, 73, 274n69;
   and Guillén, 81, 134, 161, 290n29;
   and Hughes, 73, 275n79, n82,
   276n97, 289n13; as translator, 58,
   62, 63, 71, 73–82, 85, 272n33,
   274n71, 294n90, n92
Field, Edward, 305n106
Figueira, Gastón, 62, 272n31
Filatova, Lydia, 261n34
Filreis, Alan, 202–3, 205, 303n68,
   n71, n75
"Final Curve" (poem), translation
   of, 131
Fine Clothes to the Jew, 73–74, 89,
   114, 116, 125, 185, 195; and anti-
   Semitism, 300n40; reviews of, 119;
   translations of, 62, 69, 125, 127,
   272n34
Fisher, Phil, 229, 233, 308n31
Fitts, Dudley, 134, 146, 160, 175,
   177, 288n6, 289n15, 290n28,
   296n129–32, n36; on translation,
   175, 296n128
"Florida Road Workers" (poem),
   translations of, 88, 104–5
Florit, Eugenio, 61, 66, 71, 272n29,
   273n48, 274n71, 276n90
Forbes, Jack, 289n14

Ford, Karen Jackson, 136, 289n24,
    297n156–157, 299n25
Ford, Nick Aaron, 266n47
Form, poetic: ballad, 126, 206–7,
    210, 292n49; elegy, 129; ode, 207;
    sonnet, 119, 130, 197, 211. *See also*
    Blues poetry; *Poemas-son*
Fraile Marcos, Ana María, 268n85,
    285n136
Franco, Jean, 297n142
Frank, Waldo, 92–93, 95–96, 268n79,
    279n28, 280n38; in Argentina, 96,
    280n39, n41, 281n50; and Hughes,
    98–99; and *Sur*, 96–98, 280n43,
    281n46–48, 282n77; and Toomer,
    281n52, 282n69
Freedom of speech: in Argentina, 120;
    in the USA, 188, 201, 302n59. *See
    also* Censorship
"Freedom Train" (poem), translations
    of, 125–26
Fried, Albert, 298n8
Frost, Robert, 60
Fusco, Coco, 295n103

Gáler, Julio, 59, 96, 124–25, 286n140,
    286n143–145, n150; *Langston
    Hughes. Poemas*, 58, 66, 69–71, 79,
    106, 119, 123–31, 270n12, 273n55,
    274n71, 276n90–91, 282n74, n80,
    n83, n84, n85, 286n151, n153,
    n154, 287n156, n160; *Riendo
    por no llorar*, 123; *Yo viajo por
    un mundo encantado*, 4, 48–50,
    65, 95, 123, 265n38, 266n54,
    267n64, 268n86, 285n135– 136,
    286n137, n143
Gallardo, Jorge Emilio, 280n35
García Lorca, Federico, 89, 120;
    execution of, 88, 120; Hughes's
    translations of, 5, 88, 114, 126, 135,
    260n20, 277n3, 289n18
García Márquez, Gabriel, 26, 238,
    279n34
Gardullo, Paul, 36, 264n10, 266n47,
    267n69, 300n29
Garvey, Marcus, 32, 51–52, 54
Gates, Henry Louis Jr, 24, 265n37

Gault, Webster, 266n47
Gender: and the blues, 39, *see also*
    Blues; discourses of, 48, 82, 164,
    171, 283n97; performance of, 9,
    107, 118, 149, 158, 293n82
Generation of '27, 88. *See also* Alberti,
    Rafael
Genres, literary: allegory, 165, 170–72,
    235, 261; drama, 269n90; gothic,
    98, 128; as harmless and dangerous,
    203–4; mixing of, 9, 130; novel,
    13; pastoral, 98; travelogue, 34. *See
    also* Autobiography; Form, poetic;
    Realism
Gentzler, Edwin, 281n61, 307n22
Geographies, cultural: of the Americas,
    227, 258n11, *see also* Hemisphere,
    Western; and area studies, 231–33,
    236; global, 10, 12, 14, 84, 92, 101,
    107, 227–28, 269n98; political, *see*
    Nation; racialized, 179; symbolic,
    21–22, 26, 265n29; urban, 91,
    111–12, 130, 150
Gide, André, 100
Gilbert, Gar, 146, 179
Giles, Paul, 230, 233–34, 308n34,
    309n51, 310n63
Gill, Jonathan, 284n110, 291n35
Gillman, Susan, 307n24
Gilroy, Paul, 31, 55, 236–37, 267n69,
    309n50, 310n66
Ginsburg, Allen, 219
Glissant, Edouard, 224
Glusberg, Samuel, 97, 281n46, 282n77
González, José Luis, 71, 272n42,
    274n66, n71, 276n90
González Echevarría, Roberto, 167,
    271n22, 278n21–23, 280n37,
    281n65, 291n43, 293n67, 295n107
González Tuñón, Enrique, 284n112
González Tuñón, Raúl, 69, 96, 123–
    24, 284n108–109, 284n111–113;
    "Blues de los baldíos," 111–12;
    and Borges, 111, 122, 280n37,
    283n94; "Las brigadas de choque,"
    119–20; "Calles sin nombres,"
    284n102; and Communism, 115,
    119, 122; and Hughes, 113–22,

González Tuñón, Raúl *(cont.)*
130, 278n14; "Ku Klux Klan,"
86; "Los negros de Scottsboro,"
120–21; *La rosa blindada*, 89,
277n7–8; in Spain, 89, 120, 277n8;
Todos bailan, 120, 122, 283n95,
284n103, 285n131; *El violín del
diablo*, 114, 285n124
"Good Morning, Revolution!" (poem),
66, 120, 185, 191, 194, 210; trans-
lation of, 88, 298n4
"Goodbye, Christ" (poem), 191,
194–97, 302n45–46
"The Grandfather" (poem; Hughes's
translation of "El abuelo"), 165
Grandt, Jürgen, 21, 265n24–26,
283n92
Greer, Bonnie, 257n3, 260n25
Gruesz, Kirsten Silva, 258n9, 271n20,
278n18, 307n24, 308n35, 309n59
Guillaume, Alfred, Jr, 259n18
Guillén, Nicolás, 126, 272n26; and
Afrocubanism, 56–57, 139, 270n3;
Cantos para soldados, 146; and
Communism, 69, 88, 182, 191;
"Conversation with Langston
Hughes," 80, 261n34, 276n94,
288n7; after the Cuban Revolution,
123, 220; as Cuba's poet laureate, 57, 73; *Elegías*, 94, 294n94,
295n116; English translations
of his poems, 290n28, 293n61,
296n199, 296n129, *see also Cuba
Libre;* in exile in Buenos Aires, 124,
285n126; friendship with Hughes,
87, 132–33, 137, 144, 159–61,
182–83, 287n3, 288n5–6, 288n9–
10, 290n29–30, 291n42, 292n47,
294n84, 294n86–87, n89–91, n93,
297n148, 297n150, n152; Hughes's
presumed influence on, 81–82, 85,
94, 238, 271n13, 287n4, 289n13,
292n48–49, 297n141; on poetry as
weapon, 90; "Recuerdo a Langston Hughes,"270n7, 278n12,
288n7; "Sabas," 132, 161; *Sóngoro cosongo*, 94, 137, 291n43;
in Spain, 87–88, 134; *West Indies,*

Ltd., 146. *See also Motivos de son
Poemas-son*
Guirao, Ramón, 143, 146, 291n43,
293n70
Gunn, Drewey Wayne, 273n60,
275n80
Gurley, Jennifer, 307n30, 308n36
Gutiérrez, Rosana, 285n126
Gutiérrez y Sánchez, Gustavo, 275n77

H.D. (Hilda Doolittle), 210
Hall, Stuart, 27, 55, 259n17, 309n46
Handley, George, 236, 278n20,
310n64
Handy, W.C., 54, 109–10, 283n92;
Blues, 21, 283n89; *Father of the
Blues*, 21, 265n25; "St Louis Blues,"
108, 110
"Hard Luck" (poem), 194–95, 278n14
Harlem Renaissance, 10, 18, 51, 58–
61, 80, 83, 94, 98, 139, 184, 222
Harootunian, Harry, 231–32, 243,
308n41, 309n56
Harper, Donna, 299n16
Harris, William J., 145, 148, 265n19
Harris, Wilson, 222, 225, 237,
267n60, 306n4
Haugen, Brenda, 257n3
Hayden, Robert, 62, 266n54
Hedrick, Tace, 94, 279n26
Hemenway, Robert, 18, 264n6,
265n41, 267n59
Hemingway, Ernest, 87, 93
Hemisphere, Western, 9, 75, 83, 97,
113, 222, 227–28, 231, 233, 235,
237, 239
Henestrosa, Andrés, 270n7
Herman, Arthur, 302n53
Hernández Urbina, Francisco, 370n7
Heterolingualism, 16, 33, 85, 221
"Hey!" (poem), translation of, 129
Hicks, Granville, 195
"History" (poem), 209
Hoffman, Nicholas von, 298n8,
299n26, 301n48, 302n52, 303n72,
304n95
Homes: academic, 224; and culture
shock, 230; fictionalized return to,

52–53; and homelessness, 223, 225; impossibility of return to, 41–42; remapping of, 9–10, 14, 31, 32, 102, 211. *See also* Migrancy

"Homesick Blues" (poem), translation of, 273n55

Hones, Sheila, 232, 308n45, 309n47

Hoover, Herbert, 96

Hoover, J. Edgar, 197

Hopenhayn, Martin, 307n22

Horrego Estuch, Manuel, 289n20

House on Un-American Activities Committee (HUAC), 185–86, 188, 191, 197, 201, 203, 298n5, 299n12, n16, n23, 300m36, 301n48; and the Hollywood Ten, 299n15, 304n93

Howard, J. Woodford, 302n59

Hubs, modernist: Buenos Aires, 8, 14, 85, 93, 96, 98, 111–14, 116, 122–25, 183, 285n126; Harlem, 4, 7, 14, 5, 51–52, 91, 111–14, 130, 184, 284n105; Madrid, 8, 14, 34, 85–89, 92–93, 122; Montevideo, 8, 85, 110, 124, 221; Moscow, 16, 23–24, 28, 40, 42, 92, 268n88; Paris, 14, 30, 40, 85, 87–89, 92, 114, 124; Valencia (Spain), 86–87, 89

Hughes, Langston: as autobiographer, *see The Big Sea; I Wonder As I Wander;* and anti-Semitism, 194; and black middle class, *see* Bourgeoisie, black; and the blues, *see* Blues poetry; as cultural ambassador, 59–60, 189, 271n19; and double consciousness, 26; as dramatist, 32–33, 41, 207, 267n59; as editor and marketer, *see Cuba Libre;* essays by, 18, 20, 145, 304, 264n7, 265n22, 299n21, 301n45, 305n105; *Fields of Wonder*, 118, 125; and foreign languages, 9–10, 222, *see also* Heterolingualism; *Langston Hughes Reader*, 19, 26, 195, 219; *Laughing to Keep from Crying*, 95, 123; marginalization of, 60, 91; as novelistic character, 51–52; poetics of, 2, 5, 7–9, 20, 55, 79, 102, 130, 134; popularity in the USA, 1, 222;

radical politics of, 6, 58, 69–70, 74, 185–86, 189, 191, 195, 198, 205, 210, 217–18, 220, 264n10, 304n87, *see also* Socioaesthetics; red smear campaign against, 18, 188–89; and religion, 196–97; reputation in the Hispanic Americas, 4, 57–58, 69–70, 127, 185, 270n5; reticence about personal life, 18, 263n4; *Selected Poems of*, 77, 145, 195, 216, 218–19; *Shakespeare in Harlem*, 125; *Simple Speaks His Mind*, 9, 194, 236n5, 265n39, 299n16; testimonies before McCarthy, *see* McCarthy Committee; translations of his works: in Argentina, 3–4, 48–49, 58–59, 66, 71, 89, 95–131, 183; in Chile, 4, 58, 60, 64, 66, 70, 96; in Uruguay, 4, 58–60, 65–66, 70–71, 93; into Japanese, 2, 48, 259n19; into Spanish (numbers of), 58; into Portuguese, 2, 48, 268n86, 270n10, 274n67; into Uzbek, 2, 259n19; as translator, *see* García Lorca, Federico; Guillén, Nicolás; Mistral, Gabriela; Roumain, Jacques; on victimhood and agency, 26, 218. *See also* titles of **individual poems** and poetry collections. For names of translators, *see* appendix.

Huidobro, Vicente, 94, 278n24

Huizinga, Johan, 30, 266n48, 268n81, 269n93

Hulme, Peter, 236, 310n65

Humanities, academic, 234, 310n60; and interdisciplinary work, 234–35; and survival, 239–40

Humboldt, Alexander von, 11, 221, 225, 229

Hurston, Zora Neale, 51, 184; *Dust Tracks on a Road*, 18, 263n5, 264n6, n11, 265n29; "How it Feels to be Colored Me," 26, 265n41; and Hughes, 33, 267n59; *Mules and Men*, 8, 261n30

Hutchinson, George B., 91–92, 266n51, 278n19, n23, 290n33, 291n40, 292n49, 296n127

Hybridity: cultural, 29, 223, 267n66, 306n9, and postcolonialism, 276n101; racial, 140, 142, 147, 151, 267n55, *see also* Miscegenation

I Wonder As I Wander, 10, 15; and autobiographical conventions, 15, 32, 40, 263n5, 264n12; the dozens in, 47; global cultural networks in, 55; importance of sound in, 48; omissions from, 26, 264n9; and the picaresque, 23–24, 34; plain language in, 2, 22–23; racism in, 80; reviews of, 17–18; ritualized play in, 30, 47; scenes of translation in, 16–17, 27–31, 40–41, 47–48, 87–88; and syndesis, 23, translation of, *see* Gáler, Julio; and travel writing, 19
"I, Too" (poem), 1, 212; translations of, 62–64, 70–82, 88, 101, 110, 147, 273n57, 276n99
Identity, 6, 10, 31, 76, 174, 274n62; academic, 229; and diaspora, 55; and difference(s), 27, 86; discourses of, 45, 163, 167, 172; and gender, 26, 158, 261n38; and hybridity, 266n55, 276n101; and nation, 13, 45, 49, 103, 134, 158, 171, 223, 232; and/as performance, 36, 149, 267n61; racialized, 13, 18, 29, 40, 45, 49, 73, 78, 112, 151, 155, 157, 169; and sameness, 5; and selfhood, 22; sexual, 13, 31; strategic, 36; and translation, 43, 260n28, 261n32, 281n61. *See also* Home; Misrecognition
Imperialism: academic, 230, 235; and anti-imperialism, 64, 83, 148; USAmerican, 59, 70, 115, 141, 220, 227, 229
Influence, literary and cultural, 7, 13–14, 60, 80–82, 84, 96, 98, 110, 133, 210, 237–38, 271n13
Ingram, Zell, 36, 266n47
Intent, 186; authorial, 195, 203–4; criminal, 200–3, 303n67–68, 304n77. *See also* Smith Act; U.S. Supreme Court

Interdisciplinarity, 234–35, 288n4, 309n53, n55, 309n57, n59
International Brigades, 88–8, 227n5, 277n4
Internationalism: black, 3, 5, 50–51, 55, 59, 85, 237, 239, 268n89; Communist, 87. *See also* Cosmopolitanism
Irwin, Robert, 308n35, 309n59
Iser, Wolfgang, 281n67, 306n11, 307n19

Jackson, Henry M., 299n28
Jackson, Lawrence Patrick, 305n2
Jackson, Richard L., 69, 259n16, 269n92, 271n15, n24, 273n53, n59, 275n80, 277n105, 287n4
Jacques, Geoffrey, 292n50, 307n21, 310n78
Jakobson, Roman, 100, 294n97
James, C.L.R, 33, 233
Jazz, 1, 10, 20–21, 27–28, 39, 64, 69, 208, 265n22, 284n112, 301n47. *See also* Blues
"Jazz Band in a Parisian Cabaret" (poem), translations of, 125, 274n65
"Jazzonia" (poem), translation of, 274n67
"The Jester" (poem), translation of, 130, 287n161
Johnson, Barbara, 257n6
Johnson, Charles S., 299n16
Johnson, James Weldon, 51, 61, 115, 268n88; against Negro dialect, 144, 292n50; *Black Manhattan*, 114, 284n114; *The Book of Negro Poetry*, 62, 292n49; "The Dilemma of the Negro Author," 264n7; "Negro with a Big N," 292n50; in translation, 272n27
Johnston, David, 13, 263n55, n57
Johnston, Georgia, 264n14
Johnston, Nancy, 266n50, 268n82, n84
Jones, LeRoi. *See* Baraka, Amiri
Jones, Veda Boyde, 253n3
"Joy" (poem), translations of, 125, 272n33

Joyce, James, 90, 100, 270n9, 281n63
Jrade, Cathy, 278n22
Julien, Eileen, 267n74
Julien, Isaac, 1, 261n35

Kadir, Djelal, 227, 229, 258n11,
    259n15, 307n23, n25, n29–30,
    308n44, 309n55, 310n61
Kafka, Franz, 95, 100, 281n62
Kaplan, Amy, 229, 261n37, 308n32,
    309n55
Karem, Jeff, 257n4, 272n27, 278n20,
    308n35, 309n58
Katz, Daniel, 310n72
Kaup, Monica, 276n102, 287n4,
    288n13
Kelley, Robin, 277n1
Kent, George, 263n4
King, John, 96–97, 279n34, 280n42,
    n44, 281n46, 282n70, n79,
    285n133
Kinzer, Stephen, 296n125
Kirkpatrick, Gwen, 278n22
Klein, Julie Thompson, 309n57
Knopf, Blanche, 95, 123, 124, 135,
    279n33, 285n135, 289n18–19,
    291n44
Knowledge: cultural, 23, 157–58, 165–
    66, 225; garden of, 91; hemispheric,
    222, 233; humanist, 20, 221; for
    living together, 170; of moving, 55;
    partial, 226, 235; production, 226,
    236; and survival, 108, 170, 222;
    and universality, 226
Koestler, Arthur, 27, 266n44
Kolin, Philip, 268n76
Kowalewski, Michael, 230, 308n37
Krasner, David, 266n50–51
Kronfeld, Chana, 8, 260n29
Kutzinski, Vera M., 271n22–23,
    272n38–39, 274n68, 279n27,
    293n69, n83, 303n76

Lafleur, Héctor René, 280n43,
    284n98, 285n133
Laforgue, Jules, 265n36, 282n82
Lamming, George, 33, 267n57–58
Langston, James Nathaniel, 35, 135

Language, legal, and
    translation, 202–3
Larra, Raúl, 123
"Last Night Somebody Called Me
    Darky" (poem; translation of ""Ayé
    me dijeron negro"), 82, 151–54,
    170, 173–74, 291n43
Latin America, 60, 135, 142, 183; and
    American studies, 227, 235; black dias-
    pora in, 69, 95, 101, 110; invention of,
    231; nomenclature, 83, 230, 258n11;
    studies of, 12, 227, 231–34, 308n40
Lattuca, Lisa, 309n57
Lecercle, Jean-Jacques, 162, 177,
    294n96, 296n138
"Lenin" (poem), 207
"Lenox Avenue: Midnight" (poem),
    translation of, 130, 287n159, n161
Lenz, Günter, 307n23
"Let America Be America Again"
    (poem), 211, 257n1
"Letter to the Academy"
    (poem), 120–21
Levander, Caroline, 229, 308n33
Levine, Susan Jill, 289n21
Lewis, Marvin A., 259n16, 269n97,
    271n22
Lewis, Sinclair, 272n31
Leyda, Julia, 232, 308n45, 309n47
Lincoln, Abraham, 107–10, 115
Lipschutz (Gabriel), Lucie, 124. *See
    also* Rivaud, Luisa
Literature, comparative, 12, 83, 224;
    and American studies, 232, 309n55;
    and cultural studies, 310n75
"Little Song" (poem), translation of,
    125, 272n33
Locke, Alain, 17, 51, 53, 71, 262n40,
    268n88, 275n75
Loftus, Brian, 38, 261n35, 264n14,
    265n32, 266n55, 267n65, n72,
    268n75
Longfellow, Henry Wadsworth, 3,
    57; in Spanish translation, 272n26,
    274n67
López, Mario Luis, 279n35
López Narváez, Carlos, 53–54,
    269n96

Lowenfels, Walter, 216
Lowney, John, 18, 264n7, 301n47
Lozano, Rafael, 62, 79, 94, 99, 106,
    119, 272n33, n40, n42, 274n71,
    275n89, 276n91, n93, 279n30,
    281n60, 282n83–85
Lugones, Leopoldo, 93, 98
Lynching, 44, 90, 107, 109, 120, 128,
    283n90

"Ma Man" (poem), 116–18
Maglione de Jorge, Sara, 124
Majstorovic, Gloria, 280n39–40,
    281n47, n51
Mallan, Lloyd, 135, 152, 156, 176–77,
    293n74, n76, n81, 296n134
Mallea, Eduardo, 96, 98, 280n39
Maltese, John, 302n59, 303n68
"Man into Men" (poem), translation
    of, 88
Mañach, Jorge, 293n72
Mandelik, Peer, 270n11
Mansour, Monica, 71, 272n42
"March Moon" (poem), translation of,
    73, 127
Marco, Joaquín, 286n144
Marques, Oswaldino, 270n10, 274n67
Márquez, Roberto, 296n119
Martí, José, 60, 64, 75, 93, 103, 142,
    271n25, 275n86
Martínez Estrada, Ezekiel, 98
Martin-Ogunsola, Dellita, 260n20
Martinsville Seven, 169, 295n116
Marx, Karl, 197, 224, 306n15
Marxism, 41, 124, 201, 210, 216,
    261n34, 303n68
Masiello, Francine, 270n9, 281n63
Mason, Charlotte Osgood, 42, 184–85
Master, Edgar Lee, 61, 100
Matheus, John, 146, 292n54, n59
Maupassant, Guy de, 261n33
Maurer, Christopher, 260n20
May, Barbara, 277n2
Mayakovski, Vladimir, 261n34
McCarthy, Joseph (U.S. Senator),
    187–88, 304n95; private meeting
    with Hughes, 191–92, 215–16,
    298n5; Wheeling speech, 298n8

McCarthy Committee: Army-McCarthy
    Hearings, 198, 302n53; demise
    of, 302n53; and "Dream Boo-
    gie," 302n101; and homosexuals,
    192, 266n47; Hughes about, 299;
    Hughes's public testimony before,
    187–88, 190–92, 216, 299n18,
    300n33; Hughes's secret testimony
    before, 6, 186–88, 190, 192–218,
    260n25, 299n27; Hughes's sub-
    poena to appear before, 299n17;
    its and literary translations, 217,
    298n4; mistranslations of Hughes's
    writings, 15, 195; other public hear-
    ings of, 19, 198, 302n50
McCarthyism, 9, 26, 41, 136, 139,
    186–87, 298n5, 298n8, 305n98;
    and academia, 303n66; and jazz
    musicians, 301n47; legal basis for,
    see Smith Act; and the Venona
    documents, 187
McClellan, John (U.S. Senator), 190,
    216, 298n5, 299n28, 302n55
McGuinness, Aims, 307n22
McKay, Claude, 51, 61, 115, 119,
    268n88, 271n26, 273n56, 276n98
McMillan, Terry, 269n119
McMurray, David Arthur, 287n4
Medina, Harold (U.S. Judge), 184,
    199–201, 302n59
Mejía Sánchez, Ernesto, 273n43,
    282n79
Melas, Natalie, 224, 306n14–15
Memory, 36, 107, 213; and character-
    masks, 33; cultural, 108; divest-
    ment of, 31; and travel, 10. *See also*
    Translation
"Merry-Go-Round: Colored Child at
    Carnival" (poem), translation of,
    274n66
Method(ology): formalist, 91; for
    hemispheric American studies,
    234–35, 239; and language ac-
    quisition, 230, 308n38. *See also*
    Interdisciplinarity
"Mexican Market Woman" (poem),
    translation of, 272n33
Mignolo, Walter, 308n43

Migrancy, 5, 8–9, 40, 259n19; linguistic, 42, 223

Migration, 7, 230, 280n44; literature of, 12, poetics of, 102

"Militant" (poem), translation of, 103, 105

Miller, Arthur, 124, 203, 286n144,

Miller, Christopher L., 257n5, 309n50

Miller, Jason, 283n90,

Miller, Joshua, 260n23, 278n20, 307n20, 308n37

Miller, Marilyn, 227n106, 292n52

Miller, Perry, 229, 308n32

Miller, R. Baxter, 263n4, 264n12, 266n54

Mills, C. Wright, 219

Miscegenation, 117, 119, 142; Antimiscegenation laws in the USA, 147, 167, 169; *Loving v. Virginia*, 295n108; *Perez v. Sharp*, 295n108

Misrecognition, 31, 40, 42, 227, 261n37

Mistral, Gabriela, 5, 135, 178, 279n26, 281n45, 287n16, 289n16, 296n139

Modernism: and African-American literature(s), 3–4, 12, 17, 21, 31–32, 36, 54, 91–92, 139, 240, 271n19, 292n50; Anglo-American, 8, 57, 60–61, 90–94, 145, 274n67; canons, modernist, 57, 61–62, 92, 94, 185, 210, 231, 239; European, 64, 90, 282n82; global, 12–14, 55, 89, 239, 269n98; hemispheric, 59, 92–93; high and low, 7, 90–92, 137, 179, 206, 239, 290n33; Hispanic American, 59, *see also* Modernismo; hybrid, 265; marginalized, 14, 114, *see also* Ethnopoetry; mestizo, 94; and neomodernism, 185; and political engagement, 90–92, 94, 210, 304n87, *see also* Socioaesthetics; and/as primitivism, 64, 92, 99, 139, 148, 184, 272n42; and sexuality, 264n14; transatlantic, 8, 64, 89, 92–93, 136; and translation, 237–38, 262n51. *See also* Aesthetics: modernist; Avant-gardes; Hubs, modernist.

Modernismo, 92–93, 179, 278n23. *See also* Ultraísmo; Vanguardia.

Modernity, 237, 278n19

Molina, Lucía Dominga, 279n35

Montage of a Dream Deferred (poems), 4, 89, 125, 185, 191, 301n42, 305n101

Montalvo, Berta G., 271n24, 275n77

Moore, David Chioni, 237, 259n19, 310n71

Moore-Gilbert, Bart, 264n13, 266n53

Moretti, Franco, 224, 306n16–17, 309n59

Morgan, Ted, 187, 298n5, n7–9, 299n13, n26, 302n53, 304n95

Morrison, Toni, 238

"Mother to Son" (poem), 285n120

Motivos de son (poems), 80–81, 94, 134, 137–38, 143–44, 154, 170, 290n29–30, 294n86; translations of, *see Cuba Libre*

Movement, spatial, 6–8, 10–11, 13, 20–21, 26, 34–36, 48, 78, 102, 107, 222–23, 233, 236, 283n883. *See also* Geographies; Migrancy

Muchnik, Jacobo, 286n143–144

Mudrovcic, Maria Eugenia, 279n32

Mulatto (play), 32, 123, 266n50; translation of, 262n48, 285n136

"Mulatto" (poem), translations of, 65–66, 69, 125, 276n92

Mullen, Edward J., 58, 64, 85, 259n16, 262n41, 268n86, 270n5, n11, 271n16, 272n35, n40, 273n60, 275n79, 276n97, 277n107, 270n30, 287n4, 288n7, 290n29

Multiculturalism, 174–75

Multidisciplinarity, 234–35

Multiplicity, linguistic, 11, 33, 162, 171, 203, 308n38. *See also* Heterolingualism

Music, African American: in Argentina (tango), 21, 109–10, 115, 284n112; in Cuba, 56–57, 134, 150, 165, 170, 273n62, 290n30, 292n48, *see also* Son; in the USA, 10, 19–22, 28–30, 48, 69, 108, 113, 117, 124, 265n19,

Music, African American *(cont.)*
    279n30, 284n102, n112, 301n47,
    see also Blues; Jazz
"Mystery" (poem), 191

Nation, concepts of, 7, 12, 82,
    84–85, 163, 165, 167, 170–72, 178,
    211, 221, 223, 231–32, 234–36,
    294n96, 306n7
Nationalism, cultural and political, 59,
    64–65, 88, 103, 126, 134, 165, 171,
    220, 223
Nationality, 10, 45, 48–49, 59, 158,
    168, 229, 231–232, 234; and
    literature, 12–13, 31, 90, 116, 141,
    171, 214, 222–23, 232, 236, 238,
    283n97
Navasky, Victor S., 299n15, 300n36
Nègre, 44, 260n23, 268n80, 293n73
"Negro" (poem), translations of, 62,
    65, 88, 126–27, 272n33, 273n57,
    276n93
Negro (Spanish), 4, 49–50, 56–57,
    64, 77, 79–82, 107, 134, 147, 151,
    153–54, 168, 174, 203, 276n91,
    n93, 293n74
"Negro Dancers" (poem), translation
    of, 130, 187n161
"The Negro Speaks of Rivers" (poem),
    translations of, 52–54, 62, 65, 94,
    99, 101, 107, 110, 125, 127, 129,
    272n32–33, 276n93, 283n90,
    304n90
Nelson, Cary, 185, 206, 210, 277n5,
    298n2–n3, n6, 301n43, 303n76,
    304n85
Neruda, Pablo, 69, 88–89, 94, 115,
    120, 123
Networks: academic, 232; global, 12–
    13, 35, 55, 93, 227; hemispheric, 14;
    transatlantic, 93, trans-Pacific, 233
New Criticism, 206, 239–40, 310n77
A New Song (poems), 69, 89, 185,
    195, 273, 300
Newcomb, John T., 90, 278n11
Niedlich, Florian, 267n61
Nietzsche, Friedrich, 90, 278n13
Niranjana, Tejaswini, 259n14
North, Michael, 91, 272n38, 292n51

Not Without Laughter (novel), 161,
    182, 184; translations of, *see* Ortíz
    Oderigo, Nestor R.
Novo, Salvador, 61, 94, 270n6,
    272n28, 279n30
Nuestra America, 103, 275n86,
    282n77. *See also* Martí, José
Núñez, Ana Julieta, 286n138
Nwankwo, Ifeoma C.K., 276n100,
    297n140–141

Ocampo, Silvia, 96–98, 124, 280n39–
    40, n43–44, 281n45, n49, 282n77
O'Daniel, Therman B., 292n54
Ogorzaly, Michael, 280n38, n39, n41,
    281n46, n48
Oleza, Joan, 277n2
Oliver, María Rosa, 96–97, 124
"One" (poem), translation of, 125
"One Friday Morning" (poem), 191
"One More 'S' in the U.S.A."
    (poem), 120, 185, 194, 198, 204,
    210–11, 298n3
One-Way Ticket (poems), 125, 131,
    293n64
Onomatopoeia, 28, 179, 291n43
Orality, and literature, 13, 108, 163.
    See also Vernacular
Orgambide, Pedro, 277n8, 280n37,
    283n94, 284n109, 285n125, n127,
    286n142
The Original: authority of, 100;
    fetishization of, 12; in translation,
    11–12, 54–56, 74, 101, 110, 131,
    161, 166, 172, 175, 230, 238,
    270n11, 306n9
Ortiz, Fernando, 142, 278n14,
    295n104
Ortíz Oderigo, Nestor R., 50, 95,
    123–24, 259n19, 286n141, 294n90
Ortiz-Carboneres, Salvador, 290n28
Oshinsky, David, 198, 298n5, 300n41,
    302n54
"Our Land" (poem), translations of,
    70, 101–3, 106, 115, 120, 272n33

Palumbo-Liu, David, 310n66
Pan-Africanism, 10, 36, 51, 54–55,
    59, 87

Pan-Americanism. *See* Frank, Waldo
Pardo García, Andrés, 270n7
"Parisian Beggar Woman" (poem),
  translations of, 130, 287n161
Parkinson Zamora, Lois, 310n74
"Passing Love" (poem), translations
  of, 125
Patrons, literary, 33, 42, 139, 184–85
Patterson, Anita Haya, 5, 20, 89, 91,
  102, 259n17, 262n41, n48, 265n21,
  n36, 266n43, 277n9–n10, 278n20–
  n21, 282n71, n73, n82
Pavli, Edward, 21, 36, 259n17,
  263n57, 265n27, n29, n34, 267n79,
  279n31, 310n77, n79
Paz, Octavio, 88–89, 224, 306n13
Pease, Donald E., 9, 262n37,
  308n31–32, n38
Peddie, Ian, 258n12, 299n16
Peden, Margaret Sayers, 238, 279n32
Pedrozo, Regino, 135, 288n6, 292n53,
  297n152
Pereda Valdés, Ildefonso, 59–60,
  65–66, 69–70, 94, 123–24,
  273n45–47, n49, n51, n54, 276n92,
  285n130, n135
Pereyra, Washington Luis, 286n144
Pérez, Luis, 295n111
Pérez Firmat, Gustavo, 261n32,
  293n72, 309n54
Pérez Heredia, Alexander, 287n3,
  290n29– 30, 294n86–87
Performance, 36, 114, 117, 204,
  290n25, 231; metatheatrical, 149,
  266n55, 154; and performativity,
  127, 267n61; of sexuality, 266n47;
  translational, 3, 22, 25–27, 30, 33,
  36, 39, 47, 151
Peripheries, global, 7–9, 14, 89, 91,
  93, 111, 113, 118, 122, 130, 164.
  See also Hubs, modernist
Pfeiffer, Kathleen, 281n52, n53, n55,
  n57, 282n69
Play, 30, 46–47, 49, 53, 164, 172,
  266n48, 269n93; and laughter,
  27–28, 38–39. *See also* Choteo.
  Performance
"Po' Boy Blues" (poem), 127; translations of, 273n55, 282n74

Podestá, Guido, 60, 137, 139, 174,
  258n14, 271n20–n21, 276n101,
  278n20, n24, 290n31, 291n34
"Poem 1" (poem), translations of, 70,
  102, 273n57
"Poem 2" (poem), translations of, 73,
  272n33
Poemas-son, 18–82, 94, 115, 137,
  146, 148–49, 151, 159, 161, 165,
  175, 179
Poesía negra, 95, 273n47, 274n64; anthologies of, 60–62, 65–66, 70–71,
  146, 271n26, 273n47
"Poet to Patron" (poem), 184–85
Poetics: cultural, 134; formalist, 90;
  of migration, 102; plurilingual and
  heterocultural, 2, 5, 7, 9, 55, 130;
  translational, 263n56. *See also*
  Aesthetics
Poetry, radical (protest or revolutionary), 4, 58, 66, 69–70, 74, 126,
  185–86, 189, 191, 195, 198, 205,
  210, 217–18, 258n12, 273n61,
  304n87
Poetry, USAmerican, anthologies of in
  the Hispanic Americas, 60, 62, 71,
  83, 271n26
Poetry of the Negro 1746–1949, 113,
  135, 139, 175, 177, 288n6
Polezzi, Loredana, 262n44
Pollard, Charles W., 309n58
Ponce, Martin, 261n35
"Port Town" (poem), translation of,
  272n33
Porter, Carolyn, 228–29, 232–34,
  307n28, 309n48
Postcolonialism, 7–8, 12, 14, 31–33,
  84, 100, 173, 227, 239, 266n53,
  276n101, 278n21
Pound, Ezra, 25, 60–61, 91–92, 145,
  179, 210, 237, 278n24, 284n110,
  291n35
Pratt, Mary Louise, 122, 233, 309n49
"Prayer" (poem), translations of,
  272n33
Prentice, Chris, 263n53
Prescott, Lawrence, 269n92
Proletariat, and poetry, 112, 146, 210,
  279n30

Propaganda: and art, 122, 195–96, 205, 218; USAmerican, 300n41; Communist, 122, 186, 198

Proust, Marcel, 90

Publishers: in Buenos Aires: Fabril, 123–24, 286n143; Futuro, 123; Jacobo Muchnik Editor, 124, 286n143; Lautaro, 123–24, 183, 285n143, 286n137, n139, 297n151; Losada, 124, 281n62, 285n132, 286n149; Quetzal, 123; Siglo Veinte, 123. In the USA: Dodd, Mead, 218; Doubleday, 133, 135, 288n6, 297n152; Farrar Straus, 133, 135, 291n44; Knopf, *see* Alfred A. Knopf; New Directions, 134–35, 148, 152, 293n65, n74; Putnam, 135, 289n20; Random House, 95; Ward Ritchie Press, 132–33, 160, 289n23, *see also* Anderson, Caroline

"Question" (poem), translation of, 287n161

Quiroga, Horacio, 98

Quiroga, José, 280n37

Rabassa, Gregory, 238

Race. *See* Blackness; Race relations; Racism; Whiteness

Race relations: in Cuba, 137, 144, 149–51, 157, 16, 274n69; and Jim Crow, 18, 79, 213–14; and race riots, 107, 189; in the USA, 20, 23, 31, 45–47, 59, 64, 80, 83, 115, 117, 174, 178, 184, 198, 213–15, 264n7, 285n120, 295n115, 296n119, 301n42. *See also* Segregation

Racism, antebellum 153; antiblack, 18, 46, 59, 83, 90, 168, 211, 226, 295n110; in Cuba, 83, 295n110. *See also* Lynching

Radhakrishnan, R., 276n101, 277n104

Radway, Jan, 308n38

Ramazani, Jahan, 128, 258n12, 283n88, 287n157, 306n3

Rampersad, Arnold, 1, 18, 22, 30, 39, 65, 73, 217, 260n20, 263n4,

265n32, 270n10–11, 287n1, 292n48, 295n97, 305n108

Read, Justin, 278n24, 307n26, 308n35

Realism: ethnographic, 139; magic, 26; mimetic, 36, 101, 116, 178; parodies of, 109 poetic, 26, 101

Redish, Martin H., 187, 201, 204, 298n9–10, 299n14–15, 303n61, n63, n64, n73

Reeves, Frank, 101–2, 215–16, 218–19, 302n56, 305n104

Reeves, Thomas C., 298n7

Reid, Margaret, 284n114

Repetition, 20, 22, 78–79, 110, 207, 267n65; and the blues, 69; and memory, 10, 35, 107; and play, 30; and syndesis, 21

Revolution, Bolshevik, 187, 268n88; Cuban, 114, 182, 219; Haitian, *see* Toussaint L'Ouverture; USAmerican, 208

Revueltas, Silvestre, 88

Rhythms, in poetry and narrative, 20–21, 64, 99, 107–8, 142–43, 148–49, 166, 185, 211, 236, 305n99; in translation, 69, 129, 166, 274n71

Richards, Merle, 309n59

Riffaterre, Michael, 124

Rise, Eric, 295n116

Ritchie, Donald A., 298n12

Rivaud, Luisa (pseud.), 4, 48–50, 123–24, 268n86, 286n146

Robeson, Paul, 191, 197, 200, 218

Rodó, José Enrique, 60

Rodríguez García, José María, 137, 260n24, 267n57, 269n1, 281n64, n66, 290n32

Rodríguez-Mourelo, Belén, 287n4

Roediger, David, 307n20

Rogin, Paul Michael, 298n8

Roldán, Amadeo, 88

Rolfe, Edwin, 89, 92, 277n5

Roosevelt, Franklin D., 200, 207

Rosenthal, Macha, 290n28

Rostagno, Irene, 279n32

Roumain, Jacques, 36, 288n6, 294n94; and Communism, 191, 300n29; *Gouverneurs de la rosée*, 5, 135,

260n23; "Langston Hughes" (poem), 15
Rovere, Richard, 302n41
Rowe, John Carlos, 308n31–32
"Ruby Brown" (poem), 114, 130; translations of, 287n161
Ruiz del Vizo, Hortensia, 71, 274n65

Sabsay, Fernando, 286n145
Sáenz, Gerardo, 287n4
Said, Edward, 261n36
Sakai, Naoki, 16, 263n2
Salas, Horacio, 111, 283n94
Salas Viu, Vicente, 88
Salvatore, Ricardo D., 308n40
Sandburg, Carl, 61, 100, 124, 126, 210
Sanders, Mark, 278n19, 290n33, 292n49
Sano, Seki, 40–41, 268n76
Sarlo, Beatriz, 8, 91, 116, 118, 260n29, 278n16, 280n40, n44, 281n49, n54, 283n97, 284n112, n115, 285n121, n124, n133
Sastre, Alfonso, 262n48, 274n71, 285n136
Sbardellati, John, 305n96
Scanlon, Larry, 20, 258n8, n13–14, 265n22–23, 268n82, 285n120, n123, 287n162, 288n12, 294n99, 295n101, 307n18
Schatt, Stanley, 270n11
Schine, David, 196, 198, 215–16, 301n41, 302n53, n55
Schrecker, Ellen, 298n7, 303n66
Scott, William, 11, 260n21, 262n43, n45, n48, 277n106
"Scottsboro" (poem), 66, 210, 304n83
The Scottsboro Boys (musical), 121, 285n129
Scottsboro Limited (poems), 116, 120, 194, 204, 304n83
Scottsboro trials, 120–21, 210
Scruggs, Charles, 91
"Sea Calm" (poem), translation of, 73
See, Sam, 265n35, 278n14
Segregation, 93, 212, 168, 214, 239–40; antisegregation legislation, 170, 212, 214

Sexuality, 9, 10, 103, 118, 163–64, 222, 263n4; and blackness, 216n3; and heterosexuality, 31, 261n31, 266n47; and homophobia, 18, 216; and homosexuality, 38, 103, 192, 216, 192, 216, 261n31, n35, 266n47, 302n53; and masculinity, 17, 158
Shukla, Sandhya, 307n22
Shull, Jodie, 257n3
Shulman, Robert, 297n2, 304n78, n81, n84
Sidney, Sir Philip, 205, 303n74
Sieber, Harry, 267n63
"Silence" (poem), translation of, 125
Slavery, 36, 83–84, 117, 140, 142, 150, 164–65, 285n119, 295n101; and the transatlantic slave trade, 95, 117
Smethurst, James, 185, 189, 210, 283n97, 284n101, n114, 297n1–2, 299n24, 301n42, 304n80–82, 305n99, n101
Smith, Sidonie, 264n11, n14
Smith Act, 200–1, 203, 206, 216, 302n60, 303n77
Smyth, Gerry, 306n9, 310n62
Socioaesthetics, 115–16, 130
Soja, Edward, 236, 310n62
"Soledad" (poem), translation of, 73
Solomianski, Alejandro, 280n35
Somerville, Siobhan B., 261n31
Son (Cuban), 144, 149, 165–66, 170, 172, 290n30, 292n48, 293n67
"Song" (poem), translation of, 275n74
"Song for a Dark Girl" (poem), translations of, 69
"Song in an [sic] Havana Bar" (poem, Hughes's translation of "Cantaliso en un bar"), 175, 177–78
"Song of a Revolution" (poem), 120
"Song of Spain" (poem), 88
"Song of the Cuban Drum" (poem, Hughes's translation of "Canción del Bongo"), 292n52
"Song to a Negro Washerwoman" (poem), translation of, 287n161
Soto, Isabel, 261n33, 262n48, 268n85, 277n6, 293n63

Soto, Michael, 263n57
Soviet Union, 9, 19, 23–25, 28, 30,
    59, 74, 96, 114, 120, 182, 187, 189,
    191, 193–94, 202, 208, 219, 226,
    237, 268n88
Spengler, Oswald, 95, 173, 296n123
Spicer, Eloise, 287n4, 291n61
Spivak, Gayatri Chakarvorti, 8, 260n29
Steenmeijer, Maarten, 289n20
Stein, Gertrude, 91–92, 139, 269n98
Steinberg, Peter, 302n58
Steiner, George, 287n164
Stephanides, Stephanos, 10, 107,
    257n5, 258n14, 261n39, 262n42,
    n6, 283n87, 294n96
Stepto, Robert B., 263n1, 265n29,
    266n52, 277n105
Stierle, Karlheinz, 257n5
Storni, Alfonsina, 98, 114
Suárez-Murias, Marguerite, 309n53
Subjectivity, 15, 22, 36, 40, 44, 199,
    206, 208, 225, 278n19
"Suicide's Note" (poem), translations
    of, 73, 129–30
Summers-Bremner, Eluned, 258n13
Sur (Buenos Aires), 6, 57, 62, 96–99,
    100–1, 275n73, 279n35, 280n39–
    40, n43–44, 281n46n47, 282n77–78
Survival, 18, 31, 33, 218, and the
    humanities, 239–40; knowledge
    for, 108, 170; reading for, 221–22;
    strategies in Hughes's writing, 39,
    47, 306n3
Sweatt v. Painter, 214

Taylor, Diana, 228–29, 231, 307n27
Thaggert, Miriam, 292n50
Thurston, Michael, 257n4, 268n85,
    273n54, 277n5–6, 301n46, 304n83
Tillis, Antonio, 269n90
Tittler, Jonathan, 51, 52–54,
    269n91, n94
Toomer, Jean, 93, 98, 139, 263n5,
    281n52, 282n69
Toropov, Brandon, 300n35
Toruño, Juan Felipe, 65, 71, 79, 99,
    272n42, 274n68, n71, 276 n90–91,
    281n60

Toussaint L'Ouverture, 41, 109,
    267n57
Tracy, Steven, 265n24
TransArea studies, 236, 306n10
Transculturación (transculturation),
    142, 161, 164–65, 170, 172
Translation, and anthropology, *see*
    ethnography; and/as Creolization,
    40, 267n74; and cultural differences,
    27–28, 30, 33, 55, 100–1, 163, 174,
    236, 238; definitions of, 2–3, 11,
    13, 267n56; and displacement, *see*
    Home; and ethics, 78, 100, 173–74;
    and equivalence, 2, 54, 59, 203; and
    incommensurability, 11, 224; and in-
    fidelity, 101, 295, 281n67, 283n87;
    intercultural, 16, 133, 165–66,
    169, 186, 236; interdiscursive, 163;
    interlingual, 100, 163, 165; intra-
    cultural, 166, 186; intralingual, 49,
    100, 163; and literary history, 12,
    96, 236, 239; and literary influ-
    ence, 7, 13–14, 60, 80–82, 84, 96,
    110, 133, 210, 237–38, 271n13;
    metaphors of, 12, 116, 257n6; and
    mistranslation, 16, 49, 100, 157,
    195, 218; and monolingualism,
    16, 158, 163, 230, 238; and the
    New Negro movement, 51; and/as
    performance, 22, 26–27; and recep-
    tion history, 12, 239; and sameness,
    224, 238; and source texts, 54, 101,
    110, 130–31, 165; and survival, 10,
    222; theories of, 3, 7, 11–12, 56, 74,
    84–85, 100–1, 116,, 172–74, 196,
    223, 257n6, 260n24, n28, 261n39,
    288n4, *see also* Apter, Emily; Borges,
    Jorge Luis; Benjamin, Walter; Jako-
    bson, Roman; Paz, Octavio; Steiner,
    George; Venuti, Lawrence; and
    transculturation, 161–62, 170, 172;
    ubiquity of, 224; and untranslat-
    ability, 27–28, 175, 226; and world
    literature, 7, 12–13, 222, 262n50.
    See also Heterolingualism; Modern-
    ism; Translator; Vernacular
Translator: invisibility of, 12, 238,
    310n73; role of, 147, 174, 195, 238;

as matchmaker, 172; as trickster, 24; as true liar, 281n67

Transnationalism, 11, 13, 64, 84, 93, 170, 220, 228, 232–33, 236, 287n4, 297n140, 306n10

Travel. *See* Migrancy; Movement

Truman, Harry S., 202, 216

Tuck, Jim, 299n18, 300n31, 302n50, 304n95

Turner, Catherine, 289n17

Turner, Daniel C., 258n8, n13

U.S. Senate Permanent Subcommittee on Investigations of the Committee on Government Operations. *See* McCarthy Committee

U.S. Supreme Court decisions: *Dennis v. United States*, 200–2, 300n36, 302n59, 303n64–n65; *Scales v. United States*, 303n77; *Schenck v. United States*, 303n67; *Yates v. United States*, 303n62

Ultraísmo, 6, 99, 272n42, 274n68

"Un-American Investigators" (poem), 217

Ungar, Stephen, 3, 258n7

"Union" (poem), 208, 273n53; translations of, 66, 273n54, n61

Urrutia, Gustavo E., 73, 132, 134, 144, 159–61, 274n69, 275n75, 289n13, 290n29, 292n46, 294n85, n92

"Vagabonds" (poem), translation of, 130

Vallejo, Antonio, 185n124

Vallejo, César, 179, 279n26, 297n142

Value, aesthetic, 30, 76, 101, 112, 121, 206; relative, *see* Marx, Karl

Van Vechten, Carl, 24, 50, 71, 102, 279n28, 285n135, 294n98, 297n143

Vandemarr, Lee, 91

Veiga, José J., 279n34

Venuti, Lawrence, 100, 116–17, 173–74, 177, 260n27–28; on Dudley Fitts, 296n128; *Scandals*, 84, 276n102, 277n103, 285n117,

293n62, 296n121–122, n135; *Translator's Invisibility*, 262n51, 289n15, 296n120, 296n124, 310n72–73

Verani, Hugo, 93–94, 278n23, n25

Vernacular, 10, 21–22, 145, 225, 288n12, 290n28, 292n48; Afro-Cuban, 5, 134, 147, 162; definitions and origins of, 163–64, 285n129, 294n99, 295n101; and Negro dialect, 5, 49, 137, 139, 143, 145, 147, 167, 260n23; as sociolect, 163; southern USAmerican, 37–38, 44–45; and translation, 4, 33, 49, 116–17, 137, 145, 147, 153, 158, 163, 171–72, 174, 178, 186, 282n74; urban, 146, 150; and vernacularity, 164; working-class, 210. *See also* Modernism: Anglo American

Vianello, Raul C., 274n69

Vieira, Else Ribeiro Pires, 267n56

Villaurrutia, Xavier, 57, 59, 62, 71–73, 76, 94, 272n33, 274n71, 275n72, 279n30, 287n160

Visuality, 20, 49, 110, 129, 153, 179. *See also* Gaze

Waisman, Sergio, 96, 100, 270n9, 280n36, 281n49, n61–64, 282n68

"Wait" (poem), 120, 210

Wald, Alan, 304n94, 305n98

War: between Bolivia and Paraguay, 119; Korean, 187; Spanish Civil War, 34, 86, 120; Spanish-Cuban-American, 59, 82–83; World War I, 60; World War II, 18, 41, 134, 212, 301n46. *See also* Bay of Pigs invasion; Cold War, Franco, Francisco; Hitler, Adolf; Mussolini, Benito

Ware, Vron, 307n20

Warren, Kenneth, 261n37

Warren, Roseanna, 260n26

Watkins, Alma T., 286n141

The Ways of White Folks (short stories), 123, 128, 182, 266n50

"The Weary Blues" (poem), 108, 127, 266n46, translation of, 273n55

The Weary Blues (poems), 6, 21, 24, 62, 73–74, 89, 101–2, 107–8, 112, 119, 125, 127, 130–31, 182, 185, 272n34, 274n70, 275n75, 284n112, 293n64, 294n98; in Japanese translation, 259n19
Weinberg, Gregorio, 124, 286n150
Werner, Craig, 263n5, 265n24
Westover, Jeff, 3, 258n8
Wheatley, Phyllis, 271n26
White, Walter, 60, 276n98
"The White Ones" (poem), translation of, 73
Whiteness, 10, 27, 32, 42–45, 61, 65, 74, 78, 80, 86, 91–92, 121, 126, 128, 140, 143, 149–50, 154–155, 157, 167–69, 171, 209–10, 226, 307n20
Whitfield, Stephen J., 302n49, 305n102
Whitman, Walt, 3, 26, 57, 76, 96, 98, 110, 115, 126, 143, 211, 271n26, 281n52, 291n42; *Leaves of Grass*, 34, 99, 281n59
Wiegman, Robin, 308n31, n38
Wilder, Charles, 268n77
Williams, Raymond, 261n34

Williams, William Carlos, 61, 94, 145, 210, 221, 225, 293n65
Woods, Gregory, 261n35
Woods, Jeff, 198, 299n28, 300n35, 301n48, 302n51
Woodson, Carter G., 286n141
World literature, 7, 12–13, 90, 222, 223
Wright, Jay, 269n99
Wright, Richard, 259n16, 278n17; and Communism, 203; "The Man Who Lived Underground," 36; *Native Son*, 215; review of *BS*, 17, 26, 271n19

Yanover, Hector, 283n94, 284n108, n111
Young, Robert, 297n2
"Youth" (poem), translation of, 130
Yrigoyen, Hipólito, 280n37

Zapata Olivella, Manuel, 6–7, 51–54, 238, 269n90–92, n94, 96
Zoot Suit Riots (Los Angeles, California), 189
Zuloaga, Manuel Antonio, 280n35